T0262135

Computer Science and Technology

Computer Science and Technology

Edited by Fiona Hobbs

CLANRYE
INTERNATIONAL
www.clanryeinternational.com

Clanrye International,
750 Third Avenue, 9th Floor,
New York, NY 10017, USA

Copyright © 2019 Clanrye International

This book contains information obtained from authentic and highly regarded sources. Copyright for all individual chapters remain with the respective authors as indicated. All chapters are published with permission under the Creative Commons Attribution License or equivalent. A wide variety of references are listed. Permission and sources are indicated; for detailed attributions, please refer to the permissions page and list of contributors. Reasonable efforts have been made to publish reliable data and information, but the authors, editors and publisher cannot assume any responsibility for the validity of all materials or the consequences of their use.

Trademark Notice: Registered trademark of products or corporate names are used only for explanation and identification without intent to infringe.

ISBN: 978-1-63240-780-1

Cataloging-in-Publication Data

Computer science and technology / edited by Fiona Hobbs.
p. cm.
Includes bibliographical references and index.
ISBN 978-1-63240-780-1
1. Computer science. 2. Information technology. 3. Computer engineering. 4. Computer software.
I. Hobbs, Fiona.
QA76 .C66 2019
004--dc23

For information on all Clanrye International publications
visit our website at www.clanryeinternational.com

CLANRYE
INTERNATIONAL

Contents

Preface

This book has been a concerted effort by a group of academicians, researchers and scientists, who have contributed their research works for the realization of the book. This book has materialized in the wake of emerging advancements and innovations in this field. Therefore, the need of the hour was to compile all the required researches and disseminate the knowledge to a broad spectrum of people comprising of students, researchers and specialists of the field.

Computer science studies the theory, experimentation and engineering that is fundamental to the design, development and use of computers. It adopts a scientific approach to the systematic study of the acquisition, processing and communication of information. This is achieved by developing algorithms, computational methodologies and computational systems. Computer science branches into a number of theoretical and practical disciplines. Its applications are in diverse fields such as software engineering, artificial intelligence, graphics, data storage, networking and communication, etc. This book on computer science and technology describes in detail the fundamental theories associated with the subject while elucidating the modern advancements that are taking place across all branches of this field. It also sheds light on some of the unexplored aspects of computer science and the recent researches in this domain of study. The book is appropriate for students seeking detailed information in this area as well as for experts.

At the end of the preface, I would like to thank the authors for their brilliant chapters and the publisher for guiding us all-through the making of the book till its final stage. Also, I would like to thank my family for providing the support and encouragement throughout my academic career and research projects.

Editor

1

PLORS: a personalized learning object recommender system

Hazra Imran[1] · **Mohammad Belghis-Zadeh**[1] · **Ting-Wen Chang**[2] · **Kinshuk**[1] · **Sabine Graf**[1]

Abstract Learning management systems (LMS) are typically used by large educational institutions and focus on supporting instructors in managing and administrating online courses. However, such LMS typically use a "one size fits all" approach without considering individual learner's profile. A learner's profile can, for example, consists of his/her learning styles, goals, prior knowledge, abilities, and interests. Generally, LMSs do not cater individual learners' needs based on their profile. However, considering learners' profiles can help in enhancing the learning experiences and performance of learners within the course. To support personalization in LMS, recommender systems can be used to recommend appropriate learning objects to learners to increase their learning. In this paper, we introduce the personalized learning object recommender system. The proposed system supports learners by providing them recommendations about which learning objects within the course are more useful for them, considering the learning object they are visiting as well as the learning objects visited by other learners with similar profiles. This kind of personalization can help in improving the overall quality of learning by providing recommendations of learning objects that are useful but were overlooked or intentionally skipped by learners. Such recommendations can increase learners' performance and satisfaction during the course.

✉ Hazra Imran
hazraimran@athabascau.ca; hazrabano@gmail.com

Mohammad Belghis-Zadeh
mobelghis@yahoo.ca

Ting-Wen Chang
tingwenchang@bnu.edu.cn

Kinshuk
kinshuk@athabascau.ca

Sabine Graf
sabineg@athabascau.ca

1 Athabasca University, Edmonton, Canada

2 Beijing Normal University, Beijing, China

Keywords Personalization · E-learning · Learning management systems · Recommender system · Association rule mining · Learning objects

1 Introduction

The innovation of information and communication technologies plays an important role in the popularity of e-learning. E-learning can be supported through different forms like web-based learning, computer-based learning, or virtual classrooms and content delivery via e-networks, audio or video tape, satellite TV, video conferencing, CD-ROM, i-pods, e-mails, wireless and mobile technology [1]. E-learning offers various benefits like increased accessibility to information, better content delivery, personalized instruction, content standardization, accountability, on-demand, availability, self-pacing, interactivity, confidence, and increased convenience [2]. Due to the benefits mentioned above, many educational institutions are focusing on e-learning. To organize the learning content in e-learning, learning management systems (LMSs) are typically used. Learning management system can be defined as an "infrastructure that delivers and manages instructional content, identifies and assesses individual and organizational learning or training goals, tracks the progress towards meeting those goals, and collects and presents data for supervising the learning process of an organization as a whole" [3]. Typically, the courses in LMS consists of learning objects (LOs). The IEEE Learning Technology Standards Committee (LTSC), in Learning Object

Metadata Standard, defines a LO as "any object, digital or non-digital, that may be used for learning, education or training" [4]. Generally, LMSs deliver the same kind of course structure and LOs to each learner [5–7] as teachers develop courses based on their preferable teaching methods without considering learners' characteristics. This is termed as "one size fits all" approach. But, each learner has different characteristics, and therefore, a "one size fits all" approach does not support most learners particularly well.

Personalization in LMS refers to the functionality which enables the system to uniquely address a learner's needs and characteristics such as levels of expertise, prior knowledge, cognitive abilities, skills, interests, preferences and learning styles [8] so as to improve a learner's satisfaction and performance within the course. The personalization can ensure that learners' get different attention, according to their needs. To make LMSs personalized, recommender systems can be integrated into LMSs to recommend learning material based on what worked well or was perceived as useful for similar learners. Personalization in the form of recommendations for resources and learning materials is an area that has gained significant interest from researchers recently. Recommendations exhibit prominent social behavior in day-to-day life [9]. For example, websites like Google [10], Yahoo! [11], Amazon [12], ebay [13] and Netflix [14] provide a personalized mechanism to support users by presenting information that is assumed to be more interesting to them. Often, users need some kind of support in their decisions [15] as they get overwhelmed by the huge amount of available information. Many times, users find particular information interesting if someone has provided a recommendation of it. Such successful integration of recommender systems in e-commerce has prompted researchers to explore similar benefits in the e-learning domain [16,17] since the integration of recommender systems in e-learning has high potential for achieving advanced personalization. For example, in an academic environment, the course contents are generally static. But each learner is different and has different learning needs. Therefore, recommender systems can benefit learners by providing personalized recommendations on which learning objects to focus on next. Furthermore, because of the complexity of some courses in terms of their structure, learners might overlook some of the useful learning objects. Again, recommender systems can help in such situations by suggesting to look at such learning objects, if those learning objects were found to be essential to look at by other similar learners. This is particularly helpful since in the context of e-learning, learners learn at their own pace, and have no feedback from other peers on the usefulness of learning objects. Given the high potential of recommender systems for e-learning, this paper focuses on the research question "How to integrate a recommendation approach in LMSs to find and recommend useful learning objects within a course, considering the learning object they are visiting as well as the learning objects visited by other learners with similar profiles to facilitate learner's learning?". To answer the research question, we introduce the personalized learning object recommender system (PLORS) which can be integrated into LMS to provide personalization to learners. The main key features of the system are:

- It considers learners' profiles consisting of learners' learning styles, expertise level, prior knowledge and performance to provide advanced personalization.
- It forms a neighborhood of learners based on their profile and discovers associations among learning objects (through association rule mining) that led to identifying the useful learning objects visited by other similar learners. The approach to find the neighborhood of a learner is advanced as it is considering different characteristics of the learners such as their learning styles, prior knowledge, expertise level and performance within the course. Accordingly, we get more similar learners in a neighborhood, which enables our approach to generate more suitable recommendations that fit to the learners' need more accurately.
- It creates a personalized list of recommendations of learning objects to be presented to an individual learner based on the navigation history of members of his/her neighborhood.
- Information on whether or not a certain learning object was helpful for a particular learner is retrieved through association rule mining among the learning objects visited by him/her and other similar learners instead of asking him/her to provide a rating on the visited learning objects.

The organization of this paper is as follows. The following section reviews the relevant literature on providing personalization through recommender systems. Section 3 discusses the architecture of the personalized learning object recommender system. Section 4 concludes the paper by summarizing the main contributions of our work and presenting future directions.

2 Related work

Recommender systems support individual user in making decisions from vast available choices by recommending the appropriate choice(s) based on behavior or opinions of a group with the similar characterstics/behavior. Recently, some recommender systems have been applied in the e-learning domain. This section describes such works in two directions: First, we discuss research works focusing on providing recommendations based on the activities done by learners in the course. These works mainly use association rule mining to find the associations among the activities done by learners and then provide recommendations to the individual learner.In these works, recommendations are based on learners' activities in a course rather than learner characteristics, needs and/or profiles. Second, we describe research works in which recommendations were provided to learners based on other similar learners having similar characteristics/attributes. These works either used clustering techniques which uses learners' characteristics to form groups or calculate the similarity between the learners based on the ratings provided by them. Subsequently, they looked at what worked well for other similar learners and provided respective recommendations. Research work falling under the first group used association rule mining to generate rules based on which recommendations were provided to learners. For example, Zaiane [18] built a recommender agent that provides recommendations of learning activities within a course based on learner access histories. Khribi et al. [19] developed a recommender system based on the learners' recent navigation histories, and similarities and dissimilarities among the contents of the learning materials. Markellou et al. [20] proposed a framework for personalized e-learning. The personalization is done based on the domain ontology and the association among the usage profiles. The system uses Apriori algorithm for finding association rules. The recommended learning materials were determined based on the domain ontology. Furthermore, Liu and Shih [21] used association rule mining as basis for their material recommendation system. The system analyzes the logs to look into learner's learning behavior and to identify the associations between the learning course content. The system used the behavior of previous learners to recommend the learning content.

The first group of research works mainly considers the web usage data of the learners' in a course and associations between the activities of learners in a course. These works focus on grouping similar learners based on their activities in a course. Our work is different from the above-cited works as we are grouping similar learners based on their characteristics (e.g., learning styles, prior knowledge, expertise levels and performance) as opposed to the activities, which has potential to allow for a more accurate grouping since we are considering the basic explanation behind learners' behavior (e.g., not much background knowledge, a certain learning style) rather than just the actions themselves.

The second group of research works finds similar learners based on the characteristics and then recommendations are provided based on the information from the similar learners. For example, Tang and McCalla [22] proposed an evolving web-based learning system that finds the relevant content from the web. They used a clustering technique to cluster the learners (based on their learning interests) to calculate learners' similarities for content recommendation. Tai et al. [23] proposed a course recommender system based on self-organizing maps and data mining techniques. Self-organizing maps were used to categorize learners based on similar interests into groups. Then a data mining technique was used to draw the rules of the best learning path for each group of learners. Kerkiri et al. [24] proposed a framework that uses reputation metadata in a recommender system. The reputation metadata was the ratings of learning resources provided by the learners. The system used learning object metadata and the learners profile based on PAPI [25]. The registered learners were requested to provide information for their profile including qualifications, skills, licenses, etc. The similarity between the learners was calculated using the Pearson's r correlation coefficient. Having all the information about learners and learning resources (metadata and reputation metadata), collaborative filtering was applied to recommend personalized learning resources. The recommendations of learning material were based on the learners' ratings. Their experiment shows that such recommendations help in increasing learner's satisfaction level. Yang et al. [26] proposed a personalized recommendation algorithm for curriculum resources based on semantic web technology using domain ontology. The algorithm first gathers curriculum resources of interest based on user evaluation and user browsing behavior. Yang et al. [26] assume that "different users evaluate different core concepts, according to domain knowledge, as there is a certain similarity between core concepts, so there are similarities between the user's interests". Therefore, similarity among users can be calculated from the similarity between core concepts. The users were asked to provide ratings to the learning resources. The similarity among learners was computed based on their ratings. Then the interest degree of users is calculated for each interest category of the nearest neighbors, and finally recommendations were provided based on the interest of the nearest neighborhood. Ghauth and Abdullah [27] developed an e-learning content based recommendation system. The system was based on vector space model and learners' rating. The system considered rating of only those learners who had studied learning material and got marks higher than 80 %. Mojtaba and Isa [28] proposed a recommender system to suggest e-learning material. They model the learning material in multidimensional space of material's attributes like authors' name, subject, price and educational level. The learners were modeled in a way so that the learning material attributes can be considered. To consider learning material attributes in learner profiles, learners' ratings were used. The recommendations were generated based on content-based, collaborative-based and hybrid-based methods. The research works mentioned in the second group provide recommendations based on other similar learners. However, these works mainly used the learner interest and learners' ratings as the parameter for generating groups. In the e-learning area, we generally do not have ratings for the content. If a learner is asked to provide ratings for each learning object in a course, it puts a great deal of exertions on the learner. In our work, we aim at providing automatic recommendations without requiring any additional effort from learners. Instead of using ratings to identify the usefulness of learning objects, we use associations among the learning objects visited by him/her and other similar learners.

Furthermore, our work is different as it considers learners' characteristics, including their learning styles, expertise level, skills and prior knowledge, along with their performance in the course. By recognizing similar learners based on the several characteristics, we believe to place a learner together with learners who learn in a very much alike fashion, leading to more accurate recommendations.

3 PLORS: personalized learning object recommender system

In this section, we introduce the Personalized Learning Object Recommender System (PLORS) which provides recommendations of learning objects within a course. The aim of the system is to enable LMSs to provide recommendations to learners, considering the learning object they are accessing as well as the learning objects visited by other learners with similar profiles. Currently, PLORS can provide the recommendations for the following types of learning objects (LO) but can easily be extended if needed.

1. Commentary—through commentary, learners get a brief idea on what the unit is about.
2. Content objects—these are the learning materials of the course. They are rich in content. They provide the description and the explanation of the concepts covered in the unit of the course.
3. Reflection quizzes—these contain open-ended questions about the concepts covered in the unit. These questions aim at encouraging learners to reflect about their knowledge of the learned material.
4. Self-assessment tests—these tests include several closed-ended questions about the concepts of a unit. By attempting these tests, learners can check their understanding of the concepts of the unit since they receive immediate feedback on whether their answers were correct or not.
5. Discussion forum—through discussion forums, learners can ask questions or can join/initiate a discussion topic with their peers and instructor.
6. Additional reading materials—these materials provide additional sources for reading about the topics in the unit. For example, they can include more detailed explanations of the topic or advanced concepts related to the topic.
7. Animations—animations explain the concepts of the unit in an animated multimedia format.
8. Exercises—through exercises, learners are asked to do some practical work. This helps the *learner* to practice what they have learned in the course.
9. Examples—Examples are used to illustrate the theoretical concepts in a more concrete way to make them more understandable to learners.
10. Real-life applications—these learning objects demonstrate how learners can apply the learned material in real-life situations.
11. Conclusions—summarize the topics learned in a unit.

A course can be divided into different units and unit can (but not necessarily) have several sections. In each section, there can be different number and types of LOs. Figure 1 shows an example of such a course. The course consists of seven units. Unit 0 contains only two types of LOs namely Commentary and Digital Reading Room Activity while Unit 1 consists of nine types of LOs (Commentary, Learning objectives, Additional reading materials, Examples, Real-life applications, Self-assessment quiz, Reflection quiz, Forum activity and Conclusion). The PLORS uses information about learners' behavior through accessing log data tracked by the LMS, which includes what learning objects have been visited by each learner and how much time he/she spent on each learning object. This is information that every LMS typically tracks.

In order to provide recommendations, PLORS finds the neighbors of a learner who have similar characteristics. We are making the assumption that since learners within a neighborhood are similar to each other, learning objects visited by one learner can be beneficial to other similar learners. The overall aim of PLORS is to provide recommendations of learning objects to the learner in a situation where the learner is visiting different learning objects than other similar learners. For example, a learner may be advised to consult some unread material that other similar learners have read before attempting a particular reflection quiz. PLORS has been designed to be integrated in any LMS and consists of four modules that gather information about learners (Learner Modelling Module), create neighborhoods (Neighborhood generation module), generate recommendations (recommendation generation module), and display recommendations to learners (Recommendation display module). Figure 2 depicts the architecture of PLORS. In the next subsections, the four main modules of PLORS are discussed in further detail.

3.1 Learner modelling module

The Learner Modelling Module aims at generating and updating the Learner Model. The Learner Model contains

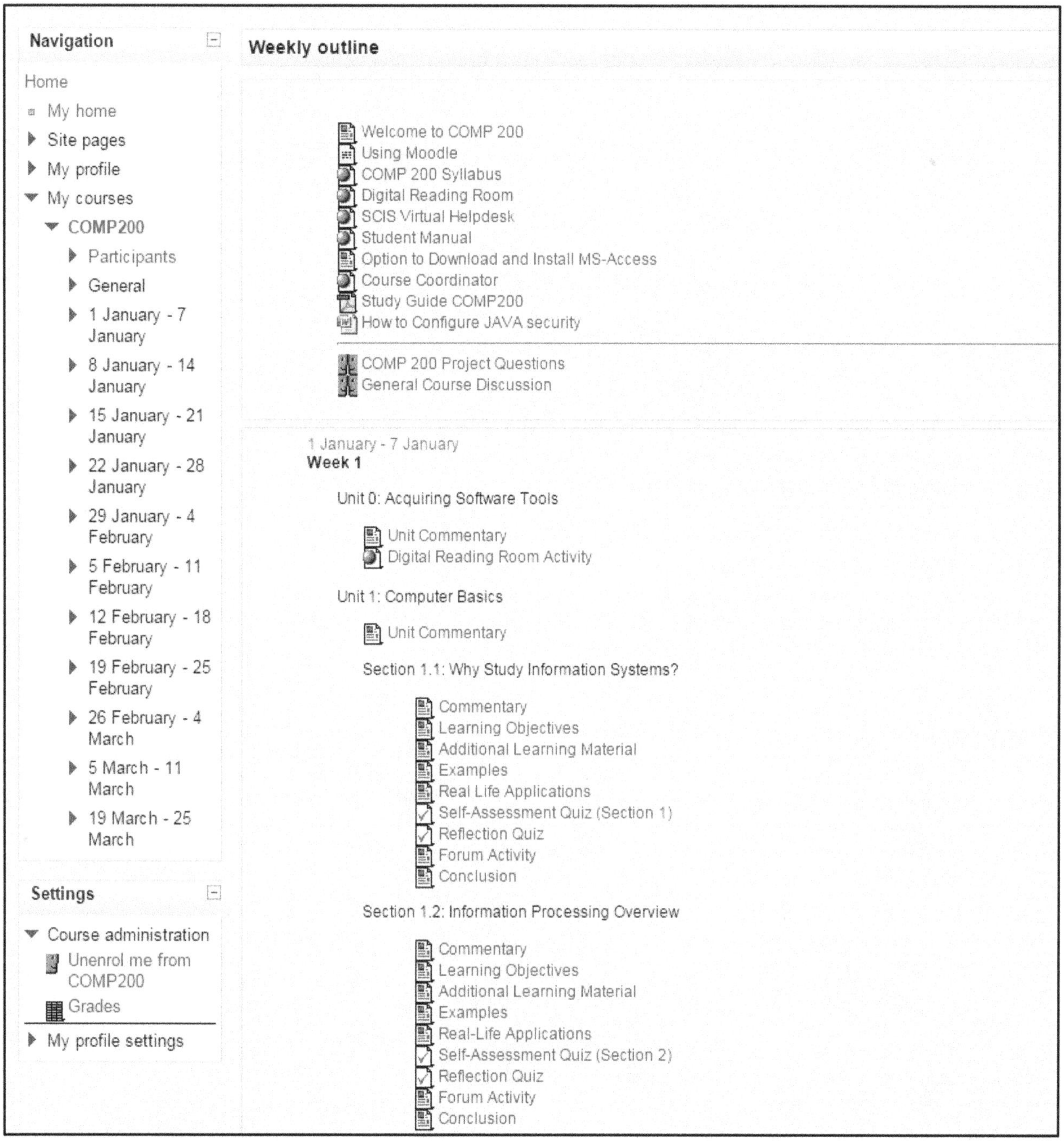

Fig. 1 Structure of a course containing different learning objects

information gathered from the learner, i.e., personal information (first name and last name), previous knowledge (related to the course), expertise level (i.e., Beginner, Intermediate or Expert), learning styles and performance. When learners register in the LMS through a registration form, the Learner Model is initialized. During the registration, learners provide personal information like first name and last name, which is stored in the Learner Model. Furthermore, once they enroll in a certain course, they are asked about their prior knowledge and expertise level specific to that course. Figure 3 shows the interface that is used to collect this information for a course on Computing and Information Systems.

In addition, the Learning Module aims at gathering information about the learning styles of learners. Every learner learns in a different and unique way, as each one has their own preferences, need and approaches toward learning. These individual differences are coined as learning styles. According to Dunn et al. [29] learningstyles can be defined as

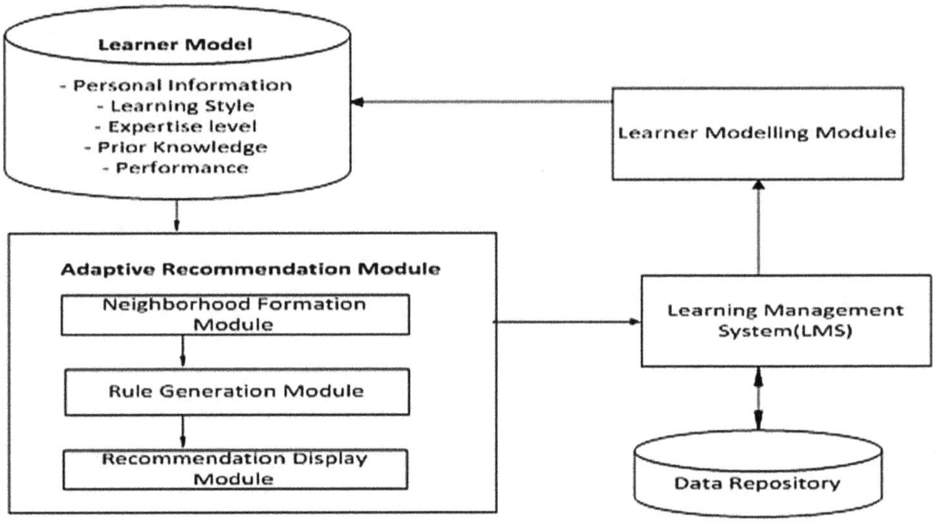

Fig. 2 Architecture of PLORS

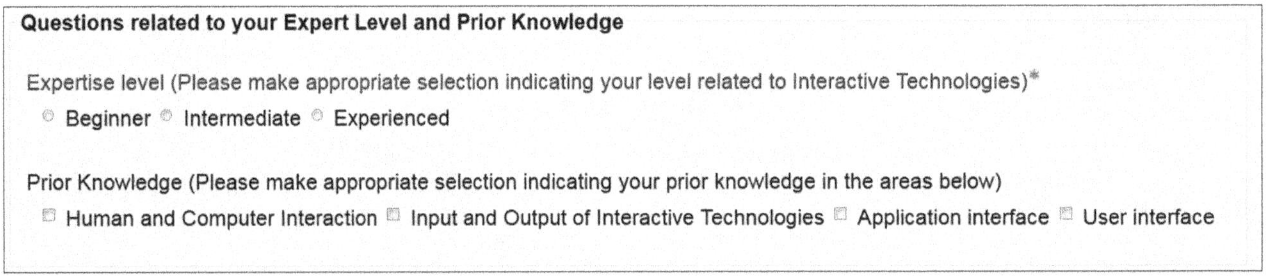

Fig. 3 Interface for gathering expertise level and prior knowledge information

"unique manners in which learners begin to concentrate on, process, absorb, and retain new and difficult information". Learning styles are important in understanding how a learner learns and participates in learning activities. More specifically, a learner's learning style is the way to gather and understand the information. There are many models about learning styles in literature like Kolb [30], Honey and Mumford [31] and Felder and Silverman [32]. To identify the learning styles, the Learner Modelling Module uses a well-investigated and commonly used questionnaire, called Index of Learning Styles (ILS) [33] developed by Felder and Solomon, which identifies the preferences of learning in four dimensions based on the Felder–Silverman Learning Style Model [32]. These four dimensions are: active/reflective, sensing/intuition, visual/verbal and sequential/global. At the time of registration, a learner is asked to fill out the ILS questionnaire, consisting of 44 questions. Based on a learner's responses, the result is calculated as four values between +11 and −11 indicating the preference on each of the four learning style dimensions. These four values are stored in the Learner Model and are used as the identified learning styles of learners.

Furthermore, performance data are stored in the Learner Model. Performance data describe a learner's performance in the course. The performance data are gathered from the learner's performance on assignments and quizzes that count towards a learner's final grade.

3.2 Adaptivity recommendation module (ARM)

This module is responsible for creating and displaying recommendations based on other similar learners' profile. ARM has three main steps: neighborhood formation, rule generation, and recommendation display. Each step is discussed in the next subsections in more detail.

Neighborhood formation module In PLORS, we assume that if a learner visits particular LOs then those LOs might be helpful to other similar learners who have not yet visited those LOs. These other similar learners build the neighborhood of a learner and are learners with similar characteristics (i.e., learning styles, prior knowledge, expertise level and performance). The purpose of the neighborhood formation module is to find such other similar learners. There were two main requirements for our algorithm to build a neighborhood: (1) the number of learners in the neighborhood of a particular learner should not be predefined but flexible and (2) the neighborhood should include the data points (learners) that are close to another. Based on the above stated requirements, our approach for finding similar learners is different from traditional clustering algorithms. Our approach does not demand the number of neighborhoods or neighbors as input a priori and can use a distance measure to place a learner only together with learners who have very similar characteristics.

To find the neighborhood, we use an algorithm that describes each learner, L_i $(i = 1, \ldots, m)$ as a vector whose components are the values of learner's learning styles, prior knowledge, expertise level and performance. Each learner vector consist of learner's four learning style values (between +11 and −11), prior knowledge in the area of Human and Computer Interaction, Input and Output of Interactive Technologies, Application Interface and User Interface (1 mean that learner have the prior knowledge in that the area and 0 mean learner does not have any prior knowledge in that area), expertise level as Beginner, Intermediate or Advanced (0 means that learner does not possess that particular expertise level and 1 mean that learner have the particular expertise level) and the learner's performance value within the course. For example learner 1 can be represented as following:

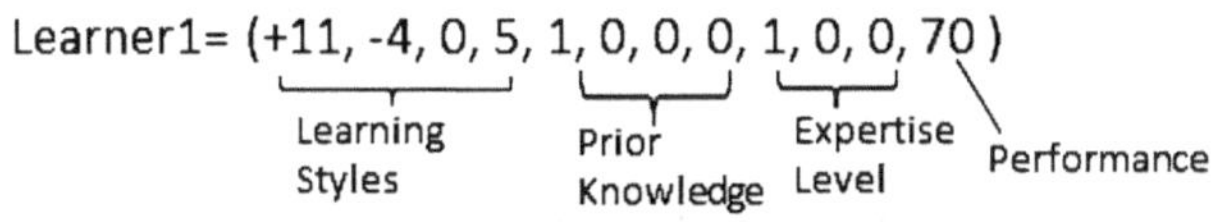
Learner1= (+11, -4, 0, 5, 1, 0, 0, 0, 1, 0, 0, 70)
Learning Styles
Prior Knowledge
Expertise Level
Performance

The number of registered learners in a specific course is denoted by m. The algorithm computes similarities between learners based on the commonly used distance measure, Euclidean distance. Euclidean distance is used because we assume that all attributes of learners are of same importance. As mentioned before, we are using different characteristics of learners including learning styles, expertise level, prior knowledge and performance. Each characteristic has a different scale of values. To ensure the equal impact of each characteristic, we normalize the data between 0 and 1. Once the characteristics values are normalized, Euclidean distance is used to compute the similarity between learners based on their characteristics. Euclidean distance (L_i, L_j) is the distance between the vectors representing two learners. The formula to calculate the Euclidean distance between two learners is shown in Formula (1).

$$\text{Euclidean\_distance}\ (L_i, L_j) = \sqrt{\sum_{k=1}^{n} (L_{ik} - L_{jk})^2}, \quad (1)$$

where L_{ik} denotes the characteristic k of learner $i$and n is the number of characteristics of the learner. In order to calculate the neighborhood of a learner, a threshold t is used as radius for the neighborhood. Accordingly, for a learner L_i, we consider every other learner L_j $(j = 1 \ldots m$ and $j! = i)$ as a member of the neighborhood if Euclidean_distance $(L_i, L_j) \leq t$. To determine a suitable value for a threshold t, we assume that two learners can be considered as similar if the difference between each characteristic is on average equal or lower than 0.25 (on a scale from 0 to 1). Accordingly, the Euclidean distance between two such learners would be 0.66. Therefore, we consider 0.66 as threshold to calculate the neighborhood.

Table 1 Example of transactions

Learner ID	Unit number	Learning objects visited by the learner
1	1	{Commentary, learning objectives, reflection quiz}
2	1	{Commentary, learning objectives, forum}
3	1	{Learning objectives, reflection quiz}
4	1	{Commentary, reflection quiz}
5	1	{Learning objectives, reflection quiz, forum}

Recommendation generation module To generate recommendations, association rule mining [34] is used. Association rule mining is a technique of finding associations and relationships among the itemsets. Given an itemset I (in our case a set of learning objects visited by the learner), and a transaction $T \subset I$ is defined as set of learning objects visited by similar learner in a unit. An association rule between two sets A and B, such that $A, B \subset I$ and where A and B are two disjoint itemsets (i.e., sets with no common items). This means that the learning objects visited in the set A in the transaction T indicates a strong probability that learning objects visited in the set $B$are also present in$T$.Such an association rule is symbolized as $A \Rightarrow B$. Table 1 shows an example of such transactions belonging to one particular unit (e.g., unit 1). For example, such rule could be {Commentary} ≥ {Learning Objectives}. The rule suggests that learners who have visited the Commentary learning object in unit 1 have also visited the Learning Objectives of unit 1.

The association rules are evaluated based on two measures namely, support and confidence. Support is defined as the percentage of the transactions containing both A and B among all transactions [34]. The formula to calculate support is shown in Formula (2).

$$\text{Support}(A => B, T) = \frac{\text{Number of transactions containing } A \cup B}{\text{Total number of transactions}} \quad (2)$$

Confidence is defined as the percentage of transactions that contain B among transactions that contain A [34]. The formula to calculate confidence is shown in Formula (3).

$$\text{Confidence}(A => B, T) = \frac{\text{Number of transactions containing } A \cup B}{\text{Number of transactions containing } A} \quad (3)$$

For example, let us consider an association rule with support 0.5 and confidence 0.7.

Sample Database	
TID	LO
T1	Commentary, Learning Objectives
T2	Forum, Exercise
T3	Commentary, Learning Objectives, Forum
T4	Learning Objectives, Reflection Quiz
T5	Learning Objectives, Forum, Exercise
T6	Commentary, Learning Objectives, Forum, Exercise
T7	Commentary, Learning Objectives, Reflection Quiz, Forum
T8	Learning Objectives, Reflection Quiz, Forum
T9	Commentary,, Exercise
T10	Commentary, Learning Objectives, Forum

Support value threshold =0.5

C_1	
Item set	Support
Commentary	0.6
Learning Objectives	0.8
Reflection Quiz	0.3
Forum	0.7
Exercise	0.4

L_1	
Item set	Support
Commentary	0.6
Learning Objectives	0.8
Forum	0.7

C_2	
Item set	Support
{Commentary, Learning Objectives}	0.5
{Commentary, Forum}	0.4
{Learning Objectives, Forum}	0.6

L_2	
Item set	Support
{Commentary, Learning Objectives}	0.5
{Learning Objectives, Forum}	0.6

C_3	
Item set	Support
{Commentary, Learning Objectives, Forum}	0.4

The algorithm will terminate as item set in C3 do not meet support threshold

Fig. 4 Process of Apriori algorithm to find large itemset

$$\{\text{Commentary, Additional Reading Material}\} \\ => \{\text{Self} - \text{Assessment Test}\}$$

This means that there is likelihood that learners who visited LOs namely, Commentary and Additional Reading Material also visited Self-Assessment Test (with confidence 70 %). The support value represents the fact that the itemset {Commentary, Additional Reading Material, and Self-Assessment Test} was present in 50 % of similar learners' transactions. Association rule discovery methods initially find sets of items occurring frequently together in transactions, satisfying a minimum support (*minsup*) criteria. Such itemsets are referred as *frequent itemsets*. The goal of association rule mining technique is to find all the rules from transactions, Thaving support $\geq$ minsup threshold and confidence $\geq$ minconf threshold [34]. We progressed to the association rule discovery by applying the Apriori algorithm [35]. The Apriori algorithm is used to control the growth of candidate itemsets based on Apriori principle, which states "Any subset of frequent itemset must be frequent" [34,35]. The candidate itemsets (denoted by *C*) are the sets of itemsets that require validation that they confirm the requirement (support $\geq$ minsup and confidence $\geq$ minconf). The frequent itemsets (denoted by *L*) are the largest possible sets, containing common items (in our case are the LOs visited by similar learners).

Apriori algorithm discovers the frequent itemsets in repeated iterations. For every similar learner, the transaction ID and each LO visited in a unit is maintained. At first step, all visited LOs are placed as candidate 1-itemset, and their support count is recorded. From Fig. 4, the large itemsets (L_1) are generated by removing LOs having minimum support (*minsup*). The large items are also called frequent 1-itemset. In the subsequent step, candidate itemset (C_k) are generated by joining $L_{k-1}X\ L_{k-1}$. The candidate itemsets whose subsets are infrequent are discarded. And the remaining C_k itemsets are used for finding frequent $k+1$ itemsets (large itemsets). An example is illustrated in Fig. 4 to show the detailed process of Apriori algorithm. This example includes a sample database, which contains ten transactions where each transaction denotes the learning objects visited by similar learners in unit 1. The minimum support value is set to be 0.5. This example shows how Apriori algorithm finds large itemsets.

After obtaining large itemsets, the association rules are generated based on minimum support and minimum confidence value. Figure 5 shows an example of finding rules. Here, minimum confidence value is 0.7.

Based on above figure, the itemset {Learning Objectives Commentary} would be discarded as the confidence value is 0.62 which is less than the minimum confidence value (0.7). Accordingly, following rules would be generated:

1. Commentary $\Rightarrow$ Learning Objectives Support $=$ 0.5; Confidence $=$ 0.83
2. Learning Objectives $\Rightarrow$ Forum Support $=$ 0.6; Con fidence $=$ 0.80
3. Forum $\Rightarrow$ Learning Objectives Support $=$ 0.6; Con fidence $=$ 0.85.

To provide recommendations to a learner, PLORS consults the association rules to check for mismatches between the learning objects visited by the current learner and the learning

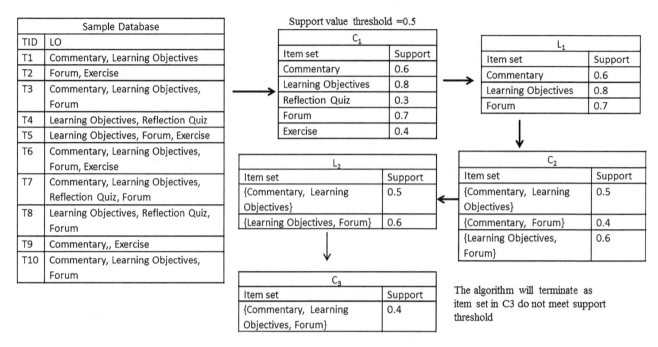

Fig. 5 Generation of association rules

L_2			
Item sets	**Support (A,B)**	**Support(A)**	**Confidence**
{Commentary, Learning Objectives}	0.5	0.6	0.83
{Learning Objectives, Forum}	0.6	0.8	0.75
{Learning Objectives, Commentary}	0.5	0.8	0.62 → Less than 0.7
{Forum, Learning Objectives}	0.6	0.7	0.85

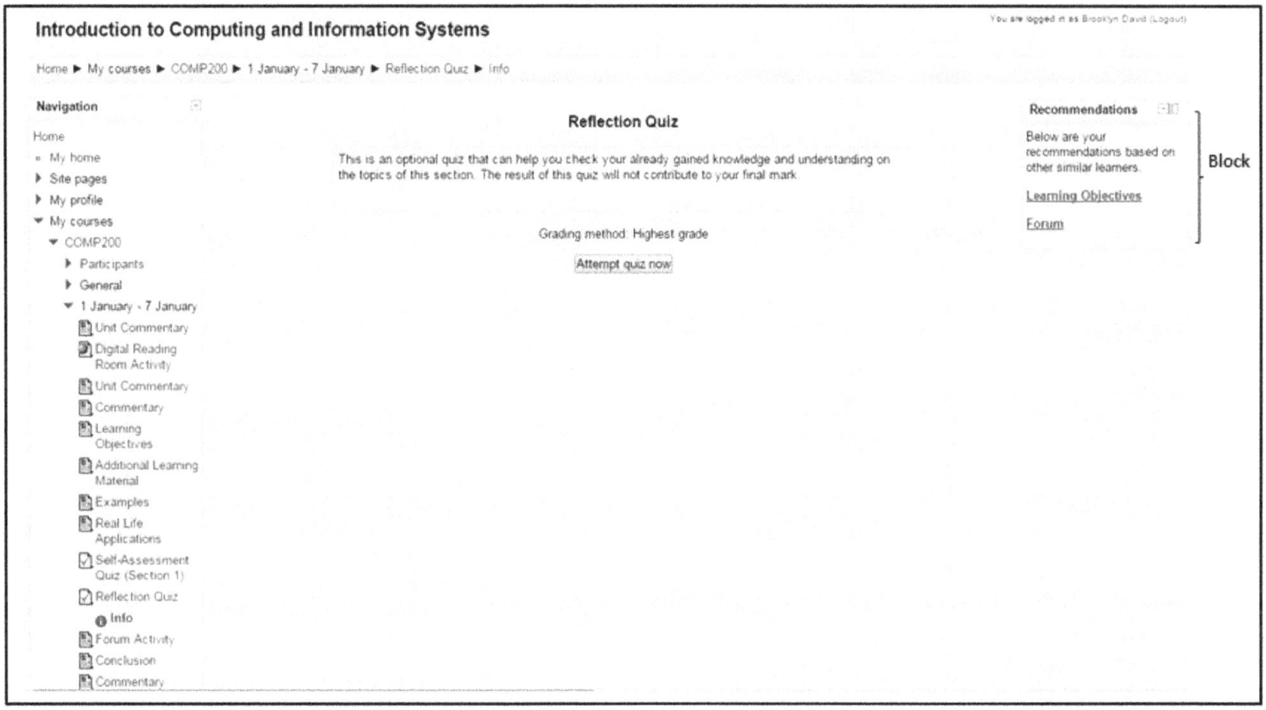

Fig. 6 Example of personalized recommendations

objects visited by the learners within the neighborhood. For example, suppose the current learner has not visited Learning Objectives yet and he/she is trying to visit Forum, but other similar learners in his/her neighborhood have visited Learning Objectives before visiting Forum. In such case, the recommendation to be provided (to the current learner) is to visit Learning Objective before Forum. Such recommendations are then passed to the recommendation display for being presented to the learner. *Recommendation display module* This module is responsible to display the personalized recommendations to the learner in an informative, precise and simple way. Recommendations are provided as a block on course page. Blocks are items that are added to the page of LMS (in our case we use Moodle LMS). The recommendation block is made sticky so that recommendations are shown on every page of the course. Recommendation block includes links to the recommended learning objects so that the learners can go to these learning objects easily. When the learner clicks on any recommended learning object link then the learning object get opened. In case, where there are no Los for recommendation then a message is shown to learner (i.e., there is no recommendation available for you. Please check back at later time!). Figure 6 shows an example of a recommendation for a learner.

In the example, when the learner tries to attempt learning object in a course (i.e. Reflection Quiz), the recommender system recommends two learning objects namely, Learning Objectives and Forum. The learner may choose to visit Learning Objective first by clicking on the respective link. In this case, Learning Objective gets open. Or, if learner wants, he/she can open all the recommendations as separate tab. When the learner tries to attempt Reflection Quiz again, then the new recommendation is generated based on other similar learners' learning experience.

4 Conclusions and future work

This paper introduces the PLORS which integrates a recommender system approach into learning management systems. PLORS provide recommendations on which learning objects within a course are more useful for learners, considering the learning object he/she is visiting as well as the learning objects visited by other learners with similar profiles. The recommendation mechanism uses association rule mining to find the association between LOs and a neighborhood algorithm. The main contributions of the work are: first, to find similar learners, our system does not consider ratings given by learners as done in most of the traditional recommender systems. Instead, it uses different characteristics/attributes of learners like learning styles, previous knowledge, expertise level, and performance to identify highly similar learners. Secondly, the usefulness of a learning object is not based on learners' rating as done in most recommender systems. Instead of that, PLORS looks into other learners' navigation history and find the set of LOs which were commonly visited by other similar learners in the course. Third, in most of the previous works similar learners are found by using a clustering approach. In our work, we consciously decided against a clustering algorithm. Clustering algorithms typically aim at assigning each learner to a group/cluster. This leads to several relevant drawbacks such as the risk of creating clusters that include data points (or learners) that are actually not too close, the risk of getting different clusters when running the same clustering algorithm again, meaning that the clustering algorithm does not always group the nearest data points (or learners), or the need for a predefined number of clusters. Since our aim is to find learners who are close to a particular learner, a neighborhood approach is more accurate and free of the above mentioned drawbacks. By using such neighborhood approach, we expect to place a learner only together with learners who learn in a very similar way, and use the experience of similar learners to provide accurate recommendations. Fourth, while most other works focus on using recommender system in particular e-learning systems, the aim of our work is to integrate a recommender system into any LMS. LMSs are commonly used by educational institutions and by enhancing LMSs with personalized functionality to provide individual recommendations, teachers can continue using the systems that they are already using for online learning and learners are receiving additionally some personalized support. The provided recommendations can help learners to better navigate the course, and therefore can improve their learning performance and satisfaction. Currently, we are providing recommendations of learning objects within a course. As a future work, we will extend the system to additionally provide recommendations of learning objects from the web based on other similar learners' profiles.

Acknowledgments The authors are grateful to MITACS for their partial financial support through the ELEVATE program. The authors acknowledge the support of Athabasca University, NSERC, iCORE, Xerox, and the research related gift funding by Mr. A. Markin.

References

1. Eke, H.N.: Modeling LIS students' intention to adopt e-learning: a case from University of Nigeria, Nsukka. Libr. Philos. Pract. **1**, 113 (2011)
2. Bhuasiri, W., Xaymoungkhoun, O., Zo, H., Rho, J.J., Ciganek, A.P.: Critical success factors for e-learning in developing countries: a comparative analysis between ICT experts and faculty. Comput. Educ. **58**(2), 843–855 (2012)
3. Szabo, M.: CMI theory and practice: historical roots of learning managment systems. World Conf. E-Learn. Corp. Gov. Healthc. High. Educ. **1**, 929–936 (2002)
4. IEEE Learning Technology Standardization Committee: Draft Standard for Learning Object Metadata (IEEE 1484.12.1-2002), New York (2002). http://ltsc.ieee.org/wg12/index.html. Accessed January 2015
5. Brusilovsky, P., Miller, P.: Course delivery systems for the virtual university. Knowl. New Inf. Technol. Emerg. Virtual Univ. 167–206 (2001)
6. Shishehchi, S., Banihashem, S.Y., Zin, N.A.M., Noah, S.A.M.: Review of personalized recommendation techniques for learners in e-learning systems. In: Proceeding of International Conference on Semantic Technology and Information Retrieval (STAIR), pp. 277–281. IEEE, New York (2011)
7. Graf, S., Kinshuk, M.C., Ives, C.:. A flexible mechanism for providing adaptivity based on learning styles in learning management systems. In: Proceedings of the International Conference on Advanced Learning Technologies (ICALT 2010), Sousse, pp. 30–34. IEEE, New York (2010)
8. Huang, M.-J., Huang, H.-S., Chen, M.-Y.: Constructing a personalized e-learning system based on genetic algorithm and case-based reasoning approach. Expert Syst. Appl. **33**(3), 551–564 (2007)
9. Tseng, C.: Cluster-Based Collaborative Filtering Recommendation Approach. Masters Thesis, Information Management Department, National Sun Yat-sen University. http://etd.lib.nsysu.edu.tw/ETD-db/ETD-search/getfile (2003)
10. Google: https://www.google.ca/. Accessed January 2015
11. Yahoo!: https://ca.yahoo.com/. Accessed January 2015
12. Amazon: http://www.amazon.com/. Accessed January 2015
13. ebay: http://www.ebay.ca/. Accessed January 2015
14. Netflix: https://www.netflix.com/. Accessed January 2015
15. Linden, G., Smith, B., York, J.: Amazon.com recommendations: item-to-item collaborative filtering. Internet Comput. IEEE **7**(1), 76–80 (2003)
16. Capuano, N., Iannone, R., Gaeta, M., Miranda, S., Ritrovato, P., Salerno, S.: A recommender system for learning goals. In: Information Systems, E-learning, and Knowledge Management Research, pp. 515–521. Springer (2013)
17. Manouselis, N., Drachsler, H., Verbert, K., Duval, E.: Recommender Systems for Learning. Springer (2013)
18. Zaíane, O.R.: Building a recommender agent for e-learning systems. In: Proceedings of the International Conference in Education, Auckland, pp. 55–59. IEEE (2002)
19. Khribi, M.K., Jemni, M., Nasraoui, O.: Automatic recommendations for e-learning personalization based on web usage mining techniques and information retrieval. In: Proceeding of the International Conference on Advanced Learning Technologies, pp. 241–245. IEEE (2008)
20. Markellou, P., Mousourouli, I., Spiros, S., Tsakalidis, A.: Using

semantic web mining technologies for personalized e-learning experiences. In: Proceedings of the Web-based Education, pp. 461–826 (2005)

21. Liu, F.-J., Shih, B.-J.: Learning activity-based e-learning material recommendation system. In: Ninth IEEE International Symposium on Multimedia Workshops, ISMW '07, pp. 343–348. IEEE, New York (2007)
22. Tang, T., McCalla, G.: Smart recommendation for an evolving e-learning system: architecture and experiment. Int. J. E-learn. **4**(1), 105–129 (2005)
23. Tai, D.W.-S., Wu, H.-J., Li, P.-H.: Effective e-learning recommendation system based on self-organizing maps and association mining. Electron. Libr. **26**(3), 329–344 (2008)
24. Kerkiri, T., Manitsaris, A., Mavridou, A.: Reputation metadata for recommending personalized e-learning resources. In: Proceedings of the Second International Workshop on Semantic Media Adaptation and Personalization, pp. 110–115. IEEE (2007)
25. PAPI: http://metadata-standards.org/Document-library/Meeting-reports/SC32WG2/2002-05-Seoul/WG2-SEL-042_SC36N0175_papi_learner_core_features.pdf. Accessed January 2015
26. Yang, Q., Sun, J., Wang, J., Jin, Z.: Semantic web-based personalized recommendation system of courses knowledge research. In: Proceedings of the International Conference on Intelligent Computing and Cognitive Informatics, pp. 214–217. IEEE (2010)
27. Ghauth, K.I., Abdullah, N.A.: Measuring learner's performance in e-learning recommender systems. Australas. J. Educ. Technol. **26**(6), 764–774 (2010)
28. Salehi, M., Kmalabadi, I.N.: A hybrid attribute-based recommender system for e-learning material recommendation. IERI Proc. **2**, 565–570 (2012)
29. Dunn, R., Dunn, K., Freeley, M.: Practical applications of the research: responding to students' learning styles-step one. Ill. State Res. Dev. J. **21**(1), 1–21 (1984)
30. Kolb, A.Y.: The Kolb learning style inventory-version 3.1 2005 technical specifications. Hay Resource Direct 200, Boston (2005)
31. Honey, P., Mumford, A.: The Learning Styles Helper's Guide. Peter Honey Maidenhead, Berkshire (2000)
32. Felder, R.M., Silverman, L.K.: Learning and teaching styles in engineering education. Eng. Educ. **78**(7), 674–681 (1988)
33. Felder, R., Soloman, B.: Index of Learning Styles Questionnaire. North Carolina State University (2001). http://www.engr.ncsu.edu/learningstyles/ilsweb.html. Accessed January 2015
34. Agrawal, R., Imieliński, T., Swami, A.: Mining association rules between sets of items in large databases. In: ACM SIGMOD Record 1993, vol. 2, pp. 207–216. ACM (1993)
35. Agrawal, R., Srikant, R.: Fast algorithms for mining association rules in large databases. In: Bocca, J.B., Jarke, M., Zaniolo, C. (eds.) Proceedings of the 20th International Conference on Very Large Data Bases, VLDB, Santiago, Chile, pp. 487–499 (1994)

2

Structure of frequent itemsets with extended double constraints

Truong Chi Tin[1] · Duong Van Hai[1] · Hoang Nguyen Thuy Ngan[1]

Abstract Frequent itemset discovering has been one essential task in data mining. In the worst case, the cardinality of the class of all frequent itemsets is of exponent which leads to many difficulties for users. Therefore, a model of constraint-based mining is necessary when their needs and interests are the top priority. This paper aims to find a structure of frequent itemsets that satisfy the following conditions: they include a subset C_{10}, contain no items of a subset C'_{11}, and have at least an item belonging to subset C'_{21}. The first new point of the paper is the proposed theoretical result that is the generalization of our former researches (Hai et al. in Adv Comput Methods Knowl Eng Sci 479:367–378, 2013). Second, based on new sufficient and necessary conditions discovered just for closed itemsets and their generators in association with the methods of creating borders and eliminating branches and nodes on the lattice, we can effectively and quickly eliminate not only a class of frequent itemsets but also one or more branches of equivalence classes of which elements are insatiate the constraints. Third, a structure and a unique representation of frequent itemsets with extended double constraints are shown by representative closed itemsets and their generators. Finally, all theoretical results in this paper are proven to be reliable and they are firm bases to guarantee the correctness and efficiency of a new algorithm, *MFS-EDC*, which is used to effectively mine all constrained frequent itemsets. Experiments show the outstanding efficiency of this new algorithm compared to modified post-processing algorithms on benchmark datasets.

Keywords Frequent itemset · Closed frequent itemset · Closed itemsets lattice · Generator · Double constraint · Extended double constraint · Constraint mining

✉ Duong Van Hai
haidv@dlu.edu.vn

Truong Chi Tin
tintc@dlu.edu.vn

Hoang Nguyen Thuy Ngan
thuyngan.dl7@gmail.com

1 Department of Mathematics and Informatics, University of Dalat, Dalat, Vietnam

1 Introduction

One of the most basic tasks in Data Mining is to discover the groups of items, products, symptoms and so on, that appear together in the given datasets. For this work, mining frequent itemset, researched first by Agrawal et al. [1] in 1993, has become more and more important and many new algorithms or improvements have been proposed to solve the problem more efficiently, such as Eclat [36], FP-Growth [18], FP-Growth* [14], BitTable-FI [12] and Index-BitTableFI [29].

A main difficulty of frequent itemset mining is that the cardinality of the solution set in the worst case is of exponent ($O(2^m)$, where $m = |A|$ and A is a set of items appearing in transactions) that can lead to the quite high computational and memory costs of mining algorithms. In fact, users can only care about a small number of them satisfying some given constraints. A model of constraint-based mining has thus been developed [5,24]. Constraints help to focus on interesting knowledge and to reduce the number of patterns extracted to those of potential interest. In addition, they are used for decreasing the search space and enhancing the mining efficiency. There are many different kinds of constraints such as knowledge-based constraints, data constraints, dimensional constraints, interestingness constraints and rule formation constraints [23]. In relation to the properties of constraints, two important types have been studied, namely anti-monotone constraints [24], denoted as $\mathcal{C}_{am}$, and monotone constraints [28], denoted as C_m. An itemset satisfies a constraint C_{am} (or C_m) if its arbitrary subset (or superset) also satisfies the constraint. C_{am} is simple and suitable with Apriori-like algorithms, so it is often integrated into them to prune candidates. On the contrary, C_m is more complicated to exploit and less effective for pruning the search space.

Most previous approaches mine frequent itemsets with either C_{am} or C_m. Mining frequent itemsets with both C_{am} and C_m is of interest because, in fact, to come closer with users' true needs, quite many various kinds are used. This can be accomplished by first mining frequent itemsets that satisfy C_{am} using algorithms, such as Apriori [1,22], Eclat [34], FP-growth [27], and then filtering the ones matching C_m in a post-processing step. This approach is inefficient because it often has to test a large number of itemsets. A more complicated solution is to integrate both C_{am} and C_m into the algorithm to find all frequent itemsets satisfying them. However, authors in [20] showed that the integration of C_m can lead to a reduction in the pruning of C_{am} since their properties are opposite. Therefore, many authors have found difficulties when facing to a quite complicated conjunction of C_{am} and C_m. An impressed approach is to combine between constraint properties and the condensed representation of frequent itemsets, such as maximal ones [11,21], closed ones or generators [7,8,26,32,33]. Instead of mining all frequent itemsets, only a small number of the condensed ones are extracted. Condensed representation has three primary advantages. First, it is easier to store because the number of condensed ones is much smaller than the size of the class of all frequent ones, especially on dense datasets. Second, we exploit it only once even when the constraints are changed. And last, the condensed representation can be used to generate all frequent ones and this generation can be performed without any access to the original dataset. In [9], the authors proposed a generic algorithm to exploit frequent itemset with both C_{am} and C_m using the minimal itemsets (like generators). They claimed that there is a tradeoff in using two of these kinds of constraints concurrently, and thus it is sometimes better to use a 'generate and test' strategy. In [10], Bucila et al. pushed both C_{am} or C_m into algorithm *DualMiner* and used the concept of positive border as a condensed representation. Unfortunately, it has to scan the dataset many times as well as perform a huge number of useless tests on long itemsets, especially when the minimum support is low. An Apriori-like algorithm, called *ExAMiner* [6], uses both of these constraints to reduce not only the input data but also the search space. However, its main difficulty is to be executed again whenever the constraints are changed. Thus, the system is hard to immediately return solution sets to users.

In this paper, we are interested in a problem that includes a conjunction of C_{am} and C_m, and each comprises of different specific constraints. Then, using closed itemsets and generators as condensed representations, we propose a new model to deal with the problem presented.

1.1 Problem statement

Before formally describing the current problem, let us present practical examples that motivate us to study and propose the new results in this paper. Let us consider searching documents on the Internet where the finding needs of users are very diverse. The datasets of information regarding documents are usually saved into the tables. Each row in a table can contain keywords, appeared in a document, the author names of the document, the type of document (Article, Book, Sort Survey, and so on) and the research area. It is common that *online users usually take interest in looking for documents that comprise of a given set of keywords. Expected documents also have to be related to a specific topic A (including one or more keywords belonging to A), but they are not involved in other topic B (not having any keywords belonging to B).* A specific example of this problem is as follows. An online user wants to look for research results from websites or search engines such as CiteSeerX, Springer and ScienceDirect. His/her need is to find the results related to keywords in the set C'_{21} = {'*sequential patterns*', '*frequent sequence*', '*web usage mining*', '*sequential rules*'}, but they are not of authors in the list C'_{11} = {'*Peter*', '*Chan*', '*Carmona*', '*Matthews*'}. In addition, the found results are also '*Article*' and belong to the area of '*Computer Science*'. Specifically, the purpose of this user is to find articles in the field of computer science (the results have to contain both words in the set C_{10} = {'*Article*', '*Computer Science*'}) that comprise of at least a keyword of C'_{21} and contain no authors in the list C'_{11}. It is clear that the need above is practical and the interest of many researchers nowadays. Other example for the current problem is when we want to build a filter to allow children searching interesting movies on the internet. Then, a compulsory key to obtain desired results is one in the set C_{10} = {*movie*}. Here, we only allow them to watch movies that belong to kinds in the list, C'_{21} = {'*Animated*', '*Cartoons*', '*Comedy*', ' *Fiction*', or '*Documentary*'}, but they are forbidden to see types of movies in the list C'_{11} = {'*Action*', '*Horror*', '*Violated*', '*Secxual*', '*Thriller*' and '*Porn*'}. In other words, the aim is to allow children to find all enjoyable and good videos (that are pulling in large audience) that are '*movie*' and follow one or more kinds in C'_{21} but are not any types in C'_{11}. In fact, it is able to see more different significant examples.

A formal statement of the problem in our current research is presented as follows.

Formal problem statement Let T be a dataset, $\mathcal{A}$ be the set of all attributes or items in T. An itemset A is a non-empty subset of $\mathcal{A}$ and a transaction in T is a set of items $t \in$

$2^{\mathcal{A}}$. The support of A, denoted as supp(A), is the number of transactions that are superset of A. Given two threshold values, s_0 and s_1, and three subsets, C_{10}, C_{11} and C_{21}, of $\mathcal{A}$ such that $0 < s_0 \leqslant s_1 \leqslant 1$, $C_{10} \subseteq C_{11} \not\subseteq C_{21}$. A is called frequent if $supp(A) \in [s_0, s_1]$. The task is to *find the class* $\mathcal{FS}_{C_{10}\subseteq C_{11},\not\supseteq C_{21}}(s_0, s_1)$ *of all the frequent itemsets that* (1) *includes a subset* C_{10}, (2) *contains no items of a subset* $C'_{11} = \mathcal{A}\backslash C_{11}$ *and* (3) *have at least an item belonging to subset* $C'_{21} = \mathcal{A}\backslash C_{21}$. In our second example above, $C_{10} =$ *movies*, $C'_{11} = L_1$ and $C'_{21} = L_2$. In other words, the goal is to discover all elements A of $\mathcal{FS}_{C_{10}\subseteq C_{11},\not\supseteq C_{21}}(s_0, s_1)$ that can be stated formally as below:

$$\mathcal{FS}_{\mathbf{C_{10}\subseteq C_{11},\not\supseteq C_{21}}}(s_0, s_1) \stackrel{\text{def}}{=} \{L' \in \mathcal{FS} : C_{10} \subseteq L' \subseteq C_{11} \quad \text{and} \quad L' \not\subseteq C_{21}\}.$$

Note that the current problem is *an extension* of many of our formerly considered problems. If $s_1 = 1$, $\mathcal{FS}$ is the class of all frequent itemsets in the traditional meaning. When $s_1 < 1$, we desire to consider frequent itemsets with supports that are not too high because they sometimes are valuable. For instance, they can help discover association rules with high confidences from abnormal phenomena appearing in frequent itemsets of which frequency is not necessary to be quite high (such as new, unusual rules for both positive and negative aspects in the field of network security or for finding out the falsehood on the figure of socioeconomic field). In addition, when the constraints are given special values, we obtain frequent itemsets without any constraint or with single constraints in simple forms, $\mathcal{FS}(s_0)$ and $\mathcal{FS}_{C_{11}}(s_0)$ in [2] or $\mathcal{FS}_{\not\subseteq C_{21}}(s_0)$ in [3] or $\mathcal{FS}_{\supseteq C_{10}}(s_0)$ in [16], or with double constraints presented in $\mathcal{FS}_{C_{10}\subseteq C_{11}}(s_0, s_1)$ [17]. So, we can find that the extended double constraint presented in this paper is more general than that, $\mathcal{FS}_{C_{10}\subseteq C_{11}}(s_0, s_1)$, shown in [17], by extending a new kind of constraint set, C_{21}, which is an arbitrary subset of $\mathcal{A}$. Indeed, when we assign $C_{21} = \varnothing$, we immediately obtain the problem $\mathcal{FS}_{C_{10}\subseteq C_{11}}(s_0, s_1)$. The extension of the new constraint C_{21} or C'_{21} has multiple practical meanings as shown in the examples above. A quite naïve thought for solving the problem $\mathcal{FS}_{\mathbf{C_{10}\subseteq C_{11},\not\supseteq C_{21}}}(s_0, s_1)$ is to filter from the results of $\mathcal{FS}_{C_{10}\subseteq C_{11}}(s_0, s_1)$ those that satisfy the constraint C_{21} in a post-processing step. However, this will do so many useless tests, and as a result, it will take much mining time. Thus, using the lattice of closed itemsets and their generators which is also used in [2,3,15–17], we study and propose a new method to effectively mine frequent itemsets with above constraints, called extended double constraints (*EDC*). *EDC* can be categorized into two kinds, $\mathcal{C}_m(supp(L') \leq s_1, C_{10} \subseteq L'$ and $L' \not\subseteq C_{21})$ and $\mathcal{C}_{am}(supp(L') \geq s_0$ and $L' \subseteq C_{11})$. Below are my contributions for the method to effectively discover frequent itemsets with *EDC*.

1.2 Contributions

The contributions of this paper are as follows. *First*, the result of the paper is the generalization of our former problems which are to find frequent itemsets without constraints or with simpler constraints. Particularly, it is an extension of the problem $\mathcal{FS}_{C_{10}\subseteq C_{11}}(s_0, s_1)$ [17] of which the result has been published in a good international journal by further considering a significant constraint, C_{21} or C'_{21}.

Second, we showed sufficient and necessary conditions for the non-emptiness of the solution set. The conditions allow us to turn checking the constraints on the very large number of frequent itemsets into testing them on representative closed itemsets of equivalence classes with quite small amount. Our lattice-based approach becomes more effective when the conditions are combined with the techniques of creating upper and under borders to quickly eliminate branches or nodes on the lattice. It also has a high sustainability in face of regular changes of the constraints following user's need. *Third*, we show a structure and a unique representation of frequent itemsets with *EDC* that help us test the conditions on the quite small number and size of generators. This representation also allows us to integrate the constraints into the process of generating constrained frequent itemsets without checks in a post-processing step. *Finally*, in practice, based on these theoretical results, we propose a new algorithm, *MFS-EDC*, to completely and distinctly exploit all frequent itemsets with *EDC*. The advantages of *MFS-EDC* are that: it quickly discovers all frequent itemsets that satisfy opposite constraints, $\boldsymbol{\mathcal{C}_{am}}$ and $\boldsymbol{\mathcal{C}_m}$, concurrently by pushing the constraints into *MFS-EDC* without direct checks on them (post-processing or naïve approaches can do this by directly testing the output results of $\mathcal{FS}_{C_{10}\subseteq C_{11}}(s_0, s_1)$ on C_{21} or the ones of $\mathcal{FS}(s_0)$ on all constraints of *EDC*); it is easy to be turned into parallel algorithms to obtain real time in mining process; it only needs to access the original dataset once, even if the constraints are changed regularly. This considerably enhances mining performance.

The rest of this paper is organized as follows. Some preliminary concepts related to the problem are reviewed in Sect. 2. Approaches to deal with the current problem are also considered in this section. Section 3 presents a rough partition and then a stricter partition of the solution set. In Sect. 4, we propose a structure of the solution set based on a necessary and sufficient condition of closed itemsets and their generators for the emptiness of $\mathcal{FS}_{C_{10}\subseteq C_{11}\not\subseteq, C_{21}}(s_0, s_1)$, and a unique representation of frequent itemsets with extended double constraint in each equivalence class based on closed itemsets and their generators. We also propose an efficient algorithm *MFS_EDC* to exploit all frequent ones with extended double constraint. Experimental results will be discussed in Sect. 5. The conclusions and future work is presented in Sect. 6. Finally, for easier to read, the proof of the theoretical results in this study is moved to "Appendix".

2 Preliminary concepts and some approaches to the problem

2.1 Preliminary concepts

For a binary dataset according to discovered data context $\mathcal{T} \stackrel{\text{def}}{=} (\mathcal{O}, \mathcal{A}, \mathcal{R})$, where $\mathcal{O}$ is a non-empty set of transactions, $\mathcal{A}$ is the set of all items appearing in those transactions and $\mathcal{R}$ is a binary relation on $\mathcal{O}x\mathcal{A}$. A set of items is called an itemset. Consider two Galois connection operators $\lambda : 2^{\mathcal{O}} \rightarrow 2^{\mathcal{A}}$ and $\rho : 2^{\mathcal{A}} \rightarrow 2^{\mathcal{O}}$ defined as follows: $\forall O, A : \varnothing \neq O \subseteq \mathcal{O}, \varnothing \neq A \subseteq \mathcal{A}, \lambda(O) \stackrel{\text{def}}{=} \{a \in \mathcal{A} | (o, a) \in \mathcal{R}, \forall o \in O\}$, $\rho(A) \stackrel{\text{def}}{=} \{o \in \mathcal{O} | (o, a) \in \mathcal{R}, \forall a \in A\}$ and, as convention, $\lambda(\varnothing) \stackrel{\text{def}}{=} \mathcal{A}$, $\rho(\varnothing) \stackrel{\text{def}}{=} \mathcal{O}$. We denote $h(A) \stackrel{\text{def}}{=} \lambda(\rho(A))$ as the closure of A (h is called the closure operation in $2^{\mathcal{A}}$). An itemset A is called closed itemset iff[1] $h(A) = A$ [25]. The support of $A \subseteq \mathcal{A}$, denoted as supp(A), is the ratio of cardinality $|\rho(A)|$ to $|\mathcal{O}|$, i.e. $supp(A) \stackrel{\text{def}}{=} |\rho(A)|/|\mathcal{O}|$. The minimum and maximum support thresholds are denoted as s_0 and s_1, respectively, where $0 < 1/n \leq s_0 \leq s_1 \leq 1$ and $n \stackrel{\text{def}}{=} |\mathcal{O}|$. We only consider non-trivial items in $\mathcal{A}^{\mathcal{F}} \stackrel{\text{def}}{=} \{a \in \mathcal{A} | supp(\{a\}) \geq s_0\}$. Let $\mathcal{CS}$ be the class of all closed itemsets together with their supports. With normal order relation "$\subseteq$" over subsets of $\mathcal{A}$, $\mathcal{LC} \stackrel{\text{def}}{=} (\mathcal{CS}, \subseteq)$ is the lattice of all closed itemsets organized by Hass diagram. A non-empty itemset A (subset of $\mathcal{A}^{\mathcal{F}}$) is called *frequent* iff $s_0 \leq$ supp(A) $\leq s_1$. Note that if s_1 is equal to 1, then the traditional frequent itemset concept is obtained. Briefly, $\mathcal{FS} \stackrel{\text{def}}{=} \mathcal{FS}(s_0, s_1) \stackrel{\text{def}}{=} \{L' : \varnothing \neq L' \subseteq \mathcal{A}, s_0 \leq supp(L') \leq s_1\}$ denotes the class of all frequent itemsets and $\mathcal{FCS} \stackrel{\text{def}}{=} \mathcal{FCS}(s_0, s_1) \stackrel{\text{def}}{=} \mathcal{FS}(s_0, s_1) \cap \mathcal{CS}$ denotes the class of all frequent closed itemsets. For any two non-empty sets $G, A : \varnothing \neq G \subseteq A \subseteq \mathcal{A}$, G is called a generator [25] of A iff $h(G) = h(A)$ and $(h(G') \subset h(G), \forall G' : \varnothing \neq G' \subset G)$. Let $\mathcal{G}(A)$ be the class of all generators of A. Since $\mathcal{G}(A)$ is non-empty and finite [4], $|\mathcal{G}(A)| = k$, all generators of A are indexed: $\mathcal{G}(A) = \{A_1, A_2, \ldots, A_k\}$. Let $\mathcal{LCG} \stackrel{\text{def}}{=} \{\langle L, supp(L), \mathcal{G}(L)\rangle | L \in \mathcal{LC}\}$ be the lattice $\mathcal{LC}$ of closed itemsets together with their generators and $\mathcal{LFCG}(s_0, s_1) \stackrel{\text{def}}{=} \{\langle L, supp(L), \mathcal{G}(L)\rangle \in \mathcal{LCG} | L \in \mathcal{FCS}(s_0, s_1)\}$ be the lattice of frequent ones and the generators.

To present an effective approach for the current problem, based on the closure operator h, we need an equivalence relation on the class of itemsets to partition the solution set into disjoint equivalence sub-classes.

[1] iff is denoted as if and only if.

Definition 1 ([31], *Equivalence relation* $\sim_{\mathcal{A}}$ over $\mathcal{FS}(s_0, s_1)$) Consider the following binary relation $\sim_{\mathcal{A}}$ on $\mathcal{FS}(s_0, s_1)$, $\forall A, B \in \mathcal{FS}(s_0, s_1)$:

$$A \sim_{\mathcal{A}} B \Leftrightarrow h(A) = h(B).$$

Obviously, $\sim_{\mathcal{A}}$ is an *equivalence relation*. For each $A \in \mathcal{FS}(s_0, s_1)$, we denote $[A] \stackrel{\text{def}}{=} \{B \in \mathcal{FS}(s_0, s_1) : h(B) = h(A)\}$ as the equivalence class of all frequent itemsets having the same closure $h(A)$ and for each $L \in \mathcal{FCS}(s_0, s_1)$, we have $[L] := \{L' \subseteq L : L' \neq \varnothing, h(L') = L\}$. Using this relation, we divide $\mathcal{FS}(s_0, s_1)$ into the disjoint equivalence classes. We have the following proposition.

Proposition 1 ([31], A partition of $\mathcal{FS}(s_0, s_1)$)

$$\mathcal{FS}(s_0, s_1) = \sum_{L \in \mathcal{FCS}(s_0, s_1)} [L].$$

For each $L \in \mathcal{FCS}(s_0, s_1)$, each equivalence class $[L]$ contains frequent itemsets having the same closure L, $\rho(L)$ and especially, the same support as supp(L). Moreover, this partition allows us to decrease the storage of the support of itemsets in each class, the production of duplicate candidates and the independent exploitation of each class by effective parallel algorithms in distributed environment. There are effective algorithms in the literature to mine the lattice $\mathcal{LCG}$ such as CHARM-L [35] *and MinimalGenerators* [34], *Touch* [30], *GENCLOSE* [4] *and CHARM-L and GDP* [19].

2.1.1 Some approaches to the problem

Two post-processing approaches For the first algorithm, *MFS-PP-EDC1*, we first find the class of all frequent itemsets $A \subseteq C_{11}$, $A \in \mathcal{FS}_{\subseteq C_{11}}(s_0)$, by one of the well-known algorithms such as *dEclat* or *FPGrowth* with the consideration of only items belonging to C_{11}. Then, the remaining constraints, $supp(A) \leq s_1$, $C_{10} \subseteq A$ and $A \nsubseteq C_{21}$, are checked to generate frequent itemsets satisfying *EDC*. For the second one, *MFS-PP-EDC1*, we additionally integrate an anti-monotonic constraint, $A \nsubseteq C_{21}$, into one of the above algorithms to obtain $\mathcal{FS}_{\subseteq C_{11}, \nsubseteq C_{21}}(s_0) = \{A \in \mathcal{FS}(s_0) | A \subseteq C_{11}$ and $A \nsubseteq C_{21}\}$ before testing the remaining monotonic constraints, supp $(A) \leq s_1$, $C_{10} \subseteq A$. Note that, in fact, we often use two dualistic constraints, $A \subseteq C_{11}$ and $A \nsubseteq C_{21}$ in the form of $A \cap C'_{11} = \varnothing$ and $A \cap C'_{21} \neq \varnothing$, where $C'_{11} = \mathcal{A} \backslash C_{11}$ and $C'_{21} = \mathcal{A} \backslash C_{21}$ with the quite small sizes of C'_{11} and C'_{21}.

The drawbacks of two these approaches are taking a lot of time for mining $\mathcal{FS}_{\subseteq C_{11}}(s_0)$ or $\mathcal{FS}_{\subseteq C_{11}, \nsubseteq C_{21}}(s_0)$ again when *EDC* is changed, and for direct check the remaining constraints on the large number of generated frequent itemsets. If we keep all frequent itemsets in the memory with $s_0 = 1/|\mathcal{O}|$, then that may need enormous storage, especially when $n = |\mathcal{O}|$ is quite large.

The approach of the paper Based on the partition (1) in the Proposition 2 (which divides the solution set into disjoint equivalence solution sub-classes), we first mine only once the *lattice* $\mathcal{LCG}$ containing closed itemsets and their generators from $\mathcal{T}$. *Second,* when *constraints are changed,* we quickly determine from $\mathcal{LCG}$ the class $\mathcal{FCS}_{C_{10}\subseteq C_{11},\not\subseteq C_{21}}(s_0, s_1)$ of all closed frequent itemsets and generators with *EDC*. Note that, with this partition, instead of checking the constraints on the so large number of frequent itemsets, we just need to do that on the quite small amount of closed frequent itemsets belonging to $\mathcal{LCG}$. In this step, based on monotone or anti-monotone properties of constraints, the parent–child relations in the lattice are used to quickly find the supersets or the subsets of a closed itemset. That helps to significantly reduce the search space when determining the elements of $\mathcal{FCS}_{C_{10}\subseteq C_{11},\not\subseteq C_{21}}(s_0, s_1)$. Moreover, another outstanding advantage of the partition is to allow us to design parallel algorithms for concurrently, independently mining each the sub-class. *Finally,* in each *equivalence sub-class* $[L]$ with $L \in \mathcal{FCS}_{C_{10}\subseteq C_{11},\not\subseteq C_{21}}(s_0, s_1)$, we *completely, quickly and distinctly generate* all *frequent itemsets* with EDC which *are represented uniquely* through L and its generators $\mathcal{G}(L)$—the *essential information of the class* $[L]$. From the theoretical results demonstrated to be reliable, we propose *MFS-EDC*, an *efficient algorithm* for mining frequent itemsets that satisfy *EDC*.

In next section, we first present an ineffective rough partition of the solution set, and then, based on above approach, we show a better strict partition for it.

3 Partitioning solution set by the equivalence relation

For each $L \in \mathcal{FCS}(s_0, s_1)$, $A \subseteq B \subseteq \mathcal{A}$, $C \subseteq \mathcal{A}$, $L_B \stackrel{\text{def}}{=} L \cap B$, we denote: $\mathcal{FS}_{A\subseteq L_B} \stackrel{\text{def}}{=} \{L' \in [L] \,|\, A \subseteq L' \subseteq L_B\} = \{L' \neq \varnothing \,|\, A \subseteq L' \subseteq L_B, h(L') = L\}$ and $\mathcal{FS}_{A\subseteq L_B,\not\subseteq C} \stackrel{\text{def}}{=} \{L' \in \mathcal{FS}_{A\subseteq L_B} \,|\, L' \not\subseteq C\}$.

3.1 The rough partition of the solution set $\mathcal{FS}_{C_{10}\subseteq C_{11},\not\subseteq C_{21},}(s_0, s_1)$

From the partition in Proposition 1, we immediately obtain the following rough partition for $\mathcal{FS}_{C_{10}\subseteq C_{11},\not\subseteq C_{21}}(s_0, s_1)$.

Proposition 2 (A rough partition of $\mathcal{FS}_{C_{10}\subseteq C_{11},\not\subseteq C_{21},}(s_0, s_1)$)

Trans	Items
1	a c e g
2	a c f h
3	a d f h
4	b c e g
5	a c e g
6	b c e g
7	a c f h

(a)

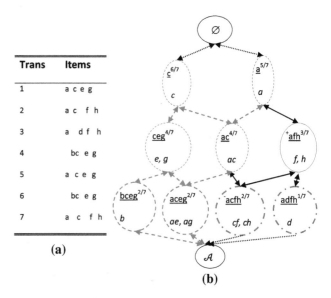

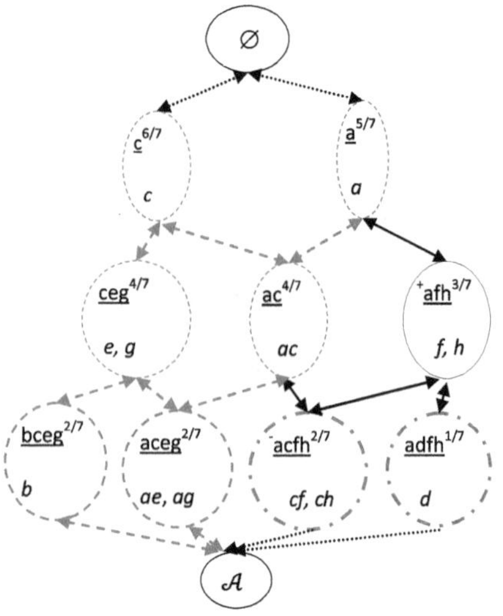

(b)

Fig. 1 **a** Example dataset and **b** the corresponding lattice of closed itemsets (*underline*), their generators (*italic*) and supports (*superscript*)

$$\mathcal{FS}_{C_{10}\subseteq C_{11},\not\subseteq C_{21},}(s_0, s_1) = \sum\nolimits_{L\in\mathcal{FCS}(s_0,s_1)} \mathcal{FS}_{C_{10}\subseteq L_{C_{11}},\not\subseteq C_{21}}. \quad (1)$$

From this partition, we can independently exploit all frequent itemsets with EDC in each equivalence class $\mathcal{FS}_{C_{10}\subseteq L_{C_{11}},\not\subseteq C_{21}}$.

Example 1 (Illustrating the disadvantage of the above rough partition) The rest of this paper considers dataset $\mathcal{T}$ shown in Fig. 1a. *Charm-L* [35] and *MinimalGenerators* [34] are used to mine a lattice of all frequent itemsets and their generators.

The results are shown in Fig. 1b. Let us consider the constraints on supports $s_0 = 2/7, s_1 = 1$. For briefness, we denote itemset $\{a_1, a_2, \ldots, a_k\}$ as $a_1a_2\ldots a_k$, for example, $\{a, f, h\}$ as *afh*. It is possible that there are many values of constraints and closed itemsets $L \in \mathcal{FCS}(s_0, s_1)$ such that $\mathcal{FS}_{C_{10}\subseteq L_{C_{11}},\not\subseteq C_{21},} = \varnothing$, even $\mathcal{FS}_{C_{10}\subseteq C_{11},\not\subseteq C_{21},}(s_0, s_1) = \varnothing$. Indeed, we consider examples as follows:

1. (i) For $C_{10} = a$, $C_{11} = adfh$ and $C_{21} = adfh$, when using the algorithm of post-processing approach based on the partition in (1), with $L = afh \in \mathcal{FCS}(s_0, s_1)$, $supp(L) = 3/7$, we have $[L] = \{f, fa, fh, fha, h, ha\}$, but $L_{C_{11}} = afh \subseteq C_{21}$, so $\mathcal{FS}_{C_{10}\subseteq L_{C_{11}},\not\subseteq C_{21},} = \varnothing$. Moreover, after generating $|\mathcal{FS}(s_0, s_1)| = 35$ itemsets and then directly testing constraints on them corresponding to all different closed frequent (*CF*) itemsets L in $\mathcal{FCS}(s_0, s_1)$, there is no itemset L' in any of 9 *CF* classes $[L]$ satisfying the constraints, so $\mathcal{FS}_{C_{10}\subseteq C_{11},\not\subseteq C_{21}} = \varnothing$ and $\mathcal{FS}_{C_{10}\subseteq L_{C_{11}},\not\subseteq C_{21}}(s_0, s_1) = \varnothing$.

(ii) We obtain the similar result $\mathcal{FS}_{C_{10}\subseteq C_{11},\not\subseteq C_{21}}(s_0, s_1) = \varnothing$ for other constraints, $C_{10} = d, C_{11} = adf$ and $C_{21} = adf$.

2. With $C_{10} = a, C_{11} = adfh$ and $C_{21} = ah$, for all $L \in \mathcal{FCS}(s_0, s_1)$, we only have one class $[L = afh]$ satisfying the constraints, $\mathcal{FS}_{C_{10}\subseteq L_{C_{11}},\not\subseteq C_{21}} = \{ahf, af\} \neq \varnothing$, since $supp(L) = 3/7, [L] = \{f, fa, fh, fha, h, ha\}$, i.e. $\mathcal{FS}_{C_{10}\subseteq C_{11},\not\subseteq C_{21}}(s_0, s_1) = \mathcal{FS}_{C_{10}\subseteq L_{C_{11}},\not\subseteq C_{21}} = \{ahf, af\} \neq \varnothing$.

Then, the post-processing approach takes quite much time to generate all frequent itemsets in equivalence sub-classes $[L]$, corresponding to closed frequent itemsets L, and then so many or even all sub-classes are eliminated because they do not satisfy the constraints. From this example, we find it is important to have sufficient and necessary conditions and then impose them on the constraints and closed itemsets L to narrow $\mathcal{FCS}(s_0, s_1)$ into $\mathcal{FS}_{C_{10}\subseteq C_{11},\not\subseteq C_{21}}(s_0, s_1)$. Here, $\mathcal{FS}_{C_{10}\subseteq C_{11},\not\subseteq C_{21}}(s_0, s_1)$ includes closed itemsets which are not only frequent but they also satisfy constraints regarding sub-items $\{C_{10}, C_{11}, C_{21}\}$ so that corresponding solution subsets are not empty, i.e. $\mathcal{FS}_{C_{10}\subseteq L_{C_{11}},\not\subseteq C_{21}} \neq \varnothing$.

3.2 Strict partition of solution set $\mathcal{FS}_{C_{10}\subseteq C_{11},\not\subseteq C_{21}}(s_0, s_1)$

To briefly present the remaining results, we consider the following lemma which will be used to prove Propositions 3 and 4 in the next section.

Lemma 1 *Let* $A, B, L', L \subseteq \mathcal{A} : L \neq \varnothing, B \neq \varnothing$,

(a)

(i) $L' \neq \varnothing \Leftrightarrow \mathcal{G}(L') \neq \varnothing$. *If* $\varnothing \subset L' \subseteq L$ *and* $h(L') = h(L)$, *then* $\mathcal{G}(L') \subseteq \mathcal{G}(L)$.

(ii) *If* $\mathcal{G}_B(L) \stackrel{\text{def}}{=} \{L_i \in \mathcal{G}(L) | L_i \subseteq B\} \neq \varnothing$, *then* $\mathcal{G}_B(L) = \mathcal{G}(L_B)$.

(iii) *Assume that* $A \subseteq B$, $\forall L \in \mathcal{FCS}_{A\subseteq B}(s_0, s_1) \stackrel{\text{def}}{=} \{L \in FCS(s_0, s_1) | L \supseteq A, \mathcal{G}_B(L) \neq \varnothing\}$. *Then,* $\forall L' \in \mathcal{FS}_{\mathbf{A\subseteq L_B}}, \forall L_i \in \mathcal{G}(L)$, *then* $\mathcal{G}(L') \subseteq \mathcal{G}_B(L)$ *and* $(hL_i) = h(L_B) = L$.

(iv) $\forall U, U \in 2^{\mathcal{A}} : \varnothing \subset U \subseteq V$, *we have* $U \cap Minimal(V) \subseteq Minimal(U)$, *i.e. if* $\exists M \in U \cap Minimal(V)$, *then* $M \in Minimal(U)$, *where the set* $Minimal(U)$ *consists of all minimal subsets of elements of* U *according to the normal order relation "*$\subseteq$*" on subsets.*

(b) *Let* $\text{Cond}(L_i)$ *be a logic condition expression related to* L_i. *Consider* $L' \subseteq \mathcal{A}, L' \neq \varnothing, L' \supseteq A, h(L') = L : \exists L_i \in \mathcal{G}(L')$ *and assume that* $\text{Cond}(L_i)$ *is true. Let* $U \stackrel{\text{def}}{=} \{K_k \stackrel{\text{def}}{=} L_k \backslash A | L_k \in \mathcal{G}(L'), \text{Cond}(L_k)\}$, $V \stackrel{\text{def}}{=} \{K_k \stackrel{\text{def}}{=} L_k \backslash A | L_k \in \mathcal{G}(L), \text{Cond}(L_k)\}$*-be finite sets. Then,* $\varnothing \subset U \subseteq V, \varnothing \subset Minimal(U) \subseteq Minimal(V)$ *and we can always assume that* i *is the minimum index such that* $K_i \in Minimal(U)$. *Moreover,* $L' \supseteq A + K_i$ *and* $K_i \in Minimal(V)$.

(c) *Let* $A \subseteq L_B \stackrel{\text{def}}{=} L \cap B \neq \varnothing, K_{\min}$ *be a non-empty class of subsets in* $L_B (\varnothing \subset K_i \subseteq L_B, \forall K_i \in K_{\min})$, $K_U^i \stackrel{\text{def}}{=} \begin{cases} \bigcup_{K_k \in K_{\min}: k \leq i} K_k, \text{if } i \geq 1 \\ \varnothing, if i = 0 \end{cases}$, $K_{U,i} \stackrel{\text{def}}{=} K_U^{i-1} \backslash K_i$ *and* $K_{-,i} \stackrel{\text{def}}{=} L_B \backslash (A + K_U^i), \forall i \geq 1$. *If* $L' = A + K_i + K_i' + K_i^{\sim}$, *where* $K_i \in K_{\min}, K_i' \subseteq K_{U,i}, K_i^{\sim} \subseteq K_{-,i}$, *then* $A \subseteq L' \subseteq L_B$. *In addition, if* $K_i \stackrel{\text{def}}{=} L_i \backslash A$ *with* $L_i \in \mathcal{G}_B(L)$, *then* $h(L') = h(L_B) = L$ *and* $L' \in \mathcal{FS}_{A\subseteq L_B}$.

Note that in general case, the reverse of the a.(iv) *above is not true. However, in the present special cases, if we add some corresponding conditions, then the reverse assertion in Lemma* 1b *is also true.*

We denote $C^+ \stackrel{\text{def}}{=} C_{11} \cap C_{21}, C_- \stackrel{\text{def}}{=} C_{10} \cap C_{21}, C^* \stackrel{\text{def}}{=} C_{11} \backslash C_{21}$ *and* $\mathcal{FCS}_{C_{10}\subseteq C_{11},\not\subseteq C_{21}}(s_0, s_1) \stackrel{\text{def}}{=} \{L \in \mathcal{FCS}(s_0, s_1) | C_{10} \subseteq L_{C_{11}} \not\subseteq C_{21}, \mathcal{G}_{C_{11}}(L) \neq \varnothing\}$. *It is obvious that* $\mathcal{FCS}_{C_{10}\subseteq C_{11},\not\subseteq C_{21}}(s_0, s_1) \subseteq \mathcal{FCS}(s_0, s_1)$, $C_- \subseteq C^+$ *and for every* $L' \in \mathcal{FS}_{C_{10}\subseteq C_{11},\not\subseteq C_{21}}(s_0, s_1) \neq \varnothing$, *then* $\varnothing \subset L' \backslash C_{21} \subseteq L_{C_{11}} \backslash C_{21} \subseteq C_{11} \backslash C_{21} \subseteq C_{11}$, $supp(C_{11}) \leqslant supp(L') \leqslant s_1$, $supp(C_{10}) \geqslant supp(L') \geqslant s_0$. *Thus, from now on, we always assume that the following hypothesis* (H_1) *is satisfied:*

$$0 < s_0 \leq s_1 \leq 1, \quad C_{10} \subseteq C_{11} \not\subseteq C_{21}, \quad supp(C_{11}) \leq s_1, \quad supp(C_{10}) \geq s_0. \qquad (\text{H}_1)$$

Proposition 3 (Necessary and sufficient conditions of $L \in \boldsymbol{\mathcal{FCS}(s_0, s_1)}$ for the emptiness of $\boldsymbol{\mathcal{FS}_{C_{10}\subseteq C_{11},\not\subseteq C_{21},}(s_0, s_1)}$ and $\boldsymbol{\mathcal{FS}_{C_{10}\subseteq L_{C_{11}},\not\subseteq C_{21}}}$, a better partition of $\boldsymbol{\mathcal{FS}_{C_{10}\subseteq C_{11},\not\subseteq C_{21},}(s_0, s_1)}$) *Assume that the above hypothesis* (H_1) *is satisfied. Then:*

(a) $\mathcal{FS}_{C_{10}\subseteq C_{11},\not\subseteq C_{21}}(s_0, s_1) \neq \varnothing \Leftrightarrow \mathcal{FCS}_{C_{10}\subseteq C_{11},\not\subseteq C_{21}}(s_0, s_1) \neq \varnothing$.

(b) *We obtain a better partition of* $\mathcal{FS}_{C_{10}\subseteq C_{11},\not\subseteq C_{21}}(s_0, s_1)$ *as follows:*

$$\mathcal{FS}_{C_{10}\subseteq C_{11},\not\subseteq C_{21}}(s_0, s_1) = \sum\nolimits_{L \in \mathcal{FCS}_{C_{10}\subseteq C_{11},\not\subseteq C_{21}}(s_0,s_1)} \mathcal{FS}_{C_{10}\subseteq L_{C_{11}},\not\subseteq C_{21}}. \quad (2)$$

The following algorithm, *MFCS-EDC*, is to extract $\boldsymbol{\mathcal{FCS}_{C_{10}\subseteq C_{11},\not\subseteq C_{21}}(s_0, s_1)}$ (the set of constrained frequent closed itemsets which is the output of the algorithm) from the input data which is the lattice $\boldsymbol{\mathcal{LCG}}$ of all closed item-

Fig. 2 MFCS-EDC algorithm

$\boldsymbol{\mathcal{FCS}}_{C_{10}\subseteq C_{11},\not\subseteq C_{21}}(s_0, s_1)$ ***MFCS-EDC***$(\mathcal{LCG}, s_0, s_1, C_{10}, C_{11}, C_{21})$
$\mathcal{FCS}_{C_{10}\subseteq C_{11},\not\subseteq C_{21}}(s_0, s_1) := \varnothing$; $C^* := C_{11} \backslash C_{21}$;
for each (<L, supp(L), $\mathcal{G}(L)$> $\in \mathcal{LCG}$) **do** {
    if ($s_0 \le$ supp(L) $\le s_1$ **and** $C_{10} \subseteq L$ **and** $L \cap C_{11} \not\subseteq C_{21}$) **then** {
        $\mathcal{G}_{C_{11}}(L) := \{L_i \in \mathcal{G}(L) \mid L_i \subseteq C_{11}\}$;
        if ($\mathcal{G}_{C_{11}}(L) \ne \varnothing$) **then** $\mathcal{FCS}_{C_{10}\subseteq C_{11},\not\subseteq C_{21}}(s_0, s_1) := \mathcal{FCS}_{C_{10}\subseteq C_{11},\not\subseteq C_{21}}(s_0, s_1)$ + <L, supp(L), $\mathcal{G}_{C_{11}}(L)$>;
    }
}
return $\mathcal{FCS}_{C_{10}\subseteq C_{11},\not\subseteq C_{21}}(s_0, s_1)$;

sets and their generators together with user constraints, $\boldsymbol{s_0}, \boldsymbol{s_1}, \boldsymbol{C_{10}}, \boldsymbol{C_{11}}$ and $\boldsymbol{C_{21}}$ (Fig. 2).

Remark 1 Methods to eliminate nodes and branches of nodes as well as to create monotonic upper borders and anti-monotonic under borders on the lattice $\boldsymbol{\mathcal{LCG}}$ to quickly determine $\boldsymbol{\mathcal{FCS}}_{C_{10}\subseteq C_{11},\not\subseteq C_{21}}(\boldsymbol{s_0}, \boldsymbol{s_1})$.

When implementing the algorithm *MFCS-EDC*, to quickly determine $\mathcal{FCS}_{C_{10}\subseteq C_{11},\not\subseteq C_{21}}(s_0, s_1)$ from $\mathcal{LCG}$, we can use the methods of eliminating nodes and branches of nodes, or creating upper and under borders while travelling the lattice. We split the constraints in $\mathcal{FCS}_{C_{10}\subseteq C_{11},\not\subseteq C_{21}}(s_0, s_1)$ into the groups: *monotonic* $\mathcal{C}_m \overset{\text{def}}{=}$ *(supp(L)* $\leqslant s_1$ *and* $C_{10} \subseteq$ *Land* $L \cap C_{11} \not\subseteq C_{21}$), *anti-monotonic* $\mathcal{C}_{am} \overset{\text{def}}{=}$ *(supp(L)* $\geqslant s_0$) and $\mathcal{C}_{\text{non}} \overset{\text{def}}{=} (\mathcal{G}_{C_{11}}(L) \ne \varnothing)$ (that is neither *monotonic* nor *anti-monotonic*. An itemset satisfies a constraint $\mathcal{C}_{\text{non}}$ if it does not satisfy both $\mathcal{C}_{am}$ and $\mathcal{C}_m$).

To use the advantages of the properties of $\mathcal{C}_m$, when travelling in the bottom-up direction of the lattice, standing at one node L, if:

(i) The constraint $\mathcal{C}_m$ is not satisfied, then we immediately wipe the branch with the root node L out of the lattice (i.e. we do not need to consider all of nodes in this branch since we know for certain that $\mathcal{C}_m$ will not meet its requirement on them), and go to other branch.
(ii) $\mathcal{C}_m$ is satisfied and $\mathcal{C}_{\text{non}}$ is not, then only L is eliminated from the lattice.
(iii) Both $\mathcal{C}_m$ and $\mathcal{C}_{\text{non}}$ are satisfied, then we still keep L on the lattice.
(iv) The conditions of $\mathcal{C}_{am}$ or $\mathcal{C}_{\text{non}}$ are not met, then L is cut out of the lattice.
(v) Both $\mathcal{C}_{am}$ and $\mathcal{C}_{\text{non}}$ are satisfied, then we put L on the list of anti-monotonic under borders. So, it does not need to check $\mathcal{C}_{am}$ on all of its predecessor nodes.

Similarly, we use five steps above when going in the top-down direction of the lattice to consider $\mathcal{C}_{am}$.

Note that we often pre-select one of two groups, $\mathcal{C}_{am}$ and $\mathcal{C}_m$, which is much more likely to be not satisfied, such as the group with more constraints in the form of AND than other. We also choose the bottom-up or the top-down first so that eliminating branches is done before borders are created. For the considering problem, it is more suitable to select $\mathcal{C}_{am}$ and go in the bottom-up direction of the lattice first.

Example 2 Illustrating the good effect of the sufficient and necessary conditions so that $\boldsymbol{\mathcal{FS}}_{C_{10}\subseteq C_{11},\not\subseteq C_{21}}(\boldsymbol{s_0}, \boldsymbol{s_1}) = \varnothing$ or $\boldsymbol{\mathcal{FS}}_{C_{10}\subseteq L_{C_{11}},\not\subseteq C_{21}} = \varnothing$ when $L \in \boldsymbol{\mathcal{FCS}}(\boldsymbol{s_0}, \boldsymbol{s_1}) \backslash \boldsymbol{\mathcal{FCS}}_{C_{10}\subseteq C_{11},\not\subseteq C_{21}}(\boldsymbol{s_0}, \boldsymbol{s_1})$ and the effectiveness of the methods of eliminating branches and nodes, and creating borders.

1. In Example 1.1(i), we just need to find one of the conditions in (H_1) which is not met: $adfh = C_{11} \not\subseteq C_{21} = adfh$, then we immediately result $\mathcal{FS}_{C_{10}\subseteq C_{11},\not\subseteq C_{21}}(s_0, s_1) = \varnothing$ and $\mathcal{FS}_{C_{10}\subseteq L_{C_{11}},\not\subseteq C_{21}} = \varnothing, \forall L \in \mathcal{FCS}(s_0, s_1)$. In Example 1.1(ii), since other condition in (H_1), $1/7 = supp(C_{10}) \ge s_0 = 2/7$, is not satisfied, we lead to the similar conclusion.
2. Consider Example 1.2, the groups of constraints $\mathcal{C}_{am}$ and $\mathcal{C}_m$ for each $L \in \mathcal{LCG}$, respectively, are $\{supp(L) \geqslant 2/7\}$ and $\{\text{supp}(L) \leqslant 1, a \subseteq L, L \cap adfh \not\subseteq ah\}$. First, we go in the bottom-up direction of $\mathcal{LCG}$ in Fig. 1b. When using the properties of monotonic constraints, the branches started at *bceg* and *aceg* (circled in red by dashed lines) all are eliminated since the constraint $\mathcal{C}_m : a \not\subseteq bceg$ and $a = aceg \cap adfh \subseteq ah$ are violated (case (i)). For $L = acfh$, the constraint $\mathcal{C}_{\text{non}}$: $\mathcal{G}_{C_{11}}(L) = \{L_i \in \{cf, ch\} | L_i \subseteq C_{11} = adfh\} = \varnothing$, is not satisfied (case (ii)), so $L \notin \mathcal{FCS}_{C_{10}\subseteq C_{11},\not\subseteq C_{21},}(s_0, s_1)$ and we cut L out of the lattice (circled by dotted, dashed lines in red); then, we only need to consider two remaining nodes on the lattice, *afh* and *adfh*. The node *adfh* (circled by dotted, dashed lines in blue) continues to be eliminated since $\mathcal{C}_{am}$: supp(*adfh*) = 1/7 < 2/7 is violated (case (iv)). Second, in $\mathcal{LCG}$ remains only one node, *afh*, and we travel in both the bottom-up and top-down directions started at $L = \overline{afh}$ (circled by red solid lines). After that, L is put into the lists of under and upper borders since it satisfies all constraints $\mathcal{C}_m : C_{10} = a \subseteq L_{C_{11}} = L = afh \not\subseteq C_{21} = ah$, $\mathcal{C}_{am}$: $supp(L) = 3/7 \geqslant 2/7$ and $\mathcal{C}_{\text{non}} : G_{C_{11}}(L) = G(L) = \{f, h\} \ne \varnothing$. Finally, we have $\mathcal{FCS}_{C_{10}\subseteq C_{11},\not\subseteq C_{21},}(s_0, s_1) = \{L = afh\} \ne \varnothing, [L] =$

$\{f, fa, fh, fha, h, ha\}$, so $\mathcal{FS}_{C_{10}\subseteq C_{11},\not\subseteq C_{21}}(s_0, s_1) = \mathcal{FS}_{C_{10}\subseteq L_{C_{11}},\not\subseteq C_{21}} = \{ahf, af\} \neq \varnothing$.

It is able to be found from this example that, for post-processing approach, we have to take a lot of time to generate all $|\mathcal{FS}(s_0, s_1)| = 35$ frequent itemsets and then check them on the constraints about sub-items. But, we only obtain two of them, *ahf* and *af*, satisfying the constraints. Meanwhile, based on the condition $L \in \mathcal{FCS}_{C_{10}\subseteq C_{11},\not\subseteq C_{21}}(s_0, s_1)$ and the methods of eliminating branches and nodes as well as creating borders on the lattice, we quickly wiped out eight of nine equivalence sub-classes (corresponding with 29 of 35 frequent itemsets), which did not meet the requirements of the constraints, and only need to check one node.

Note that, in the final sub-class $[L = afh]$, after generating six frequent itemsets, we have to check them on the constraints in the post-processing step which can still consume time a lot. In next section, we will show the way to partition $\mathcal{FS}_{C_{10}\subseteq L_{C_{11}},\not\subseteq C_{21}}$ into two disjoint solution subsets based on dividing the generators in $\mathcal{G}_{C_{11}}(L)$ into two parts according to C_{21}.

4 Structure of the solution set $\mathcal{FS}_{C_{10}\subseteq C_{11},\not\subseteq C_{21}}(s_0, s_1)$ and algorithm MFS-EDC

4.1 Partition and explicit structure of each equivalence class $\mathcal{FS}_{C_{10}\subseteq L_{C_{11}},\not\subseteq C_{21}}$

Going on the idea of partition, for $\forall L \in \mathcal{FCS}_{C_{10}\subseteq C_{11},\not\subseteq C_{21}}(s_0, s_1)$, we divide each equivalence class $\mathcal{FS}_{C_{10}\subseteq L_{C_{11}},\not\subseteq C_{21}} \overset{\text{def}}{=} \{L' \in [L] | C_{10}\subseteq L' \subseteq L_{C_{11}}, L' \not\subseteq C_{21}\}$ into two disjoint parts based on the partition of generators in $\mathcal{G}_{C_{11}}(L)$ as follows, $\mathcal{G}_{C_{11}}(L) = \mathcal{G}_{C^+}(L) + \mathcal{G}_{C_{11},\not\subseteq C_{21}}(L)$, where $\mathcal{G}_{C^+}(L) \overset{\text{def}}{=} \{L_i \in \mathcal{G}(L) : L_i \subseteq C^+\} = \{L_i \in \mathcal{G}_{C_{11}}(L) : L_i \subseteq C_{21}\}$, $\mathcal{G}_{C_{11},\not\subseteq C_{21}}(L) \overset{\text{def}}{=} \{L_i \in \mathcal{G}_{C_{11}}(L) : L_i \not\subseteq C_{21}\}$.

We first number all $K_i \in K_{\min,C_-\subseteq L_{C^+}} \overset{\text{def}}{=} Minimal\{K_i \overset{\text{def}}{=} L_i\backslash C_-, L_i \in \mathcal{G}_{C^+}(L), 1 \leq i \leq M\}$ from 1 to M if $\mathcal{G}_{C^+}(L) \neq \varnothing$ or set M = 0, if $\mathcal{G}_{C^+}(L) = \varnothing$. Then, we continue to number, from $M + 1$, subsets in $K_{\min,C_{10}\subseteq L_{C_{11}},G\not\subseteq C_{21}} \overset{\text{def}}{=} \text{Minimal } \{K_i \overset{\text{def}}{=} L_i\backslash C_{10}, L_i \in \mathcal{G}_{C_{11},\not\subseteq C_{21}}(L), \forall i > M\}$ and denote $K^+_{\min,C_{10}\subseteq L_{C_{11}},\not\subseteq C_{21}} \overset{\text{def}}{=} K_{\min,C\subseteq L_{C^+}} \cup K_{\min,C_{10}\subseteq L_{C_{11}},G\not\subseteq C_{21}}$.

Note that if $\mathcal{G}_{C^+}(L) = \varnothing$ (like when $C^+ = \varnothing$), then we set

$$\mathcal{FS}^*_{C_-\subseteq L_{C^+},+L_{C^*}} \overset{\text{def}}{=} \lfloor L \rfloor_{C_-\subseteq L_{C^+},+L_{C^*}} \overset{\text{def}}{=} \varnothing.$$

Otherwise, if $\mathcal{G}_{C^+}(L) \neq \varnothing$, we define: $\lfloor L \rfloor_{C_-\subseteq L_{C^+},+L_{C^*}} \overset{\text{def}}{=} \{L' \in \mathcal{FS}_{C_{10}L_{C_{11}},\not\subseteq C_{21}} | \exists L_i \in \mathcal{G}_{C^+}(L) : L' \supseteq L_i\}$ and $2^{[C_{10}\backslash C_{21}\subseteq L_{C^*}]*} \overset{\text{def}}{=} \{L^\sim \neq \varnothing | C_{10}\backslash C_{21}\subseteq L^\sim \subseteq L_{C^*}\}$, $K^i_{U,C_-\subseteq L_{C^+}} \overset{\text{def}}{=} \bigcup_{K_k\in K_{\min,C_-\subseteq L_{C^+}},k\leq i} K_k$, $K_{U,C_-\subseteq L_{C^+},i} \overset{\text{def}}{=} \begin{cases} K^{i-1}_{U,C_-\subseteq L_{C^+}}\backslash K_i, & \text{if } i \geq 2 \\ \varnothing, & \text{if } i = 1 \end{cases}$, $K_{-,C_-\subseteq L_{C^+},i} \overset{\text{def}}{=} L_{C^+}\backslash (C_- + K^i_{U,C_-\subseteq L_{C^+}}) = L_{C^+}\backslash(C_{10} \cup K^i_{U,C_-\subseteq L_{C^+}})$ and $\mathcal{FS}^*_{C_-\subseteq L_{C^+}} \overset{\text{def}}{=} \{L'' \overset{\text{def}}{=} C_- + K_i + K'_i + K^\sim_i | K_i \in K_{\min,C_-\subseteq L_{C^+}}, K'_i \subseteq K_{U,C_-\subseteq L_{C^+},i}, K^\sim_i \subseteq K_{-,C_-\subseteq L_{C^+},i}$ and $(K_k \not\subseteq K_i + K'_i, \forall K_k \in K_{\min,C_-\subseteq L_{C^+}} : 1 \leq k < i)^{(*)}, 1 \leqslant i \leqslant M\}$.

$$\mathcal{FS}^*_{C_-\subseteq L_{C^+},+L_{C^*}} \overset{\text{def}}{=} \left\{L' \overset{\text{def}}{=} L'' + L^\sim | L'' \in \mathcal{FS}^*_{C_-\subseteq L_{C^+}}, L^\sim \in 2^{[C_{10}\backslash C_{21}\subseteq L_{C^*}]*}\right\}. \tag{3a}$$

And if $\mathcal{G}_{C_{11},\not\subseteq C_{21}}(L) = \varnothing$ then we assign $\mathcal{FS}^*_{C_{10}\subseteq L_{C_{11}},C_{20}\not\subseteq,G\not\subseteq C_{21}} \equiv \lfloor L \rfloor_{C_{10}\subseteq L_{C_{11}},C_{20}\not\subseteq,G\not\subseteq C_{21}} \overset{\text{def}}{=} \varnothing$. On the contrary, we denote $\lfloor L \rfloor_{C_{10}\subseteq L_{C_{11}},G\not\subseteq C_{21}} \overset{\text{def}}{=} \{L' \in \mathcal{FS}_{C_{10}\subseteq L_{C_{11}},\not\subseteq C_{21}} | (\exists L_i \in \mathcal{G}_{C_{11},\not\subseteq C_{21}}(L) : L' \supseteq L_i)$ and $(L_k \not\subseteq L', \forall L_k \in \mathcal{G}_{C^+}(L))\}$, $K^i_{U,C_{10}\subseteq L_{C_{11}}} \overset{\text{def}}{=} \bigcup_{K_k\in K^+_{\min,C_{10}\subseteq L_{C_{11}},\not\subseteq C_{21}},k\leq i} K_k$,

$K_{U,C_{10}\subseteq L_{C_{11}},i} \overset{\text{def}}{=} \begin{cases} K^{i-1}_{U,C_{10}\subseteq L_{C_{11}}}\backslash K_i, \text{if } i \geq 2 \\ \varnothing, \text{if } i = 1 \end{cases}$,

$K_{-,C_{10}\subseteq L_{C_{11}},i} \overset{\text{def}}{=} L_{C_{11}}\backslash(C_{10} + K^i_{U,C_{10}\subseteq L_{C_{11}}})$ and:

$$\mathcal{FS}^*_{C_{10}\subseteq L_{C_{11}},G\not\subseteq C_{21}} \overset{\text{def}}{=} \{L' \overset{\text{def}}{=} C_{10} + K_i + K'_i + K^\sim_i | K_i \in K_{\min,C_{10}\subseteq L_{C_{11}},G\not\subseteq C_{21}}, K'_i \subseteq K_{U,C_{10}\subseteq L_{C_{11}},i}, K^\sim_i \subseteq K_{-,C_{10}\subseteq L_{C_{11}},i} \text{ and } (K_k \not\subseteq K_i + K'_i, \forall K_k \in K^+_{\min,C_{10}\subseteq L_{C_{11}},\not\subseteq C_{21}} : 1 \leq k < i)^{(**)}, \forall i > M\}. \tag{3b}$$

Finally, we denote $\mathcal{FS}^*_{C_{10}\subseteq L_{C_{11}},\not\subseteq C_{21}} \overset{\text{def}}{=}$

$$\mathcal{FS}^*_{C_-\subseteq L_{C^+},+L_{C^*}} + \mathcal{FS}^*_{C_{10}\subseteq L_{C_{11}},rmG\not\subseteq C_{21}}. \tag{3c}$$

Obviously, $\mathcal{FS}_{C_{10}\subseteq L_{C_{11}},\not\subseteq C_{21}}, = \lfloor L \rfloor_{C_-\subseteq L_{C^+},+L_{C^*}} + \lfloor L \rfloor_{C_{10}\subseteq L_{C_{11}},G\not\subseteq C_{21}}$.

Proposition 4 (Partition, explicit structure and unique representation of $\boldsymbol{\mathcal{FS}_{C_{10}\subseteq L_{C_{11}},\not\subseteq C_{21}}}$) *Assume that the hypothesis* (H_1) *is satisfied and let* $L \in \mathcal{FCS}_{C_{10}\subseteq C_{11},\not\subseteq C_{21}}(s_0, s_1)$, *then*

(i) *All frequent itemsets in* $\mathcal{FS}^*_{C_-\subseteq L_{C^+}}$, $\mathcal{FS}^*_{C_{10}\subseteq L_{C_{11}},G\not\subseteq C_{21}}$, *and thus, all ones in* $\mathcal{FS}^*_{C_-\subseteq L_{C^+},+L_{C^*}}$ *and* $\mathcal{FS}^*_{C_{10}\subseteq L_{C_{11}},\not\subseteq C_{21}}$ *have a unique representation and are generated distinctly;*

(ii)

$$\mathcal{FS}_{C_{10}\subseteq C_{11},\not\subseteq C_{21}} = \mathcal{FS}^*_{C_{10}\subseteq C_{11},\not\subseteq C_{21}}. \quad (4)$$

(i.e. each constrained sub-class $\mathcal{FS}_{C_{10}\subseteq L_{C_{11}},\not\subseteq C_{21}}$ *is partitioned into two disjoint subsets* $\mathcal{FS}^*_{C_-\subseteq L_{C^+},+L_{C^*}}$, $\mathcal{FS}^*_{C_{10}\subseteq L_{C_{11}},G\not\subseteq C_{21}}$*).*

Example 3 (Illustrating disjoint partition and structure of $\mathcal{FS}_{C_{10}\subseteq L_{C_{11}},\not\subseteq C_{21}}$) According to Example 2.1, for $L = afh \in \mathcal{FS}_{C_{10}\subseteq C_{11},\not\subseteq C_{21}}(s_0, s_1)$, $\mathcal{G}_{C_{11}}(L) = \{f, h\}$, we will illustrate the direct generation of two constrained frequent itemsets $\{fa, fha\}$ in $\mathcal{FS}_{C_{10}\subseteq L_{C_{11}},\not\subseteq L_{C_{21}}}$, using (4) based on the splitting of $\mathcal{G}_{C_{11}}(L) = \mathcal{G}_{C^+}(L)+\mathcal{G}_{C_{11},\not\subseteq C_{21}}(L)$, where $C^+ = L_{C^+} = ah$, $\mathcal{G}_{C^+}(L) = \{h\}$, $\mathcal{G}_{C_{11},\not\subseteq C_{21}}(L) = \{f\}$. Besides, $C_- = a$, $L_{C^*} = \{f\}$, $K_{\min,C_-\subseteq L_{C^+}} = \{K_1 = h\}$, $K_{U,C_-\subseteq L_{C^+},1} = \varnothing$, $K_{-,C_-\subseteq L_{C^+},1} = \varnothing$, $2^{[C_{10}\backslash C_{21}\subseteq L_{C^*}]*} = \{f\}$, $\mathcal{FS}^*_{C_-\subseteq L_{C^+},+L_{C^*}} = \{L' \stackrel{\text{def}}{=} L'' + L^{\sim} = a + h + f = ahf\}$; $K_{\min,C_{10}\subseteq L_{C_{11}},G\not\subseteq C_{21}} = \{K_2 = f\}$, $K_{U,C_{10}\subseteq L_{C_{11}},2} = \{h\}$, $K_{-,C_{10}\subseteq L_{C_{11}},2} = afh\backslash\{a + hf\} = \varnothing$, $\mathcal{FS}^*_{C_{10}\subseteq L_{C_{11}},G\not\subseteq C_{21}} = \{L' = a+f+K'_2+\varnothing | \varnothing \subseteq K'_2 \subseteq \{h\}$ and $(K_1 \not\subseteq K_2 + K'_2)\} = \{af, \text{with} K'_2 = \varnothing\} = \{af\}$, since with $K'_2 = h$, then $h = K_1 \subseteq K_2 + K'_2 = fh$. So we reject $L' = afh$ (as this itemset was belong to $\mathcal{FS}^*_{C_-\subseteq L_{C^+},+L_{C^*}}$) already). Thus, $\mathcal{FS}_{C_{10}\subseteq L_{C_{11}},\not\subseteq C_{21}} = \mathcal{FS}^*_{C_-\subseteq L_{C^+},+L_{C^*}} + \mathcal{FS}^*_{C_{10}\subseteq L_{C_{11}},G\not\subseteq C_{21}} = \{ahf, af\}$.

Remark 2 (An effective way to calculate subsets $K_{U,i}$, $K_{-,i}$ when finding sets in $\mathcal{FS}^*$)

(a) To calculate $\mathcal{FS}^*_{C_-\subseteq L_{C^+}}$ more effectively, we set $K^i_U \stackrel{\text{def}}{=} K^i_{U,C_-\subseteq L_{C^+}}$, $K_{U,i} \stackrel{\text{def}}{=} K^{i-1}_U\backslash K_i$, $K_{-,i} \stackrel{\text{def}}{=} L_{C^+}\backslash(C_- + K^i_U)$ and then find that $K_{U,i} = [(K^{i-2}_U\backslash K_{i-1}) + K_{i-1}]\backslash K_i = (K_{U,i-1} + K_{i-1})\backslash K_i$, $K_{-,i} = K_{-,i-1}\backslash K_i$, $\forall i \geq 1$ and $K_0 \stackrel{\text{def}}{=} K_{U,0} \stackrel{\text{def}}{=} \varnothing$, $K_{-,0} \stackrel{\text{def}}{=} L_{C^+}\backslash C_-$. Thus, $K_{U,i} = \begin{cases}(K_{U,i-1} + K_{i-1})\backslash K_i, \text{if } 1 \leqslant i \leqslant M \\ \varnothing, \text{if } i = 0\end{cases}$, $K_{-,i} = \begin{cases}K_{-,i-1}\backslash K_i, \text{if } 1 \leqslant i \leqslant M \\ L_{C^+}\backslash C_-, \text{if } i = 0\end{cases}$ và $K_0 \stackrel{\text{def}}{=} \varnothing$.

(b) Similarly, we also have more effective recursive expressions for $\mathcal{FS}^*_{C_{10}\subseteq L_{C_{11}},G\not\subseteq C_{21}}$. If we set $K^i_U \stackrel{\text{def}}{=} K^i_{U,C_{10}\subseteq L_{C_{11}}}$, $K_{U,i} \stackrel{\text{def}}{=} K^{i-1}_U\backslash K_i$, $K_{-,i} \stackrel{\text{def}}{=} L_{C_{11}}\backslash(C_{10} + K^i_U)$, then, for $\forall i \geqslant M+1 \geqslant 2$: $K_{U,i} = (K_{U,i-1} + K_{i-1})\backslash K_i$, $K_{-,i} = \begin{cases}K_{-,i-1}\backslash K_i, \text{if } i \geqslant M+2 \\ [(L_{C^*}\backslash C_{10}) + K_{-,M}]\backslash K_{M+1}, \text{if } i = M+1\end{cases}$. Indeed, for $L_{C^*} = L \cap C_{11}\backslash C_{21}$, since $K_{-,M+1} = L \cap C_{11}\backslash(C_{10} + K^{M+1}_U) = [L_{C^*}\backslash(C_{10} + K^M_U)\backslash K_{M+1}] + [L \cap C_{11} \cap C_{21}\backslash(C_{10}+K^M_U)\backslash K_{M+1}] = [L_{C^*}\backslash C_{10}\backslash K_{M+1}]+[L\cap C_{11}\cap C_{21}\backslash(C_{10} \cap C_{21} + K^M_U\backslash K_{M+1}] = [L_{C^*}\backslash C_{10}\backslash K_{M+1}] + [L_{C^+}\backslash(C_- + K^M_U)\backslash K_{M+1}] = [(L_{C^*}\backslash C_{10}) + K_{-,M}]\backslash K_{M+1}$. *Especially, if* $M = 0$, *then* $K_{-,1} = [(L_{C^*}\backslash C_{10}) + K_{-,0}]\backslash K_1 = [(L_{C^*}\backslash C_{10}) + (L_{C^+}\backslash C_-)]\backslash K_1 = [(L_{C^*}\backslash C_{10}) + (L_{C^+}\backslash C_{10})]\backslash K_1 = L_{C_{11}}\backslash(C_{10} + K_1)$.

* In brief, for $\forall M \geqslant 0$ ($If\, \mathcal{G}_{C^+}(L) \neq \varnothing$, then $M > 0$; else $M = 0$), if we set

$$.K_{\min} \stackrel{\text{def}}{=} \begin{cases}K_{\min,1} = K_{\min,C_-\subseteq L_{C^+}}, & if\ Begin = 0 \\ K_{\min,2} = K_{\min,C_{10}\subseteq L_{C_{11}},G\not\subseteq C_{21}}, & if\ Begin = M\end{cases},$$

$$K^+_{\min} \stackrel{\text{def}}{=} K_{\min,1} + K_{\min,2},$$

$$K^+_{\min\_} \stackrel{\text{def}}{=} \begin{cases}K_{\min,1}, & if\ Begin = 0 \\ K^+_{\min}, & if\ Begin = M\end{cases};$$

$$.K_{U,i} = \begin{cases}(K_{U,i-1} + K_{i-1})\backslash K_i, & if i \geqslant 2 \\ , & if i = 1\end{cases}, \forall Begin \in \{0; M\} and K_{U,0} = \varnothing;$$

$$.K_{-,i} = \begin{cases}K_{-,i-1}\backslash K_i, & if\ i \geqslant Begin + 2 \\ First\_\backslash K_i, & if\ i = Begin + 1\end{cases} .\forall Begin \geq 0 \text{ where } First\_ = \begin{cases}L_{C^+}\backslash C_-, & if\ Begin = 0 \\ (L_{C^*}\backslash C_{10}) + K_{-,M}, & if\ Begin = M\end{cases}$$

and

$$K_{-,0} \stackrel{\text{def}}{=} L_{C^+}\backslash C_-;$$

$$.\ Sub\_L = \begin{cases}C_-, & if\ Begin = 0 \\ C_{10}, & if\ Begin = M\end{cases}.$$

Then, we can calculate $L''in\mathcal{FS}^*_{C_-L_{C^+}}, and$ $L'in\mathcal{FS}^*_{C_{10}\subseteq L_{C_{11}},G\not\subseteq C_{21}}$ as follows

$L' \stackrel{\text{def}}{=} Sub\_L + K_i + K'_i + K^{\sim}_i$, where $K_i \in K_{\min,M}$, $K'_i \subseteq K_{U,i}$, $K^{\sim}_i \subseteq K_{-,i}$ and $(K_k \not\subseteq K_i + K'_i, \forall K_k \in K_{\min}, C_{10} \subseteq L_{C_{11}}, \not\subseteq C^+_{21} : 1 \leq k < i), \forall i \geqslant Begin + 1$, using the general algorithm below.

$$\mathcal{FS}_{Sub\_L}{}^* = \boldsymbol{MFS - EDC - SubClass}$$
$$(Sub\_L, K_{\min}, \&Begin, \&K_{U,\text{Begin}}, \&K_{\_,Begin}, K^+_{\min\_}).$$

Then

$$\mathcal{FS}^*_{C_-\subseteq L_{C^+}} = \textbf{MFS-EDC-SubClass}$$
$$(C_-, K_{\min,1}, Begin = 1, KUBegin, K\_Begin, K_{\min,1})$$

And after the algorithm finishes, we obtain $Begin = M$, $KUBegin = K_{U,M}$, $K\_Begin = K_{-,M}$. After that, we calculate new values, $Begin = M + 1$, $KUBegin = (K_{U,M} + K_M)\backslash K_{M+1}$, $K\_Begin = K_{-,M}\backslash K_{M+1}$, to find $\mathcal{FS}^*_{C_{10}\subseteq L_{C_{11}},G\not\subseteq C_{21}} =$ **MFS-EDC-SubClass**$(C_{10}, K_{\min,2}, Begin = M + 1, K_{U,Begin}, K_{-,Begin}, K^+_{\min})$.

(c) Note that, the condition (**) is not satisfied if $\exists K_i \in K_{\min,C_{10}\subseteq L_{C_{11}},G\not\subseteq C_{21}} \cap K_{\min,C_-\subseteq L_{C^+}}$. Thus,

```
FS*_Sub_L MFS-EDC-SubClass(Sub_L, K_min, &Beg, &KUBeg, &K_Beg, K+_min_)
FS*_Sub_L := ∅;
if (K_min) then return ∅;
K_U,Beg := KUBeg; K_-,Beg := K_Beg;                  // remark 2.b
for (i=Beg+1; K_i ∈ K_min; i++) do {
   K_U,i := (K_U,i-1+K_i-1)\K_i;                     // remark 2.b
   for each (K'_i ⊆ K_U,i) do {
      IsDuplicate := false;               // saving only once A ≝ K_i + K'_i
      for (j=1; K_j ∈ K+_min_, j < i; j++) do
         if (K_j ⊆ K_i+K'_i) then {
            IsDuplicate := true; break;
         }
      if (not(IsDuplicate)) then {
         K_-,i := K_-,i-1\K_i;                       // remark 2.b
         for each (K~_i ⊆ K_-,i) do
            FS*_Sub_L := FS*_Sub_L + {Sub_L + K_i + K'_i + K~_i};
      }
   } // for each K'_i
} // for i
Beg = i-1; KUBeg := K_U,Beg; K_Beg := K_-,Beg;
return FS*_Sub_L;
```

Fig. 3 MFS-EDC-SubClass algorithm

$K_{\min,C_{10}\subseteq L_{C_{11}},G\not\subset C_{21}}$ and $K^+_{\min,C_{10}\subseteq L_{C_{11}},\not\subset C_{21}}$ can be replaced by $K_{\min,C_{10}\subseteq L_{C_{11}},G\not\subseteq C_{21}} \stackrel{\text{def}}{=} Minimal\{K_i \stackrel{\text{def}}{=} L_i\backslash C_{10},\ L_i \in \mathcal{G}_{C_{11},\not\subseteq C_{21}}(L), \forall i > M\}\backslash K_{\min,C_-\subseteq L_{C^+}}$ and $K^+_{\min,C_{10}\subseteq L_{C_{11}},\not\subseteq C_{21}} \stackrel{\text{def}}{=} K_{\min,C_-\subseteq L_{C^+}} + K_{\min,C_{10}\subseteq L_{C_{11}},G\not\subseteq C_{21}}$, respectively (Fig. 3).

(d) Since K_k and K_i are two minimal subsets belonging to different sets $K_{\min,C_-\subseteq L_{C^+}}$ and $K_{\min,C_{10}\subseteq L_{C_{11}},G\not\subseteq C_{21}}$, respectively, so they can still get equal values and we are unable to replace the sign $\not\subset$ in $^{(**)}$ by $\not\subseteq$, i.e. if $K_k = K'_i + K^\sim_i$, then we still eliminate K'_i. Indeed, consider the example in [4,16], for $L = acdfh, \mathcal{G}(L) = \$\{cd, acf\}, supp(L) = 1/6, C_{10} = afd, C_{11} = acdf, C_{21} = cd, s_0 = 1/6, s_1 = 1$. Then, we have $C^+ = cd, C_- = d, L_{C^*} = af, \mathcal{G}_{C_{11}}(L) = \mathcal{G}(L), \mathcal{G}_{C^+}(L) = \{L_1 = cd\}, \mathcal{G}_{C_{11},\not\subseteq C_{21}}(L) = \{L_2 = caf\}, K_{\min,C_-\subseteq L_{C^+}} = \{K_1 = c\}, K_{\min,C_{10}\subseteq L_{C_{11}},G\not\subseteq C_{21}} = \{K_2 = c\}, \varnothing \subset af \subseteq L^\sim \subseteq af, K_{U,C_-\subseteq L_{C^+},1} = \varnothing, K_{-,C_-\subseteq L_{C^+},1} = acdf\backslash(afd + c) = \varnothing, \mathcal{FS}^*_{C_-L_{C^+},+L_{C^*}} = \{L'' + L^\sim = (d + c + \varnothing + \varnothing) + af\} = \{dcaf\}; K'_2 \subseteq K_{U,C_{10}\subseteq L_{C_{11}},2} = K_1\backslash K_2 = \varnothing, K^\sim_2 \subseteq K_{-,C_{10}\subseteq L_{C_{11}},2} = acdf\backslash(afd + c) = \varnothing, K'_2 = \varnothing, K^\sim_2 = \varnothing, K_1 = K_2 + \varnothing = c$ and then obtain a frequent itemset $L' = afd + c = afdc$ which coincides with $L' = dcaf$ in $\mathcal{FS}^*_{C_-L_{C^+},+L_{C^*}}$. Therefore, we still wipe out L' corresponding with $K'_2 = \varnothing$ and $\mathcal{FS}^*_{C_{10}\subseteq L_{C_{11}},G\not\subseteq C_{21}} = \varnothing$. Hence, $\mathcal{FS}^*_{C_{10}\subseteq L_{C_{11}},G\not\subseteq C_{21}} = \mathcal{FS}^*_{C_-\subseteq L_{C^+},+L_{C^*}} = \{dcaf\}$.

Theorem 1 (Structure of the solution set $\mathcal{FS}_{C_{10}\subseteq C_{11},\not\subseteq C_{21}}(s_0, s_1)$)

Assume that the hypothesis (H$_1$) *is satisfied. Then*

$$\mathcal{FS}_{C_{10}\subseteq C_{11},\not\subseteq C_{21},}(s_0, s_1) = \sum\nolimits_{L\in\mathcal{FCS}_{C_{10}\subseteq C_{11},\not\subseteq C_{21}}(s_0,s_1)} \times\mathcal{FS}^*_{C_{10}\subseteq L_{C_{11}},\not\subseteq C_{21}}. \quad (5)$$

Proof It is a consequence of (2) in Proposition 3 and (4) in Proposition 4. □

Remark 3 (Some typically special cases) When the constraints are gotten special values, we obtain better results than those known in out former papers (since the way of calculating sets K^i_U, $K_{U,i}$ and $K_{-,i}$ to find solution sub-classes in this new version will take time less and thus more effective than the former one, according to Remark 2).

(i) To show the structure of frequent itemsets with simple double constraint $\mathcal{FS}_{C_{10}\subseteq C_{11}}(s_0, s_1)$ in [17], we choose $C_{21} = \varnothing$, with conditions changed as follows: $C^* = C_{11} \neq \varnothing, C^+ = C_- = \varnothing, \mathcal{FCS}_{C_{10}\subseteq C_{11}}(s_0, s_1) \stackrel{\text{def}}{=} \{L \in \mathcal{FCS}(s_0, s_1)|C_{10} \subseteq L_{C_{11}}, L_{C_{11}} \neq \varnothing, \mathcal{G}_{C_{11}}(L) \neq \varnothing\}$. Since $\mathcal{G}_{C^+}(L) = \varnothing$, $K_{\min,C_-\subseteq L_{C^+}} = \varnothing, M = 0$, so $\mathcal{G}_{C_{11}}(L) \equiv \mathcal{G}_{C_{11},\not\subseteq\varnothing}(L)$, $\mathcal{FS}^*_{C_-L_{C^+},,+L_{C^*}} = \varnothing$, let $K_{\min,C_{10}\subseteq L_{C_{11}}} \stackrel{\text{def}}{=} K^+_{\min,C_{10}\subseteq L_{C_{11}},\not\subseteq\varnothing} = K_{\min,C_{10}\subseteq L_{C_{11}},G\not\subset\varnothing} = Minimal\{K_i \stackrel{\text{def}}{=} L_i\backslash C_{10}, L_i \in \mathcal{G}_{C_{11}}(L), i \geqslant 1\}$ and $\mathcal{FS}^*_{C_{10}\subseteq L_{C_{11}}} \stackrel{\text{def}}{=} \mathcal{FS}^*_{C_{10}\subseteq L_{C_{11}},,G\not\subseteq\varnothing} = \{L' \stackrel{\text{def}}{=} C_{10} + K_i + K'_i + K^\sim_i | K_i \in K_{\min,C_{10}\subseteq L_{C_{11}}}, K'_i \subseteq K_{U,i}, K^\sim_i \subseteq K_{-,i}$ and $(K_k \not\subseteq K_i + K'_i, \forall K_k \in K_{\min,C_{10}\subseteq L_{C_{11}}} : 1 \leq k < i)\}$, vói $K_{U,i} = \begin{cases}(K_{U,i-1} + K_{i-1})\backslash K_i, if\ i \geqslant 1\\ \varnothing, if\ i = 0\end{cases}$, $K_{-,i} = \begin{cases}K_{-,i-1}\backslash K_i, if\ i \geqslant 1\\ L_{C_{11}}\backslash C_{10}, if\ i = 0\end{cases}$ and $K_0 \stackrel{\text{def}}{=} \varnothing$ (see Remark 2).

(ii) To obtain the results presented in [16] or in [2] with single constraints $\mathcal{FS}_{C_{10}\subseteq}(s_0, s_1)$ or $\mathcal{FS}_{C_{11}}(s_0, s_1)$, respectively, we only need to not consider ones C_{11} or C_{10} in (i) which can be performed by assigning $C_{11} = \mathcal{A}$ or $C_{10} = \varnothing$, respectively.

(iii) When $C_{10} = C_{21} = \varnothing, C_{11} = \mathcal{A}, s_1 = 1$, we have the structure of frequent itemsets without constraints, $\mathcal{FS}^*(s_0) = \mathcal{FS}^*_{\varnothing\subseteq\mathcal{A},\not\subseteq\varnothing}(s_0, s_1)$. Then, $\mathcal{G}_{C_{11}}(L) = \mathcal{G}(L), \forall L \in \mathcal{FCS}_{\varnothing\subseteq\mathcal{A},\not\subseteq\varnothing}(s_0, s_1) = \mathcal{FCS}(s_0) = \{L \in \mathcal{CS} : \varnothing\neq L, supp(L) \geqslant s_0\}$ and $\mathcal{FS}^*_{\subseteq L} \stackrel{\text{def}}{=} \{L' \stackrel{\text{def}}{=} L_i + L'_i + L^\sim_i | L_i \in \mathcal{G}(L), L'_i \subseteq L_{U,i}, L^\sim_i \subseteq L_{-,i}$ and $(L_k \not\subseteq L_i + L'_i, \forall L_k \in \mathcal{G}(L): 1 \leq k < i)\}$, where $K_{U,i} = \begin{cases}(K_{U,i-1}+K_{i-1})\backslash K_i, if\ i\geqslant 1\\ \varnothing, if\ i=0\end{cases}$, $K_{-,i} = \begin{cases}K_{-,i-1}\backslash K_i, if\ i \geqslant 1\\ L, if\ i = 0\end{cases}$ and $K_0 \stackrel{\text{def}}{=} \varnothing$.

(iv) To show the structure of frequent itemsets with the dualistic constraint $\mathcal{FS}_{\not\subseteq C_{21}}(s_0, s_1) \stackrel{\text{def}}{=} \{A \in \mathcal{FS}(s_0, s_1)|A \not\subseteq C_{21}\}$ in [3], we choose $C_{10} = \varnothing, C_{11} = \mathcal{A}$. Conditions are changed as follows: $C^* = \mathcal{A}\backslash C_{21} \neq \varnothing, supp(\mathcal{A}) \leqslant s_1, C^+ = C_{21}, C_- = \varnothing, \mathcal{FCS}_{C_{10}\subseteq C_{11}}(s_0, s_1) \stackrel{\text{def}}{=} \{L \in \mathcal{FCS}(s_0, s_1)|L \not\subseteq C_{21}\}, \mathcal{G}(L) = \mathcal{G}_{C_{21}}(L) + \mathcal{G}_{\not\subseteq C_{21}}(L)$,

Fig. 4 MFS-EDC algorithm

$\mathcal{FS}_{C_{10}\subseteq C_{11},\not\subseteq C_{21}}(s_0,s_1)$ **MFS-EDC**($\mathcal{LCG}$, s_0, s_1, C_{10}, C_{11}, C_{21})
1. $\mathcal{FS}_{C_{10}\subseteq C_{11},\not\subseteq C_{21}}(s_0,s_1) := \varnothing$; $C^* := C_{11}\backslash C_{21}$;
2. **if** ($s_0>s_1$ **or** supp(C_{10})$<s_0$ **or** supp(C_{11})$>s_1$ **or** $C_{10}\backslash C_{11} \neq \varnothing$ **or** $C^* = \varnothing$) **then** **return** $\varnothing$; // (H_1) is not true
3. $\mathcal{FCS}_{C_{10}\subseteq C_{11},\not\subseteq C_{21}}(s_0,s_1) := $ **MFCS_EDC**($\mathcal{LCG}$, s_0, s_1, C_{10}, C_{11}, C_{21});
4. **for each** (<L, supp(L), $\mathcal{G}_{C_{11}}(L)$> $\in\mathcal{FCS}_{C_{10}\subseteq C_{11},\not\subseteq C_{21}}(s_0,s_1)$) **do** {
5. $\quad L_{C_{11}} := $ L$\cap C_{11}$;
6. $\quad \mathcal{FS}^*_{C_{10}\subseteq L_{C_{11}},\not\subseteq C_{21},} := $ **MFS_EDC_OneClass**(C_{10}, C_{11}, C_{21}, $\mathcal{G}_{C_{11}}(L)$);
7. $\quad \mathcal{FS}_{C_{10}\subseteq C_{11},\not\subseteq C_{21}}(s_0,s_1) := \mathcal{FS}_{C_{10}\subseteq C_{11},\not\subseteq C_{21}}(s_0,s_1) + \mathcal{FS}^*_{C_{10}\subseteq L_{C_{11}},\not\subseteq C_{21}}$;
8. }
9. **return** $\mathcal{FS}_{C_{10}\subseteq C_{11},\not\subseteq C_{21}}(s_0,s_1)$;

Fig. 5 **a** MFS-EDC-OneClass algorithm. **b** MFS-EDC-FirstSubClass algorithm. **c** MFS-EDC-SecondSubClass algorithm

$\mathcal{FS}^*_{C_{10}\subseteq L_{C_{11}},\not\subseteq C_{21},}$ **MFS-EDC-OneClass**(C_{10}, C_{11}, C_{21}, L, $\mathcal{G}_{C_{11}}(L)$):
1. $\mathcal{G}_{C^+}(L) = \{L_i\in\mathcal{G}_{C_{11}}(L)| L_i\subseteq C_{21}\}$; $\mathcal{G}_{C_{11},\not\subseteq C_{21}}(L) := \{L_i\in\mathcal{G}_{C_{11}}(L) | L_i\not\subseteq C_{21}\}$;
2. $K_{min,1} = $ Minimal $\{K_i \overset{\text{def}}{=} L_i\backslash C_-, L_i\in\mathcal{G}_{C^+}(L), 1\leqslant i\leqslant M\}$; // if $\mathcal{G}_{C^+}(L)$ khac=$\varnothing$, then $M\geqslant 1$, else $M=0$
3. $K_{min,2}= $ Minimal$\{K_i \overset{\text{def}}{=} L_i\backslash C_{10}, L_i\in\mathcal{G}_{C_{11},\not\subseteq C_{21}}(L), i\geqslant M+1\}\backslash K_{min,C_-\subseteq L_{C^+}}$;   // Remark 2.c
4. $K^+_{min} = K_{min,1}+K_{min,2}$;
5. $\mathcal{FS}^*_{C_-\subseteq L_{C^+},+L_{C^*}} := $ **MFS_EDC_FirstSubClass**(C_{10}, C_{11}, C_{21}, L, $K_{min,1}$, Beg, KUBeg, K_Beg);
6. $\mathcal{FS}^*_{C_{10}\subseteq L_{C_{11}},G\not\subseteq C_{21}} := $ **MFS_EDC_SecondSubClass**(C_{10}, C_{11}, C_{21}, L, $K_{min,2}$, Beg, KUBeg, K_Beg, K^+_{min});
7. $\mathcal{FS}^*_{C_{10}\subseteq L_{C_{11}},\not\subseteq C_{21}} := \mathcal{FS}^*_{C_-\subseteq L_{C^+},+L_{C^*}} + \mathcal{FS}^*_{C_{10}\subseteq L_{C_{11}},G\not\subseteq C_{21}}$;
8. **return** $\mathcal{FS}^*_{C_{10}\subseteq L_{C_{11}},\not\subseteq C_{21}}$;

(a)

$\mathcal{FS}^*_{C_-\subseteq L_{C^+},+L_{C^*}}$ **MFS_EDC_FirstSubClass**(C_{10}, C_{11}, C_{21}, L, $K_{min,1}$, &Beg, &KUBeg, &K_Beg)
1. $\mathcal{FS}^*_{C_-\subseteq L_{C^+},+L_{C^*}} := \varnothing$; $K_0=\varnothing$; $K_{\_0}=L_{C^+}\backslash C_-$; Beg=0; KUBeg=$\varnothing$; K_Beg=$K_{\_0}$;
2. $L_{C^*} := (L\cap C_{11})\backslash C_{21}$; $C_* := C_{10}\backslash C_{21}$; $C_- := C_{10}\cap C_{21}$; $C^+ := C_{11}\cap C_{21}$; $L_{C^+}=$L$\cap C^+$;
3. **If** ($K_{min,1}\neq\varnothing$) **then** {
4. $\quad$ Beg=1; First =$L_{C^+}\backslash C_-$; K_Beg= First$\backslash K_{Beg}$;
5. $\quad \mathcal{FS}^*_{C_-\subseteq L_{C^+}} = $ **MFS_EDC_SubClass**(C_-, $K_{min,1}$, Beg, KUBeg, K_Beg, $K_{min,1}$);
6. $\quad$ **for each** (L'' $\in\mathcal{FS}^*_{C_-\subseteq L_{C^+}}$) **do**
7. $\quad\quad$ **for each** (L$^\sim\subseteq L_{C^*}$ | $C_*\subseteq$ L$^\sim$ and L$^\sim\neq\varnothing$) **do**
8. $\quad\quad\quad \mathcal{FS}^*_{C_-\subseteq L_{C^+},+L_{C^*}} := \mathcal{FS}^*_{C_-\subseteq L_{C^+},+L_{C^*}} + \{L''+L^\sim\}$;
9. }
10. **return** $\mathcal{FS}^*_{C_-\subseteq L_{C^+},+L_{C^*}}$;

(b)

$\mathcal{FS}^*_{C_{10}\subseteq L_{C_{11}},G\not\subseteq C_{21}}$ **MFS_EDC_SecondSubClass**(C_{10}, C_{11}, C_{21}, L, $K_{min,2}$, Beg, KUBeg, K_Beg, K^+_{min})
1. First = (($L\cap C_{11}$)$\backslash C_{21}\backslash C_{10}$)+K_Beg; Beg=Beg+1;
2. K_Beg= First$\backslash K_{Beg}$; $KUBeg =(KUBeg+K_{Beg-1})\backslash K_{Beg}$;
3. $\mathcal{FS}^*_{C_{10}\subseteq L_{C_{11}},G\not\subseteq C_{21}} = $ **MFS_EDC_SubClass**(C_{10}, $K_{min,2}$, Beg, KUBeg, K_Beg, K^+_{min});
4. **return** $\mathcal{FS}^*_{C_{10}\subseteq L_{C_{11}},G\not\subseteq C_{21}}$;

(c)

$\mathcal{FS}^*_{\subseteq L_{C_{21}},+L\backslash C_{21}} \overset{\text{def}}{=} \{L' \overset{\text{def}}{=} L'' + L^\sim|L'' \in \mathcal{FS}^*_{\subseteq L_{C_{21}}},$ $\varnothing \subset L^\sim \subseteq L\backslash C_{21}\}$, $\mathcal{FS}^*_{\subseteq L,G\not\subseteq C_{21}} \overset{\text{def}}{=} \mathcal{FS}^*_{\varnothing\subseteq L,G\not\subseteq C_{21}}$ and $\mathcal{FS}^*_{\not\subseteq L_{C_{21}}} = \mathcal{FS}^*_{\subseteq L_{C_{21}},+L\backslash C_{21}} + \mathcal{FS}^*_{\subseteq L,G\not\subseteq C_{21}}$.

According to Propositions 3 and 4, we obtain two procedures *MFS-EDC-FirstSubClass* and *MFS-EDC-SecondSubClass* (pseudo code shown in Fig. 5a, b) to produce constrained frequent itemsets in two sub-classes $\mathcal{FS}^*_{C_-\subseteq L_{C^+},+L_{C^*}}$ and $\mathcal{FS}^*_{C_{10}\subseteq L_{C_{11}},G\not\subseteq C_{21}}$, respectively, and then the procedure *MFS-EDC-OneClass* (see in Fig. 5) to generate all constrained frequent itemsets in an equivalence class. Using Theorem 1 and these procedures, the algorithm *MFS-EDC* is proposed, shown in Fig. 4, for mining all frequent itemsets with *EDC*.

5 Experiments

Experiments were performed on a PC with an i5-2400 CPU, 3.10 GHz@ 3.09 GHz PC and 3.16 GB of memory, running on Windows XP. The algorithms were coded in C#. To compare the performance, the source code for *Charm-L* [35], *MinimalGenerators* [34] and *dEclat* [36] was converted to C#. *Charm-L* and *MinimalGenerators* were used to mine the lattice of the closed itemsets and their generators. *dEclat* was used to exploit all frequent itemsets.

To test and evaluate our new proposed algorithm, **MFS-EDC**, we compare its performance to those of two different new post-processing algorithms. The first one is called *MFS-E-EDC* that is a new modified version of *dEclat* for mining frequent itemsets with the extended double constraint. *MFS-E-EDC* is done by integrating constraints s_0 and C_{11} into *dEclat* algorithm to discover only frequent itemsets satisfying two these constraints. Then, *MFS-E-EDC* implements a post-processing step to filter frequent itemsets satisfying the remaining constraints, s_1, C_{10} and C_{21}. The second new post-processing algorithm is named *MFS-PP-EDC* that is a modification of *Gen_Itemsets* [2]. *MFS-PP-EDC* includes two steps. In the first step, it uses *Gen_Itemsets* to mine all frequent itemsets without constraints. The second one is to directly check all generated frequent itemsets on the constraints to filter frequent itemsets satisfying extended double constraint.

We chose benchmark datasets in FIMDR [13] including Pumsb, Connect, Mushroom, Chess, and T40I10D100K to test the algorithms in performance. Pumsb, Connect, Chess, and Mushroom are real and dense, i.e. they produce many long frequent itemsets even for very high support values. The other is synthetic and sparse. Table 1 shows their characteristics.

We keep the support threshold s_1 unchanged at 0.9. Assuming that the size of C_{10} is m, then C_{11} with the size of $m + d{*}|A^F|/100(d. \in [1, 100])$ is chosen. For each pair of datasets (DB) and minimum support (MS), m ranges from 10 to 28 % of $|A^F|$ (step 2 %) and $d = 60$. For each pair of C_{10}'s size and C_{11}'s size, there are 10 value triples of C_{10}, C_{11} and C_{21} randomly selected from A^F (the size of C_{21} is also chosen randomly).

Table 1 Dataset characteristics

Dataset	#Items	#Records	Avg. length
Connect (C)	129	67,557	43
Mushroom (M)	119	8124	23
Pumsb (P)	7117	49,046	74
Chess (Ch)	75	3196	37
T40I10D100K (T40)	1000	100,000	40

Table 2 Time reductions of *MFS-EDC* compared to *MFS-PP-EDC* and *MFS-E-EDC*

DS-MS	R_PP (%)	R_E (%)	DS-MS	R_PP (%)	R_E (%)
M-14	1.50	6.32	Ch-76	33.06	17.58
M-12	1.44	6.86	Ch-72	25.73	27.86
M-10	0.60	9.82	C-82	4.48	5.12
M-8	0.53	10.40	C-80	23.62	6.71
M-6	0.34	11.97	C-78	13.01	5.73
P-82	65.87	5.89	C-76	9.11	6.20
P-78	26.06	9.62	C-72	4.03	6.27
P-76	17.70	12.80	T40-1	45.27	5.41
P-74	11.71	16.17	T40-0.8	42.23	5.12
P-72	8.57	23.24	T40-0.6	41.12	4.87
Ch-84	3.51	2.94	T40-0.4	39.23	4.13
Ch-82	7.54	5.82	T40-0.2	38.01	3.98
Ch-80	2.85	2.90			

Let *T_EDC*, *T_PP_EDC*, and *T_E_EDC* be the average execution times of *MFS-EDC*, *MFS-PP-EDC*, and *MFS-E-EDC* for 100 selected extended double constraints.

Table 2 shows the experimental evaluation of *MFS-EDC* against *MFS-PP-EDC* and *MFS-E-EDC*, where column *DS-MS* denotes the dataset *DS* with the minimum support *MS* (for example, $M - 14$ means the dataset Mushroom with the minimum support of 14 %), column *R_PP* shows the ratios of *T_EDC* and *T_PP_EDC*, and column *R_E* reveals the rates of *T_EDC* and *T_E_EDC*. Compared to *MFS-PP-EDC*, *MFS-EDC* is faster for all selected datasets. The time is reduced by 65.87–0.34 %. *MFS-EDC* is also much faster than *MFS-E-EDC* for all datasets with the time reduction from 27.86 to 2.90 %.

We found that the reason for the reduction in the mining time of *MFS-EDC* in comparison with *MFS-PP-EDC* and *MFS-E-EDC* is because there are a large number of candidates which fail the last test of both *MFS-PP-EDC* and *MFS-E-EDC*, leading to their lower performance. Note that, for sparse dataset T10, the time reduction of *MFS-EDC*, compared to *MFS-PP-EDC*, in general, is not high (over 54.73 %) because the number of frequent itemsets is small and their size is small too, leading to a low cost for testing the constraints. However, when compared to *MFS-E-EDC* for this dataset, the figure is quite high, accounting for over 94.59 %. This can be explained that when constraints are changed, *MFS-E-EDC* have to re-scan the original dataset, which will take a lot of mining time, while *MFS-EDC* only needs to travel back to the lattice.

Figure 6a, b show the comparisons of the average execution times for various support values. The performance and scalability of *MFS-EDC* are superior to those of *MFS-PP-EDC* and *MFS-E-EDC*.

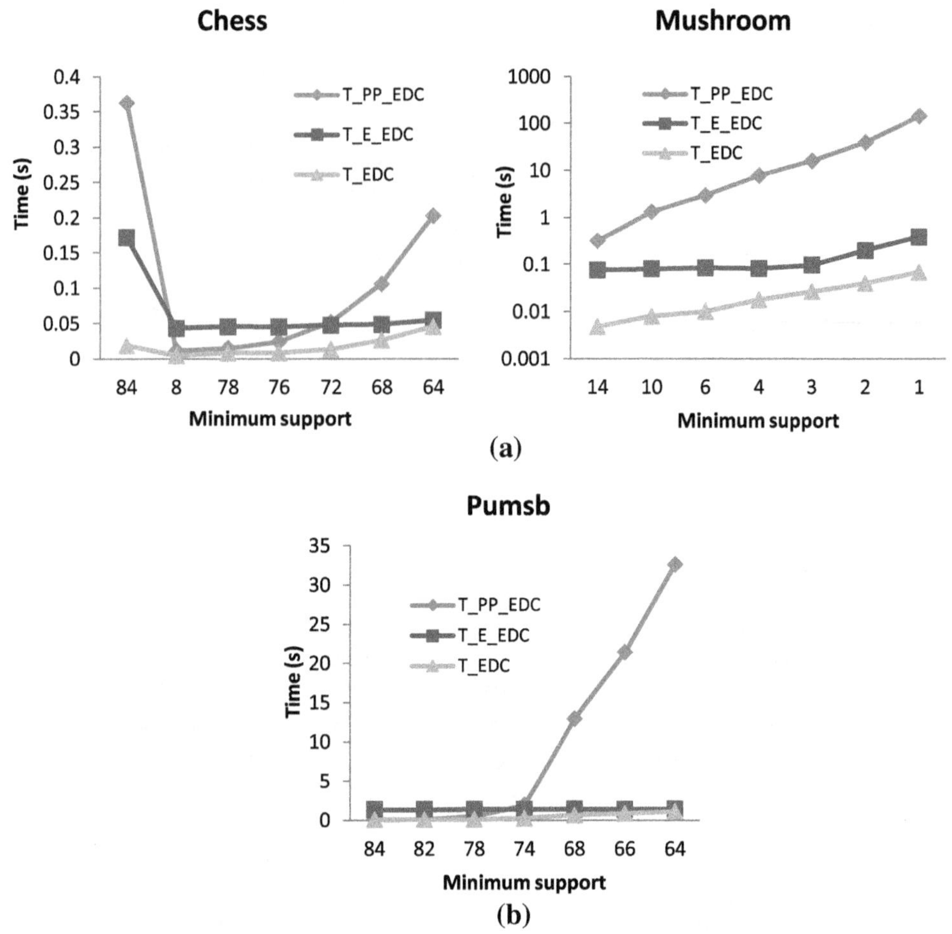

Fig. 6 **a** Performance results for Chess and Mushroom. **b** Performance results for Pumsb

Figure 7a, b show the results in the average execution time of different numbers of constraints. We realize that the performance gap between *MFS-EDC* and *MFS-E-EDC* increases along with the number of constraints (*#Constraints*). The main reason is that, when the extended double constraints changes, *MFS-EDC* executes without creating the lattice of closed itemset and their generators again from the dataset.

In general, *MFS-EDC* outperforms both *MFS-PP-EDC* and *MFS-E-EDC*, especially when the minimum support is lower and the number of constraints is high.

6 Conclusion and future work

In this paper, in theory, checking the general constraints was performed directly on the lattice of closed itemsets and their generators based on partitioning solution set into disjoint equivalence sub-classes. Instead of eliminating an enormous amount of itemsets not satisfying the constraints by so many direct checks, the partition helps to test and eliminate redundant, candidate equivalence classes only based on the necessary conditions. Thereby, the structure and explicit representation of $\mathcal{FS}_{C_{10}\subseteq C_{11},\not\subseteq C_{21}}(s_0, s_1)$ were shown and proven to be reliable. On the basis of the theoretical results, on practice, the corresponding algorithm, *MFS-EDC*, to find solution set without generating any redundant candidate was obtained. Its efficiency was verified and compared to several post-processing algorithms on a lot of benchmark datasets in the domain.

Based on saving a not too large number of the lattice of closed itemsets and their generators, the approach of the paper is sustainable through the regular changes of constraints given by online users. In addition, these generally theoretical results are also the reliable basis for designing parallel algorithms that efficiently mine frequent itemsets with more general constraints in real time.

Appendix

Appendix 1: Proof of Proposition 2

Obviously, $\forall L' \in \mathcal{FS}_{C_{10}\subseteq C_{11},\not\subseteq C_{21},}(s_0, s_1) \subseteq \mathcal{FS}(s_0, s_1)$, we have $L \stackrel{\text{def}}{=} h(L') \in \mathcal{FCS}(s_0, s_1)$, $\mathcal{FS}_{C_{10}\subseteq C_{11},\not\subseteq C_{21},}(s_0, s_1) = \sum_{L\in\mathcal{FCS}(s_0,s_1)}\{[L] \cap \mathcal{FS}_{C_{10}\subseteq C_{11},\not\subseteq C_{21},}(s_0, s_1)\}$ and $[L] \cap \mathcal{FS}_{C_{10}\subseteq C_{11},\not\subseteq C_{21},}(s_0, s_1) = \{L' \in [L] | C_{10} \subseteq L' \subseteq$

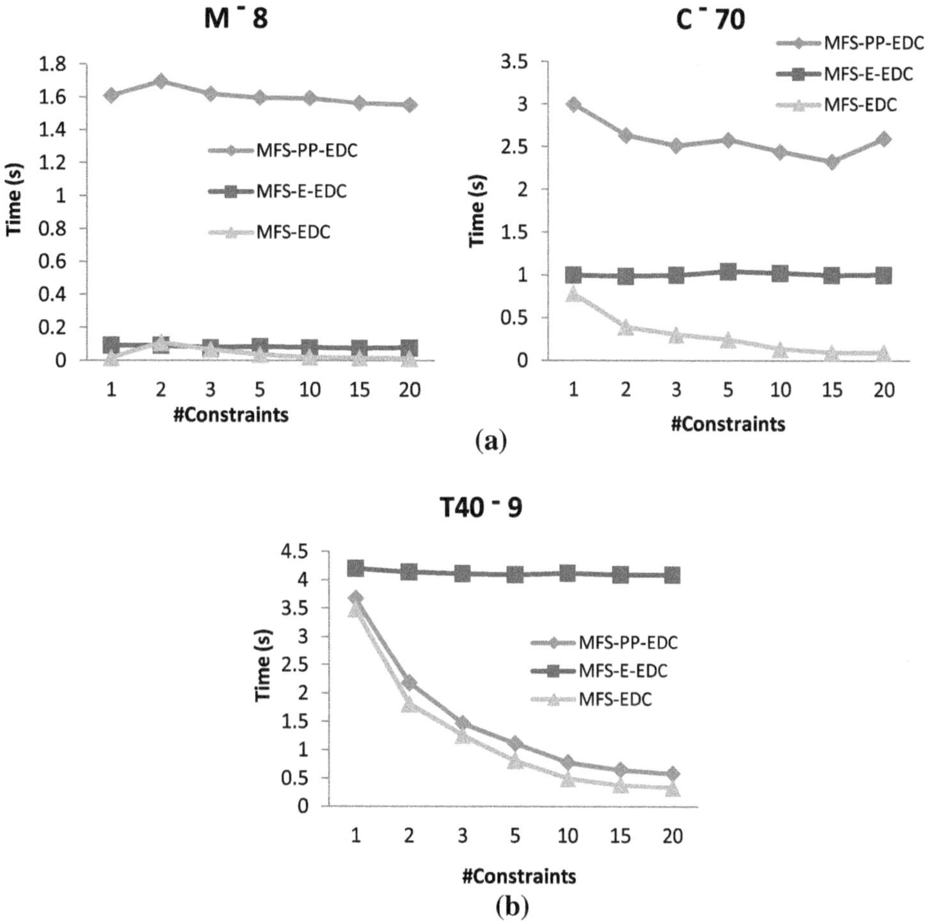

Fig. 7 **a** Performance results for M-8 (Mushroom, minsup = 8 %) and C-70 (Connect, minsup = 70 %). **b** Performance results for T40-9 (T40I10D100K, minsup = 9 %) for various numbers of constraints

$L_{C_{11}}, L' \nsubseteq C_{21}\} = \{L' \in \mathcal{FS}_{C_{10}\subseteq L_{C_{11}}} | L' \nsubseteq C_{21}\} = \mathcal{FS}_{C_{10}\subseteq L_{C_{11}}, \nsubseteq C_{21}}$. □

Appendix 2: Proof of Lemma 1 (a)

(i) We need only prove that $\mathcal{G}(L') \neq \varnothing \Rightarrow L' \neq \varnothing$, the remain of the assertion could see in [4]. Indeed, if $\mathcal{G}(L') \neq \varnothing$, then $\exists L_i \in \mathcal{G}(L') : \varnothing \subset L_i \subseteq L'$, i.e. $L' \neq \varnothing$.

(ii) "$\subseteq$": $\forall L_k \in G_B(L) : L_k \in \mathcal{G}(L), L_k \subseteq B$, we have $L_k \subseteq L_B \subseteq L, L = h(L_k) = h(L_B)$, thus, $L_k \in \mathcal{G}(L_B)$.
."$\supseteq$": Conversely, $\forall L_k \in \mathcal{G}(L_B)$, then $L_k \subseteq L_B \subseteq B, h(L_k) = h(L_B)$; since $\mathcal{G}_B(L) \neq \varnothing$, so $\exists L_i \in G(L) : L_i \subseteq B, L_i \subseteq L_B \subseteq L$ and $L = h(L_i) = h(L_B) = h(L_k)$, i.e. $L_k \in G(L) : L_k \subseteq B$ or $L_k \in \mathcal{G}_B(L)$.

(iii) Since $\mathcal{G}_B(L) \neq \varnothing, so\ \exists L_j \in \mathcal{G}(L) : L_j \subseteq L_B \stackrel{\text{def}}{=} L \cap B \subseteq L$, so $h(L_j) = L = h(L_B)$. Denote $L* \stackrel{\text{def}}{=} A \cup L_j$, then $A \subseteq L*, \varnothing \subset L_j \subseteq L* \subseteq L_B \subseteq L, L = h(L_j) = h(L*) = h(L_B)$ and $L* \in FS_{A\subseteq L_B} \neq \varnothing$. Moreover, $\forall L' \in FS_{A\subseteq L_B}, \forall L_i \in \mathcal{G}(L)$, since $L' \neq \varnothing$, by (i), then for any $L_i \in \mathcal{G}(L') \neq \varnothing$, we have $L_i \subseteq L' \subseteq L_B \subseteq B, h(L_i) = h(L') = L$, thus $L_i \in \mathcal{G}_B(L), \mathcal{G}(L') \subseteq \mathcal{G}_B(L)$ and $h(L_i) = L = h(L_B)$.

(iv) Since $\varnothing \subset U \subseteq V, U$ and $V$are finite, so there exist $Minimal(U)$ and $Minimal(V)$. If $\exists M \in U \cap Minimal(V)$, and assume that $M \notin Minimal(U)$, so $\exists K \in Minimal(U) \subseteq V$ such that $K \subset M$. It contradicts the hypothesis $M \in Minimal(V)$!

(b) Consider $\forall L' \subseteq A : L' \neq \varnothing, L' \supseteq A, h(L') = L : \exists L_i \in \mathcal{G}(L'), Cond(L_i)$. Then, $K_i \stackrel{\text{def}}{=} L_i \backslash A \in U$ and $U \neq \varnothing$. For any $K_k \stackrel{\text{def}}{=} L_k \backslash A \in U : L_k \in \mathcal{G}(L') \subseteq \mathcal{G}(L), Cond(L_k)$, then $L_k \in \mathcal{G}(L)$ and $K_k \in V$, thus, $U \subseteq V$. Due to $\varnothing \subset U \subseteq V, U$ and V is finite, then $Minimal(V) \neq \varnothing, Minimal(U) \neq \varnothing$. Consider $\forall K_j \in Minimal(U)$, then $L' \supseteq A \cup L_j = A + K_j$ and $K_j \in Minimal(V)$. Indeed, assume $K_j \notin Minimal(V)$, then $\exists K_k \stackrel{\text{def}}{=} L_k \backslash A \in Minimal(V) : K_k \subset K_j, L_k \in \mathcal{G}(L)$ and $Cond(L_k)$; since $L_k \subseteq A + K_k \subseteq A + K_j \subseteq L' \subseteq L$, so $L = h(L_k) = h(L'), L_k \in \mathcal{G}(L'), K_k \in U \cap Minimal(V)$, thus $K_k \in Minimal(U)$: it is a contradiction of the facts $K_j \in Minimal(U)$ and $K_k \subset K_j$! Hence, $Minimal(U) \subseteq Minimal(V)$. We can always assume that i is the minimum index in all ones of K_i in $Minimal(U)$.

(c) If $L' = A + K_i + K'_i + K^{\sim}_i$, where $K_i \in K_{\min}$, $K'_i \subseteq K_{U,i}$, $K^{\sim}_i \subseteq K_{-,i}$, then, since $K_i \subseteq L_B$, $K_{-,i} \subseteq L_B$,so $K_{U,i} \subseteq K_U^{i-1} \subseteq L_B$. Hence, $A \subseteq L' \subseteq L_B$. If $K_i \stackrel{\text{def}}{=} L_i \backslash A$, with $L_i \in \mathcal{G}(L)$, then $\varnothing \subset L_i \subseteq A + K_i \subseteq L' \subseteq L_B \subseteq L$, so $L' \neq \varnothing, L = h(L') = h(L_i) = h(L_B)$ and $L' \in FS_{A \subseteq L_B}$.

□

Appendix 3: Proof of Proposition 3

+"(a). ⇒ và b. ⊆": $\forall L' \in \mathcal{FS}_{C_{10} \subseteq C_{11}, \nsubseteq C_{21}}, (s_0, s_1)$, $L' \in \mathcal{FS}(s_0, s_1), C_{10} \subseteq L' \subseteq C_{11}, L' \nsubseteq C_{21}$, call $L = h(L')$, $L_i \in \mathcal{G}(L') \subseteq \mathcal{G}(L)$ (by Lemma 1a(i)) then $supp(L) = supp(L') \in [s_0, s_1], C_{10} \subseteq L' \subseteq L_{C_{11}}, \varnothing \subset L_i \subseteq L_i \cup C_{10} \subseteq L' \subseteq L_{C_{11}} \subseteq L$ and $L = h(L_i) = h(L') = h(L_{C_{11}})$. Due to $\varnothing \subset L' \backslash C_{21} = L' \backslash L_{C_{21}} \subseteq L_{C_{11}} \backslash C_{21}$, then $L' \in \mathcal{FS}_{C_{10} \subseteq L_{C_{11}}, \nsubseteq C_{21}}$, $L \in \mathcal{FCS}(s_0, s_1), C_{10} \subseteq L_{C_{11}} \nsubseteq C_{21}$ and $L_i \in \mathcal{G}_{C_{11}}(L) \neq \varnothing$, i.e. $L \in \mathcal{FCS}_{C_{10} \subseteq C_{11}, \nsubseteq C_{21}}$, $(s_0, s_1) \neq \varnothing$.

"(a). ⇐" :$\forall L \in \mathcal{FCS}_{C_{10} \subseteq C_{11}, \nsubseteq C_{21}}, (s_0, s_1), C_{10} \subseteq L_{C_{11}} \nsubseteq C_{21}, \mathcal{G}_{C_{11}}(L) \neq \varnothing$, let $L_i \in \mathcal{G}_{C_{11}}(L) \subseteq \mathcal{G}(L) : L_i \subseteq C_{11}$ and $L' \stackrel{\text{def}}{=} (C_{10} \cup L_i) \cup \{a\}$, where $a \in L_{C_{11}} \backslash C_{21} \neq \varnothing$. Then, $a \in L' \backslash C_{21} \neq \varnothing$, so $C_{10} \subseteq L' \subseteq L_{C_{11}} \subseteq C_{11}, L' \nsubseteq C_{21}, \varnothing \subset L_i \subseteq L' \subseteq L_{C_{11}} \subseteq L$ and $L = h(L_i) = h(L') = h(L_{C_{11}}), supp(L') = supp(L) \in [s_0, s_1], L' \in \mathcal{FS}(s_0, s_1)$. Thus, $L' \in \mathcal{FS}_{C_{10} \subseteq C_{11}, \nsubseteq C_{21}}$ $(s_0, s_1) \neq \varnothing$.

+"b. ⊇": It is a consequence of Proposition 2 and $\mathcal{FCS}_{C_{10} \subseteq C_{11}, \nsubseteq C_{21}}, (s_0, s_1) \subseteq \mathcal{FCS}(s_0, s_1)$. □

Appendix 4: Proof of Proposition 4

Note that, $\mathcal{FS}_{C_{10} \subseteq C_{11}, \nsubseteq C_{21}} = \lfloor L \rfloor_{C_- \subseteq L_{C^+}}, + \lfloor L \rfloor_{C^*} + L_{C_{10} \subseteq C_{11}, G \nsubseteq C_{21}}$. Consider $\forall L \in \mathcal{FCS}_{C_{10} \subseteq C_{11}, \nsubseteq C_{21}}, (s_0, s_1)$.

(i) + *The uniqueness in the representation of* $L'' \in \mathcal{FS}^*_{C_- \subseteq L_{C^+}}$:

Assume that L' has two representations: $L'' = C\_ + K_k + K'_k + K^{\sim}_k = C\_ + K_i + K'_i + K^{\sim}_i$, where $1 \leq k < i$, K_k and $K_i \in K_{\min, C_- \subseteq L_{C^+}}$, $K'_i \subseteq K_{U,\min,C_- \subseteq L_{C^+},i}$, $K^{\sim}_i \subseteq K_{-,C_- \subseteq L_{C^+} i}$, $K'_k \subseteq K_{U,C_- \subseteq L_{C^+},k}$, $K^{\sim}_k \subseteq K_{-,C_- \subseteq L_{C^+},k}$. Then, $K_k \subseteq K_i + K'_i + K^{\sim}_i$, but due to $K_k \subseteq K^k_{U,C_- \subseteq L_{C^+}} \subseteq K^i_{U,C_- \subseteq L_{C^+}}$, $K^{\sim}_i \cap K^i_{U,C_- \subseteq L_{C^+}} = \varnothing$,so $K_k \cap K^{\sim}_i = \varnothing$ and $K_k \subset K_i + K'_i$ (the equality does not happen, because K_k and K_i are two different minimal sets in $K_{\min, C \subseteq L_{C^+}}$) : it is a contradiction of the selection of K_i!

+ *The uniqueness in the representation of* $L' \in \mathcal{FS}^*_{C_{10} \subseteq L_{C_{11}}, G \nsubseteq C_{21}}$: Assume that L' have two representations: $L' = C_{10} + K_k + K'_k + K^{\sim}_k = C_{10} + K_i + K'_i + K^{\sim}_i$, where $M \leq k < i$, $K_i \in K_{\min, C_{10} \subseteq L_{C_{11}}, G \nsubseteq C_{21}}$, $K_k \in K_{\min, C_{10} \subseteq L_{C_{11}}, G \nsubseteq C_{21}} \subseteq K^+_{\min, C_{10} \subseteq L_{C_{11}}, \nsubseteq C_{21}}$, $K_k \neq K_i$, $K'_i \subseteq K_{U, C_{10} \subseteq L_{C_{11}}, \nsubseteq C_{21}, i}$, $K^{\sim}_i \subseteq K_{-, C_{10} L_{C_{11}}, \nsubseteq C_{21}, i}$, $K'_k \subseteq K_{U, C_{10} L_{C_{11}}, \nsubseteq C_{21}, k}$, $K^{\sim}_k \subseteq K_{-, C_{10} \subseteq L_{C_{11}}, \nsubseteq C_{21}, k}$. Then, $K_k \subseteq K_i + K'_i + K^{\sim}_i$, but since $K_k \subseteq K^k_{U, C_{10} \subseteq L_{C_{11}}, \nsubseteq C_{21}} \subseteq K^i_{U, C_{10} \subseteq L_{C_{11}}, \nsubseteq C_{21}}$, $K^{\sim}_i \cap K^i_{U, C_{10} \subseteq L_{C_{11}}, \nsubseteq C_{21}} = \varnothing$, so $K_k \cap K^{\sim}_i = \varnothing$ and $K_k \subset K_i + K'_i$ ((the equality does not also happen, because K_k and K_i are two different minimal sets in $K_{\min, C_{10} \subseteq L_{C_{11}}, G \nsubseteq C_{21}}$): it contradicts the selection of K_i!

(ii) + "$\mathcal{FS}_{C_{10} \subseteq L_{C_{11}}, \nsubseteq C_{21}} \subseteq \mathcal{FS}^*_{C_{10} \subseteq L_{C_{11}}, \nsubseteq C_{21}}$": We will prove that $\lfloor L \rfloor_{C_- \subseteq L_{C^+}, +L_{C^*}} \subseteq \mathcal{FS}^*_{C_- \subseteq L_{C^+}, +L_{C^*}}$ and $\lfloor L \rfloor_{C_{10} \subseteq L_{C_{11}}, G \nsubseteq C_{21}} \subseteq \mathcal{FS}^*_{C_{10} \subseteq L_{C_{11}}, \nsubseteq C_{21}}$, thus, $\mathcal{FS}_{C_{10} \subseteq L_{C_{11}}, \nsubseteq C_{21}} \subseteq \mathcal{FS}^*_{C_{10} \subseteq C_{11}, \nsubseteq C_{21}}$.

. "$\lfloor L \rfloor_{C_- L_{C^+}, +L_{C^*}} \subseteq \mathcal{FS}^*_{C_- L_{C^+}, +L_{C^*}}$": $\forall L' \in \mathcal{FS}_{C_{10} \subseteq C_{11}, \nsubseteq C_{21}}, \exists L_i \in \mathcal{G}_{C^+}(L) \subseteq \mathcal{G}(L) : L_i \subseteq L'$, then $L' \neq \varnothing$ and $L' \supseteq C_{10}, L_i \subseteq L' \subseteq L_{C_{11}} \subseteq C_{11}, L_i \subseteq C^+ \subseteq C_{21}$. Since $L' \subseteq L_{C_{11}}$, so based on C_{21}, we can partition L' into disjoint subsets $L' \stackrel{\text{def}}{=} L'' + L^{\sim}$, where $C_- \subseteq L'' \stackrel{\text{def}}{=} L' \cap C_{21} \subseteq L_{C_{11}} \cap C_{21} = L_{C^+} \subseteq L_{C_{21}}$ and $C_{10} \backslash C_{21} \subseteq L^{\sim} \stackrel{\text{def}}{=} L' \backslash C_{21} \subseteq L_{C_{11}} \backslash C_{21} = L_{C^*}$. Moreover, due to $L'' \backslash C_{21} = \varnothing, L^{\sim} \cap C_{21} = \varnothing, L' \nsubseteq L_{C_{21}}$, so $\varnothing \subset L' \backslash L_{C_{21}} = L^{\sim} \backslash L_{C_{21}} = L^{\sim}, L^{\sim} \in 2^{[C_{10} \backslash C_{21} \subseteq L_{C^*}]*}$. We need to prove that $L'' \in \mathcal{FS}^*_{C_- \subseteq L_{C^+}}$. Let $K_i \stackrel{\text{def}}{=} L_i \backslash C\_ = L_i \backslash C_{10}$(vì $L_i \subseteq C_{21}$), $Cond(L_k) \stackrel{\text{def}}{=} (L_k \subseteq C^+)$, $U \stackrel{\text{def}}{=} \{K_k \stackrel{\text{def}}{=} L_k \backslash C\_ | L_k \in \mathcal{G}(L''), Cond(L_k)\}$, $V \stackrel{\text{def}}{=} \{K_k \stackrel{\text{def}}{=} L_k \backslash C\_ | L_k \in \mathcal{G}(L), Cond(L_k)\} = \{K_k \stackrel{\text{def}}{=} L_k \backslash C\_ | L_k \in \mathcal{G}_{C^+}(L)\}$, then $L_i \subseteq C\_ + K_i = C\_ \cup L_i \subseteq L'' \subseteq L, h(L_i) = h(L'') = L$ and $L_i \in \mathcal{G}(L'')$, thus, $K_i \in U \subseteq V$, $K_{\min, C_- \subseteq L_{C^+}} = Minimal(V)$. From Lemma 1b, we can always assume that i is the minimum index such that $K_i \in Minimal(U)$. Then, $K_i \in Minimal(V)$ và $L'' \supseteq C\_ + K_i$. We can represent L'' as follows: $L'' \stackrel{\text{def}}{=} C\_ + K_i + K'_i + K^{\sim}_i$, where $K'_i \stackrel{\text{def}}{=} [L'' \backslash (C\_ + K_i)] \cap K^i_{U, C_- \subseteq L_{C^+}} \subseteq K^i_{U, C_- \subseteq L_{C^+}} \backslash K_i = K_{U, C_- \subseteq L_{C^+}, i}$, $K^{\sim}_i \stackrel{\text{def}}{=} [L'' \backslash (C\_ + K_i) \backslash K^i_{U, C_- \subseteq L_{C^+}} \subseteq K_{-, C_- \subseteq L_{C^+}, i}$. Finally, assume that the condition $^{(*)}$ is false, i.e. $\exists K_k \equiv L_k \backslash C\_ \in K_{\min, C_- \subseteq L_{C^+}}: 1 \leq k < i$ and $K_k \subset K_i + K'_i$, then $L_k \in \mathcal{G}_{C^+}(L) \subseteq \mathcal{G}(L), L_k \subseteq C\_ + K_k \subseteq C\_ + K_i + K'_i \subseteq L'' \subseteq L$ and $L_k \in \mathcal{G}(L'')$. Hence, $K_k \in U \cap Minimal(V)$, $K_k \in Minimal(U)$ and $k < i$: it contradicts the selection of the index i! Thus, $L'' \in \mathcal{FS}^*_{C_- L_{C^+}}$.

. "$\lfloor L \rfloor_{C_{10} \subseteq L_{C_{11}}, G \nsubseteq C_{21}} \subseteq \mathcal{FS}^*_{C_{10} \subseteq L_{C_{11}}, G \nsubseteq C_{21}}$": cxv $\forall L' \in \lfloor L \rfloor_{C_{10} \subseteq L_{C_{11}}, G \nsubseteq C_{21}}$, we have $L' \in \mathcal{FS}_{C_{10} \subseteq L_{C_{11}}, \nsubseteq C_{21}}$, $\exists L_i \in \mathcal{G}_{C_{11}, \nsubseteq C_{21}}(L) \subseteq G(L) : L_i \subseteq L'$, so $L' \neq \varnothing$, $L' \supseteq C_{10}, L_i \subseteq L' \subseteq L_{C_{11}} \subseteq C_{11}, L_i \nsubseteq C_{21}$ and $(L_k \nsubseteq L', \forall L_k \in \mathcal{G}_{C^+}(L))^{(-)}$. From Lemma 1a, we have $h(L') = L$ and $L_i \in \mathcal{G}(L')$. Let $Cond'(L_k) \stackrel{\text{def}}{=} (L_k \nsubseteq C_{21}, L_k \subseteq C_{11})$, $U \stackrel{\text{def}}{=} \{K_i \stackrel{\text{def}}{=} L_i \backslash C_{10} | L_k \in \mathcal{G}(L'), Cond'(L_k)\}$,

$V \stackrel{def}{=} \{K_i \stackrel{def}{=} L_i \backslash C_{10} | L_k \in \mathcal{G}(L), Cond'(L_k)\} = \{K_i \stackrel{def}{=} L_i \backslash C_{10} | L_k \in \mathcal{G}_{C_{11}, \not\subseteq C_{21}}(L)\}$. From Lemma 1b, due to $K_i \stackrel{def}{=} L_i \backslash C_{10} \in U$, then $\varnothing \neq U \subseteq V$ and we can choose the minimum index i such that $K_i \in Minimal(U)$. Then, $L' \supseteq C_{10} + K_i$ and $K_i \in Minimal(V) \equiv K_{\min, C_{10} \subseteq L_{C_{11}}, G \not\subseteq C_{21}} \neq \varnothing$. Since $C_{10} + K_i \subseteq L' \subseteq L_{C_{11}}$, call $L''_i \stackrel{def}{=} L' \backslash (C_{10} + K_i) \subseteq L_{C_{11}} \backslash (C_{10} + K_i)$, so $L' = (C_{10} + K_i) + L''_i = C_{10} + K_i + K'_i + K^{\sim}_i$, where $K'_i = L''_i \cap K^{i-1}_{U, C_{10} \subseteq L_{C_{11}}} \subseteq K^{i-1}_{U, C_{10} \subseteq L_{C_{11}}} \backslash K_i = K_{U, C_{10} \subseteq L_{C_{11}}, i}$, $K^{\sim}_i = L''_i \backslash K^{i-1}_{U, C_{10} \subseteq L_{C_{11}}} \subseteq L_{C_{11}} \backslash (C_{10} + K^i_{U, C_{10} \subseteq L_{C_{11}}}) = K_{-, C_{10} \subseteq L_{C_{11}}, i}$. Finally, assume that the condition $^{(**)}$ is not true, i.e. $\exists K_i \stackrel{def}{=} L_i \backslash C_{10} \in K_{\min}, C_{10} \subseteq L_{C_{11}}, C^{+}_{21}: 1 \leq k < i$ and $K_k \subseteq K_i + K'_i$, then $L_k \in \mathcal{G}_{C_{11}}(L) \subseteq \mathcal{G}(L), L_k \subseteq C_{11}, L_k \subseteq C_{10} + K_k \subseteq C_{10} + K_i + K'_i \subseteq L' \subseteq L$ and $h(L_k) = h(L') = L$. Hence, $L_k \in (L')$, $L_k \not\subseteq C_{21}$ (because if $L_k \subseteq C_{21}$, then $L_k \subseteq C^{+}$ and $L_k \in \mathcal{G}_{C^{+}}(L)$: it contradicts the above condition $^{(-)}$!). Moreover, $L_k \in \mathcal{G}_{C_{11}, \not\subseteq C_{21}}(L)$, $K_k \in K_{\min}$, $C_{10} \subseteq L_{C_{11}}$, $G \not\subseteq C_{21} \cap U$, $K_k \in Minimal(U)$ and $k < i$: it is a contradiction of the selection the minimum index i such that $K_i \in Minimal(U)$! Thus, the condition $^{(**)}$ in $\mathcal{FS}^{*}_{C_{10} \subseteq L_{C_{11}}, G \not\subseteq C_{21}}$ is true and $L' \in \mathcal{FS}^{*}_{C_{10} \subseteq L_{C_{11}}, G \not\subseteq C_{21}}$.

+ "$\mathcal{FS}^{*}_{C_{10} \subseteq L_{C_{11}}, \not\subseteq C_{21},} \subseteq \mathcal{FS}_{C_{10} \subseteq L_{C_{11}}, \not\subseteq C_{21}}$" We will prove that $\mathcal{FS}^{*}_{C_{-} \subseteq L_{C^{+}}, +L_{C^{*}}} \subseteq \lfloor L \rfloor_{C_{-} \subseteq L_{C^{+}}, +L_{C^{*}}}$ and $\mathcal{FS}^{*}_{C_{10} \subseteq L_{C_{11}}, G \not\subseteq C_{21}} \subseteq \lfloor L \rfloor_{C_{10} \subseteq L_{C_{11}}, G \not\subseteq C_{21}}$, thus, $\mathcal{FS}^{*}_{C_{-} \subseteq L_{C^{+}}, +L_{C^{*}}} \cap \mathcal{FS}^{*}_{C_{10} \subseteq L_{C_{11}}, G \not\subseteq C_{21}} = \varnothing$ an $\mathcal{FS}^{*}_{C_{10} \subseteq L_{C_{11}}, \not\subseteq C_{21},} \subseteq \mathcal{FS}_{C_{10} \subseteq L_{C_{11}}, \not\subseteq C_{21}}$.

. "$\mathcal{FS}^{*}_{C_{-} \subseteq L_{C^{+}}, +L_{C^{*}}} \subseteq \lfloor L \rfloor_{C_{-} \subseteq L_{C^{+}}, +L_{C^{*}}}$": $\forall L' \stackrel{def}{=} L'' + L^{\sim} \in \mathcal{FS}^{*}_{C_{-} \subseteq L_{C^{+}}, +L_{C^{*}}}$, $L'' \stackrel{def}{=} C_{-} + K_i + K'_i + K^{\sim}_i \in \mathcal{FS}^{*}_{C_{-} \subseteq L_{C^{+}}}$, $L^{\sim} \in 2^{[C_{10} \backslash \not\subseteq C_{21} \subseteq L_{C^{*}}]*}$, where $K_i \stackrel{def}{=} L_i \backslash C_{-} = L_i \backslash C_{10}$ (because $L_i \in \mathcal{G}_{C^{+}}(L) \subseteq \mathcal{G}(L)$, $L_i \subseteq C^{+} \subseteq\not\subseteq C_{21}$) and from Lemma 1c, $L'' \in \mathcal{FS}_{C_{-} \subseteq L_{C^{+}}}$. On the other hand, since $C_{10} = (\neq) + (C_{10} \not\subseteq C_{21}) \subseteq L' = L^{\sim} + L'' \subseteq L_{C^{*}} + L_{C^{+}} = L_{C_{11}}$, $L_i \subseteq C_{-} + K_i \subseteq L'' \subseteq L' \subseteq L_{C_{11}} \subseteq L$, $h(L_{C_{11}}) = h(L') = h(L_i) = L$, $\varnothing \subset L^{\sim} = L^{\sim} \backslash C_{21} \subseteq L' \backslash C_{21}$, then $L' \not\subseteq C_{21}$. Hence, $L' \in \mathcal{FS}_{C_{10} \subseteq L_{C_{11}}, \not\subseteq C_{21}}$ and $L' \in L_{C_{-}L_{C^{+}}, +L_{C^{*}}}$.

."$\mathcal{FS}^{*}_{C_{10} \subseteq L_{C_{11}}, G \not\subseteq C_{21}} \subseteq \lfloor L \rfloor_{C_{10} \subseteq L_{C_{11}}, G \not\subseteq C_{21}}$" : $\forall L' \stackrel{def}{=} C_{10} + K_i + K'_i + K^{\sim}_i \in \mathcal{FS}^{*}_{C_{10} \subseteq L_{C_{11}}, G \not\subseteq C_{21}}$, $K_i \stackrel{def}{=} L_i \backslash C_{10}$, $L_i \in \mathcal{G}_{C_{11}, \not\subseteq C_{21}}(L)$ and $(K_k \not\subseteq K_i + K'_i, \forall K_k \in K^{+}_{\min, C_{10} \subseteq L_{C_{11}}, \not\subseteq C_{21}} : 1 \leq k < i)^{(**)}$, then from Lemma 1a and c, due to $\mathcal{G}_{C_{11}, \not\subseteq C_{21}}(L) \subseteq \mathcal{G}(L)$, we obtain $h(L') = L$, $L' \in \mathcal{FS}_{C_{10} \subseteq L_{C_{11}}}$ and $L' \backslash C_{21} \supseteq L_i \backslash C_{21} \supset \varnothing$, $L_i \subseteq K_i + C_{10} \subseteq L'$, thus $L' \in \mathcal{FS}_{C_{10} \subseteq L_{C_{11}}, \not\subseteq C_{21}}$. To prove $L' \in \lfloor L \rfloor_{C_{10} \subseteq L_{C_{11}}, G \not\subseteq C_{21}}$, in addition, we need to test the condition $^{(-)}$: $(L_k \not\subseteq L', \forall L_k \in \mathcal{G}_{C^{+}}(L))$ by contradiction. Assume that $\exists L_k \in \mathcal{G}_{C^{+}}(L) \subseteq \mathcal{G}_{C_{11}}(L) \subseteq \mathcal{G}(L) : L_k \subseteq L' = C_{10} + K_i + K'_i + K^{\sim}_i \subseteq L, L_k \subseteq L_{C^{+}} \subseteq\not\subseteq C_{21}$, then $L_k \in \mathcal{G}(L')$ and $k \leqslant M < i$ (from the above indexing k of K_k). Using Lemma 1b, with $U'' \stackrel{def}{=} \{K_i \stackrel{def}{=} L_i \backslash C_{10}, L_i \in \mathcal{G}(L'), \mathrm{Cond}(L_k)\}$ and $K_i \stackrel{def}{=} L_i \backslash C_{10} = L_k \backslash C_{-} \in U'' \neq \varnothing, U'' \subseteq V$, we can choose the minimum index k such that $K_k \in Minimal(U'')$ and $K_k \in Minmal(V) = K_{\min, C_{-} \subseteq L_{C^{+}}} \subseteq K^{+}_{\min, C_{10} \subseteq L_{C_{11}}, C_{21}}$. Since $K_k \subseteq L' \backslash C_{10} = K_i + K'_i + K^{\sim}_i$, $K_k \subseteq K^{k}_{U, C_{-} \subseteq L_{C^{+}}} = K^{k}_{U, C_{10} \subseteq L_{C_{11}}} \subseteq K^{i}_{U, C_{10} \subseteq L_{C_{11}}}$ and $K^{\sim}_i \cap K^{i}_{U, C_{10} \subseteq L_{C_{11}}} = \varnothing$, so $K_k \cap K^{\sim}_i = \varnothing$ and $K_k \subseteq K_i + K'_i$: It is a contradiction of the selection of the index i in $^{(**)}$! Thus, the condition $^{(-)}$ is true.

Finally, all itemsets in $\mathcal{FS}_{C_{10} \subseteq L_{C_{11}}, \not\subseteq C_{21}}$ have a unique representation and are generated completely and distinctly by itemsets in $\mathcal{FS}^{*}_{C_{10} \subseteq L_{C_{11}}, \not\subseteq C_{21}}$. □

References

1. Agrawal, R., Imielinski, T., Swami, N: Mining association rules between sets of items in large databases. In: Proceedings of the ACM SIGMOID, pp. 207–216 (1993)
2. Anh, T., Hai, D., Tin, T., Bac, L.: Efficient algorithms for mining frequent Itemsets with constraint. In: Proceedings of the Third International Conference on Knowledge and Systems Engineering, pp. 19–25 (2011)
3. Anh, T., Hai, D., Tin, T., Bac, L.: Mining frequent itemsets with dualistic constraints. In: Proceedings PRICAI 2012, LNAI, vol. 7458, pp. 807–813 (2012)
4. Anh, T., Tin, T., Bac, L.: Simultaneous mining of frequent closed itemsets and their generators: foundation and algorithm. Int. J. Eng. Appl. Artif. Intell. (EAAI) **36**, 64–80 (2014)
5. Bayardo, R.J., Agrawal, R., Gunopulos, D.: Constraint-based rule mining in large, dense databases. Proc. Data Min. Knowl. Discov. **4**, 217–240 (2000)
6. Bonchi, F., Giannotti, F., Mazzanti, A., Pedreschi, D.: Examiner: optimized level-wise frequent pattern mining with monotone constraints. In: Proceedings IEEE ICDM'03, pp. 11–18 (2003)
7. Bonchi, F., Lucchese, C.: On closed constrained frequent pattern mining. In: Proceedings IEEE ICDM'04, pp. 35–42 (2004)
8. Boulicaut, J.F., Bykowski, A., Rigotti, C.: Free-sets: a condensed representation of boolean data for the approximation of frequency queries. Data Min. Knowl. Dis. **7**, 5–22 (2003)
9. Boulicaut, J.F., Jeudy, B.: Using constraints during set mining: should we prune or not. In: Actes des Seizime Journes Bases de Donnes Avances BDA'00, Blois, pp. 221–237 (2000)
10. Bucila, C., Gehrke, J.E., Kifer, D., White, W.: Dualminer: a dual-pruning algorithm for itemsets with constraints. Data Min. Knowl. Dis. **7**, 241–272 (2003)
11. Burdick, D., Calimlim, M, Gehrke, J.: MAFIA: A maximal frequent itemset algorithm for transactional databases. In: Proceedings IEEE ICDE'01, pp. 443–452 (2001)
12. Dong, J., Han, M.: BitTable-FI: an efficient mining frequent itemsets algorithm. Int. J. Knowl. Based Sys. **20**, 329–335 (2007)

13. Frequent Itemset Mining Dataset Repository (FIMDR). http://fimi.cs.helsinki.fi/data/. Accessed 2009
14. Grahne, G., Zhu, J.: Fast algorithms for frequent itemset mining using fp-trees. Proc. IEEE Trans. Knowl. Data Eng. **17**, 1347–1362 (2005)
15. Hai, D., Tin, T.: An efficient method for mining association rules based on minimum single constraints. Vietnam J. Comput. Sci. **2**, 67–83 (2015)
16. Hai, D., Tin, T., Bac, L.: An efficient algorithm for mining frequent itemsets with single constraint. Adv. Comput. Methods Knowl. Eng. Sci. **479**, 367–378 (2013)
17. Hai, D., Tin, T., Bay, V.: An efficient method for mining frequent itemsets with double constraints. Int. J. Eng. Appl. Artif. Intell. (EAAI) **27**, 148–154 (2014)
18. Han, J., Pei, J., Yin, Y.: Mining frequent patterns without candidate generation. In: SIGMOD'00, pp. 1–12 (2000)
19. Huy, P., Tin, T.: An efficient lattice-based approach for generator mining. Int. J. Adv. Comput. Res. **4**, 741–751 (2014)
20. Jeudy, B., Boulicaut, J.F.: Optimization of association rule mining queries. Intell. Data Anal. **6**, 341–357 (2002)
21. Lin, D.I., Kedem, Z.M.: Pincer search: an efficient algorithm for discovering the maximum frequent sets. IEEE Trans Knowl. Data Eng. **14**, 553–566 (2002)
22. Mannila, H., Toivonen, H.: Levelwise search and borders of theories in knowledge discovery. Data Min. Knowl. Dis. **1**, 241–258 (1997)
23. Mashoria, V., Singh, A.: A survey of mining association rules using constraints. Int. J. Comput. Technol. **7**, 620–625 (2013)
24. Nguyen, R.T., Lakshmanan, V.S., Han, J., Pang, A.: Exploratory mining and pruning optimizations of constrained association rules. In: Proceedings of the 1998 ACM-SIG-MOD International Conference on the Management of Data, pp. 13–24 (1998)
25. Pasquier, N., Bastide, Y., Taouil, R., Lakhal, L.: Efficient mining of association rules using closed itemset lattices. Inf. Syst. **24**(1), 25–46 (1999)
26. Pasquier, N., Taouil, R., Bastide, Y., Stumme, G., Lakhal, L.: Generating a condensed representation for association rules. Intell. Inf. Syst. **24**, 29–60 (2005)
27. Pei, J., Han, J.: Constrained frequent pattern mining: a pattern-growth view. Proc. ACM SIGKDD Explor. **4**, 31–39 (2002)
28. Pei, J., Han, J., Lakshmanan, L.V.S.: Mining frequent itemsets with convertible constraints. In: Proceedings IEEE ICDE'01, pp. 433–442 (2001)
29. Song, W., Yang, B., Xu, Z.: Index-BitTableFI: an improved algorithm formining frequent itemsets. Int. J. Knowl. Based Syst. **21**, 507–513 (2008)
30. Szathmary, L., Valtchev, P., Napoli, A.: Efficient vertical mining of frequent closed itemsets and generators. IDA **2009**, 393–404 (2013)
31. Tin, T., Anh, T.: Structure of set of association rules based on concept lattice. In: Advances in Intelligent Information and Database Systems, SCI, vol. 283, pp. 217–227. Springer (2010)
32. Vo, B., Hong, T.P., Le, B.: A lattice-based approach for mining most generalization association rules. Knowl. Based Syst. **45**, 20–30 (2013)
33. Vo, B., Hong, T.P., Le, B.: DBV-Miner: a dynamic bit-vector approach for fast mining frequent closed itemsets. Expert Syst. Appl. **39**, 7196–7206 (2012)
34. Zaki, M.J.: Mining non-redundant association rules. Data Min. Knowl. Discov. **9**(3), 223–248 (2004)
35. Zaki, M.J., Hsiao, C.J.: Efficient algorithms for mining closed itemsets and their lattice structure. IEEE Trans. Knowl. Data Eng. **17**, 462–478 (2005)
36. Zaki, M.J., Parthasarathy, S., Ogihara, M., Li, W.: New algorithms for fast discovery of association rules. In: Proceedings of the 3rd International Conference on Knowledge Discovery and Data Mining (KDD'97), pp. 283–296 (1997)

3

Using hyper populated ant colonies for solving the TSP

Andrzej Siemiński[1]

Abstract The paper discusses the application of hyper populated ant colonies to the well-known traveling salesman problem (TSP). The ant colony optimization (ACO) approach offers reasonably good quality solutions for the TSP, but it suffers from its inherent non-determinism and as a consequence the processing time is unpredictable. The paper tries to mitigate the problem by a substantial increase in the number of used ants. This approach is called ant hyper population and it could be obtained by increasing the number of ants in a single colony assigning more than one colony to solve the same task or both. In all cases the level of non-determinism decreases and thus the number iterations could be reduced. Parallel implementation of the ACO makes it possible to reduce drastically the processing time. The paper compares two ways of implementation of the parallelism using the sockets or the RMI—remote method invocation mechanisms. The paper concentrates on the classical static version of the TSP, but preliminary experiments indicate that such an approach could be even more useful for dynamic TPSs.

Keywords Ant colony optimization · Traveling salesmen problem · Parallelization strategies for ACO · Ant colony community (ACC)

1 Introduction

The aim of the paper is to discuss the problem of optimizing the performance of the ant colony optimization (ACO) used for the traveling salesman problem (TSP). Metaheuristics such as the ACO solve a complex problem by iteratively improving candidate solutions. They do not guarantee the selection of an optimum or even a satisfactory near-optimal solution. In the case of the NP-hard or even NP-complete problems they are often the only available choice that we have.

Usually the quality of solutions is measured by exclusively by the length of the selected route. The ACO works in a non-deterministic way. Usually a predefined number of iterations are executed and the best found solution is selected. The quality of solutions improves with time, but the process is not uniform. A high quality solution could be found after a few thousands of iterations, but it is not uncommon that we can have it after just a few dozens of them. Therefore, it is so hard to tell when to stop the operation of the ACO. There is a great incentive to prolong the execution time. The reported experiment results look more impressive. This is certainly possible in an university environment. It may not be the case for the real life applications. The time needed to execute a great number of iterations may simply not be available. Moreover, the longer we run the ACO, the solution updates are the less and less frequent. This demerit is even more acute for the dynamic TSP. In that case the ACO may not be able to catch up with the changing environment.

The paper addresses the problem using a drastically increased number of ants. In what follows such ACOs are called hyper populated Ant Colonies. They come in two flavors. In the first one the ant number increases in just one colony and in the second we have a number of cooperating colonies—the so-called ant colony community (ACC). In both cases the results converge faster so the number of iterations could be limited. The main contribution of the paper is a detailed presentations of a model for the ACC and verification of its efficiency. The Socket mechanism was used to

✉ Andrzej Siemiński
Andrzej.Sieminski@pwr.edu.pl

[1] Faculty of Computer Science and Management, Wroclaw University of Technology, Wroclaw, Poland

implement the model and its advantages over the competing RMI mechanism are discussed. The complexity of interactions between individual ants or even ant colonies make a theoretical analysis extremely hard even with a number of simplifying assumptions. Therefore, this paper demonstrates empirically the performance and convergence aspects of the proposed model.

The paper is organized as follows. The second Section briefly introduces the TSP. The next one is devoted to the ACO—a metaheuristics commonly used to solve it. This section presents its general operational principles and the role played by its parameters. Attempts to optimize their values are also mentioned. It ends with the discussion of the stopping conditions. In the fourth Section we provide experiment results that justify the increase in the number of used ants. The prolonged execution time resulting from increasing of ant population could be mitigated by the parallel implementation of the ACO. The fifth Section contains the taxonomy of parallel ACOs and introduces the coarse-grained ACC proposed in the paper. The conducted experiments, their results with the criteria used to evaluate them are presented in the 6th Section. The paper concludes with the resume of research work done so far and the plans for future investigation.

2 Traveling salesman problem specification

The TSP could be stated in a remarkably simple way: given a list of cities and the distances separating them what is the shortest possible route that visits each city exactly once and returns to the origin city? For the first time the problem was stated as early as in 1800's. At that time it was treated as a recreational puzzle, papers printed graphs and prized best solution sent by readers. Nowadays it has many practical implications in areas as diverse as optimizing scheduling of a route of the drill machine used to drill holes in a printed circuit board or minimizing material wasted in the cutting-stock problem.

The number of all possible different routes for a graph with n nodes is equal to (n-1)!/2. The number is estimated by $\sqrt{2\pi n}(\frac{n}{e})^n$ and even for relatively small values of n like 50 the value is just staggering. It is equal approximately to 3,04141E+64 which is far exceeds the mass of an observable steady-state universe is 1,45E+53 kg. This clearly calls for heuristic solutions as the complete search is not feasible.

The TSP is now one of the established, classical problems of Artificial Intelligence and serves as a touchstone for many general heuristics devised for combinatorial optimization. in 1970's it was proved to be a NP-hard problem. A recent comparison of metaheuristics used for TSP could be found in [1]. The paper discusses: genetic algorithms, simulated annealing, tabu search, quantum annealing, particle swarm optimization, harmony search, a greedy 2-opt interchange algorithm and the last, but not the least the ACO.

In a classical statement of the problem the distances between nodes are symmetric and do not change. This seems to match the real life where the road structure remains relatively static. Having said that we should bear in mind that minimizing the distance is not what we have really interest in. In more practical objectives include, e.g., the traveling time which is subject to the ever changing road conditions and therefore is inherently dynamic. The Dynamic TSP was introduced for the first time by Psarafits [2] and various aspects of the DTSP are now the subject of intensive study [3–5].

3 Ant colony optimization

Scientists were for a long-time puzzled by way the in which tiny, week and blind creatures, e.g., the termites, were capable of building and operating extremely complex, city like structures such as termite nests. The explanation was proposed in late 50' of the previous centaury by the French biologist Pierre-Paul Grassé. He coined the term stigmergy to describe a mechanism of indirect coordination between agents or actions. In the real world it could produce complex, seemingly intelligent structures, without the need for any planning, control, or even direct communication between the agents. The agents have very little or no memory. They lack intelligence or even awareness of each other. What makes them so capable is the pheromone trail that is deposited in the environment. The extreme simplicity of ants combined with their apparent ability to produce complex structures make them very attractive for computer science.

The ACO technique was introduced by Dorigo in as early as in 1992 [6]. Until now he remains one of the key researchers in this area. His extensive and fairly recent account of the ACO state of the art is presented in [7]. An ant colony consists of ants which are extremely simple agents. All they can do is to move from one node to another laying a pheromone trail on their way. They are also capable of detecting their current position, remembering the nodes that were already visited and sensing the direct distances from its current position to other nodes as well as the amount of pheromone laid upon them. The colony works in iterations. At the start of each iteration the ants are placed randomly on the graph. Each ant works on its own, completing a route that connects all nodes. In each step of an iteration an ant, sensing the distance and pheromone levels placed on routes connecting nodes, selects the next node to visit. The iteration stops when all cities are visited by all ants. The pheromone matrix harvests the collective experience gained by the ants. This general idea has many variants such as ant systems, ant colony systems, Max–Min ant systems. They differ mainly in exact way pheromone is deposited and the role played by the colony. In each case the colony remembers the BSF (Best So Far) route, the current iteration number and the iterations' best route. The colony is responsible also for global pheromone updating.

3.1 Operation details

The distances between the cities (nodes) are represented by a square matrix of floating point numbers. The number of rows or columns is denoted by N. The element in row r and column s is denoted by $\delta(r, s)$ and is known also as a cost measure. The matrix is symmetric so $\delta(r, s) = \delta(s, r)$ and additionally for all nodes r $\delta(r, r) = 0$.

The pheromone levels are stored in an another matrix of floating point numbers which has the same size of the distances matrix. Its elements are denoted by $\tau(r, s)$ and are referred to as the desirability measure. The algorithm guaranties, that allays $\tau(r, s) > 0$. The ACO initializes all elements of the matrix are with the same value at the beginning of its work. Pheromone levels are preserved from one iteration to another.

There are three rules that define the operation of the ACO:

- the State Transition Rule that specifies the next node an ant selects, see Formulas 1 and 2;
- the Local Updating Rule which updates the pheromones as an ant moves from one node to another, see Formula 3;
- the Global Updating Rule which defines the way in which the pheromones are updated when all ants have constructed whole route, see Formula 5.

The operation of the ACO is controlled by five parameters. They are shown in the Table 1. The complexity of the ACO operation so great that it is impossible to provide an analytical way of selecting their optimal values. Therefore, they are usually chosen in an experimental manner. The table contains also their recommend used by many researches, e.g., by Chirico [8].

Table 1 ACO parameter description

Name	Description	Suggested value
N	Number of ants	Number of nodes
Q0	Probability of selecting exploitation over exploration	0.8
α	Aging factor used in the global updating rule	0.1
β	Moderating factor for the cost measure function	2.0
ρ	Aging factor in the local updating rule	0.1

An ant selects the next node using one of two possible operation modes: exploitation and exploration. In the exploitation mode an ant works in a deterministic manner. Staying in the r node an it selects the node t which maximizes the route quality function qf:

$$qf(r, t) = \tau(r, t) * \eta(r, t)^{\beta}. \tag{1}$$

The pheromone levels represent the collective knowledge of all ants. The influence of the distance depends of the parameter β. It is greater than 1. The distance between two nodes is always ≤ 1 therefore increasing β gives more prominence to pheromone level. Note, that to find the next node the values of the $qf(r, t)$ function for all possible (not yet visited) nodes have to be calculated.

By contrast, the exploration is a non-deterministic process. It selects the next t node with the probabilities defined by the Formula 2:

$$pr(r, t) = \frac{qf(r, t)}{\sum_{u \in A(r)} qf(r, u)} \tag{2}$$

The exploration algorithm prefers to choose nodes with the highest value of the qf function but it could, with a lesser probability, select any other available node. Their set is denoted by $A(r)$. Exploration is used to search for alternative solutions and to mitigate the danger of a colony being trapped in a local minimum. The parameter Q0 specifies the probability of selecting the exploitation mode of operation. The selection of operation mode is done each time a node is to be selected. As you can see the operation of the ACO is non-deterministic. A random number generator is used both for the selection of the operating mode and to select a node in the exploration mode. Usually the ants are implemented as threads and this is also introduces non-determinism.

Due to the sheer number of time-consuming floating point operations that are necessary to select the next node the ACO algorithm is relatively slow.

The pheromone levels are changed applying local and global updating rules. The local updating rule is used on the fly by each ant as it moves from one node to another. The global updating is done by the colony after an iteration step was completed. Let BSF (Best So Far) denote the best path found so far by any ant and L(BSF) denote its length. The Formula F3 defines the local updating rule:

$$\tau(r, s) = (1 - \rho) * \tau(r, s) + \rho * \Delta(r, s) \tag{3}$$

where:

$$\Delta(r, s) = \begin{cases} \frac{L(BSF)^{-1} \quad \text{if}(r, s) \in \text{global-best-tour}}{0 \quad \text{otherwise}} \end{cases}. \tag{4}$$

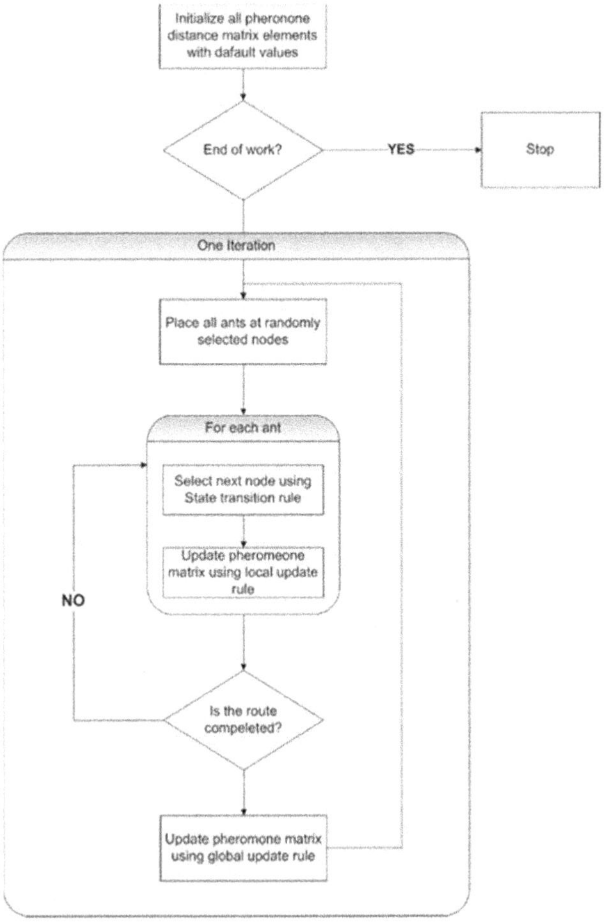

Fig. 1 Schema of the ACO operation

Taking a route that does not belong to the BSF results in decreasing the level of its pheromone. This simulates the process of pheromone evaporation. Otherwise the range of modification depends on the quality of the BSF solution. The shorter it is, the more impact it has on the resulting pheromone level. The evaporating intensity is controlled by the parameter ρ.

The global updating function is evoked after each iteration, It changes the pheromone level on all routs in the graph. The Formula 5 specifies the level modification:

$$\tau(r, s) = (1 - \alpha) * \tau(r, s) + \alpha * \Delta(r, s). \quad (5)$$

The Formula 5 is very much like the Formula 3, the only difference is that it evaporation intensity is controlled by still another parameter α. For $\alpha = 1$ the ACO has no memory of previous results. With consecutive numbers of iterations the value of $\Delta(r, s)$ increases and therefore ACO favors exploration at start of its work and later the found solution become more and more stable as the exploitation becomes more prominent.

The initial values of the pheromone level for all paths (τ_0) of a network with n nodes are not parameterized and are calculated using the Formula 6:

$$\tau_0 = \frac{2n}{\sum \delta(r, s)}. \quad (6)$$

The operation of an ant colony is shown on the Fig. 1. The end of work condition usually tests the total number of completed iterations or checks if no shortening of the BSF route has been reported over a predefined number of iterations.

3.2 ACO Optimization

Although the operation of each ant is simple their interplay is complex. Therefore, the selection of the values for the parameters from the Table 1 is not possible in any analytic manner. The paper [9] reports that their strikingly different values could lead to solutions of similar quality. What makes the process even more complex is the non-deterministic character of the ACO. The solutions found for the same static graph and the same set of parameter values could differ even after many thousands of iterations.

The recommended parameter values have round values like 0.8 or 2.0. This gives rise to an assumption that they are not optimal. Various attempts to identify values offering better results were described, e.g., in [10] or [11]. They include algorithms inspired by evolutionary programming (EP), simulated annealing (SA) or a statistical analysis of a large collection of gathered results. The results are not quite satisfactory. It possible to find values that lead to better results than the results achieved with recommended values, but it was not possible to correlate them to the properties of the environment. In each particular case has to be treated individually and the optimization of parameters values requires time-consuming experiments.

The route length is not the only quality measure. The other one is the execution time. In the study reported in this paper we examine the way in which the number of used ants and their organization impacts the processing time and route length.

3.3 Stopping Problem

No matter what the parameter values are used the processing has to be stopped at same point of time. When to stop is a question that is rarely raised in the discussion of the ACO. The frequency of changes of the BSF route lessens as the number of iterations increases. This means that the computational effort needed to execute subsequent iterations is less and less profitable. This is clearly visible on the Fig. 2 which illustrates the typical performance of an ACO.

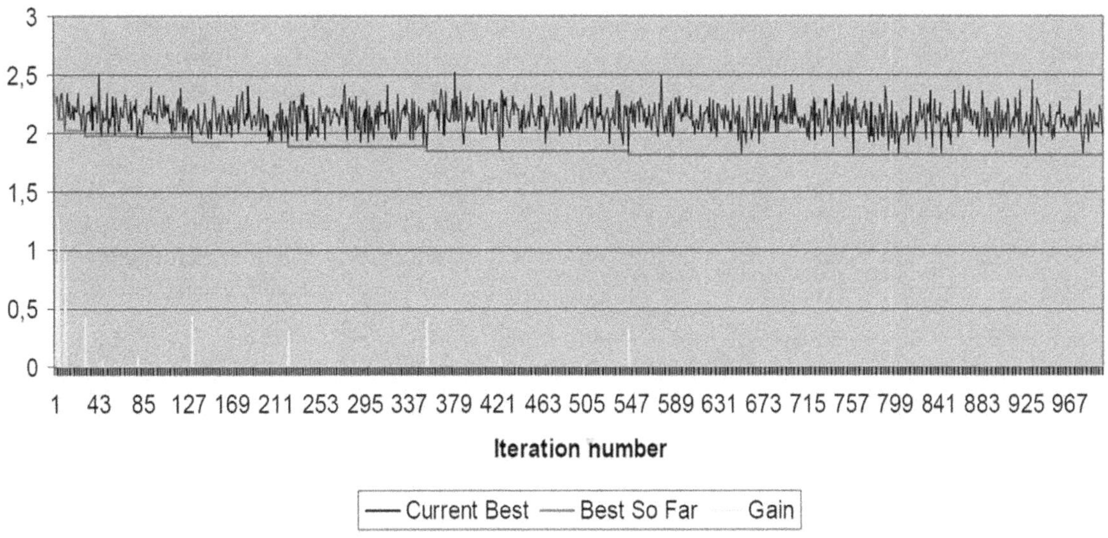

Fig. 2 The performance of a standard version of ACO [18]

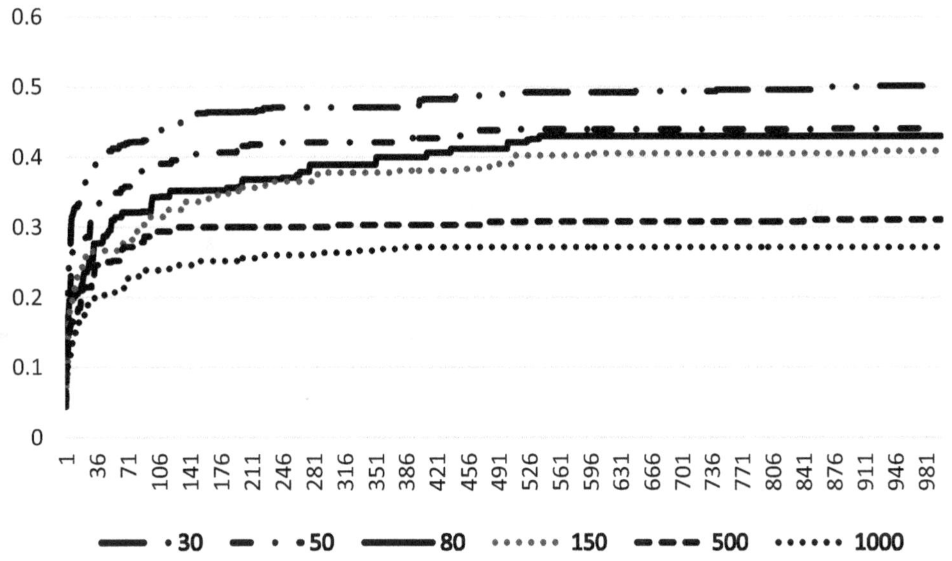

Fig. 3 The cumulative gain in consecutive iterations for colonies with the number of ants in the range from 30 to 1000 [18]

The jigsaw upper line represents the best solution for consecutive iterations. There seems to be no clear pattern in its behavior. This makes extremely hard to predict the quality of the solution which the next iteration delivers. The lower, while spikes mark iterations for which there was a change in the BSF route length and their height is proportional to the shortening of L(BSF). They are more predictable. With the increasing number of iterations the spikes are less and less frequent. Note also that in the above example almost half of the processing time was not productive at all. There was no spike and hence no shortening of the BSF path after the iteration number 547.

To have a deeper insight into the performance of ACO we introduce the Cumulative Gain defied by the Formula 7. It describes the how much the solutions improve.

$$CG(i) = \left(\sum_{r=0}^{R} (\text{len}(r, 0) - \text{len}(r, i)) \right) / R \tag{7}$$

where R is the number of runs, i is the iteration number, len(r, i) is the BSF route length for the iteration i in the test run number r.

The Fig. 3 shows what impact the different sizes of an Ant Colony have on the Cumulative Gain.

The cumulative gain is the measure of the shortening of route not of its length. Therefore, the best performer (disregarding complexity of operation) is the colony with 1000 ants represented by the lower, dotted line. The sooner the values converge the better. Over populating the colonies offers a reasonable solution to the stopping problem. The routes length converge faster and there is much less incentive to extend the

Table 2 Observed average BSF route for varying colony populations, number of iterations, number of runs 30

Ant colony size	BSF fixed size	BSF normalized
30	1.82 [1000]	1.80 [1666]
50	1.81 [1000]	1.81 [1000]
80	1.80 [1000]	1.80 [625]
120	1.80 [1000]	1.85 [417]
150	1.79 [1000]	1.80 [333]
1000	1.78 [1000]	1.78 [50]

number of iterations. Note that in the above example for the 1000 ant colony there is hardly any improvement after the 320 iteration.

4 Increasing the number of ants

Many experiments have proven that the standard values of parameters provide a stable and reasonable good performance over a wide spectrum of input data. The recommended number of ants is equal to the number of nodes. For that reason the solution proposed in the paper keeps their standard values and studies the impact that the changes in the number of ants have on the performance of the ACO. The Fig. 1 suggests that the increase in the population size could be offset by the decrease in the number of iterations that are necessary to obtain stable and reasonably good results. In particular we are interested in using ant numbers that substantially exceed the recommended values. There are two ways in which the number is increased: single colony and multi-colony approaches.

Experiments conducted on a matrix with 50 nodes are reported in the Table 2 confirm that it is really possible to benefit from that phenomena. The Table shows average values of the BSF for different sizes of colony and varying number of iterations. The number of iterations is shown in square brackets. The iteration numbers in the BSF normalized column ware selected in such a way as to preserve the same the computational complexity of each raw.

The over populating of a single ant colony does not offer a significant reduction in route length. The middle column contains the route lengths obtained after 1000 iterations for all colonies. The slight decrease in route length, e.g., for the colony of size 1000 does not compensate the 20-fold increase in processing time. Observe, however, that the last column with the normalized values for the BSF. Increasing if the ant's number is compensated by lowering the number of iterations. For the hugely overpopulated colony with 1000 ants the number of iterations is as small 50. The decrease in the BSF is not impressive, but the small number of iterations paves the way for parallel implementation of the ACO.

In the multi-colony approach the ants are distributed over more than one colony. Their number in a single colony could also exceed regular values as well. Using many colonies working in parallel brings up two problems:

- The necessary communication overhead must not diminish the advantages of speed up due to parallelism.
- The lack or reduction of cooperation of ants from different colonies must have not much effect upon the quality of the resulting solution.

The first problem could be analyzed theoretically. Let us assume that the colony is implemented by a number of node computers and one host computer that coordinates their work. The operation of a parallel colony is characterized by the following factors:

- n – the number of ants.
- k – the number of node computers.
- m – the number of chunks of data.
- t_i – time required to process one chunk of data by one ant.
- t_d – time necessary to transmit data to and from the host and a node.
- t_c - time for the establishing the initial connection between the host and a node.

A parallel implementation reduces the processing time only if the number of node computers satisfies the inequity:

$$k > \frac{nt_i}{nt_i - t_d - \frac{t_c}{m}} \tag{8}$$

and

$$nt_i - t_d - \frac{t_c}{m} > 0 \tag{9}$$

For a continues mode of operation which is typical for dynamic environments the value of t_c/m is negligible. What is really required is that the local one node processing time is less than the time necessary to transmit the necessary data.

The study on the second phenomena is for more complex and is delayed until the Sect. 6. This Section describes the details of the proposed approach and interprets the obtained experimental results. The following Sect. 5 describes related work on parallel implementations of the ACO.

5 Parallel implementations of ACO

No matter what is the number of used ants, the ACO metaheuristic needs relatively long time to provide a solution. Therefore, the first attempts to shorten the processing time by parallel implementation of the ACO were presented just a few years after the its introduction. The ACO depends on cooperation of individual ants. The main problem is: in what way to preserve some level of their cooperation in a parallel environment.

5.1 Performance measures

The efficient, algorithmic solutions for many complex real life problems are not known. Solving NP-hard optimization problems is compute-intensive. Therefore, often we have to resolve to parallel implementations. The reasons for that are twofold [12]. First they take benefit of using several computing elements to speed up the processing. Second we may introduce new exploration patterns that are not workable for the sequential implementations. In parallel algorithms that require a close cooperation between individual agents there is a need for specially designed hardware that can support it. Therefore, the parallel ACO is mainly implemented on traditional supercomputers, clusters of workstations, multicore processors and grid environments and recently graphics processing units [13].

The most common metrics used to evaluate the performance of parallel algorithms are the speed up (s_m) and the efficiency (e_m). The speed up indicates how much faster a parallel algorithm is than its corresponding sequential algorithm. In the case of non-deterministic implementations the mean values are used, see Formula 10 and

$$S_m = \frac{T_1}{T_m} \tag{10}$$

or for non-deterministic case

$$S_m = \frac{E\left[T_1\right]}{E\left[T_m\right]} \tag{11}$$

where T_1 and T_m denote the execution time of sequential algorithm and its parallel version using m processors.

The efficiency is the normalized version of the speed up and is introduced to enable the comparison of implementations using non-identical computing platforms.

$$e_m = \frac{S_m}{m}. \tag{12}$$

There are two factors that usually restrict the value of e_m to values less than 1. First is the well-known Amdahl's law [14] which limits the performance of any parallel application by the sequential part of the code. The second is the communication time overhead which could be quite considerable even on a specialized hardware. There were, however, reports, that for some specific problems, taking into advantage specialized hardware architecture and dedicated algorithm design it is possible to achieve the values of $e_m > 1$ [15].

In the paper [12] we have a comprehensive, up to date taxonomy of parallel ACO. The taxonomy consists of two broad categories: Master-slave model and Cellular model.

5.2 Taxonomy of parallel ACO

5.2.1 Master-slave model

This is a strictly a hierarchical parallel model in which a master process manages the global information including, e.g., the pheromone matrix or best-so-far solution. It also controls the slave processes that are responsible performing the actual search of the solution space. The model has three subcategories. The classification criterion is the granularity level that is the amount of work performed by each slave process.

- Coarse-grain master-slave model. The master manages the pheromone matrix and the interaction with the slaves is based on complete solutions. Each slave has one or more ants, and they compute complete solutions which are then communicated back to the master. The master can receive just one or many solutions from a slave. It selects the best solution or merges them.
- Medium-grain master-slave model. The key feature is the domain decomposition. The slave processes solve work on each sub-problem independently. The master process is responsible for managing the overall problem information and constructing a complete solution from the partial solutions reported by the slaves.
- Fine-grain master-slave model. The model requires the parallel evaluation of solution elements. The slaves perform minimum granularity tasks, e.g., selecting the next node. It is characterized by the frequent communications between the master and the slaves.

5.2.2 Cooperative models

In this group the colonies cooperate directly without the need of a master.

- Cellular model. The model uses follows the guidelines specified by the diffusion model employed in cellular evolutionary algorithm. A single colony is structured in small neighborhoods. Each one has its own pheromone matrix. The trail pheromone update in each matrix considers only the solutions constructed by the ants in its neighborhood. The model uses overlapping neighborhoods. This makes it possible to spread gradually high quality solutions from the place of their origin to other neighborhoods.

Table 3 Characteristics of the models in the new taxonomy [12]

Model	Population organization	# Colonies	# Pheromone matrices	Communication frequency
Coarse-grain master-slave	Hierarchical, non-cooperative	One	One	Medium
Medium-grain master-slave	Hierarchical, non-cooperative	One	One	Medium-high
Fine-grain master-slave	Hierarchical	One	One	High
Cellular	Structured, cooperative	One	Many	Medium
Parallel independent runs	Distributed, non-cooperative	Several	Several	Zero
Multi-colony	Distributed, cooperative	Several	Several	Low
Hybrids	Hierarchical	D/P	D/P	D/P

- Parallel independent runs model. The cooperation between colonies is not required. Several sequential ACOs are concurrently executed on a set of processors. The individual ACO can use identical or different parameters. The executions are completely independent.
- Multi-colony model. Several colonies explore in this model the search space using their own pheromone matrices. The colonies periodically exchange information.
- Hybrid models. Some papers describe algorithms that feature characteristics from more than one parallel model. This may include approaches that combine master-slave models or that introduce hierarchical structure into the basic model.

The basic features of the taxonomy are summarized in the Table 3. The D/P abbreviation stands for depending on proposal.

5.3 Examples of fine-grain implementations of ACO

The approach taken in this study is an example of coarse-grain master-slave model. We think, however, that is instructive to confront it with two fine-grain approaches. This makes apparent the consequences of using a particular model.

In the implementation proposed by Randall and Lewis [16] each ant is assigned to a separate processor. It is therefore extremely fine-grained implementation. The client works in a loop in which it receives the pheromone matrix form the server, selects the next node and passes back the choice to the server. This involves massive data exchange. The problem of it is not only just amount of the data, but also frequency of data synchronization. The ants are allowed to modify the pheromone matrix at the same time. In traditional approaches the synchronization of matrix access by different threads is done, e.g., by the standard lock mechanism of Java. The locks are part of the core of the JVM and therefore they are very efficient. The synchronization of different processes if much more time consuming. There are two drawbacks of the solution. The number of ants is limited by the available hardware. In the experiment their number was in the range from 2 to 8.

Table 4 Comparing the efficiency (*Sm*) of message passing and sharing of memory for parallel ACO's [17]

Node number	Number of processors						
	Message passing						
	2	3	4	5	6	7	8
318	0.60	0.48	0.36	0.32	0.27	0.22	0.20
442	0.71	0.54	0.48	0.44	0.38	0.33	0.29
657	0.83	0.65	0.58	0.58	0.54	0.47	0.41
	Shared memory						
318	0.83	0.80	0.77	0.73	0.69	0.66	0.60
442	0.86	0.82	0.81	0.80	0.76	0.75	0.69
657	0.87	0.87	0.85	0.82	0.80	0.77	0.77

All papers advocate more numerous ant colonies and some of them describe even the advantages of overpopulating of the colonies. The second is long time necessary to synchronize numerous modifications of the pheromone matrix. To communicate the processors use the messages.

The solution proposed by Delisle et al. [17] eliminates some on the above deficiencies by relaxing the onerous pheromone matrix update. In this solution each client looks for the route separately updating the pheromones levels locally. Only after completing the route it is passed to the server. The server is responsible for finding the best solution, preforming the global pheromone level update and sending the results to the clients. Each client can host several ants. Best results, both in the terms of speed up and the solution quality were obtained with the value of 40—the maximal number of ants being allocated to a processor. The communication is based on sheared memory model. The Table 4 compares the efficiency measured by S_m of the two approaches.

The results speak clearly for the second approach. In all reported cases the efficiency lowers with increasing number of processors and increases with the number of nodes. The shared memory approach is superior to message passing on every instance. The difference is remarkably high for the lowest number of nodes and eight processers. Note also that the efficiency raises significantly with the increase of node number.

The communication overhead and need for synchronization of pheromone matrix could severely limit the benefits of parallelization. In the first from above examples the size of transferred data is small, but it is very frequent. The second approach makes the transfer less frequent, but the size of data increases. It is well known that memory sharing is the fastest way of communication between processes. The size of data is not critical factor. The impact of synchronizing read-write access to common memory has more severe impact.

The low level approaches described above have two deficiencies. The necessity of frequent updates diminishes the speed up factor and they require dedicated hardware. The hardware configurations are hardly scalable and are not popular. On the other hand they duplicate or closely mimic the operation of a single colony. Therefore, they can directly exploit the extensive research work on the ACO area.

5.4 Coarse-grain implementation

In a contrast to the fine-grained models the coarse-grain models communicate less frequently. They can be implemented on a number of different types of standard computers. This is the approach taken in this paper. It has two advantages. The structure of the implementation is flexible, could adopt itself to needs or changing environment. Computers with different processing power could cooperate easily. It even enables us to harvest the spare computer power which is available for free on almost all computers. Up to date multicore processors have processing power exceeding that of mainframes from mid-90's. Computers working in a typical network have processor utilization less than 5 % most all the time. The rest is consumed by the idle process of operating system and thus is available for free.

The implementation uses the Sockets mechanism. It keeps permanent connection between two processes until one of them closes it or stops operation. They communicate over network addresses. This ensures a great deal of flexibility as we are not constrained by the physical structure of a computer. The processes could be run on one computer using local host address or over a network. The socket stream-based mode of operation used in the experiments ensures reliable transfer of data on the physical level.

In a previous work the communication between the server and clients used the Java Remote Method Invocation which is a relatively high level mechanism [18]. It offers the developer many advantages. Once the connection has been established the code for handling local and remote objects is almost identical. This gives the developer full compiler support. The implementation and debugging of network programs are not much different from traditional programming. The complexity of organizing the data flow is handled by the compiler.

Table 5 Time necessary to perform basic operations for the RMI and sockets

Operation	RMI network	Sockets	
		Local server	Network server
Initialization if the connection	1.30 s	0.75 s	0.45 s
Passing parameter (one double value)	0.01 s	0.01 s	0.23 s
Passing distance matrix (50 Nodes)	1.60 s	0.03 s	0,26 s

Using the RMI is therefore most beneficial when the interaction pattern is complex.

The RMI enable us to have a parallel implementation with just one remote colony object that resides on a server and hosts the distance and pheromone matrixes. The individual ants could be located on client computers. Once the connection between processes has been established the source code for such an implementations differs not much from its original, sequential version. The RMI could be easily used for fine-grained parallelization approaches.

The RMI approach looks attractive at first, but it is less useful when it comes to an actual implementation. The time necessary for a remote procedure call to fetch a double value is approximately equal to 0.39 ms even when the client and the server reside on the same machine. In contrast fetching the same value from a local object is equal to 0,001785 ms so it is two orders of magnitude faster. Calling a methods with a single double parameter to on network object is much slower—it takes 10 ms, see Table 5. The passing of a pheromone matrix takes almost 2 s.

The RMI mechanism makes it possible to have a straightforward implementation of a fine-grained parallel ant colony, but the performance of such a solution is poor. The access to pheromone matrix is many orders of magnitude slower than for traditional thread-based sequential implementations. For the coarse-grained parallel implementation the communication burden is not prohibitive. Transmitting a whole matrix takes a few seconds, but a colony needs a few minute to process it.

In the case of the coarse-grained parallel implementation of the ACC the data flow pattern is straightforward and it could be implemented without using remote objects. All we need is pure data transfer. That functionality is offered by sockets. The low level socket mechanism provides a connection-oriented service. The protocol used for transmission is the TCP. The Community uses stream-based sockets to establish a connection between two processes. While it is in place, data flow between the processes in continuous streams.

Unlike the RMI the sockets do not provide remote objects and offers only means for data transfer. The programmer

Table 6 Time necessary for the sockets to transfer a given number of floating point numbers (in milliseconds)

Connection type	Number of doubles	Mean time	Std. dev.	Rate
Local	100	11.13	6.48	8.98
	1200	34.99	7.054	34.31
	4900	136.31	12.35	35.95
	19800	511.37	96.89	38.72
Network	100	228.75	12.55	0.44
	1200	261.27	39.37	4.59
	4900	342.85	31.13	14.29
	19800	726.55	330.26	27.25

is solely responsible for ensuring the correctness of data flow that is making sure that both the server and the client expect the same type of data. As the real life communication between a server and a client requires many types of messages being transferred and this may sound prohibitive. Fortunately enough the JVM supports the transfer of any serializable object what makes the task less daunting. Using serialized objects by the socket mechanism does not mean that we have access to objects methods. Only the data are transferred.

The data in the Table 5 show the difference in performance between the RMI an Sockets. The RMI is optimized for parameter passing what is common for method evocation, but are less efficient for passing large amounts of data.

The time that is necessary for initializing connection is shorter than for the RMI, but this is not crucial as it happens only once. The sockets mechanism is optimized for transferring large blocks of data over the network as is clearly visible from the measurements that are shown in the Table 6. The transfer rate steadily increases with the size of data being transmitted and for the largest block there is not much difference between local and network transfer.

In the traditional client—server mode of operation thin clients call a server for performing complex calculations or to obtain data from a centralized database. In the parallel implementation of the ACO the configuration is reversed. The bulk of computations is done by the clients. The obtained results are passed to the server which is responsible for evaluating the individual solutions obtained by the clients, selecting solutions to propagate and sending tasks to servers. The kind of task depends on the granularity level of parallelization.

The server is a multi-threaded process with each thread being attached to a unique client. The number of threads is limited only by the memory available on the server. For a computer with 12 Gb of memory is no limit to their number from the practical point of view. Usually a client colony works on a dedicated computer as a separate process. It is also possible to locate a few of clients running on a single machine.

5.5 Presentation of ant colony community

The ACC consists of a number of colonies controlled by a server. The initial version of the ACC was presented in [18]. The older version of the ACC used the RMI mechanism and its structure was rigid. In an apparent contrast to its predecessor the structure of the ACC presented here uses Sockets and its structure is highly flexible. It could change at runtime.

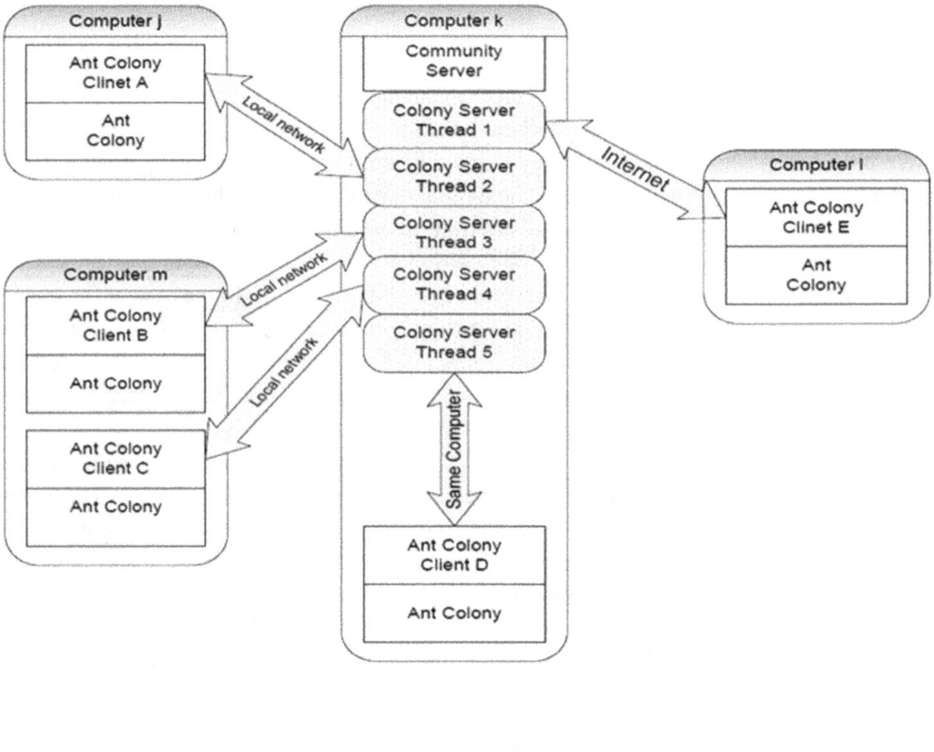

Fig. 4 An example of an ant colony community

Table 7 The message passing between a server and a client colony

Community server operation	Ant colony client operation	Remarks
Stop if work is accomplished		The stopping criteria are described in Sect. 3.3
	← Register client	A separate thread is created to handle the client. Register data include: client identifier and location, current time. They are stored in a server's registry
Initialization data→		Colony operational parameters distance matrix specification
Loop data →	Using data from server the client creates an ant colony and starts its operation	Community best so far solution [distance matrix][pheromone matrix]
	←Found solution	Distance of the best path, sequence of visited nodes, [pheromone] matrix
Result Integration		

The colonies could run a single computer, many computers in a local network or on computers on internet servers. It is possible also to have any combination of this locations. An exemplary structure with four computers and five Ant Colonies is presented on the Fig. 4.

The CS (community server) awaits for calls from ACCs (ant colony clients). The CS after receiving a request from the ACC, registers it in its repository and creates a separate thread for handling data transmission. In the next step the CS passes parameters and data to the appropriate ACC. Depending on the type of Community Server the data can contain distance matrix, pheromone matrix as well as previously found routes. After that, the CS waits for the a solution from any ACC. The ACC in turn after receiving data from the CS a colony creates a local ant colony and feeds it with the data from the server and then starts it operation. An Ant Colony produces solution and passes it to ACC which transmits it further to the Community server.

The descried above structure is relatively simple and at the same time robust and flexible. The complex task of finding solutions is separated from the rest of the implementation. Replacing one type of an ant colony by another is relatively simple. The communication process is initiated by an Ant Colony Client and the Community adopts itself automatically to different processing power or connection transfer rate. The "slower" clients, hosted, e.g., on a remote Internet server are just less frequently assigned tasks by the Colony Server. Even dropping out of a computer from the Community does not disintegrate its operations. The processing just slows down as more tasks are allocated to the remaining clients. The ACCs are separate processes. To obtain reliable measurements of the execution time they were started by a cron-like utility during the tests. A single computer can host many ACCs. We have found that running more than six ACCs on a computer without a SSD drains the recourses of a typical personal computer.

The processing ends when the stopping condition has been met. This happens when the server has already received a specified number of solutions or the predefined processing time has elapsed. The stopping criteria and their substantiation are described in the Sect. 3.3. In either case the server breaks connection to all clients what eventually leads to killing all processes that are executed on the client side.

The Table 7 shows the operation synchronization of the Community Server and Client. The elements enclosed in [ ] are optional. The operations written in bold are performed in a loop, separate for each client.

6 Analysis of ACC operation

To evaluate the performance of the proposed solution a number of experiments were performed.

6.1 Experimental setup

The experiments were run on a network of four computers with codenames from Ca to Cd. All of them have minimum 4 Gb of memory. They were equipped with different processors. The Ca computer was the fastest one. It had Intel i7-4700MQ 2.4 GHz 2.4 Ghz. The Cc with processor Inter Core2Quad D6600 computer was the slowest one. The difference in computing power had an impact on the structure of the communities.

Each colony runs as a separate process. All of the computers were powerful enough to host many of them. The data in the Table 8 show how efficient it could be. The table shows the time used to run various number of an ACO tasks simul-

Table 8 The efficiency of hosting many colonies on a single computer with a SSD drive

Number of colonies	Total time	Time per colony
1	81	81.0
2	83	41.5
3	86	28.7
4	89	22.2
5	100	20.0
6	115	19.8

Table 9 Structure of ant communities

Code	Number of ant colonies	Computer/colony number
A	1	Cb /1
B	3	Ca/3
C	7	Ca/4; Cb/3
D	12	Ca/6; Cb/4; Cd/2

taneously on the computer Cc. Running simultaneously five colonies has increased the processing time by mere 25 % from 81 to 100 seconds. This means that the time per colony has dropped fourfold. For greater number colonies the time per colony increases due to memory swapping and frequent context switching. The data reported in the Table 8 refer to a computer equipped with a SSD drive. For computers with traditional hard disk drives the time per colony starts to increase for smaller number of colonies.

During the tests reported in this table the computer run only ant colony applications. The processor power was fully utilized. This kind of performance could not be sustained if a computer runs any other resource demanding a or an interactive application. This is not a serious limitation as the processor workload of computers in a typical network exceeds single digit values only occasionally. The ant colony application could be started if the processor workload does not exceed a predefined value.

It turned out that assigning many colonies to slower computers, although technically possible has resulted in a notable drop in quality of obtained results. The allocation of colonies to computers was done according to the rule of a thumb and was not the result of any optimization process. The aim of the study was to measure the relationship between the number of Ant Colonies and the achieved route length and not to optimize the Ant Communities structure. The structure of the used communities used in the experiment is presented in the next Table 9. The last column shows the computers and the maximal number of ant colonies that they could host. The Cd computer was used as a server. The Cb computer, ranked in the middle according to processor power was used for reference purposes.

Table 10 Ranking of communities, an example

Community	$Len(C_x T_k)$					$PRV(C_x, T_k)$					$RV(C_x)$
	1	2	3	4	5	1	2	3	4	5	
C1	2.4	2.1	3.0	2.3	2.1	1	2	0	0	2	5
C2	2.5	1.9	2.2	2.1	2.7	0	3	2	2	1	8
C3	2.1	2.4	1.9	2.2	1.8	3	0	3	1	3	10
C4	2.3	2.2	2.6	1.9	2.8	2	1	1	3	0	7

In the study only one server was used, but it is possible to build a more complex, multilayer structure in which lower layer server pass found solutions to a server located higher in the structure hierarchy.

6.2 Evaluating the efficiency of the TSP ACO

The TSP had started as a recreational puzzle and the solutions were assessed according to one criteria: the length of route. This simplistic approach is not sufficient when we try to evaluate ACO algorithms used for solving the problem. There are several reasons for that:

- As stated in the Sect. 3.1 the exploitation mode of work uses random function to select the next node. The selection of the mode of work is also controlled by a random function. As the result the ACO is non-deterministic by nature. The same algorithm working with identical set of parameters and processing the same distance matrix produces usually different results every time it is activated. We must therefore consider not a single result, but their arithmetic mean, other statistical measures could be also considered.
- A single solution, even a very good one, is not a decisive factor in evaluating a Community. It is very much possible that the next found solution will be not as good.
- Measuring the performance using mean values is not entirely justified due to the dispersion of results obtained in consecutive runs.
- For parallel implementations the computational complexity should be augmented or even replaced by duration of execution.
- It is important not only what solution was found, but also how may iterations we executed. It is true for both parallel and sequential implementations. For the dynamic TSP good quality solutions must be found quickly enough to catch up with the changing distances matrix.

Bearing all this in mind all these above factors we have decided to propose a more complex schema for ranking Ant Colony Communities. The process respects the following principles:

- To evaluate a community we run test it several times using the same distance matrix.
- Instead of using mean of route lengths we used ranks of route lengths.
- Two criteria for stopping the run are used:
  - Equal complexity—the computational complexity measured by the number of node selection operations is the same for all Colonies. The time needed to find a solution could be different and depends on the architecture of the Community.
  - Equal time—the clock time given to all Colonies is the same. The complexity of operation could be different and it is the sum of the complexities of individual Colonies that make up a Community.

Let Len(C_{xk}) denote the length of the best route length found by the Community x in the k-th run.

The process of ranking the communities starts the calculation of PRV($C_x T_k$)—Partial Ranking Value for each test run and each community, see the Formula 13. To rank the Communities we use the PR(C_x) which is sum their ranking values of their tasks, see the Formula 14.

$$\mathrm{PRV}(C_x T_k) = \sum_{i=1}^{N} \left\{ \frac{1 : \mathrm{ifLen}(C_x T_k) < \mathrm{Len}(C_i T_k)}{0 : \mathrm{otherwize}} \right\} \quad (13)$$

where N is the number of communities.

$$\mathrm{RV}(C_x) = \sum_{i=1}^{M} \mathrm{PRV}(C_x T_i) \quad (14)$$

where M is the number of test runs.

The process of ranking of Communities is illustrated by the Table 10.

The equal complexity criteria do not need much justification. It is well established in the computer science. It does not mean that it should be the only one used. Two Communities could have similar ranking values, but could differ substantially in their processing time. In this case the physical structure of a community does not have here any importance.

The equal time criteria are used to select a Community that is most likely to find the best solution in a given period of time. On many occasions the processing time is more important than the difference in route length. For Dynamic TSPs a Community has to find solutions fast enough to adopt to changes in the route matrix. The proposed solution scales very easily and so adding more Colonies could sufficiently seed up the processing.

6.3 The experiment results

During the experiments we ranked Ant Communities using both using the Equal Distances criteria and Equal Time criterion. The Communities used in an experiment are identified by their code (upper case letter) that refers to their structure (see Table 9) and an optional index that differentiates between distinct set of parameters: ant number and iteration number.

6.3.1 Equal complexity criterion

The reference community (code name A) consisted of one colony with standard set of operational parameters with 50 ants and iteration number of 800. All the other communities have preserved the level of computational complexity: the lower values of iteration number were compensated by the increase in the number of colonies and the number of ants in a colony. The actual number of used colonies could be lower that the maximal possible values.

The Table 11 shows the ranking of Communities according the Equal Complexity criterion. The good performance of the Standard Colony comes not as a surprise. Its parameters were carefully chosen after running many experiments and are not manually selected as in the case of the other Communities. Judging the performance of the Standard Community presented in the first row we should not forget that it is much slower than the rest of colonies. The winner, although not a clear one, is the Community B which doubles the number of colonies and keeps relatively large number of iterations. It looks like the iteration number close to 400 is required to achieve acceptable results. Further decreasing of the number of iterations could not be offset by the increase of number of Ants.

Table 11 Ranking of communities according the equal complexity criterion

Comm. code	Colony num.	Ant num.	Iter. #	1	2	3	4	5	6	7	9	8	10	RV
A	1	50	800	5	5	3	5	3	4	0	1	4	1	31
B	2	50	400	1	0	5	3	5	5	4	4	1	5	33
C	2	100	200	0	3	1	0	1	1	3	2	3	0	14
D_1	4	50	200	4	1	2	1	0	2	1	3	5	3	22
D_2	8	50	100	2	2	0	2	4	3	2	5	2	1	23
D_3	8	75	67	3	4	3	4	2	0	5	0	0	4	25

Table 12 Ranking of Communities according the Equal Time criterion

Comm. code	Iter. no.	Ant no.	Colony no.	1	2	3	4	5	6	7	8	9	10	RV
A	800	50	1	0	1	3	0	0	3	0	1	0	0	8
B	350	50	3	1	3	4	3	3	1	4	4	2	4	29
C	350	50	7	5	5	5	5	5	5	5	2	4	4	45
D_1	100	50	12	3	4	1	4	4	3	3	3	4	3	32
D_2	50	100	12	4	2	0	1	2	0	1	4	3	2	19
D_3	100	100	12	2	0	1	2	1	2	2	0	1	1	12

6.3.2 Equal time criterion

In the Equal Time test the structure of the Communities has a great impact on the achieved results. As a reference value we have used the time span necessary for the Cb computer to complete standard run (800 iterations, 50 ants). During the test all colonies were activated at the same time and were allowed to run for the mentioned above time span. After that they were stopped and the best found solution was recorded. Running more colonies on a single computer slows the execution and therefore the number of iterations was lowered from 400 to 350. This was to enable an Ant colony to complete a task within the allowed time period. That percussion measure was needed for the test runs with relative large number of iterations.

The allocation of colonies to computers was done according to the rule of a thumb and was not the result of any optimization process. The aim of the study was to measure the relationship between the number of Ant Colonies and the achieved route length and not to optimize the Ant Communities structure.

The achieved results are presented in the Table 12. The performance looks strikingly different from the previous test. The Standard A community is this time the looser. The difference between the B and C is not a surprise, increasing almost twice the number of Colonies has to result in better solutions. What is, however, worth noting is the performance of the D_1 community. It has a relatively small number of ants, very small amount of iterations and still it the occupies the second position in the ranking. This means that each test takes short time to accomplish. This makes the community a good choice for dynamic TSP.

7 Conclusions and future work

The paper presents initial studies in the performance of Ant Communities. An Ant Community is a coarse-grained parallel implementation of the ACO algorithm. An Ant community has a very flexible structure and the server could coordinate the work of practically any number of individual colonies located upon one or many servers. It uses low level Socket mechanism and is implemented in Java. Both of the features guarantee a fast data transfer. The TSP is a computational demanding process and completion of a typical task could well take almost a minute. Therefore, it allows us to locate many Colonies on one computer or spread them over local or global network and the change the amount of data being transferred between the server and client computers.

The experiments were done with a coarse-grained parallel implementation. The flexible structure of the Ant Community and relatively short transmission overhead allows us to manipulate the granularity level. Further study on that area are necessary. The obtained results show that the Communities could improve the basic, static performance of the TSP ACO. They also provide many clues that they will be much more useful for the dynamic version of the TSP. The tests described in [18], although were obtained using a different approach and implementation technology, also support such a claim.

The ACC was used to coordinate the work of standard Ant Colonies. It is, however, possible to apply the ACC to other related problems, in particular more specific versions of the ACO. Any success on that area would be a proof of the validity of the Ant Colony Communities idea.

References

1. Antosiewicz, M., Koloch, G., Kaminski, B.: Choice of best possible metaheuristic algorithm for the travelling salesman problem with limited computational time: quality, uncertainty and speed. J Theor Appl Comput Sci **7**(1), 46–55 (2013)
2. Psarafits, H.N.: Dynamic Vehicle Routing: Status and Prospects. National technical annals of operations research. University of Athens, Greece (1995)
3. Sieminski, A.: Using ACS for Dynamic Traveling Salesman Problem, New Re-search in Multimedia and Internet Systems. Advances in intelligent systems and computing. Springer, Berlin (2015)
4. Schaefer, R., et al.: Ant Colony Optimization with Immigrants Schemes. In: Schaefer, R., Cotta, C., Kolodziej, J., Rudolph, G. (eds.) PPSN XI, Part II, LNCS 6239, pp. 371–380. Springer, Berlin (2010)
5. Song Y., Qin Y.: Dynamic TSP Optimization Base on Elastic Adjustment. In: IEEE Fifth International Conference on Natural Computation, pp. 205–210 (2009)
6. Dorigo M.,: Optimization, learning and natural algorithms, PhD thesis, Politecnico di Mila-no, Italie (1992)

7. Dorigo M., Stuetzle T.: Ant colony optimization: overview and recent advances, IRIDIA—Technical Report Series, Technical Report No. TR/IRIDIA/2009-013 (2009)
8. Chirico U.: A Java Framework for Ant Colony Systems. Technical report, Siemens Informatica S.p.A (2004)
9. Sieminski, A.: TSP/ACO parameter Optimization. Information Systems Architecture and Technology; System Analysis Approach to the Design, Control and Decision Support, pp. 151–161. Oficyna Wydawnicza Politechniki Wroclawskiej, Wroclaw (2011)
10. Gaertner, D., Clark, K. L.: On optimal parameters for ant colony optimization algorithms. In: IC-AI, pp. 83–89 (2005)
11. Sieminski A.: Ant colony optimization parameter evaluation. In: Multimedia and internet systems: theory and practice. Advances in Intelligent Systems and Computing, ISSN 2194-5357, vol. 183, pp. 143–153
12. Pedemonte, M., Nesmachnow, S., Cancela, H.: A survey on parallel ant colony optimization. Appl. Soft Comput. **11**, 5181–5197 (2011)
13. Delévacq, A., Delisle, P., Gravel, M., Michaël Krajecki, M.: Parallel ant colony optimization on graphics processing units. J. Parallel Distrib. Comput. **73**, 52–61 (2013)
14. G. Amdahl: Validity of the single processor approach to achieving large scale computing capabilities. In: Proceedings of the spring joint computer conference, ACM, New York, USA, pp. 483–485 (1967)
15. Alba, E., Tomassini, M.: Parallelism and evolutionary algorithms. IEEE Trans. Evol. Comput. **6**(5), 443–462 (2002)
16. Randall, M., Lewis, A.: A parallel implementation of ant colony optimization. J. Parallel Distrib. Comput. **62**, 1421–1432 (2002)
17. Delisle, P., Gravel, M., Krajecki, M., Gagne, C., Price, W.: Comparing parallelization of an ACO: message passing vs. shared memory, hybrid metaheuristics. Proc. Lect. Notes Comput. Sci. **2005**(3636), 1–11 (2005)
18. Sieminski, A.: Potentials of Hyper Populated Ant Colonies, 7th Asian Conference, ACIIDS 2015. Lecture Notes in Artificial Intelligence **9011**, 408–417 (2015)
19. Michel, R., Middendorf, M.: An ant system for the shortest common supersequence problem. In: Corne, D., Dorigo, M., Glover, F. (eds.) New ideas in optimization, pp. 51–61. McGraw-Hill Ltd., UK (1999)
20. Gharehchopogh, F.S., Maleki I., Farahmandian M.: New approach for solving dynamic travelling salesman problem with hybrid genetic algorithms and ant colony optimization. Int. J. Comput. Appl. **53**(1), 39–44 (2012)

4

Making kernel-based vector quantization robust and effective for incomplete educational data clustering

Thi Ngoc Chau Vo[1] · Hua Phung Nguyen[1] · Thi Ngoc Tran Vo[2]

Abstract Nowadays, knowledge discovered from educational data sets plays an important role in educational decision making support. One kind of such knowledge that enables us to get insights into our students' characteristics is cluster models generated by a clustering task. Each cluster model presents the groups of similar students by several aspects such as study performance, behavior, skill, etc. Many recent educational data clustering works used the existing algorithms like *k*-means, expectation–maximization, spectral clustering, etc. Nevertheless, none of them considered the incompleteness of the educational data gathered in an academic credit system although incomplete data handling was figured out well with several different general-purpose solutions. Unfortunately, early in-trouble student detection normally faces data incompleteness as we have collected and processed the study results of the second-, third-, and fourth-year students who have not yet accomplished the program as of that moment. In this situation, the clustering task becomes an inevitable incomplete educational data clustering task. Hence, our work focuses on an incomplete educational data clustering approach to the aforementioned task. Following kernel-based vector quantization, we define a robust effective simple solution, named VQ_fk_nps, which is able to not only handle ubiquitous data incompleteness in an iterative manner using the nearest prototype strategy but also optimize the clusters in the feature space to reach the resulting clusters with arbitrary shapes in the data space. As shown through the experimental results on real educational data sets, the clusters from our solution have better cluster quality as compared to some existing approaches.

Keywords Incomplete data clustering · Educational data mining · Kernel-based vector quantization · Nearest prototype strategy · Non-spherical cluster

✉ Thi Ngoc Chau Vo
chauvtn@cse.hcmut.edu.vn

Hua Phung Nguyen
phung@cse.hcmut.edu.vn

Thi Ngoc Tran Vo
vtntran@hcmut.edu.vn

1 Faculty of Computer Science and Engineering, Ho Chi Minh City University of Technology, Vietnam National University, Ho Chi Minh City, Vietnam

2 School of Industrial Management, Ho Chi Minh City University of Technology, Vietnam National University, Ho Chi Minh City, Vietnam

1 Introduction

Educational data mining is nowadays well known worldwide for discovering knowledge hidden in educational data to support educational decision making. As one of the widely used mining tasks, educational data clustering has been considered with many different student-related aspects in [4,5,11–13,15,18,20–22,26] for many various purposes. For example, discovering the groups of similar students is based on study performance in [11], learning behavior in [15], skill in [18], preference in [26], etc. A variety of data have been collected and processed for clustering the students. For example, Bogarín et al. [4] used data of the undergraduate students in an online course using Moodle and Zakrzewska [26] got data about the undergraduate and graduate students participating in the experiments in online collaboration also on Moodle, Refs. [5,11,20] clustered the data of undergraduate students and courses in a few years, Jayabal and Ramanathan [12] analyzed the 10th grade data, Kerr and Chung [13] extracted the student performance features from log data in educational video games and simulations, Li and Yoo [15] used the data recorded from each student's actual lab experience, and so on. Among these related works, only Inyang and Joshua [11] has presented the handling of incomplete data by deleting the missing results in the courses while the others had no mention of incomplete data issues. If the number of missing values is small, ignoring them might have no impact on the performance of the clustering task. Otherwise, the effectiveness of the clustering task might be influenced by data insufficiency. In addition, incomplete data are ubiquitous in the data gathered in an academic credit system, especially in the case we would like to provide any appropriate support to the students as soon as possible in the second, third, or fourth year of their study period. So, our work in this paper is dedicated to a clustering task on incomplete educational data.

Despite such a lack of incomplete data handling for an educational data clustering task, we are aware of many existing works on incomplete data clustering in general such as [1,2,7–9,23,25,27]. Among these works, Refs. [1,2,9,23, 27] updated incomplete data while doing data clustering, Wang [25] translated incomplete data into so-called fuzzy observations before generating clusters, and Refs. [7,8] estimated incomplete data after attaining clusters. Thus, it can be seen that Wang [25] handled incomplete data in the preprocessing phase of the clustering task, Refs. [1,2,9,23,27] tackled incomplete data in the clustering phase of the clustering task, and Refs. [7,8] performed post-processing incomplete data after the clustering task was done. Furthermore, some existing works such as Refs. [9,27] have constrained the resulting shapes of the clusters. Fuzzy c-means, mean-shift clustering, and the self-organizing map (SOM) learning algorithm are some examples which have been enhanced for incomplete data clustering. Nonetheless, it is hard for us to foresee which incomplete data handling techniques are certainly appropriate for a particular application domain and also work well with any existing learning algorithms. Therefore, a study of handling incomplete data in a clustering task is needed to attain an effective cluster model in general and in the education domain.

Based on the motivations stated previously, we concentrate on a solution to the incomplete educational data clustering task in an academic credit system. In particular, we define a kernel-based vector quantization approach to effectively clustering incomplete educational data where incompleteness can be present in any data record at any dimension. Indeed, this work is an extended version of the work previously proposed in [24] where we focused on an effective algorithmic framework for incomplete educational data clustering and illustrated the applicability of the framework with the two proposed algorithms: K_nps and S_nps. K_nps followed the partitioning approach while S_nps did the neural network-based approach. Both of them utilized the nearest prototype strategy for incomplete data updates while do clustering within our proposed algorithmic framework. Like K_nps and S_nps, this work is also based on the proposed framework in [24]; however, defines a new approach using kernel-based vector quantization proposed in [10] and the nearest prototype strategy to handle the ubiquity of incomplete data. The resulting algorithm, named VQ_fk_nps, is our novel incomplete educational data clustering approach as compared to the algorithms K_nps and S_nps which have been achieved in [24]. As compared to K_nps and S_nps, VQ_fk_nps is capable of forming the groups of the similar students which are the clusters with non-spherical shapes in the data space corresponding to the spherical clusters in the feature space. Via the experimental results on real educational data sets with internal clustering validation measures, VQ_fk_nps is confirmed to outperform several existing approaches and thus, be effective for incomplete educational data clustering. Besides, the incomplete data sets that become completed after the data clustering task can be utilized in other mining tasks such as classification and association analysis.

2 Kernel-based vector quantization for incomplete educational data clustering

2.1 Incomplete educational data clustering task definition

To be self-contained, an incomplete educational data clustering task is re-stated in this subsection although first introduced in [24]. This task is a performance-based student clustering task in an academic credit system.

Our educational data mining is dedicated to regular undergraduate students being studying at a university using an academic credit system. During the period of study time, each student has a study status and might face many difficult problems that would influence their study and then make them fail to get a degree from the university. Therefore, we would like to support the current undergraduate students appropriately by examining the cases of the similar students in the past. This leads us to the necessity of grouping the students according to their similar study results, i.e. *a performance-based student clustering task* considered in this paper.

The input of the task is a set $\boldsymbol{D}$ of data vectors each of which represents a student. Dimensions of each vector correspond to the subjects each student has to successfully study to accomplish the program. A value of each vector at a dimension is a grade that the student gets after taking a subject. If the student has not yet taken a subject, its grade is not available and its value at the corresponding dimension is incomplete. Thus, the study performance of each student is reflected through the values of the corresponding vector. In general, $\boldsymbol{D}$ is specified with n data vectors in a p-dimensional data space: $\boldsymbol{D} = \{X_1, X_2, \ldots, X_n\}$ where $X_j = (x_{j,1}, x_{j,2}, \ldots, x_{j,p})$ for $j = 1, \ldots, n$.

The output of the task is a collection of clusters each of which has some similar data vectors. Indeed, each cluster represents a group of the students who have similar study performance. Therefore, they can be considered in the similar cases.

In practice, data gathered in a flexible academic credit system are incomplete. Such data incompleteness is the peculiarity that makes our task challenging. As discussed in [24], *incomplete data can exist in any vector at any dimension in the educational data sets archived within an academic credit system*. That is: $\forall j = 1..n, \exists dim = 1..p, x_{j,dim} \neq$ NULL and $\forall dim = 1..p, \exists j = 1..n, x_{j,dim} \neq$ NULL where NULL is an incomplete value in a given data set $\boldsymbol{D}$. This situation shows the ubiquity of incomplete data in the data we gathered and processed in order to perform a clustering task and thus, requires a clustering solution to pay attention to such data incompleteness.

Unfortunately, no existing educational data mining work has taken data incompleteness into account thoroughly except for [24]. In this paper, our work follows the kernel-based approach with vector quantization and the nearest prototype strategy by proposing a robust and effective incomplete educational data clustering algorithm, named VQ_fk_nps, where we tackle data incompleteness in the data space while doing clustering in the feature space. The reasons for choosing kernel-based vector quantization are given as follows. First, it uses a competitive learning mechanism for grouping the similar objects into several single clusters in the entire data space in a simple but intuitive way. Second, it follows a kernel-based approach that is capable of generating the resulting clusters with non-spherical shapes inherent in the data space corresponding to spherical clusters in the feature space. Finally, it is an iterative clustering algorithm that enables us to embed an incomplete data update phase in an elegant manner without breaking the original clustering procedure.

2.2 Making kernel-based vector quantization robust and effective for incomplete educational data clustering

In this section, a kernel-based approach with vector quantization and the nearest prototype strategy is proposed to effectively clustering incomplete educational data. The resulting algorithm is named VQ_fk_nps (*V*ector *Q*uantization for data clustering in a *F*eature space using the Gaussian *K*ernel function and the *N*earest *P*rototype *S*trategy).

The foundations of a robust kernel-based approach with vector quantization for effectively clustering incomplete educational data

The foundations of our approach are based on the framework proposed in [24] which is the generalization of OCSFCM and NPSFCM algorithms in [9]. This is because Hathaway and Bezdek [9] has taken into account the ubiquity of incomplete data in the same way as we found in the educational data sets earlier discussed in Sect. 2.1. Besides, Hathaway and Bezdek [9] defined a gentle objective-based approach for both clustering and incomplete data handling towards the best resulting clusters in an iterative manner. Moreover, Hathaway and Bezdek [9] has embedded the fuzzy c-means algorithm in steps 2–4 of OCSFCM algorithm completely in the original state in each epoch. These characteristics facilitate the task with any existing iterative algorithms in various clustering approaches.

As previously defined along with the framework in [24], K_nps is an incomplete data clustering version of the k-means algorithm and S_nps is the one of the self-organizing algorithm, both using the nearest prototype strategy. K_nps and S_nps have been tested with the generalization of OCSFCM and NPSFCM algorithms. Experimental results have shown that the proposed framework and its algorithms seem to be appropriate for clustering educational incomplete data sets.

Similarly, in this paper, which is an extended version of [24], VQ_fk_nps is proposed and also dedicated to the education domain. VQ_fk_nps is an incomplete data clustering version of kernel-based vector quantization using the nearest prototype strategy. The main difference between VQ_fk_nps and our previous incomplete educational data clustering algorithms, K_nps and S_nps, is the formulation of the clusters of the similar objects in the feature space with the Gaussian kernel function instead of that in the data space. This approach will enable us to find the non-spherical clusters truly based on the nature of the objects in the data space by means of the simple, efficient, and intuitive unsupervised learning procedure of vector quantization in the feature space. Therefore, we expect to achieve the resulting clusters of better quality in terms of compactness and separation. Besides, we generalize the incomplete data handling approach in the preprocessing phase as well as in the post-processing phase in the proposed algorithm. As a generalized version of the incomplete data handling approach in the preprocessing phase, VQ_fk_nps starts clustering the objects with data completeness after the initial updates on incomplete data using some existing data cleaning method such as attribute means. As a generalized version in the post-processing phase, VQ_fk_nps performs the updates on incomplete data using the nearest prototype strategy after the movement of the reference vectors closer to their members. Furthermore, incomplete data update is made in an iterative manner so that our incomplete data handling process is optimized along with the optimization of the clustering process for better clusters with an approximation of incomplete data.

VQ_fk_nps: a kernel-based vector quantization approach to incomplete data clustering using the nearest prototype strategy

In the following, we describe our incomplete educational data clustering algorithm, VQ_fk_nps, using kernel-based vector quantization proposed in [10]. VQ_fk_nps based on the framework in [24] is composed of four main phases: initialization phase, cluster update phase, incomplete data update phase, and termination phase.

In the initialization phase, we replace all missing values with the attribute means in the complete data subspace so that the initial clusters can be generated by vector quantization with the corresponding data vectors which are now complete. Phase 2 is a cluster update phase where the clustering procedure is run in the feature space to find the clusters with non-linear boundaries in the data space. This phase is mainly employed from [10] where the mean vectors are not explicitly computed. Instead, the clustering procedure keeps track of their members by means of a distance matrix d ($k \times n$ where k is the number of clusters and n is the number of objects). Different from an entire distance update on the distance matrix in [10], our work defines an incremental distance update on an individual cell of the distance matrix. As we check the convergence in step 2.2 right after the update of the clusters in the feature space, the convergence of the clustering procedure is preserved and guaranteed in our algorithm. It is based on the stability of the resulting clusters reflected by the stability of the distance matrix in the feature space. In phase 3, we handle incomplete data directly in an iterative way using their clusters in the data space each of which includes the similar data vectors. Thus, our scheme can conduct incomplete data handling towards the final clusters. In phase 4, we prepare for termination of the algorithm by returning the resulting clusters as several groups of the similar data vectors that are now completed.

Our incomplete educational data clustering algorithm, VQ_fk_nps, is defined as:

Input:

- ***D***: an input data set where incomplete data are present. There are n data vectors each of which is $X_j = (x_{j,1}, x_{j,2}, \ldots, x_{j,p})$ for $j=1..n$ and p is the number of dimensions in the data space.
- σ: the width of the Gaussian kernel function K
- k: the number of clusters
- lr_0: an initial learning rate which is a positive value (lr_0<1.0); used to define the learning rate lr according to the function: $lr = lr_0$/the current number of *iterations*
- *threshold*: a value for the stopping criterion

Output:

- ***C***: a set of the k resulting clusters each of which has a reference vector $C_i = (c_{i,1}, c_{i,2}, \ldots, c_{i,p})$ where $i = 1..k$ and p is the number of dimensions in the data space. In the feature space, k clusters are embodied in the distance matrix d (kxn) with k rows and n columns. Each cell in the matrix d is a distance between C_i and a data vector X_j in the feature space.
- ***D***: the input data set that has incomplete data imputed

Algorithm:

1. Initialization phase

1.1. Fill the incomplete data in ***D*** using the attribute means (am) in the complete data subspace: $am_1, am_2, \ldots, am_p$.

For each vector $X_j = (x_{j,1}, x_{j,2}, \ldots, x_{j,p})$ in ***D*** for $j=1..n$

Update the incomplete value at each dimension *dim* for $dim=1..p$ with the value of the attribute mean at the same dimension using the incomplete data update rule:

$$x_{j,dim} = am_{dim}. \quad (1)$$

1.2. Initialize k reference vectors each of which C_i is a reference vector of a corresponding cluster obtained by roughly clustering the data vectors with vector quantization in the complete data space.

1.3. Initialize the distance matrix d in the feature space using the Gaussian kernel function K for each cell in the matrix as follows:

$$d_{ij} = 2*(1-K(C_i, X_j)) \text{ for } i=1..k \text{ and } j=1..n. \quad (2)$$

2. Cluster update phase

2.1. Update each cluster in the feature space based on the membership of each data vector in ***D*** by updating the distance matrix d.
For each data vector $X_j = (x_{j,1}, x_{j,2}, \ldots, x_{j,p})$ in ***D***:
2.1.1. Find the cluster that X_j belongs to based on the nearest distance between X_j and its corresponding reference vector C_l in the distance matrix d in the feature space.

$$C_l = \text{argmin}_i\ d_{ij}\ (C_i, X_j) \text{ for } i = 1..k \quad (3)$$

2.1.2. Update the distance between the vector X_j and the corresponding reference vector C_l to favor the membership of the vector X_j as follows:

$$d_{lj} = (1\text{-}lr)*d_{lj}^{prev}\text{-}lr*(1\text{-}lr)*d_{ll}^{prev} + 2*lr*(1\text{-}K(X_j,X_l)) \quad (4)$$

Where d_{lj}^{prev} and d_{ll}^{prev} are the previous distance between the reference vector C_l and the vector X_j and the one between the reference vector C_l and the vector X_l, respectively, in the previous iteration. The update of the distance d_{lj} is made to move the reference vector C_l closer to its member in the feature space while there is no change on the reference vectors of the other clusters. More details about this update of d_{lj} can be found in [10].
2.2. If the distance matrix d in the feature space is not stable with respect to *threshold*, then go to phase 3.

3. Incomplete data update phase

For each vector $X_j = (x_{j,1}, x_{j,2}, \ldots, x_{j,p})$ in ***D***:
3.1. Find the nearest cluster whose reference vector $C^* = (c^*_1, c^*_2, \ldots, c^*_p)$ in the data space based on the minimum distance in the distance matrix in the feature space where C^* is obtained as a mean vector in the complete data space using all the data vectors belonging to the same cluster in the feature space as the vector X_j.

$$C^* = \text{argmin}_i\ d_{ij}(C_i, X_j) \text{ for } i = 1..k. \quad (5)$$

3.2. Update the incomplete value at each dimension *dim* for the vector X_j with the value of the nearest reference vector C^* at the same dimension using the incomplete data update rule in the nearest prototype strategy:

$$x_{j,dim} = c^*_{dim}. \quad (6)$$

3.3. Update the learning rate: $lr = lr_0$/the current number of *iterations*
3.4. Go back to phase 2.

4. Termination phase

4.1. Derive k clusters based on the distance matrix between the reference vectors of the clusters and the data vectors.
4.2. Return ***D*** with no more incomplete data.

An evaluation of the proposed approach from the theoretical perspectives

In this subsection, we would like to highlight the properties of our proposed approach from the theoretical perspectives as follows:

- Regarding the complexity of the proposed algorithm, an incremental update is performed to adjust the distance d_{1j} in the distance matrix with respect to the best matching between a current data vector X_j and its corresponding reference vector C_1 as specified in (4) at step 2.1.2 of the cluster update phase. This update follows a stochastic gradient descent instead of standard gradient descent which allows an entire update on the distance matrix after all the objects are assigned to their appropriate clusters. As a result, our learning process carries out an incremental update at a finer and faster pace as soon as we found the correct cluster of each object in each epoch. This might avoid stepping over the actual converging point and increasing the computational cost of cluster formulation through updating the distance matrix. Indeed, in our algorithm, the total number of distance updates in each epoch is n because there is one update for the cluster assignment of each object. This is quite efficient as compared to the total number of distance updates on the entire distance matrix in each epoch which is $k \times n$.

- Reducing the randomness in initialization by means of the clustering procedure with vector quantization is considered in the initialization phase of our proposed algorithm. Consequently, our initial reference vectors in the data space are the resulting reference vectors from vector quantization in the complete data space. Such an initialization helps stabilizing the convergence of VQ_fk_nps speedily.
- In our opinion, the incomplete data update approach in the nearest prototype strategy is a special case of that in the optimal completion strategy regardless of fuzziness for the membership of each vector. Therefore, for incomplete data update, we prefer the nearest prototype strategy for hard clustering to the optimal completion strategy for fuzzy clustering. The reason from the practical point of view is that in our education clustering task, we need to distinguish the in-trouble students from the others so that appropriate support can be provided to the students. In addition, the employed clustering algorithm which is kernel-based vector quantization belongs to the category of hard clustering algorithms. Thus, our choice of the nearest prototype strategy is made appropriately.
- As presented previously, our VQ_fk_nps algorithm has an important inheritance from kernel-based vector quantization to reach the resulting non-spherical clusters in the data space in a simple, intuitive, and efficient learning scheme. Above all, there is no need of a concrete explicit mapping between the data space and the feature space. This leads to no need of any explicitly transformed version of either data vectors or their corresponding clusters while the clustering procedure iteratively formulates the clusters of the similar data vectors in the feature space. In order to remain the effectiveness and efficiency of kernel-based vector quantization, VQ_fk_nps has kept its spirit in tact in each epoch and simply enhanced the clustering procedure with the aforementioned incomplete data handling mechanism. Thus, VQ_fk_nps can be regarded as an incomplete data clustering version of kernel-based vector quantization.

3 Experimental results

For further evaluation from the empirical perspectives, we present several experimental results in this section. The experiments were performed on educational data including study results of the undergraduate students enrolled in 2005–2008 following the program in Computer Science in the academic credit system at Faculty of Computer Science and Engineering, Ho Chi Minh City University of Technology, Vietnam, [3]. Three data sets were prepared corresponding to 3 years of study from year 2 to year 4: data set "Year 2" for second-year students, "Year 3" for third-year students, and "Year 4" for fourth-year students. Each data set includes the study results of 1334 students (i.e., $n = 1334$). Each vector of a data set representing a student has 43 dimensions (i.e., $p = 43$) corresponding to 43 subjects. Missing grades appear corresponding to incomplete subjects as detailed in Table 1 where the percentage of missingness in data set "Year 2" is the highest and the one in "Year 4" is the lowest.

Table 1 Distribution of incomplete subjects over study years

Year of study		Year 2	Year 3	Year 4
Incomplete subjects	Total number	28,874	18,225	11,553
	Percentage (%)	50.34	31.77	20.14

As for the algorithms, we used the following algorithms for comparison with our proposed algorithm, VQ_fk_nps:

- **K_an** K_an is an algorithm that handles incomplete data in the data preprocessing phase by replacing incomplete data with the mean value at each dimension and then uses k-means [17] on the resulting data set.
- **VQ_an** VQ_an is an algorithm similar to K_an using vector quantization instead of k-means.
- **ImpSOM** ImpSOM is based on the self-organization map learning algorithm [14]. It tackles data incompleteness in the post-processing phase by means of the mean value at each dimension of each cluster for missing data in the same cluster after performing the self-organizing map on the incomplete data set in the complete data subspace. This algorithm is adapted from one in [7].
- **NPSFCM** NPSFCM is the algorithm proposed in [9] using the nearest prototype strategy for updating incomplete data while data clustering in the entire data space.
- **OCSFCM** OCSFCM is the algorithm proposed in [9] using the optimal completion strategy for incomplete data updates while clustering in the data space.
- **rmVQ_fk_nps** a variant of VQ_fk_nps is obtained by using random vectors in step 1.2 of the initialization phase as originally defined in vector quantization and using an entire update on the distance matrix after the cluster assignment of all the data vectors in step 2.1 of the cluster update phase as originally proposed in kernel-based vector quantization in [10]. We include this variant in order to check if our improvement on both vector quantization and kernel-based vector quantization is empirically appropriate.
- **mVQ_fk_nps** also as a variant of VQ_fk_nps, mVQ_fk_nps is obtained by using an entire update on the distance matrix after the cluster assignment of all the

Table 2 Averaged results of 30 runs from each algorithm

Algorithm	Xie_Beni			S_Dbw		
	Year 2	Year 3	Year 4	Year 2	Year 3	Year 4
K_an	1.11*	0.93*	1.24	0.57*	0.54*	0.46*
S_an	0.68*	1.2*	1.01	0.56*	0.56*	0.49*
VQ_an	0.68*	1.17*	1.12	0.56*	0.56*	0.49*
ImpSOM	0.58	1.07*	1.33	0.51*	0.44	0.45*
NPSFCM	2.36*	1.7*	2.07*	0.52*	0.46*	0.47*
OCSFCM	0.98*	0.96*	1.1	0.47*	0.48*	0.45*
rmVQ_fk_nps	0.83*	2.34*	6*	0.38*	0.48*	0.54*
mVQ_fk_nps	1.68*	2.73*	5.21*	0.4*	0.54*	0.59*
rVQ_fk_nps	0.91*	1.63*	5.13*	0.43*	0.48*	0.53*
kVQ_fk_nps	0.53	0.88	0.96	0.33	0.46*	0.38
VQ_fk_nps	0.31	0.56	0.82	0.33	0.43	0.37

* Average values with significance level at 0.05 as compared with VQ_fk_nps

data vectors in step 2.1 of the cluster update phase as originally proposed in kernel-based vector quantization in [10]. Different from rmVQ_fk_nps, we include the VQ-based initialization phase for this variant in order to check if our improvement on kernel-based vector quantization is empirically appropriate.

- **rVQ_fk_nps** a variant of VQ_fk_nps is obtained by using random vectors in step 1.2 of the initialization phase as originally defined in vector quantization. We include this variant in order to check if our initialization is empirically appropriate for reducing the unstability of the converged clusters stemming from random initialization in various runs of the kernel-based vector quantization procedure.
- **kVQ_fk_nps** similarly, a variant of VQ_fk_nps is obtained by using mean vectors from the k-means algorithm in step 1.2 of the initialization phase. This variant will help us figure out the appropriateness of our choice of vector quantization to determine the starting point of our clusters in the feature space.

As an extended version of the work in [24], we re-used the choices of the parameter values for NPSFCM and OCSFCM where the number c (or k) of clusters is 5 and the weighting exponent m is 1.25. As for other parameter values of an initial learning rate lr_0 and the bandwidth σ, we used a trial-and-error scheme which is quite tedious and thus, they will be automatically determined in our future work. The value of lr_0 is 0.9 and the value of σ for "Year 2" data set is 1.15, σ for "Year 3" data set is 2.11, and σ for "Year 4" data set is 2.02. In addition, the stopping criterion is set for all the experiments based on the stability of the resulting clusters or the distance matrix in kernel-based vector quantization which is exactly the same as one in [9], which is 10^{-5}. In order to avoid randomness in initialization, each experimental result for comparison in Table 2 is an averaged value calculated from 30 runs of each algorithm. Their corresponding standard deviations are given in Table 3. Besides, several results for K_an, ImpSOM, NPSFCM, and OCSFCM in Table 2 are inherited from the corresponding results of our previous work in [24].

Regarding examining how well VQ_fk_nps clusters incomplete educational data, we also used two internal clustering validation measures well-known in unsupervised learning: Xie_Beni and S_Dbw. Examined in [19], Xie_Beni is popularly used for fuzzy cluster validity with the inter-cluster separation defined as the minimum square distance between cluster centers and the intra-cluster compactness defined as the mean square distance between each object and its cluster center. The smaller Xie_Beni, the better the resultant clusters are. As analyzed in [16], S_Dbw is a measure that can examine the separation and compactness of the resulting clusters with respect to monotonicity, noise, density, subclusters, and skewed distributions in data. The smaller S_Dbw, the better the clusters are. More details about Xie_Beni and S_Dbw can be found in [16]. In addition, One-Way ANOVA was conducted with equal variances assumed for post hoc multiple comparisons with Bonferroni at the 0.05 level of significance. Levene Statistic is also included for a test of homogeneity of variances. In Table 2, a star (*) is used to denote the mean difference significant at the 0.05 level in comparison with the averaged results of VQ_fk_nps.

Presented in Table 2, the values of Xie_Beni and S_Dbw from our algorithm, VQ_fk_nps, are always the smallest ones with a very much difference from the results of the other algorithms. In particular, the difference between the fuzzy approaches and ours can be explained in such a way that our educational data sets have many distinct groups of similar students and thus, a choice of the nearest prototype strategy is appropriate. This result is also consistent with such a fact that we have got a small value (1.25) for the

Table 3 Standard deviations corresponding to the averaged results of 30 runs from each algorithm in Table 2

Algorithm	Xie_Beni			S_Dbw		
	Year 2	Year 3	Year 4	Year 2	Year 3	Year 4
K_an	0.22	0.34	0.24	0.19	0.01	0.03
S_an	≈0	≈0	≈0	≈0	≈0	≈0
VQ_an	≈0	≈0	≈0	≈0	≈0	≈0
ImpSOM	0.26	≈0	≈0	0.09	≈0	≈0
NPSFCM	0.07	≈0	0.33	≈0	≈0	≈0
OCSFCM	0.31	0.38	0.59	0.08	0.06	0.07
rmVQ_fk_nps	0.85	1.7	5.34	0.04	0.09	0.12
mVQ_fk_nps	2.39	2.67	2.97	0.04	0.11	0.17
rVQ_fk_nps	0.91	1.2	3.62	0.06	0.04	0.12
kVQ_fk_nps	0.41	0.4	0.22	0.02	0.05	0.03
VQ_fk_nps	0.02	0.12	0.05	0.02	0.02	0.03

weighting exponent m in [24]. Considering the variance at each individual measure, we observe a quite large range for Xie_Beni and a small one for S_Dbw from different approaches and algorithms except for VQ_fk_nps. Xie_Beni shows the clearer distinction between the algorithms while S_Dbw shows that distinction a little. Almost the differences between VQ_fk_nps and the other approaches are significant through a statistical test at the 0.05 level. Therefore, it can be concluded that VQ_fk_nps is suitable for educational data sets as compared to the others which have been examined. Besides, Table 3 gives us the standard deviations corresponding to the averaged results of 30 runs from each algorithm in Table 2. Via the values of those standard deviations, there is no much variance in the results from many various executions of VQ_fk_nps as compared to other variants of VQ_fk_nps, leading to the fact that VQ_fk_nps is more stable than its variants. Nevertheless, the most stable algorithms with almost no variance are S_an and VQ_an. Such a stability of S_an and VQ_an stems from the nature of the self-organizing learning process. As our algorithm performs the clustering of data vectors in the feature space and tackles the incomplete data handling in the data space, its stability might be influenced although we considered this feature by reducing the randomness in initialization.

As compared to the resulting clusters from the variants of VQ_fk_nps, the resulting clusters from VQ_fk_nps are more compact and separate from each other. In addition, all the differences between these variants except for kVQ_fk_nps are statistically significant. Such differences prove that the design of our proposed algorithm, VQ_fk_nps, is empirically sound. Regarding the statistically insignificant difference from the results from kVQ_fk_nps, it is understood that the initialization with k-means and the one with vector quantization are quite similar to each other. It seems to be certain as the resulting clusters from both K_an and VQ_an have the similar compactness and separation via the values of Xie_Beni and S_Dbw measures. Hence, stabilizing the initial clusters instead of random data vectors for the initial clusters helps us to obtain the clusters of better quality. Regarding the appropriateness of a distance update scheme in the feature space, VQ_fk_nps much outperforms rmVQ_fk_nps and mVQ_fk_nps. So, our choice of an incremental distance update scheme on only the distance associated with the winning cluster is confirmed to be more appropriate than a standard distance update scheme on an entire distance matrix.

Generally speaking, VQ_fk_nps can perform the data clustering task effectively on incomplete educational data and produce the non-spherical clusters with higher compactness and better separation in the data space through the internal clustering validation measures such as Xie_Beni and S_Dbw. As VQ_fk_nps always has the lowest values for Xie_Beni and S_Dbw, such experimental results have confirmed the robustness and effectiveness of VQ_fk_nps, for handling different amounts of incomplete data in educational data sets. Using the resulting clusters, several concrete groups of the 2nd-year students (or 3rd-year students or 4th-year students) at the same level of study performance can be determined and our support can be planned and provided appropriately for each group of the similar students. Besides, the resulting completed data can play a role of a good input for other mining tasks including educational data classification and association analysis.

4 Related works

For further comparison with the related works, this section examines several existing works such as [1,2,7–9,23,25,27] in incomplete data clustering. Among these works, Refs. [1,2,9,23] updated incomplete data while doing data clustering, Wang [25] translated incomplete data into so-called fuzzy observations before generating clusters, and Cottrell and Letrémy [7] estimated incomplete data after attaining clusters.

As one of the first works, Hathaway and Bezdek [9] developed four different strategies handling incomplete data in fuzzy clustering: the whole data strategy (WDS), the partial distance strategy (PDS), the optimal completion strategy (OCS), the nearest prototype strategy (NPS) similar to OCS except for using the nearest prototypes. As a kernel-based extension to OCSFCM, a kernel-based fuzzy c-means algorithm (KFCM) was proposed in [27] using a kernel-induced metric in the data space instead of the conventional Euclidean metric and the optimal completion strategy for incomplete data handling. In comparison, VQ_fk_nps is different from NPSFCM and OCSFCM in [9] and KFCM in [27] in the following aspects. In Initialization phase, we suggested to use a mean of all the known values at each dimension to fill in incomplete data in VQ_fk_nps while OCSFCM and NPSFCM algorithms had no mention of such a particular initialization. In addition, VQ_fk_nps uses a kernel-based approach to produce the clusters with arbitrary shapes while those algorithms used a partitioning-based approach forming only the hyper-spherical shapes of the resulting clusters. Based on OCS and fuzzy SOM algorithm, Abidi and Yahia [2] proposed OCS-FSOM and an extension of OCS-FSOM called Multi-OCSFSOM. In these algorithms, a learning rate is used as a fuzzy membership value of the current input vector in the output cluster. Besides, the algorithms in [2] require the maximal iteration number for the learning process. This might lead to an early convergence. Differently, our work does not fix the number of iterations.

Wang [25] is another work based on SOM algorithm by transforming incomplete data into so-called fuzzy observations. This approach depended on the domains at the dimensions where missing values exist and a large number of fuzzy observations would be generated for each input. Based on SOM, Cottrell and Letrémy [7] clustered incomplete data in the complete data subspace by ignoring the dimensions with missing values during the learning process. After the learning process, missing value estimation is performed using the (weighted) mean values of the class of each vector. For a comparison with Cottrell and Letrémy [7], we adapted this approach to obtain a simplified algorithm ImpSOM in the previous section. However, Cottrell and Letrémy [7] might lose the details of the vectors to be clustered if the number of dimensions with missing values gets larger. Moreover, the missing data imputation was not tightly involved in the cluster forming process.

As one of the most recent works, Vatanen [23] has proposed a revision of handling missing values to the batch SOM algorithm which is called Imputation SOM. Unlike Refs. [7,23] did not ignore the missing values in the learning process. Indeed, Vatanen [23] used the current value of the corresponding prototype, i.e. a mean value, to fill each missing component of a vector. To some extent, the missing value updates in [23] are similar to that of VQ_fk_nps. Differently, instead of using the current prototype, VQ_fk_nps uses the nearest prototype of each vector after the update of all reference vectors via the update of the distance matrix has been done in the feature space. In [8], a SOM-based method has been introduced for data imputation in incomplete data matrices. Although not focusing on the resulting clusters, Folguera et al. [8] is somewhat related to a SOM-based incomplete data clustering approach. Their method needs a part of complete data vectors to pre-train a SOM and then impute incomplete data. Thus, Folguera et al. [8] is not applicable to our work because the educational application domain has the data sets where there is no such a set of complete data vectors from the 2nd-year, 3rd-year, and 4th-year students in an academic credit system. Using the mean shift algorithm as introduced in [6], AbdAllah and Shimshoni [1] considered handling incomplete data by means of so-called MD_E distance; but did not supply any incomplete data handling scheme.

Finally, among a large number of the existing works, it is hard to foresee which incomplete data handling techniques are certainly appropriate for a particular domain and also work well with any existing unsupervised learning algorithms. So, a study of handling incomplete data in a clustering task is needed for obtaining an effective cluster model in general and in the education domain particularly. In addition, VQ_fk_nps has the merit of discovering the non-spherical clusters of better quality in the incomplete educational data sets by means of a kernel-based clustering process in the feature space. This approach has not yet been supported by any existing works.

5 Conclusion

For educational decision making support, we would like to early detect and support the in-trouble students who have just spent two years, three years, or four years studying in an academic credit system. This situation asks us to collect their study results as soon as possible, leading to data incompleteness that is one of the troublesome characteristics of the data in analysis and mining tasks. Therefore, our work has to deal with a so-called incomplete educational data clustering task to discover some groups of the similar students based on their study performance at different points in study time. As a solution to the task, a robust and effective clustering approach based on kernel-based vector quantization is determined along with the nearest prototype strategy. The resulting clustering algorithm, VQ_fk_nps, is elaborated and discussed in comparison with several different approaches based on k-means, SOM, fuzzy c-means, kernel fuzzy c-means, etc. Different from the existing general-purpose solutions, VQ_fk_nps is more effective on the real educational data sets at various levels of data incompleteness via internal clustering validation. It can generate the non-spherical clusters based on the clusters resulted in the feature space by a kernel-based vector quantization approach. In addition, the data sets which got completed after clustered can be utilized in other mining tasks.

As of this moment, we focus on which incomplete data clustering approach is appropriate for our educational domain by making kernel-based vector quantization robust and effective. In the future, we will further evaluate our approach for a more diversity of complete data sets. It is also interesting to consider obtaining a parameter-free kernel-based vector quantization approach whose parameter values are automatically derived from the inherent characteristics of each data set.

Acknowledgments This paper is funded by Ho Chi Minh City University of Technology, Vietnam National University at Ho Chi Minh City, under the Grant number T-KHMT-2015-27.

References

1. AbdAllah, L., Shimshoni, I.: Mean shift clustering algorithm for data with missing values. In: Proceedings of DAWAK, pp. 426-438 (2014)
2. Abidi, B., Yahia, S.B.: A new algorithm for fuzzy clustering handling incomplete dataset. Int. J. Artif. Intell. Tools **23**(4), 1–21 (2014)
3. Academic Affairs Office, Ho Chi Minh City University of Technology, Vietnam, http://www.aao.hcmut.edu.vn/dhcq.html (2014)
4. Bogarín, A., Romero, C., Cerezo, R., Sánchez-Santillán, M.: Clustering for improving educational process mining. In: Proceedings of LAK'14, pp. 1–5 (2014)
5. Campagni, R., Merlini, D., Verri, M.C.: Finding regularities in courses evaluation with k-means clustering. In: Proceedings of the 6th International Conference on Computer Supported Education, pp. 26–33 (2014)
6. Comaniciu, D., Meer, P.: Mean shift: a robust approach toward feature space analysis. IEEE Trans. Pattern Anal. Mach. Intell. **24**(5), 603–619 (2002)
7. Cottrell, M., Letrémy, P.: Missing values: processing with the Kohonen algorithm. In: Proceedings of applied stochastic models and data analysis, pp. 489–496 (2005)
8. Folguera, L., Zupan, J., Cicerone, D., Magallanes, J.F.: Self-organizing maps for imputation of missing data in incomplete data matrices. Chemometr. Intell. Lab. Syst. **143**, 146–151 (2015)
9. Hathaway, R.J., Bezdek, J.C.: Fuzzy c-means clustering of incomplete data. IEEE Trans. Syst. Man Cybernet. Part B Cybernet. **31**(5), 735–744 (2001)
10. Inokuchi, R., Miyamoto, S.: LVQ clustering and SOM using a kernel function. In: Proceedings of the 2004 IEEE International Conference on Fuzzy Systems, vol. 3, pp. 1497–1500 (2004)
11. Inyang, U.G., Joshua, E.E.: Fuzzy clustering of students' data repository for at-risks students identification and monitoring. Comput. Inf. Sci. **6**(4), 37–50 (2013)
12. Jayabal, Y., Ramanathan, C.: Clustering students based on student's performance—a partial least squares path modeling (PLS-PM) study. In: Proceedings of MLDM, LNAI 8556, pp. 393–407 (2014)
13. Kerr, D., Chung, G.K.W.K.: Identifying key features of student performance in educational video games and simulations through cluster analysis. J. Educ. Data Min. **4**(1), 144–182 (2012)
14. Kohonen, T.: The self-organizing map. Proc. IEEE **78**(9), 1464–1480 (1990)
15. Li, C., Yoo, J.: Modeling student online learning using clustering. In: Proceedings of ACM SE'06, pp. 1–6 (2006)
16. Liu, Y., Li, Z., Xiong, H., Gao, X., Wu, J.: Understanding of internal clustering validation measures. In: Proceedings of the 2010 IEEE International Conference on Data Mining, pp. 911–916 (2010)
17. MacQueen, J.: Some methods for classification and analysis of multivariate observations. In: Proceedings of the 5th Berkeley Symp. Math. Stat. Prob., vol. 1, pp. 281–297 (1967)
18. Nugent, R., Dean, N., Ayers, E.: Skill set profile clustering: the empty k-means algorithm with automatic specification of starting cluster centers. In: Proceedings of the 3rd International Conference on Educational Data Mining, pp. 151–160 (2010)
19. Pal, N.R., Bezdek, J.C.: On cluster validity for the fuzzy c-means model. IEEE Trans. Fuzzy Syst. **3**(3), 370–379 (1995)
20. Pardos, Z.A., Trivedi, S., Heffernan, N.T., Sárközy, G.N.: Clustered knowledge tracing. In: Proceedings of ITS, LNCS 7315, pp. 405–410 (2012)
21. Shih, B., Koedinger, K.R., Scheines, R.: Unsupervised discovery of student learning tactics. In: Proceedings of the 3rd International Conference on Educational Data Mining, pp. 201–210 (2010)
22. Tanai, M., Kim, J., Chang, J.H.: Model-based clustering analysis of student data. In: Proceedings of ICHIT 2011, LNCS 6935, pp. 669–676 (2011)
23. Vatanen, T., Osmala, M., Raiko, T., Lagus, K., Sysi-Aho, M., Orešič, M., Honkela, T., Lähdesmäki, H.: Self-organization and missing values in SOM and GTM. Neurocomputing **147**, 60–70 (2015)
24. Vo, T.N.C., Nguyen, H.P., Vo, T.N.T.: A robust and effective algorithmic framework for incomplete educational data clustering. In: Proceedings of the 2nd National Foundation for Science and Technology Development Conference on Information and Computer Science (NICS), pp. 65–70 (2015)
25. Wang, S.: Application of self-organising maps for data mining with incomplete data sets. Neural Comput. Appl. **12**, 42–48 (2003)
26. Zakrzewska, D.: Cluster analysis in personalized e-learning systems. Intel. Syst. Knowl. Manag. SCI **252**, 229–250 (2009)
27. Zhang, D.-Q., Chen, S.-C.: Clustering incomplete data using kernel-based fuzzy c-means algorithm. Neural Process. Lett. **18**, 155–162 (2003)

5

Similarity search for numerous patterns over multiple time series streams under dynamic time warping which supports data normalization

Bui Cong Giao[1] · Duong Tuan Anh[1]

Abstract A huge challenge in nowadays' data mining is similarity search in streaming time series under Dynamic Time Warping (DTW). In the similarity search, data normalization is a must to obtain accurate results. However, data normalization on the fly and the DTW calculation cost a great deal of computational time and memory space. In the paper, we present two methods, SUCR-DTW and ESUCR-DTW, which conduct similarity search for numerous prespecified patterns over multiple time-series streams under DTW supporting data normalization. These two methods utilize a combination of techniques to mitigate the aforementioned costs. The efficient methods inherit the cascading lower bounds introduced in UCR-DTW, a state-of-the-art method of similarity search in the static time series, to admissibly prune off unpromising subsequences. To be adaptive in the streaming setting, SUCR-DTW performs incremental updates on the envelopes of new-coming time-series subsequences and incremental data normalization on time-series data. However, like UCR-DTW, SUCR-DTW retrieves only similar subsequences that have the same length as the patterns. ESUCR-DTW, an extension of SUCR-DTW, can find similar subsequences whose lengths are different from those of the patterns. Furthermore, our proposed methods exploit multi-threading to have a fast response to high-speed time-series streams. The experimental results show that SUCR-DTW obtains the same precision as UCR-DTW and has lower wall clock time. Besides, the experimental results of SUCR-DTW and ESUCR-DTW reveal that the extended method has higher accuracy in spite of longer wall clock time. Also, the paper evaluates the influence of incremental z-score normalization and incremental min–max normalization on the obtained results.

✉ Bui Cong Giao
giao.bc@cb.sgu.edu.vn

Duong Tuan Anh
dtanh@cse.hcmut.edu.vn

1 Faculty of Computer Science and Engineering, Ho Chi Minh City University of Technology, Ho Chi Minh City, Vietnam

Keywords Similarity search · Time series stream · Dynamic time warping · Data normalization

1 Introduction

A time-series stream is a sequence of data collected in a continuous manner as time progresses. In recent years, due to accelerated technology developments, there have been more and more applications related to data mining in streaming time series, ranging from monitoring of sensor networks [1] and environmental signals [2], to trading stocks online [3]. In such applications, similarity search for prespecified patterns in streaming time series is a critical subroutine, yet the time taken for the task is almost a hurdle, since time-series streams might transfer huge amount of data at steady high-speed rates. Hence, time-series streams are potentially unbounded in size within a short period and the system runs out of memory soon. Consequently, if a data point of time-series stream has been processed, it is quickly discarded and cannot be retrieved so that it yields to a new-coming one. To achieve real-time response, methods of similar search in streaming time series need to have one-pass scan and low computational time, yet available methods used to manage static time series are hardly able to satisfy the above requirements as they commonly need to scan time-series sequences many times and often have high computation cost. Therefore, according to Yang and Wu [4], high-speed data streams is the second ranking challenge among the ten top challenging problems in the present day' s data mining. Furthermore, Fu [5] has recently conducted a

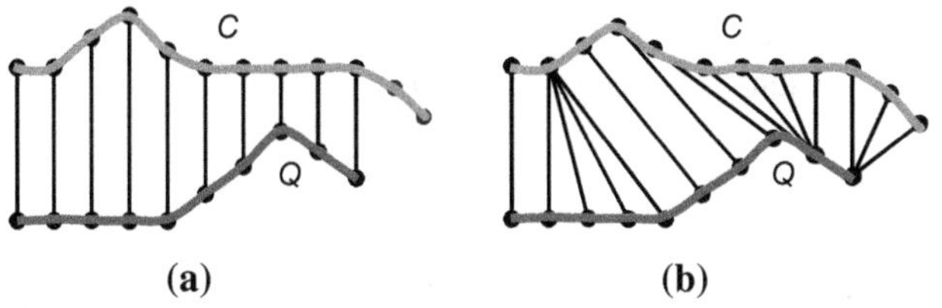

Fig. 1 Matching points of **a** the Euclidean distance and **b** the DTW distance

review on time-series data mining and claimed that mining on streaming time series is a fascinating research direction.

There are two popular distance metrics for similarity search in time-series data, the Euclidean distance and the Dynamic Time Warping (DTW) [6] distance. DTW, which originated in the speech community [7], is a robust distance measure, because the distance measure can find similar time-series sequences though they are misaligned and different in length, whereas the Euclidean metric can hardly do this. Therefore, results obtained from DTW are more accurate than those from the Euclidean metric. Figure 1 illustrates the difference between the two distance metrics in matching among points to calculate the distance between two time-series sequences C and Q. The applicability of DTW is not only in pattern discovery by similarity search over time-series data, but also in other time-series data-mining tasks such as classification [8] and clustering [9].

Data normalization is very important for similarity search over time-series data. Many researchers [10,11] reckoned that this preprocessing step is necessary to have meaningful results. For example, when two time series are analyzed concurrently, one collects rainfall, whereas another records humidity. Since these values are measured on different offsets, they cannot be compared meaningfully. Another example is given in Fig. 2 to justify the reason that data normalization is required for similarity search over time-series data. In Fig. 2b, the time-series sequence is a segment extracted from a real EEG data set [12]. We define a time-series pattern for query as in Fig. 2a, so as to retrieve similar subsequences in the time-series sequence. The result is that only one similar subsequence is found as shown in Fig. 2b and two other similar subsequences are missed due to shifting.

DTW is not only used for static time series but also for streaming time series, yet some accelerating techniques for the DTW calculation in similarity search over time-series streams work only on the un-normalized data (e.g. [13,14]); consequently, the obtained results are not accurate. Recently, Rakthanmanon et al. [11] have introduced UCR-DTW, a method of similarity search for patterns, which are prespecified time-series sequences, in static time series under DTW. The authors paid due attention to data normalization prior to any computation of the DTW distance. The experimental results of UCR-DTW reveal that the method has low computational time and high accuracy. The method, however, works only on static time series and requires two sequences of the same length while computing the DTW distance, so it leaves many things open in similarity search over time-series streams.

Motivated by the above observation, in this paper we will present two methods, SUCR-DTW and ESUCR-DTW, of similarity search for prespecified patterns in streaming time series under DTW, which support data normalization. We introduced SUCR-DTW in [15], which is a modification of UCR-DTW to be adaptive in the streaming context. In the work, we will describe SUCR-DTW in more detail and introduce ESUCR-DTW for the first time. ESUCR-DTW is an extension of SUCR-DTW for retrievals of similar subsequences whose lengths are likely to be different from those of the corresponding patterns. Besides, in ESUCR-DTW, the lengths of expectative similar subsequences can be prespecified within a valid domain for each pattern. The two methods can be used with any type of data normalization such as z-score normalization and min–max normalization provided that these data normalization types can be incrementally calculated, so as to mitigate the high computational time due to the course of data normalization in the streaming setting. More specifically, these two methods can deal with an important scenario in streaming applications where incoming data are from multiple concurrent time-series streams at high-speed rates, and there are numerous prespecified patterns for query.

As regards technical aspect, both of the proposed methods have salient characteristics as follows.

- Applicability of *multi-threading* for similarity search over multiple time-series streams.

Fig. 2 An example illustrates why data normalization is required for similarity search over time-series data

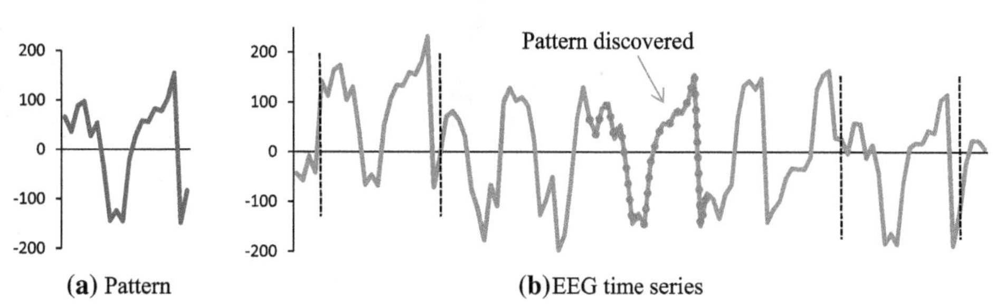

- Incremental update on the envelopes of new-coming time-series subsequences so that these envelopes can be immediately used in a lower bounding function.

We conducted a large number of experiments to evaluate the efficacy of SUCR-DTW and ESUCR-DTW. Firstly, SUCR-DTW is compared with UCR-DTW in terms of precession and wall clock time. Next, ESUCR-DTW is compared with SUCR-DTW in terms of accuracy and wall clock time. Then, for the first time, the results obtained by ESUCR-DTW using incremental z-score normalization are compared with those done by ESUCR-DTW using incremental min–max normalization. Finally yet importantly, ESUCR-DTW is compared with SPRING, a well-known method of similarity search in streaming time series, combined with incremental min–max normalization in terms of wall clock time and the quality of similar subsequences.

The rest of paper is organized as follows. Section 2 describes DTW, techniques to speedup DTW, data normalization, and typical tasks of similarity search in streaming time series. Section 3 reviews related work. Afterwards, Sect. 4 describes our two proposed methods. Section 5 goes into the experimental evaluation, and Sect. 6 gives conclusions and future work.

2 Background

2.1 Dynamic Time Warping

This nonlinear distance measure allows time-series sequences to be stretched along the time axis to minimize the distance between the sequences. The DTW distance is calculated by dynamic programming as follows. Consider two time-series sequences $C = c_1, c_2, \ldots, c_m$ and $Q = q_1, q_2, \ldots, q_n$. The DTW distance between C and Q is defined as:

$$DTW(C, Q) = f(m, n)$$

$$f(m, n) = d(c_i, q_j) + \min \begin{cases} f(i, j-1) \\ f(i-1, j) \\ f(i-1, j-1) \end{cases} \quad (1)$$

$$f(0, 0) = 0, \quad f(i, 0) = f(0, j) = \infty$$
$$(1 \le i \le m, 1 \le j \le n)$$

where $d(c_i, q_j) = (c_i - q_j)^2$ is the Euclidean distance between two numerical values, c_i and q_j. Notice that any choice (e.g. $d(c_i, q_j) = |c_i - q_j|$) would be fine. Our proposed methods are completely independent of such choices. To align C and Q using DTW, an n-by-m accumulated cost matrix whose (ith, jth) cell contains the value of $f(c_i, q_j)$ is constructed. An optimal warping path P is a sequence of continuous cells in the matrix, which defines a mapping between C and Q such that $f(m, n)$ is minimum.

The calculation of the DTW distance can be expressed by a simpler way. Matching points of C and Q as in Fig. 1b creates an optimal warping path P as in Fig. 3a. Let the kth element of P be $p_k = (i, j)_k$. We have $P = p_1, p_2, \ldots, p_k, \ldots, p_K$, where $\max(m, n) \le K \le m + n - 1$. The DTW distance between C and Q is a cumulative addition along P, which minimizes the warping cost as follows:

$$DTW(C, Q) = \sqrt{\sum_{k=1}^{K} d(p_k)}. \quad (2)$$

Because DTW uses a dynamic programming algorithm whose time and space complexity are $\mathcal{O}(mn)$, the distance

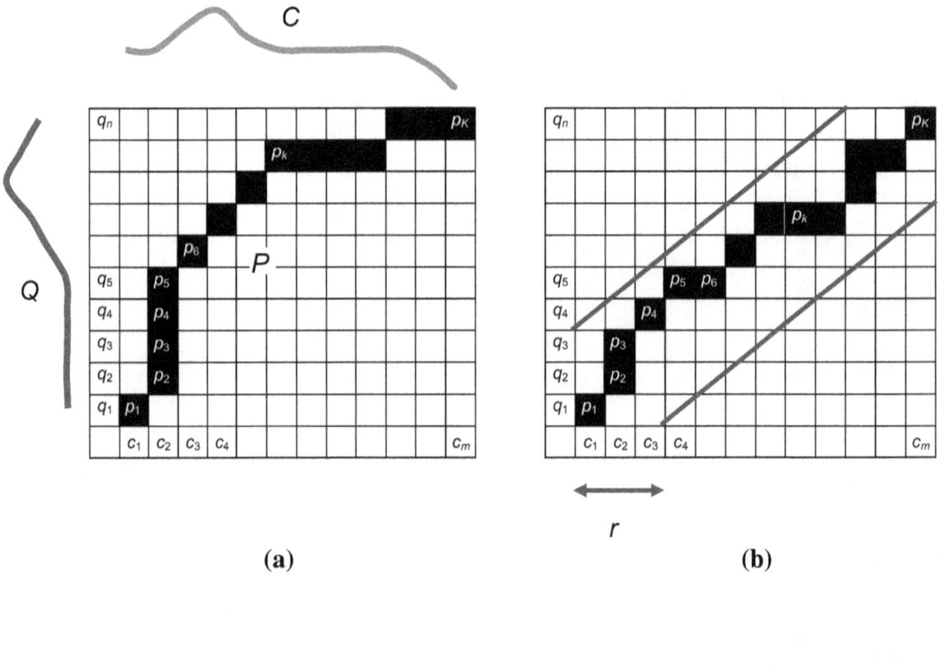

Fig. 3 **a** To align C and Q, a warping path P, shown with *solid squares*, is constructed. **b** The Sakoe–Chiba band with a width r is used as a global constraint to limit the scope of P

measure is almost very slow, especially for long time-series sequences. For that reason, there have been many incessant researches to speed up DTW, since Berndt and Clifford introduced the distance metric in 1994 [6].

2.2 Techniques to speedup Dynamic Time Warping

The techniques to speedup DTW often fall into three categories:

- *Constraints* The technique aims to limit the number of cells evaluated in the accumulated cost matrix. Figure 3b depicts a Sakoe–Chiba band [16] that prevents pathological warping paths, where a data point in one time-series sequence matches too many data points of another as in Fig. 1b. The Sakoe–Chiba band constrains a warping window in the area defined by two lines parallel to the diagonal. Keogh and Ratanamahatana [10] showed that restricting the size of the warping windows not only speedups computation, because only a part of the accumulated cost matrix needs computing, but also tightens the lower bounding property.
  The Sakoe–Chiba band works well in domains where an optimal warping path is expected to be close to the diagonal of the accumulated cost matrix. The constraint works poorly if time series are of events that start and stop at extremely different times because the warping path can stray very far from a linear warping path and nearly the entire matrix must be evaluated to find an optimal warping path.
- *Lower bounding* The technique uses cheap-to-compute lower bounding functions to reduce the number of times computing the DTW distance for finding the time-series sequence that is nearly similar to a given time-series pattern.
  Let F be a function of dimension reduction or feature extraction of a time-series sequence. A lower bounding function d_F is of the lower bounding property as follows.

$$d_F(F(C), F(Q)) \leq DTW(C, Q). \quad (3)$$

The efficiency of d_F is evaluated in terms of time complexity and pruning power. The pruning power of d_F is competence for early detection of unpromising sequences so as not to use the naive DTW calculation on these sequences in the post-processing phase. Let g be the number of unpromising sequences which d_F identifies, and G be the total number of sequences which are performed in a similarity search. The pruning power of d_F is

$$\frac{100 \times g}{G} \%. \quad (4)$$

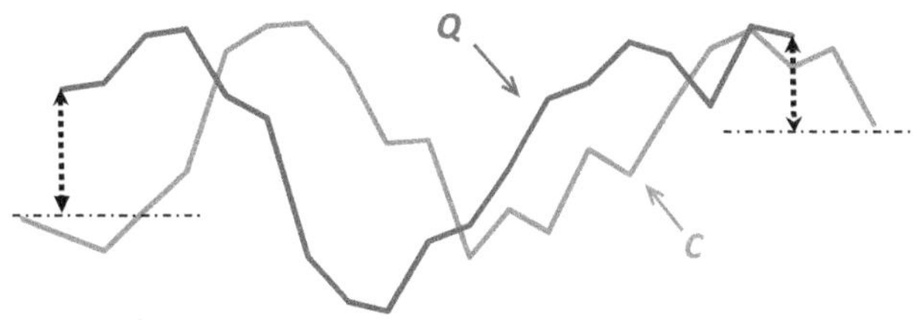

Fig. 4 LB_{Kim} on Q and C, which are normalized

In this work, we applied two efficient lower bounding functions that will be briefly described as follows. Firstly, the lower bounding measure proposed by Kim et al. [17] (hereafter, referred to as LB_{Kim}), uses the four-tuples features from each sequence. The features are the first and last data points of the sequence, together with the maximum and minimum values. However, Rakthanmanon et al. [11] believed that as time-series sequences are normalized, the distance values of these extra two-tuples (the maximum and minimum vectors) tend to be very small, so we may ignore them. As a result, the computation complexity of LB_{Kim} reduces from $\mathcal{O}(n)$ to $\mathcal{O}(1)$. Figure 4 depicts an illustration of LB_{Kim} using the first points and last ones of Q and C.

Secondly, Keogh and Ratanamahatana [10] introduced another lower bounding technique (referred to as LB_{Keogh}). The technique exploits the fact that most DTW applications use global path constraints while comparing two time-series sequences, that is, i and j in $p_k = (i, j)_k$ are constrained to $j - r \leq i \leq j + r$, where r is independent of i in case of the Sakoe–Chiba band. Using the fact, two time series U and L (for upper and lower bounds) are constructed, such that they define an envelope that Q must lie in, regardless of how much it is skewed under all possible warping paths that are allowed under the global path constraint. Time-series data points of U and L are

$$\begin{aligned} u_i &= \max(q_{i-r} : q_{i+r}) \\ l_i &= \min(q_{i-r} : q_{i+r}). \end{aligned} \quad (5)$$

Figure 5 shows the computation of LB_{Keogh} on Q and C with U and L of Q. The lower bounding function computes the sum of the distances of the data points of C beyond the envelope of Q. The authors [10] reckoned two time-series sequences of the same length and constrained amount of warping produces no false dismissals. Thus, DTW has become a very powerful tool in time-series data mining since then. Having Q and C of same length, and U and L of Q, LB_{Keogh} is defined as follows:

$$LB\_{Keogh}(Q, C) = \sqrt{\sum_{i=1}^{n} \begin{cases} (c_i - u_i)^2 & \text{if } c_i > u_i \\ (l_i - c_i)^2 & \text{if } c_i < l_i \\ 0 & \text{otherwise.} \end{cases}} \quad (6)$$

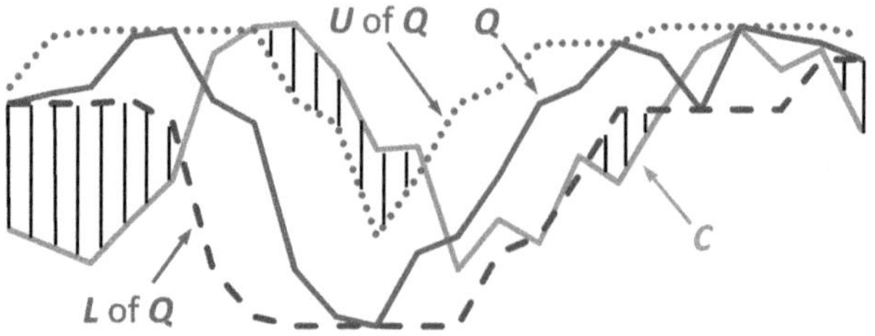

Fig. 5 $LB_{\_Keogh}$ on Q and C whose length is n, so the computation complexity is $\mathcal{O}(n)$

- *Early abandoning* The technique is based on a comparison of distances with a threshold ε. Similarity search over two time-series sequences C and Q needs to check $f(i, j)$ in the formula (1), such that $f(i, j) \leq \varepsilon$. If the value of f exceeds ε, then C is not similar to Q and the course to compute $DTW(C, Q)$ is stopped immediately. Some works using the technique to accelerate the DTW calculation are [11,18]. Notice that early abandoning with a threshold ε can also be used in the calculation of the Euclidean distance. Moreover, the $LB_{\_Keogh}$ lower bound can be used for early abandoning of the DTW calculation as follows. While the classical DTW calculation is being incrementally computed from left to right of two sequences Q and C (e.g. from 1 to k), if the partial DTW accumulation with the $LB_{\_Keogh}$ contribution from $k+1$ to n exceeds ε, then the naive DTW calculation is aborted right away, since the sum of

$$DTW(Q_{1:k}, C_{1:k}) + LB_{\_Keogh}(Q_{k+1:n}, C_{k+1:n})$$

is a lower bound of $DTW(Q_{1:n}, C_{1:n})$. Hence, on the occasion of the calculation of $LB_{\_Keogh}(Q, C)$, an array of cumulative bounds is got from the lower bounding function. The kth element of the array of cumulative bounds is $LB_{\_Keogh}(Q_{k:n}, C_{k:n})$.

2.3 Data normalization

Data normalization makes the results of data-mining tasks more accurate. Two common ways to normalize time-series data are min–max and z-score. Let X denote a time-series sequence, $X = x_1, x_2, \ldots, x_n$.

Min–max normalization maps a value x of X to x_{norm} by computing

$$x_{norm} = \frac{x - x_{min}}{x_{max} - x_{min}}, \tag{7}$$

where x_{min} and x_{max} are the minimum and the maximum values of time-series X. x_{min} and x_{max} are referred to as min–max coefficients.

Z-score normalization maps a value x of X to x_{norm} by computing

$$x_{norm} = \frac{x - \mu}{\sigma} \tag{8}$$

with $\mu = \frac{1}{n} \sum_{i=1}^{n} x_i \tag{9}$

and $\sigma^2 = \frac{1}{n} \sum_{i=1}^{n} x_i^2 - \mu^2. \tag{10}$

μ and σ are referred to as z-score coefficients.

Z-score normalization is often used in data-mining tasks on time-series data, since normalized time-series sequences follow the shape of original time-series ones more closely; however, z-score normalization does not make sure that normalized time-series sequences are of the same amplitude. For instance, in image processing, pixel intensities have to be normalized to fit within a range from 0 to 255 for the RGB colour range. Also, a typical algorithm of neural network requires data on a 0–1 scale, so min–max normalization can be utilized to get values within the range. Furthermore, min–max normalization is of low computational time. Thus, there have been many recent time-series applications (e.g. [19,20]) using min–max normalization.

2.4 Typical tasks of similarity search in streaming time series

A time-series stream X is a discrete, semi-infinite time-series sequence of real numbers $x_1, x_2, \ldots, x_n$, where x_n is the most recent value. In other words, X is a univariate time series, which is evolving with an increase of n after each time tick. Let $X[x_s : x_e]$ be the subsequence starting from time tick s, and ending at e; and $NX[nx_s : nx_e]$ be the normalized subsequence of $X[x_s : x_e]$. Let $Y[y_0 : y_{m-1}]$ be a time-series pattern of length m, and $NY[ny_0 : ny_{m-1}]$ be the normalized sequence of Y. Three typical tasks of similarity search for Y over X until the most recent time tick n are:

- *Best-so-far search*: Finding such an NX that is most similar to NY. That means $DTW(NX, NY)$ is smallest. The smallest value, which is recorded until time tick n, is the *best-so-far* value, and X is the *best-so-far* subsequence of Y.
- *Range search*: Given a threshold ε, finding any NX such that $DTW(NX, NY) \leq \varepsilon$. Notice that ε is also referred to as a range radius of Y. It is likely that similar subsequences are overlapped, so *Range search* is modified to *Disjoint query*. This means that given all overlapped resultant NXs, *Disjoint query* chooses the one with the smallest $DTW(NX, NY)$.

- *k-nearest neighboring (k-NN) search*: Given a positive integer k, finding a set of k NXs similar to NY, the set is referred to as kS, such that if there is $NX' \notin kS$, then $\forall NX \in kS, DTW(NX, NY) \leq DTW(NX', NY)$. Note that if $k = 1$, the similarity search type becomes *best-so-far search*.

3 Related work

There have been a few typical research efforts dealing with similarity search over streaming time series under DTW. The first is SPRING introduced by Sakurai et al. [13]. The method is very impressive in the computational time. The authors claimed that SPRING is up to 650,000 times faster than using the naive calculation of the DTW distance. However, SPRING cannot work on z-score normalization, since at each time tick the z-score coefficients (mean and standard deviation) change frequently. When the z-score coefficients change, reusing computed results at previous time ticks is virtually impossible to SPRING. Hence, SPRING cannot be used to compare with our methods. Recently, Gong et al. [21] have introduced NSPRING, an extension of SPING supporting z-score normalization. However, since NSPRING computes current data, created from the current z-score coefficients, and then combines these data with the previous data, created from the previous z-score coefficients, in our opinion the method is inaccurate. With an incessant effort, we have recently developed ISPRING [22], an improved variant of SPRING. ISPRING is SPRING equipped with incremental min–max normalization (see Sect. 4.1). We choose min–max normalization rather than z-score normalization for ISPRING, because the min–max coefficients (minimum and maximum values) of evolving subsequences in streaming time series are occasionally changed, whereas the z-score coefficients of the subsequences are almost changed whenever there is a new-coming data point. For the reason, ISPRING using incremental min–max normalization can use current normalized data with previous normalized data to compute the DTW distance between a new-coming time-series subsequence and a specific time-series pattern if the min–max coefficients of the evolving subsequence are not changed. To extract the min–max coefficients of the new-coming subsequence of one streaming time series on the spot, ISPRING uses a monitoring window anchored at the entry of the time-series stream. The experiments in [21] demonstrated that the size of the monitoring window should be the same length as the pattern. We will compare ESUCR-DTW using incremental min–max normalization with ISPRING in Sect. 5.

Next, Rodpongpun et al. [23] proposed a lower bounding function, referred to as LB_GUN, under global constraint, uniform scaling, and z-score normalization. LB_GUN inher-

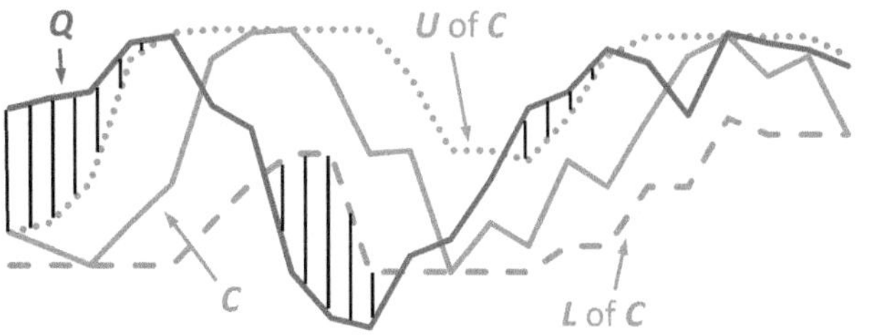

Fig. 6 Reversed $LB_{\_Keogh}$ on C and Q

its from $LB_{\_Keogh}$ and is expanded to deal with uniform scaling. Since we assume that time-series data are uniformly scaled already in our methods, it is not suitable to compare our methods with LB_GUN.

Last but not least, UCR-DTW [11] is a method of similar search in static time series under DTW supporting z-score normalization. The method is of low computational time and high accuracy, so we will be compare SUCR-DTW with UCR-DTW in Sect. 5. UCR-DTW will be reviewed in the following paragraphs.

The spirit of UCR-DTW is using $LB_{\_Kim}$, $LB_{\_Keogh}$, reversed $LB_{\_Keogh}$, and the naive computation of DTW in a cascading fashion. Reversed $LB_{\_Keogh}$ is an exchange of the role of query/data in $LB_{\_Keogh}$; this means that query Q is compared with the envelope of time-series sequence C. Reversed $LB_{\_Keogh}$ is computed in a *just-in-time* fashion, only if $LB_{\_Kim}$ and $LB_{\_Keogh}$ fail to prune. Therefore, UCR-DTW costs a negligible time overhead for reversed $LB_{\_Keogh}$ to prune off more classical DTW calculations. Figure 6 shows reversed $LB_{\_Keogh}$ that contrasts with $LB_{\_Keogh}$ illustrated as in Fig. 5. Besides, UCR-DTW uses the Sakoe–Chiba band as a global constraint to support $LB_{\_Keogh}$, reversed $LB_{\_Keogh}$, and the classical DTW calculation for reduction of the running time.

UCR-DTW is briefly described in Algorithm *UCR-DTW* for *best-so-far* search with some notations defined in Table 1. There are some noticeable issues in the algorithm. At first, the lower bounding functions, which are $LB_{\_Kim}$ (line 6), $LB_{\_Keogh}$ (line 8), reversed $LB_{\_Keogh}$ (line 10), and the procedure *DTW* (lines 13 and 15) all use $q.bsf$ as an upper bound for early abandoning of these functions. Next, it is likely that the length of T is very large, so it is necessary to read T into many big sections (e.g. 100,000 data points) (line 2). The construction of E_s (line 3) is carried out using the method of Lemire [24] and then E_s is used in reversed $LB_{\_Keogh}$ (line 10). In line 4, c extracted from s is stored in a circular buffer whose length is double that of $q.l$. The z-score coefficients of c are got in line 5; and at the moment, the data points of nc had not been determined yet. Thanks to these z-score coefficients, the data points of nc, which are required in $LB_{\_Kim}$ (line 6) and $LB_{\_Keogh}$ (line 8), are computed in a *just-in-time* fashion. $LB_{\_Kim}$ in line 6 is expanded to cal-

Table 1 Notations for UCR-DTW

Notation	Meaning
T	A static time series
s	A big section of T
q	A time-series pattern for query
nq	The normalized pattern of q
$q.l$	The length of q
$q.r$	The width r of the Sakoe–Chiba band of q
E_s	The envelope of s constructed with $q.r$
$q.bsf$	The *best-so-far* value of q over T
c	A new-coming subsequence of S, corresponding with q
$coef$	The normalization coefficients of c
nc	The normalized pattern of c
$cb1, cb2$	Two arrays of cumulative bounds

culate on the first three data points and the last three ones of nq and nc. In line 8, LB_{Keogh} uses the available envelope of nq. If the algorithm reaches line 10, then the data points of nc are completely determined at the moment, so reversed LB_{Keogh} does not need to recalculate them. The computation of LB_{Keogh} on nq and nc in line 8 returns one lower bounding distance between the two normalized time-series sequences, LB_{Keogh1}, and one array of cumulative bounds, $cb1$. Similarly, in line 10, the calculation of reversed LB_{Keogh} on nc and nq returns LB_{Keogh2} and $cb2$. The procedure DTW in lines 13 and 15 uses $cb1$ and $cb2$ for early abandoning of DTW.

Algorithm $UCR\text{-}DTW(T, q)$

1. $q.bsf \leftarrow \infty$
2. Get each s of T
3.   Construct E_s
4.   Use a sliding window whose width is $q.l$ to slide over s. The operation extracts c for every sliding step.
5. $coef \leftarrow$ Incremental z-score normalize c
6. $lb\_{Kim} \leftarrow LB\_{Kim}(nq, nc, q.bsf)$
7.   **if** $lb\_{Kim} < q.bsf$ **then**
8. $(lb\_{Keogh1}, cb1) \leftarrow LB\_{Keogh}(nq, nc, q.bsf)$
9.   **if** $lb\_{Keogh1} < q.bsf$ **then**
        // reversed LB_{Keogh}
10. $(lb\_{Keogh2}, cb2) \leftarrow LB\_{Keogh}(nc, nq, q.bsf)$
11.   **if** $lb\_{Keogh2} < q.bsf$ **then**
12.   **if** $lb\_{Keogh1} > lb\_{Keogh2}$ **then**
13. $d \leftarrow DTW(nq, nc, q.bsf, cb1)$
14.   **else**
15. $d \leftarrow DTW(nc, nq, q.bsf, cb2)$
16.   **if** $d < q.bsf$ **then**
17. $q.bsf \leftarrow d$

It is obvious that UCR-DTW combines all the techniques mentioned in Sect. 2.2 so as to accelerate the similarity search; therefore, the method is of low computational time with respect to theoretical evaluation. We also note that the algorithm can be expanded for range search and *k-NN* search, and can be adjusted to process numerous patterns at every sliding step over *T*.

Since Rakthanmanon et al. [11] reckoned that the speedup techniques used in UCR-DTW dwarf the improvements gained by multi-threading, we want to check the claim and so propose our methods working on multicores. To evaluate the accuracy and execution time of the proposed methods, we adjust the methods for range search and each pattern has its own range radius.

4 The proposed methods

In the section, we present incremental data normalization to support data normalization in the streaming setting and then give the problem definition. After that, the two proposed methods, SUCR-DTW and ESUCR-DTW, are proposed to solve the problem.

4.1 Incremental data normalization

Since time-series sequences change continuously in the streaming setting, data normalization becomes a burden for pre-processing time-series data prior to subsequence matching. Therefore, it is necessary to have a complementary technique for data normalization in the streaming context. We propose incremental data normalization to get normalization coefficients, which are min–max and z-score coefficients, on the fly. Incremental min-max normalization and z-score normalization are presented as follows.

- *Incremental min–max normalization* In the beginning, an ascending numeric array is created from the data points of X with the algorithm of *Quicksort*, so $x_{\min}$ is the first element and $x_{\max}$ is the last one of the ordering array. When there is a new-coming data point, the oldest data point of X is deleted out of the array, and then the new data point is inserted into the array. The course of the deletion and insertion must preserve the ascending order of the array, so the algorithm of *Binary search* is used to find the element that needs deleting and the suitable position in the array to insert the new data point. As *Quicksort* is carried out once when the array of new-coming data points is full at the beginning of the course of the similarity search, and since then *Binary search* is invoked for every new-coming data point afterward, the time complexity of incremental min–max normalization is $\mathcal{O}(\log(n))$.

- *Incremental z-score normalization*

Let us define $$x^2 = \sum_{i=1}^{n} x_i^2. \quad (11)$$

Equation (10) can be expressed as: $$\sigma^2 = \frac{x^2}{m} - \mu^2. \quad (12)$$

At first, Eq. (9) is used to compute μ and Eq. (11) is used to compute $x2$. Next, when there is a new-coming data point x_{n+1} deriving from the evolution of X, we compute

$$\mu_{\text{new}} = \mu + \frac{x_{n+1} - x_1}{n} \quad (13)$$

$$\text{and} \quad x_{\text{new}}^2 = x^2 + x_{n+1}^2 - x_1^2. \quad (14)$$

Therefore, we do not need to compute μ_{new} and x_{new}^2 completely. Note that the time complexity of incremental z-score normalization is higher than that of incremental min–max normalization, since the complex arithmetic operators, which are the square to compute x_{new}^2 and the square root to compute σ, are used in incremental z-score normalization.

Notice that because of the accumulation of the floating-point error in the implementation of the incremental z-score normalization, μ_{new} and x_{new}^2 will be completely calculated by Eqs. (9) and (11), respectively, to flush out any accumulated error for once every 100,000 coming data points of a time-series stream.

4.2 Problem definition

The problem is that numerous prespecified time-series patterns need to conduct one of the tasks of similarity search, which is mentioned in Sect. 2.4, over multiple concurrent time-series streams at high-speed rates under DTW and data normalization. The multi-threading technique is proposed to use to support the solution of the problem. The solution consists of two phases:

Phase 1 The patterns are normalized and their envelopes are constructed.

Phase 2 Each threading process deals with one time-series stream. When there is a new-coming data point of the time-series stream, for each pattern the matching procedure will determine whether the new-coming time-series subsequence is a candidate in case of SUCR-DTW or many new-coming time-series subsequences are candidates in case of ESUCR-DTW. The matching procedure works nearly the same as for UCR-DTW. With respect to range search, a similar subsequence has the DTW distance between its normalized subsequence and the normalized pattern within the range radius of the pattern.

Table 2 Additional notations

Notation	Meaning
$QSet$	The set of patterns
$q.ep$	The range radius of q
$q.RSet$	The range set of q
S	A streaming time series
T_n	The new-coming data value at time point n of S
T_{n-1}	The new-coming data value at time point $n-1$ of S
E_c	The envelope of c

There are some following supplementary ideas for the similarity search. As regards data normalization, the similarity search makes a choice between incremental z-score normalization and incremental min–max normalization to get normalization coefficients. Using whichever data normalization is dependent on the requirement of applications. Next, to accelerate the similarity search, data points of one time-series stream are stored in a circular buffer whose length is longer than the length of the longest pattern.

As for one time-series stream, if the similarity search is conducted over one new-coming time-series subsequence of the same length as the pattern, we propose SUCR-DTW, which stands for Streaming UCR-DTW; otherwise, ESUCR-DTW standing for Extended SUCR-DTW is proposed to carry out the similarity search over many new-coming time-series subsequences. Combined with Table 1, Table 2 shows some additional notations, which we will use in the proposed two methods afterwards.

4.3 SUCR-DTW

The working environment of the method is illustrated as in Fig. 7. Given one pattern q, SUCR-DTW conducts the similarity search over the new-coming subsequence c of the time-series stream S and c having length of $q.l$. Therefore, the method has a delay of $q.l$ time ticks at the beginning

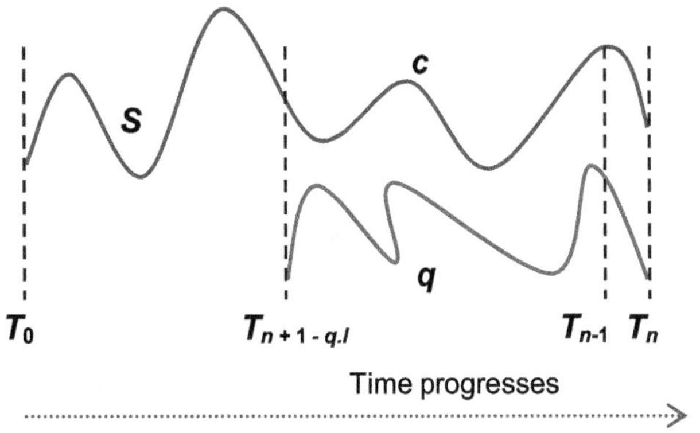

Fig. 7 SUCR-DTW extracts c and normalizes it, and then compares nc with nq under DTW

of the similarity search for q. In addition, when there is a new-coming data point of the time-series stream, the method needs to construct the envelope of c, which is E_c. Notice that q also has its own envelope, which is created in Phase 1, and the data structure to store the envelope is a pair of conventional arrays. In UCR-DTW, the construction of the envelope of c is carried out once for each big section of static time series (line 3 of Algorithm *UCR-DTW*), while in the streaming context, E_c can be created in a *just-in-time* fashion; that is, E_c can be created from scratch, right from the moment at which it is needed. However, SUCR-DTW uses another way to construct E_c, which performs incremental updates on E_c. SUCR-DTW thus uses two circular buffers of the same length as the pattern to store the upper and lower bounds of E_c. In Sect. 5.1, we will compare the performance of the two cases in constructing E_c.

SUCR-DTW implementing Phase 2 is presented in Algorithm *SUCR-DTW* for range search. We have some remarks on the algorithm. Firstly, the algorithm handles many patterns in succession (line 1), and every pattern q has its own subsequence c of the streaming time series S (line 3). Next, construction of E_c is carried out once (line 5), and after that E_c is incrementally updated (line 7). E_c is used in reversed LB_{Keogh} (line 13). Line 20 indicates that if c is a disjoint query in the set *q.RSet*, then c is a valid similar subsequence of q. Similar to the role of *q.bsf* in Algorithm *UCR-DTW*, *q.ep* is an upper bound for early abandoning in LB_{Kim} (line 9), LB_{Keogh} (line 11), reversed LB_{Keogh} (line 13), and the procedure *DTW* (lines 16 and 18).

Algorithm *SUCR-DTW(S)*

```
When there is a new-coming data of S, T_n
 1. foreach( q in QSet)
 2.    if n ≥ q.l − 1 then
 3.       Get c
 4.       if n = q.l − 1 then
 5.          Construct E_c
 6.       else
 7.          Incrementally update E_c
 8.       coef ← Incrementally normalize c
 9.       lb_Kim ← LB_Kim(nq, nc, q.ep)
10.       if lb_Kim ≤ q.ep then
11.          (lb_Keogh1, cb1) ← LB_Keogh(nq, nc, q.ep)
12.          if lb_Keogh1 ≤ q.ep then
             // reversed LB_Keogh
13.          (lb_Keogh2, cb2) ← LB_Keogh(nc, nq, q.ep)
14.          if lb_Keogh2 ≤ q.ep then
15.             if lb_Keogh1 > lb_Keogh2 then
16.                d ← DTW(nq, nc, q.ep, cb1)
17.             else
18.                d ← DTW(nc, nq, q.ep, cb2)
19.             if d ≤ q.ep then
20.                if DisjoinQuery(c, q.RSet) then
21.                   Add c into q.RSet
22. end foreach
```

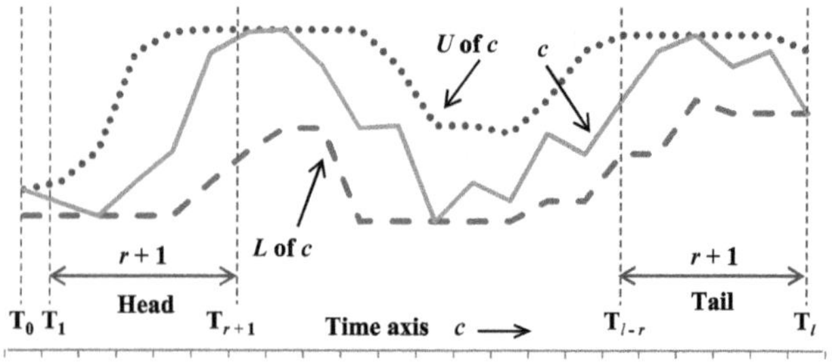

Fig. 8 The parts of *Head* and *Tail* of $E_c = \{U, L\}$ need updating

Next, we will depict how to update E_c incrementally. When a data point of S newly arrives, we can imagine that c slides rightwards along the time axis. Let l be the length of c, and r be the width of the Sakoe–Chiba band of q ($r \ll l$). In other words, $q.l$ is referred to as l, and $q.r$ is referred to as r. For the sake of illustration, we assume that c slides from time tick 0 to 1, and l is the most recent time tick. That means $c = \{T_1, T_2, \ldots, T_l\}$. Let $U = \{u_1, u_2, \ldots, u_l\}$ be the upper bound of c, and $L = \{l_1, l_2, \ldots, l_l\}$ be the lower bound of c. That means $E_c = \{U, L\}$. Deduced from the formula (5), U and L keep the same values from time points $r + 2$ to $l - r - 1$. Let *Head* be values of E_c from time point 1 to $r + 1$ and *Tail* be values of E_c from time point $l - r$ to l. *Head* and *Tail* need updating when c slides over the time axis. Figure 8 depicts the envelope E_c, and its *Head* and *Tail* when c slides from time tick 0 to 1.

It is obvious that if E_c is completely constructed for each sliding step, the time complexity of the task is $\mathcal{O}(l)$; however, if E_c is incrementally updated at its *Head* and *Tail*, the time complexity reduces to $\mathcal{O}(r)$. Furthermore, due to the features of the upper and lower bounds of E_c, updating *Head* and *Tail* can be early abandoned. Updates on *Head* and *Tail* are detailed in Algorithm *UpdateTail* and Algorithm *UpdateHead*, respectively. Line 7 of Algorithm *SUCR-DTW* implements *UpdateTail* as well as *UpdateHead*.

Algorithm *UpdateTail*

```
u_l ← max(T_{l−r}, T_{l−r+1}, ..., T_l)        // update U
for (i = 1; i ≤ r; i++)
   if u_{l−i} ≥ u_l then
      break
   u_{l−i} ← u_l
end for
l_l ← min(T_{l−r}, T_{l−r+1}, ..., T_l)        // update L
for (i = 1; i ≤ r; i++)
   if l_{l−i} ≤ l_l then
      break
   l_{l−i} ← l_l
end for
```

```
Algorithm UpdateHead
1.  if T0 = u0 then                              // update U
2.      u1 ← max(T1, T2, ..., Tr+1)
3.      umax ← u1
4.      for (i = 2; i ≤ r + 1; i++)
5.          if Tr+i > umax then
6.              umax ← Tr+i
7.          ui ← umax
8.      end for
9.  if T0 = l0 then                              // update L
10.     l1 ← min(T1, T2, ..., Tr+1)
11.     lmin ← l1
12.     for (i = 2; i ≤ r + 1; i++)
13.         if Tr+i < lmin then
14.             lmin ← Tr+i
15.         li ← lmin
16.     end for
```

Note that if the condition in line 3 of Algorithm *UpdateTail* is satisfied, updating U will be immediately stopped. Similarly, early abandoning takes place for L if the condition in line 9 of the algorithm is true. As regards Algorithm *UpdateHead*, we note that $u_0 = \max(T_0, T_1, \ldots, T_r)$ and $l_0 = \min(T_0, T_1, \ldots, T_r)$ for the present. Updating U in *Head* occurs only if T_0 is u_0 (line 1). Similarly, updating L in *Head* takes place only if T_0 is equal to l_0 (line 9). Notice that *UpdateTail* and *UpdateHead* need adjusting slightly in the general case where c slides from time tick h to $h+1$ with $h \geq 0$.

To evaluate the effectiveness and efficiency of the incremental updates on E_c, we make two different variants of SUCR-DTW. Both of them do not have lines 4–7 of Algorithm *SUCR-DTW*. The first variant creates E_c at the right time at which E_c is needed (between lines 12 and 13 of Algorithm *SUCR-DTW*). Let us denote the variant by SUCR-DTW-1. The second variant does not use E_c, so reversed LB_{Keogh} is omitted (lines 13, 14, 15, 17, and 18 are ignored). Let us denote the second variant by SUCR-DTW-2. Besides, we also modify UCR-DTW so that the algorithm can accommodate with multi-threaded programming, in which each threading process handles a static time-series sequence. Let TUCR-DTW be UCR-DTW equipped with multi-threading.

4.4 ESUCR-DTW

The method is an extension of SUCR-DTW from the following observation. Given a pattern q, the subsequences at the entry of one streaming time series can be matched with the pattern under DTW provided that the lengths of these subsequences are within a range of $[q.l - q.r : q.l + q.r]$. The reason is that because of the characteristic of the Sakoe–Chiba band, LB_{Keogh}, reversed LB_{Keogh}, and the procedure *DTW* can work with q and a time-series subsequence whose length is within this range. Figure 9 indicates

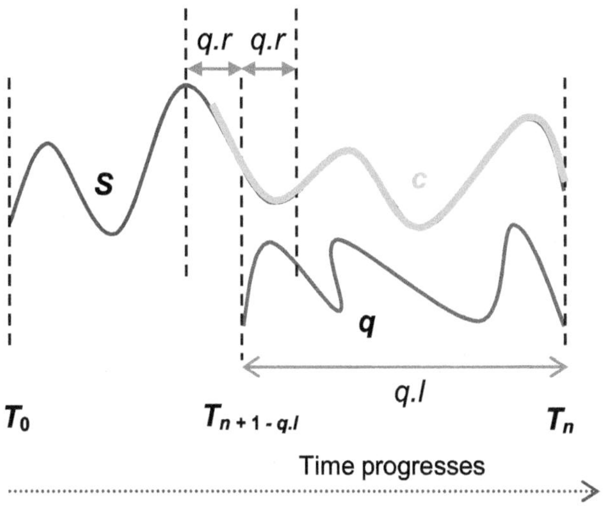

Fig. 9 A new-coming subsequence c whose length is within a range of $[q.l - q.r : q.l + q.r]$ can be matched with pattern q by ESUCR-DTW

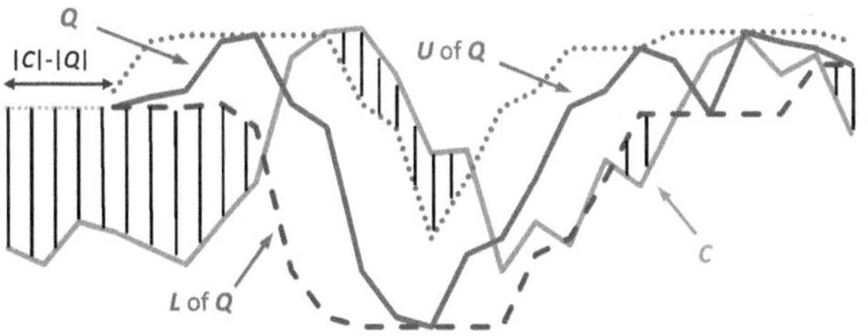

Fig. 10 Using LB_{Keogh} in case of $0 \leq |C| - |Q| \leq r$

that a subsequence c can be matched with q as the length of c is within the range. ESUCR-DTW can find many more similar subsequences than SUCR-DTW does, because the latter performs similarity search only over one new-coming subsequence of length $q.l$. The trade-off of finding many more similar subsequences by ESUCR-DTW is that the running time of ESUCR-DTW is much longer than that of SUCR-DTW, directly proportional to the number of subsequences matched with q at a time tick. The maximum number of subsequences that are performed by the similarity search for every pattern q over one time series stream at a time tick is $2 \times q.r + 1$.

Original LB_{Keogh} works only on two time-series sequences of the same length, so to deal with two time-series sequences whose lengths are different within a width r of the Sakoe–Chiba band, the lower bounding function needs a slight change in the two following cases.

Figure 10 illustrates the first case in which C is longer than Q. Let $m = |Q|$, $n = |C|$, and $w = n - m$. Suppose that $w \leq r$. It is intuitive that $c_1, c_2, \ldots, c_w$ can be measured with the first couple of the envelope of Q (i.e. u_1 and l_1). The formula (6) is thus changed to

$$LB\_{Keogh}(Q,C) = \sqrt{\sum_{i=1}^{n} \begin{cases} (c_i - u_1)^2 & \text{if } i \le w \text{ and } c_i > u_1 \\ (l_1 - c_i)^2 & \text{if } i \le w \text{ and } c_i < l_1 \\ (c_i - u_{i+1-w})^2 & \text{if } i > w \text{ and } c_i > u_{i+1-w} \\ (l_{i+1-w} - c_i)^2 & \text{if } i > w \text{ and } c_i < l_{i+1-w} \\ 0 & \text{otherwise.} \end{cases}} \quad (15)$$

Figure 11 shows the second case in which Q is longer than C, which means $w < 0$. The formula (6) becomes

$$LB\_{Keogh}(Q,C) = \sqrt{\sum_{i=1}^{n} \begin{cases} (c_i - u_{i+1-w})^2 & \text{if } i > w \text{ and } c_i > u_{i+1-w} \\ (l_{i+1-w} - c_i)^2 & \text{if } i > w \text{ and } c_i < l_{i+1-w} \\ 0 & \text{otherwise.} \end{cases}} \quad (16)$$

Let $q.cS$ denote the set of new-coming subsequences, which are performed the similarity search for q, of streaming time series S. Also, given $\alpha, \beta \in N$ and $\alpha, \beta \le q.r$, all the subsequences of $q.cS$ have their lengths within a range of $[q.l - \alpha : q.l + \beta]$. ESUCR-DTW implementing Phase 2 is described in Algorithm *ESUCR-DTW*. There are some comments on the algorithm as follows. Line 2 implies that the similarity search has a delay of $q.l - q.r$ time ticks. At the time tick $q.l - q.r - 1$, the envelope E_c of a new-coming subsequence of length $q.l - q.r$ is created (line 4). This envelope is used in reserved LB_{Keogh} for all subsequences in $q.cS$. Notice that E_c does not have its *Head* at this moment (line 4), so in the following time ticks from $q.l - q.r$ to $q.l + q.r - 1$, only *Tail* of E_c is updated (line 6). At time tick $q.l + q.r - 1$, E_c is fully made; this means E_c has *Tail* as well as *Head*. Thus, *Head* of E_c is also updated since time tick $q.l + q.r$ (line 8). Line 9 gets all new-coming subsequences of $q.cS$. The similarity search is then performed on every subsequence c in $q.cS$ for pattern q in the same course of the similarity search in Algorithm *SUCR-DTW* (line 11). Note that the maximum number of the elements in $q.cS$ is $2 \times q.r + 1$ and, if $(\alpha, \beta) = (0, 0)$, then ESUCR-DTW becomes SUCR-DTW.

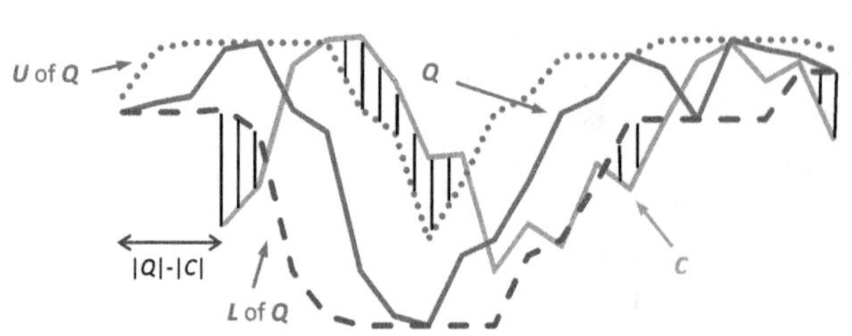

Fig. 11 Using LB_{Keogh} in case of $0 \le |Q| - |C| \le r$

Algorithm *ESUCR-DTW(S)*

When there is a new-coming data of S, T_n

1. **foreach**(q **in** $QSet$)
2. **if** $n \ge q.l - q.r - 1$ **then**
3. **if** $n = q.l - q.r - 1$ **then**
4. Construct E_c
5. **else**
6. $UpdateTail$ for E_c
7. **if** $n > q.l + q.r - 1$ **then**
8. $UpdateHead$ for E_c
9. Get $q.cS$
10. **foreach**(c **in** $q.cS$)
11. Reuse lines 8-21 of Algorithm *SUCR-DTW*
12. **end foreach**
13. **end foreach**

5 Experimental evaluation

The section demonstrates experiments on the methods of similarity search to evaluate their effectiveness and efficiency. All the experiments were conducted on an Intel Dual Core i3 M350 2.27 GHz, 4GB RAM PC. The programming language is C# as the language is powerful for multi-threading. For the sake of fairness, all threading processes are of the same priority.

5.1 Evaluation of SUCR-DTW

Table 3 presents Dataset 1 that consists of five time-series text files used as input for five time-series sequences. The sources of the time-series files are given in [25,26]. Except for the first time-series file, the four remaining time-series files are for time-series classification and clustering, but not time-series subsequences matching. Thus, we revised the data format of these four time-series files slightly as follows. Each time-series file consists of a set of time-series sequences $\{S_1, S_2, \ldots, S_n\}$ and label l_i(s) of the sequences. We connect all the sequences $S_1, S_2, \ldots, S_n$ together as a whole sequence S. That means the labels l_i(s) in the time-series file are removed.

We created three pattern sets from the above time-series files, and the number of patterns in each pattern set is 100. In

Table 3 Dataset 1 simulates time-series sequences

No.	Time-series file	Length
1	Data.txt to demonstrate UCR Suite	1,000,000
2	Revised CinC_ECG_torso_TEST	2,261,820
3	Revised InlineSkate_TEST	1,035,100
4	Revised NonInvasiveFatalECG_Thorax1TEST	1,271,250
5	Revised uWaveGestureLibrary_X_TEST	1,128,330
	Total points	6,695,500

each pattern set, the number of patterns created from a time-series file is directly proportional to the number of data points in the file. The lengths of the patterns for query vary from 50 to 550. The patterns were extracted from random positions in the time-series files. Next, all data points of a pattern were added by a numerical constant, and then the data points were virtually increased or decreased by a relatively small numeric value (e.g. 0.3 or −0.3). Finally, 33 % of the data points were changed by which they got the value of the preceding data point or successive one, or the mean of neighboring ones. The total number of data points was 28,762 for the pattern set 1; 28,927 for the pattern set 2; and 33,219 for the pattern set 3.

We developed UCR-DTW for *best-so-far* search as well as range search for numerous prespecified patterns in multiple static time series. After that, we implemented UCR-DTW for *best-so-far* search of each pattern set over Dataset 1 and recorded the *best-so-far* value of every pattern. The *best-so-far* value is used as a range radius of this pattern for range search. In this way, we created three pattern sets for range search over Dataset 1. The other parameters of the testbed are as follows. The circular buffers of the time-series streams have the size of 1024. Since the authors in [7] claimed that 10 % constraint on warping inherited from speech community is actually much higher than the constraint needed for data-mining applications, the methods of similarity search takes 5 % constraint on warping in their implementation. For example, if the length of a time-series pattern is 500, then the width r of the Sakoe–Chiba band is 25.

Then we implemented UCR-DTW for range search of the three pattern sets. The results are 100 hits for each pattern set, and all the patterns have one hit. After that, we carried out SUCR-DTW, SUCR-DTW-1, SUCR-DTW-2, and TUCR-DTW for the three pattern sets. Notice that all the methods in the experiments use incremental z-score normalization mentioned in Sect. 4.1. The results of the methods are same as those of UCR-DTW, so the precision and recall of the methods are 100 %. As regards wall clock time, the obtained results are illustrated as in Fig. 12. The figure shows that the performance of SUCR-DTW is better than those of SUCR-DTW-1 and SUCR-DTW-2. This means that incrementally updating the envelope E_c of a time-series subsequence c and then using E_c in reversed LB_{Keogh} make similarity search faster than completely constructing E_c, or not using E_c. UCR-DTW is slowest; however, TUCR-DTW, which is UCR-DTW equipped with multi-threading, has the least wall clock time. Note that TUCR-DTW is not suitable for the streaming setting, because the method requires available time-series sequences before the similarity search is done, whereas time-series data points of a time-series stream are only collected at every time tick, unknown beforehand. Finally, with regard to SUCR-DTW, we recorded the average CPU times to process a new-coming data point of 2835 ticks for the pattern set 1; 2944 ticks for the pattern set 2; and 3208 ticks for the pattern set 3. These results present the usability of SUCR-DTW in real-time applications that need to perform the similarity search at high-speed rates.

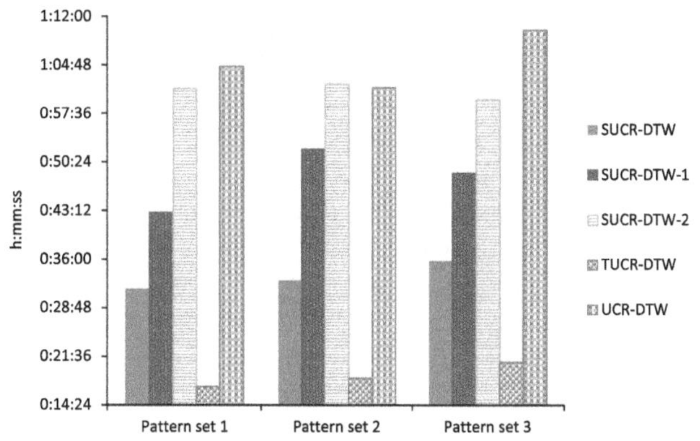

Fig. 12 Statistic of the wall clock times for range search

Table 4 Pruning powers of the lower bounding functions

	LB_{Kim} (%)	LB_{Keogh} (%)	Reversed LB_{Keogh} (%)
Pattern set 1			
SUCR-DTW	54.66	34.67	9.95
UCR-DTW	54.67	34.66	9.90
Pattern set 2			
SUCR-DTW	55.45	34.41	9.44
UCR-DTW	55.45	34.40	9.39
Pattern set 3			
SUCR-DTW	51.47	39.17	8.69
UCR-DTW	51.47	39.17	8.65

Finally, there are two noticeable remarks on pruning powers of the three lower bounding functions used in SUCR-DTW and UCR-DTW. In the two methods, LB_{Kim}, LB_{Keogh}, and reversed LB_{Keogh} are arranged in the ascending tightness of the lower bounding property, such that front lower bounding functions with low time complexities rule out most unpromising subsequences. As a result, the number of post-checking times using the classical DTW so as to determine if a candidate subsequence is a true hit is very tiny. Table 4 indicates that LB_{Kim}, whose time complexity is $\mathcal{O}(1)$, takes charge of the most pruning. After that, LB_{Keogh}, whose time complexity is $\mathcal{O}(n)$, prunes off remaining unpromising subsequences, and then reversed LB_{Keogh}, whose time complexity is highest, tries to prune off unpromising subsequences which LB_{Kim} and LB_{Keogh} cannot detect. In addition, Table 4 shows that the pruning power of reversed LB_{Keogh} in SUCR-DTW is larger than that in UCR-DTW, roughly 0.05 %. This implies that the envelopes, which are incrementally updated in SUCR-DTW, are tighter than those which are constructed once, in UCR-

Table 5 Dataset 2 simulates time-series sequences

No.	Time-series file	Length
1	Revised Adiac_TEST	68,816
2	Revised Adiac_TRAIN	68,640
3	Revised FISH_TEST	81,025
4	Revised FISH_TRAIN	81,025
5	Revised MedicalImages_TEST	75,240
	Total points	374,746

Table 6 The number of same similar subsequences of the two incremental data normalization

(α, β)	# of same similar subsequences
(1, 1)	8
(2, 2)	6
(3, 3)	9
(4, 4)	4
(5, 5)	2

DTW. In SUCR-DTW, more tightness is shown at both ends of the envelopes of new-coming subsequences.

5.2 Evaluation of ESUCR-DTW

To evaluate ESUCR-DTW, we used Dataset 2 depicted as in Table 5. The dataset consists of five time-series files [25] revised in the same way as the four time-series files done in Dataset 1. The reason using Dataset 2 rather than Dataset 1 is that the time complexity of ESUCR-DTW is much larger than that of SUCR-DTW, so experiments on ESUCR-DTW with Dataset 1 will have wall clock times too long. Although the size of Dataset 2 is smaller than that of Dataset 1, the experimental results on Dataset 2 are also significant, because the second dataset has a comparatively large scale.

Next, a pattern set was created from the revised time-series files of Dataset 2. The number of patterns in the set is 100 and the lengths of the patterns vary from 128 to 512. These patterns were created in the same way as the patterns constructed in Sect. 5.1. The total number of data points of the pattern set is 34,404. Three next experiments on Dataset 2 and the pattern set were carried out to evaluate ESUCR-DTW.

At first, ESUCR-DTW was compared with SUCR-DTW in terms of accuracy and wall clock time. In the experiment, both the methods use incremental z-score normalization. As regards ESUCR-DTW, we set $(\alpha, \beta) = (1, 1)$. At the beginning of the comparison, we implemented an original UCR-DTW on the pattern set and recorded the *best-so-far* value of every pattern. The *best-so-far* value is used as a range radius of the pattern for range search. We thus created the pattern set for range search over Dataset 2. After that, SUCR-DTW and ESUCR-DTW were implemented. With regard to SUCR-DTW, the results are 100 hits, and all patterns have 1 hit. The wall clock time of SUCR-DTW is roughly 8:56.95 min. With respect to ESUCR-DTW, the results are 111 hits, and the patterns have one or many hits. However, the wall clock time of ESUCR-DTW is about 26:28.02 min. In the experiment, ESUCR-DTW is three times as slow as SUCR-DTW, since for each pattern q, ESUCR-DTW must perform similarity search over three new-coming subsequences, whose lengths are $q.l - 1$, $q.l$, and $q.l + 1$, respectively, of one streaming time series at a time tick. It is obvious that ESUCR-DTW is more accurate than SUCR-DTW, yet the former costs much more time than the latter.

The second experiment illustrates the correlation between the obtained results with incremental z-score normalization and those with incremental min-max normalization. At first, ESUCR-DTW is changed from range search to *best-so-far* search, and then the method employs incremental z-score normalization with the cases of 2-tuple (α, β) be (0, 0), (1, 1), (2, 2), (3, 3), (4, 4), and (5, 5). After that, the method uses incremental min–max normalization with the same above cases of (α, β). Table 6 presents the number of same *best-so-far* subsequences obtained by ESUCR-DTW using incremental z-score normalization and ESUCR-DTW using incremental min–max normalization for each case of (α, β). These results show that if the search scope of new-coming subsequences increases in ESUCR-DTW (i.e. from (1, 1) up to (5, 5)), the number of same similar subsequences of the two cases tends to decrease. As a whole, the *best-so-far* subsequences obtained with incremental z-score normalization rarely coincide with those done with incremental min–max normalization. Notice that in case of *best-so-far* search implemented with SUCR-DTW or ESUCR-DTW, a threading process can compete with others to update the *best-so-far* value of one pattern at a time, so the system must lock the shared property and check the *best-so-far* value again before the update can be done.

Other fascinating statistics of the second experiment also is unfolded. We reuse the conventional symbols as follows. Let q be a time-series pattern for query and c be the *best-so-far* subsequence of q. Figure 13 depicts the number of cases where *best-so-far* subsequences are shorter than patterns ($|c| < |q|$), longer than patterns ($|c| > |q|$), and the same length as patterns ($|c| = |q|$) for each case of (α, β). ESUCR-DTW uses incremental z-score normalization and incremental min–max normalization in turn. The figure reveals that ESUCR-DTW often returns similar subsequences longer than patterns. With regard to both incremental data normalizations, the number of cases of $|c| = |q|$ is relatively low; especially for incremental z-score normalization, the value is from four to five cases. Next, the number of

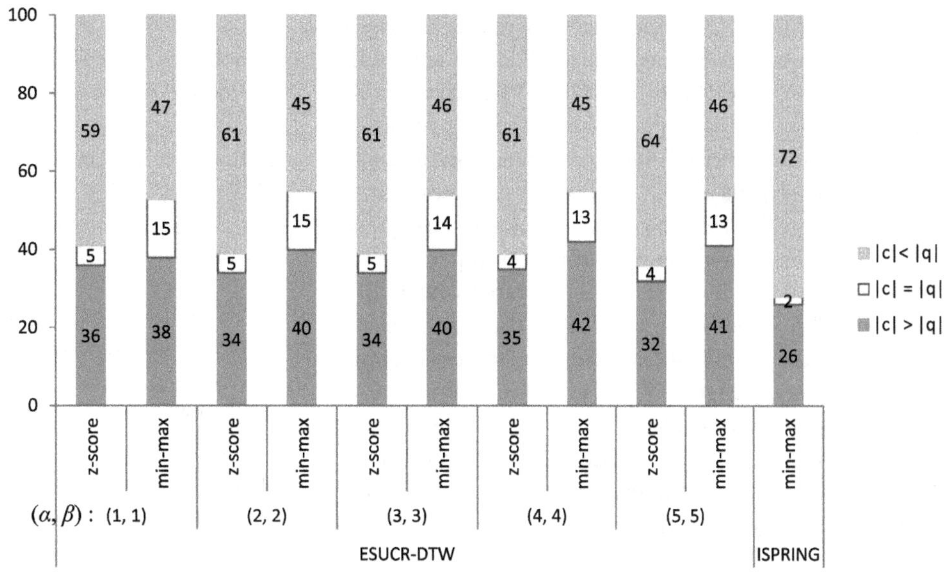

Fig. 13 Evaluate *best-so-far* subsequences with their patterns in terms of length in 100 cases

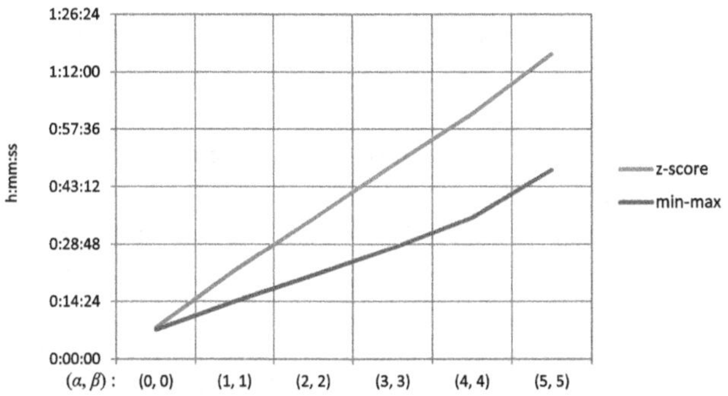

Fig. 14 The wall clock times of ESUCR-DTW for each case of (α, β) with the two incremental data normalizations

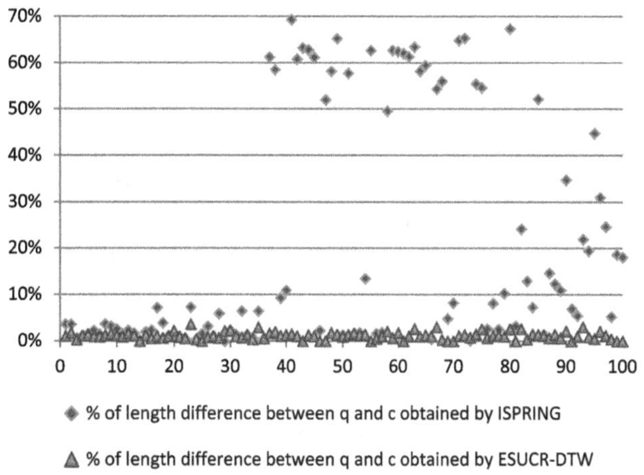

Fig. 15 The distribution of the percentages of length difference between the 100 patterns and the 100 corresponding *best-so-far* subsequences obtained by ISPRING and ESUCR-DTW

cases of $|c| > |q|$ with incremental min–max normalization is larger than that with incremental z-score normalization.

Figure 14 indicates the wall clock times of ESUCR-DTW for every case of (α, β) with the two incremental data normalizations. Note that if ESUCR-DTW is degraded to SUCR-DTW due to $(\alpha, \beta) = (0, 0)$, the wall clock time of ESUCR-DTW using incremental z-score normalization and that of ESUCR-DTW using incremental min–max normalization are nearly the same. Figure 14 also depicts that the wall clock times of ESUCR-DTW using incremental min–max normalization are smaller than those of ESUCR-DTW using incremental z-score normalization. However, this does not mean that ESUCR-DTW supports incremental min–max normalization better than incremental z-score normalization. Incremental min–max normalization takes low computational time evidently, $\mathcal{O}((\log(n)))$, so the technique mitigates the running time of ESUCR-DTW significantly; whereas incremental z-score normalization is of higher computational time, ESUCR-DTW has longer wall clock time. Furthermore, the wall clock times of ESUCR-DTW using incremental z-score normalization are nearly directly proportional to the number of new-coming subsequences of one streaming time series, which are matched with a pattern at a time tick. For instance, the wall clock times are 7:57.41 min in case of $(\alpha, \beta) = (0, 0)$, and 1:16:33.94 h in case of $(\alpha, \beta) = (5, 5)$. The increase of approximately ten times in wall clock time relates to the increase in the number of new-coming subsequences on which the similarity search is performed with a specific pattern at a time tick, of one time-series stream, from 1 up to $5 + 1 + 5 = 11$.

The third experiment is to compare ESUCR-DTW and ISPRING in terms of wall clock time and the quality of similar subsequences. *Best-so-far* search using min–max normalization is implemented in the two methods. We use again results obtained by ESUCR-DTW with $(\alpha, \beta) = (5, 5)$. The wall clock times of ESUCR-DTW and ISPRING are 47:27.75 min, 1:37:13.88 h, respectively. Thus, ESUCR-DTW is roughly twice as fast as ISPRING in the testbed.

With respect to similar subsequences, there are 91 cases in which *best-so-far* values obtained by ISPRING are smaller (i.e. better) than those done by ESUCR-DTW. The two methods have the same *best-so-far* values in the nine remaining cases. As regards ISPRING, there are two remarks on lengths of similar subsequences. Firstly, Fig. 13 indicates that the probability by which ISPRING returns a similar subsequence whose length is shorter than that of the corresponding pattern is very high, 72 % of ISPRING compared with 46 % of ESUCR-DTW. Secondly, the patterns and their similar subsequences often have a huge difference of lengths. For example, there is a pattern of length 479, and ISPRING returns its *best-so-far* subsequence of length 186; the percentage of length difference in this case is 61.17 %. ESUCR-DTW returns similar subsequences whose lengths are dependent on (α, β), so the similar subsequences always have lengths in a domain prespecified by users. Figure 15 shows that with respect to ISPRING, the maximum percentage of length difference is 69.3 %, whereas the value is 3.68 % as for ESUCR-DTW. If the length of a similar subsequence is too different from that of the corresponding pattern, it is because ISPRING does not use any constraint on the warping path in the accumulated cost matrix. It is likely that a point of one pattern matches with too many points of its similar subsequence, or vice versa. Consequently, ISPRING can create a pathological warping path in the accumulated cost matrix and this is a shortcoming of this method.

6 Conclusions and future work

The paper has presented two methods of similar search for numerous prespecified patterns in multiple time-series streams under DTW. The both methods conduct data normalization before the DTW distance between two normalized time-series sequences is computed. To be adaptive in the streaming setting, these methods use either incremental z-score normalization or incremental min–max normalization. The first method, SUCR-DTW [15], is a modification of UCR-DTW, a state-of-the-art method of similar search for prespecified patterns in static time series, so that SUCR-DTW can cope with difficulties and complexities of similarity search in streaming time series. Furthermore, SUCR-DTW can deal with multiple concurrent time-series streams at high-speed rates, because the method employs multi-threading and a combination of techniques so as to accelerate the performance of the similarity search. One of these techniques is that the envelopes of new-coming time-series subsequences are incrementally updated with low computational time, so these envelopes can be immediately used in reversed LB_{Keogh}, a lower bounding function to prune off more unpromising subsequences. However, like UCR-DTW, SUCR-DTW returns similar subsequences of the same length as the patterns. We thus introduce the second method, ESUCR-DT, which is an extension of SUCR-DTW for finding similar subsequences whose lengths are likely different from those of the patterns. Some major conclusions are drawn from the experiments on SUCR-DTW, ESUCR-DTW, and ISPRING, and another method of similar search over time-series streams, as follows.

- SUCR-DTW has the same precision as UCR-DTW and runs faster than the original UCR-DTW without multi-threading.
- The envelopes incrementally updated in SUCR-DTW are tighter than those constructed once in UCR-DTW.
- Similar subsequences obtained by ESUCR-DTW are better than those done by SUCR-DTW, yet the former must spend more time than the latter.
- With regard to ESUCR-DTW, the *best-so-far* subsequences obtained with incremental z-score normalization rarely coincide with those done with incremental min–max normalization.
- ESUCR-DTW often returns similar subsequences longer than the patterns.
- In addition, ESUCR-DTW using incremental z-score normalization is slower than ESUCR-DTW using incremental min–max normalization.
- *Best-so-far* values obtained by ISPRING are less than or equal to those done by ESUCR-DTW, yet ISPRING often returns *best-so-far* subsequences whose lengths are unreasonable. This means that many similar subsequences obtained by ISPRING are too short in comparison to the lengths of the patterns.

In future work, we plan to study how to identify common local patterns of coevolving time-series sequences under DTW and data normalization in light of the outcomes obtained from this work.

Acknowledgments We specially thank the authors in [11] for providing the source code and datasets of the UCR suite on the website [26]. Thanks to the valuable resources, our work was quickly progressed.

References

1. Borgne, Y.-A., Santinib, S., Bontempi, G.: Adaptive model selection for time series prediction in wireless sensor networks. Signal Process. **87**(12), 3010–3020 (2007)
2. Zhu, Y., Shasha, D.: Efficient elastic burst detection in data streams. In: Proceedings of the 2003 ACM SIGMOD International Conference on Management of Data, Washington, DC, USA, pp. 181–192 (2003)
3. Wu, H., Salzberg, B., Zhang, D.: Online event driven subsequence matching over financial data streams. In: Proceedings of the 2004 ACM SIGMOD International Conference on Management of Data, New York, USA, pp. 23–34 (2004)

4. Yang, Q., Wu, X.: 10 challenging problems in data mining research. Int. J. Inf. Technol. Decis. Mak. 5(4), 597–604 (2006)
5. Fu, T.-C.: A review on time series data mining. J. Eng. Appl. Artif. Intell. **24**, 164–181 (2011)
6. Bemdt, D., Clifford, J.: Using Dynamic Time Warping to find patterns in time series. In: Proceedings of AAAI Workshop on Knowledge Discovery in Databases, Seattle, Washington, USA, pp. 359–370 (1994)
7. Ratanamahatana, C., Keogh, E.: Everything you know about Dynamic Time Warping is wrong. In: 3rd Workshop on Mining Temporal and Sequential Data, in Conjunction with 10th ACM SIGKDD International Conference Knowledge Discovery and Data Mining (KDD-2004), Seattle, WA, USA (2004)
8. Petitjean, F., Forestier, G., Webb, G., Nicholson, A., Chen, Y., Keogh, E.: Dynamic Time Warping averaging of time series allows faster and more accurate classification. In: ICDM 2014: IEEE International Conference on Data Mining, Shenzhen, China, pp. 470–479 (2014)
9. Zakaria, J., Mueen, A., Eamonn Keogh, E.: Clustering time series using unsupervised-shapelets. In: ICDM 2012: IEEE International Conference on Data Mining, Brussels, Belgium, pp. 785–794 (2012)
10. Keogh, E., Ratanamahatana, C.: Exact indexing of Dynamic Time Warping. Knowl. Inf. Syst. **7**(3), 358–386 (2004)
11. Rakthanmanon, T., Campana, B., Mueen, A., Batista, G., Westover, B., Zhu, Q., Zakaria, J., Keogh, E.: Searching and mining trillions of time series subsequences under Dynamic Time Warping. In: The 18th ACM SIGKDD Conference on Knowledge Discovery and Data Mining (KDD'12), Beijing, China, pp. 262–270 (2012)
12. West, M.: http://www.isds.duke.edu/mw/data-sets/ts_data/. Accessed Dec 2013
13. Sakurai, Y., Faloutsos, C., Yamamuro, M.: Stream monitoring under the time warping distance. In: The IEEE 23rd International Conference on Data Engineering, Istanbul, Turkey, pp. 1046–1055 (2007)
14. Capitani, P., Ciaccia, P.: Warping the time on data streams. Data Knowl. Eng. **62**(3), 438–458 (2007)
15. Giao, B., Anh, D.: Similarity search in multiple high speed time series streams under Dynamic Time Warping. In: Proceedings of 2015 2nd National Foundation for Science and Technology Development Conference on Information and Computer Science (NICS 2015), Ho Chi Minh City, Vietnam, pp. 82–87 (2015)
16. Sakoe, H., Chiba, S.: Dynamic programming algorithm optimization for spoken word recognition. IEEE Trans. Acoust. Speech Signal Process. **26**(1), 43–49 (1978)
17. Kim, S.-W., Park, S.: An index-based approach for similarity search supporting time warping in large sequence databases. In: Proceedings of the 17th IEEE International Conference on Data Engineering, Heidelberg, Germany, pp. 607–614 (2001)
18. Junkui, L., Yuanzhen, W.: Early abandon to accelerate exact Dynamic Time Warping. Int. Arab J. Inf. Technol. **6**(2), 144–152 (2009)
19. Tan, S., Lau, P., Yu, X.: Finding similar time series in sales transaction data. In: Proceedings of 28th International Conference on Industrial, Engineering and Other Applications of Applied Intelligent Systems, IEA/AIE 2015, Seoul, South Korea, pp. 645–654 (2015)
20. Vinh, V., Anh, D.: Constraint-based MDL principle for semi-supervised classification of time series. In: Proceedings of 2015 Seventh International Conference on Knowledge and Systems Engineering, Ho Chi Minh City, Vietnam, pp. 43–48 (2015)
21. Gong, X., Fong, S., Chan, J., Mohammed, S.: NSPRING: the SPRING extension for subsequence matching of time series supporting normalization. J. Supercomput., pp. 1–25 (2015). doi:10.1007/s11227-015-1525-6
22. Giao, B., Anh, D.: Improving SPRING Method in similarity search over time series streams by data normalization. In: Proceedings of 2nd EAI International Conference on Nature of Computation and Communication, Rach Gia, Vietnam (2016). http://ictcc.org/2016/show/program-final
23. Rodpongpun, S., Niennattrakul, V., Ratanamahatana, C.: Efficient subsequence search on streaming data based on time warping distance. Comput. Inf. Technol. **5**(1), 2–8 (2011)
24. Lemire, D.: Faster retrieval with a two-pass Dynamic-Time-Warping lower bound. Pattern Recognit. **42**(9), 2169–2180 (2009)
25. Keogh, E.: In: The UCR classification/clustering page. http://www.cs.ucr.edu/~eamonn/time_series_data/. Accessed Aug 2013
26. Keogh, E.: In: The UCR Suite. http://www.cs.ucr.edu/~eamonn/UCRsuite.html. Accessed Dec 2014

6

Ontology-based disease similarity network for disease gene prediction

Duc-Hau Le[1] · **Vu-Tung Dang**[2]

Abstract Finding underlying molecular mechanisms of diseases is one of the important issues in biomedical research. In which, prediction of novel disease-associated genes is mostly focused. Many methods have been proposed based on biological networks and shown effectively for the problem. These network-based methods are usually relied on a "disease module" principle that functionally similar genes are associated with similar phenotypes or diseases. Among them, methods solely based on gene/protein networks only exploit that principle by structural modules in the gene/protein networks. Meanwhile, others based on integration of these networks with a disease similarity network better exploit the principle and consequently result in higher prediction performance. In these studies, the disease similarity network is extracted from a disease similarity matrix which was calculated using text mining techniques on OMIM records. Considering that diseases have been recently well annotated by human phenotype ontology (i.e., a controlled vocabulary database) and semantic similarity measures can be used to calculate similarities among them. Therefore, it would be more accurate to construct disease similarity network based on semantic similarity measures on phenotype ontology database. In this study, we constructed such network and integrated them with several kinds of gene/protein networks. Experiment results show that the ontology-based disease similarity network much improves the prediction performance compared to the one based on OMIM records, irrespective of gene/protein networks. In addition, we show ability of our method in predicting novel Alzheimer's disease-associated genes, in which 19 out of top 100 ranked candidate genes are supported with evidences from literature.

✉ Duc-Hau Le
hauldhut@gmail.com

Vu-Tung Dang
tung_dv@yahoo.com

1 School of Computer Science and Engineering, Water Resources University, 175 Tay Son, Dong Da, Hanoi, Vietnam

2 Department of Information Technology, Vietnam Youth Academy, 58 Nguyen Chi Thanh, Dong Da, Hanoi, Vietnam

Keywords Disease-associated gene · Human phenotype ontology · Semantic similarity · Random walk with restart algorithm · RWR · Alzheimer's disease

1 Introduction

Disease gene prediction, the task of identifying the most plausible candidate disease genes, is an important issue in biomedical research and many studies have been done for this [1,2]. Identification of disease-associated genes also leads to more effective researches about therapies for genetic diseases and gradually approaches a future of personalized medicine [3–5]. In past decades, linkage analysis was usually used to identify novel disease genes, in which susceptible loci including hundreds of genes are investigated, and thus it is much costly for doing many experiments in wet lab. Therefore, ranking/prioritization methods for such candidate genes are introduced (i.e., genes are ranked by their relevance to a disease of interest). Highly ranked genes are further investigated to find out associated biomedical evidences. And therefore, the goal of gene ranking/prioritization is to predict novel disease-associated genes.

The prediction of novel disease-associated genes are usually approached by three main directions: (1) functional annotation based; (2) machine learning based; and (3) network based. In which, functional annotation-based methods have prioritized candidate genes by measuring the degree of similarity of each candidate genes to a set of known disease genes based on profiles which were built from many functional annotation data sources [6–8]. Therefore, those methods mostly focused on the integration of various biological datasets to obtain more accurate similarity. However, those approaches are limited in that functional annotation data sources have not covered whole human genome yet. For the second approach, many learning techniques have been applied to predict disease-associated genes. In which, the problem is considered as a classification one, where a classifier is learned from training data; then the learned classifier is used to predict whether or not a test/candidate gene is a disease gene. Briefly, at the early, machine learning-based studies usually approached disease gene prediction as a binary classification problem [9], where the learning samples are comprised of positive training samples and negative training samples [9] such as decision trees (DT) [10,11] *k*-nearest neighbor (kNN) [12], naive Bayesian classifier [13,14], binary support vector machine classifier [15–17], artificial neural network (ANN) techniques [18] and random forest (RF) [9]. In these binary classifier-based methods, positive training samples are constructed from known disease genes, whereas negative training samples are the remaining which are not known to be associated with diseases. This is the limitation of binary classifier-based solutions for the disease gene prediction problem, since the negative training set should be actual non-disease genes. However, construction of this set is nearly impossible in biomedical researches. Therefore, more advanced machine learning techniques, which do not require to define a the negative training set, have been recently introduced for this problem [19]. However, the problem was still formulated as a classification, while it should be a ranking/prioritization one. Therefore, methods for prediction of disease-associated genes have extended to network-based ones [20,21] and shown to outperform functional annotation- and machine learning-based ones [22,23]. These network-based methods are mostly based on biological networks, which are constructed based on various kinds of biomedical data, and therefore they are not limited by the coverage of functional annotation data sources. In addition, these methods can be considered as positive and unlabeled learning techniques where the rankings of candidate genes are estimated based on their relative similarities to known disease ones and others. Moreover, the dominance of network-based methods is also because they are based on a principle of "disease module" (e.g., functionally similar genes are associated with similar phenotypes or diseases). Among methods solely based on gene/protein networks, a method using a random walk with restart (RWR) algorithm [22,24,25] is more dominant compared to other methods such as nearest neighbor, shortest path and clustering [26]. Because this algorithm calculates a global similarity among candidate and known disease genes on whole network and therefore not only genes directly connected to disease genes are considered, but also indirect ones. This algorithm has been successfully applied to other problems such as prediction of disease-associated miRNAs [27] and protein complexes [28]. However, this method can only exploit the "disease module" in the gene/protein network (i.e., genes/proteins associated with the same or similar diseases usually form functional/physical modules on gene/protein interaction networks [29–31]).

Recently, a variant of RWR algorithm, namely RWRH, was proposed for a heterogeneous network. This algorithm was then applied to predict disease-associated genes on a heterogeneous network of proteins and disease phenotypes [32]. This network was constructed by integrating a disease similarity network based on text mining algorithms on OMIM records [33] and a protein interaction network. As a result, it was reported that RWRH better exploit "disease module" principle than RWR [22] since then OMIM-based disease similarity network was additionally integrated [32]. More importantly, the RWRH algorithm can be extended to use any network of genes/proteins as well as disease similarity one. Indeed, a recent RWRH-based method has used a semantic similarity network of genes instead of the protein interaction network [34] and shown to outperform the original one [32]. We also note that a disease similarity network can be constructed based on shared disease gene [30], shared pathways [35], shared miRNA [36], shared protein complex [37], shared disease ontology [38] and disease comorbidity [39]. Similarly to RWR, RWRH algorithm has been successfully applied to other problems such as prediction of novel drug–target interactions [40] as well as novel disease-associated miRNAs [41] and long non-coding RNAs [42].

In this study, we extended the use of RWRH algorithm to the prediction of disease-associated gene by integrating semantic similarities among diseases and a gene/protein network. More specifically, considering that disease phenotypes have been recently annotated by human phenotype ontology (shortly called HPO) [43] (i.e., controlled vocabulary database) and a number of semantic similarity measures have been proposed to calculate the similarity between annotated biomedical objects [44], it would be more accurate to calculate the similarity among diseases based on such the measures. Therefore, we constructed a disease similarity network using a semantic similarity measure on HPO. Then, this network was integrated with a gene/protein network by known disease phenotype–gene associations. We compared our method with the one relied on the OMIM-based disease similarity network as in [32,34]. In which, the gene/protein network can be the protein interaction network as in [32], the gene semantic similarity network as in [34] as well as one constructed based on expression profiles of

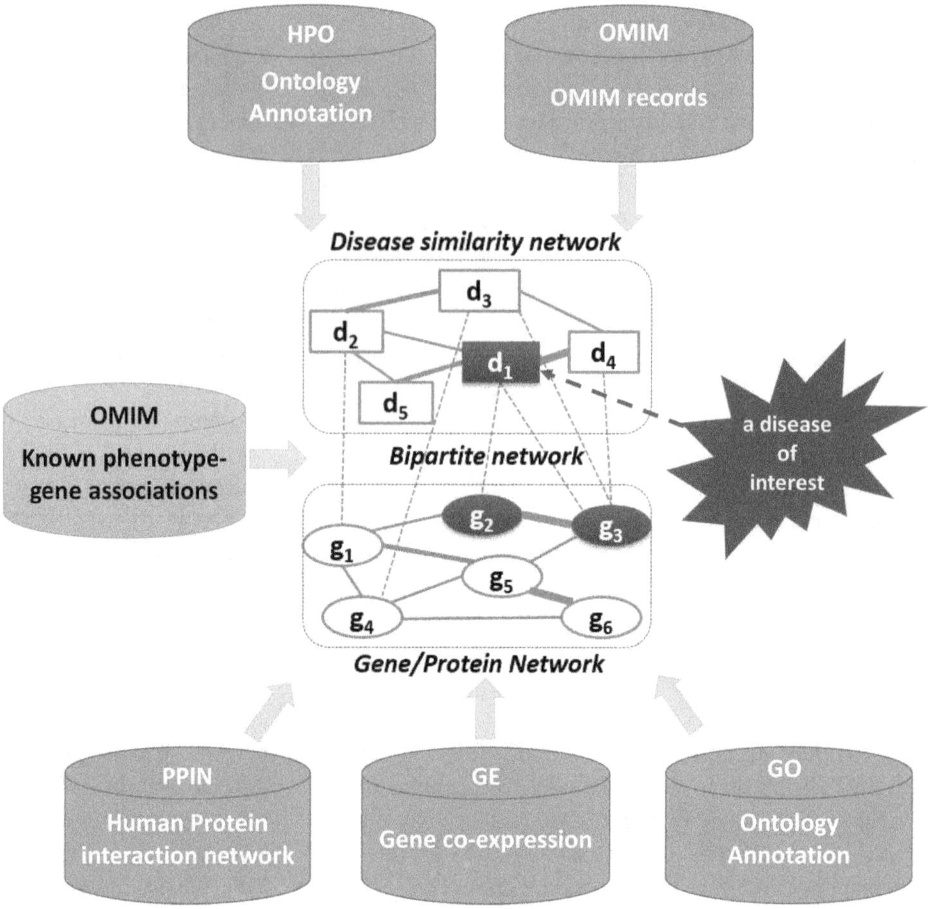

Fig. 1 Construction of heterogeneous networks of genes/proteins and diseases. Disease similarity network and gene/protein network are connected by a bipartite network of known disease-gene associations

genes. Experimental results show that the performance of our method is better than that based on the OMIM-based disease similarity network irrespective of the gene/protein networks. This indicates that HPO-based similarity calculation of diseases improves the performance of RWRH algorithm for the prediction of disease-associated genes. In addition, we used our method to find novel genes associated with Alzheimer's disease. The evidence search from literature about the associations between 100 highly ranked candidate genes and Alzheimer's disease confirmed 19 of them, which are not yet recorded in public disease–gene association database.

2 Methods

2.1 Construction of heterogeneous networks of diseases and genes

To build heterogeneous networks of diseases and genes, we constructed two kinds of networks: (1) gene/protein network, which connects genes/proteins by functional interactions; (2) disease similarity network, where a link between two diseases is specified by their similarity. Then, we connected these two networks by a bipartite network consisting of known disease–gene associations. Figure 1 shows construction of such heterogeneous networks of genes/proteins and diseases.

Gene/protein networks

Protein–protein interaction network

First, we collected a human protein interaction network (shortly called PPINet) containing 10,486 genes and 50,791 interactions from NCBI FTP repository.[1] Proteins in this network are connected by physical interactions. Therefore, we considered PPINet as an unweighted network.

Gene expression-based similarity network

Second, we constructed a weighted gene network based on gene expression data (shortly called GENet). More specifically, a gene co-expression database comprising 19,777 human genes was downloaded from COXPRESSdb [45]. To measure the similarity between a pair of genes, we employed the mutual rank method, which evaluates the strength of co-expression [46]. The mutual rank ranges from 0 to 19,776 and the normalized value $w_{ij} = \frac{(19{,}776-MR(v_i,v_j))}{19{,}776}$, where $MR(v_i, v_j)$ denotes the mutual rank between gene v_i and v_j. The GENet was constructed by replacing the original weight of each link in the PPINet network with the normal-

[1] ftp://ftp.ncbi.nlm.nih.gov/gene/GeneRIF/interactions.gz.

Table 1 Size of gene/protein networks and number of testing disease phenotypes for corresponding heterogeneous networks

#	Gene/protein network	Size (number of genes/proteins, number of interactions)	Number of testing disease phenotypes
1	PPINet	(10,486, 50,791)	2639
2	GENet	(9852, 49,404)	2533
3	GONet	(7897, 41,466)	2345

ized mutual rank value of gene pairs that participate in the network.

Gene ontology-based similarity network

Third, we constructed another weighted gene network based on gene ontology data (shortly called GONet). To construct this network, we used the UniProtKB [47] corpus in the GO annotation database [48]. There were 18,245 *Homo sapiens* proteins in total. Among them, there were 15,576 proteins annotated with molecular function terms, 14,911 proteins annotated with biological process terms, and 16,983 proteins annotated with cellular component terms. Then, to construct the network, we first needed to introduce the information content (IC). The IC of a term e in the corpus is defined as follows:

$$\mathrm{IC}(e) = -\log\left(p(e)\right),$$

where $p(e)$ is the probability of e occurring in the corpus, i.e., $p(e) = \frac{f(e)}{f(\mathrm{root})}$ such that $f(e) = \mathrm{Annot}(e) + \sum_{c \in \mathrm{Children}(e)} f(c)$. In this formula, Annot(e) means the number of proteins annotated with e in the corpus, Children(e) represents the set of children terms of e in the GO graph and root is root term of the GO graph. Then, the semantic similarity between the two GO terms, e_i and e_j, based on the most informative common ancestor approach [49], is calculated as follows:

$$\mathrm{simTerm}(e_i, e_j) = \max_{c \in P(e_i, e_j)} (\mathrm{IC}(c)),$$

where $P(e_i, e_j)$ is the set of shared ancestors of e_i and e_j. The functional similarity between a pair of genes v_i and v_j is calculated as the maximum of simTerm values between all possible pairs of terms as follows:

$$\mathrm{simGene}(v_i, v_j) = \max_{e_i \in T(v_i),\, e_j \in T(v_j)} \left(\mathrm{simTerm}(e_i, e_j)\right),$$

where $T(v)$ represents the set of terms annotating v. This value is normalized in range [0, 1] to account for an unequal number of GO terms for both genes as follows:

$$w_{ij} = \frac{2 \times \mathrm{simGene}(v_i, v_j)}{\mathrm{simGene}(v_i, v_i) + \mathrm{simGene}(v_j, v_j)}.$$

By employing the sub-ontology databases of biological process, cellular component and molecular function individually (i.e., root terms for these gene sub-ontology graphs are biological process, cellular component and molecular function, respectively), three GO-based weighted networks were constructed, in which the original weight of each link in the PPINet network was replaced by the normalized similarity value w_{ij} of two genes participating in each link. We referred to these as the BPNet, CCNet and MFNet networks, respectively. Finally, we integrated them using "per-edge average" method to construct GONet network as follows:

$$\bar{w}_{ij} = \frac{1}{M} \sum_{k=1}^{M} (w_{ij})_k$$

where M is number of networks containing interaction between gene v_i and v_j. $(w_{ij})_k$ is the weight of interaction between v_i and v_j in network k.

After selecting most connected component, we finally obtained PPINet, GENet and GONet networks with size as shown in Table 1.

2.2 Disease similarity networks

OMIM-based disease similarity network

First, following the same procedure as in [32,34], we collected a phenotypic disease similarity matrix from [50], where an element of the matrix represents degree of similarity between two phenotypes. The similarities in this matrix were calculated based on various text mining algorithms on OMIM records, which describe diseases using natural language [33]. By selecting only five neighbors which have largest similarities for each node, we constructed a phenotypic disease similarity network (shortly called OMIMNet) consisting of 19,791 interactions among 5080 phenotypes.

HPO-based disease similarity network

Second, to construct another disease similarity network, we calculated similarity among disease phenotypes based on human phenotype ontology (HPO, a controlled vocabulary database) [43] (i.e., root term for this ontology graph is All). More specifically, we collected HPO terms and corresponding annotation data at Human Phenotype Ontology database [2] [43]. Then, we followed the same procedure as for

[2] http://www.human-phenotype-ontology.org/.

gene ontology-based similarity networks to calculate similarity between every pair of disease phenotypes. Similarly, by selecting only five neighbors which have largest similarities for each node, we constructed a HPO-based disease similarity network (shortly called HPONet) consisting of 34,476 interactions among 6521 phenotypes.

2.3 A bipartite network

The bipartite network are known disease–gene associations collected from NCBI FTP repository.[3] This connects a total of 3284 diseases and 2761 genes.

2.4 RWRH-based method

Given a connected weighted graph G(V, E) with a set of nodes $V = \{v_1, v_2, \ldots, v_N\}$ and a set of links $E = \{(v_i, v_j)|v_i, v_j \in V\}$, a set of source/seed nodes $S \subseteq V$ and a $N \times N$ adjacency matrix W of link weights. Here, we are going to introduce algorithms for measuring relative importance of node v_i to S. By modeling a heterogeneous network of genes and diseases as a graph, ranking/prioritization of candidate genes/diseases is to predict novel genes/diseases associated with a disease of interest (d). The rankings of candidate genes/diseases are based on their relative importance to a set of known d-associated genes and d. This value also measures how much a candidate gene/disease is associated with d.

2.5 Random walk with restart (RWR) algorithm

Random walk with restart (RWR) is a variant of the random walk and it mimics a walker that moves from a current node to a randomly selected adjacent node or goes back to source nodes with a back-probability $\gamma \in (0, 1)$. RWR can be formally described as follows:

$$P^{t+1} = (1-\gamma)W' P^t + \gamma P^0,$$

where P^t is a $N \times 1$ probability vector of $|V|$ nodes at a time step t of which the ith element represents the probability of the walker being at node $v_i \in V$, and P^0 is the $N \times 1$ initial probability vector. W' is the transition matrix of the graph, the (i, j) element in W', denotes a probability with which a walker at v_i moves to v_j among $V \backslash \{v_i\}$. All nodes in the network are eventually ranked according to the steady-state probability vector P^∞. The steady state of each node represents its relative importance to the set of source nodes S.

This algorithm was used for disease gene prediction based on a homogeneous network of genes/proteins [22,24]. In which, the transition matrix W' is defined as follows:

$$(W')_{ij} = \frac{(W_G)_{ij}}{\sum_j (W_G)_{ij}},$$

where W_G is adjacency matrix of the network of genes/proteins.

In addition, the set of source nodes (S) was specified by genes known to be associated with d. Therefore, the initial probability vector was defined as follows:

$$P^0 = \begin{cases} \frac{1}{|S|} & \text{if } v_i \in S \\ 0 & \text{otherwise.} \end{cases}$$

2.6 Random walk with restart on heterogeneous network (RWRH) algorithm

This algorithm can be considered a variant of the RWR algorithm, since it was defined in the same formula as for RWR. The difference is construction of transition matrix W'. More specifically, W' was defined as follows:

$$W' = \begin{bmatrix} W'_G & W'_{GD} \\ W'_{DG} & W'_D \end{bmatrix},$$

where W'_G and W'_D are intra-subnetwork transition matrices of a network of genes/proteins and a disease similarity network, respectively. W'_{GD}, W'_{DG} are inter-subnetwork transition matrices. Let λ be the jumping probability the random walker jumps from the network of genes/proteins to the disease similarity network or vice versa. Then, these matrices were defined as follows:

$$(W'_{GD})_{i,j} = p(d_j|g_i) = \begin{cases} \frac{(\lambda W_{GD})_{ij}}{\sum_j (W_{GD})_{ij}} & \text{if } \sum_j (W_{GD})_{ij} \neq 0 \\ 0 & \text{otherwise,} \end{cases}$$

$$(W'_{DG})_{i,j} = p(g_j|d_i) = \begin{cases} \frac{\lambda (W_{GD})_{ji}}{\sum_j (W_{GD})_{ji}} & \text{if } \sum_j (W_{GD})_{ji} \neq 0 \\ 0 & \text{otherwise,} \end{cases}$$

$$(W'_G)_{i,j} = \begin{cases} \frac{(W_G)_{ij}}{\sum_j (W_G)_{ij}} & \text{if } \sum_j (W_{GD})_{ij} = 0 \\ \frac{(1-\lambda)(W_G)_{ij}}{\sum_j (W_G)_{ij}} & \text{otherwise,} \end{cases}$$

$$(W'_D)_{i,j} = \begin{cases} \frac{(W_D)_{ij}}{\sum_j (W_D)_{ij}} & \text{if } \sum_j (W_{GD})_{ji} = 0 \\ \frac{(1-\lambda)(W_D)_{ij}}{\sum_j (W_D)_{ij}} & \text{otherwise,} \end{cases}$$

where W_D and W_{GD} are adjacency matrices of the disease similarity and the bipartite networks.

By letting η be the parameter to weight the importance of each network, the initial probability vector was defined as follows:

[3] http://ftp.ncbi.nlm.nih.gov/gene/DATA/mim2gene_medgen.

$$P^0 = \begin{cases} (1-\eta)\frac{1}{|S|} & \text{if} v_i \in S \\ \eta & \text{if } v_i \equiv d \\ 0 & \text{otherwise.} \end{cases}$$

In case we are interested in a disease class/group, which contains set of diseases (D), P^0 was defined as follows:

$$P^0 = \begin{cases} (1-\eta)\frac{1}{|S|} & \text{if } v_i \in S \\ \eta\frac{1}{|D|} & \text{if } v_i \in D \\ 0 & \text{otherwise.} \end{cases}$$

For these two algorithms, all remaining genes in the networks, which are not known to be associated with d or D, were selected as candidates for ranking.

3 Results and discussion

3.1 Performance comparison

Note that, our method was based on the construction of heterogeneous networks by integrating HPONet network with a gene/protein network. Therefore, three heterogeneous networks were constructed for our method, i.e., HPONet-PPINet, HPONet-GENet and HPONet-GONet. Meanwhile, heterogeneous networks in [32,34] were OMIMNet-GONet and OMIMNet-PPINet, respectively. In addition to these five heterogeneous networks, we constructed OMIMNet-GENet for the comparison. To compare the performance of our method with that of others, we used leave-one-out cross-validation (LOOCV) method for each disease phenotype in a set of disease phenotypes which associates with at least one gene in the gene/protein networks. Due to the differences in size of gene/protein networks, the number of testing disease phenotypes was little different for different heterogeneous networks as shown in Table 1. Based on results of RWRH algorithm for prediction of disease-associated genes [32,34] and prediction of disease-associated miRNAs [41], we set back-probability (i.e., γ), jumping probability (i.e., λ) and subnetwork importance weight (i.e., η) to 0.5, 0.6 and 0.7, respectively. For each disease phenotype (d), in each round of LOOCV, we held out one known d-associated gene. The rest of known d-associated genes and d were used as seed nodes. The held-out gene and remaining genes in the homogeneous network, which were not known to be associated with d, were ranked by the methods. Then, we plotted the receiver operating characteristic (ROC) curve and calculated the area under the curve (AUC) to compare the performance of the methods. This curve represents the relationship between sensitivity and (1−specificity), where sensitivity refers to the percentage of known d-associated genes that were ranked above a particular threshold and specificity refers to the percentage of genes which were not known to be associated top ranked below this threshold. Figure 2 shows that the performance of our method (i.e., HPONet-PPINet, HPONet-GENet and HPONet-GONet) was better than that of study [34] (i.e., OMIMNet-GONet), study [32] (i.e., OMIMNet-PPINet) and OMIMNet-GENet. In addition, the performance of heterogeneous networks, which were based on HPO, were comparable (i.e., AUC values for HPONet-PPINet, HPONet-GENet and HPONet-GONet were 0.927, 0.926 and 0.926, respectively). Similarly, the performance of heterogeneous networks, which were based on OMIM, were comparable (i.e., AUC values for OMIMNet-PPINet, OMIMNet-GENet and OMIMNet-GONet were 0.736, 0.73 and 0.71, respectively). These results indicate that HPO-based calculation of the disease similarity network (i.e., HPONet) better reflects functional relations among diseases than that based on text mining algorithms on OMIM records for the prediction of disease-associated genes.

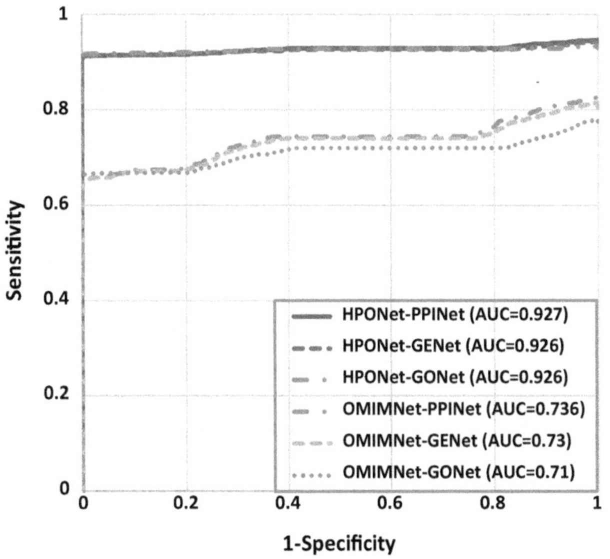

Fig. 2 Performance comparison. Our method is represented by HPONet-PPINet, HPONet-GENet and HPONet-GONet; and others by OMIMNet-PPINet, OMIMNet-GENet and OMIMNet-GONet

3.2 Case study: Alzheimer's disease

In this experiment, we tried to predict novel genes associated with Alzheimer's disease (Shortly called AD) (MIM ID is 104300). AD is a multi-factorial and fatal neurodegenerative disorder for which the mechanisms leading to profound neuronal loss are incompletely recognized. There are 16 genes are known to be associated with AD [33]; however only eleven of them are available in the gene/protein networks. To predict novel genes associated with this disease, we selected the heterogeneous network comprising HPONet and GENet. Then we used these eleven genes and the MIM ID of AD

Table 2 Nineteen evidenced Alzheimer's disease-associated genes in top 100 ranked candidate genes

Rank	Gene Entrez ID	Gene symbol	PubMed ID
1	6622	SNCA	19022350, 21056999, 22836259, 23820587
2	348	APOE	11803456, 12000192, 12232782, 12498968, 12876259, 12960780, 14741429, 15165699, 15181247, 15184600, 15184629, 15455263, 16165272, 16796589, 17050040, 17089130, 17101827, 17374951, 17474819, 17524782, 17613540, 17659844, 17854398, 18058831, 18083276, 18205760, 18416843, 18505684, 18525129, 19116453, 19199875, 19339712, 19398704, 20198498, 20473139, 20479234, 20535486, 20538374, 21143177, 21283692, 21297273, 21297948, 21409287, 21556001, 21803501, 22016362, 22179327, 22269984, 22383234, 22502727, 22596266, 22712640, 22815080, 22899317, 23050006, 23183136, 23293020, 23571587, 23581910, 23627755, 23663404, 23668794, 23771217, 23948883, 24312462, 24388797, 24446209, 24473795, 24599963, 24603451
3	5621	PRNP	18349519, 19556894
9	1312	COMT	15488308, 22483294, 23034259, 24477323
21	4137	MAPT	15848182, 16165272, 16182262, 17920160, 18431250, 18431254, 18586097, 18806919, 19153649, 19523877, 19524111, 19560101, 20473135, 20678074, 21342022, 21348938, 21442128, 21489990, 23554879, 23597931, 25378699
24	7329	UBE2I	19765634
28	1508	CTSB	23024364
29	5663	PSEN1	12668610, 15159497, 15622541, 17229472, 17594345, 18028191, 18479822, 18525293, 19667325, 19796846, 22133015, 23850332
34	627	BDNF	12192623, 15838855, 15935057, 16054753, 19088493, 19522715, 22212405, 22364688, 24334212
37	5054	SERPINE1	19604604
38	5327	PLAT	22027013
41	4035	LRP1	15048651, 18706476, 22027013
42	5329	PLAUR	11814408
50	1815	DRD4	23034259
53	7345	UCHL1	16626667, 22660851, 22726800
73	5071	PARK2	19716418
83	6667	SP1	16378688, 23435408
94	5340	PLG	22027013
95	3952	LEP	21633502

as source nodes, and other genes in the homogeneous network as candidates. After all candidate genes were ranked, we selected 100 highly ranked candidates for evidence search about the association between them and AD from literature on PubMed using Entrez Programming Utilites [51]. Table 2 shows 19 evidenced candidate genes. For instance, study [52] (PubMed ID: 16378688) showed that SP1 deposition in hyper-phosphorylated tau deposits may have functional consequences in the pathology of AD. In addition, it was suggested that UBE2I polymorphisms might be associated with a risk of AD [53] (PubMed ID: 19765634). Also, low protein levels of UCHL1 are associated with high protein levels of BACE1 in sporadic AD brains [54] (PubMed ID: 22726800). Finally, enhancing CTSB activity could lower Abeta, especially Abeta42, in AD patients with or without familial mutations [55] (PubMed ID: 23024364). Other not yet evidenced genes in the top 100 genes can be good candidates for biologists for further investigation (see Online Resource 1).

4 Conclusions

It was reported in previous studies that disease similarity improves the performance of prediction of novel disease-associated genes, since it better exploits the "disease module" principle. Based on this, methods on a heterogeneous networks comprising a disease similarity network and a gene/protein network are superior to those which are solely based on the gene/protein network. However, construction of the disease similarity network in previous studies are limited since they mostly based on an out-of-date disease similarity matrix, which was constructed using text mining algorithms on OMIM records. Considering that human phenotype ontology is now available and it well annotates to disease phenotypes, disease similarity can be semantically calculated based on such the controlled vocabulary using semantic-based similarity measures. Therefore, in this study, instead of using the OMIM-based disease similarity network, we construct a HPO-based one using a semantic similarity measure. Using the random walk with restart algorithm on a heterogeneous network, we compared the performance of the heterogeneous network built based on our method with that based on the OMIM-based disease similarity network. Simulation results show that our method is better irrespective of gene/protein networks. This indicates that the HPO-based disease similarity network better exposed functional similarities among diseases than that of OMIM-based one. A case study on Alzheimer's disease has been done to show the ability of our method in predicting novel disease-associated genes. We also note that, many other semantic similarity measures proposed to calculate similarity between annotated biomedical entities can be used to construct disease similarity networks. In addition, these networks can be constructed based on shared pathways [35], shared miRNA [36], shared protein complex [37], shared disease ontology [38] and disease comorbidity [39]. Therefore, it would be interesting for future studies to test which one is best for the prediction of novel disease-associated genes.

Acknowledgments This research is funded by Ministry of Education and Training (MOET) under Grant Number B2014-01-84.

References

1. Kann, M.G.: Advances in translational bioinformatics: computational approaches for the hunting of disease genes. Brief. Bioinform. **11**(1), 96–110 (2009). doi:10.1093/bib/bbp048
2. Tranchevent, L.-C., Capdevila, F.B., Nitsch, D., De Moor, B., De Causmaecker, P., Moreau, Y.: A guide to web tools to prioritize candidate genes. Brief. Bioinform. **12**(1), 22–32 (2010). doi:10.1093/bib/bbq007
3. Fernald, G.H., Capriotti, E., Daneshjou, R., Karczewski, K.J., Altman, R.B.: Bioinformatics challenges for personalized medicine. Bioinformatics **27**(13), 1741–1748 (2011). doi:10.1093/bioinformatics/btr295
4. Jones, D.: Steps on the road to personalized medicine. Nat. Rev. Drug Discov. **6**(10), 770–771 (2007)
5. Reynolds, K.S.: Achieving the promise of personalized medicine. Clin. Pharmacol. Ther. **92**(4), 401–405 (2012). doi:10.1038/clpt.2012.147
6. Adie, E.A., Adams, R.R., Evans, K.L., Porteous, D.J., Pickard, B.S.: SUSPECTS: enabling fast and effective prioritization of positional candidates. Bioinformatics **22**(6), 773–774 (2006). doi:10.1093/bioinformatics/btk031
7. Aerts, S., Lambrechts, D., Maity, S., Van Loo, P., Coessens, B., De Smet, F., Tranchevent, L.-C., De Moor, B., Marynen, P., Hassan, B., Carmeliet, P., Moreau, Y.: Gene prioritization through genomic data fusion. Nat. Biotechnol. **24**(5), 537–544 (2006)
8. Chen, J., Xu, H., Aronow, B., Jegga, A.: Improved human disease candidate gene prioritization using mouse phenotype. BMC Bioinform. **8**(1), 392 (2007)
9. Le, D.-H., Xuan Hoai, N., Kwon, Y.-K.: A Comparative study of classification-based machine learning methods for novel disease gene prediction. In: Nguyen, V.-H., Le, A.-C., Huynh, V.-N. (eds.) Knowledge and Systems Engineering, vol. 326. Advances in Intelligent Systems and Computing, pp. 577–588. Springer International Publishing (2015)
10. Lospez-Bigas, N., Ouzounis, C.A.: Genome-wide identification of genes likely to be involved in human genetic disease. Nucleic Acids Res. **32**(10), 3108–3114 (2004)
11. Adie, E., Adams, R., Evans, K., Porteous, D., Pickard, B.: Speeding disease gene discovery by sequence based candidate prioritization. BMC Bioinform. **6**(1), 55 (2005)
12. Xu, J., Li, Y.: Discovering disease-genes by topological features in human protein-protein interaction network. Bioinformatics **22**(22), 2800–2805 (2006). doi:10.1093/bioinformatics/btl467
13. Calvo, S., Jain, M., Xie, X., Sheth, S.A., Chang, B., Goldberger, O.A., Spinazzola, A., Zeviani, M., Carr, S.A., Mootha, V.K.: Systematic identification of human mitochondrial disease genes through integrative genomics. Nat. Genet. **38**(5), 576–582 (2006)
14. Lage, K., Karlberg, E.O., Storling, Z.M., Olason, P.I., Pedersen, A.G., Rigina, O., Hinsby, A.M., Tumer, Z., Pociot, F., Tommerup, N., Moreau, Y., Brunak, S.: A human phenome-interactome network of protein complexes implicated in genetic disorders. Nat. Biotech. **25**(3), 309–316 (2007)
15. Smalter, A., Lei, S.F., Chen, X.: Human disease-gene classification with integrative sequence-based and topological features of protein-protein interaction networks. In: IEEE International conference on bioinformatics and biomedicine (BIBM), pp. 209–216 (2007)
16. Radivojac, P., Peng, K., Clark, W.T., Peters, B.J., Mohan, A., Boyle, S.M., Mooney, S.D.: An integrated approach to inferring gene-disease associations in humans. Proteins Struct. Funct. Bioinform. **72**(3), 1030–1037 (2008). doi:10.1002/prot.21989
17. Keerthikumar, S., Bhadra, S., Kandasamy, K., Raju, R., Ramachandra, Y.L., Bhattacharyya, C., Imai, K., Ohara, O., Mohan, S., Pandey, A.: Prediction of candidate primary immunodeficiency disease genes using a support vector machine learning approach. DNA Res. **16**(6), 345–351 (2009)
18. Jiabao, S., Patra, J.C., Yongjin, L.: Functional link artificial neural network-based disease gene prediction. In: International joint conference on neural networks (IJCNN), 14–19 June 2009, pp. 3003–3010 (2009)
19. Le, D.-H., Nguyen, M.-H.: Towards more realistic machine learning techniques for prediction of disease-associated genes. In: Proceedings of the sixth international symposium on information and communication technology, Hue City, 2833269, ACM, pp. 116–120 (2015)
20. Wang, X., Gulbahce, N., Yu, H.: Network-based methods for human disease gene prediction. Brief. Funct. Genomics **10**(5), 280–293 (2011). doi:10.1093/bfgp/elr024
21. Barabasi, A.-L., Gulbahce, N., Loscalzo, J.: Network medicine: a network-based approach to human disease. Nat. Rev. Genet. **12**(1), 56–68 (2011)
22. Kohler, S., Bauer, S., Horn, D., Robinson, P.: Walking the Interactome for prioritization of candidate disease genes. Am. J. Hum. Genet. **82**(4), 949–958 (2008)
23. Chen, J., Aronow, B., Jegga, A.: Disease candidate gene identification and prioritization using protein interaction networks. BMC Bioinform. **10**(1), 73 (2009)
24. Le, D.-H., Kwon, Y.-K.: GPEC: a Cytoscape plug-in for random walk-based gene prioritization and biomedical evidence collection. Comput. Biol. Chem. **37**, 17–23 (2012)
25. Le, D.-H., Kwon, Y.-K.: Neighbor-favoring weight reinforcement to improve random walk-based disease gene prioritization. Comput. Biol. Chem. **44**, 1–8 (2013). doi:10.1016/j.compbiolchem.2013.01.001
26. Navlakha, S., Kingsford, C.: The power of protein interaction networks for associating genes with diseases. Bioinformatics **26**(8), 1057–1063 (2010). doi:10.1093/bioinformatics/btq076
27. Le, D.-H.: Network-based ranking methods for prediction of novel disease associated microRNAs. Comput. Biol. Chem. **58**, 139–148 (2015). doi:10.1016/j.compbiolchem.2015.07.003
28. Le, D.-H.: A novel method for identifying disease associated protein complexes based on functional similarity protein complex networks. Algo. Mol. Biol. **10**(1), 14 (2015)

29. Feldman, I., Rzhetsky, A., Vitkup, D.: Network properties of genes harboring inherited disease mutations. Proc. Natl. Acad. Sci. **105**(11), 4323–4328 (2008). doi:10.1073/pnas.0701722105
30. Goh, K.-I., Cusick, M.E., Valle, D., Childs, B., Vidal, M., Barabási, A.-L.: The human disease network. Proc. Natl. Acad. Sci. **104**(21), 8685–8690 (2007). doi:10.1073/pnas.0701361104
31. Oti, M., Brunner, H.G.: The modular nature of genetic diseases. Clin. Genet. **71**(1), 1–11 (2007). doi:10.1111/j.1399-0004.2006.00708.x
32. Li, Y., Patra, J.C.: Genome-wide inferring gene-phenotype relationship by walking on the heterogeneous network. Bioinformatics **26**(9), 1219–1224 (2010). doi:10.1093/bioinformatics/btq108
33. Amberger, J., Bocchini, C.A., Scott, A.F., Hamosh, A.: McKusick's online Mendelian inheritance in man (OMIM). Nucleic Acids Res. **37**(suppl 1), D793–D796 (2009). doi:10.1093/nar/gkn665
34. Jiang, R., Gan, M., He, P.: Constructing a gene semantic similarity network for the inference of disease genes. BMC Syst. Biol. **5**(Suppl 2), S2 (2011)
35. Li, Y., Agarwal, P.: A pathway-based view of human diseases and disease relationships. PLoS ONE **4**(2), e4346 (2009)
36. Lu, M., Zhang, Q., Deng, M., Miao, J., Guo, Y., Gao, W., Cui, Q.: An analysis of human microRNA and disease associations. PLoS ONE **3**(10), e3420 (2008)
37. Markou, M., Singh, S.: Novelty detection: a review—part 2: neural network based approaches. Signal Process. **83**(12), 2499–2521 (2003)
38. Li, J., Gong, B., Chen, X., Liu, T., Wu, C., Zhang, F., Li, C., Li, X., Rao, S., Li, X.: DOSim: an R package for similarity between diseases based on disease ontology. BMC Bioinform. **12**(1), 266 (2011)
39. Lee, D.S., Park, J., Kay, K.A., Christakis, N.A., Oltvai, Z.N., Barabasi, A.L.: The implications of human metabolic network topology for disease comorbidity. Proc. Natl. Acad. Sci. **105**(29), 9880–9885 (2008). doi:10.1073/pnas.0802208105
40. Chen, X., Liu, M.-X., Yan, G.-Y.: Drug-target interaction prediction by random walk on the heterogeneous network. Mol. Biosyst. **8**(7), 1970–1978 (2012). doi:10.1039/C2MB00002D
41. Le, D.-H.: Disease phenotype similarity improves the prediction of novel disease-associated microRNAs. In: 2015 2nd National Foundation for Science and Technology Development conference on information and computer science (NICS), 16–18 Sept 2015, pp. 76–81 (2015)
42. Zhou, M., Wang, X., Li, J., Hao, D., Wang, Z., Shi, H., Han, L., Zhou, H., Sun, J.: Prioritizing candidate disease-related long non-coding RNAs by walking on the heterogeneous lncRNA and disease network. Mol. Biosyst. **11**(3), 760–769 (2015). doi:10.1039/C4MB00511B
43. Köhler, S., Doelken, S.C., Mungall, C.J., Bauer, S., Firth, H.V., Bailleul-Forestier, I., Black, G.C.M., Brown, D.L., Brudno, M., Campbell, J., FitzPatrick, D.R., Eppig, J.T., Jackson, A.P., Freson, K., Girdea, M., Helbig, I., Hurst, J.A., Jähn, J., Jackson, L.G., Kelly, A.M., Ledbetter, D.H., Mansour, S., Martin, C.L., Moss, C., Mumford, A., Ouwehand, W.H., Park, S.M., Riggs, E.R., Scott, R.H., Sisodiya, S., Vooren, S.V., Wapner, R.J., Wilkie, A.O.M., Wright, C.F., Vulto-van Silfhout, A.T., Leeuw, N., de Vries, B.B.A., Washingthon, N.L., Smith, C.L., Westerfield, M., Schofield, P., Ruef, B.J., Gkoutos, G.V., Haendel, M., Smedley, D., Lewis, S.E., Robinson, P.N.: The Human Phenotype Ontology project: linking molecular biology and disease through phenotype data. Nucleic Acids Res. **42**(D1), D966–D974 (2014). doi:10.1093/nar/gkt1026
44. Pesquita, C., Faria, D., Falcão, A.O., Lord, P., Couto, F.M.: Semantic similarity in biomedical ontologies. PLoS Comput. Biol. **5**(7), e1000443 (2009)
45. Obayashi, T., Kinoshita, K.: COXPRESdb: a database to compare gene coexpression in seven model animals. Nucleic Acids Res. **39**(suppl 1), D1016–D1022 (2011). doi:10.1093/nar/gkq1147
46. Obayashi, T., Kinoshita, K., Nakai, K., Shibaoka, M., Hayashi, S., Saeki, M., Shibata, D., Saito, K., Ohta, H.: ATTED-II: a database of co-expressed genes and cis elements for identifying co-regulated gene groups in *Arabidopsis*. Nucleic Acids Res. **35**(suppl 1), D863–D869 (2006). doi:10.1093/nar/gkl783
47. UniProt Consortium: The Universal Protein Resource (UniProt) in 2010. Nucleic Acids Res. **38**, D142–D148 (2010)
48. Barrell, D., Dimmer, E., Huntley, R.P., Binns, D., O'Donovan, C., Apweiler, R.: The GOA database in 2009—an integrated Gene Ontology Annotation resource. Nucleic Acids Res. **37**(suppl 1), D396–D403 (2009). doi:10.1093/nar/gkn803
49. Resnik, P.: Using information content to evaluate semantic similarity in a taxonomy. Paper presented at the 14th international joint conference on artificial intelligence, vol. 1, Montreal
50. van Driel, M.A., Bruggeman, J., Vriend, G., Brunner, H.G., Leunissen, J.A.M.: A text-mining analysis of the human phenome. Eur. J. Hum. Genet. **14**(5), 535–542 (2006)
51. Maglott, D., Ostell, J., Pruitt, K.D., Tatusova, T.: Entrez gene: gene-centered information at NCBI. Nucleic Acids Res. **39**(suppl 1), D52–D57 (2011). doi:10.1093/nar/gkq1237
52. Santpere, G., Nieto, M., Puig, B., Ferrer, I.: Abnormal Sp1 transcription factor expression in Alzheimer disease and tauopathies. Neurosci. Lett. **397**(1–2), 30–34 (2006). doi:10.1016/j.neulet.2005.11.062
53. Ahn, K., Song, J.H., Kim, D.K., Park, M.H., Jo, S.A., Koh, Y.H.: Ubc9 gene polymorphisms and late-onset Alzheimer's disease in the Korean population: a genetic association study. Neurosci. Lett. **465**(3), 272–275 (2009). doi:10.1016/j.neulet.2009.09.017
54. Guglielmotto, M., Monteleone, D., Boido, M., Piras, A., Giliberto, L., Borghi, R., Vercelli, A., Fornaro, M., Tabaton, M., Tamagno, E.: Aβ1-42-mediated down-regulation of Uch-L1 is dependent on NF-κB activation and impaired BACE1 lysosomal degradation. Aging Cell **11**(5), 834–844 (2012). doi:10.1111/j.1474-9726.2012.00854.x
55. Wang, C., Sun, B., Zhou, Y., Grubb, A., Gan, L.: Cathepsin B degrades amyloid-β in Mice expressing wild-type human amyloid precursor protein. J. Biol. Chem. **287**(47), 39834–39841 (2012). doi:10.1074/jbc.M112.371641

7

A classification framework for data marketplaces

Florian Stahl[1,2] · Fabian Schomm[1] · Gottfried Vossen[1,2] · Lara Vomfell[1]

Abstract Trading data as a commodity has become increasingly popular in recent years, and data marketplaces have emerged as a new business model where data from a variety of sources can be collected, aggregated, processed, enriched, bought, and sold. They are effectively changing the way data are distributed and managed on the Internet. To get a better understanding of the emergence of data marketplaces, we have conducted several surveys in recent years to systematically gather and evaluate their characteristics. This paper takes a broader perspective and relates data marketplaces as currently discussed in computer science to the neoclassical notions of market and marketplace from economics. Specifically, we provide a typology of electronic marketplaces and discuss their approaches to the distribution of data. Finally, we provide a distinct definition of data marketplaces, leading to a classification framework that can provide structure for the emerging field of data marketplace research.

Keywords Data-as-a-Service · Data marketplace · Data marketplace survey · Data marketplace development · Classification · Economics · Computer Science

✉ Gottfried Vossen
vossen@uni-muenster.de; vossen@waikato.ac.nz

Florian Stahl
florian.stahl@uni-muenster.de; fstahl@waikato.ac.nz

Fabian Schomm
fabian.schomm@uni-muenster.de

Lara Vomfell
lara.vomfell@unimuenster.de

1 ERCIS, University of Münster, Münster, Germany

2 The University of Waikato Management School, Hamilton, New Zealand

1 Introduction

The Internet allows for almost ubiquitous transactions, access to and exchange of information, and instant communication. Due to the unprecedented supply of data, the Internet has altered how people relate to and access information or data, respectively. Besides the emergence of new markets, this wealth of information has also led to a major transformation of existing markets. Prior to the Web 2.0 development, the market for data could be characterized as a private large-scale information exchange between major companies [17]. However, in light of the newly available abundance of data sources as well as the variety of storage and processing options, it is not surprising that data are increasingly supplied and demanded publicly on the Internet. Besides (partially) free platforms such as Wikipedia or Wolfram Alpha, commercial data marketplaces have emerged; examples include http://knoema.com, Microsoft Azure, Freebase, or http://datamarket.com (recently acquired by Qlik). In this paper, we develop a classification framework for data marketplaces.

In recent years, we have conducted several surveys in the area of data marketplaces, to gain an understanding of their offerings, their functionality, their business models, and their dynamics [35,36]. During this analysis, we found that a clear definition of data marketplaces and the market for data is still missing. This paper aims at closing this gap, by providing such a definition and presenting a classification framework for data market places. Every emerging market is characterized by a number of participants entering and leaving, while developing resolutions and strategies for the number of challenges that new markets or products entail. The high number of providers eventually leaving the field of trading data in the past few years illustrates that data marketplaces seem to be particularly challenging. Interviews with founders of the visualization tool Swivel[1] yielded that, aside from the "usual" management issues, the main obstacle to their business was that users were willing to pay for the services in the "single-digit" area only [14]. The Internet, the very medium that led to the transformation of data markets in the first place, is also one of the major threats to their business model; indeed, users are accustomed to have constant access to information for free which results in a rather low willingness to pay for data. Thus, companies with a focus on data provisioning need to find suitable strategies to generate revenue with their offerings.

Considering how much those strategies are an alluring field of research for business administration and information systems and how much the concept of a data market is discussed in the blogosphere, the lack of formal research on this topic is surprising. On the Internet, informal evaluations by journalists and platform operators can easily be found. Informative examples are [7,10,16,17,22].[2] The only studies of the market with formalized standards are by SCHOMM, STAHL, and VOSSEN who surveyed the data market on a selected sample size in 2012 and 2013. They characterize the market through an increasing "proliferation of data as a commodity" and identify several trends, most notably a trend towards high-quality data [35,36].

The theoretical and empirical research concerning data, data markets, and data marketplaces is filled with a number of different, partly contradictory terms: electronic markets, e-hubs, or data vendors [15]. Most of these terms do not properly describe the underlying concepts concerned with data exchange. Providing a definition for data marketplaces allows us to relate this development to traditional markets and marketplaces as known from the field of economics. Furthermore, it allows to provide clarity whenever the term is used, which is currently not the case—as the term *data market* may refer to the overall market for data, an online platform facilitating the trading of data, or even vendors. A clear definition also allows for further studies to clearly include and exclude providers of marketplaces, as we have done in the latest iteration of our data marketplaces study [37].

The remainder of this paper is organized as follows: After a short review of existing classification models from neo-classical economics in Sect. 2, our own model of categorizing electronic marketplaces is presented as a framework for provider characterization in Sect. 3; additionally, the obstacles to the marketability of information goods are presented: the difficulty of value attribution, information asymmetries, and the particular cost structure of information goods. How those can be overcome in the case of data and how data are distributed and allocated on electronic marketplaces are discussed in Sect. 4. A consideration of the relevance to our study is given in Sect. 5, where we outline our latest survey results. Section 6 concludes the paper.

[1] Swivel shut down business in 2010.

[2] It should be noted that several of the offerings discussed there are already out of business.

2 Markets and marketplaces

In everyday language, the terms *market* and *marketplace* are commonly used synonymously without taking their differences into account. However, to understand data marketplaces, it is important to define the terms for the purpose of establishing a common understanding. Neo-classical economics—the currently widely accepted economic model—consider marketplaces to be the physical or virtual implementation of markets. *Markets* are defined as the concrete place where the interactions of buyers and sellers determine the price and the quantity of a good or a service [21,32]. This implies that a market commonly focuses on one product [3]. In contrast, the term *marketplace* for a given good is the explicit place of encounter in terms of time and location where market participants prepare and execute transactions, i.e., it provides the infrastructure for trading [13]. An examples is a marketplace focusing on flowers, e.g., Dutch tulips. The marketplace can be considered the real interpreter of supply and demand that coordinates output [33]. This means that the difference between a market and a marketplace can be attributed to the level of abstraction. A marketplace is the infrastructure that enables the abstract concept of a market. Indeed, the sum of all market-based transactions, e.g., selling and buying a specific good in a specific region, constitute a market [26]. For instance, one could investigate the PC market in the UK, which is constituted by all PC-related transactions in the country through various channels, such as online and offline marketplaces.

On a market, the abstract place of trade, potential and realized trading relationships determine the economic equilibrium of price and quantity of a product [32]. Both the entirety or segments of the economic structure can be addressed with the term "market" [33]. It serves three main functions:

1. *Institution* The market as an institution is a framework of rules that governs the behavior of the participating agents. It assigns the roles of the agents (e.g., intermediary, seller, etc.) and sets expectations and protocols on their behavior. Further, participants willing to trade find a medium allowing them to satisfy their exchange goals [28].
2. *Transaction* The market is constituted by the sum of all market-based transactions. In turn, the market defines the process of transactions [31]. The transaction itself is, according to [27], constituted by four distinct phases: (1) the *information phase* where agents collect informa-

tion on products and form concrete exchange intentions in the form of bids and offers; (2) the *negotiation phase* where negotiations on the product, the contract terms, and the price are carried out and which ends in a contract; (3) the *transaction phase* where the contract is fulfilled and the commodity is exchanged; and (4) the *after-sales phase* where customer service is crucial to individualize and enhance the customer's satisfaction and commit them. Other authors use different phases, for example [31] splits the information phase into an information and intention phase while aggregating the transaction and after-sales phase. In order to be considered part of an electronic market, at least one transaction phase needs to be performed electronically. Most researchers consider the information phase to be the minimal requirement as in this phase demand and supply are matched globally and immediately [31].

3. *Pricing mechanism* Markets are a mechanism through which buyers and sellers interact to set prices. To be more precise, the price is the equalizing element that coordinates the actions of buyers and sellers on a market. Furthermore, prices signal the conditions of exchange to other participants [32]. The market as a pricing mechanism is closely linked to the efficient market hypothesis: once supply and demand have equalized by the optimal price that clears the market, the allocation of goods is pareto-optimal and social welfare is maximized [19,32].

3 Information technology, data, marketplaces

The rapid development of modern information and communication technology (ICT) also constitutes the development of a new medium through which market relations, transactions, and information can be processed and realized [31]. This new medium enabled by ICT is an electronic infrastructure which companies, individuals, and governments can use to create virtual marketplaces where they previously did not exist [5]. Indeed, ICT has led to the creation of virtual trading areas where products, services, and information are sold [27]. Furthermore, due to the on-demand availability of large computing power, high-capacity storage as a service from the cloud, and application service provisioning, completely new categories of *goods* have emerged, most notably *data*. Data in various forms (raw, aggregated, processed in various forms, etc.) can nowadays be traded just like any other good, and platforms supporting this resemble marketplaces for traditional goods.

Moreover, ICT integration has entailed several configurations of traditional market mechanisms like more flexible price setting or faster transaction performance, but its defining new quality is the mechanization of information processing, leading to a drastic increase in information production [28].

This reshaping is not without consequences to the current set of definitions. The position of electronic markets in the existing framework is not self-evident, and up to date no commonly agreed upon definition of electronic markets and marketplaces has been established. A patchwork of several definitions—ranging from electronic markets as *agora*[3] [31] to *information systems* [9]—hampers respective research. We suggest the relationship between electronic markets and electronic marketplaces to be analogous to the (often neglected) distinction between their real-world counterparts.

3.1 Electronic markets

As implied above, "the electronic market as an electronic medium is based on the new digital communication and transaction infrastructure" [31]. Accordingly, electronic markets are submarkets qualified by the electronic infrastructure they are based upon [3]. Analogously to the economic market definition, an electronic market is the abstract summary of all market-based allocation on the basis of electronic media [33].

Understood as a submarket, the three main market functions defined above—institution, transaction, and pricing mechanism—remain unchanged on electronic markets. Electronic markets deviate from the traditional realization mainly in two regards: the implementation of the institution function is more complex because the ubiquitous nature of electronic markets makes the assignment of rules and language difficult, and it deviates in pricing [31]. As in traditional markets, pricing is the principal signal of the value and conditions of the good offered. Price composition with regard to transaction costs and the cost structure of virtual goods may be different. Since transaction costs are one of the main elements in pricing, the facilitation via ICT typically leads to a drastic drop in the costs of a good [2].

Electronic markets are often discussed in terms of their transformation power and can be considered a convergence of the market towards a perfect market [13]. With respect to higher accessibility, lower entry barriers, and their ubiquity, electronic markets carry a high advantage over traditional markets [31]. Given their higher transparency, electronic markets are usually attributed an improved allocation coordination [31]. These advancements give electronic markets an advantage over traditional forms of market organization. Especially transaction cost theory asserts that by implementing an electronic infrastructure the transaction costs become negligible, improving the competition and almost completing the conversion towards a perfect market [34].

[3] Agora refers to the central meeting point and marketplace in ancient Greek cities.

3.2 Electronic marketplaces

Following the previously introduced distinction between markets and marketplaces, an electronic marketplace is the concrete agency or infrastructure that allows participants to meet and perform the market transactions, translated into an electronic medium. Yet, the term is often used to describe various concepts of e-commerce and market organization or as a synonym for electronic markets. Wang and Archer [39] present a summary of prevalent definitions and group them concept-wise. They outline two fundamental types in the mass of definitions: electronic marketplaces as governance structures and as business models which can be characterized as follows:

The *Business Model* dimension is effectively the definition of an electronic marketplace: the concrete virtual institution and place of exchange that brings together supply and demand and supports the trade between providers and customers, i.e., transferring the market function into an electronic infrastructure. Any type of business action on online platforms or any type of electronic venture falls into this dimension with no regard to whether they are based on competition or on collaboration [39].

Definitions covered by the *Governance Structure* dimension actually refer to electronic markets in the abstract sense. As such, these definitions do not really reference electronic marketplaces.

3.3 Typology of electronic marketplaces

Electronic marketplaces manifest in different shapes and can be categorized along various dimensions. As a result of the overlapping definitions of electronic marketplaces, the categorizations are equally confusing. Each model uses different definitions which makes a general classification of the various forms of business models difficult.

In their literature review, [39] find nine common categories of electronic marketplaces: number of participants; relationship dimension; participant behavior; ownership; industry scope; market mechanism; products; power asymmetries and fee structure. Some models implement all or most of these categories, e.g., [1,13,30,33]. Although those models are capable of reflecting every particular manifestation of specific platforms, they do not allow for meaningful conclusions on the prevalence of categories in quantitative empirical research. For example, the application of the model by [1] in a study with 31 samples returned zero findings in six categories, which illustrates that simpler models with less categories enable a more concise typology.

Other models, e.g., [8,12,24,27], differentiate providers based on the relationship dimension into buyer-biased, seller-biased, and neutral. Those simpler models, however, often merge several dimensions, especially the ownership and the relationship dimension, without specifying that they are indeed distinct dimensions. Concerning the evaluation of data marketplaces, an examination of the prevalent forms of electronic marketplaces with respect to the relationship dimension and the market/hierarchy differentiation is most interesting. On the markets, market forces are allowed to operate freely; in contrast, in a hierarchy model—i.e., in an exchange of goods within organizational boundaries—the operator of the infrastructure, be it supplier or demander, has an advantage over the other party involved.

All transactions between suppliers and buyers can be classified as either hierarchical or market-based. In the market, the quantity and price of a good are determined by market forces among competitive offerings while hierarchical relations are characterized by pre-determined limitations for a specific price and specific buyers or suppliers. The relative advantages of the strategies depend on the transaction costs and the structure of the good [20].

As no comprehensive model incorporating all of the above has yet been developed, we present a new model, illustrated in Fig. 1, incorporating the market/hierarchy divide as well as the correlations between the nine categories identified by [39]. The high correlations between the number of participants, the relationship dimension and market mechanism as well as the correlation between ownership and power asymmetries allow for an aggregation of categories [39].

First, providers are placed on a scale between *hierarchy* and *market*. Furthermore, marketplaces are categorised based on their *ownership*, which can be (a) private, i.e., owned by a single company (seller or buyer); (b) consortia-based, i.e., owned by a small number of companies (seller or buyer); and (c) independent, i.e., the marketplace is run as a platform without any connection to sellers or buyers. The differentiation between vendor-based and marketplace-based electronic marketplaces has some implications. While marketplaces as platforms are inherently independent, marketplaces driven by vendors (or buyers) are likely to be biased in their respective favour.

Based on these dimensions, our model differentiates six business models. At the hierarchy level, privately owned platforms typically facilitate the procurement or selling of its owner (a company) in closed systems and only allow for one-to-many or many-to-one relations. In between hierarchy and market, consortia-based platforms implement many-to-few or vice versa relations and are typically a collaboration of several companies in the same industry that seek to facilitate their sales or procurement processes. Those platforms are closed because the entry into the platform (into the consortium) is only theoretically possible.

At the market level, many-to-many marketplaces are usually operated by an independent intermediary and only have minimal entry restrictions. Many-to-many platforms on which operators are also trading their own products and ser-

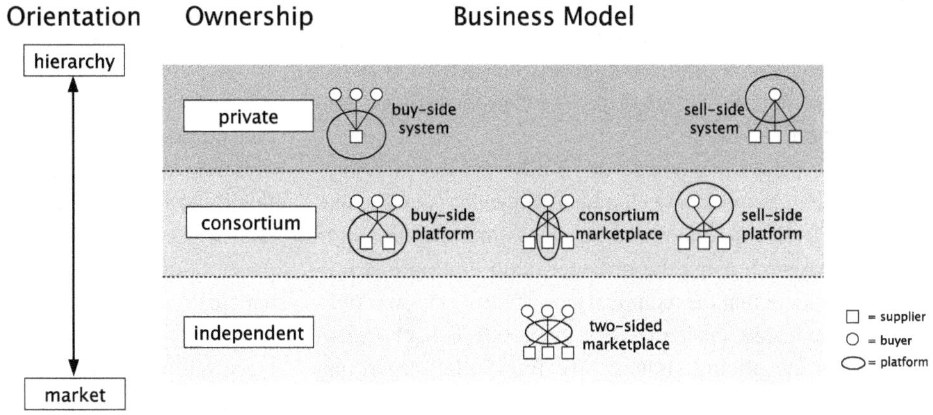

Fig. 1 A model of electronic marketplaces discerning between three ownership types, inspired by [27] and [8], cited from [40]

vices are a special case. These platforms are not independent and neutral because operators run them with the biased interest of facilitating their sales [15]. In this case, operators and competing suppliers form the supply side even though the association between the agents may not be formalized. For the purpose of our model, they are consortium marketplaces because they operate in a similar way to real consortia. The competition on consortium platforms is higher than on purely hierarchical systems but still lower than on marketplaces due to the entry restrictions [32].

This model, depicted in Fig. 1, intends to close the gap between theoretical models that are hard to apply in empirical studies and simpler models with little explanatory power and a simplified focus on the ownership. Through the aggregation of ownership, power asymmetries, and number of participants into six different business models the number of types is manageable while allowing for meaningful conclusions.

4 Discussion

Following the integration of electronic data marketplaces into the existing neo-classical framework for markets, several qualifiers and disqualifiers can be developed to allow for a clear identification and characterization of data marketplaces as *electronic* marketplaces. In particular, the following criteria are defined:

1. Having established that markets and marketplaces are shaped by the goods they focus on, a provider's primary business model needs to be providing data and/or related services to be a data marketplace.
2. Data marketplace providers need to offer an infrastructure that allows customers to upload, browse, download, buy, and sell machine-readable (e.g., RDF or XML) data. The data have to be hosted by the providers and it needs to be clear whether the specific data come from the community or the operator to classify as an electronic marketplace in the narrow sense.

Moreover, this has some implications regarding side constraints. As already indicated, marketplaces should focus on one particular good. For data marketplace this good is data and data-related services. However, to be indeed well exchangeable, automatically processable and hence useful, it has to be in machine-readable format. This rule applies, for example, to Wikipedia: its infrastructure allows users to freely upload and/or access information, which is not easily machine-processable though. Data vendors only linking to data locations without hosting the data proper (such as the list of data sets on `KDnuggets.com`) are also excluded because this type of provider offers a directory rather than data itself.

Despite meeting the above criteria, offerings from government agencies or non-governmental organizations (NGOs) providing free data are not regarded as data marketplaces because publishing and trading data is not their core business. If at all, they are only remotely relevant, as they publish data as a side effect of their general purpose and are not set on commoditizing data or even finding an appropriate business model. A large number of cities, provinces, and countries—the Global Open Data Index counts 79 countries—participate in the Open Government movement [11]. This movement aims at publishing government data to allow for more transparent and citizen-oriented participation and innovation [23]. Transnational organizations such as the United Nations or the World Bank and NGOs like `interaction.org` promote their objectives by sharing their findings. The research on this emerging field is still developing; two notable works are [6,29].

5 Relevance

The purpose of defining data marketplaces is to closely monitor relevant real-world implementations of the opportunities offered by recent technical innovations, such as cloud infrastructures. Empirical research on this emerging field is still scarce. Three surveys on data marketplaces have been conducted by several of the authors between 2012 and 2014. The most current one has employed the classification system presented here [35–37].

This last survey has looked at 72 different data marketplaces and data providers to characterize the data market and to identify trends in data-related business models. Through empirical research using the provider definition outlined, it becomes evident that the technical side of information provisioning is far less severe than its economic side, e.g., choosing the appropriate pricing strategy. We found that, regarding the pricing models, flat rates enjoy a clear advancement over pay-per-use models among the surveyed data providers, often combined with freemium models. Whether this is to accommodate customers or to make use of lock-in effects should be subject to future research. Customers might be unsatisfied with granular pricing models that also restrict unfocused data exploration and prefer simpler subscriptions. Up to now, flat rates remain the most attractive pricing model for providers because of the more stable revenue generated by subscription plans without additional costs due to the practically non-existing marginal costs. Furthermore, pay-per-use models have not (yet) reached the necessary level of sophistication to prevent arbitrage exploitation. Research is currently conducted to find technical and policy amendments [4]. Until then, the trend towards flat rates is not surprising and most likely indicates a rather low competition among the providers so that they still have plenty of options for differentiation and no need for price competitions.

The study presented in [37] suggests two distinct scenarios with very different data access requirements. In the first scenario, data are used as a type of manufacturing input and customers expect complete, formatted, and reliable data. In order to process the acquired data further and use it as a basis for the production of another good, its quality must be extremely high and the access to it must be reliable. However, it does not need to be very specific and pre-analyzed. In the second scenario, data are considered as add-on in the process of decision making and a specialized product that can be spot-purchased whenever necessary or may be acquired on a regular basis. Its quality is not of crucial importance compared to the importance of its specificity. In the add-on scenario, customers do not depend on the data quality, but rather expect a higher individuality of the product to match their particular wishes. In contrast, data buyers in the first scenario would more likely expect a constant standard which they can depend on. Examples of the first scenario are the financial data APIs offered by Xignite, Bloomberg PolarLake, or Interactive Data. The specialized inputs in the second scenario could be some enrichment services like CrowdSource, crawling services like 80legs or address sellers like xDayta [18].

In general, hierarchical structures are more prevalent among the providers than intermediate platforms [37]. This could possibly be linked to the reach/ scope hypothesis touched upon in Sect. 3.3. A possible explanation may be, considering that the data market is mainly a B2B market, that hierarchical relationships are easier to implement which is a favorable feature in a B2B market. Also, private customers tend to have a lower willingness to pay for data [25]. The observations hint that the data market is developing towards a mainstream market also targeting non-technical companies and users: a high number of providers offer several access possibilities but limit the number of data formats. The restriction to mostly standard formats such as reports or CSV files probably aims to reduce the presuppositions for data usage.

6 Conclusion

The development of IT has brought about innovations in both technical and commercial areas which have led to the emergence of new business models for data exchange. The question of how to make data provisioning profitable is relevant to entrepreneurs and academic research alike. Still, the successful distribution of data is impeded by complex pricing mechanisms combined with a generally low willingness to pay on the buyers' side. Well-studied economical principles for markets and marketplaces can help to explain and mitigate those concerns which make an integration of electronic data marketplaces into the existing economic framework necessary. The provision of such a theoretical foundation as in this paper complements previous studies by ourselves and others regarding the dynamics when selling data and data-related services. It allows for further research regarding the business models of data providers, pricing strategies, and the distribution of data.

As pointed out earlier, the Internet has enabled a number of service developments in recent years. Many of these resemble traditional phenomena from the real world, or try to transform such phenomena to the virtual world, often even without realizing what is going on. It then happens that only after a while the originators of such a transition discover that what they considered "new" in the virtual world has had quite a tradition in the real world already, and there are indeed underpinnings that could help to better understand the virtual world.

It is our conviction that this paper, which tries to bridge the gap between computer science and economics, can help to avoid unnecessary explorations of what has been explored already in other domains. At the same time, this study provides a common language to facilitate the comprehension of what is happening on the data market and on data marketplaces.

As a result, several topics for further research arise. Indeed, the obstacles and concerns raised in the proliferation of data on data marketplaces should lead to research concerning cloud sourcing of data. Pricing strategies such as ones based on data quality [38], trading options, or auctioning systems are all to be reconsidered for data marketplaces, and to be adapted to the digital nature of the goods being at stake. Moreover, as any market, data markets will undergo, and partially have already undergone, a diversification into "black" and "white" markets, where data are traded illegally in the former. To this end, it will be both interesting and relevant how to detect this and how to protect data from being traded on a black market.

References

1. Alt, R., Caesar, M.A., Grau, J.: Collaboration in the consumer products goods industry—analysis of marketplaces. In: Proceedings of the10th European Conference on Information Systems (ECIS). Gdansk, Poland, 582–595 (2002)
2. Bakos, J.Y.: Reducing buyer search costs: implications for electronic marketplaces. Manag. Sci. **43**(12), 1676–1692 (1997)
3. Bieberbach, F., Hermann, M.: Die Substitution von Dienstleistungen durch Informationsprodukte auf elektronischen Märkten. In: Nüttgens, M., Scheer, A.-W. (eds.) Electronic Business Engineering, pp. 67–81. Springer, Berlin (1999)
4. Balazinska, M., Howe, B., Suciu, D.: Data markets in the cloud: an opportunity for the database community. In: Proceedings of the VLDB Endowment, vol. 4, pp. 1482–1485 (2011)
5. Coppel, J.: E-commerce: impacts and policy challenges. Economics Department Working Paper 252, OECD Publishing (2000)
6. Chun, S.A., Shulman, S., Sandoval, R., Hovy, E.: Government 2.0: making connections between citizens, data and government. Inf. Polity **15**(1/2), 1–9 (2010)
7. Dumbill, E.: Data markets compared (2012). Last Accessed: 2014-11-24
8. Fischer, T., Winkler, M.: e-Business Modelle: Kategorien, Einflüsse und Entwicklungen. Internal research report, Gruppe Management Forschung (2002)
9. Grewal, R., Comer, J.M., Mehta, R.: An investigation into the antecedents of organizational participation in business-to-business electronic markets. J. Mark. **65**(3), 17–33 (2001)
10. Gislason, H.: The emerging field of data markets—our competitive landscape (2011). Last Accessed: 2014-11-24
11. Global open data index (2014). Last Accessed: 2014-10-21
12. Ganesh, J., Madanmohan, T.R., Jose, P.D., Seshadri, S.: Adaptive strategies of firms in high-velocity environments: the case of B2B electronic marketplaces. J. Glob. Inf. Manag. **12**(1), 41–59 (2004)
13. Grieger, M.: Electronic marketplaces: a literature review and a call for supply chain management research. Eur. J. Oper. Res. **144**(2), 280–294 (2003)
14. Kosara, R.: The rise and fall of swivel.com (2010). Last Accessed: 2014-11-20
15. Luomakoski, J.: Why did electronic B2B marketplaces fail? Case study of an agricultural commodity exchange. Dissertation, University of Jyväskylä (2012)
16. Miller, P.: Podcasts (2012). Last Accessed: 2014-11-24
17. Miller, P.: Nurturing the market for data markets (2012). Last Accessed: 2014-11-24
18. Muschalle, A., Stahl, F., Löser, A., Vossen, G.: Pricing approaches for data markets. In: Castellanos, M., Dayal, U., Rundensteiner, E.A. (eds.) Enabling Real-Time Business Intelligence, pp. 129–144. Springer, Berlin (2013)
19. Mankiw, N.G., Taylor, M.P.: Grundzüge der Volkswirtschaft, 5th edn. Schäffer-Poeschel Verlag, Stuttgart (2012)
20. Malone, T.W., Yates, J., Benjamin, R.I.: Electronic markets and electronic hierarchies. Commun. ACM **30**(6), 484–497 (1987)
21. Nieschlag, R., Dichtl, E., Hörschgen, H.: Marketing, 17th edn. Duncker & Humboldt, Berlin (1994)
22. O'Grady, S.: What's holding back the age of data (2011). Last Accessed: 2014-11-24
23. O'Reilly, T.: Government as a platform. In: Lathrop, D., Ruma, L. (eds.) Open Government: Collaboration, Transparency, and Participation in Practice, pp. 11–40. O'Reilly Media, Sebastopol (2010)
24. Ordanini, A.: What drives market transactions in B2B exchanges? Commun. ACM **49**(4), 89–93 (2006)
25. Potoglou, D., Patil, S., Gijón, C., Palacios, J.F., Feijóo, C.: The value of personal information online: results from three stated preference discrete choice experiments in the UK. In: ECIS 2013 Completed Research (2013)
26. Pindyck, R.S., Rubinfeld, D.L.: Microeconomics, 8th edn. Pearson College Division, London (2012)
27. Richter, K., Nohr, H.: Elektronische Marktplätze: Potenziale. Funktionen und Auswahlstrategien, Shaker (2002)
28. Schmid, B.F.: Elektronische Märkte. In: Handbuch Electronic Business, 2nd edn, pp. 211–239. Gabler, Wiesbaden (2002)
29. Scholl, H.J., Janssen, M., Wimmer, M.A., Moe, C.E., Flak, L.S.: Electronic Government. Springer, Berlin (2012)
30. Skjøtt-Larsen, T., Kotzab, H., Grieger, M.: Electronic marketplaces and supply chain relationships. Ind. Mark. Manag. **32**(3), 199–210 (2003)
31. Schmid, B.F., Lindemann, M.A.: Elements of a reference model for electronic markets. In: Proceedings of the 31st HICSS Conference, vol. 4, pp. 193–201 (1998)
32. Samuelson, P.A., Nordhaus, W.D.: Economics, 19th edn. McGraw-Hill Education, New York (2009)
33. Schwickert, A.C., Pfeiffer, E.: Elektronische Marktplätze–Formen, Beteiligte, Zutrittsbarrieren.Arbeitspapier WI 5, Lehrstuhl für allg. BWL und Wirtschaftsinformatik Mainz (2000)
34. Strader, T.J., Shaw, M.J.: Characteristics of electronic markets. Decis. Support Syst. **21**(3), 185–198 (1997)
35. Schomm, F., Stahl, F., Vossen, G.: Marketplaces for data: an initial survey. ACM SIGMOD Rec. **42**(1), 15–26 (2013)
36. Stahl, F., Schomm, F., Vossen, G.: Data marketplaces: an emerging species. In: Haav, H.-M., Kalja, A., Robal, T. (eds.) Databases and Information Systems VIII, pp. 145–158. IOS Press, Amsterdam (2014)
37. Stahl, F., Schomm, F., Vomfell, L., Vossen, G.: Marketplaces for digital data: quo vadis?, vol. 24. ERCIS Working Papers (2015)
38. Stahl, F., Vossen, G.: Data quality scores for pricing on data marketplaces. In: Proceedings of the 8th International Conference on Intelligent Information and Database Systems (ACIIDS). LNAI, vol. 9621, Springer, Berlin (2016)
39. Wang, S., Archer, N.P.: Electronic marketplace definition and classification: literature review and clarifications. Enterp. Inf. Syst. **1**(1), 89–112 (2007)
40. Winkler, M.: Electronic Business in traditionellen Strukturen – Neue Dienste als Wegbereiter der Kooperation am Beispiel eines Textildesign-Netzwerkes. Dissertation, Universität Stuttgart (2005)

8

Maximal assortative matching for real-world network graphs, random network graphs and scale-free network graphs

Natarajan Meghanathan[1]

Abstract We define the problem of maximal assortativity matching (MAM) as a variant of the maximal matching problem wherein we want to maximize the similarity between the end vertices (with respect to any particular measure for node weight) constituting the matching. The MAM algorithm (with a targeted assortative index value of 1) works on the basis of the assortative weight of an edge, defined as the product of the number of uncovered adjacent edges and the absolute difference of the weights of the end vertices of the edge. The MAM algorithm prefers to include the edge with the smallest assortativity weight (the assortative weight of the edges is updated for each iteration) until all the edges in the graph are covered. We show that the MAM algorithm can be easily adapted to be used for maximal dissortative matching (MDM) with a targeted assortative index of -1 for the matching as well as for maximal node matching (MNM) algorithm to maximize the percentage of nodes matched. We illustrate the execution of the MAM, MDM and MNM algorithms on complex network graphs such as the random network graphs and scale-free network graphs as well as on real-world network graphs and analyze the tradeoffs.

Keywords Maximal matching · Assortative matching · Dissortative matching · Assortativity index · Complex networks · Independent edge set · Node similarity · Random networks · Scale-free networks

✉ Natarajan Meghanathan
natarajan.meghanathan@jsums.edu

1 Jackson State University, Jackson, MS 39217, USA

1 Introduction

A matching M for a graph $G = (V, E)$ is a subset of the edges E such that no two edges in M have a common vertex. A maximal matching is a set of independent edges such that the inclusion of any additional edge to the set violates the property of matching (no common vertex between any two edges of the set). A matching for a graph is said to be maximum if every vertex in the graph could be matched with another vertex of the graph through a set of edges such that no two edges in the set have a common vertex. There may exist maximal matching of various sizes for the vertices of a graph; but, every maximal matching need not be a maximum matching; on the other hand, a maximum matching of the vertices in a graph is the largest possible maximal matching for the vertices of the graph. Accordingly, we refer to the maximum matching problem as a problem of finding the largest set of independent edges whose end vertices form the non-overlapping node pairs such that the maximum number of node pairs is $\frac{V}{2}$ if the number of vertices V is even and is $\frac{V}{2} - 1$ if the number of vertices V is odd.

A well-known algorithm for finding the maximum set of independent edges for maximum node matching in arbitrary network graphs is the Blossom algorithm [1] of time-complexity $O(V^4)$ on a graph of V vertices. Several improvements (e.g., [2]) to the Blossom algorithm have been proposed in the literature. A weakness of all these algorithms is that in pursuit of maximum node matching, little consideration is given to the similarity between the vertices that are matched. As observed in the simulations of this paper, a maximum or maximal node matching of the vertices in a complex network graph need not match vertices of comparable node weight (e.g., node degree). The motivation for the research presented in the paper stems from this observation. We want to determine a maximal matching (need not be the maximum matching, but close enough to the maximum matching) of the vertices that are very similar to each other (or very dissimilar from each other). This amounts to maximizing (or minimizing) a metric called the assortativity index of the edges that constitute the matching. Until now in the literature for complex network graphs, assortativity has been considered only at the network level [3] and node level [4,5], but not with respect to the matching of the vertices. Ours is the first paper in this direction.

The assortativity index of a set of edges (with respect to any particular measure of node weight-like the node degree) is a quantitative measure of the similarity between the end vertices of the edges that are part of the set [6]. The assortativity index values can range from -1 to 1. If the assortativity index of a set of edges calculated with respect to a particular measure of node weight is close to 1, then it implies the end vertices of the edges that form the set are very similar to each other with respect to the particular measure of node weight (for example, a high-degree vertex matched to another high-degree vertex, a low-degree vertex matched to another low-degree vertex, etc). If the assortativity index is close to 0, then the pairing of the vertices in the edge set is arbitrary with respect to the node weight. On the other hand, if the assortativity index of the set of the edges with respect to a measure of node weight is close to -1, then it implies that most of the node pairs constituting the edge set are not similar to each other with respect to the node weight (for example, if node degree is used as the node weight, then an assortativity index of -1 of a set of edges implies that most of the node pairings in this set involve a high degree vertex matched to a low degree vertex and vice-versa).

For social networks and other complex real-world networks where peer-to-peer interaction and collaboration are preferred, it might be useful to pair vertices that are very similar (or very dissimilar) to each other as part of a maximal matching of the vertices in the network. A maximal matching that is arbitrary with respect to the weight of the vertices being matched need not be preferred in social networks. For example, a researcher who already has some accomplishments to his/her credit may want to pair with another researcher who also has a similar research profile (say quantified in terms of the number of peer-reviewed publications in a research area) so that they can mutually collaborate and benefit from each other. On the other hand, a newly joining researcher to a social forum (like researchgate.net or linkedin.com) may want to pair with an accomplished researcher. If each node in a social network can be matched with only one another node at a time, then it is imperative to match the nodes that are either dissimilar to each other or similar to each other (depending on the application of interest); an arbitrary matching of the vertices in a social network may not be of any practical benefit. To the best of our knowledge, we have not come across a maximal matching algorithm that maximizes the assortativity index (for matching nodes that are similar to each other) or minimizes the assortativty index (for matching nodes that are very different from each other) in complex network graphs.

In this paper, we propose a maximal matching algorithm that can be used to maximize or minimize the assortativity index of the edges constituting the matching determined in complex network graphs where the nodes have weights (the smaller the difference in the node weights, the more similar are the nodes and vice-versa). An edge that is part of a matching is said to cover itself as well as cover the edges adjacent to it in the original graph and these edges cannot be part of the matching. We define a metric called the assortativity weight of an edge as the product of the number of uncovered edges adjacent to the edge in the graph and the absolute value of the difference in the weights of the end vertices constituting the edge. The maximal matching algorithm for maximizing the assortativity index (hereafter, referred to as the maximal assortative matching algorithm, MAM) prefers to include edges that have lower assortativity weight as part of the matching. The algorithm runs in iterations. In each iteration, we determine a ranking of the uncovered edges in the graph based on the assortativity weight metric defined above and choose the edge with the smallest value for the assortativity weight metric and include it among the edges constituting the matching. We continue the iterations until all edges in the graph are covered. An edge with the smallest value for the assortativity weight is likely to have fewer adjacent edges as well as comprise of end vertices with close-enough node weights. Our hypothesis is that by choosing such edges with smaller values for the assortativity weight, for graphs that are sufficiently dense, we can simultaneously maximize the assortativity index of the matching as well as maximize the number of edges chosen as part of the matching. The proposed algorithm would be very useful for matching vertices in social networks and other real-world networks for peer-to-peer interaction and collaboration.

Ours will be the first such algorithm to determine a maximal matching of the vertices based on the notion of assortative weight of the edges and does not use the notion of augmenting paths [7], as used by most of the existing matching algorithms. We evaluate the performance of the proposed maximal assortative matching (MAM) algorithm on six real-world network graphs whose degree distribution range from Poisson (random networks) [8] to Power-law (scale-free networks) [9] as well as run the algorithm on complex networks simulated from theoretical models such as the Erdos–Renyi model (for random networks) [10] and Barabasi–Albert model (for scale-free networks) [11]. We observe the MAM algorithm to determine a maximal matching of the nodes (the end vertices of each node pair are similar to each other) and the overall assortativity index of the matching is significantly larger than a matching of the nodes determined with the objective of just maximizing the number of nodes matched.

The focus of the paper is on presenting the proposed maximal assortative matching algorithm for maximizing the assortativity index of the matching. Towards the end of the paper, we also show that the algorithm can be used to minimize the assortativity index of the matching (maximum dissortative matching) by simply including the edges with the largest assortativity weight as part of the matching in each iteration (no other modifications are required). The rest of the paper is organized as follows: Sect. 2 presents the maximal assortative matching (MAM) algorithm for an arbitrary graph and discusses its flexibility to be used as a maximal matching algorithm for maximizing the number of nodes matched (hereafter referred to as the maximal node matching algorithm, MNM). Section 3 presents the results of the execution of the MAM and MNM algorithms on real-world network graphs with degree distribution ranging from Poisson to Power-law. Sections 4 and 5 present the results of the execution of the MAM and MNM algorithms on random networks generated according to the Erdos–Renyi model with the node degree as node weights and random node weights, respectively. Section 6 presents the results of the execution of the MAM and MNM algorithms on scale-free networks generated according to the Barabasi–Albert model. Section 7 presents a modification of the maximal assortativity matching algorithm (referred to as the maximal dissortative matching algorithm, MDM) to determine a matching with an objective of minimizing the assortativity index and presents results of execution of the MDM algorithm on network graphs considered in Sects. 3–6. Section 8 discusses related work and highlights the contribution of the research presented in this paper. Section 9 concludes the paper. Throughout the paper, the terms 'node' and 'vertex', 'link' and 'edge' as well as 'pair' and 'match' are used interchangeably. They mean the same.

2 Maximal assortative matching (MAM) Algorithm

2.1 Network model and definitions

We model the input network graph $G = (V, E)$ as a set of vertices V and undirected edges E wherein each vertex $v \in V$ has a weight $w(v) \in \mathbb{R}$. We say an edge (p, q) is adjacent to an edge (r, s) if $p, q, r, s \in V$ and either $p = r$ or $p = s$ or $q = r$ or $q = s$. That is, two edges (p,q) and (r, s) are said to be adjacent to each other if they have one common end vertex. The degree of a vertex $u \in V$ is the number of edges incident on u (i.e., the number of edges that have vertex u as one of the two end vertices). Though the edges are undirected, for the sake of discussion, we refer to the first vertex (vertex u) indicated in an edge (u, v) as the upstream vertex and the second vertex (vertex v) indicated in an edge (u, v) as the downstream vertex. Also, since the edges are undirected, we conveniently adopt a convention to represent the edges: the ID of the upstream vertex of an edge (u, v) is always less than the ID of the downstream vertex of the edge (i.e., $u < v$).

A matching M of the vertices in a graph $G = (V, E)$ is a subset of the set of edges E such that no two edges in the set M have a common end vertex [7]. We refer to the edges that are part of a matching as a set of independent edges. A maximal matching is a set of independent edges of the graph such that the inclusion of an additional edge to the set violates the property of matching (i.e., no two edges of a matching have a common end vertex) [12]. A maximum node matching is the largest set of independent edges such that the number of vertices that could be paired is the maximum. The maximum node matching for a graph is one of the maximal matchings of the graph, but not vice-versa. We refer to maximal node matching as a matching determined with the objective of maximizing the number of nodes matched, but the size of the matching is not guaranteed to be that of the maximum node matching.

For a set of edges M constituting a matching of the vertices V in the graph G, the assortativity index of M is a quantitative measure of the similarity (or equivalently the dissimilarity) of the end vertices of the edges in M [6]. The assortativity index for a set M of edges (AI_M) with respect to the node weights $w(v)$ for every vertex $v \in V$ is calculated using the formula (1) given below, where $\overline{U}$ and $\overline{D}$ are, respectively, the average weight of the upstream and downstream vertices of the edges constituting the set M.

$$AI_M = \frac{\sum_{(p,q)\in M}\left[w(p)-\overline{U}\right]\left[w(q)-\overline{D}\right]}{\sqrt{\sum_{(p,q)\in M}\left[w(p)-\overline{U}\right]^2}\sqrt{\sum_{(p,q)\in M}\left[w(q)-\overline{D}\right]^2}};$$
$$\overline{U} = \frac{1}{|M|}\sum_{(p,q)\in M} w(p); \quad \overline{D} = \frac{1}{|M|}\sum_{(p,q)\in M} w(q) \qquad (1)$$

The assortativity index for a set of edges M (AI_M) could range from -1 to 1. If AI_M is close to 1, it indicates that the end vertices of the edges in M are similar to each other with respect to the node weight used in calculating the assortativity index. If AI_M is close to -1, it indicates that the end vertices of the edges in M are very much different from each other with respect to the node weight used in calculating the assortativty index. If AI_M is close to 0, it indicates that the matching of the vertices is quite arbitrary with respect to the node weight used in calculating the assortativity index.

Fig. 1 Pseudo-code for the maximal assortativity matching (MAM) algorithm

```
Input: Graph G = (V, E), where weight w(v) ∈ ℝ is the weight of node v for every v ∈ V
Output: Maximal Assortativity Matching, MAM
Auxiliary Variables: UncoveredEdges
Initialization: UncoveredEdges = E; MAM = ϕ
Begin MAM Algorithm
    FindAssortativityWeights(UncoveredEdges)
    while (UncoveredEdges ≠ ϕ) do
        Edge (u, v) = { (p,q) | Min_{(p,q)∈UncoveredEdges}[AssortativityWeight(p,q)] }
        MAM = MAM ∪ {(u, v)}
        UncoveredEdges = UncoveredEdges - {(u, v)}
        RemoveEdges( (u, v), UncoveredEdges)
        FindAssortativityWeights(UncoveredEdges)
    end while
    return MAM
End MAM Algorithm
```

2.2 Assortativity weight of an edge and hypothesis

We say an edge (u, v) included in a matching covers itself as well as covers the edges that are adjacent to it. An uncovered edge is an edge in the graph that is not yet covered by an edge in the matching. We define the assortativity weight of an edge (u, v) to be the product of the number of uncovered edges that are adjacent to it and the absolute value of the difference in the weights of the end vertices u and v. The number of uncovered edges adjacent to an edge (u, v) is the number of uncovered edges incident on each of the end vertices u and v. The proposed maximal assortative matching (MAM) algorithm for maximizing the assortativty index of the matching (to be as close to 1 as possible) proceeds in iterations. In each iteration, we include the uncovered edge with the smallest assortativty weight as one of the edges constituting the matching and consider it to have covered itself as well as its adjacent edges. Our hypothesis is that by giving preference to edges with lower assortativity weight (as defined above), we choose edges whose end vertices have weights that are as close as possible (primary objective) as well as be able to maximize the number of independent edges that are chosen to be part of the matching (secondary objective). As observed in Sects. 3–7, it may not be possible to simultaneously accomplish both the above objectives (especially for sparse graphs); there could exist a tradeoff—as the primary objective of the MAM algorithm is to give preference to edges whose end vertices have close-enough weights, the size of the maximal assortative matching could be less than the size of a maximal node matching (MNM). On the other hand (as observed in the results of Sects. 3–6), the assortativity index of an MAM for a graph could be significantly larger than the assortativity index of an MNM for the same graph. Note that the MAM algorithm could be easily transformed to an MNM algorithm by setting the assortative weight of an edge (u, v) to be simply the number of uncovered edges adjacent to it and giving preference to edges that have lower assortativity weight for inclusion to the MNM.

2.3 Description of the algorithm for maximal assortative matching

The MAM algorithm employs a greedy strategy and at the beginning of each iteration, the algorithm chooses the uncovered edge with the smallest assortativity weight. The pseudo-code for the algorithm to determine maximal assortative matching (MAM) is outlined in Fig. 1; the pseudo-code for the two sub routines used in the algorithm is given in Fig. 2. The algorithm maintains the set of uncovered edges (*UncoveredEdges*) that are yet to be covered by an edge in the MAM. The set *UncoveredEdges* is initialized to the set of all edges E for the input graph G.

To start with, the assortativity weight of the edges in the set *UncoveredEdges* is determined and the edge (u, v) that has the smallest assortativity weight among the edges in *UncoveredEdges* is selected for inclusion in the MAM. An edge (u, v) selected for inclusion to the MAM is said to cover itself as well as cover its adjacent edges; accordingly, all these newly covered edges are removed from the set *UncoveredEdges*. The assortativity weight of the edges in the updated set of *UncoveredEdges* is recalculated and the edge with the smallest assortativity weight is selected for inclusion in the MAM. The above procedure is repeated as a sequence of iterations until the set of *UncoveredEdges* is empty. At this stage, we have found a maximal matching of the vertices in the graph.

The run-time complexity of the MAM algorithm depends on the time complexity to update the set of *UncoveredEdges* in each iteration. As the algorithm proceeds, with each edge added to the MAM, we expect the size of the set of *UncoveredEdges* to reduce significantly. For optimal run-time, we suggest maintaining the set of *UncoveredEdges* as a minimum heap [7] that can be constructed in $O(E)$ time for the

Fig. 2 Pseudo-code for the subroutines used by the maximal assortativity matching algorithm

```
Subroutine FindAssortativityWeights(UncoveredEdges)
    for every edge (u, v) ∈ UncoveredEdges do
        numUncoveredAdjacentEdges(u, v) = 0
        for every edge (u, p) ∈ UncoveredEdges AND p != v do
            numUncoveredAdjacentEdges(u, v) = numUncoveredAdjacentEdges(u, v) + 1
        end for
        for every edge (v, q) ∈ UncoveredEdges AND q != u do
            numUncoveredAdjacentEdges(u, v) = numUncoveredAdjacentEdges(u, v) + 1
        end for
        AssortativityWeight(u, v) = numUncoveredAdjacentEdges(u, v) * |w(u) − w(v)|,
            where w(u) and w(v) are the weights of nodes u and v respectively
    end for
End Subroutine

Subroutine RemoveEdges(Edge (u, v), UncoveredEdges)
    for every edge (u, v) ∈ UncoveredEdges do
        for every edge (u, p) ∈ UncoveredEdges AND p != v do
            UncoveredEdges = UncoveredEdges - {(u, p)}
        end for
        for every edge (v, q) ∈ UncoveredEdges AND q != u do
            UncoveredEdges = UncoveredEdges - {(v, q)}
        end for
    end for
End Subroutine
```

E edges of the graph. Each update to the minimum heap (like removing an edge or updating the assortativity weight of an edge) takes $O(\log E)$ time. The MAM algorithm can run at most for $V/2$ iterations for a graph of V vertices. During each such iteration, there would have to be at most E updates to the heap (one update or removal for each edge, depending on the case), incurring a worst-case time complexity of $O(E\log E)$ per iteration. Considering that there could be at most $V/2$ iterations, the overall run-time complexity of the MAM algorithm is $O(EV\log E)$. For sparse graphs ($E = O(V)$), the run-time complexity of the MAM algorithm would be $O(V^2\log V)$; for dense graphs ($E = O(V^2)$), the run-time complexity of the MAM algorithm would be $O(V^3\log V)$.

2.4 Algorithm for maximal node matching (MNM)

The MAM algorithm can be easily adapted to be used as an algorithm for maximal node matching (MNM). In this pursuit, the assortativity weight of an uncovered edge (u, v) in Subroutine *FindAssortativityWeights* could be simply set as the number of uncovered adjacent edges of the edge (u, v). There would be no other change required in the pseudo-code of the MAM algorithm, as illustrated in Figs. 1 and 2. This modification would be sufficient to maximize the number of independent edges that can get selected as part of the matching. Note that the MNM algorithm is independent of the node weights as the assortativity weight for an edge is measured simply to be the number of uncovered adjacent edges; thus, the maximal node matching obtained using the MNM algorithm for a given graph would be the same irrespective of the criterion used for node weights. By iteratively giving preference to including edges that have the lowest number of uncovered edges into the MNM, we are maximizing the chances of accommodating as many independent edges as possible into the MNM and it would be apt to call such a matching as maximal node matching. Our hypothesis is further vindicated by the results observed in Sects. 3–6.

2.5 Example for maximal assortative matching and maximal node matching

Figure 3 presents an example to illustrate the execution of the maximal assortative matching algorithm on a graph wherein the node weights are random numbers generated in the range 0–1. All the edges in the input graph and the initialization graph are uncovered edges. The initialization graph displays the assortative weight of the edges as a tuple. For an edge (u, v), we indicate a tuple representing (number of uncovered adjacent edges and the absolute value of the difference in the node weights of the end vertices u and v) as well as the assortativity weight of the edge, which is the product of the two entries in the tuple. In the first iteration, the algorithm encounters a tie between edges (3, 6) and (4, 7)—both of which have the lowest assortative weight of 0.6; the algorithm breaks the tie arbitrarily by including edge (3, 6) to the maximal assortative matching (MAM). As part of the inclusion of the edge (3, 6) into the MAM, all its adjacent edges are considered to be covered and are removed from the graph. We reevaluate the assortativity weight of the uncovered edges in the graph; edge (4, 7) with the currently lowest assortative weight of 0.3 is the second edge to be picked for inclusion to the MAM

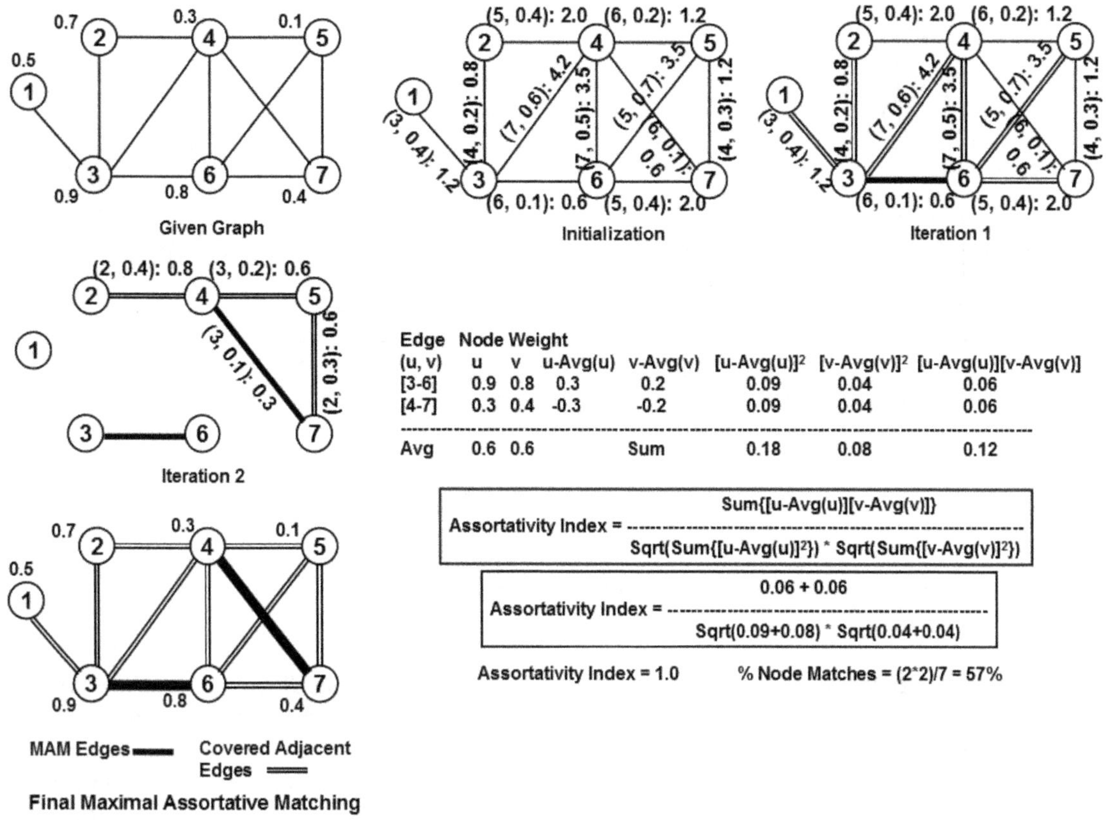

Fig. 3 Example to illustrate the execution of the algorithm for maximal assortative matching

and all its adjacent edges are removed from the graph. At the end of the second iteration, all edges in the graph are either in the MAM or covered by an edge in the MAM. The node weights of the end vertices that are included into the MAM are (0.9, 0.8) and (0.3, 0.4) for the edges (3, 6) and (4, 7), respectively. The difference in the node weights of the end vertices for both the edges in the MAM is the bare minimum that we could get for the input graph considered (as one can notice, all the nodes in the input graph have unique weights). The % of nodes matched in the MAM is $4/7 = 57\,\%$ and the assortative index of the matching (based on node weights) is 1.0; the calculations are illustrated as part of Fig. 3.

Figure 4 presents an example to illustrate the execution of the maximal node matching (MNM) algorithm on the same graph used in Fig. 3. The initialization graph displays the assortativity weight of the edges and in the case of MNM, it is simply the number of uncovered adjacent edges. The first edge to be picked for inclusion in the maximal node matching (MNM) is edge (1, 3) that has three uncovered adjacent edges. As a result of this selection, the three adjacent edges of (1, 3) are said to be covered and removed from the graph. In the next iteration, we determine the number of uncovered adjacent edges for each of the remaining uncovered edges in the graph and select edge (2, 4) with three uncovered adjacent edges as the next edge for inclusion to the MNM. Finally, in the third iteration, we have a tie between the three edges (5, 6), (5, 7) and (6, 7)—we break the tie arbitrarily by choosing edge (5, 6). The maximal node matching thus consists of the three edges {(1, 3), (2, 4), (5, 6)} and their node weights are, respectively, {(0.5, 0.9), (0.7, 0.3), (0.1, 0.8)}. Unlike the MAM, we can see the difference in the node weights of the vertices in the MNM to be arbitrary (neither all low nor all high). The calculation for the assortative index is illustrated on the right side of Fig. 4. The assortative index (based on the node weights) of the MNM is -0.55 and the % of node matches is $6/7 = 86\,\%$. On the other hand, the assortative index of the MAM is 1.0 and the % of node matches is 57 %. Thus, the toy example considered in Figs. 3 and 4 gives sufficient hints of the tradeoff between assortativity and maximal node matching (especially for sparse graphs) and this is further vindicated through the results presented and analyzed in Sects. 3–6.

Though the expected value for the assortative index of an MNM is 0 (to vindicate that the maximal node matching is independent of node weights); the assortativity index value of -0.55 observed for the graph in Fig. 4 is still far from -1 (an assortative index value of -1 would indicate the matching algorithm pairs nodes that are very dissimilar). Thus, the MNM for this toy example could still be considered somewhat neutral with respect to node weights. The maxi-

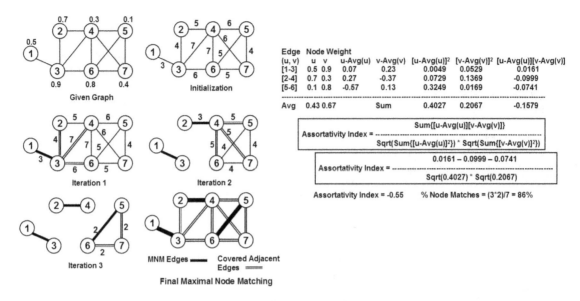

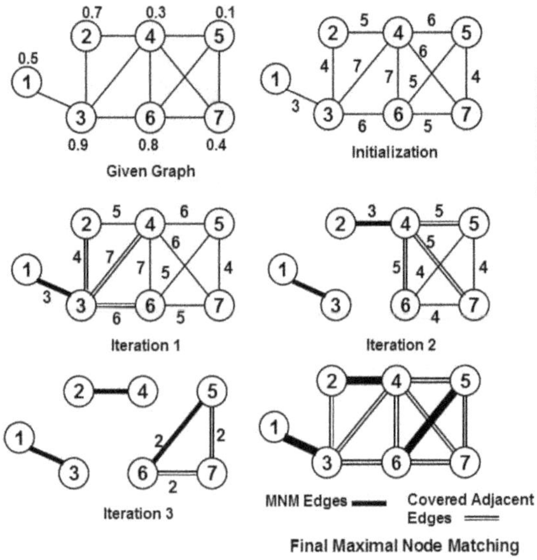

Edge (u, v)	Node Weight u	Node Weight v	u-Avg(u)	v-Avg(v)	[u-Avg(u)]^2	[v-Avg(v)]^2	[u-Avg(u)][v-Avg(v)]
[1-3]	0.5	0.9	0.07	0.23	0.0049	0.0529	0.0161
[2-4]	0.7	0.3	0.27	-0.37	0.0729	0.1369	-0.0999
[5-6]	0.1	0.8	-0.57	0.13	0.3249	0.0169	-0.0741
Avg	0.43	0.67		Sum	0.4027	0.2067	-0.1579

Assortativity Index = Sum{[u-Avg(u)][v-Avg(v)]} / (Sqrt(Sum{[u-Avg(u)]^2}) * Sqrt(Sum{[v-Avg(v)]^2}))

Assortativity Index = (0.0161 – 0.0999 – 0.0741) / (Sqrt(0.4027) * Sqrt(0.2067))

Assortativity Index = -0.55 % Node Matches = (3*2)/7 = 86%

Fig. 4 Example to illustrate the execution of the algorithm for maximal node matching

mal node matching for the random graphs (generated based on the Erdos–Renyi model) with randomly assigned node weights (results analyzed in Sect. 5) incur an assortativity index close to 0 to vindicate that the maximal node matching is indeed independent of node weights.

3 Analysis of real-world network graphs

In this section, we present the results of the execution of the MAM and MNM algorithms on six real-world network graphs whose degree distribution ranges from Poisson (random networks) to Power-law (scale-free networks). The real-world networks are modeled as graphs with the nodes represented as vertices and links between any two nodes represented as edges (all edges are undirected). The implementation can work for any real-world network. The input to the implementation is an adjacency list of the real-world network wherein we store a list of edges (u, v) where $u < v$ (just as a convention we store the pair of vertices constituting an undirected edge in this format). A brief description of the six real-world networks available as .gml files at: http://www-personal.umich.edu/~mejn/netdata/ is as follows: (i) US College Football Network [13] is a network of 115 football teams that played the Fall 2000 Football season in the US; each team is a node and there exists an edge between two nodes if and only if the corresponding teams have competed against each other in the earlier seasons. (ii) Dolphin Social Network [14] is a social network of 62 Dolphins living in the Doubtful Sound fjord of New Zealand; each Dolphin is modeled as a node and there exists an edge between two nodes if and only if the corresponding Dolphins are seen associated with each other. (iii) US Politics Books Network [15] is a network of 105 books on US politics sold in amazon.com; each book is modeled as a node and there exists an edge between two nodes u and v if and only if customers who bought the book corresponding to node u also bought the book corresponding to node v and vice-versa. (iv) Zachary's Karate Club [16] is a network of 34 members of a Karate club at a US university in the 1970s; each member of the club is modeled as a node and there exists an edge between two nodes if and only if the corresponding members are friends. (v) Word Adjacencies Network [17] is a network of 112 words (adjectives and nouns) selected from the novel "David Copperfield" by Charles Dickens; each word is modeled as a node and there exists an edge between two words if and only if the two words have appeared adjacent to each other at least once in the book. (vi) US Airports 1997 Network [18] is a network of 332 airports; each airport is modeled as a node and there exists an edge between two nodes if and only if there is at least one direct flight connection between the corresponding airports. All the real-world networks are modeled as undirected graphs.

We characterize the nature of the degree distribution in these graphs on the basis of a metric, called the spectral radius ratio, for node degree [19]—defined as the ratio of the principal Eigenvalue (largest Eigenvalue) [8] of the adjacency matrix of the graph to that of the average node degree. The principal Eigenvalue of the adjacency matrix of a graph maximally captures the variation in the node degree. For networks that are completely random (i.e., there could exist an edge between any two vertices with a certain probability), the variation in the degree of the vertices in the graph is minimal and the spectral radius ratio for node degree is close to 1.0; on the other hand, for networks that exhibit a power-law degree distribution (majority of the nodes have low degree; but few

Table 1 Real-world networks and their degree distribution

#	Real-world network	# nodes	# edges	$k_{\min}$	$k_{\max}$	k_{avg}	λ_k
(i)	US College Football Network	115	613	7	12	10.66	1.01
(ii)	Dolphins' Social Network	62	159	1	12	5.13	1.40
(iii)	US Politics Books Network	105	441	2	25	8.40	1.41
(iv)	Karate Club Network	34	78	1	17	4.59	1.46
(v)	Word Adjacencies Network	112	425	1	49	7.59	1.73
(vi)	US Airports 1997 Network	332	2126	1	140	12.81	3.22

Table 2 Real-world networks and their analysis for maximal matching

#	Real-world network	Network A.index	MNM		MAM		$\text{Diff}_{\text{A.Index}} = MAM_{\text{A.Index}} - \text{MNM}_{\text{A.Index}}$
			% Node matches	A.Index	% Node matches	A.Index	
(i)	US College Football Net.	−0.04	99	0.51	95	0.81	0.30
(ii)	Dolphins' Social Net.	−0.04	93	−0.23	73	0.82	1.05
(iii)	US Politics Books Net.	−0.02	99	0.22	86	0.71	0.49
(iv)	Karate Club Net.	−0.48	76	−0.43	71	−0.13	0.30
(v)	Word Adjacencies Net.	−0.10	96	−0.18	78	0.50	0.68
(vi)	US Airports 1997 Net.	−0.21	83	−0.15	68	0.87	1.02

hub nodes have significantly larger degree), the variation in the degree of the vertices in the graph would be high and the spectral radius ratio for node degree would be far above 1.0. Table 1 lists the real-world networks analyzed in the increasing order of their spectral radius ratio for node degree (λ_k). We denote the minimum, maximum and average node degree for the graphs as $k_{\min}$, $k_{\max}$ and k_{avg}, respectively.

As can be seen from Table 1, the US College Football Network exhibits a degree distribution that is very close to that of a random network (spectral radius ratio for node degree close to 1.0)—this is as expected, because other than the knock out games, each football team is more likely to play against all the other teams of the tournament in the round-robin games and thus, the number of football teams that each team has played against is quite close to the average number of teams that every team has played against. On the other hand, the US Airports network exhibits a scale-free distribution for node degree—indicating that there are few airports with degree as large as 140 (i.e., connections to 140 other airports in the network) while majority of the airports have fewer connections, leading to an average of 12.81 connections per airport. The other four real-world networks fall in between these two extremes.

We assume the node weights as node degree and calculate the assortativity index (hereafter, shortly referred to as A.Index) of the network (considering the set of all edges) and the assortativity index of the maximal matching obtained with the MAM and MNM algorithms. For all the six real-world networks, the A.Index values for each of the network graphs are negative, but majority of them are more close to 0 (indicating that the difference in the degrees of the end vertices of the edges is arbitrary and is neither too low nor too high). The A.Index values of the networks get more negative as the networks get increasingly scale-free, as is observed in the case of the Karate Club network, Word Adjacencies network and the US Airports network. We ran the MAM and MNM algorithms on each of the six real-world network graphs 100 times and averaged the results (presented in Table 2); this is to weed out any bias in the results due to the arbitrary breaking of ties among contending edges for inclusion to the set of edges constituting the maximal matching for both the MNM and MAM algorithms.

For each of the six real-world graphs, the MAM algorithm yielded a maximal matching that had a significantly larger A.Index compared to the matching obtained with the MNM algorithm. Neglecting the negative A.Index values obtained for the maximal matching to the Karate Club network under both the algorithms, the range of A.Index values obtained with the MAM algorithm across the other five real-world network graphs is 0.50–0.87, whereas the range of A.Index values obtained with the MNM algorithm across these real-world network graphs is −0.23 to 0.51. The median value for the A.Index of the maximal matching obtained with the MAM algorithm across the six real-world network graphs is 0.76, while the median value for the A.Index of the maximal matching obtained with the MNM algorithm is −0.17. As the A.Index values can range only from −1 to 1, a difference in the median A.Index values of 0.76 − (−0.17) = 0.95 is very significant (as the difference in the A.Index values can be only

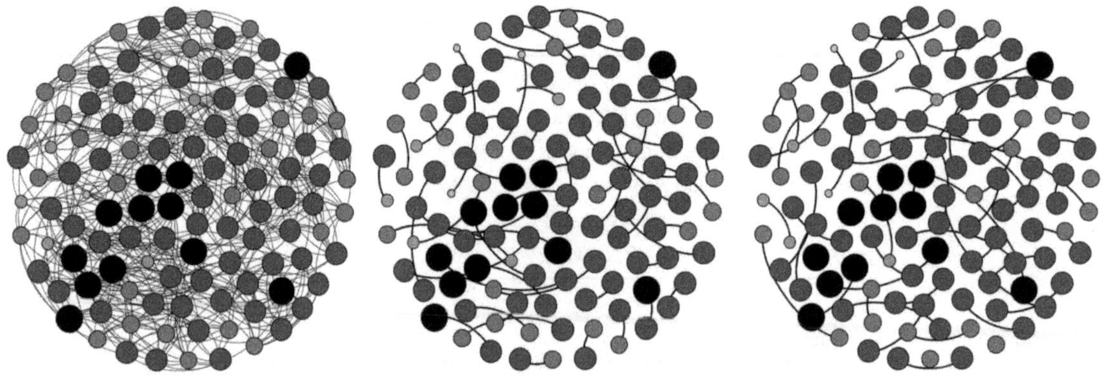

Original Network [A. Index: -0.04] | Maximal Node Matching [% Matches: 99%; A. Index: 0.51] | Maximal Assortative Matching [% Matches: 95%; A. Index: 0.81]

Fig. 5 US College Football Network: 115 nodes and 613 edges [spectral radius ratio: 1.01]

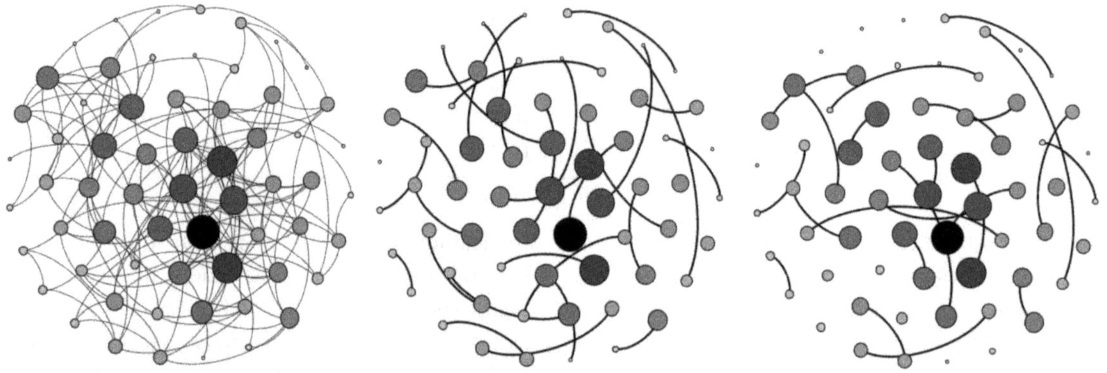

Original Network [A. Index: -0.04] | Maximal Node Matching [% Matches: 93%; A. Index: -0.23] | Maximal Assortative Matching [% Matches: 73%; A. Index: 0.82]

Fig. 6 Dolphins' Social Network: 62 nodes and 159 edges [spectral radius ratio: 1.40]

on a scale of 0–2). As a tradeoff for larger A.Index, we had expected the MAM algorithm to incur a relatively fewer node matches compared to that of the MNM algorithm. The results for the analysis of the real-world network graphs indicate that the tradeoff is indeed not very significant. We observe the % node matches for the MAM algorithm to range from 68 to 98 %, with a median of 75 %, whereas the % node matches for the MNM algorithm ranges from 76 to 99 %, with a median of 95 %. The difference in the median values for the % node matches is 20 % (on a scale of 0–100 %).

Figures 5, 6, 7, 8, 9 and 10 illustrate the maximal matching obtained for each of the real-world network graphs with respect to both maximal node matching and maximal assortative matching. The visualization is generated through Gephi [20]; the layout of these networks is based on the Fruchterman Reingold algorithm [21]. The larger and darker the node circles, the larger the degree for the node. As can be seen in the figures for all the six real-world network graphs, the maximal assortative matching (MAM) has a larger fraction of edges whose end vertices are more likely to have degrees close enough to each other. On the other hand, we could observe some nodes remaining unpaired in the figures for the MAM, attributed to the relatively lower % of node matches.

The Gephi software package does not include algorithms for maximal matching. We primarily use Gephi for visualization; the implementations of the maximal matching algorithms proposed in this paper have been done from scratch through object-oriented programming in Java. The outputs of the algorithms (the edges chosen for maximal matching), saved as .csv files, are ported to Gephi through the "Data Laboratory" user interface for visualization. Gephi has a .jar toolkit at https://gephi.org/toolkit/. One could download this toolkit to their programming environment (say: NetBeans, https://netbeans.org/), transform the code for maximal matching algorithms to an API and integrate the API as a plug-in to Gephi.

The US Airports Network is the largest network (332 nodes and 2126 edges) we have analyzed in this paper. On a Dell Precision M4600 computer (Intel i7-2620M CPU @ 2.70 GHz; 8 GB RAM), the execution time of the MAM and MNM algorithms for the US Airports Network are, respec-

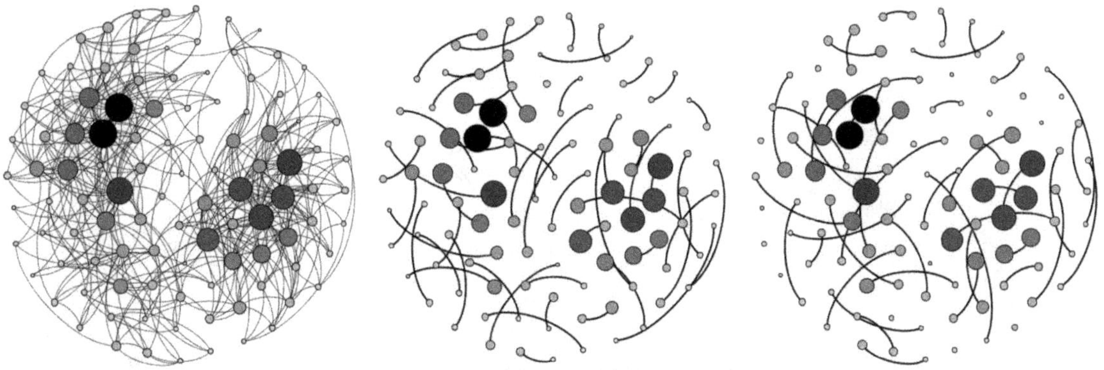

Original Network [A. Index: -0.02] | Maximal Node Matching [% Matches: 99%; A. Index: 0.22] | Maximal Assortative Matching [% Matches: 86%; A. Index: 0.71]

Fig. 7 US Politics Books Network: 105 nodes and 441 edges [spectral radius ratio: 1.41]

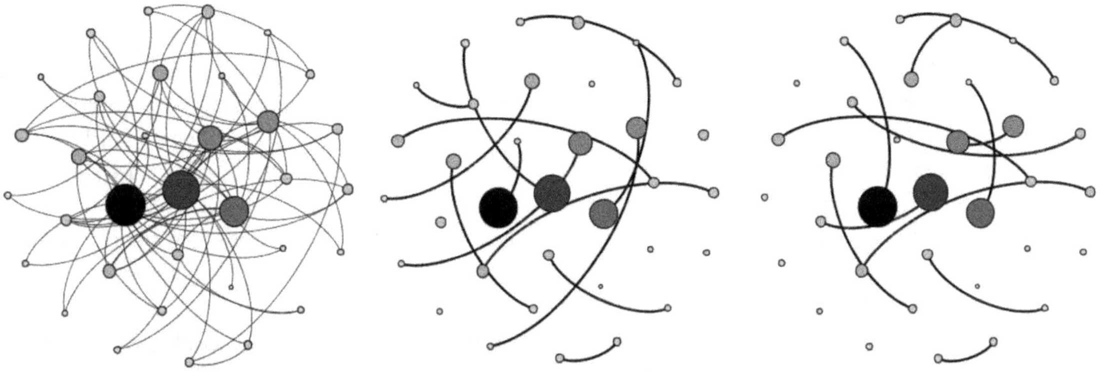

Original Network [A. Index: -0.48] | Maximal Node Matching [% Matches: 76%; A. Index: -0.43] | Maximal Assortative Matching [% Matches: 71%; A. Index: -0.13]

Fig. 8 Karate Club Network: 34 nodes and 78 edges [spectral radius ratio: 1.46]

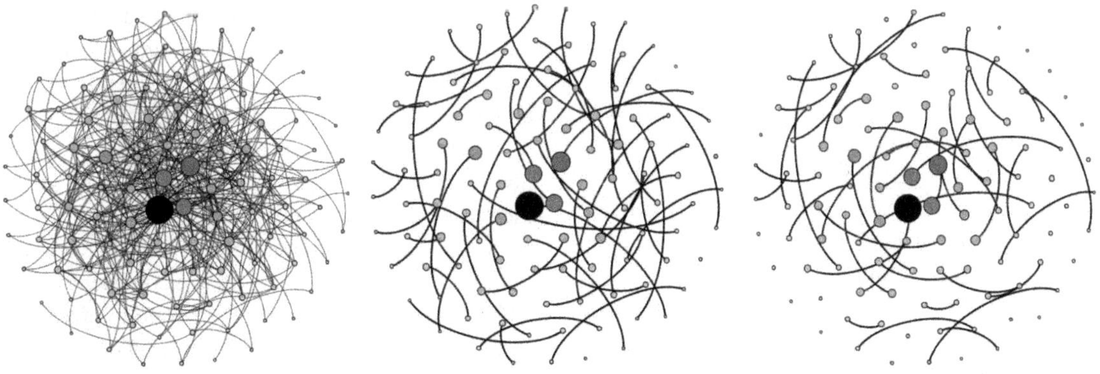

Original Network [A. Index: -0.10] | Maximal Node Matching [% Matches: 96%; A. Index: -0.18] | Maximal Assortative Matching [% Matches: 78%; A. Index: 0.50]

Fig. 9 Word Adjacency Network: 112 nodes and 425 edges [spectral radius ratio: 1.73]

tively, 0.23 and 0.19 ms. With a polynomial-time complexity O($EV\log E$) and actual execution times (in milliseconds, as observed above), we are confident that the proposed maximal matching algorithms are easily scalable for very large real-world networks of several hundreds and even thousands of nodes. As mentioned earlier, the results of our maximal matching algorithms can be ported to any network visualization tool and the edges chosen for matching could be visualized; the resolution of the visualization is limited only to the tool being used.

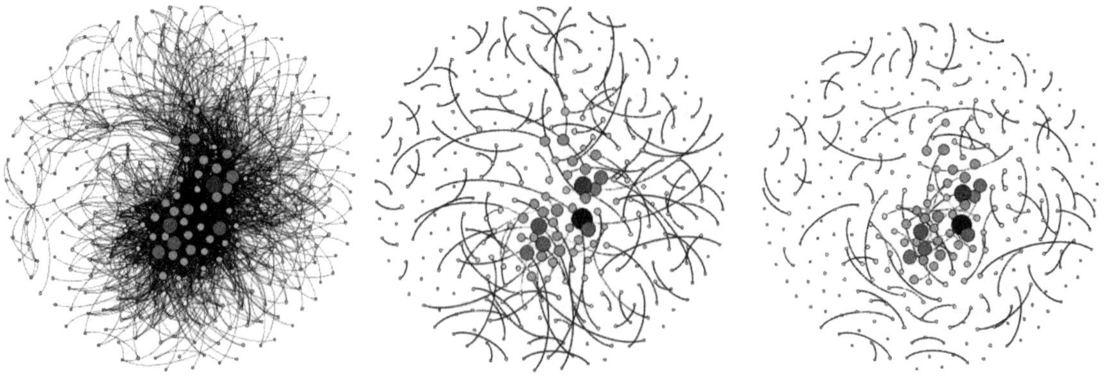

Fig. 10 US Airports (1997) Network: 332 nodes and 2126 edges [spectral radius ratio: 3.22]

Out of the results obtained for 100 trials, we pick the results of the trial that lie very close to that of the average values obtained for the assortativity of the network as well as the % node matches and the assortativity index for both the MAM and MNM. In this pursuit, we normalize the values for each of the above five metrics for each of the 100 trials as well as normalize the average values of the metrics for all the trials; for each trial, we determine the sum of the squares of the difference between the normalized values for the above five metrics and the normalized average values; we use the maximal assortative matching and maximal node matching of the trial that has the lowest error for the sum of the squares of the differences (as calculated above). The network graphs and the matching shown in Figs. 5, 6, 7, 8, 9 and 10 correspond to the graphs of the trials chosen as explained above.

With regard to the impact of the type of network on assortativty, we observe the random networks to incur larger A.index values for both MAM and MNM and this could be attributed to the relatively fewer number of adjacent edges per edge and the edges are evenly distributed across the entire network. On the other hand, for scale-free networks, a significant fraction of the edges are incident on the hubs and relatively lower fraction of the edges connect two non-hub nodes. As a result, the inclusion of an edge incident on a hub into a maximal matching leads to the coverage of a larger fraction of the uncovered edges as well as results in a low-degree node being paired with a high-degree node. Such scenarios are more evident in the case of maximal node matching, leading to much smaller negative A.Index values (reasonably lower than 0). The MAM algorithm is much more successful in identifying and including edges between two non-hub nodes (low-moderate degree nodes) as part of the maximal matching.

Compared to the other real-world network graphs, the relatively poor performance of both the maximal assortative matching and maximal node matching for the Karate Club network could be attributed to the sparse and scale-free nature of the graph (34 nodes and 78 edges; the average node degree is 4.59 and the maximum node degree is 17); as a result, the inclusion of an edge in the MAM or MNM is more likely to result in the coverage of several other adjacent uncovered edges as well as result in the more likely pairing of a low-degree node with a high-degree node.

4 Analysis of random network graphs with node degree as node weights

In Sects. 4 and 5, we simulate the evolution of random network graphs generated using the well-known Erdos–Renyi model [10]. The model inputs two parameters: the total number of nodes (N) and the probability of a link (p_{link}) between any two nodes in the graph. As we simulate the evolution of an undirected random network, the links are bi-directional and we could assume that the end vertices of each link could be represented as an ordered pair (u, v) where u and v are the node IDs and $u < v$. We assume there are no self-loops and there is no more than one edge in the network. For an N node network, the maximum number of undirected links possible in the network is $N(N-1)/2$. We consider every such possible link in the network and generate a random number to decide whether to include the link in the network or not. If the random number generated for a pair (u, v) is less than or equal to p_{link}, then we include the link (u, v) in the network; otherwise, not. As it is obvious, the larger the value of p_{link}, the larger the number of links in the random network graph as well as larger the chances for the network to have a degree distribution wherein the degree of each node is closer to the average node degree.

The total number of nodes considered in the simulations for this section is $N = 100$ nodes. The values used for the probability of link between any two nodes in the network

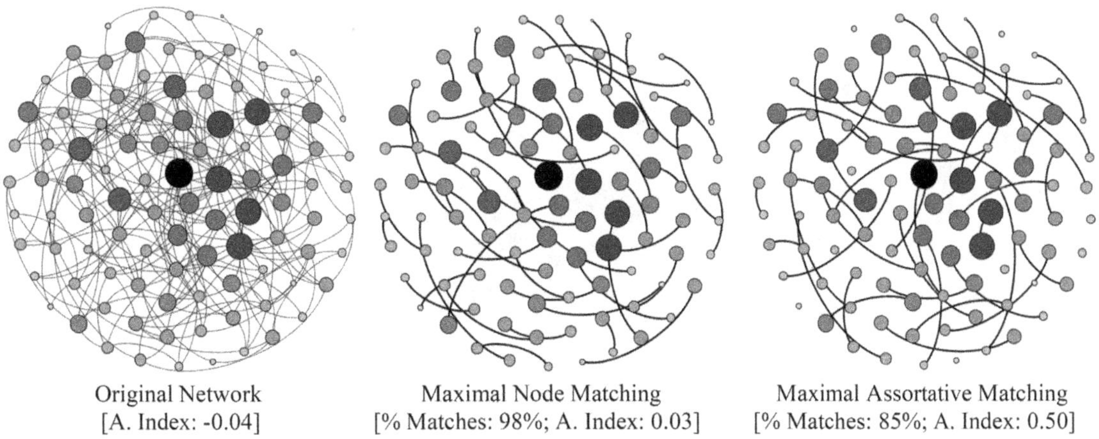

Fig. 11 Random network: 100 nodes; probability of link between any two nodes—0.05

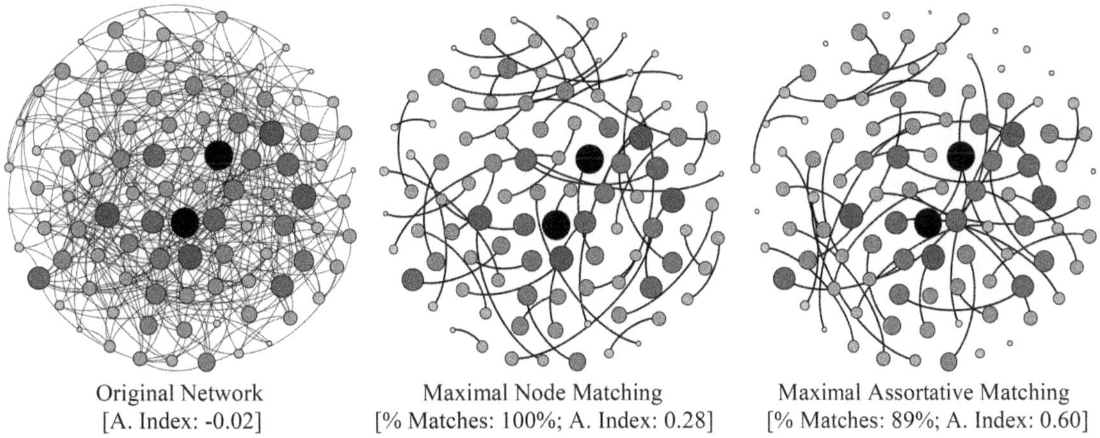

Fig. 12 Random network: 100 nodes; probability of link between any two nodes—0.07

(p_{link}) are 0.05, 0.07, 0.10, 0.15, 0.20, 0.30, 0.40 and 0.50. For each p_{link} value, we run 100 trials of the network evolution and analyze the assortatvity of the network as well as evaluate the % of node matches and assortativity of the maximal matching obtained with both the MAM and MNM algorithms. In this section, node degree is used as node weight for the assortativity calculations.

As explained in Sect. 3, we pick the trial network whose values for the above five metrics lie close to the average values for these metrics across all the 100 trials (according to the sum of the squares of the differences between the normalized values of the metrics for the individual trials and the overall normalized average values) and represent in Figs. 11, 12, 13, 14, 15, 16, 17 and 18 the network graph and maximal matching (with respect to both MAM and MNM) obtained for the network graph of the chosen trial.

We observe that the random networks for all the 100 trials generated with $p_{\text{link}} \geq 0.05$ to be connected. Even though the number of links in the network increases with increasing p_{link} values, the assortativity of the set of all edges in a random network remains close to 0 for all the p_{link} values. This vindicates the random nature of the distribution of the edges among the vertices as per the Erdos–Renyi model.

With regard to the % of node matches, we start observing a 100 % node match with the MNM algorithm with p_{link} values of 0.07 or above, whereas the % of node matches with the MAM algorithm is 85 % for p_{link} value of 0.05 and reaches 99 % for p_{link} value of 0.5; the % of node matches for MAM crosses 95 % when p_{link} is 0.15. However, the tradeoff is quite high with respect to the assortativity index (A.Index). The A.Index of the maximal node matching is significantly low compared to that of the maximal assortative matching. The A.Index of MNM and MAM are, respectively, 0.03 and 0.5 when p_{link} is 0.05 and reaches 0.60 and 0.84 when p_{link} value is 0.3. The A.Index does not increase appreciably for both the MAM and MNM (especially for the MNM) as we further increase the p_{link} value. The average A.Index values observed for the MNM and MAM are, respectively, 0.64 and 0.90 when the p_{link} value is 0.90. This is a significant observation that has been hitherto not reported in the literature for random

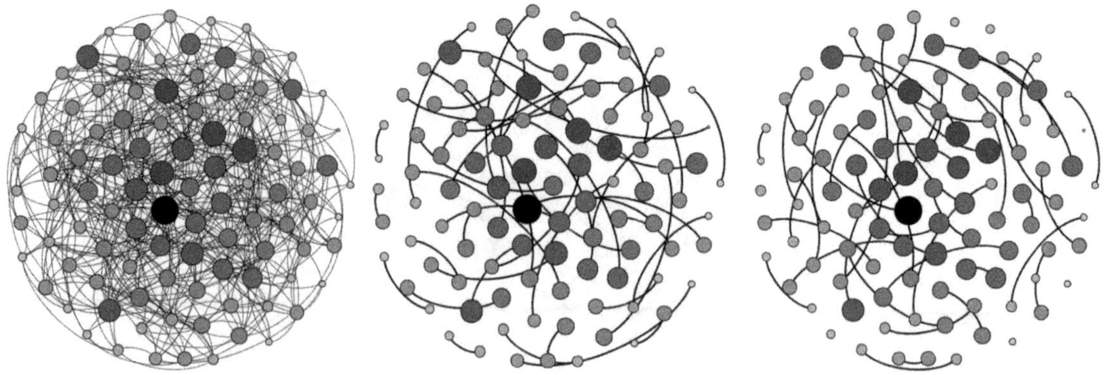

Fig. 13 Random network: 100 nodes; probability of link between any two nodes—0.10

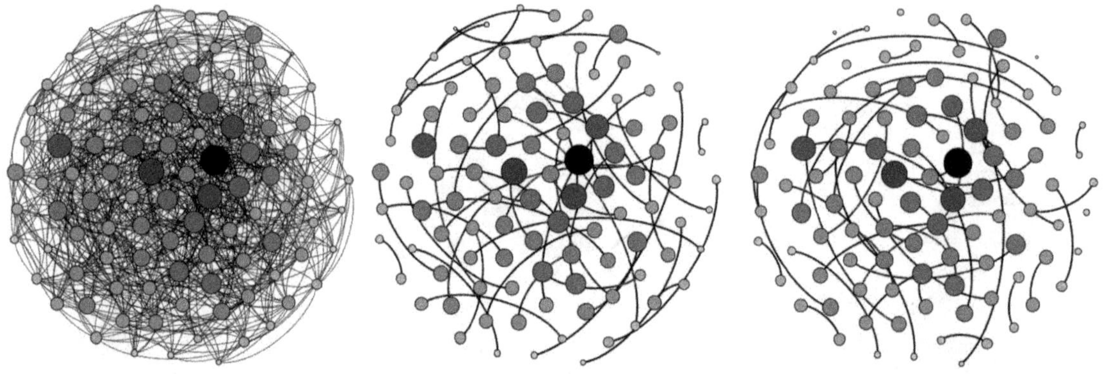

Fig. 14 Random network: 100 nodes; probability of link between any two nodes—0.15

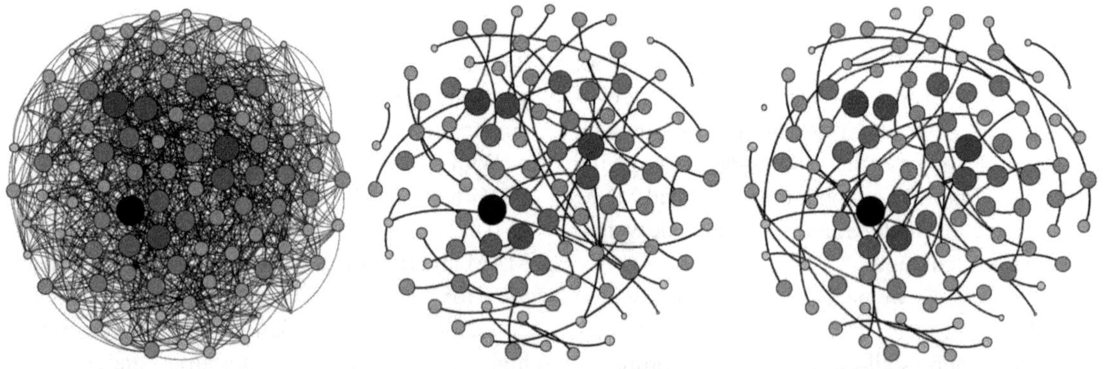

Fig. 15 Random network: 100 nodes; probability of link between any two nodes—0.20

networks. Figure 19 illustrates the nature of increase in % of node matches and the assortativity index values as we increase the p_{link} values from 0.05 to 0.50 as explained above. The values reported in Fig. 19 are the average values obtained from the 100 trial runs for each p_{link} value.

5 Analysis of random network graphs with random node weights

In this section, we present the results for the percentage of node matches and assortativity index incurred with the max-

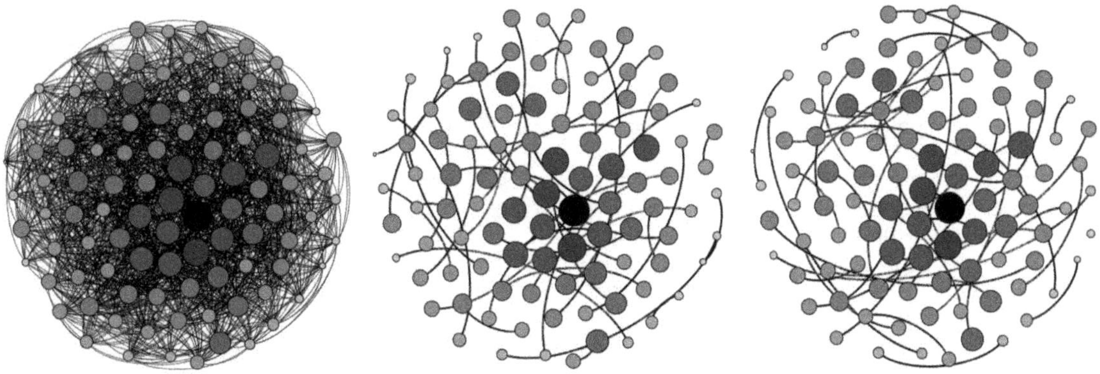

Original Network [A. Index: -0.02] | Maximal Node Matching [% Matches: 100%; A. Index: 0.60] | Maximal Assortative Matching [% Matches: 98%; A. Index: 0.84]

Fig. 16 Random network: 100 nodes; probability of link between any two nodes—0.30

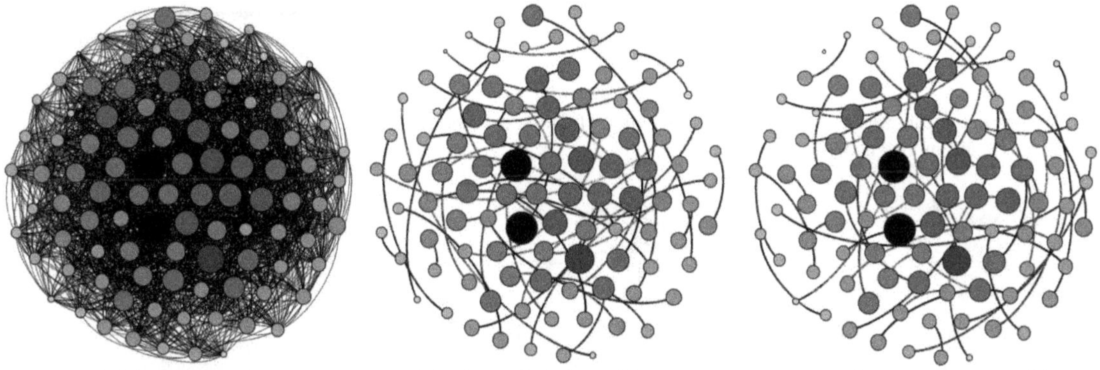

Original Network [A. Index: -0.02] | Maximal Node Matching [% Matches: 100%; A. Index: 0.61] | Maximal Assortative Matching [% Matches: 98%; A. Index: 0.85]

Fig. 17 Random network: 100 nodes; probability of link between any two nodes—0.40

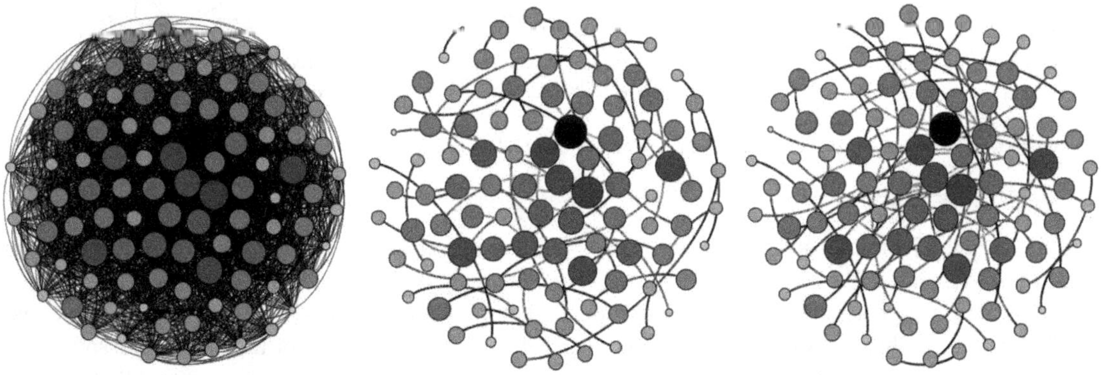

Original Network [A. Index: -0.02] | Maximal Node Matching [% Matches: 100%; A. Index: 0.62] | Maximal Assortative Matching [% Matches: 99%; A. Index: 0.86]

Fig. 18 Random network: 100 nodes; probability of link between any two nodes—0.50

imal node matching and maximal assortative matching for random networks generated under the Erdos–Renyi model wherein the node weights are random numbers generated from 0 to 1. We conducted the simulations with 100 trials for each p_{link} value and averaged the results for the network assortativity as well as the % of node matches and assortativity index for both the maximal node matching and maximal assortative matching. The results presented in Fig. 20 indicate the average values for these metrics from the 100 trials. Also, the network graphs presented in Figs.

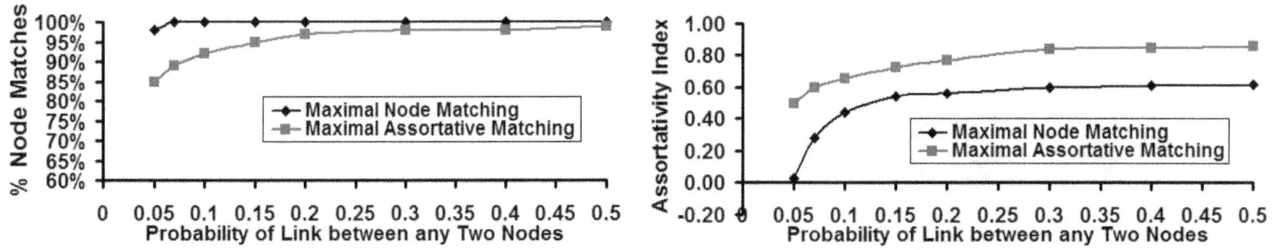

Fig. 19 Random networks with node degree as node weights: distribution of the percentage of node matches and assortativity index as a function of the probability of link between any two nodes

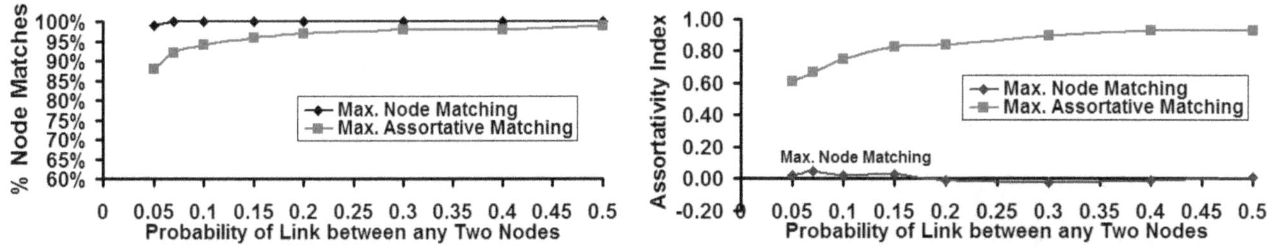

Fig. 20 Random networks with random node weights: distribution of the percentage of node matches and assortativity index as a function of the probability of link between any two nodes

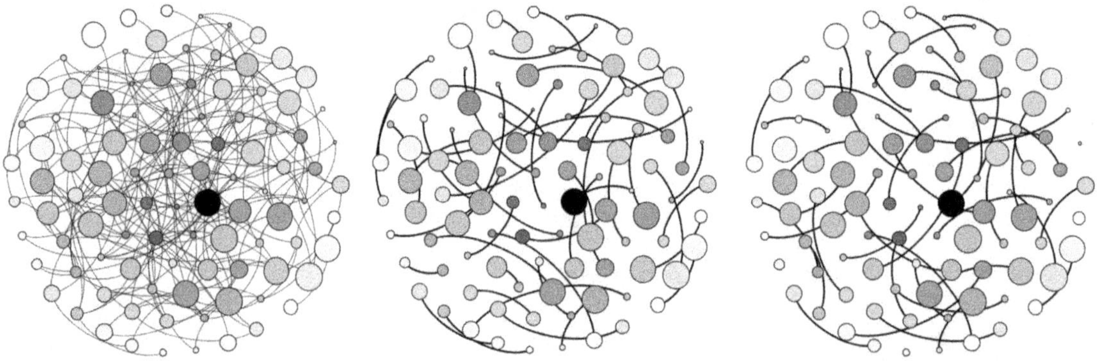

Original Network [A. Index: 0.01] | Maximal Node Matching [% Matches: 99%; A. Index: 0.02] | Maximal Assortative Matching [% Matches: 88%; A. Index: 0.61]

Fig. 21 Random network: 100 nodes; probability of link between any two nodes—0.05

21, 22, 23, 24, 25, 26, 27 and 28 are representative network graphs whose values for the above five metrics are close to that of the average values observed for these metrics in the 100 trials such that the sum of the squares of the difference in the normalized values for these metrics is the minimum. In Figs. 21, 22, 23, 24, 25, 26, 27 and 28, the size of the node circles is a measure of the node weight (the larger the node weight, the larger is the size of a node and vice-versa); on the other hand, the darkness of a node circle is a measure of the node degree (the more darker—black—a node is, the larger is its node degree).

As explained in Sects. 1 and 2, the maximal node matching is independent of node weights; as a result, we expect the assortativity index of maximal node matching to be close to 0 for all values of p_{link} and it is confirmed through the simulations. On the other hand, though it was not obvious before the simulations, for a given p_{link} value, we observe the assortativity index of the maximal assortative matching (with random node weights) to be slightly higher (the difference is as large as 0.1 in a scale of 0–2) than the assortative index of the maximal assortative matching with node degree as node weights. Though the difference in the assortativity index values for maximal assortative matching with the above two categories of node weights could be observed for all p_{link} values, the difference is relatively more prominent for random networks with lower p_{link} values and reduces as the p_{link} value increases. As can be observed from Fig. 20, the curve for the assortativity index for maximal assortative matching with random node weights becomes flat starting

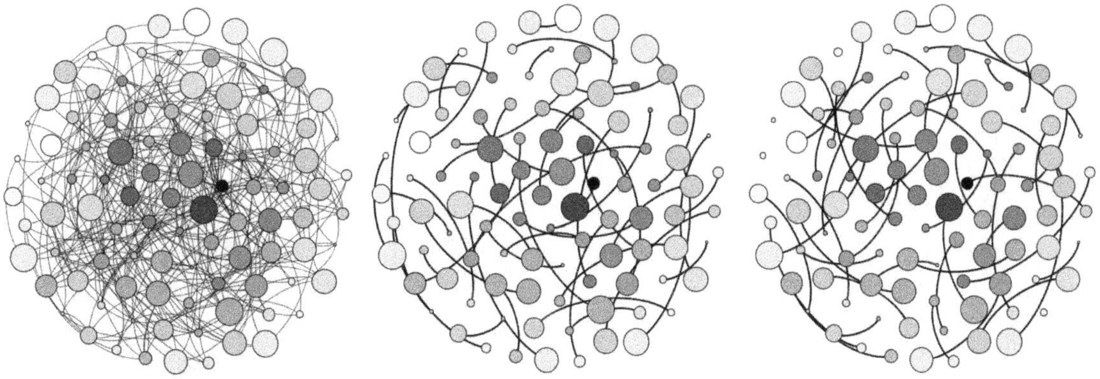

Original Network [A. Index: 0.00] | Maximal Node Matching [% Matches: 100%; A. Index: 0.05] | Maximal Assortative Matching [% Matches: 92%; A. Index: 0.67]

Fig. 22 Random network: 100 nodes; probability of link between any two nodes—0.07

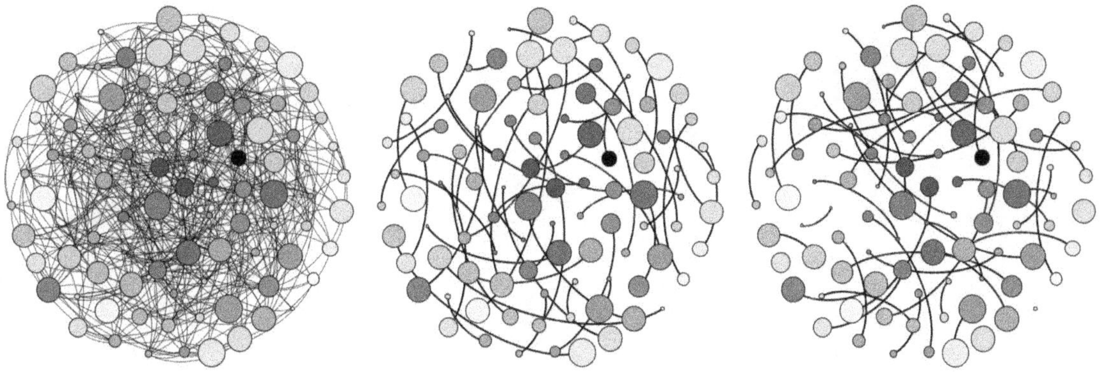

Original Network [A. Index: 0.00] | Maximal Node Matching [% Matches: 100%; A. Index: 0.02] | Maximal Assortative Matching [% Matches: 94%; A. Index: 0.75]

Fig. 23 Random network: 100 nodes; probability of link between any two nodes—0.10

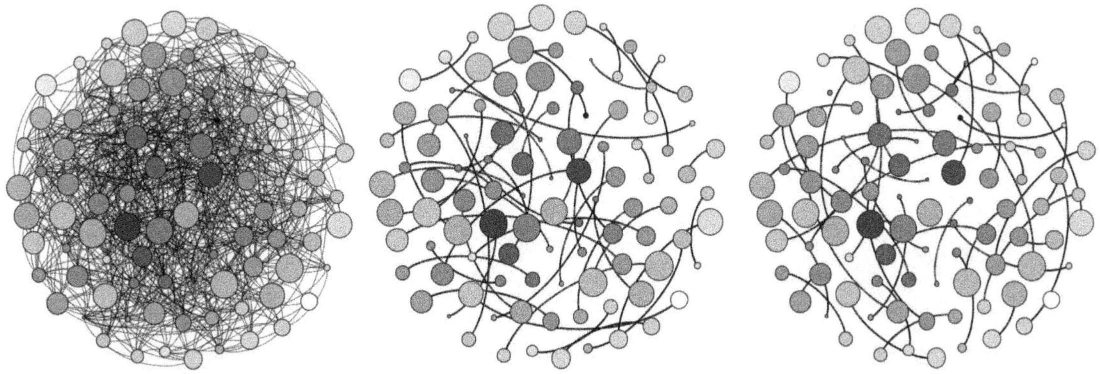

Original Network [A. Index: 0.00] | Maximal Node Matching [% Matches: 100%; A. Index: 0.03] | Maximal Assortative Matching [% Matches: 96%; A. Index: 0.83]

Fig. 24 Random network: 100 nodes; probability of link between any two nodes—0.15

from p_{link} value of 0.40 (the assortativity index curve for the MAM with node degree as node weights became flat starting from p_{link} value of 0.30).

An interesting observation is that (in addition to incurring a relatively larger assortativity index) the % of node matches obtained with the MAM algorithm for random network graphs with random node weights is even slightly larger than the % of node matches obtained with the MAM algorithm for random network graphs with node degree as node weights, especially for networks formed with lower

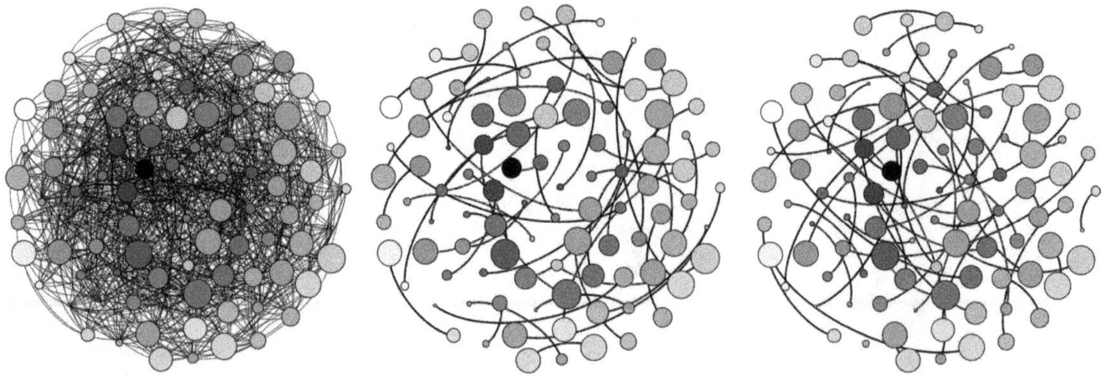

Fig. 25 Random network: 100 nodes; probability of link between any two nodes—0.20

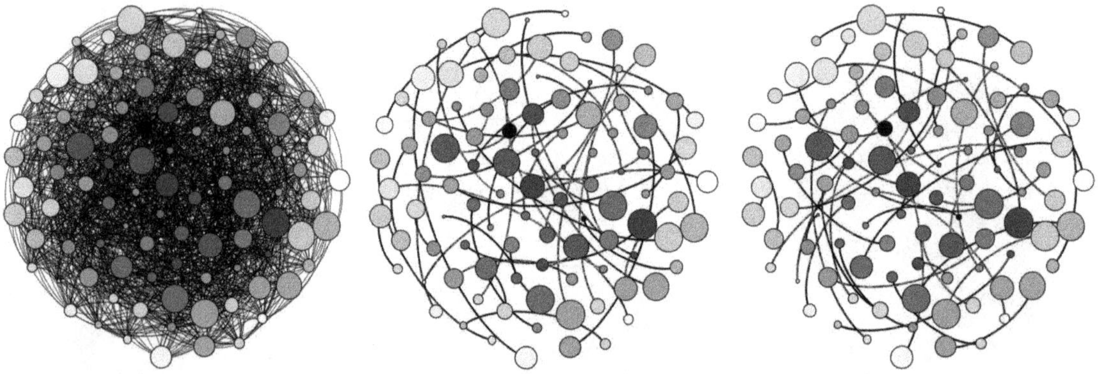

Fig. 26 Random network: 100 nodes; probability of link between any two nodes—0.30

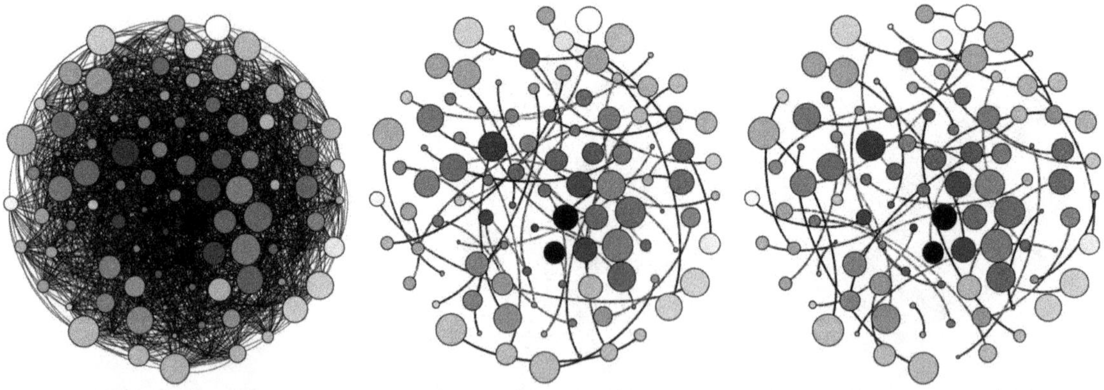

Fig. 27 Random network: 100 nodes; probability of link between any two nodes—0.40

p_{link} values. Overall, the maximal assortative matching algorithm could give even relatively better optimal results (with respect to both assortativity index and % of node matches) for random network graphs with random node weights and the tradeoff in the values incurred for the above two metrics is relatively less pronounced than what is observed in random network graphs with node degree as node weights.

As we expect node weights in social networks to be not only a measure of the node degree, the MAM algorithm could be very useful to match vertices with any measure of node weights, especially in social network graphs that are not very

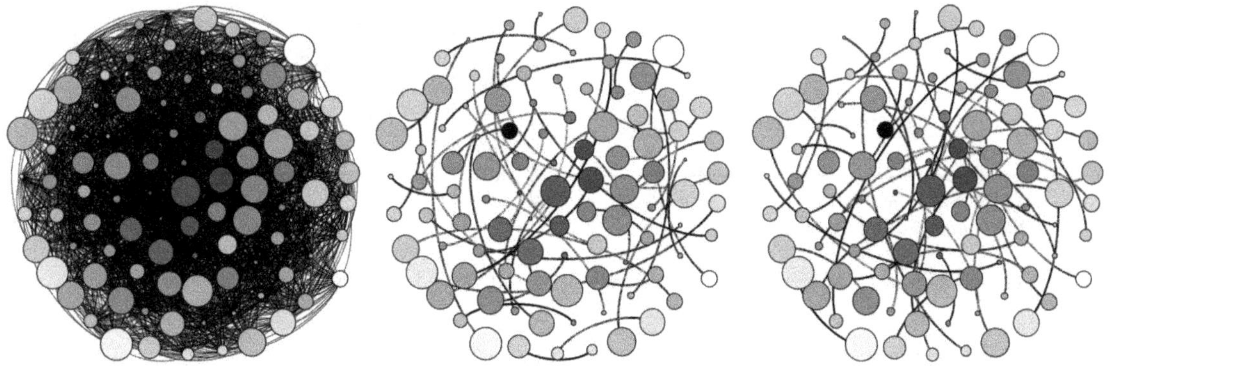

Fig. 28 Random network: 100 nodes; probability of link between any two nodes—0.50

dense. This vindicates the wider scope of application of the proposed maximal assortative matching (MAM) algorithm; the algorithm could give even better optimal results (with respect to assortativity) for random graphs with node weights that are independent of node degree.

6 Analysis of scale-free network graphs with node degree as node weights

In this section, we present the results of the execution of the maximal assortative matching and maximal node matching algorithms on scale-free network graphs that are generated with the well-known Barabasi–Albert (BA) model [11]. The evolution of a scale-free network under the BA model is explained briefly below: We start with an initial number of nodes (n_{init}) and setup links between them in such a way that each node has at least one link. The node IDs are assigned as $1, 2, \ldots, n_{\text{init}}$. After this initialization, we start a timer ($t = n_{\text{init}} + 1, n_{\text{init}} + 2, \ldots, n_{\text{total}}$) introducing new nodes to the network, one at a time (with IDs corresponding to the time of introduction of the node). We setup $links_{\text{new}}$ links to a newly introduced node (connecting it to the existing nodes in the network; not more than one link per node). If $links_{\text{new}}$ is greater than or equal to the total number of nodes existing in the network at the time of introduction of a node, then the newly introduced node is simply connected to each of the existing nodes (one link per node). If $links_{\text{new}}$ is less than the total number of nodes existing in the network at the time of introduction of a node, then the existing nodes are chosen for a link probabilistically according to the formulation explained below. The idea is to give preference for nodes that have a relatively higher degree (i.e., the BA model follows the rich-gets-richer preferential attachment phenomenon).

The probability for an existing node$i$ to be chosen to have a link with a newly introduced node j is proportional to the degree of the node i at the time of introduction of node j (since node i has been already introduced to the network at the time of introduction of node j, going by the above convention, $j > i$ and the IDs of all the existing nodes in the network will be $1, 2 \ldots, j-1$). Let t_j denote the time of introduction of node j. Let $k_i^{t_j-1}$ be the degree of node i just before the introduction of node j to the network (i.e., at the end of the time of introduction of node $j-1$). Before any new link is added due to the introduction of node j, we compute the unnormalized probability $P_i^{j,\text{unnorm}} = \frac{k_i^{t_j-1}}{\sum_{id=1}^{j-1} k_{id}^{t_j-1}}$ with which an existing node i gets a link.

To decide which of the $1, 2, \ldots, j-1$ nodes get the first link to node j, we divide the range $(0\ldots1]$ proportionally among the $j-1$ nodes such that node 1 gets the sub range $(0, \ldots, P_1^{j,\text{unnorm}}]$, node 2 gets the sub range $(P_1^{j,\text{unnorm}}, \ldots, P_2^{j,\text{unnorm}}]$, etc., and node $j-1$ gets the sub range $(P_{j-1}^{j,\text{unnorm}}, \ldots, 1]$. We generate a random number in the range $(0, \ldots, 1]$ and depending on which sub range the random number falls into, the corresponding node is selected to have the first link to the newly introduced node j; the chosen node is not considered for the inclusion of any other new link (among the $links_{\text{new}}$ links) to be added during the introduction of node j. Let *Neighbors*(j) be the set of nodes that have already had a link with the newly introduced node j. To decide which of the $\{1, 2, \ldots, j-1\}$-*Neighbors*(j) candidate nodes get a link with node j, we normalize the unnormalized probability of the candidate nodes $i \in \{1, 2, \ldots, j-1\}$-*Neighbors*($j$) as follows: $\forall i \in \{1, 2, \ldots, j-1\}$-*Neighbors*($j$), $P_i^{j,\text{norm}} = \frac{P_i^{j,\text{unnorm}}}{\sum_{id \in \{1,2,\ldots,j-1\}-Neighbors(j)} P_{id}^{j,\text{unnorm}}}$. We divide the range $(0, \ldots, 1]$ proportionally among the candidate nodes $i \in \{1, 2, \ldots, j-1\}$-*Neighbors*($j$) according to the $P_i^{j,\text{norm}}$ values, similar to what was explained for the introduction of the first link. We generate a random number in the range

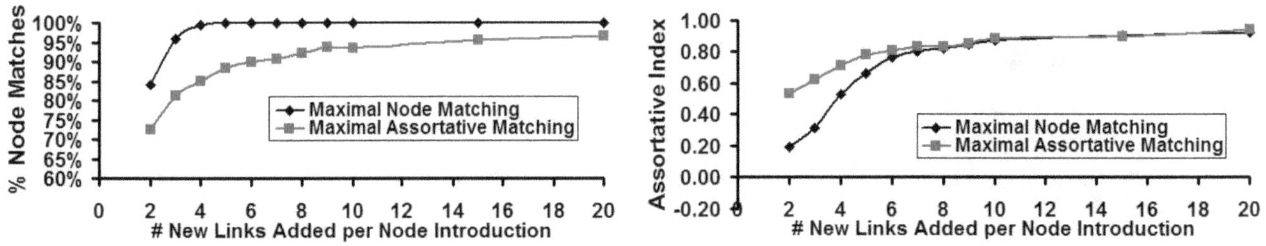

Fig. 29 Scale-free networks: average values for % of node matches and assortativity index (initial # nodes: 3; total nodes: 100)

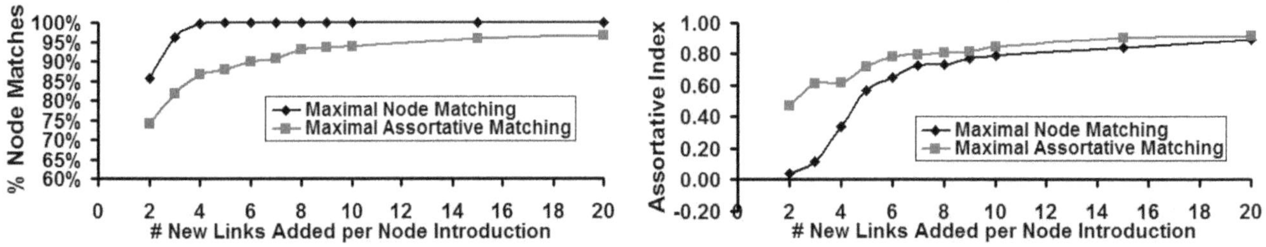

Fig. 30 Scale-free networks: average values for % of node matches and assortativity index (initial # nodes: 10; total nodes: 100)

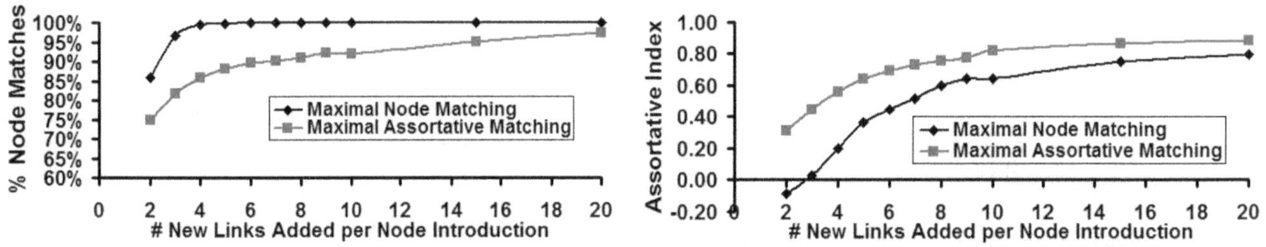

Fig. 31 Scale-free networks: average values for % of node matches and assortativity index (initial # nodes: 20; total nodes: 100)

(0, . . ., 1] and whichever candidate node falls in the normalized range of probabilities, that node gets the new link. We repeat the above procedure until all of the $links_{\text{new}}$ links are added to a newly introduced node j.

To conduct the assortativity analysis, we simulate the evolution of a scale-free network under the above explained BA model with a total of 100 nodes (n_{total}): varied the initial number of nodes (n_{init}) with values of 3, 10 and 20, and varied the initial number of links per node at the time of its introduction ($links_{\text{new}}$) with values of 2, 3, 4, 5, 6, 7, 8, 9, 10, 15 and 20. We ran 100 trials of the simulations for each combination of n_{init} and $links_{\text{new}}$ values and averaged the results for network assortativity, % of node matches and assortativity index (A.Index) with respect to both maximal node matching (MNM) and maximal assortativity matching (MAM). Figures 29, 30 and 31 illustrate the averaged values for the % of node matches and A.Index for each combination of n_{init} and $links_{\text{new}}$ values listed above. Figures 32, 33, 34, 35, 36, 37, 38, 39 and 40 illustrate the scale-free networks evolved using n_{init} values of 3, 10 and 20 and $links_{\text{new}}$ values of 2, 5 and 20. Node degree is used as node weight in the assortativity calculations. The larger and darker is the circle for a node in Figs. 32, 33, 34, 35, 36, 37, 38, 39 and 40, the larger is its degree and vice-versa.

Some interesting observations can be made from the results presented in Figs. 29 and 31. For a given number of new links added per node introduction, the % of node matches does not appreciably change for both the MAM and MNM as we increase the initial number of nodes from 3 to 10 and further to 20. On the other hand, for a given number of new links added per node introduction, the assortativity index for both the MNM and MAM decreases significantly as we increase the initial number of nodes from 3 to 10 and further to 20 (especially, for lower values of the number of new links added per node introduction). This could be attributed to the relatively sparse nature of the scale-free networks and a larger variation in node degree (refer to Figs. 32, 33, 34, 35, 36, 37, 38, 39, 40) as we increase the initial number of nodes (for a fixed value of the initial number of links added per node introduction), especially for lower values of the number of new links added per node introduction.

The initial number of nodes setup during the evolution of the scale-free network form the core of the network to which the newly introduced nodes get attached to. As a result,

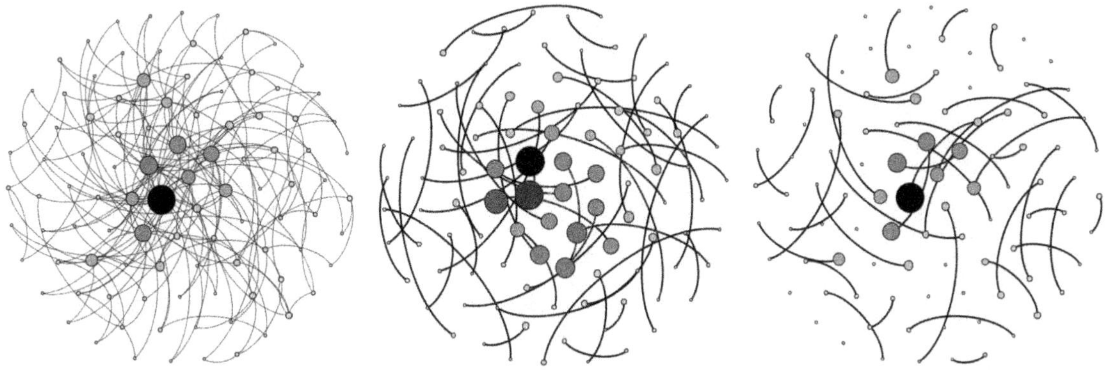

Original Scale-Free Network [A. Index: 0.23] | Maximal Node Matching [% Matches: 85%; A. Index: 0.13] | Maximal Assortative Matching [% Matches: 74%; A. Index: 0.53]

Fig. 32 Scale-free network (100 nodes)—BA model: initial—3 nodes; 2 links per node addition [spectral radius ratio for node degree: 1.78]

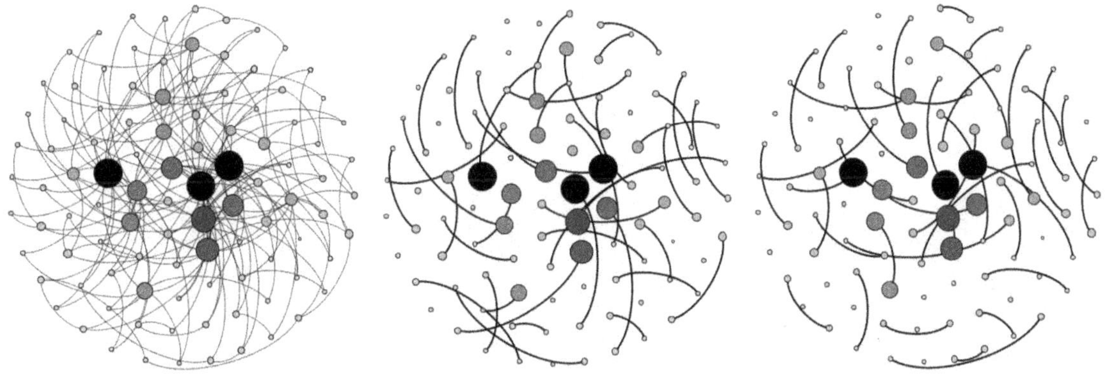

Original Scale-Free Network [A. Index: 0.15] | Maximal Node Matching [% Matches: 86%; A. Index: 0.04] | Maximal Assortative Matching [% Matches: 75%; A. Index: 0.43]

Fig. 33 Scale-free network (100 nodes)—BA model: initial—10 nodes; 2 links added per node introduction [spectral radius ratio for node degree: 1.62]

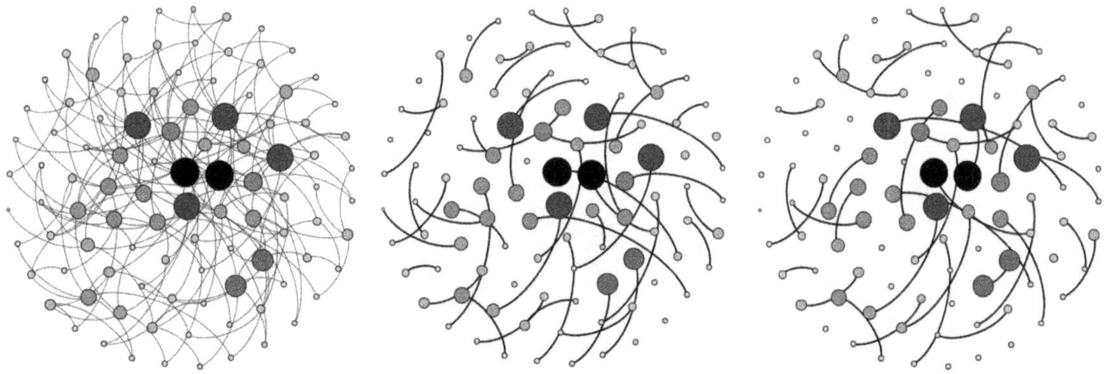

Original Scale-Free Network [A. Index: 0.10] | Maximal Node Matching [% Matches: 85%; A. Index: -0.05] | Maximal Assortative Matching [% Matches: 73%; A. Index: 0.40]

Fig. 34 Scale-free network (100 nodes)—BA model: initial—20 nodes; 2 links added per node introduction [spectral radius ratio for node degree: 1.49]

the initial set of nodes are bound to have a considerably larger degree than the newly introduced nodes (especially for smaller values of new links added per node introduction). If the initial number of nodes is high and the number of new links added per node is low, the network is more sparse and also relatively more scale-free (vindicated by larger values for the spectral radius ratio for node degree, as in Figs. 32, 33, 34): with a concentration of only few hubs, most of the

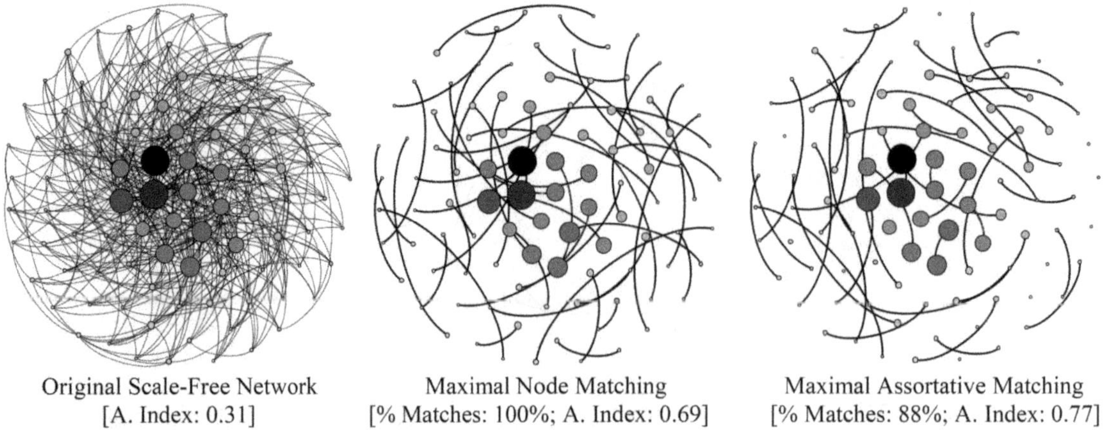

Fig. 35 Scale-free network (100 nodes)—BA model: initial—3 nodes; 5 links added per node introduction [spectral radius ratio for node degree: 1.46]

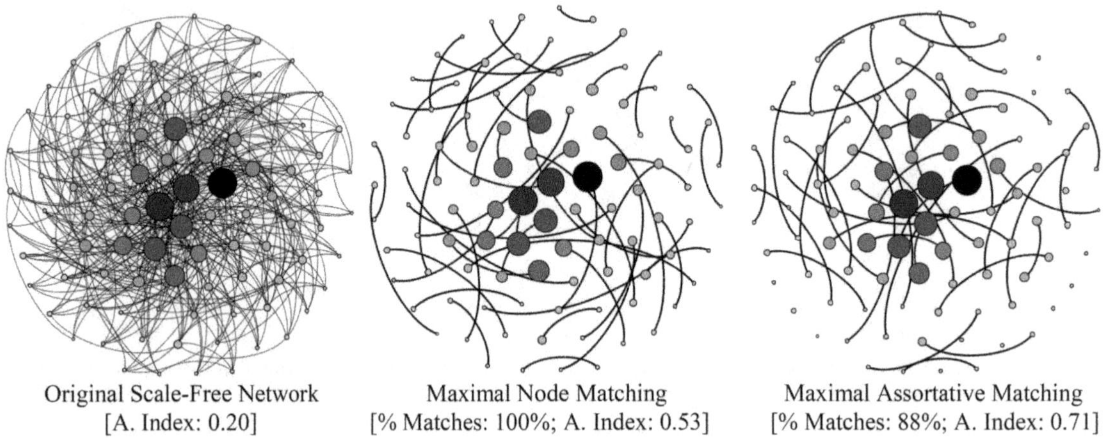

Fig. 36 Scale-free network (100 nodes)—BA model: initial—10 nodes; 5 links added per node introduction [spectral radius ratio for node degree: 1.35]

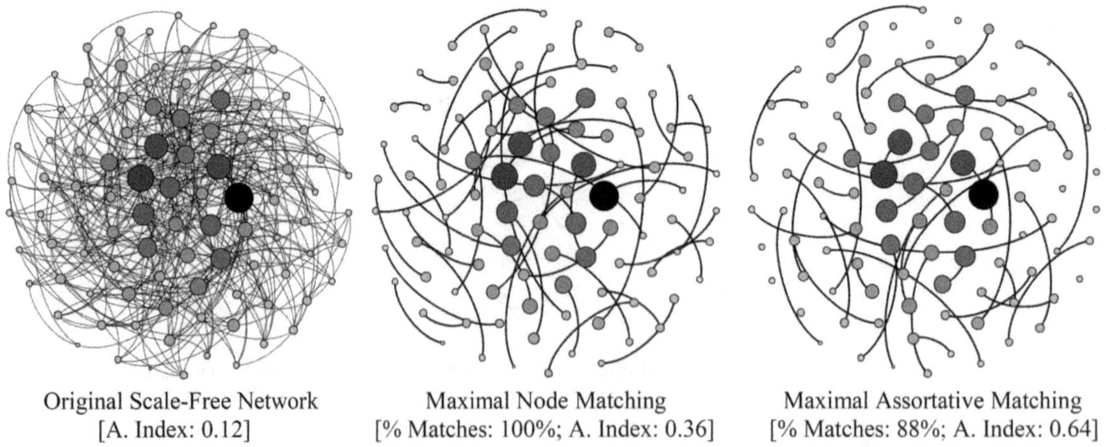

Fig. 37 Scale-free network (100 nodes)—BA model: initial—20 nodes; 5 links added per node introduction [spectral radius ratio for node degree: 1.29]

links are links involving a low-degree node connected to a high-degree node (results in a lower assortativity index for the matching algorithms).

As we increase the initial number of nodes and/or the number of new links added per node introduction, the number of high-degree nodes increases and the variation in the degree

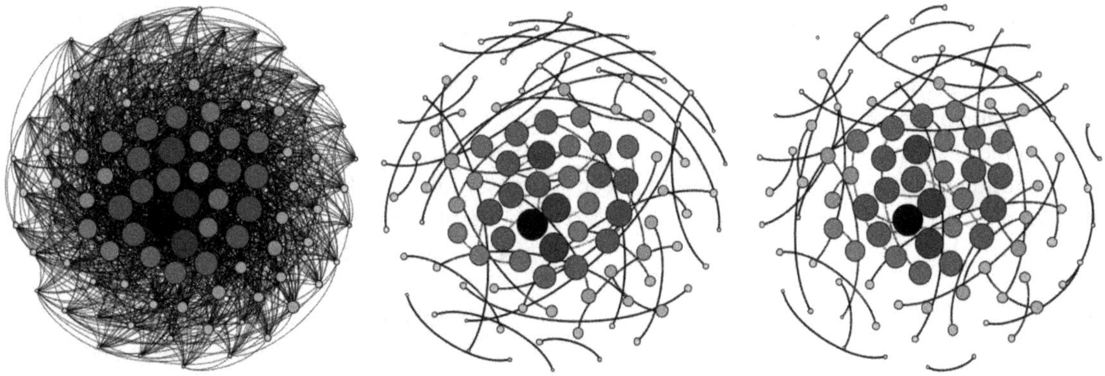

Original Scale-Free Network [A. Index: 0.39] | Maximal Node Matching [% Matches: 100%; A. Index: 0.93] | Maximal Assortative Matching [% Matches: 97%; A. Index: 0.94]

Fig. 38 Scale-free network (100 nodes)—BA model: initial—3 nodes; 20 links added per node introduction [spectral radius ratio for node degree: 1.16]

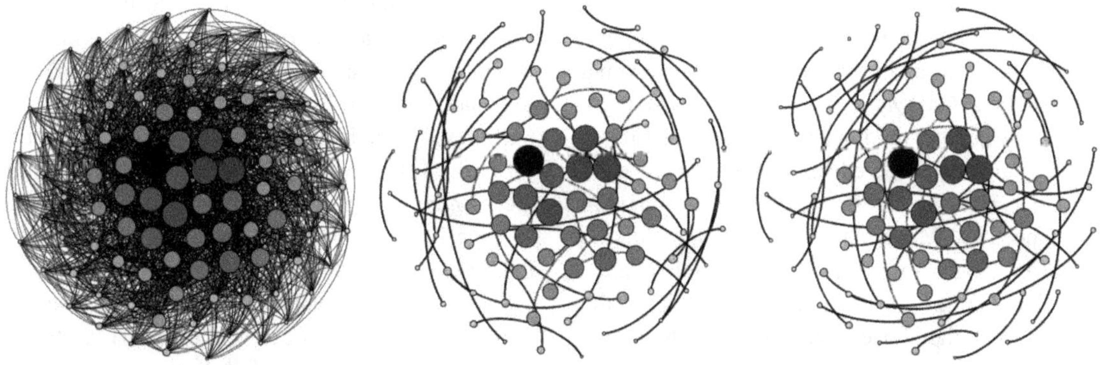

Original Scale-Free Network [A. Index: 0.26] | Maximal Node Matching [% Matches: 100%; A. Index: 0.89] | Maximal Assortative Matching [% Matches: 98%; A. Index: 0.93]

Fig. 39 Scale-free network (100 nodes)—BA model: initial—10 nodes; 20 links added per node introduction [spectral radius ratio for node degree: 1.14]

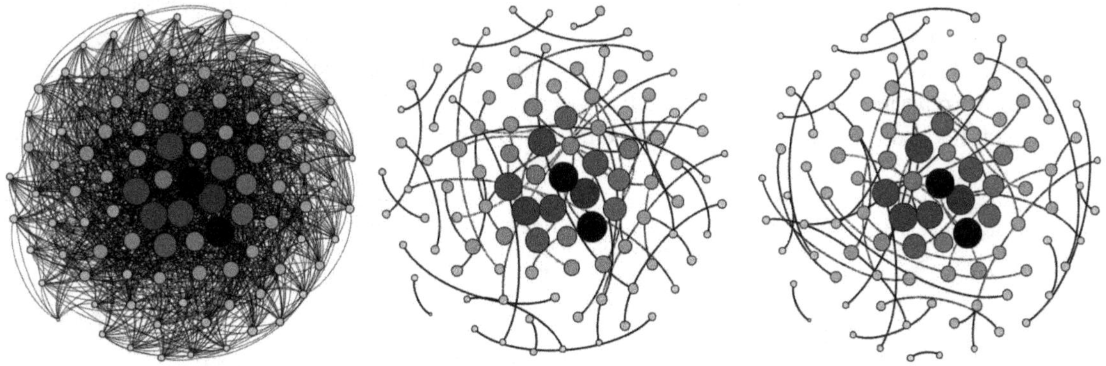

Original Scale-Free Network [A. Index: -0.01] | Maximal Node Matching [% Matches: 100%; A. Index: 0.80] | Maximal Assortative Matching [% Matches: 97%; A. Index: 0.88]

Fig. 40 Scale-free network (100 nodes)—BA model: initial—20 nodes; 20 links added per node introduction [spectral radius ratio for node degree: 1.13]

of the nodes decreases (vindicated by relatively lower values for the spectral radius ratio for node degree, as in Figs. 35, 36, 37, 38, 39, 40), facilitating the two algorithms (especially, the MAM algorithm) to pair similar nodes (with respect to node degree). The A.Index of the MAM is significantly larger than that of the MNM for scale-free networks that have a lower number of new links added per node introduction (as large as by a difference of 0.4); as we increase the number of links added per node introduction, the A.Index of MNM approaches to that of the MAM. Though there is a tradeoff expected between A.Index and the % of node matches, the % of node matches incurred with the MAM is only about 3–9 % low compared to the % of node matches incurred with the MNM (the larger differences are observed when the number of new links added per node introduction is low).

7 Maximal dissortative matching

Though the focus and objective of this paper is to develop an algorithm to find a maximal matching whose assortative index is maximum (close to 1), in this section, we want to illustrate that the proposed maximal assortative matching (MAM) algorithm (of Sect. 2) can also be used to determine a maximal matching whose assortative index is minimum (close to -1). We refer to the problem of finding a maximal matching with minimum assortative index as the maximal dissortative matching (MDM) problem. The MAM algorithm has to be only slightly modified to determine an MDM: instead of preferring to include edges with a lower assortative weight (to maximize the assortative index of the maximal matching), we need to include the uncovered edge with the largest assortative weight (to minimize the assortative index of the maximal matching) in each iteration. We refer to the MAM algorithm with the above modification as the MDM algorithm. The definition of the assortative weight remains the same as before, that is, the assortative weight of an uncovered edge (u, v) is the product of the number of uncovered edges adjacent to (u, v) and the absolute value of the difference in the node weights for the end vertices u and v.

The pseudo-code for the MDM algorithm to minimize the assortative index is shown in Fig. 41. The sub routines *FindAssortativeWeights* and *RemoveEdges* remain the same as before (see Sect. 2). We repeated the simulations of Sects. 3–6 for the MDM algorithm and averaged the results as we did before in these sections. The results are presented in Table 3 (for real-world network graphs) and in Figs. 42, 43, 44, 45 and 46 for the theoretical models-based complex networks. Since the maximal node matching (MNM) algorithm works independent of the node weights, we do not show any comparison of the MDM algorithm with the MNM algorithm. The results presented in the earlier sections comparing the MAM (for maximizing the assortative index) with that of the MNM algorithm and the results presented in this section (comparing the MDM and MAM) would be sufficient to draw conclusions about the relative performance of the MDM vis-a-vis the MNM.

7.1 Analysis for real-world network graphs

The results presented in Table 3 illustrate that for four of the six real-world network graphs, the maximal dissortative matching algorithm is not effective as the maximal assortative matching algorithm in optimizing the assortative index (A.Index). Though the assortative index values for the MDM for each of the six real-world network graphs are negative, the A.Index values for four of the six network graphs (US College Football Network, Dolphins' Social Network, US Politics Books Network, US Airports Network) are not that close to the optimal value of -1 compared to the proximity of the A.Index values observed for the MAM to the optimal value of 1. For the Karate Club Network and the Word Adjacencies Network, the assortativity index values observed for the MDM are relatively more closer or at the same distance to the targeted optimal value (-1) vis-a-vis the MAM to the targeted optimal value of 1. Except the Dolphins' Social Network for which the Maximal Dissortative Matching sustained a % of node matches that is 10 % larger than that incurred with maximal assortative matching, for all the other five real-world network graphs, the difference in the % of node matches between the two maximal matching strate-

Fig. 41 Pseudo-code for the maximal dissortative matching (MDM) algorithm

Input: Graph $G = (V, E)$, where weight $w(v) \in \mathbb{R}$ for every $v \in V$
Output: Maximal Dissortativity Matching, *MDM*
Auxiliary Variables: *UncoveredEdges*
Initialization: *UncoveredEdges* = *E*; *MDM* = ϕ
Begin *MDM Algorithm*
    FindAssortativityWeights(*UncoveredEdges*)
    while (*UncoveredEdges* $\neq \phi$) **do**
        $\text{Edge } (u, v) = \left\{ (p,q) \mid \underset{(p,q) \in UncoveredEdges}{Max}[AssortativityWeight(p,q)] \right\}$
        $MDM = MDM \cup \{(u, v)\}$
        $UncoveredEdges = UncoveredEdges - \{(u, v)\}$
        RemoveEdges((u, v), *UncoveredEdges*)
        FindAssortativityWeights(*UncoveredEdges*)
    end while
    return *MDM*
End *MDM Algorithm*

Table 3 Analysis of real-world networks for maximal dissortative and maximal assortative matching

#	Real-world network	Network A.Index	Maximal assortative matching (MAM)		Maximal dissortative matching (MDM)	
			% Node matches	A.Index	% Node matches	A.Index
(i)	US College Football Net.	−0.04	95	0.81	93	−0.48
(ii)	Dolphins' Social Net.	−0.04	73	0.82	83	−0.78
(iii)	US Politics Books Net.	−0.02	86	0.71	84	−0.51
(iv)	Karate Club Net.	−0.48	71	−0.13	70	−0.56
(v)	Word Adjacencies Net.	−0.10	78	0.50	79	−0.50
(vi)	US Airports 1997 Net.	−0.21	68	0.87	66	−0.24

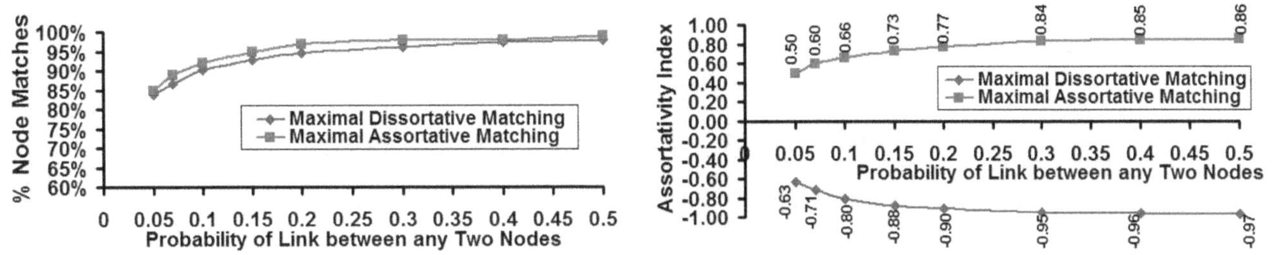

Fig. 42 Random networks: comparison of maximal dissortative matching and maximal assortative matching [node degree as node weights]

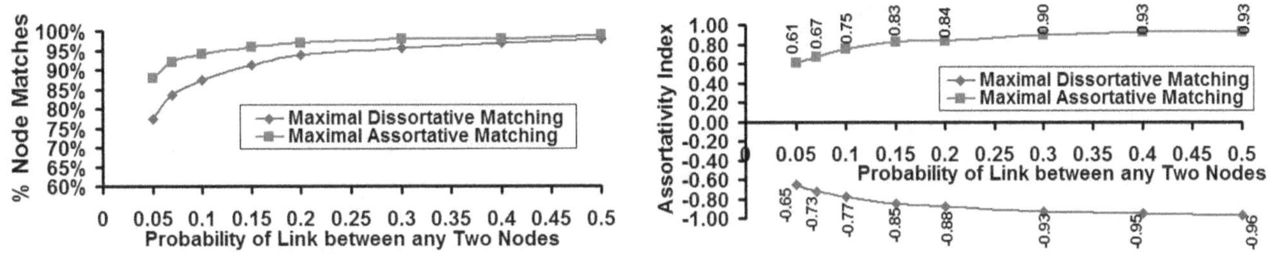

Fig. 43 Random networks: comparison of maximal dissortative matching and maximal assortative matching [random node weights]

gies (MAM and MDM) is only within a ±2 % difference. The study conducted here could be used as a framework to decide which of the two maximal matching strategies (maximal assortative matching or maximal dissortative matching) would be relatively more effective/optimal (with respect to the proximity of the assortative index to the targeted optimal value) for a real-world network graph and accordingly the particular matching strategy could be applied.

7.2 Analysis for random network graphs

The results presented for random network graphs with node degree as node weights (Fig. 42) illustrate that the assortative index values obtained with maximal dissortative matching (MDM) is more close to the targeted optimal value (−1) compared to the closeness of the assortative index values obtained with the maximal assortative matching (MAM) to the targeted optimal value (1). On the other hand, though the % of node matches obtained with maximal dissortative matching appears to be less than that obtained with the maximal assortative matching, the difference in the % of node matches is within 2–3 % for all values of p_{link} and by observing the nature of the increase in the % of node matches with the two maximal matching strategies, we could say that the difference in the % of node matches would only further narrow down with increase in the p_{link} value. The results of Fig. 42 thus illustrate that for random network graphs with node degree as node weights, it would be more apt to target a maximal dissortative matching compared to a maximal assortative matching on the basis of the proximity of the assortative index to the targeted optimal value (−1 for MDM and +1 for MAM).

When we run the MDM algorithm on random network graphs (that evolved using the Erdos–Renyi model) with randomly generated node weights in the range (0, …, 1], we observe (from Fig. 43) the assortativity index values for the maximal dissortative matching to be very close to that of the assortativity index values illustrated in Fig. 42 for the

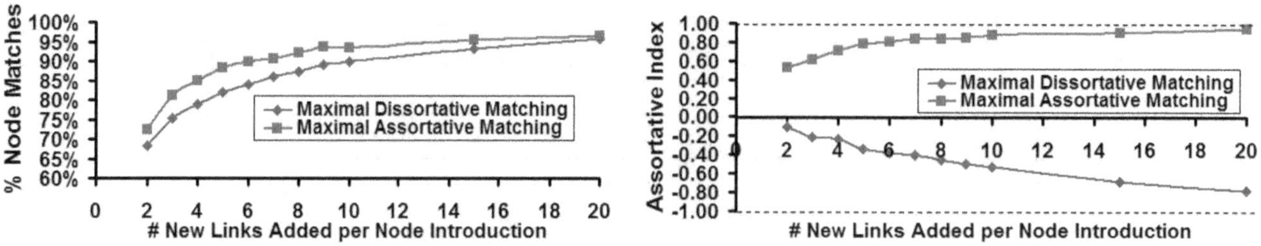

Fig. 44 Scale-free networks: comparison of maximal dissortative matching and maximal assortative matching (initial # nodes: 3; total nodes: 100)

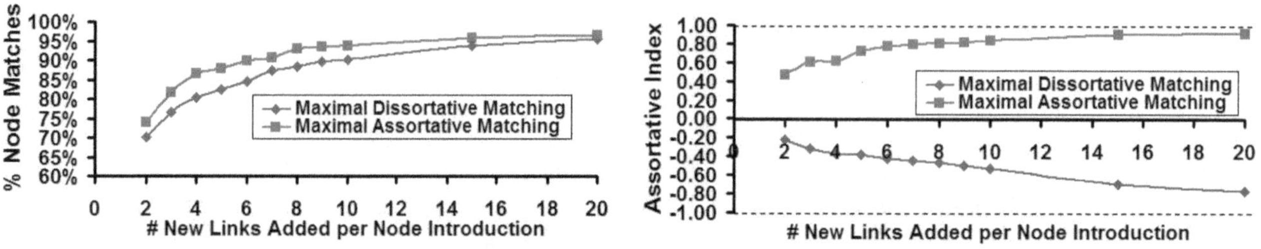

Fig. 45 Scale-free networks: comparison of maximal dissortative matching and maximal assortative matching (initial # nodes: 10; total nodes: 100)

maximal dissortative matching obtained on random network graphs with node degree as node weights (the difference in A.Index is within ± 0.03); the % of node matches obtained for the maximal dissortative matching with random node weights is at most 7 % lower than that obtained for the maximal dissortative matching with node degree as node weights.

While comparing the results obtained for the maximal assortative matching and maximal dissortative matching obtained on random network graphs with random node weights, we observe the assortativity index values of the maximal dissortative matching to be relatively more closer to the targeted optimal value of -1 compared to that of the closeness of the assortativity index values of the maximal assortative matching to its targeted optimal value of 1. Thus (like in the case of random network graphs with node degree as node weights), we could still say that for random network graphs with random node weights, it would be more apt to aim for a maximal dissortative matching compared to a maximal assortativity matching on the basis of the proximity of the assortative index to the targeted optimal value.

7.3 Analysis for scale-free network graphs

Figures 44, 45 and 46 present the results of the execution of the MDM and MAM algorithms on scale-free network graphs that evolve from the BA model (described in Sect. 6); the node degree is used as node weights for the assortativity calculations. The simulation conditions are the same as those used in Sect. 6: the values for the initial number of nodes (n_{init}) are 3, 10 and 20; the values for the number of new links added per node introduction ($links_{\text{new}}$) are: 2, 3, 4, 5, 6, 7, 8, 9, 10, 15 and 20. The results presented in Figs. 44, 45 and 46 are the average of 100 trial runs of the simulations for each of the above combinations of the n_{init} and $links_{\text{new}}$ values. Overall, for a given operating condition (n_{init}, $links_{\text{new}}$), we observe the assortativity index values for a maximal assortative matching to be relatively more closer to the targeted optimal value of 1 vis-a-vis the closeness of the assortativity index values for a maximal dissortative matching to the targeted optimal value of -1. Likewise, the % of node matches observed with the maximal assortative matching is slightly larger than that obtained with the maximal dissortative matching for all operating conditions (the difference could be at most 7 %). For a given n_{init}, the % of node matches between the two maximal matching strategies is larger at lower values of $links_{\text{new}}$ and the difference narrows down as we increase the value of $links_{\text{new}}$. Thus, overall, maximal assortative matching would be relatively more apt for scale-free networks with respect to the proximity towards the targeted optimal value for the assortative index vis-a-vis the maximal dissortative matching (1 for MAM; -1 for MDM).

With regard to the nature of increase or decrease with respect to the each of the two operating parameters, we observe the following: For a given value of $links_{\text{new}}$, as we increase the n_{init} value, the values for the assortativity index for a maximal dissortative matching get more closer to the targeted optimal value of -1. This is contrary to what has been observed for maximal assortative matching: for a given value of $links_{\text{new}}$, as we increase the n_{init} value, the values for the assortativity index for a maximal assortative matching move farther away from the targeted optimal value of 1. On the contrary, for a given n_{init} value, as we increase $links_{\text{new}}$, we observe the assortativity index values for the maximal assortative matching to get relatively more

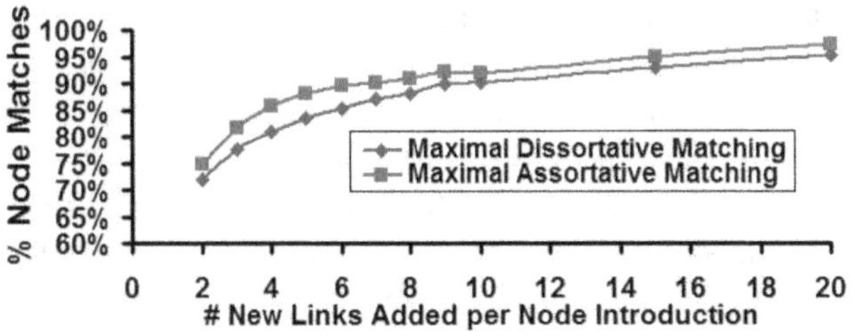

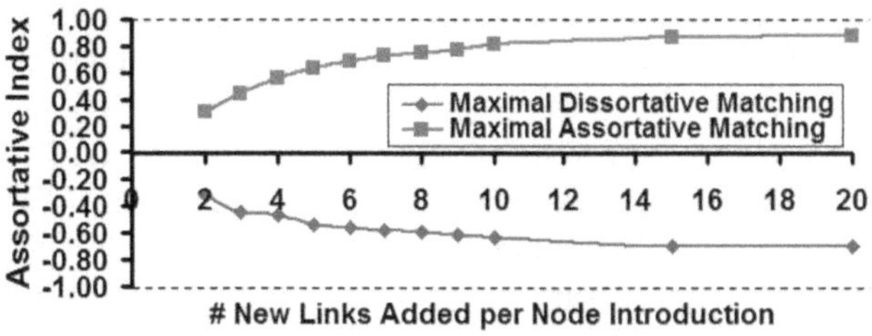

Fig. 46 Scale-free networks: comparison of maximal dissortative matching and maximal assortative matching (initial # nodes: 20; total nodes: 100)

closer to the targeted optimal value (1) compared to what is observed for the assortativity index values for the maximal dissortative matching with respect to the target optimal value (−1).

7.4 Correlation with the degree distribution for real-world networks and scale-free networks

An interesting observation from the results presented in Figs. 44, 45, 46 and Table 3 is that the larger the magnitude of the difference in the assortativity index (A.Index) values for the MAM and MDM (i.e., $\text{A.Index}_{\text{MAM}} - \text{A.Index}_{\text{MDM}}$) with respect to node degree, the smaller the spectral radius ratio for node degree (i.e., the smaller the variation in the node degree) for the corresponding network and vice-versa. For example, in Table 3, the magnitude of difference in the assortativity index values between the MAM and MDM of the US College Football network (with a spectral radius ratio for node degree 1.01) is $0.81 - (-0.48) = 1.29$; on the other hand, for the Karate Club network (with a spectral radius ratio for node degree 1.46), the magnitude of the difference between the assortativity index values for the MAM and MDM is $-0.13 - (-0.56) = 0.43$.

For a given initial number of nodes (n_{init}) during the evolution of a scale-free network, we could observe that the difference in the assortative index values for the MAM and MDM gets larger with increase in the values for the number of new links ($links_{\text{new}}$) added per node introduction (which leads to a decrease in the spectral radius ratio for node degree). To get a better understanding of this relationship, we compiled the results observed for the assortative index (A.Index) of MAM and MDM obtained for scale-free networks with different n_{init} and $links_{\text{new}}$ values used in the simulations, and plotted the difference ($\text{A.Index}_{\text{MAM}} - \text{A.Index}_{\text{MDM}}$) vs. the Spectral radius ratio for node degree in a single plot: we observe an inverse relationship (see Fig. 47) between the spectral radius ratio for node degree and the difference between the assortativity index values for MAM and MDM; the correlation coefficient is −0.90. Note that the larger the difference between the A.Index values for MAM and MDM, the more closer the A.Index values of the respective maximal matching to their targeted optimal values (−1 for MDM and 1 for MAM) and vice-versa. Hence, the correlation discussed here between the spectral radius ratio for node degree and the difference between the A.Index values for the maximal a(di)ssortative matching indicate that for scale-free networks with a larger variation in node degree, it is less likely for the assortative index of a maximal assortative or maximal dissortative matching to be closer to the targeted optimal value, and vice-versa.

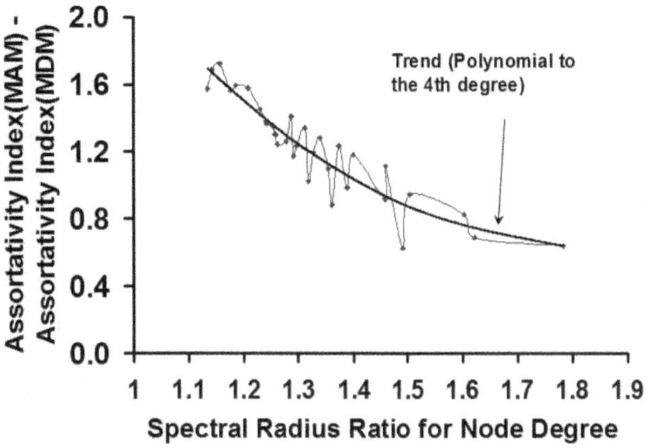

Fig. 47 Scale-free networks: correlation between spectral radius ratio for node degree and the difference between the assortativity index values for maximal assortative matching (MAM) and maximal dissortative matching (MDM)

In the case of theoretically generated random networks (from the Erdos–Renyi model), since the spectral radius ratio for node degree is more likely to be close to its minimum value of 1.0 and less variation is expected among the nodes with respect to degree, we do not attempt to correlate the spectral radius ratio for node degree and the difference in the assortativity index values between the MAM and MDM for random networks.

8 Related work

Before the spurge in interest for social network analysis, the graphs considered for maximum matching are typically bipartite graphs wherein there exists two sets of vertices (with no edges between vertices in the same set) and the edges connect the vertices from one set to the other set. Given a bipartite graph with no edge weights, the maximum matching problem would be about determining the maximum number of matches between the vertices across the two sets of the graph. If the edges of a bipartite graph have weights, the maximum matching problem would be about determining the set of matching edges (no two edges in the set have overlapping vertices) such that the sum of the edge weights is the maximum. The maximum matching problem for bipartite graphs could be optimally solved using well-known polynomial-time algorithms such as the Edmonds–Karp algorithm [22].

The maximal assortative matching problem has been so far not considered in the literature for bipartite graphs. Instead, a related problem, called the stable matching problem, was considered for bipartite graphs and is defined as follows: given a set of preferences for each vertex of the two partitions of a bipartite graph, a matching of the vertices from one partition to another partition is considered to be stable if there does not exist any pair of vertices (A, B) such that A is matched to some other vertex that is less preferred than B and likewise, B is matched to some other vertex that is less preferred than A. The Gale–Shapley algorithm [23] is a well-known algorithm for stable matching in bipartite graphs with an equal number of vertices in both the partitions. We do not see any possible extension of this algorithm or any other stable matching algorithm proposed for bipartite graphs to determine maximal assortative or maximal dissortative matching for arbitrary network graphs.

If a maximum matching is needed for directed network graphs, the common strategy in the literature is to get the bipartite equivalent of the network graph and apply the Edmonds–Karp or any other algorithm for determining maximum matching in bipartite graphs. The problem of determining the bipartite equivalent for a directed graph is an NP-hard problem [24]. A well-known heuristic using clique covering has been proposed in [25] for transforming a directed graph to a bipartite graph. In [26], an alternate strategy was proposed using the concept of structural controllability [27] to determine maximum matching in directed complex network graphs, bypassing the need to first transform to a bipartite graph. This algorithm is targeted at maximizing the number of nodes that are part of a matching and is not designed to maximize or minimize the assortativity index.

In [28], the authors showed that for networks with binomial degree distribution, the maximum and minimum assortativity vary with the density of the networks. Motivated by this observation, the authors in [29] introduced an algorithm to compute a network with maximal or minimal assortativity given a vector of valid node degrees using degree-preserving rewiring [30] and weighted b-matching [31]. Degree-preserving link rewiring is effective in decreasing or increasing the assortativity of a network graph without affecting the degree distribution of the vertices. However, neither the work in [28] nor in [29] could be extended to determine a maximal a(di)ssortative matching of the edges of the graph. It was also shown in [28] that for networks whose degree distribution is binomial (like the Erdos–Renyi model-based random network graphs), the maximum assortativity and minimum assortativity are asymptotically anti-symmetric. This observation correlates well with our observation in Sect. 7 that the values for the assortative index for maximum assortative matching are comparable enough to the absolute values of the assortative index for maximum dissortative matching, especially in the case of the random network graphs with random node weights as well as with node degree as node weights.

In [5,32], Piraveenan et al. explore degree assortativity in complex networks and propose that a perfect degree assortativity is possible if the network could be fragmented into sub networks, whereby each sub network is a complete network; on the other hand, perfect degree assortativity has been considered to be relatively more difficult to achieve in complex networks, except the case of complete bipartite graphs [33] (like a star graph). Even though perfect degree assortativity and perfect degree dissortativity are difficult to be observed in all kinds of complex networks, in this paper, we show that it is possible to find a matching of the vertices such that the assortative index is significantly close to the optimal value (especially in the case of maximal assortative matching).

In [34], the authors repeatedly employed degree-preserving link rewiring on a given complex network graph (generated from a theoretical model) to obtain an ensemble of graphs and measured the range of values for the assortativity and clustering coefficient for the ensemble of graphs; the broader the range of the values for the assortativity and clustering coefficient, the narrower the degree distribution of the original graph and vice-versa. In Sect. 7.4, we discuss the correlation between the difference in the assortativity index values (calculated based on node degree) for the MAM and MDM vis-a-vis the spectral radius ratio for node degree in a scale-free network. We show that instead of additionally considering clustering coefficient (as in [34]), the assortativity index values of the maximal assortative matching and maximal dissortative matching alone could be used to characterize the variation in the degree distribution for scale-free networks.

The problem of determining a maximal matching with minimum cardinality for the set of edges constituting the matching is an NP-hard problem [35]. It is equivalent to the problem of finding a minimum edge dominating set [36]—to find the smallest set of edges of the graph such that each edge in the set covers itself and covers one or more adjacent edges as well as satisfies the matching constraint (no two edges in the set have a common end vertex). The computational time-complexity of the heuristics [35–37] to determine approximations to the minimum edge dominating set is $O((E + V)\log E)$ for a graph of V vertices and E edges. Similarly, another related problem: the problem of determining a connected dominating set of minimum size (to find the smallest set of connected vertices such that each vertex in the set covers itself and one or more of its adjacent vertices) is also a NP-hard problem. Efficient heuristics [38,39] of computational-time complexity $O((E + V)\log V)$ have been proposed in the literature to determine approximations to minimum connected dominating sets for complex network graphs. Though the heuristics for both the minimum edge dominating set and minimum node connected dominating set problems have a computational time-complexity that is smaller than our proposed $O(EV\log V)$ heuristic for maximal assortative matching, these heuristics cannot be applied for the problem of focus in this paper.

The problem of focus in this paper is the maximal independent edge set problem [7] wherein we want to find the largest set of independent edges such that no two edges have a common end vertex. Note that heuristics (e.g., [37]) for the minimum edge dominating set problem cannot be applied to determine the maximal node matching and the maximal a(di)ssortative matching because heuristics for the minimum edge set problem are more likely to determine the set of edges such that each edge in the set covers a larger number of adjacent edges. Similarly, heuristics for the minimum connected dominating set problem prefer to include nodes that could cover several adjacent nodes (and the associated edges). Hence, using the heuristics for minimum edge dominating set or minimum connected dominating set for determining a maximal node matching or maximal assortative matching of the edges would only reduce the number of independent edges that become part of the matching. The maximal matching algorithms developed in this paper take the approach of preferring to include edges that cover a smaller number of adjacent edges so that the number of independent edges determined could be as large as possible. To the best of our knowledge, we have not come across a maximal matching algorithm that is aimed at simultaneously maximizing the a(di)ssortativity of the matching as well as maximizing the cardinality of the matching for complex network graphs. In this perspective, the maximal assortative matching and maximal dissortative matching algorithms proposed in this paper are significant contributions to the literature for complex network graphs and analysis.

9 Conclusions

The results of the execution of the maximal assortative matching (MAM), maximal dissortative matching (MDM) and maximal node matching (MNM) algorithms on the complex network graphs generated from theoretical models as well as on the real-world network graphs convey useful insights. We observe that the MAM and MDM algorithms could be, respectively, used to determine maximal assortative matching and maximal dissortative matching (matching nodes of similar weights or dissimilar weights, depending on the application) for various complex network graphs (including social networks) without any significant loss in the % of node matches vis-a-vis the maximal node matching. On the other hand, we observe the assortative index of a maximal node matching to be far away from the targeted optimal values of -1 and 1 (indicating that maximal node matching is more arbitrary with respect to the pairing of the vertices); however, such an arbitrary matching is of no use for networks that require the users (nodes) to be matched to other nodes of similar or dissimilar weights, as in the case of social networks. In the case of the complex network graphs generated from theoretical models, we have also identified which of the two maximal matching strategies (MAM or MDM) are likely to incur an assortativity index that is closer to their targeted optimal values (1 for MAM and -1 for MDM). We observe the random network graphs (generated from the Erdos–Renyi model) to be more apt for a maximal dissortative matching (MDM) and the scale-free network graphs (generated from the Barabasi–Albert model) to be more apt for a maximal assortative matching (MAM). We also observe that the difference between the assortative index values for an MAM and MDM is negatively correlated to the variation in the node degree for scale-free networks generated according to the BA model as well as for the real-world network graphs studied in this paper.

References

1. Edmonds, J.: Paths, trees, and flowers. Can. J. Math. **17**, 449–467 (1965)
2. Micali, S., Vazirani, V.: An $O(V^{1/2}E)$ Algorithm for Finding Maximum Matching in General Graphs. In: Proceedings of the 21st Annual Symposium on Foundations of Computer Science, pp. 17–27, Syracuse, NY, USA (1980)
3. Newman, M.E.J.: Assortative mixing in networks. Phys. Rev. Lett. **89**, 208701 (2002)
4. Piraveenan, M., Prokopenko, M., Zomaya, A.: Local assortativeness in scale-free networks. Europhys. Lett. **84**(2), 28002 (2008)
5. Piraveenan, M., Prokopenko, M., Zomaya, A.: Assortative mixing in directed biological networks. IEEE/ACM Trans. Comput. Biol. Bioinform. **9**(1), 66–78 (2012)
6. Newman, M.E.J.: Networks: An Introduction, 1st edn. Oxford University Press, Oxford (2010)
7. Cormen, T.H., Leiserson, C.E., Rivest, R.L., Stein, C.: Introduction to Algorithms, 3rd edn. MIT Press, Cambridge (2009)
8. Strang, G., Linear Algebra and Its Applications, 4th edn. Brooks Cole, Pacific Grove (2006)
9. Caldarelli, G.: Scale-Free Networks: Complex Webs in Nature and Technology, 1st edn. Oxford University Press, Oxford (2007)

10. Erdos, P., Renyi, A.: On random graphs. Publ. Math. **6**, 290–297 (1959)
11. Barabasi, A.-L., Albert, R.: Emergence of scaling in random networks. Science **286**(5439), 509–512 (1999)
12. Demange, M., Ekim, T.: Minimum maximal matching is NP-hard in regular bipartite graphs. Theory and Applications of Models of Computation. Lecture Notes in Computer Science, vol. 4978, pp. 364–374 (2008)
13. Girvan, M., Newman, M.: Community structure in social and biological networks. Proc. Natl. Acad. Sci. U. S. A. **19**(12), 7821–7826 (2002)
14. Lusseau, D., Schneider, K., Boisseau, O.J., Haase, P., Slooten, E., Dawson, S.M.: The bottlenose dolphin community of Doubtful Sound features a large proportion of long-lasting associations. Behav. Ecol. Sociobiol. **54**, 396–405 (2003)
15. Krebs, V.: Working in the connected world: book network. J. Inst. Health Rec. Inf. Manag. **4**(1), 87–90 (2000)
16. Zachary, W.W.: An information flow model for conflict and fission in small groups. J. Anthropol. Res. **33**(4), 452–473 (1977)
17. Newman, M.: Finding community structure in networks using the eigenvectors of matrices. Phys. Rev. E **74**, 036104 (2006)
18. Pajek Datasets: http://vlado.fmf.uni-lj.si/pub/networks/data/map/USAir97.net. Last accessed 25 May 2015
19. Meghanathan, N.: Spectral Radius as a Measure of Variation in Node Degree for Complex Network Graphs. In: Proceedings of the 3rd International Conference on Digital Contents and Applications, pp. 30–33, Hainan, China (2014)
20. Cherven, K.: Network Graph Analysis and Visualization with Gephi, 1st edn. Packt Publishing, Birmingham (2013)
21. Fruchterman, T.M.J., Reingold, E.M.: Graph drawing by force-directed placement. Softw. Pract. Exp. **21**(11), 1129–1164 (1991)
22. Edmonds, J., Karp, R.M.: Theoretical improvements in algorithmic efficiency for network flow problems. J. ACM **19**(2), 248–264 (1972)
23. Shoham, Y., Leyton-Brown, K.: Multiagent Systems: Algorithmic, Game-Theoretic, and Logical Foundations, 1st edn. Cambridge University Press, Cambridge (2009)
24. Kalman, R.E.: Mathematical description of linear dynamical systems. J. Soc. Ind. Appl. Math. Ser. A Control **1**(2), 152–192 (1963)
25. Guillaume, J.-L., Latapy, M.: Bipartite graphs as models of complex networks. Physica A Stat. Mech. Appl. **371**(2), 795–813 (2006)
26. Chatterjee, A., Das, D., Naskar, M.K., Pal, N., Mukherjee, A.: Heuristic for Maximum Matching in Directed Complex Networks. In: Proceedings of the International Conference on Advances in Computing, Communications and Informatics, pp. 1146–1151 (2013)
27. Liu, Y.-Y., Slotine, J.-J., Barabasi, A.-L.: Controllability of complex networks. Nature **473**, 167–173 (2011)
28. Wang, H., Winterbach, W., Van Mieghem, P.: Assortativity of complementary graphs. Eur. Phys. J. B **83**(2), 203–214 (2011)
29. Winterbach, W., de Ridder, D., Wang, H.J., Reinders, M., Van Mieghem, P.: Do greedy assortativity optimization algorithms produce good results? Eur. Phys. J. B **5**, 151–160 (2012)
30. Maslov, S., Sneppen, K.: Specificity and stability in topology of protein networks. Science **296**(5569), 910–913 (2002)
31. Muller-Hannemann, M., Schwartz, A.: Implementing weighted b-matching algorithms: insights from a computational study. Algorithm Engineering and Computation. Lecture Notes in Computer Science, vol. 1619, pp. 18–36 (1999)
32. Piraveenan, M., Prokopenko, M., Zomaya, A.: Assortativeness and information in scale-free networks. Eur. Phys. J. B **67**(3), 291–300 (2009)
33. Van Mieghem, P., Wang, H., Ge, X., Tang, S., Kuipers, F.: Influence of assortativity and degree-preserving rewiring on the spectra of networks. Eur. Phys. J. B **76**(4), 643–652 (2010)
34. Holme, P., Zhao, J.: Exploring the assortativity-clustering space of a network's degree sequence. Phys. Rev. E **75**, 046111 (2007)
35. Yannakakis, M., Gavril, F.: Edge dominating sets in graphs. SIAM J. Appl. Math. **38**(3), 364–372 (1980)
36. Horton, J.D., Kilakos, K.: Minimum edge dominating sets. SIAM J. Discrete Math. **6**(3), 375–387 (1993)
37. Cardinal, J., Labbe, M., Langerman, S., Levy, E., Melot, H.: A Tight Analysis of the Maximal Matching Heuristic. Lecture Notes in Computer Science, vol. 3595, pp. 701–709 (2005)
38. Meghanathan, N.: Centrality-based connected dominating sets for complex network graphs. Int. J. Interdiscip. Telecommun. Netw. **6**(2), 1–19 (2014)
39. Erciyes, K.: Complex Networks: An Algorithmic Perspective, 1st edn. CRC Press, Boca Raton (2014)

9

Verification of temporal-causal network models by mathematical analysis

Jan Treur[1]

Abstract Usually dynamic properties of models can be analysed by conducting simulation experiments. But sometimes, as a kind of prediction properties can also be found by calculations in a mathematical manner, without performing simulations. Examples of properties that can be explored in such a manner are:

- whether some values for the variables exist for which no change occurs (stationary points or equilibria), and how such values may depend on the values of the parameters of the model and/or the initial values for the variables
- whether certain variables in the model converge to some limit value (equilibria) and how this may depend on the values of the parameters of the model and/or the initial values for the variables
- whether or not certain variables will show monotonically increasing or decreasing values over time (monotonicity)
- how fast a convergence to a limit value takes place (convergence speed)
- whether situations occur in which no convergence takes place but in the end a specific sequence of values is repeated all the time (limit cycle)

Such properties found in an analytic mathematical manner can be used for verification of the model by checking them for the values observed in simulation experiments. If one of these properties is not fulfilled, then there will be some error in the implementation of the model. In this paper some methods to analyse such properties of dynamical models will be described and illustrated for the Hebbian learning model, and for dynamic connection strengths in social networks. The properties analysed by the methods discussed cover equilibria, increasing or decreasing trends, recurring patterns (limit cycles), and speed of convergence to equilibria.

1 Introduction

Usually dynamic properties of dynamic models can be analysed by conducting simulation experiments. But sometimes, as a kind of prediction properties can also be found by calculations in a mathematical manner, without performing simulations. Examples of properties that can be explored in such a manner are:

- whether some values for the variables exist for which no change occurs (stationary points or equilibria), and how such values may depend on the values of the parameters of the model and/or the initial values for the variables
- whether certain variables in the model converge to some limit value (equilibria) and how this may depend on the values of the parameters of the model and/or the initial values for the variables
- whether or not certain variables will show monotonically increasing or decreasing values over time (monotonicity)
- whether situations occur in which no convergence takes place but in the end a specific sequence of values is repeated all the time (limit cycle)

Mathematical techniques addressing such questions have been developed, starting with Poincaré [12,13]; see also[3,9, 11], and [7] for a historical perspective. Such types of prop-

✉ Jan Treur
j.treur@vu.nl

1 VU University Amsterdam, Behavioral Informatics Group, Amsterdam, The Netherlands

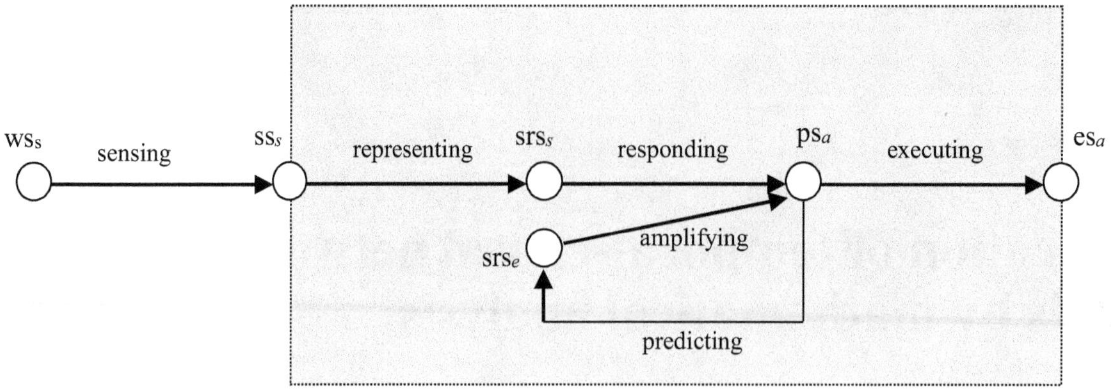

Fig. 1 Conceptual representation of an example model

erties found in an analytic mathematical manner can be used for verification of the model by checking them for the values observed in simulation experiments. If one of these properties is not fulfilled, then there will be some error in the implementation of the model. This particular use of mathematical analysis is the focus of this paper. In this paper some methods to analyse such properties of temporal-causal network models will be described and illustrated for some example models, including a Hebbian learning model, and a model for dynamic connection strengths in social networks. The properties analysed by the methods discussed cover equilibria, increasing or decreasing trends, and recurring patterns: limit cycles.

To get the idea, first the general set up is discussed in Sect. 2. This is illustrated in Sect. 3 by an analysis of a simple example as discussed in [17], Section 2.4.1, using sum and identity combination functions. In simulations it is observed for this example model that when a constant stimulus level occurs in the world, for each state its activation value increases from 0 to some value that is then kept forever, until the stimulus disappears: an equilibrium state. In subsequent sections three more general examples of this type of analysis for which equilibrium states occur are addressed: for a scaled sum combination function (Sect. 4), for Hebbian learning (Sect. 5), and for dynamic networks based on the homophily principle (Sect. 6). In Sect. 7 the analysis is discussed for a case in which no equilibrium state occurs, but instead a limit cycle pattern emerges.

2 How to verify a temporal-causal network model by mathematical analysis

A stationary point of a state occurs at some point in time if for this time point no change occurs: the graph is horizontal at that point. Stationary points are usually maxima or minima (peaks or dips) but sometimes also other stationary points may occur. An equilibrium occurs when for all states no change occurs. From the difference or differential equations describing the dynamics for a model it can be analysed when stationary points or equilibria occur. Moreover, it can be found when a certain state is increasing or decreasing when a state is not in a stationary point or equilibrium. First a definition for these notions is expressed; for example, see [3,9,11–13].

Definition (*increase, decrease, stationary point and equilibrium*) Let Y be a state

- Y has a *stationary point* at t if $\mathbf{d}Y(t)/\mathbf{d}t = 0$
- Y is *increasing* at t if $\mathbf{d}Y(t)/\mathbf{d}t > 0$
- Y is *decreasing* at t if $\mathbf{d}Y(t)/\mathbf{d}t < 0$

The model is in *equilibrium* a t if every state Y of the model has a stationary point at t.

To illustrate these notions, consider the example from [17], with conceptual representation depicted here in Fig. 1, and an example simulation shown in Fig. 2.

The systematic transformation from a conceptual representation of a temporal-causal model (as depicted in Fig. 1) into a numerical representation of this temporal-causal model works as follows [17]:

- At each time point t each state Y in the model has a real number value in the interval [0, 1], denoted by $Y(t)$
- At each time point t each state X connected to state Y has an *impact* on Y defined as $\mathbf{impact}_{X,Y}(t) = \omega_{X,Y} X(t)$ where $\omega_{X,Y}$ is the weight of the connection from X to Y
- The *aggregated impact* of multiple states X_i on Y at t is determined using a *combination function* $\mathbf{c}_Y(..)$:

$$\begin{aligned}\mathbf{aggimpact}_Y(t) &= \mathbf{c}_Y(\mathbf{impact}_{X_1,Y}(t), \ldots, \mathbf{impact}_{X_k,Y}(t)) \\ &= \mathbf{c}_Y(\omega_{X_1,Y} X_1(t), \ldots, \omega_{X_k,Y} X_k(t))\end{aligned}$$

where X_i are the states with connections to state Y

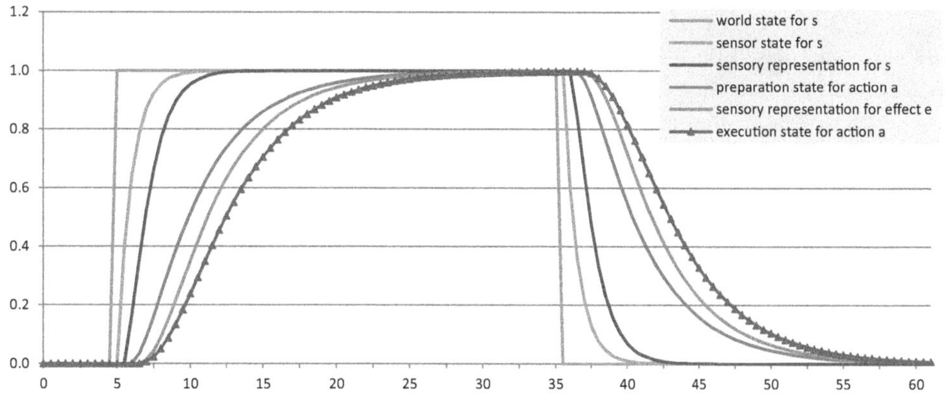

Fig. 2 Simulation example for the model depicted in Fig. 1 using identity and sum combination functions for all states

- The effect of $\mathbf{aggimpact}_Y(t)$ on Y is exerted over time gradually, depending on *speed factor* η_Y:

$$Y(t + \Delta t) = Y(t) + \eta_Y[\mathbf{aggimpact}_Y(t) - Y(t)]\Delta t$$

or

$$\mathbf{d}Y(t)/\mathbf{d}t = \eta_Y[\mathbf{aggimpact}_Y(t) - Y(t)]$$

- Thus, the following *difference* and *differential equation* for Y are obtained:

$$\begin{aligned} Y(t+\Delta t) &= Y(t) \\ &\quad + \eta_Y[\mathbf{c}_Y(\omega_{X_1,Y}X_1(t), \ldots, \omega_{X_k,Y}X_k(t)) - Y(t)]\Delta t \\ \mathbf{d}Y(t)/\mathbf{d}t &= \eta_Y[\mathbf{c}_Y(\omega_{X_1,Y}X_1(t), \ldots, \omega_{X_k,Y}X_k(t)) - Y(t)] \end{aligned}$$

For more details, see [17].

Combination functions used in this simple example are the scaled sum function and the identity function, and all connections have weight 1, except the connections to ps_a, which have weight 0.5.

In Fig. 2 it can be seen that as a result of the stimulus all states are increasing until time point 35, after which they start to decrease as the stimulus disappears. Just before time point 35 all states are almost stationary. If the stimulus is not taken away after this time point this trend is continued, and an equilibrium state is approximated. The question then is whether these observations based on one or more simulation experiments are in agreement with a mathematical analysis. If it is found out that they are in agreement with the mathematical analysis, then this provides some extent of evidence that the implemented model is correct. If they turn out not to be in agreement with the mathematical analysis, then this indicates that probably there is something wrong, and further inspection and correction has to be initiated.

Considering the differential equation for a temporal-causal network model more specific criteria can be found:

$$\mathbf{d}Y(t)/\mathbf{d}t = \eta_Y[\mathbf{aggimpact}_Y(t) - Y(t)]$$

with

$$\mathbf{aggimpact}_Y(t) = \mathbf{c}_Y(\omega_{X_1,Y}X_1(t), \ldots, \omega_{X_k,Y}X_k(t))$$

and $X_1, \ldots, X_k$ the states connected toward Y
For example, it can be concluded that

$$\begin{aligned} \mathbf{d}Y(t)/\mathbf{d}t > 0 &\Leftrightarrow \eta_Y[\mathbf{aggimpact}_Y(t) - Y(t)] > 0 \\ &\Leftrightarrow \mathbf{aggimpact}_Y(t) > Y(t) \\ &\Leftrightarrow \mathbf{c}_Y(\omega_{X_1,Y}X_1(t), \ldots, \omega_{X_k,Y}X_k(t)) > Y(t) \end{aligned}$$

In this manner the following criteria can be found.

2.1 Criteria for a temporal-causal network model: increase, decrease, stationary point and equilibrium

Let Y be a state and $X_1, \ldots, X_k$ the states connected toward Y. Then the following hold

Y has a stationary point at t	$\Leftrightarrow$	$\mathbf{aggimpact}_Y(t) = Y(t)$	$\Leftrightarrow$	$\mathbf{c}_Y(\omega_{X_1,Y}X_1(t), \ldots, \omega_{X_k,Y}X_k(t)) = Y(t)$
Y is increasing at t	$\Leftrightarrow$	$\mathbf{aggimpact}_Y(t) > Y(t)$	$\Leftrightarrow$	$\mathbf{c}_Y(\omega_{X_1,Y}X_1(t), \ldots, \omega_{X_k,Y}X_k(t)) > Y(t)$
Y is decreasing at $t < 0$	$\Leftrightarrow$	$\mathbf{aggimpact}_Y(t) < Y(t)$	$\Leftrightarrow$	$\mathbf{c}_Y(\omega_{X_1,Y}X_1(t), \ldots, \omega_{X_k,Y}X_k(t)) < Y(t)$
The model is in equilibrium a t	$\Leftrightarrow$	$\mathbf{aggimpact}_Y(t) = Y(t)$ for every state Y		
	$\Leftrightarrow$	$\mathbf{c}_Y(\omega_{X_1,Y}X_1(t), \ldots, \omega_{X_k,Y}X_k(t)) = Y(t)$ for every state Y		

These criteria can be used to verify (the implementation of) the model based on inspection of stationary points or equilibria in the following two different manners. Note that in a given simulation the stationary points that are identified are usually approximately stationary; how closely they are approximated depends on different aspects, for example on the step size, or on how long the simulation is done.

2.2 Verification by checking the criteria through substitution values from a simulation in the criteria

1. Generate a simulation
2. For a number of states Y identify stationary points with their time points t and state values $Y(t)$
3. For each of these stationary points for a state Y at time t identify the values $X_1(t), \ldots, X_k(t)$ at that time of the states $X_1, \ldots, X_k$ connected toward Y
4. Substitute all these values $Y(t)$ and $X_1(t), \ldots, X_k(t)$ in the criterion $\mathbf{c}_Y(\omega_{X_1,Y} X_1(t), \ldots, \omega_{X_k,Y} X_k(t)) = Y(t)$
5. If the equation holds (for example, with an accuracy < 10^{-2}), then this test succeeds, otherwise it fails
6. If this test fails, then it has to be explored were the error can be found

This verification method can be illustrated for the example of Figs. 1 and 2 as follows. For example, consider state ps_a with numerical representation

$$\begin{aligned}\text{ps}_a(t + \Delta t) = \text{ps}_a(t) \\ + \eta_{\text{ps}_a}[\omega_{\text{responding}}\text{srs}_s(t) \\ + \omega_{\text{amplifying}}\text{srs}_e(t) - \text{ps}_a(t)]\Delta t\end{aligned}$$

The equation expressing that a state of ps_a is stationary at time t is

$$\omega_{\text{responding}}\text{srs}_s(t) + \omega_{\text{amplifying}}\text{srs}_e(t) = \text{ps}_a(t)$$

At time point $t = 35$ (where all states are close to stationary) the following values occur: $\text{ps}_a(35) = 0.99903$, $\text{srs}_s(35) = 1.00000$ and $\text{srs}_e(35) = 0.99863$; moreover $\omega_{\text{responding}} = \omega_{\text{amplifying}} = 0.5$. All these values can be substituted in the above equation:

$$0.5 \times 1.00000 + 0.5 \times 0.99863 = 0.99903$$
$$0.999315 = 0.99903$$

It turns out that the equation is fulfilled with accuracy < 10^{-3}. This gives some evidence that the model as implemented indeed does what it was meant to do. If this is done for all other states, similar outcomes are found. This gives still more evidence. The step size Δt for the simulation here was 0.5, which is even not so small. For still more accurate results it is advisable to choose a smaller step size. So, having the equations for stationary points for all states provides a means to verify the implemented model in comparison to the model description. The equations for stationary points themselves can easily be obtained from the model description in a systematic manner.

Note that this method works without having to solve the equations, only substitution takes place; therefore, it works for any choice of combination function. Moreover, note that the method also works when there is no equilibrium but the values of the states fluctuate all the time, according to a recurring pattern (a limit cycle). In such cases for each state there are maxima (peaks) and minima (dips) which also are stationary. The method can be applied to such a type of stationary points as well; here it is still more important to choose a small step size as each stationary point occurs at just one time point. In Sect. 7 it will be discussed how the approach can be applied to such limit cycles.

There is still another method possible that is sometimes proposed; this method is applied for the case of an equilibrium (where all states have a stationary point simultaneously), and is based on solving the equations for the equilibrium values first. This can provide explicit expressions for equilibrium values in terms of the parameters of the model. Such expressions can be used to predict equilibrium values for specific simulations, based on the choice of parameter values. This method provides more than the previous method, but a major drawback is that it cannot be applied in all situations. For example, when logistic combination functions are used it cannot be applied. However, in some cases it still can be useful. The method goes as follows.

2.3 Verification by solving the equilibrium equations and comparing predicted equilibrium values to equilibrium values in a simulation

1. Consider the equilibrium equations for all states Y:

   $$\mathbf{c}_Y(\omega_{X_1,Y} X_1(t), \ldots, \omega_{X_k,Y} X_k(t)) = Y(t)$$

2. Leave the t out and denote the values as constants

   $$\mathbf{c}_Y(\omega_{X_1,Y}\underline{\mathbf{X}}_1, \ldots, \omega_{X_k,Y}\underline{\mathbf{X}}_k) = \underline{\mathbf{Y}}$$

   An equilibrium is a solution $\underline{\mathbf{X}}_1, \ldots, \underline{\mathbf{X}}_k$ of the following set of n equilibrium equations in the n states $X_1, \ldots, X_n$ of the model:

   $$\mathbf{c}_{X1}(\omega_{X_1,X_1}\underline{\mathbf{X}}_1, \ \ldots, \omega_{X_n,X_1}\underline{\mathbf{X}}_n) = \underline{\mathbf{X}}_1$$
   $$\ldots$$
   $$\mathbf{c}_{Xn}(\omega_{X_1,X_n}\underline{\mathbf{X}}_1, \ \ldots, \omega_{X_n,X_n}\underline{\mathbf{X}}_n) = \underline{\mathbf{X}}_n$$

3. Solve these equations mathematically in an explicit analytical form: for each state X_i a mathematical formula

$\underline{\mathbf{X}}_i = \ldots$ in terms of the parameters of the model (connection weights and parameters in the combination function $\mathbf{c}_{Xi}(..)$, such as the steepness σ and threshold τ in a logistic sum combination function); more than one solution is possible
4. Generate a simulation
5. Identify equilibrium values in this simulation
6. If for all states Y the predicted value $\underline{\mathbf{Y}}$ from a solution of the equilibrium equations equals the value for Y obtained from the simulation (for example, with an accuracy $<10^{-2}$), then this test succeeds, otherwise it fails
7. If this test fails, then it has to be explored where the error can be found

In Sect. 2.3 it will be illustrated how this method works for the example depicted in Figs. 1 and 2. In general, whether or not the equilibrium equations can be solved in an explicit analytical manner strongly depends on the form of the combination functions $\mathbf{c}_Y(\ldots)$. In a number of specific cases explicit analytical solutions can be found. Three examples of this are addressed in subsequent sections:

- for a (scaled) sum combination function (Sects. 3 and 4)
- for Hebbian learning (Sect. 5)
- for dynamic networks based on the homophily principle (Sect. 6)

However, there are also many cases in which an explicit analytical solution cannot be determined, for example, when logistic combination functions are used. In such cases equilibria can only be determined either by numerically solving the equations by some numerical approximation method, or by observing the behaviour of the model in simulation experiments. But in the latter case verification is not possible, as then only simulation results are available. An additional drawback is that in such cases specific values for the parameters of the model have to be chosen, whereas in the case of an explicit analytical solution a more generic expression can be obtained which depends, as a function, on the parameter values. For example, for the cases described in Sects. 3–6 expressions can be found for the equilibrium values in terms of the connection weights (for which no specific values are needed at forehand).

3 Mathematical analysis for equilibrium states: an example

Are there cases in which the types of behaviour considered above can be predicted without running a simulation? In particular, can equilibrium values be predicted, and how they depend on the specific values of the parameters of the model (e.g. connection weights, speed factors)? Below, these questions will be answered for a relatively simple example. Indeed it will turn out that in this case it is possible to predict the equilibrium values from the connection weights (the equilibrium values turn out to be independent of the speed factors, as long as these are nonzero). As a first step, consider the sensor state ss_s.

LP$_{\mathrm{ss}_s}$ Sensing a stimulus: determining values for state ss_s

$$\mathbf{d}\mathrm{ss}_s(t)/\mathbf{dt} = \eta_{\mathrm{ss}_s}[\omega_{\mathrm{sensing}}\mathrm{ws}_s(t) - \mathrm{ss}_s(t)]$$

Having an equilibrium value means that no change occurs at t: $\mathbf{d}\mathrm{ss}_s(t)/\mathbf{dt} = 0$. As it is assumed that η_{ss_s} is nonzero, this is equivalent to the following equilibrium equation for state ss_s, with $\underline{\mathbf{ws}}_s$ and $\underline{\mathbf{ss}}_s$ the equilibrium values for the two states ws_s and ss_s.

$$\omega_{\mathrm{sensing}}\underline{\mathbf{ws}}_s = \underline{\mathbf{ss}}_s$$

In a similar manner this can be done for the other states, resulting in the following equations:

Equilibrium of state	Equilibrium criterion
ss_s	$\omega_{\mathrm{sensing}}\underline{\mathbf{ws}}_s = \underline{\mathbf{ss}}_s$
srs_s	$\omega_{\mathrm{representing}}\underline{\mathbf{ss}}_s = \underline{\mathbf{srs}}_s$
ps_a	$\omega_{\mathrm{responding}}\underline{\mathbf{srs}}_s + \omega_{\mathrm{amplifying}}\underline{\mathbf{srs}}_e = \underline{\mathbf{ps}}_a$
srs_e	$\omega_{\mathrm{predicting}}\underline{\mathbf{ps}}_a = \underline{\mathbf{srs}}_e$
es_a	$\omega_{\mathrm{executing}}\underline{\mathbf{ps}}_a = \underline{\mathbf{es}}_a$

These are five equations with six unknowns $\underline{\mathbf{ws}}_s$, $\underline{\mathbf{ss}}_s$, $\underline{\mathbf{srs}}_s$, $\underline{\mathbf{ps}}_a$, $\underline{\mathbf{srs}}_e$, $\underline{\mathbf{es}}_a$; however, the variable $\underline{\mathbf{ws}}_s$ can be considered given as it indicates the external stimulus. So the five equations can be used to find expressions for the equilibrium values for the five other states in terms of the connection weights and $\underline{\mathbf{ws}}_s$. Note that for the sake of simplicity here it is assumed that $\omega_{\mathrm{amplifying}}$ and $\omega_{\mathrm{predicting}}$ are not both 1. Then this can be solved in an explicit analytical manner as follows. First two of them (the first two equations) are expressed in the externally given value $\underline{\mathbf{ws}}_s$:

$$\underline{\mathbf{ss}}_s = \omega_{\mathrm{sensing}}\underline{\mathbf{ws}}_s$$

$$\underline{\mathbf{srs}}_s = \omega_{\mathrm{representing}}\underline{\mathbf{ss}}_s = \omega_{\mathrm{representing}}\omega_{\mathrm{sensing}}\underline{\mathbf{ws}}_s$$

Moreover, the third and fourth equation can be solved as follows:

$$\omega_{\mathrm{responding}}\underline{\mathbf{srs}}_s + \omega_{\mathrm{amplifying}}\underline{\mathbf{srs}}_e = \underline{\mathbf{p}}_a$$

$$\omega_{\mathrm{predicting}}\underline{\mathbf{ps}}_a = \underline{\mathbf{srs}}_e$$

Substitute $\omega_{\mathrm{predicting}}\,\underline{\mathbf{ps}}_a$ for $\underline{\mathbf{srs}}_e$ in the third equation, resulting in the following equation in $\underline{\mathbf{ps}}_a$ and $\underline{\mathbf{srs}}_s$:

$$\omega_{\mathrm{responding}}\underline{\mathbf{srs}}_s + \omega_{\mathrm{amplifying}}\omega_{\mathrm{predicting}}\underline{\mathbf{ps}}_a = \underline{\mathbf{ps}}_a$$

This can be used to express $\underline{\mathbf{ps}}_a$ in $\underline{\mathbf{srs}}_s$, and subsequently in $\underline{\mathbf{ws}}_s$:

$$\omega_{\text{responding}}\underline{\mathbf{srs}}_s = (1 - \omega_{\text{amplifying}}\omega_{\text{predicting}})\underline{\mathbf{ps}}_a$$

$$\begin{aligned}\underline{\mathbf{ps}}_a &= \omega_{\text{responding}}\underline{\mathbf{srs}}_s/(1 - \omega_{\text{amplifying}}\omega_{\text{predicting}}) \\ &= \omega_{\text{responding}}\omega_{\text{representing}} \\ &\quad \times \omega_{\text{sensing}}\underline{\mathbf{ws}}_s/(1 - \omega_{\text{amplifying}}\omega_{\text{predicting}})\end{aligned}$$

Moreover, by the fourth equation it is found

$$\begin{aligned}\underline{\mathbf{srs}}_e &= \omega_{\text{predicting}}\underline{\mathbf{ps}}_a = \omega_{\text{predicting}}\omega_{\text{responding}}\omega_{\text{representing}} \\ &\quad \times \omega_{\text{sensing}}\underline{\mathbf{ws}}_s/(1 - \omega_{\text{amplifying}}\omega_{\text{predicting}})\end{aligned}$$

Based on these, the fifth equation can be used to get an expression for $\underline{\mathbf{es}}_a$:

$$\begin{aligned}\underline{\mathbf{es}}_a &= \omega_{\text{executing}}\underline{\mathbf{ps}}_a = \omega_{\text{executing}}\omega_{\text{responding}}\omega_{\text{representing}} \\ &\quad \times \omega_{\text{sensing}}\mathbf{ws}_s/(1 - \omega_{\text{amplifying}}\omega_{\text{predicting}})\end{aligned}$$

Summarizing, all equilibrium values have been expressed in terms of the external state $\underline{\mathbf{ws}}_s$ and the connection weights:

$$\begin{aligned}\underline{\mathbf{ss}}_s &= \omega_{\text{sensing}}\underline{\mathbf{ws}}_s \\ \underline{\mathbf{srs}}_s &= \omega_{\text{representing}}\omega_{\text{sensing}}\mathbf{ws}_s \\ \underline{\mathbf{ps}}_a &= \omega_{\text{responding}}\omega_{\text{representing}} \\ &\quad \times \omega_{\text{sensing}}\mathbf{ws}_s/(1 - \omega_{\text{amplifying}}\omega_{\text{predicting}}) \\ \underline{\mathbf{srs}}_e &= \omega_{\text{predicting}}\omega_{\text{responding}}\omega_{\text{representing}} \\ &\quad \times \omega_{\text{sensing}}\mathbf{ws}_s/(1 - \omega_{\text{amplifying}}\omega_{\text{predicting}}) \\ \underline{\mathbf{es}}_a &= \omega_{\text{executing}}\omega_{\text{responding}}\omega_{\text{representing}} \\ &\quad \times \omega_{\text{sensing}}\mathbf{ws}_s/(1 - \omega_{\text{amplifying}}\omega_{\text{predicting}})\end{aligned}$$

For example, if the external stimulus $\underline{\mathbf{ws}}_s$ has level 1 this becomes:

$$\begin{aligned}\underline{\mathbf{ss}}_s &= \omega_{\text{sensing}} \\ \underline{\mathbf{srs}}_s &= \omega_{\text{representing}}\ \omega_{\text{sensing}} \\ \underline{\mathbf{ps}}_a &= \omega_{\text{responding}}\ \omega_{\text{representing}}\ \omega_{\text{sensing}}/ \\ &\quad (1 - \omega_{\text{amplifying}}\ \omega_{\text{predicting}}) \\ \underline{\mathbf{srs}}_e &= \omega_{\text{predicting}}\ \omega_{\text{responding}}\ \omega_{\text{representing}} \\ &\quad \times \omega_{\text{sensing}}/(1 - \omega_{\text{amplifying}}\ \omega_{\text{predicting}}) \\ \underline{\mathbf{es}}_a &= \omega_{\text{executing}}\ \omega_{\text{responding}}\ \omega_{\text{representing}} \\ &\quad \times \omega_{\text{sensing}}/(1 - \omega_{\text{amplifying}}\ \omega_{\text{predicting}})\end{aligned}$$

Moreover, if all connection weights are 1, except that $\omega_{\text{responding}} = 0.5$ and $\omega_{\text{amplifying}} = 0.5$, as in the example simulation shown in [17], Section 2.4.1, the values become:

$$\begin{aligned}\underline{\mathbf{ss}}_s &= 1 \\ \underline{\mathbf{srs}}_s &= 1 \\ \underline{\mathbf{ps}}_a &= 0.5/0.5 = 1 \\ \underline{\mathbf{srs}}_e &= 0.5/0.5 = 1 \\ \underline{\mathbf{es}}_a &= 0.5/0.5 = 1\end{aligned}$$

Indeed in the example simulation in [17], Section 2.4.1 Fig. 11 it can be seen that all values go to 1. The solution of the equilibrium equations in terms of the connection weights can be used to predict that when the connection weights have different values, also these equilibrium values will turn out different. Recall that the cases $\omega_{\text{amplifying}} = 1$ and $\omega_{\text{predicting}} = 1$ was excluded. In that case the combined third and fourth equation becomes trivial, as $\underline{\mathbf{ps}}_a$ is lost from the equation:

$$\begin{aligned}&\omega_{\text{responding}}\underline{\mathbf{srs}}_s + \omega_{\text{amplifying}}\omega_{\text{predicting}}\underline{\mathbf{ps}}_a = \underline{\mathbf{ps}}_a \\ &\omega_{\text{responding}}\underline{\mathbf{srs}}_s + \underline{\mathbf{ps}}_a = \underline{\mathbf{ps}}_a \\ &\omega_{\text{responding}}\underline{\mathbf{srs}}_s = 0 \\ &\underline{\mathbf{srs}}_s = 0\end{aligned}$$

Here in the last step it is assumed that $\omega_{\text{responding}} > 0$. As a consequence by the first two equations also $\underline{\mathbf{ss}}_s$ and $\underline{\mathbf{ws}}_s$ are 0, and by the fourth and fifth equation also the values for the other states. It turns out that in this case there can only be an equilibrium if there is no stimulus at all. As soon as there is a nonzero stimulus in this case that $\omega_{\text{amplifying}} = 1$ and $\omega_{\text{predicting}} = 1$, the values of ps_a, srs_e and es_a increase indefinitely to larger and larger values (and in particular do not stay within the interval [0, 1]), as can be seen from simulations. Note that there was an additional assumption made that $\omega_{\text{responding}} > 0$. If, in contrast, $\omega_{\text{responding}} = 0$, then still more possibilities for equilibria are available. For example, in that case $\underline{\mathbf{ps}}_a$ and $\underline{\mathbf{srs}}_e$ can have any value, but they have to be equal due to the fourth equation, but this value is independent of the values of $\underline{\mathbf{ws}}_s$, $\underline{\mathbf{ss}}_s$ and $\underline{\mathbf{srs}}_s$, as there is no nonzero connection between these parts of the graph. So, this would not be a very relevant case.

The analysis above can also be done to find out whether or not the activation level of a state is increasing. As a first step, again consider the sensor state ss_s.

LP_{ss_s} Sensing a stimulus: determining values for state ss_s

$$\mathbf{d}\text{ss}_s(t)/\mathbf{d}t = \eta_{\text{ss}_s}[\omega_{\text{sensing}}\text{ws}_s(t) - \text{ss}_s(t)]$$
$$\text{ss}_s(t + \Delta t) = \text{ss}_s(t) + \eta_{\text{ss}_s}[\omega_{\text{sensing}}\text{ws}_s(t) - \text{ss}_s(t)]\Delta t$$

The activation value increases mean

$$\mathbf{d}\text{ss}_s(t)/\mathbf{dt} > 0 \quad \text{or} \quad \text{ss}_s(t + \Delta t) > \text{ss}_s(t)$$

This is equivalent to:

$\omega_{\text{sensing}} \text{ws}_s(t) - \text{ss}_s(t) > 0$

This in turn is equivalent to the criterion that the impact on ss_s is higher than the current activation value:

$\omega_{\text{sensing}} \text{ws}_s(t) > \text{ss}_s(t)$

For example, when $\text{ws}_s(t) = 1$ and $\omega_{\text{sensing}} = 1$, then the criterion $\omega_{\text{sensing}}\ \text{ws}_s(t) > \text{ss}_s(t)$ indicates the activation of state ss_s will increase as long as it did not reach the value 1 yet. This gives as additional information that the equilibrium value 1 of sensor state ss_s is *attracting*: the value goes in that direction as long as it was not reached.

In a similar manner this can be done for the other states, thus obtaining the following criteria:

State	is increasing if and only if
ss_s	$\omega_{\text{sensing}} \text{ws}_s(t) > \text{ss}_s(t)$
srs_s	$\omega_{\text{representing}} \text{ss}_s(t) > \text{srs}_s(t)$
ps_a	$\omega_{\text{responding}} \text{srs}_s(t) + \omega_{\text{amplifying}} \text{srs}_e(t) > \text{ps}_a(t)$
srs_e	$\omega_{\text{predicting}} \text{ps}_a(t) > \text{srs}_e(t)$
es_a	$\omega_{\text{executing}} \text{ps}_a(t) > \text{es}_a(t)$

4 Mathematical analysis for equilibrium states: scaled sum combination function

The approach described above can be applied easily for the case of a scaled sum combination function $c_i(\ldots)$ for each state X_i; such a scaled sum function $\mathbf{ssum}_{\lambda_i}(\ldots)$ with scaling factor λ_i is defined as

$$\mathbf{ssum}_{\lambda_i}(V_1, \ldots, V_k) = (V_1 + \cdots + V_k)/\lambda_i$$

Suppose the differential equation for some state X_i connected to states X_j is given by

$$\mathbf{d}X_i/\mathbf{d}t = \eta_i[\mathbf{aggimpact}_i(X_1, \ldots, X_k) - X_i]$$

where

$$\begin{aligned}\mathbf{aggimpact}_i(X_1, \ldots, X_k) &= c_i(\omega_{1,i}X_1, \ldots, \omega_{k,i}X_k)\\ &= \mathbf{ssum}_{\lambda_i}(\omega_{1,i}X_1, \ldots, \omega_{k,i}X_k)\\ &= (\omega_{1,i}X_1 + \cdots + \omega_{k,i}X_k)/\lambda_i\end{aligned}$$

with $\omega_{j,i}$ the specific weights for the connections from X_j to X_i. In this case the following holds:

$$\begin{aligned}&\text{Increasing } X_i : X_i(t + \Delta t) > X_i(t)\\ &\quad\Leftrightarrow (\omega_{1,i}X_1(t) + \cdots + \omega_{k,i}X_k(t))/\lambda_i > X_i(t)\end{aligned}$$

$$\begin{aligned}&\text{Equilibrium of } X_i : X_i(t + \Delta t) = X_i(t)\\ &\quad\Leftrightarrow (\omega_{1,i}X_1(t) + \cdots + \omega_{k,i}X_k(t))/\lambda_i = X_i(t)\end{aligned}$$

$$\begin{aligned}&\text{Decreasing } X_i : X_i(t + \Delta t) < X_i(t)\\ &\quad\Leftrightarrow (\omega_{1,i}X_1(t) + \cdots + \omega_{k,i}X_k(t))/\lambda_i < X_i(t)\end{aligned}$$

In particular, the equilibrium equations for the states X_i are

$$(\omega_{1,1}\underline{\mathbf{X_1}} + \cdots + \omega_{k,1}\underline{\mathbf{X_k}})/\lambda_1 = \underline{\mathbf{X_1}}$$
$$\cdots$$
$$(\omega_{1,k}\underline{\mathbf{X_1}} + \cdots + \omega_{k,k}\underline{\mathbf{X_k}})/\lambda_k = \underline{\mathbf{X_k}}$$

This means that in an equilibrium state the value $\underline{\mathbf{X}}_i$ for a state X_i may be a weighted average of the equilibrium values $\underline{\mathbf{X}}_j$ for the states X_j, in particular when

$$\lambda_i = \omega_{1,i} + \cdots + \omega_{k,i}$$

Note that always at least one solution exists: when all are 0. But it is usually more interesting to know whether nonzero solutions exist.

The equilibrium equations are equivalent to

$$\omega_{1,1}\underline{\mathbf{X_1}} + \cdots + \omega_{k,1}\underline{\mathbf{X_k}} = \lambda_1\underline{\mathbf{X_1}}$$
$$\cdots$$
$$\omega_{1,k}\underline{\mathbf{X_1}} + \cdots + \omega_{k,k}\underline{\mathbf{X_k}} = \lambda_k\underline{\mathbf{X_k}}$$

or

$$(\omega_{1,1} - \lambda_1)\underline{\mathbf{X_1}} + \omega_{2,1}\underline{\mathbf{X_2}} + \cdots + \omega_{k,1}\underline{\mathbf{X_k}} = 0$$
$$\cdots\cdots$$
$$\begin{aligned}&\omega_{1,i}\underline{\mathbf{X_1}} + \cdots + \omega_{i-1,i}\underline{\mathbf{X_{i-1}}} + (\omega_{i,i} - \lambda_i)\underline{\mathbf{X_i}}\\ &\quad + \omega_{i+1,i}\underline{\mathbf{X_{i+1}}} + \cdots + \omega_{k,i}\underline{\mathbf{X_k}} = 0\end{aligned}$$
$$\cdots\cdots$$
$$\omega_{1,k}\underline{\mathbf{X_1}} + \cdots + \omega_{k-1,k}\underline{\mathbf{X_{k-1}}} + (\omega_{k,k} - \lambda_k)\underline{\mathbf{X_k}} = 0$$

In general these linear equilibrium equations can be solved analytically, which in principle can provide symbolic expressions for the equilibrium values of X_j in terms of the connection weights $\omega_{j,i}$ and the scaling factor λ_i. However, for more than two states ($k > 2$) such expressions may tend to become more and more complex, but this depends on the number of these $\omega_{j,i}$ which are nonzero, i.e. how many connections between the states exist. For example, if all states have only one incoming and one outgoing connection (a cascade or loop), then these equations can easily be solved. In some cases no nonzero solution exists. This happens, for example, when the values of the parameters are such that two of the equations in a sense contradict each other, as in the equations $X_1 - 2X_2 = 0$ and $X_1 - 3X_2 = 0$.

In some cases some properties of equilibrium values can be derived. For well-connected temporal-causal network models based on scaled sum functions with as scaling factor the sum of the weights of the incoming connections it can be derived that all states have the same equilibrium value.

Definition 1 A network is called *strongly connected* if for every two nodes A and B there is a directed path from A to B and vice versa.

Lemma 1 *Let a temporal-causal network model be given based on scaled sum functions:*

$$\mathbf{d}Y/\mathbf{d}t = \eta_Y[\Sigma_{X,\omega_{X,Y}>0}\omega_{X,Y}X/\Sigma_{X,\omega_{X,Y}>0}\omega_{X,Y} - Y]$$

Then the following hold.

(a) *If for some state Y at time t for all states X connected toward Y it holds $X(t) \geq Y(t)$, then $Y(t)$ is increasing at t : $\mathbf{d}Y(t)/\mathbf{d}t \geq 0$; if for all states X connected toward Y it holds $X(t) \leq Y(t)$, then $Y(t)$ is decreasing at t : $\mathbf{d}Y(t)/\mathbf{d}t \leq 0$.*

(b) *If for some state Y at time t for all states X connected toward Y it holds $X(t) \geq Y(t)$, and at least one state X connected toward Y exists with $X(t) > Y(t)$ then $Y(t)$ is strictly increasing at t: $\mathbf{d}Y(t)/\mathbf{d}t > 0$. If for some state Y at time t for all states X connected toward Y it holds $X(t) \leq Y(t)$, and at least one state X connected toward Y exists with $X(t) < Y(t)$ then $Y(t)$ is strictly decreasing at t : $\mathbf{d}Y(t)/\mathbf{d}t < 0$.*

Proof of Lemma 1 (a) From the differential equation for $Y(t)$

$$\begin{aligned}\mathbf{d}Y/\mathbf{d}t &= \eta_Y[\Sigma_{X,\omega_{X,Y}>0}\omega_{X,Y}X/\Sigma_{X,\omega_{X,Y}>0}\omega_{X,Y} - Y]\\ &= \eta_Y[\Sigma_{X,\omega_{X,Y}>0}\omega_{X,Y}X\\ &\quad - \Sigma_{X,\omega_{X,Y}>0}\omega_{X,Y}Y]/\Sigma_{X,\omega_{X,Y}>0}\omega_{X,Y}\\ &= \eta_Y[\Sigma_{X,\omega_{X,Y}>0}\omega_{X,Y}(X - Y)]/\Sigma_{X,\omega_{X,Y}>0}\omega_{X,Y}\end{aligned}$$

it follows that $\mathbf{d}Y(t)/\mathbf{d}t \geq 0$, so $Y(t)$ is increasing at t. Similar for decreasing.

(b) In this case it follows that $\mathbf{d}Y(t)/\mathbf{d}t > 0$, so $Y(t)$ is strictly increasing. Similar for decreasing. □

Theorem 1 (convergence to one value) *Let a strongly connected temporal-causal network model be given based on scaled sum functions:*

$$\mathbf{d}Y/\mathbf{d}t = \eta_Y[\Sigma_{X,\omega_{X,Y}>0}\omega_{X,Y}X/\Sigma_{X,\omega_{X,Y}>0}\omega_{X,Y} - Y]$$

Then for all states X and Y the equilibrium values $\underline{\mathbf{X}}$ and $\underline{\mathbf{Y}}$ are equal: $\underline{\mathbf{X}} = \underline{\mathbf{Y}}$. Moreover, this equilibrium state is attracting.

Proof of Theorem 1 Take a state Y with highest value $\underline{\mathbf{Y}}$. Then for all states X it holds $\underline{\mathbf{X}} \leq \underline{\mathbf{Y}}$. Suppose for some state X connected toward Y it holds $\underline{\mathbf{X}} < \underline{\mathbf{Y}}$. Take a time point t and assume $Z(t) = \underline{\mathbf{Z}}$ for all states Z. Now apply Lemma 1b) to state Y. It follows that $\mathbf{d}Y(t)/\mathbf{d}t < 0$, so $Y(t)$ is not in equilibrium for this value $\underline{\mathbf{Y}}$. This contradicts that this $\underline{\mathbf{Y}}$ is an equilibrium value for state Y. Therefore, the assumption that for some state X connected toward Y it holds $\underline{\mathbf{X}} < \underline{\mathbf{Y}}$ cannot be true. This shows that $\underline{\mathbf{X}} = \underline{\mathbf{Y}}$ for all states connected toward Y.Now this argument can be repeated for all states connected toward Y instead of X. By iteration every other state in the network is reached, due to the strong connectivity assumption; it follows that all other states X in the temporal-causal network model have the same equilibrium value $\underline{\mathbf{X}}$ as $\underline{\mathbf{Y}}$. From Lemma 1b) it follows that such an equilibrium state is attracting: if for any state the value is deviating it will move to the equilibrium value. □

5 Mathematical analysis for equilibrium states: Hebbian learning

It can also be analysed from the difference or differential equation when a Hebbian adaptation process (e.g. [2,4–6,8,15,16]) has an equilibrium and when it increases or decreases. More specifically, assume the following dynamic model (also see [5]) for Hebbian learning for the strength ω of a connection from a state X_1 to a state X_2 with maximal connection strength 1, learning rate $\eta > 0$, and extinction rate $\zeta \geq 0$ (here $X_1(t)$ and $X_2(t)$ denote the activation levels of the states X_1 and X_2 at time t; sometimes the t is left out of $X_i(t)$ and simply X_i is written)

$$\omega(t + \Delta t) = \omega(t) + [\eta X_1(t)X_2(t)(1 - \omega(t)) - \zeta\omega(t)]\Delta t$$
$$\mathbf{d}\omega(t)/\mathbf{d}t = \eta X_1X_2(1 - \omega(t)) - \zeta\omega(t)$$

Note that also for the states X_1 and X_2 equations may be given, but here the focus is on ω.

From the expressions for ω it can be analysed when each of the following cases occurs:

$$\text{Increasing } \omega: \ \mathbf{d}\omega(t)/\mathbf{d}t > 0 \Leftrightarrow \eta X_1X_2(1 - \omega(t)) - \zeta\omega(t) > 0$$

$$\text{Equilibrium of } \omega: \ \mathbf{d}\omega(t)/\mathbf{d}t = 0 \Leftrightarrow \eta X_1X_2(1 - \omega(t)) - \zeta\omega(t) = 0$$

$$\text{Decreasing } \omega: \ \mathbf{d}\omega(t)/\mathbf{d}t < 0 \Leftrightarrow \eta X_1X_2(1 - \omega(t)) - \zeta\omega(t) < 0$$

5.1 Analysis of increase, decrease or equilibrium for Hebbian learning without extinction

To keep things a bit simple for a first analysis, for the special case that there is no extinction ($\zeta = 0$), this easily leads to the following criteria

$$\begin{aligned}\text{Increasing } \omega:\ & \eta X_1 X_2(1-\omega(t)) > 0\\ & \Leftrightarrow \omega(t) < 1 \text{ and both } X_1 > 0 \text{ and } X_2 > 0\end{aligned}$$

$$\begin{aligned}\text{Equilibrium of } \omega:\ & \eta X_1 X_2(1-\omega(t)) = 0\\ & \Leftrightarrow \omega(t) = 1 \text{ or } X_1 = 0 \text{ or } X_2 = 0\end{aligned}$$

$$\begin{aligned}\text{Decreasing } \omega:\ & \eta X_1 X_2(1-\omega(t)) < 0\\ & \text{this is never the case, as always } X_i \geq 0\\ & \text{and } \omega(t) \leq 1\end{aligned}$$

So, in case that there is no extinction, the only equilibrium is when $\omega = 1$, and as long as this value was not reached yet and both $X_1 > 0$ and $X_2 > 0$, the value of ω increases: the equilibrium is attracting. Note that when $X_1 = 0$ or $X_2 = 0$, also an equilibrium for ω can be found: no (further) learning takes place; the value of ω stays the same independent of which value it has, so in this case any value is an equilibrium value. In simulations this indeed can be observed: as long as both $X_1 > 0$ and $X_2 > 0$ the value of ω keeps on increasing until it reaches 1, but if $X_1 = 0$ or $X_2 = 0$ then ω always stays the same.

5.2 Analysis of increase, decrease or equilibrium for Hebbian learning with extinction

As a next step this analysis is extended to the case with extinction $\zeta > 0$. In this case the analysis requires slightly more work; here for convenience the *t* is left out of the expressions.

$$\begin{aligned}\textbf{Increasing } \omega:\ & \eta X_1 X_2(1-\omega) - \zeta\omega > 0\\ & \Leftrightarrow \eta X_1 X_2 - \eta X_1 X_2 \omega - \zeta\omega > 0\\ & \Leftrightarrow \eta X_1 X_2 - (\zeta + \eta X_1 X_2)\omega > 0\\ & \Leftrightarrow (\zeta + \eta X_1 X_2)\omega < \eta X_1 X_2\\ & \Leftrightarrow \omega < \frac{\eta X_1 X_2}{\zeta + \eta X_1 X_2}\\ & \Leftrightarrow \omega < \frac{1}{1+\zeta/(\eta X_1 X_2)}\\ & (\text{when both } X_1 > 0 \text{ and } X_2 > 0)\end{aligned}$$

Note that when $X_1 = 0$ or $X_2 = 0$, the value of ω is never increasing. Similarly the following criteria can be found.

$$\begin{aligned}\textbf{Equilibrium of } \boldsymbol{\omega}:\ & \eta X_1 X_2(1-\omega) - \zeta\omega = 0\\ & \Leftrightarrow \omega = \frac{\eta X_1 X_2}{\zeta + \eta X_1 X_2}\\ & \Leftrightarrow \omega = \frac{1}{1+\zeta/\eta(X_1 X_2)}\\ & (\text{when both } X_1 > 0 \text{ and } X_2 > 0)\\ & \eta X_1 X_2(1-\omega) - \zeta\omega = 0\\ & \Leftrightarrow \omega = 0\\ & (\text{when } X_1 = 0 \text{ or } X_2 = 0, \text{ and } \zeta > 0)\end{aligned}$$

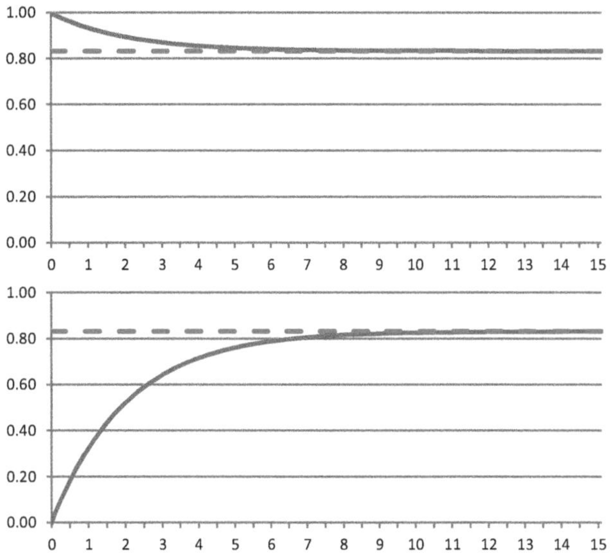

Fig. 3 Hebbian learning for $\eta = 0.4$, $\zeta = 0.08$, $\Delta t = 0.1$, and activation levels $X_1 = 1$ and $X_2 = 1$ Equilibrium value 0.83 (*dotted line*)

$$\begin{aligned}\textbf{Decreasing } \boldsymbol{\omega}:\ & \eta X_1 X_2(1-\omega) - \zeta\omega < 0\\ & \Leftrightarrow \omega > \frac{\eta X_1 X_2}{\zeta + \eta X_1 X_2}\\ & \Leftrightarrow \omega > \frac{1}{1+\zeta/(\eta X_1 X_2)}\\ & (\text{when both } X_1 > 0 \text{ and } X_2 > 0)\\ & \eta X_1 X_2(1-\omega) - \zeta\omega < 0\\ & \Leftrightarrow \text{always}\\ & (\text{when } X_1 = 0 \text{ or } X_2 = 0, \text{ and } \zeta > 0, \omega > 0)\end{aligned}$$

In this more general case with extinction, depending on the values of X_1 and X_2 there may be a positive equilibrium value (when both $X_1 > 0$ and $X_2 > 0$) but when $\zeta > 0$ this value is < 1. Also 0 is an equilibrium value (when $X_1 = 0$ or $X_2 = 0$). This looks similar to the case without extinction. Moreover, as before, the value of ω increases when it is under the positive equilibrium value and it decreases when it is above this value (it is an attracting equilibrium); for example patterns, see Figs. 3 and 4.

Note that this time this positive equilibrium value (indicated by the dotted line) is lower than 1. It may be close to

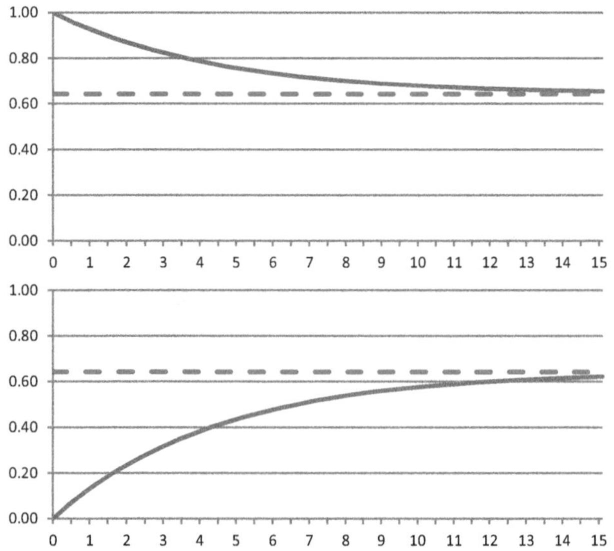

Fig. 4 Hebbian learning for $\eta = 0.4$, $\zeta = 0.08$, $\Delta t = 0.1$, and activation levels $X_1 = 0.6$ and $X_2 = 0.6$ Equilibrium value 0.64 (*dotted line*)

1, but when $\zeta > 0$ it never will be equal to 1. In fact the maximal value of this equilibrium is when both $X_1 = 1$ and $X_2 = 1$, in which case the equilibrium value is

$$\frac{1}{1 + \zeta/\eta}$$

For example, for $\eta = 0.4$, $\zeta = 0.02$, and $X_1 = 1$ and $X_2 = 1$, the positive equilibrium value for ω is about 0.95. Another example is $\eta = 0.4$, $\zeta = 0.08$, and $X_1 = 1$ and $X_2 = 1$, in which case the equilibrium value is 0.83. The graphs in Fig. 2 show what happens below this equilibrium and above it. If for the same settings for η and ζ, the activation levels are lower ($X_1 = 0.6$ and $X_2 = 0.6$), then the equilibrium value is lower too (0.64), and the learning is much slower, as is shown in Fig. 3.

So, it is found that the positive equilibrium value occurs for $X_1 > 0$ and $X_2 > 0$, and in that case this equilibrium is attracting. In contrast, the equilibrium value 0 does not occur for $X_1 > 0$ and $X_2 > 0$, but it does occur for $X_1 = 0$ or $X_2 = 0$, in which case no positive equilibrium value occurs. In this case pure extinction occurs: ω is attracted by the equilibrium value 0; this pattern is different from the case without extinction. For an example of such a pure extinction process, see Fig. 5. Note that, given the lower value of the extinction rate ζ, the extinction process takes a much longer time than the learning process.

5.3 How much activation of X_1 and X_2 is needed to let ω increase?

From a different angle, another question that can be addressed is for a given value of ω, how high the value X_1X_2 should be

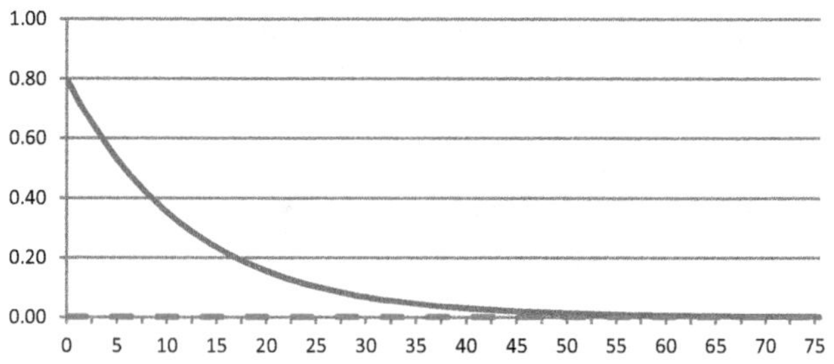

Fig. 5 Pure extinction for $\eta = 0.4$, $\zeta = 0.08$, $\Delta t = 0.1$, and activation levels $X_1 = X_2 = 0$; equilibrium value 0

to let ω become higher. This can be determined in a similar manner as follows:

$$\textbf{Increasing } \omega: \ \omega < \frac{1}{1 + \zeta/(\eta X_1 X_2)}$$
$$\Leftrightarrow (1 + \zeta/\eta X_1 X_2)\omega < 1$$
$$\Leftrightarrow 1 + \zeta/(\eta X_1 X_2) < 1/\omega$$
$$\Leftrightarrow \zeta/(\eta X_1 X_2) < 1/\omega - 1 = (1 - \omega)/\omega$$
$$\Leftrightarrow 1/(X_1 X_2) < \frac{\eta}{\zeta}(1 - \omega)/\omega$$
$$\Leftrightarrow X_1 X_2 > \frac{\zeta}{\eta}\omega/(1 - \omega)$$

So, for activation levels X_1 and X_2 with $X_1X_2 > \frac{\zeta}{\eta}\omega/(1-\omega)$, further learning takes place, and below this value extinction dominates and will decrease the level of ω.

6 Mathematical analysis for equilibrium states: dynamic network connections

The connections between agents in a social network may change over time based on the *homophily principle*: the closer the states of the interacting agents, the stronger the connections of the agents will become. This principle may be formalized with as a general template

$$\mathbf{d}\omega_{A,B}/\mathbf{d}t = \eta_{A,B}[c_{A,B}(X_A, X_B, \omega_{A,B}) - \omega_{A,B}]$$

for some combination function $c_{A,B}(V_1, V_2, W)$ for which it is assumed that $c_{A,B}(V_1, V_2, 0) \geq 0$ and $c_{A,B}(V_1, V_2, 1) \leq 1$. The example used in this section is

$$c_{A,B}(V_1, V_2, W) = W + (\tau_{A,B}^2 - (V_1 - V_2)^2)W(1 - W)$$

In this case

$$\mathbf{d}\omega_{A,B}/\mathbf{d}t = \eta_{A,B}(\tau_{A,B}^2 - (X_A - X_B)^2)\omega_{A,B}(1 - \omega_{A,B})$$

In this section it is analysed which equilibrium values $\underline{\boldsymbol{\omega}}_{A,B}$ can occur for $\omega_{A,B}(t)$ and when $\omega_{A,B}(t)$ is increasing or decreasing.

The standard approach is to derive an inequality or equation from the differential equation by putting $\mathbf{d}\omega_{A,B}(t)/\mathbf{d}t = 0$, $\mathbf{d}\omega_{A,B}(t)/\mathbf{d}t \geq 0$ or $\mathbf{d}\omega_{A,B}(t)/\mathbf{d}t \leq 0$. For this case this provides

$$\text{Increasing } \omega_{A,B} \quad \mathbf{d}\omega_{A,B}(t)/\mathbf{d}t \geq 0 \;\Leftrightarrow\; \eta_{A,B}(\tau_{A,B}^2 - (X_A - X_B)^2) \times \omega_{A,B}(1-\omega_{A,B}) > 0$$

$$\text{Equilibrium of } \omega_{A,B} \quad \mathbf{d}\omega_{A,B}(t)/\mathbf{d}t = 0 \;\Leftrightarrow\; \eta_{A,B}(\tau_{A,B}^2 - (X_A - X_B)^2) \times \omega_{A,B}(1-\omega_{A,B}) = 0$$

$$\text{Decreasing } \omega_{A,B} \quad \mathbf{d}\omega_{A,B}(t)/\mathbf{d}t \leq 0 \;\Leftrightarrow\; \eta_{A,B}(\tau_{A,B}^2 - (X_A - X_B)^2) \times \omega_{A,B}(1-\omega_{A,B}) < 0$$

For $\omega_{A,B} = 0$ or $\omega_{A,B} = 1$ the middle condition is fulfilled. This means that $\underline{\omega}_{A,B} = 0$ and $\underline{\omega}_{A,B} = 1$ are equilibrium values. Now assume $0 < \omega_{A,B} < 1$. Then $\omega_{A,B}(1-\omega_{A,B}) > 0$, and therefore this factor can be left out, and the same applies to $\eta_{A,B} > 0$; this results in:

$$\text{Increasing } \omega_{A,B} \quad \tau_{A,B}^2 - (X_A - X_B)^2 > 0 \;\Leftrightarrow\; |X_A - X_B| < \tau_{A,B}$$

$$\text{Equilibrium of } \omega_{A,B} \quad \tau_{A,B}^2 - (X_A - X_B)^2 = 0 \;\Leftrightarrow\; |X_A - X_B| = \tau_{A,B}$$

$$\text{Decreasing } \omega_{A,B} \quad \tau_{A,B}^2 - (X_A - X_B)^2 < 0 \;\Leftrightarrow\; |X_A - X_B| > \tau_{A,B}$$

This shows that for cases that $|X_A - X_B| < \tau_{A,B}$ the connection keeps on becoming stronger until $\omega_{A,B}$ becomes in equilibrium at 1. Similarly for cases that $|X_A - X_B| > \tau_{A,B}$ the connection keeps on becoming weaker until $\omega_{A,B}$ comes in equilibrium at 0. This implies that the equilibria $\underline{\boldsymbol{\omega}}_{A,B} = 0$ and $\underline{\boldsymbol{\omega}}_{A,B} = 1$ can both become attracting, but under different circumstances concerning the values of X_A and X_B.

In exceptional situations it could be the case that $|X_A - X_B| = \tau_{A,B}$ in which case $\omega_{A,B}$ is also in equilibrium, with $\omega_{A,B}$ having any value. So in principle the equilibrium equation has three solutions

$$\underline{\boldsymbol{\omega}}_{A,B} = 0 \quad \text{or} \quad \underline{\boldsymbol{\omega}}_{A,B} = 1 \quad \text{or}$$
$$|\underline{\mathbf{X}}_A - \underline{\mathbf{X}}_B| = \tau_{A,B} \quad \text{and} \quad \underline{\boldsymbol{\omega}}_{A,B} \text{ has any value}$$

The analysis above can also be done for similar but slightly more complex variants of the model, of which the quadratic variant is described in [14]:

$$\begin{aligned}
\mathrm{c}_{A,B}(V_1, V_2, W) &= \boldsymbol{W} + \mathrm{Pos}(\eta_{A,B}(\tau_{A,B} - |V_1 - V_2|))(1 - W) \\
&\quad - \mathrm{Pos}(-\eta_{A,B}(\tau_{A,B} - |V_1 - V_2|))W \\
\mathrm{c}_{A,B}(V_1, V_2, W) &= \boldsymbol{W} + \mathrm{Pos}(\eta_{A,B}(\tau_{A,B}^2 - (V_1 - V_2)^2))(1 - W) \\
&\quad - \mathrm{Pos}(-\eta_{A,B}(\tau_{A,B}^2 - (V_1 - V_2)^2))W \\
\mathrm{c}_{A,B}(V_1, V_2, W) &= \boldsymbol{W} + \mathrm{Pos}(\eta_{A,B}(0.5 - 1/(1 \\
&\quad + \mathrm{e}^{-\sigma A,B(|V1 - V2| - \tau A,B)})))(1 - W) \\
&\quad - \mathrm{Pos}(-\eta_{A,B}(0.5 - 1/(1 + \mathrm{e}^{-\sigma A,B(|V1 - V2| - \tau A,B)})))W
\end{aligned}$$

where $\mathrm{Pos}(x) = (|x| + x)/2$, which returns x when x is positive and 0 when x is negative. These models make that the approaching of the boundaries 0 and 1 of the interval [0, 1] of ω is slow, thus making ω not cross these boundaries, but ω departing from the neighbourhood of these boundaries is not slow. In [14] an analysis and example simulations can be found using the second, quadratic model. As part of the analysis, there it is also shown that different equilibrium values $\underline{\mathbf{X}}_A$ and $\underline{\mathbf{X}}_B$ have a distance of at least $\tau_{A,B}$, which implies that at most $1/\tau_{A,B}$ clusters can emerge.

7 Mathematical analysis for behaviour ending up in a limit cycle pattern

Sometimes the values of the states of a model do not end up in an equilibrium value, but instead keep on fluctuating all the time, and after some time they do this according to a repeated pattern, called a *limit cycle*; for example, see [3,9,11–13]. The example model shown in Figs. 1 and 2 can be extended to show such behaviour; see Fig. 6. In this case it is assumed that action *a* directs the person (e.g. his or her gaze) away from the stimulus *s*, so that after (full) execution of *a* stimulus *s* is not sensed anymore. This type of behaviour can occur as a form of emotion regulation to down-regulate a stressful emotion triggered by *s*. The effect of this is as follows. The presence of stimulus *s* leads to high activation levels of sensor state and sensory representation for *s*, and subsequently for the preparation state and execution state of action *a*. But then the action leads to its effect in the world which is suppression of the sensor state for *s*. As a consequence the sensor state and sensory representation for *s*, and also the preparation state and execution state of action *a* get low activation levels. The effect is that there is no suppression of sensing the stimulus anymore and, therefore, all activation levels become high again. And so it goes on and on, forever (see also Fig. 8). At a longer timescale this type of pattern may also occur in so-called on-again-off-again relationships. This type of behaviour can be achieved by the following additions to the example model (see Fig. 6):

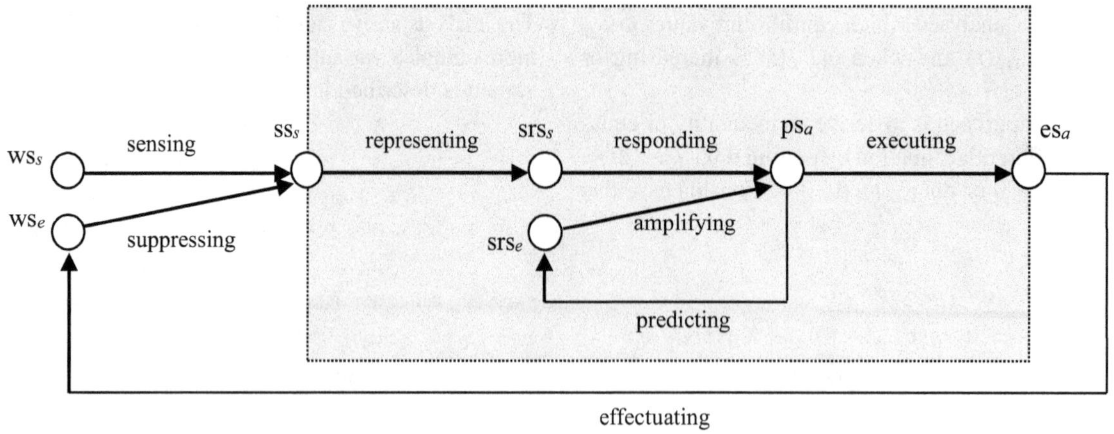

Fig. 6 Simple example model incorporating suppression of sensing

- a connection from the execution state es_a of a to the world state ws_e for effect e of action a
- a connection from this world state ws_e for e to the sensor state ss_s of s
- a combination function for the sensor state ss_s of s that models that ws_e makes that s is not sensed

The aggregation used for ss_s is modelled by the following combination function $\mathbf{c}_{ss_s}(V_1, V_2)$, where V_1 refers to the impact $\omega_{ws_s,ss_s}\, ws_s(t)$ from ws_s on ss_s and V_2 to the impact $\omega_{ws_e,ss_s}\, ws_e(t)$ from ws_e on ss_s:

$$c_{ss_s}(V_1, V_2) = V_1(1 + V_2)$$

Since the connection weight ω_{ws_e,ss_s} is chosen negative (it is a suppressing link), for example -1, this function makes the sensing of stimulus s inversely proportional to the extent $ws_e(t)$ of avoidance; e.g. sensing s becomes 0 when avoidance e is 1, and V_1 when avoidance e is 0. According to this combination function the difference and differential equation for ss_s are as follows:

$$ss_s(t + \Delta t) = ss_s(t) + \eta_{ss_s}[\omega_{ws_s,ss_s} ws_s(t)(1 - \omega_{ws_e,ss_s} ws_e(t)) - ss_s(t)]\Delta t$$

$$\mathbf{d}ss_s/\mathbf{d}t = \eta_{ss_s}[\omega_{ws_s,ss_s} ws_s(t)(1 - \omega_{ws_e,ss_s} ws_e(t)) - ss_s(t)]$$

The combination functions for all states with only one connection toward it are the identity function, except for es_a in which case the advanced logistic function $\mathbf{alogistic}_{\sigma,\tau}(\ldots)$ is used. The combination function for ps_a is also the advanced logistic function $\mathbf{alogistic}_{\sigma,\tau}(\ldots)$.

In Fig. 8 an example simulation with the model depicted in Fig. 7 clearly shows how a limit cycle pattern emerges, with period 18.5.

Here all connection weights are 1, except the weight of the suppressing connection from ws_e to ss_s, which is -1. Moreover, the steepness σ and threshold τ for ps_a are 4 and 0.9, respectively, and for es_a they are 40 and 0.7. The step size Δt was 0.1 and the speed factors η for es_a and ws_e were 0.4, and for the other (internal) states η was1.

For this simulation an analysis of the stationary points has been performed for the maxima and minima in the final stage for all states. Recall from Sect. 2 that the equation expressing that a state Y is stationary at time t is

$$\mathbf{aggimpact}_Y(t) = Y(t)$$

which is equivalent to

$$\mathbf{c}_Y(\omega_{X_1,Y} X_1(t), \ldots, \omega_{X_k,Y} X_k(t)) = Y(t)$$

For example, for state ps_a the combination function is the sum function, so the aggregated impact is

$$\mathbf{aggimpact}_Y(t) = \omega_{\text{responding}} srs_s(t) + \omega_{\text{amplifying}} srs_e(t)$$

Then the stationary point equation expressing that state ps_a is stationary at time t is

$$\omega_{\text{responding}} srs_s(t) + \omega_{\text{amplifying}} srs_e(t) = ps_a(t)$$

It is this equation that has been checked for the minima and maxima for each of the states in the final stage of the simulation. The results are shown in Table 1. Here both for the maxima and for the minima the first rows show the time points at which the stationary point occurs. The next row (state value) shows the values of the right-hand side of the above equation, followed by rows (aggregated impact) showing the left-hand sides of this equation, and then a row with the absolute deviation between the values in the two rows above it.

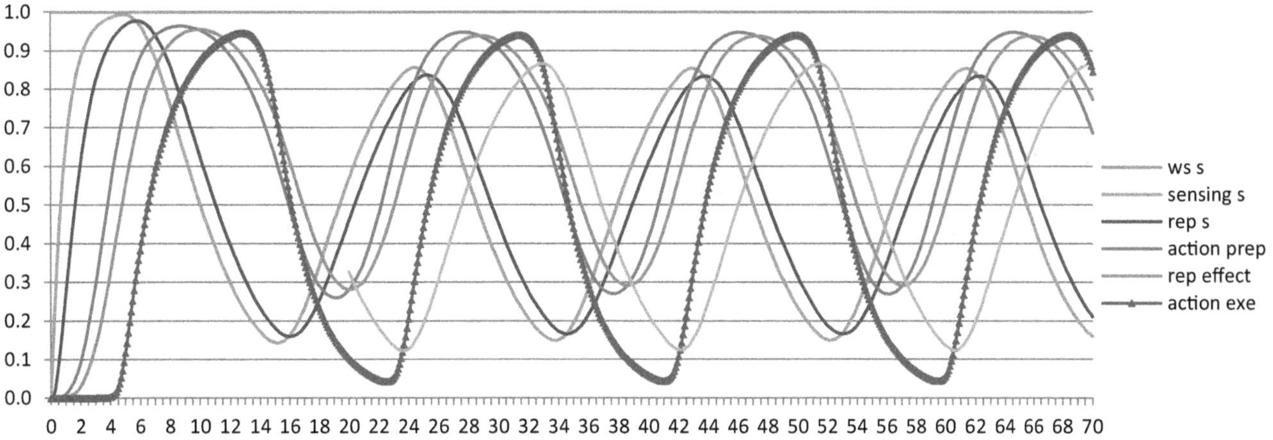

Fig. 7 Example simulation showing a limit cycle

Table 1 Overview of the outcomes of a mathematical analysis for stationary points in a limit cycle

	ws_e	ss_s	srs_s	srs_e	ps_a	es_a
Maxima						
Time point	69.9	61.4	62.2	65.8	64.6	68.3
State value	0.86700	0.85401	0.83455	0.93859	0.94754	0.93975
Aggregated impact	0.86105	0.85001	0.83325	0.93713	0.94703	0.94012
Absolute deviation	0.00595	0.00400	0.00131	0.00146	0.00051	0.00037
Minima						
Time point	60.6	52.2	53.0	57.1	56.1	59.4
State value	0.12553	0.14993	0.16699	0.29153	0.27012	0.04400
Aggregated impact	0.13033	0.15168	0.16689	0.29480	0.27159	0.04317
Absolute deviation	0.00480	0.00175	0.00009	0.00327	0.00147	0.00083

It turns out that the stationary point equations are fulfilled with an average accuracy over all states and stationary points of 0.002 and a maximal accuracy of 0.006, which both is $< 10^{-2}$. This provides evidence that the implemented model is correct in comparison to the model description. In Table 1 the more specific numbers are shown for the different states. For the maxima the average deviation is 0.00226, and the maximal absolute deviation is 0.00595 (which occurs for state ws_e). For the minima the average absolute deviation is 0.00204, and the maximal absolute deviation is 0.00480 (which again is for state ws_e). Taken minima and maxima together, the overall average absolute deviation is 0.00215, and the maximal absolute deviation is 0.00595 (for the maxima of state ws_e).

As another type example of the emergence of limit cycle behaviour, consider that in a realistic context stimuli can be present for some time, but also may be absent for certain periods according to fixed periods, for example, day/night rhythms. As an example, for Hebbian learning, for activations based on stimuli that return from time to time an analysis can be made about when there is enough stimulation over time to achieve or maintain a value for the weight ω of some connection. As an example, see the pattern in Fig. 7, where the upper graph shows the levels of both X_1 and X_2 (alternating between 0 and 1) and the lower graph shows how due to these activation periods, the periods of learning ($d_1 = 5$ time units) and pure extinction ($d_0 = 15$ time units) alternate. It turns out that there is a form of convergence not to one specific value of ω, but to a recurring pattern that repeats itself; this is a specific case of a limit cycle, in this case induced by environmental fluctuations.

8 Discussion

In this paper it was discussed how mathematical analysis can be used to find out some properties of a model. An advantage is that this is done without performing simulations. This advantage makes that it can be used as an additional source of knowledge, independent of a specific implementation of the model. By comparing properties found by mathematical analysis and properties observed in simulation experiments

Fig. 8 Limit cycle for $d_1 = 5$ (learning), $d_0 = 15$ (pure extinction), and $\eta = 0.2$, $\zeta = 0.04$ Equilibrium value 0.83, $\omega_{max} = 0.72$, $\omega_{min} = 0.39$ (*dotted lines*)

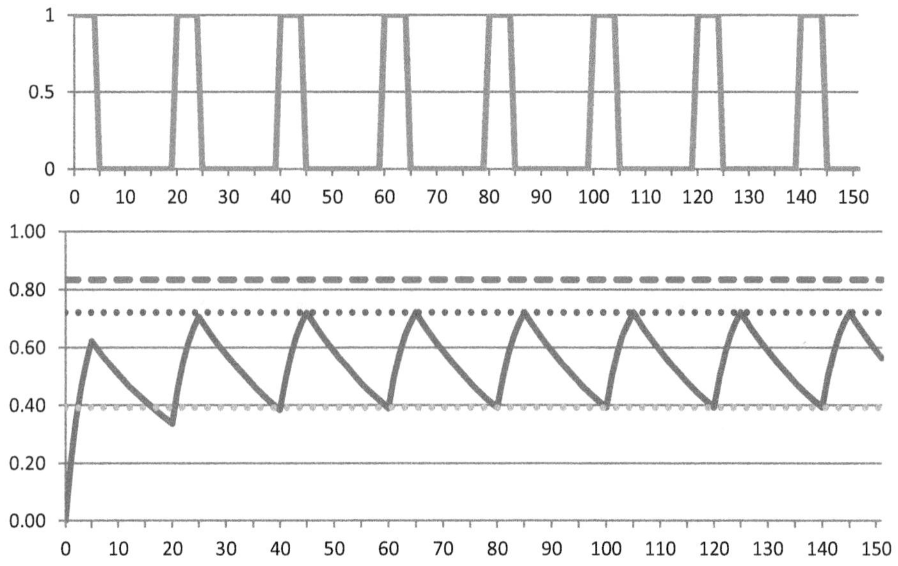

some form of verification can be done. If a discrepancy is found, for example, in the sense that the mathematical analysis predicts a certain property but some simulation does not satisfy this property, this can be a reason to inspect the implementation of the model carefully (and/or check whether the mathematical analysis is correct). Having such an option can be fruitful during a development process of a model, as to acquire empirical data for validation of a model may be more difficult or may take a longer time.

The techniques used for such mathematical analysis were adopted from [3,9,11–13]. In this literature many more techniques can be found than those covered in the current paper, for example, for the convergence speed (e.g. [10]) for attracting equilibria, but also for other types of properties. For example, there is underlying theory that proves the existence of certain patterns, for example, theorems from Poincaré (1881–1882) and Bendixson (1901) that state that under certain circumstances for two-dimensional systems (described by only two differential equations) limit cycles will occur. These are beyond the scope of this paper.

Mathematical analysis is not always easy or feasible. For example, linear equilibrium equations (for example, obtained when using scaled sum combination functions) in principle can be solved analytically in a generic form, thereby obtaining expressions for the equilibrium values in terms of the parameters of the model, but equilibrium equations involving logistic functions cannot be solved in such a manner. Nevertheless, for such cases often specific instances can be solved. Moreover, as discussed in Sect. 2, verification of a model does not depend on finding explicit analytical solutions of the equilibrium equations. For verification it is already sufficient if the equilibrium equations have been identified, which is always possible from the difference or differential equations. Then for each simulation trace observed equilibrium values can be substituted in these equations and by this it is checked whether they satisfy the equations. Therefore, in general, mathematical analysis still can add some value, in addition to systematic simulation experiments. However, a limitation is that although verification is always possible, prediction is not. For prediction without having any simulation, it is needed to find explicit analytical solutions of the equilibrium equations, and in many realistic models this is not feasible.

References

1. Bendixson, I.: Sur les courbes définies par des équations différentielles. Acta Math. **24**, 1–88 (1901)
2. Bi, G., Poo, M.: Synaptic modification by correlated activity: Hebb's postulate revisited. Annu. Rev. Neurosci. **24**, 139–166 (2001)
3. Brauer, F., Nohel, J.A.: Qualitative Theory of Ordinary Differential Equations. Benjamin, Amsterdam (1969)
4. Garagnani, M., Wennekers, T., Pulvermueller, F.: A neuroanatomically grounded Hebbian-learning model of attention-language interactions in the human brain. Eur. J. Neurosci. **27**(2008), 492–513 (2008)
5. Gerstner, W., Kistler, W.M.: Mathematical formulations of Hebbian learning. Biol. Cybern. **87**, 404–415 (2002)
6. Hebb, D.: (1949) The Organisation of Behavior. Wiley, New York (1949)
7. Hirsch, M.W.: The dynamical systems approach to differential equations. Bull. (New Series) Am. Math. Soc. **11**, 1–64 (1984)
8. Keysers, C., Perrett, D.I.: Demystifying social cognition: a Hebbian perspective. Trends Cognit. Sci. **8**(2004), 501–507 (2004)
9. Lotka, A.J.: Elements of Physical Biology. Williams and Wilkins Co. (1924), Dover Publications, 2nd ed. (1956)
10. Mathunjwa, J.S., Temple, J. (2006). Convergence behaviour in exogenous growth models. Discussion Paper No. 06/590, Department of Economics, University of Bristol
11. Picard, E.: Traité d'Analyse, vol. 1 (1891), vol. 2 (1893)

12. Poincaré, H.: Mémoire sur les courbes défine par une équation différentielle (1881–1882) (On curves defined by differential equations)
13. Poincaré, H.: New methods of celestial mechanics, vol. 3 (1892–1899) English translation (1967)
14. Sharpanskykh, A., Treur, J.: Modelling and analysis of social contagion in dynamic networks. Neurocomputing J. **146**(2014), 140–150 (2014)
15. Treur, J.: (2011a) A computational agent model for Hebbian learning of social interaction. In: Lu, B.-L., Zhang, L., Kwok, J. (eds.) Proceedings of the 18th international conference on neural information processing, ICONIP'11, Part I. Lecture Notes in Artificial Intelligence, vol. 7062, pp. 9–19. Springer, Berlin (2011)
16. Treur, J.: (2011b) Dreaming your fear away: a computational model for fear extinction learning during dreaming. In: Lu, B.-L., Zhang, L., Kwok, J. (eds.) Proceedings of the 18th international conference on neural information processing, ICONIP'11, Part III. Lecture Notes in Artificial Intelligence, vol. 7064, pp. 197–209. Springer, Berlin (2011)
17. Treur, J. (2016) Dynamic modeling based on a temporal-causal network modeling approach. Biologically Inspired Cognitive Architectures, 2016, ResearchGate https://www.researchgate.net/publication/289193241_Dynamic_Modeling_Based_on_a_Temporal-Causal_Network_Modeling_Approach **(to appear)**

10

Mixture of hyperspheres for novelty detection

Duy Nguyen[1] · Vinh Lai[1] · Khanh Nguyen[1] · Trung Le[1]

Abstract In this paper, we present a mixture of support vector data descriptions (mSVDD) for one-class classification or novelty detection. A mixture of optimal hyperspheres is automatically discovered to characterize data. The model includes two parts: log likelihood to control the fit of data to model (i.e., empirical risk) and regularization quantizer to control the generalization ability of model (i.e., general risk). Expectation maximization (EM) principle is employed to train our proposed mSVDD. We demonstrate the advantage of the proposed model: if learning mSVDD in the input space, it simulates learning a single hypersphere in the feature space and the accuracy is thus comparable, but the training time is significantly shorter.

Keywords Mixture of experts · Mixture model · Kernel method · One-class classification

1 Introduction

Novelty detection is an interesting research topic in many data analytics and machine learning tasks ranging from video security surveillance, network abnormality detection, and detection of abnormal gene expression sequence to name a few. Different from the binary classification which focuses mainly on balance dataset, novelty detection aims to learn from imbalance dataset where a majority in the dataset is normal data, and abnormal data or outliers constitute a minor portion of dataset. The purpose of novelty detection is to find patterns in data that do not conform to expected behaviors [5]. To obtain this aim, a data description is constructed to capture all characteristics of normal data, and subsequently this description is used to detect abnormal data which cannot fit it well. These anomaly patterns are interesting because they reveal actionable information, the known unknowns and unknown unknowns. Notable real-world applications of novelty detection include intrusion detection [10], fraud detection (credit card fraud detection, mobile phone fraud detection, insurance claim fraud detection) [7], industrial damage detection [2], and sensor network data processing [13].

Probability density-based and neural network-based approaches have been proposed to address novelty detection problems. Another notable solution is the kernel-based approach. At its crux, data are mapped into the feature space with very high or infinite dimension via a transformation. In this space, a simple geometric shape is learned to discover the domain of novelty [16,20,21]. One-class support vector machine (OCSVM) [20] uses an optimal hyperplane, which separates the origin from data samples, to distinguish abnormality from normality. The domain of novelty in this case is certainly a positive region of the optimal hyperplane with maximal margin, the distance from the origin to the hyperplane. In another approach, support vector data description (SVDD) [21], the novelty domain of the normal data, is defined as an optimal hypersphere in the feature space, which becomes a set of contours tightly covering the normal data when mapped back to the input space.

Data in real-world applications are often collected from many different data sources. Such a heterogeneous dataset requires a mixture of individual data descriptions. A mixture of experts refers to the problem of using and combining many experts (e.g., classification or regression models) for classification or prediction purpose [12]. Two challenging obstacles that need to be addressed include: (1) how to automatically

✉ Trung Le
trunglm@hcmup.edu.vn

1 Faculty of Information Technology, HCMc University of Pedagogy, Ho Chi Minh City, Vietnam

discover the appropriate number of experts in use or automatically do model selection; (2) how to train an individual expert with reference to others.

In this paper, we present a mixture of support vector data descriptions (mSVDD) for the novelty detection task. The idea of mSVDD is to use a set of hyperspheres as a data description for normal data. In mSVDD, we leverage the probabilistic framework with kernel-based method, where the model comprises two quantities: log likelihood to control the fit of data to the model (i.e., empirical error) and regularization quantizer to control the generalization capacity of the model (i.e., general error). The EM algorithm is used to train the model and the model is guaranteed to gradually converge to an appropriate set of optimal hyperspheres that well describes data. In the model, for each hypersphere (expert), a quantity, which expresses the total fit of data to this hypersphere, is utilized for model selection. We start with a maximal number of hyperspheres and step by step the redundant hyperspheres are eliminated. In the experimental section, we demonstrate the advantage of mSVDD: although learning in the input space, the set of hyperspheres offered by mSVDD is able to approximate a set of contours formed by a single optimal hypersphere in the feature space. In particular, our experiment on several benchmark datasets shows that mSVDD often yields a comparable classification accuracy while achieving a significant speed-up compared with the baselines.

To summarize, the contribution of the paper consists of the following points:

- We have viewed the problem of mixture of hyperspheres under the probabilistic perspective and proposed a mixture of support vector data description (mSVDD) for novelty detection. We have employed the EM algorithm to train mSVDD. The resultant model can automatically discover the appropriate number of experts in use and the weight of each expert.
- We have conducted the experiments on several benchmark datasets. The results have showed that mSVDD can learn mixture of hyperspheres in the input space which can approximately represent the set of contours generated by the traditional SVDD in the feature space. While the accuracy of mSVDD is comparable, the training time of mSVDD is faster than the kernelized baselines, since all computations are performed directly in the input space.
- Compared with the conference version [15], we have introduced two new strategies, i.e., approximate SVDD (amSVDD) and probabilistic mSVDD (pmSVDD), to improve the training time and accuracy compared with the general mSVDD. We have also conducted more experiments to evaluate these two new strategies and investigated the behaviors of the proposed algorithms.

2 Related work

We review the studies on a mixture of experts closely related to our work. These works can be divided into two branches: mixture of hyperplanes and mixture of hyperspheres. The works presented in [6,12,14] applied divide-and-conquer strategy to partition the input space into many disjoint regions, and in each region, a linear or nonlinear SVM can be employed to classify data. In [19], multiple hyperplanes were used for learning to rank. It also follows up the divide-and-conquer strategy and the final rank is aggregated by the ranks offered by the hyperplanes. Multiple hyperplane was brought into play in [1,24] for multiclass classification where each class was characterized by a set of hyperplanes. In [9], a mixing of linear SVMs was used to simulate a nonlinear SVM. This approach has both the efficiency of linear SVM and the power of nonlinear SVM for classifying data. Recently, a Dirichlet process mixture of large-margin kernel machine was proposed in [27] for multi-way classification. This work conjoined the advantages of Bayesian nonparametrics in automatically discovering the underlying mixture components and maximum entropy discrimination framework in integrating large-margin principle with Bayesian posterior inference.

Yet another approach to combine linear classifiers for nonlinear classification is ensemble methods including bagging [3], boosting [8], and random forests [4]. They implement a strong classifier by integrating many weak classifiers. However, since ensemble methods tend to use a great number of base classifiers and for stable model like SVM, the training is quite robust to data perturbation. Hence, the classifiers obtained at different stages are usually highly correlated and this would increase the number of iterations required for convergence and also bring the negative effect to the performance of combination scheme with such classifiers used as weak learners.

Mostly related to ours are the works of [17,18,25], which are shared with us the idea of using a set of hyperspheres as the domain of novelty. In [25], the procedure to discover a set of hyperspheres is ad hoc, heuristic and does not conform to any learning principle. The works of [17,18] are driven by the principle learning with minimum volume. However, the main drawback in those works is that the model selection cannot be performed automatically and the number of hyperspheres in use must be declared a priori.

3 Background

3.1 Expectation maximization principle

The main task in machine learning problems is to find the optimal parameter θ of the model given a training set D. In probabilistic perspective, it is described as a maximization of log likelihood function. However, estimating parameters using maximum-likelihood principle is very hard if there are some missing data or latent variables (i.e., cannot be observed). The expectation maximization principle [11], for short EM, was proposed to overcome this obstacle. EM is an iterative method, in which each iteration consists of expectation step (E-step) followed by the maximization step (M-step). The basic idea of EM is described as follows.

Let $\{x_n\}_{n=1}^N$ be the observed data and $\{z_n\}_{n=1}^N$ the latent variables; the log likelihood function is given as follows:

$$l(\theta) = \sum_{n=1}^{N} \log p(x_n \mid \theta) = \sum_{n=1}^{N} \log \left[\sum_{z_n} p(x_n, z_n \mid \theta) \right].$$

As can be seen, the log cannot be pushed inside the sum; hence it is hard to find the maximum of $l(\theta)$. Instead of finding maximum likelihood, EM involves the complete data log likelihood as follows:

$$l_c(\theta) = \sum_{n=1}^{N} \log p(x_n, z_n \mid \theta).$$

In the E-step, the expected complete data log likelihood $Q(\theta, \theta^{t-1})$ is computed by formulation as follows:

$$Q\left(\theta, \theta^{t-1}\right) = \mathbb{E}\left[l_c(\theta) \mid D, \theta^{t-1}\right].$$

Then, in the M-step, θ^t is found by optimizing the Q function w.r.t θ

$$\theta^t = \arg\max\ Q\left(\theta, \theta^{t-1}\right).$$

3.2 Weighted support vector data description

Given the training set $D = \{(x_n, y_n)\}_{n=1}^N$ where $x_n \in \mathbb{R}^d$ and $y_n \in \{-1; 1\}$, $n = 1, \ldots, N$ including normal (labeled by 1) and abnormal (labeled by -1) observations. To find the domain of novelty, weighted SVDD [26] learns an optimal hypersphere which encloses all normal observations with tolerances. Each observation x_n is associated with a weight $C\lambda_n$ and a smaller value for the weight implies that the correspondent observation is allowed to have a bigger error. The optimization problem of weighted SVDD is defined as follows:

$$\min_{c,R,\xi} \left(R^2 + C \sum_{n=1}^{N} \lambda_n \xi_n \right)$$

$$\text{s.t. : } \|x_n - c\|^2 \le R^2 + \xi_n,\ n = 1, \ldots, N;\ y_n = 1 \quad (1)$$

$$\|x_n - c\|^2 \ge R^2 - \xi_n,\ n = 1, \ldots, N;\ y_n = -1$$

$$\xi_n \ge 0,\ n = 1, \ldots, n$$

where R, c are the radius and center of the optimal hypersphere, respectively.

It follows that the error at the observation x_n is given as

$$\xi_n = \max\left\{0,\ y_n\left(\|x_n - c\|^2 - R^2\right)\right\}$$

and the optimization problem in Eq. (1) can be rewritten as follows:

$$\min_{c,R}\left(R^2 + C \sum_{n=1}^{N} \lambda_n \max\left\{0,\ y_n\left(\|x_n - c\|^2 - R^2\right)\right\}\right).$$

4 Mixture of support vector data descriptions

4.1 Idea of mixture of support vector data descriptions

Let us denote the latent variable which specifies the expert of x_n by $z_n \in \{0; 1\}^m$. The latent variable z_n, a bit pattern of size m where only its jth component is 1 and others are 0, means that the jth expert (i.e., the jth SVDD) is used to classify the observation x_n. The graphical model of mSVDD is shown in Fig. 1.

In mSVDD, we describe normal data using a set of m hyperspheres denoted by $\mathbb{S}_j(c_j, R_j)$, $j = 1, \ldots, m$. Given the jth hypersphere and the observation x_n, the conditional probability to classify x_n w.r.t the jth hypersphere is given as follows:

$$\begin{aligned} p(\text{normal} \mid x_n, \mathbb{S}_j) &= p(y_n = 1 \mid x_n, \mathbb{S}_j) \\ &= p\left(y_n = 1 \mid x_n, z_n^j = 1, \theta\right) = s\left(R_j^2 - \left\|x_n - c_j\right\|^2\right) \\ p(\text{abnormal} \mid x_n, \mathbb{S}_j) &= p(y_n = -1 \mid x_n, \mathbb{S}_j) \\ &= p\left(y_n = -1 \mid x_n, z_n^j = 1, \theta\right) = s\left(\left\|x_n - c_j\right\|^2 - R_j^2\right), \end{aligned} \quad (2)$$

where $s(x) = \frac{1}{1+e^{-x}}$ is the sigmoid function and θ is the model parameter.

Intuitively, $p(\text{normal} \mid x_n, \mathbb{S}_j)$ is exactly $\frac{1}{2}$ if x_n locates at the boundary of the hypersphere $\mathbb{S}_j$ and increases to 1 when x_n resides inside the hypersphere or decreases from 0 when

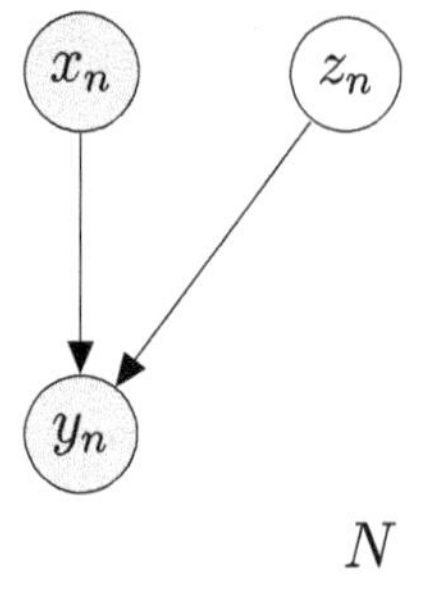

Fig. 1 Graphical model of a mixture of SVDD

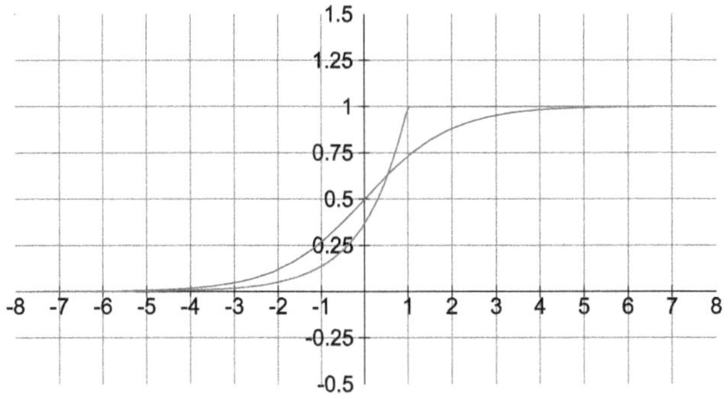

Fig. 2 Plots of two functions on the same coordinate when $\delta = 0$

x_n resides outside the hypersphere and moves apart from it. Because it is difficult to handle the log of $s(x) = \frac{1}{1+e^{-x}}$, we approximate $s(x)$ as follows:

$$s(x) = \frac{1}{1+e^{-x}} \approx e^{-\max\{0;\delta - x\}}. \tag{3}$$

To visually see how tight the approximation is, we plot the above two functions on the same coordinate when $\delta = 1$. As can be seen in Fig. 2, the blue line (presenting function $\frac{1}{1+e^{-x}}$) is close to the green line (presenting function $e^{-\max\{0;\delta-x\}}$). Therefore, the function $e^{-\max\{0;\delta-x\}}$ is a good approximation of the sigmoid function $s(x)$.

The marginal likelihood is given as: $p(Y|X,\theta) = \prod_{n=1}^{N} p(y_n \mid x_n, \theta)$, where $X = [x_n]_{n=1}^{N} \in \mathbb{R}^{d\times N}$, $Y = [y_n]_{n=1}^{N} \in \mathbb{R}^{N}$, and $\theta = (\theta_1, \theta_2, \ldots, \theta_m)$ encompass the parameters of all experts.

4.2 Optimization problem

To take into account both the general and empirical risks, the following optimization problem is proposed:

$$\max_{\theta} \left(-\sum_{j=1}^{m} R_j^2 + C \times \log p(Y \mid X, \theta) \right). \tag{4}$$

In the optimization problem as shown in Eq. (4), we minimize $\sum_{j=1}^{m} R_j^2$ to maximize the generalization capacity of the model. In the meanwhile, we maximize the log marginal likelihood $\log p(Y \mid X, \theta)$ to boost the fit of the model to the observed data X. The trade-off parameter C is used to control the proportion of the first and second quantities or to govern the balance between overfitting and underfitting.

To efficiently solve the optimization problem in Eq. (4), we make use of EM principle by iteratively performing two steps: E-step and M-step.

4.2.1 E-step

Given $z = (z_1, z_2, \ldots, z_N)$, we first compute the complete log likelihood as

$$l_c(\theta \mid D) = \log p(Y, \mathbf{z} \mid X, \theta) = \sum_{n=1}^{N} \log p(y_n, z_n | x_n, \theta). \tag{5}$$

It is clear that (cf. [15] for details)

$$\begin{aligned}
&\log p(y_n, z_n \mid x_n, \theta) \\
&= \log \left(\prod_{j=1}^{m} \left(p\left(y_n \mid z_n^j = 1, x_n, \theta\right) p\left(z_n^j = 1 \mid x_n, \theta\right) \right)^{z_n^j} \right) \\
&= \sum_{j=1}^{m} z_n^j \left(-\xi_j(x_n) + \log \alpha_j\right),
\end{aligned} \tag{6}$$

where $\alpha_j \triangleq p\left(z_n^j = 1 \mid \theta\right)$ is interpreted as the mixing proportion of the jth expert and satisfies $\sum_{j=1}^{m} \alpha_j = 1$. Because it is difficult to compute the log of $p\left(y_n \mid x_n, z_n^j = 1, \theta\right)$, as mentioned before, we approximate $p\left(y_n \mid x_n, z_n^j = 1, \theta\right)$ as

$$\begin{aligned}
&p\left(y_n \mid x_n, z_n^j = 1, \theta\right) \\
&= e^{-\xi_j(x_n)} = e^{-\max\left\{0;\delta - y_n\left(R_j^2 - \|x_n - c_j\|^2\right)\right\}}.
\end{aligned}$$

Therefore, we have

$$\log p(y_n, z_n \mid x_n, \theta) = \sum_{j=1}^{m} z_n^j \left(-\xi_j(x_n) + \log \alpha_j\right).$$

Substituting Eq. (6) in Eq. (5), we gain the following:

$$\begin{aligned}
l_c(\theta \mid D) &= \sum_{n=1}^{N} \sum_{j=1}^{m} z_n^j \left(-\xi_j(x_n) + \log \alpha_j\right) \\
&= \sum_{j=1}^{m} \sum_{n=1}^{N} z_n^j \left(-\xi_j(x_n) + \log \alpha_j\right).
\end{aligned}$$

To fulfill the E-step, we compute the following conditional expectation when $\mathbf{z}$ is varied (cf. [15] for details):

$$\begin{aligned}
\mathbb{E}(\theta) &= \left\langle -\sum_{j=1}^{m} R_j^2 + C l_c(\theta \mid D) \right\rangle_{z/D,\theta^{(t)}} \\
&= -\sum_{j=1}^{m} R_j^2 + C \sum_{j=1}^{m} \sum_{n=1}^{N} \left\langle z_n^j \right\rangle_{z/D,\theta^{(t)}} \left(-\xi_j(x_n) + \log \alpha_j\right)
\end{aligned}$$

$$= -\sum_{j=1}^{m} R_j^2 + C \sum_{j=1}^{m} \sum_{n=1}^{N} \tau_{jn}^{(t)} \left(-\xi_j(x_n) + \log \alpha_j\right),$$

where $\theta^{(t)}$ is the value of parameter θ at t^{th} iteration and $\tau_{jn}^{(t)} \triangleq p\left(z_n^j = 1 \mid x_n, y_n = 1, \theta^{(t)}\right)$ can be computed by the Bayes formula as follows:

$$\tau_{jn}^{(t)} \triangleq p\left(z_n^j = 1 \mid x_n, y_n, \theta^{(t)}\right) = \frac{p\left(y_n \mid z_n^j = 1, x_n, \theta^{(t)}\right)\alpha_j^{(t)}}{\sum_{k=1}^{m} p\left(y_n \mid z_n^k = 1, x_n, \theta^{(t)}\right)\alpha_k^{(t)}}.$$

4.2.2 M-step

In this step, we need to find $\theta = (\theta_1, \theta_2, \ldots, \theta_m)$ where $\theta_j = (\alpha_j, c_j, R_j)$, which maximizes $\mathbb{E}(\theta)$. To this end, we rewrite this function as

$$\mathbb{E}(\theta) = -\sum_{j=1}^{m}\left(R_j^2 + \sum_{n=1}^{N} C\tau_{jn}^{(t)}\xi_j(x_n)\right) + C\sum_{j=1}^{m}\tau_j^{(t)}\log \alpha_j$$
$$= -E_1(\mathbf{R}, \mathbf{c}) + CE_2(\boldsymbol{\alpha}),$$

where $\tau_j^{(t)} \triangleq \sum_{n=1}^{N} \tau_{jn}^{(t)}$, $\mathbf{R} = \left[R_j\right]_{j=1}^{m}$, $\mathbf{c} = \left[c_j\right]_{j=1}^{m}$, and $\boldsymbol{\alpha} = \left[\alpha_j\right]_{j=1}^{m}$.

It is obvious that the two following optimization problems need to be solved. The first becomes

$$\max_{\boldsymbol{\alpha}} \left(\sum_{j=1}^{m} \tau_j^{(t)} \log \alpha_j\right)$$
$$\text{s.t.}: \sum_{j=1}^{m} \alpha_j = 1,\ \alpha_j \geq 0,\ j = 1, \ldots, m.$$

The rule to update $\boldsymbol{\alpha}$ is given as: $\alpha_j^{(t+1)} = \frac{\tau_j^{(t)}}{\sum_{k=1}^{m} \tau_k^{(t)}}$.

The second is given as:

$$\min_{c_j, R_j}\left(R_j^2 + \sum_{n=1}^{N} C\tau_{jn}^{(t)} \max\left\{0, \delta - y_n\left(R_j^2 - \left\|x_n - c_j\right\|^2\right)\right\}\right)$$

where $j = 1, \ldots, m$.

If we choose $\delta = 0$, the second is indeed split into m independent weighted SVDD problems as

$$\min_{c_j, R_j}\left(R_j^2 + \sum_{n=1}^{N} C\tau_{jn}^{(t)} \max\left\{0, y_n\left(\left\|x_n - c_j\right\|^2 - R_j^2\right)\right\}\right)$$

where $j = 1, \ldots, m$. (7)

4.3 How to do model selection in mixture of SVDDs

We start with the number of hyperspheres $m = m_{\max}$ and make use of the criterion $\alpha_j^{(t+1)} < \lambda$, where $\lambda > 0$ is a threshold, for decision to eliminate the jth hypersphere. The small value for the mixing proportion $\alpha_j^{(t+1)}$ of the jth hypersphere implies that $\tau_j^{(t)}$ is too small as compared to others. The quantity $\tau_j^{(t)} = \sum_{n=1}^{N} p(z_n^j = 1 \mid x_n, y_n = 1, \theta^{(t)})$ is interpreted as the sum of the relevance levels of observations to the jth hypersphere and its small value implies that this hypersphere is redundant and has a too small radius.

4.4 The approaches to make a decision in mSVDD

In mSVDD, a natural way to classify a new observation x is to examine whether it belongs to at least one of m hyperspheres. The decision function is given as follows:

$$f(x) = \max\left\{\text{sign}\left(R_1^2 - \|x - c_1\|^2\right), \ldots, \text{sign}\left(R_m^2 - \|x - c_m\|^2\right)\right\}$$

where R_j, c_j are radius and center of the jth hypersphere, respectively.

The above decision function can be regarded as a hard way to decide the normality or abnormality. To take advantage of the probabilistic perspective of mSVDD, we propose a probabilistic approach to make a decision. This approach decides an observation x as a normal data point if more than k experts (e.g., $k = 0.8m$) classify it as normal data with a confidence level over ρ, that is

$$f(x) = \begin{cases} 1 & \text{if } \exists j: p\left(\text{normal} \mid x, \mathbb{S}_j\right) = 1 \\ 1 & \text{if } \left|\left\{j: p\left(\text{normal} \mid x, \mathbb{S}_j\right) \geq \rho\right\}\right| \geq k, \\ -1 & \text{otherwise} \end{cases}$$

where the second case means that x is classified as normal if there are more than k experts that predict it as normal with a confidence level over ρ.

Table 1 Statistics of experimental datasets

Datasets	#Train	#Dim	Domain
a9a	26, 049	123	Social survey
usps	5833	256	OCR images
Mushroom	6500	112	Biology
Shuttle	34, 800	9	Physical
Splice	800	60	Biology

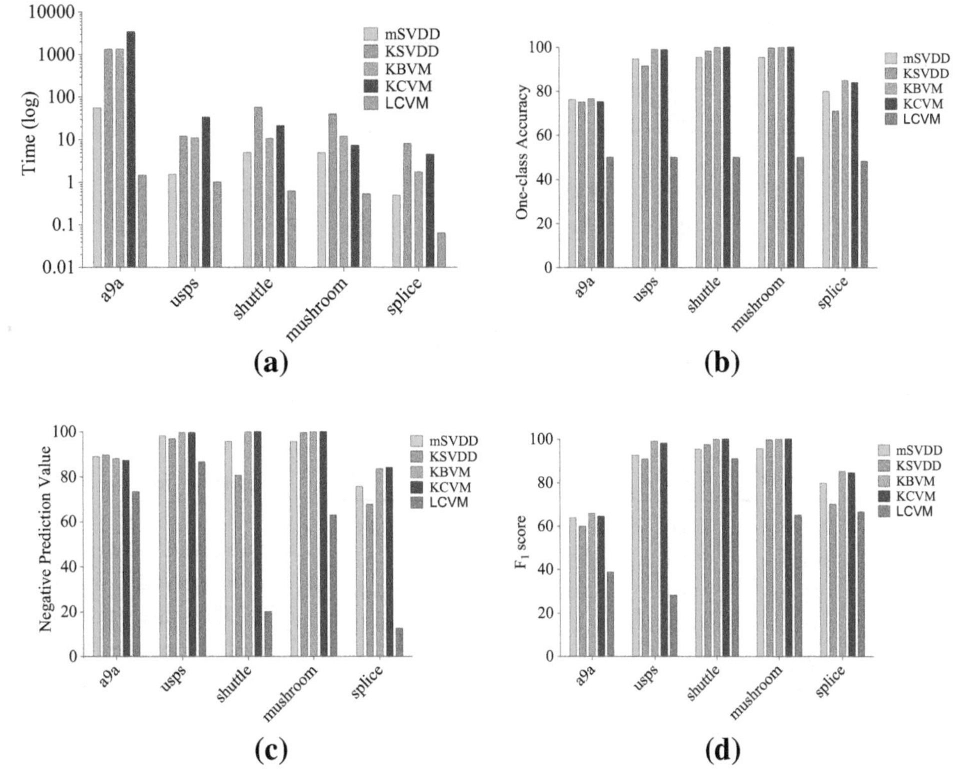

Fig. 3 Experimental results on the datasets. **a** Training times, **b** One-class accuracy, **c** negative prediction value, **d** F_1 score

4.5 Approximate mixture of SVDDs

According to Eq. (7), M-step requires the solutions of m weighted SVDD problems, each of which requires training the whole training set. It is also noteworthy that the variable $\tau_{jn}^{(t)}$ governs the influence of data point x_n to the jth hypersphere. A large value of $\tau_{jn}^{(t)}$ highly affects the determination of the jth hypersphere and vice versa, and a small value of $\tau_{jn}^{(t)}$ slightly affects the determination of the jth hypersphere. Therefore, the data point x_n with a small value of $\tau_{jn}^{(t)}$ can be eliminated when training the jth hypersphere without possibly changing the learning performance. In return, the training time of a mixture of SVDDs would be improved because training each SVDD now possibly involves a small subset of the training set. To realize this idea, we define the parameter $\mu \in (0, 1)$ as a threshold to eliminate data point x_n in the determination of the jth hypersphere (i.e., $\tau_{jn}^{(t)} < \mu$).

5 Experiment

5.1 Experimental settings

We establish the experiments over five datasets.[1]

[1] All datasets can be downloaded at the URL http://www.csie.ntu.edu.tw/~cjlin/libsvmtools/datasets.

The statistics of the experimental datasets is given in Table 1. To form the imbalanced datasets, we choose a class as the positive class and randomly select the negative data samples from the remaining classes such that the proportion of positive and negative data samples is 10 : 1. We make a comparison of our proposed mSVDD with ball vector machine (BVM) [22], core vector machine (CVM) [23] and support vector data description (SVDD) [21]. All codes are implemented in C/C++. All experiments are run on the computer with core I3 2.3GHz and 16GB in RAM.

5.2 How fast and accurate the proposed method compares with the baselines

We do experiments to investigate the performance of our proposed mSVDD in the input space compared with BVM, CVM and SVDD in the feature space with RBF kernel, named KBVM, KCVM, and KSVDD, respectively. To prove the necessity of mSVDD, we also compare mSVDD with CVM using the linear kernel (i.e., LCVM). We wish to validate that with mixture model dataset, a single hypersphere offered by LCVM cannot be sufficiently robust to classify it. We apply fivefold cross-validation to select the trade-off parameter C for KBVM, LCVM, KCVM, KSVDD, mSVDD and the kernel width parameter γ for KBVM, KCVM and KSVDD. The considered ranges are $C \in \{2^{-3}, 2^{-1}, \ldots, 2^{29}, 2^{31}\}$ and $\gamma \in \{2^{-3}, 2^{-1}, \ldots, 2^{29}, 2^{31}\}$. With mSVDD and LCVM, the linear kernel given by $K(x, x') = \langle x, x' \rangle$ is used, whereas

Table 2 One-class accuracy (in %) comparison

Dataset	One-class accuracy				
	mSVDD	SVDD	KBVM	KCVM	LCVM
a9a	76.18	75.06	76.62	75.24	50.00
usps	94.81	91.65	99.15	98.89	50.02
Shuttle	95.43	98.24	99.99	99.99	50.00
Mushroom	95.48	99.75	100	100	50.10
Splice	80.00	70.98	84.92	83.84	48.28

Table 3 Negative prediction value (in %) comparison

Dataset	Negative prediction value				
	mSVDD	KSVDD	KBVM	KCVM	LCVM
a9a	88.99	89.80	88.13	87.24	73.44
usps	98.20	96.84	99.67	99.58	86.67
Shuttle	95.68	80.63	99.99	99.97	20.00
Mushroom	95.61	99.64	100	100	62.86
Splice	75.70	67.52	83.60	84.11	12.50

Table 4 F_1 score (in %) comparison

Dataset	F_1 score				
	mSVDD	KSVDD	KBVM	KCVM	LCVM
a9a	63.76	59.75	65.91	64.30	38.76
usps	92.60	90.82	99.07	98.04	28.14
Shuttle	95.40	97.45	100	99.99	90.99
Mushroom	95.76	99.74	100	100	65.02
Splice	79.80	69.96	85.24	84.59	66.44

with kernel versions, the RBF kernel given by $K\left(x, x'\right) = e^{-\gamma\|x-x'\|^2}$ is employed. It is certainly true that the computation cost of the linear kernel is much lower than that of the RBF kernel. We fix $\delta = 0$ in all experiments; then in Sect. 5.4 we will investigate the behavior of mSVDD when δ is varied. We repeat each experiment five times and compute the means of the corresponding measures. We report training times (cf. Table 5 and Fig. 3a), the one-class accuracy (cf. Table 2 and Fig. 3b), the negative prediction values (NPVs) (cf. Table 3 and Fig. 3c) and F_1 score (cf. Table 4 and Fig. 3d) corresponding to the optimal values of C, γ.

In addition, the one-class accuracy is computed by $acc = \frac{\%TP+\%TN}{2} = \frac{acc^{+}+acc^{-}}{2}$. This measure is appropriate for one-class classification, since it is required to achieve high values for both acc^{+} and acc^{-} to produce a high one-class accuracy. The negative prediction values (NPVs) are computed by $NPV = \frac{TN}{TN+FN}$. This formulation indicates that a less number of false negative (FN) produces a higher value of NPV. F_1 score is the harmonic mean of precision and recall and is computed by $F_1 = \frac{2.precision.recall}{precision+recall}$ where $precision = \frac{TP}{TP+FP}$ and $recall = \frac{TP}{TP+FN}$. F_1 score can be rewritten as $F_1 = \frac{2.TP}{2.TP+FP+FN}$ which shows that a higher value of F_1 score is caused by a less number for both false negative and false positive.

Table 5 Training time (in s) comparison

Dataset	Training time				
	mSVDD	KSVDD	KBVM	KCVM	LCVM
a9a	55.48	1,334.75	1,342.05	3,396.91	1.45
usps	1.53	11.92	10.95	33.30	1.02
Shuttle	5.00	57.11	10.55	20.92	0.62
Mushroom	5.00	39.36	11.90	7.29	0.53
Splice	0.50	8.10	1.75	4.47	0.06

As observed from the experimental results, our proposed mSVDD is faster than others (except LCVM) on all datasets. This observation is reasonable since mSVDD learns m hyperspheres in the input space and, hence, is slower than learning only one hypersphere in the input space. However, mSVDD is faster than the kernel versions because of its lower kernel computation cost. Regarding the measures involving the learning performance, mSVDD is comparable or a little less than others especially KBVM and KCVM. The reason is that in mSVDD, each component hypersphere in the input space can simulate a contour generated by mapping back the optimal hypersphere of KSVDD, KBVM, and KCVM in the feature space into the input space. The slightly lower accuracy and NPVs of mSVDD compared to the kernel versions comes from the fact the hyperspheres of mSVDD may be less robust than its representative contours.

To visually support the above reason, we design experiments on 2-D datasets as displayed in Figs. 4 and 5. In Fig. 4, mSVDD recommends two hyperspheres in the input space to approximate two contours formed by a single hypersphere in the feature space. In Fig. 5, mSVDD offers three simple hyperspheres which can be visually seen to sufficiently simulate the set of contours formed by a single hypersphere in the feature space. The results of LCVM in all cases are worse, because it learns a single hypersphere in the input space which cannot sufficiently represent the contours formed by a single hypersphere in the feature space.

5.3 How approximate and probabilistic approaches improve mSVDD

We empirically compare mSVDD with its two variations which are approximate approach (amSVDD) and probability approach (pmSVDD). In amSVDD, we use the threshold $\mu = 0.8$ to eliminate data points for reducing training size

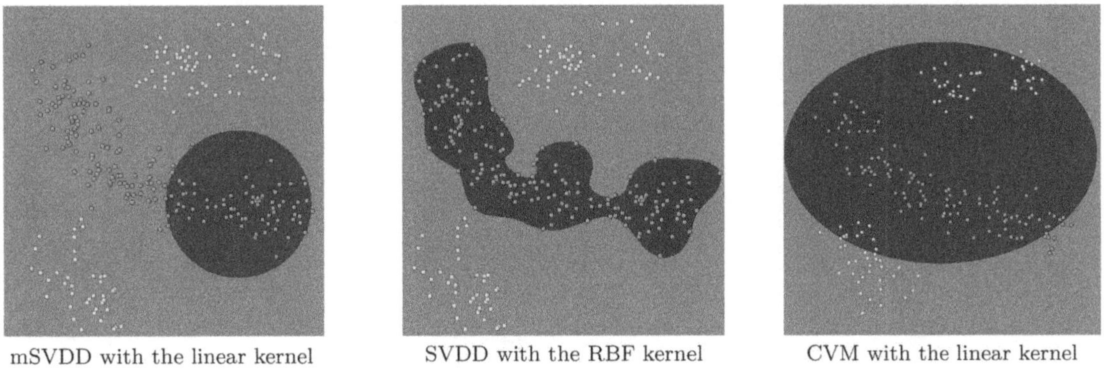

Fig. 4 Comparison of mSVDD with the linear kernel, SVDD with the RBF kernel, and CVM with the linear kernel

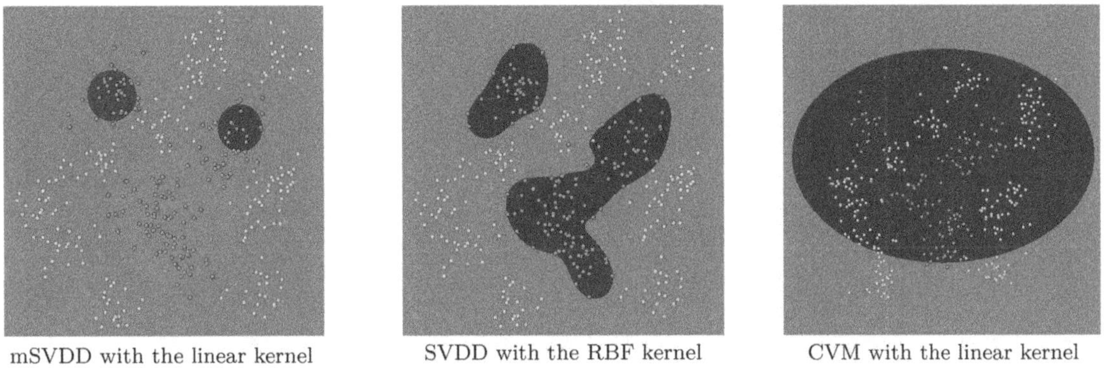

Fig. 5 Comparison of mSVDD with the linear kernel, SVDD with the RBF kernel, and CVM with the linear kernel

Table 6 One-class accuracy (in %) and training time (in s) comparison

Dataset	One-class accuracy			Training time		
	mSVDD	amSVDD	pmSVDD	mSVDD	amSVDD	pmSVDD
a9a	76.18	77.42	77.43	55.48	60.89	58.77
usps	94.81	93.29	95.20	1.53	1.41	1.09
Mushroom	95.48	92.74	92.35	5.00	4.74	5.39
Australian	81.39	81.06	82.57	0.06	0.02	0.06
Breast-cancer	96.44	94.51	96.75	0.02	0.01	0.02

Table 7 Negative prediction value (in %) and F_1 score (in %) comparison

Dataset	Negative prediction value			F_1 score		
	mSVDD	amSVDD	pmSVDD	mSVDD	amSVDD	pmSVDD
a9a	88.99	90.77	90.78	63.76	63.49	63.49
usps	98.20	97.77	98.36	92.60	89.85	92.68
Mushroom	95.61	92.14	91.42	95.76	92.25	91.79
Australian	83.02	84.69	84.12	79.23	79.90	80.66
Breast-cancer	92.37	86.59	94.19	97.13	95.14	97.54

in each SVDD problem. Our pmSVDD applies probability perspective and allows experts to vote when predicting new data. We set the parameter k to 2 and the parameter ρ to 0.8. Tables 6, 7 and Fig. 6 summarize the performance measures of mSVDD, amSVDD, and pmSVDD. The results show that pmSVDD achieves higher accuracies on all datasets, except mushroom, in comparison to mSVDD. This demonstrates that the probability approach really improves mSVDD by allowing a voting scheme and using probabilistic perspective. For amSVDD, its training time is usually less than others in

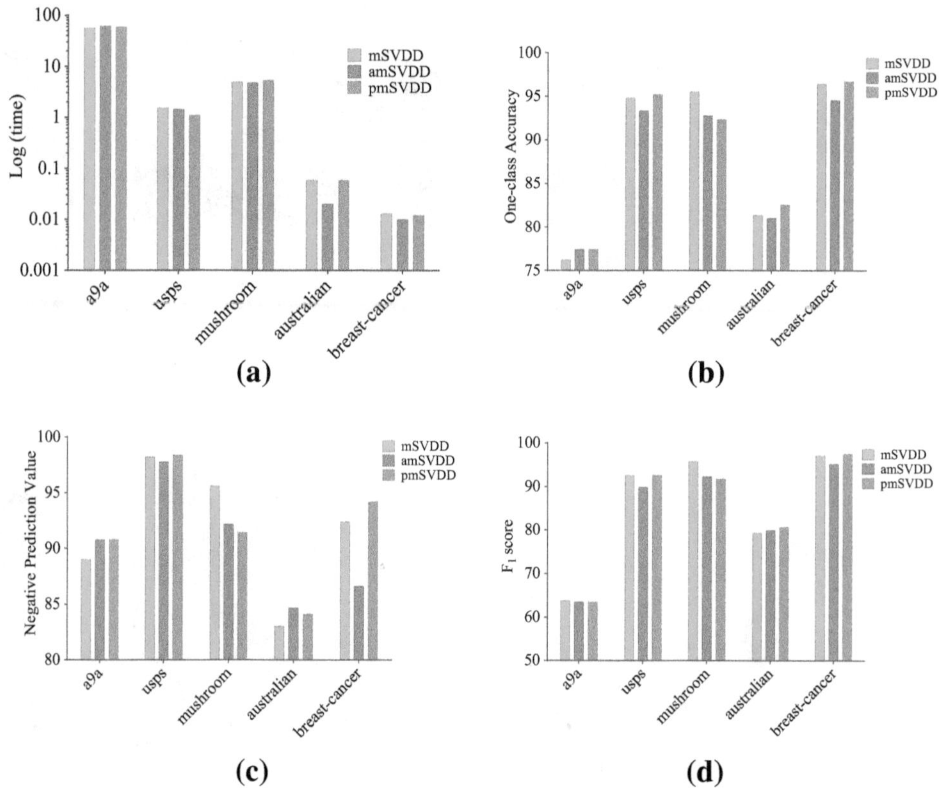

Fig. 6 Experimental results of the datasets on cross-validation. **a** Training times, **b** One-class accuracy, **c** negative prediction value, **d** F_1 score

Table 8 The one-class accuracy when parameter δ is varied

$\delta =$	**–1**	**–0.75**	**–0.50**	**–0.25**	**0**	**0.25**	**0.50**	**0.75**
a9a	74.93	76.08	75.54	74.78	74.32	75.69	75.07	75.41
usps	93.96	95.011	92.68	93.51	93.41	94.46	93.50	92.57
Mushroom	95.55	95.30	96.20	95.83	95.86	95.00	95.05	95.55
Australian	78.90	79.04	79.08	77.12	78.94	78.06	77.42	77.49
Diabetes	67.99	68.40	68.30	72.78	72.70	71.69	74.03	73.21

Table 9 The negative prediction value when parameter δ is varied

$\delta =$	**–1**	**–0.75**	**–0.50**	**–0.25**	**0**	**0.25**	**0.50**	**0.75**
a9a	87.86	88.83	88.56	87.69	87.49	88.39	88.00	88.14
usps	98.01	98.37	97.56	97.79	97.68	98.08	97.78	97.52
mushroom	95.61	96.12	96.19	95.24	96.29	94.45	95.02	94.82
australian	79.73	79.21	80.00	77.30	79.87	78.62	77.34	76.74
diabetes	49.28	50.73	51.88	51.78	52.99	52.42	54.21	52.10

all datasets, except a9a. Obviously, it comes from the reasonable reduction in training size of each SVDD problem at each step. This allows amSVDD to run faster than others while still preserving the accuracy.

5.4 How variation of the parameter δ influences accuracy

To analyze how parameter δ affects the one-class accuracy and negative prediction value, we conduct the experiment where δ is varied and other parameters are kept fixed. As observed from Tables 8 and 9, when δ is varied in ascending order, the accuracy at first increases to its peak and then gradually decreases. This fact may be partially explained as δ is altered and also changes the probability function of the observed data to classify them with respect to a particular hypersphere. When δ decreases, the component hypersphere tends to absorb more data outside it and, consequently, the hypersphere becomes bigger. Therefore, some abnormal data points can be misclassified. Reversely,

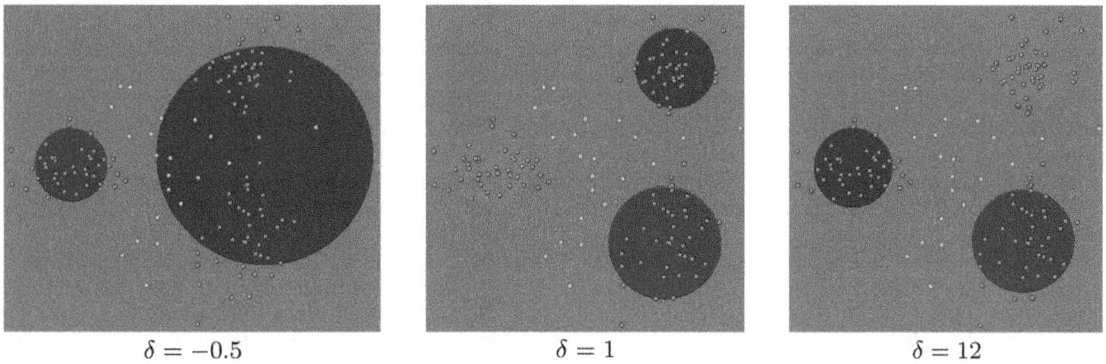

Fig. 7 Behavior of mSVDD when parameter δ is varied

the component hypersphere tends to be smaller and would not give a very high probability to data located inside the hypersphere and near the boundary. This prevents the model from misclassifying abnormal data points, but have the side effect of increasing the misclassification of normal data.

To visually manifest the above reason, we also provide simulation study on $2 - D$ datasets, as displayed in Fig. 7. When we set $\delta = -0.5$ and start with 3 hyperspheres, the hyperspheres tend to become bigger; as a result, two of them overlap each other. In the meanwhile, we increase δ to 1 and get a better solution which induces 90 % one-class accuracy. However, if we continue to increase δ to 12, the hypersphere is too small to describe normal data and, thus, the one-class accuracy declines to 88.75 %.

6 Conclusion

Leveraging on the expectation maximization principle, we propose a mixture of support vector data descriptions for one-class classification or novelty detection problem. Instead of learning the optimal hypersphere in the feature space involving costly RBF kernel computation, mSVDD learns a set of hypersphere(s) in the input space. Each component hypersphere is able to simulate a contour generated by mapping back the optimal hypersphere in the feature space into the input space. The experiments established on the benchmark datasets show that the mSVDD obtains shorter training time while achieving comparable one-class classification accuracies compared with other methods operated in the feature space.

References

1. Aiolli, F., Sperduti, A.: Multiclass classification with multi-prototype support vector machines. J. Mach. Learn. Res. **6**, 817–850 (2005)
2. Basu, S., Meckesheimer, M.: Automatic outlier detection for time series: an application to sensor data. Knowl. Inf. Syst. **11**(2), 137–154 (2007)
3. Breiman, L.: Bagging predictors. Mach. Learn. **24**(2), 123–140 (1996)
4. Breiman, L.: Random forests. Mach. Learn. **45**(1), 5–32 (2001)
5. Chandola, V., Banerjee, A., Kumar, V.: Anomaly detection: A survey. ACM Comput. Surv. **41**(3), 1–58 (2009)
6. Collobert, R., Bengio, S., Bengio, Y.: A parallel mixture of svms for very large scale problems. Neural Comput. **14**(5), 1105–1114 (2002)
7. Fawcett, T., Provost, F.: Activity monitoring: Noticing interesting changes in behavior. In: Proceedings of the fifth ACM SIGKDD international conference on knowledge discovery and data mining, 53–62 (1999)
8. Freund, Y., Schapire, R.E.: A decision-theoretic generalization of on-line learning and an application to boosting. J. Comput. Syst. Sci. **55**(1), 119–139 (1997)
9. Fu, Z., Robles-Kelly, A., Zhou, J.: Mixing linear SVMs for nonlinear classification. Neural Netw. IEEE Trans. **21**(12), 1963–1975 (2010)
10. Gwadera, R., Atallah, M.J., Szpankowski, W.: Reliable detection of episodes in event sequences. Knowl. Inf. Syst. **7**(4), 415–437 (2005)
11. Hartley, H.O.: Maximum likelihood estimation from incomplete data. Biometrics **14**(2), 174–194 (1958)
12. Jacobs, R.A., Jordan, M.I., Nowlan, S.J., Hinton, G.E.: Adaptive mixtures of local experts. Neural Comput. **3**(1), 79–87 (1991)
13. Janakiram, D., Reddy, V. A., Kumar, A. V. U. P.: Outlier detection in wireless sensor networks using bayesian belief networks. In: Proceedings of the 1st international conference on communication system software and middleware (Comsware), pp 1–6 (2006)
14. Krnger, S.E., Schafföner, M., Katz, M., Andelic, E., Wendemuth, A.: Mixture of support vector machines for hmm based speech recognition. ICPR **4**, 326–329 (2006)
15. Lai, V., Nguyen, D., Nguyen, K., Le, T.: Mixture of support vector data descriptions. In: Information and computer science (NICS), 2015 2nd national foundation for science and technology development conference, IEEE, pp 135–140 (2015)
16. Le, T., Tran, D., Ma, W., Sharma, D.: An optimal sphere and two large margins approach for novelty detection. Int Joint Conf Neural Netw IJCNN **2010**, 1–6 (2010)
17. Le, T., Tran, D., Ma, W., Sharma, D.: A theoretical framework for multi-sphere support vector data description. Lecture Notes in Computer Science, vol. 6444, pp. 132–142. Springer, Heidelberg (2010)
18. Le, T., Tran, D., Ma, W., Sharma, D.: Fuzzy multi-sphere support vector data description. In: FUZZ-IEEE, IEEE, pp. 1–5. (2012)

19. Qin, T., Zhang, X-D., Wang, D-S., Liu, T-Y., Lai, W., Li, H.: Ranking with multiple hyperplanes. In: Proceedings of the 30th annual international ACM SIGIR conference on research and development in information retrieval, SIGIR '07, 279–286. (2007)
20. Schölkopf, B., Platt, J.C., Shawe-Taylor, J.C., Smola, A.J., Williamson, R.C.: Estimating the support of a high-dimensional distribution. Neural Comput. **13**(7), 1443–1471 (2001)
21. Tax, D.M.J., Duin, R.P.W.: Support vector data description. J. Mach. Learn. Res. **54**(1), 45–66 (2004)
22. Tsang, I. W., Kocsor, A., Kwok, J. T.: Simpler core vector machines with enclosing balls. In: Proceedings of the 24th international conference on machine learning, ICML '07, pp. 911–918 (2007)
23. Tsang, I.W., Kwok, J.T., Cheung, P., Cristianini, N.: Core vector machines: fast SVM training on very large data sets. J Mach Learn Res **6**, 363–392 (2005)
24. Wang, Z., Djuric, N., Crammer, K., Vucetic, S.: Trading representability for scalability: Adaptive multi-hyperplane machine for nonlinear classification. In: Proceedings of the 17th ACM SIGKDD international conference on knowledge discovery and data mining, KDD '11, ACM, pp. 24–32. (2011)
25. Xiao, Y., Liu, B., Cao, L., Wu, X., Zhang, C., Hao, Z., Yang, F., Cao, J.: Multi-sphere support vector data description for outliers detection on multi-distribution data. In: ICDM Workshops, pp. 82–87. (2009)
26. Yan, J., Wang, Y., Cao, C., Zheng, H.: Example error weighted support vector data description. Comput. Eng. **2**, 009 (2005)
27. Zhu, J., Chen, N., Xing, E. P.: Infinite svm: a dirichlet process mixture of large-margin kernel machines. In: ICML, pp. 617–624. Omnipress, Madison (2011)

11

Language representability of finite place/ transition Petri nets

Roberto Gorrieri[1]

Abstract Finite-net multi-CCS is a CCS-like calculus which is able to model atomic sequences of actions and, together with parallel composition, also multi-party synchronization. This calculus is equipped with a labeled transition system semantics and also with an unsafe P/T Petri net semantics, which is sound w.r.t. the transition system semantics. For any process p of the calculus, the net associated to p by the semantics has always a finite number of places, but it has a finite number of transitions only for so-called well-formed processes. The main result of the paper is that well-formed finite-net multi-CCS processes are able to represent all finite, statically reduced, P/T Petri nets.

Keywords Operational semantics · Process algebra · Petri nets

1 Introduction

Finite-state labeled transition systems (i.e., LTSs with finitely many states and transitions) can be expressed by the CCS [25] sub-calculus of *finite-state processes*, i.e., the sequential processes generated from the empty process $\mathbf{0}$, prefixing $\mu.p$, alternative composition $p_1 + p_2$ and a finite number of process constants C, each one equipped with a defining equation of the form $C \stackrel{\text{def}}{=} p$. More precisely, the semantics of any finite-state CCS process is a finite-state LTS and, conversely, given a reduced, finite-state LTS TS, it is possible to define a finite-state CCS process p_{TS} such that the operational semantics for p_{TS} generates an LTS isomorphic to TS. Hence, this famous result of Milner offers a process calculus to represent, up to isomorphism, all and only finite-state LTSs.

This paper addresses the same language representability problem for finite labeled Place/Transition Petri nets without capacity bounds on places. We single out a fragment (called *finite-net processes*) of an extension of CCS (called multi-CCS, fully described in [19]), such that not only all processes of this fragment generate finite P/T nets, but also for any finite (statically reduced) P/T net we can find a term of the calculus that generates it. This solves the open problem of providing a process calculus representing finite P/T Petri nets, and opens interesting possibilities of cross-fertilization between the areas of Petri nets and process calculi. In particular, it is now possible, on the one hand, (i) to define any (statically reduced) finite P/T net compositionally and (ii) to study algebraic laws for net-based behavioral equivalences (such as net isomorphism) over such a class of systems; on the other hand, it is now possible (iii) to reuse all the techniques and decidability results available for finite P/T nets [12] also for this fragment of multi-CCS, as well as (iv) to continue the study of non-interleaving semantics, typical of Petri nets (e.g., [11,27,29]), also for process algebras (initiated in [8,28]), in particular for finite-net multi-CCS.

Finite-net multi-CCS includes the operator $\underline{\alpha}.s$ of *strong prefixing* (in contrast to normal prefixing $\mu.t$), which states that the visible action α is the initial part of an atomic sequence that continues with the sequential process s. So, by strong prefixing, a transition can be labeled with a sequence of visible actions. This operator, introduced in [16,17] with a slightly different semantics, is also at the base of multi-party synchronization, obtained as an atomic sequence of binary CCS-like synchronizations. In finite-net multi-CCS, parallel composition may occur inside the body of a recursively

---

✉ Roberto Gorrieri
roberto.gorrieri@unibo.it

1 Dipartimento di Informatica, Scienza e Ingegneria, Università di Bologna, Mura A. Zamboni, 7, 40127 Bologna, Italy

defined constant C; on the contrary, the restriction operator (νa) is not allowed in the body of C. So, a finite-net process may be represented as $(\nu L)t$, where L is a set of actions (if L is empty, the restriction operator is not present) and t a restriction-free process.

We equip our calculus with a net semantics that, differently from the approach by Degano et al. [8–10,28], uses *unsafe* P/T nets, as done in [13,15] for a CCS sub-calculus without restriction, and in [5] for the π-calculus, where however inhibitor arcs are used to model restriction. The extension of the approach to restriction and strong prefixing is not trivial and passes through the introduction of an auxiliary set of *restricted* actions i.e., actions which are only allowed to synchronize. We prove that the net semantics associates a P/T net Net(p) to any finite-net multi-CCS process p, such that Net(p) has finitely many places; if p is *well-formed*, then Net(p) has also finitely many transitions; intuitively, process p is well-formed if the sequences that p may generate via strong prefixing have never the possibility to synchronize. We also provide a soundness result, i.e., p and Net(p) are bisimilar [25]. Finally, we also prove the *representability theorem*: for any finite, statically reduced, P/T net N, we can find a well-formed, finite-net multi-CCS process p_N such that Net(p_N) and N are isomorphic.

The paper is organized as follows. Section 2 contains some basic background on LTSs and Petri nets. Section 3 introduces the process calculus called *finite-net multi-CCS*, its interleaving semantics in terms of LTSs, the well-formedness condition on its processes, and also the concurrent readers/writers example. Section 4 defines the operational net semantics for the calculus and presents the finiteness theorem (for any well-formed process p, Net(p) is finite) and some examples of net construction. Section 5 provides the soundness theorem (p and Net(p) are bisimilar). Section 6 proves the language expressibility theorem, i.e., the representability theorem mentioned above. Finally, some conclusions are drawn in Sect. 7, together with a comparison with related literature, in particular with the earlier version [18] of this paper. This paper is the full version of the extended abstract [14].

2 Background

2.1 Labeled transition systems and bisimulation

Definition 1 A *labeled transition system* (or *LTS* for short) is a triple $TS = (Q, A, \rightarrow)$ where

- Q is the countable set of states,
- A is the countable set of labels,
- $\rightarrow \subseteq Q \times A \times Q$ is the transition relation.

In the following $q \xrightarrow{a} q'$ denotes $(q, a, q') \in \rightarrow$. A *rooted* LTS is a pair (TS, q_0) where $\mathrm{TS} = (Q, A, \rightarrow)$ is a transition system and $q_0 \in Q$ is the *initial state*; a rooted LTS is usually represented as $\mathrm{TS} = (Q, A, \rightarrow, q_0)$. A *path* from q_1 to q_{n+1} is a sequence of transitions $q_1 \xrightarrow{a_1} q_2 \xrightarrow{a_2} \ldots q_n \xrightarrow{a_n} q_{n+1}$. We say that q' is *reachable* from q if there exists a path from q to q'. A rooted LTS $(Q, A, \rightarrow, q_0)$ is *reduced* if all the states in Q are reachable from the initial state q_0.

Definition 2 Given two LTSs $\mathrm{TS}_1 = (Q_1, A, \rightarrow_1)$ and $\mathrm{TS}_2 = (Q_2, A, \rightarrow_2)$ a *bisimulation* between TS_1 and TS_2 is a relation $R \subseteq (Q_1 \times Q_2)$ such that if $(q_1, q_2) \in R$ then for all $a \in A$

- $\forall q_1'$ such that $q_1 \xrightarrow{a}_1 q_1'$, $\exists q_2'$ such that $q_2 \xrightarrow{a}_2 q_2'$ and $(q_1', q_2') \in R$
- $\forall q_2'$ such that $q_2 \xrightarrow{a}_2 q_2'$, $\exists q_1'$ such that $q_1 \xrightarrow{a}_1 q_1'$ and $(q_1', q_2') \in R$.

If $\mathrm{TS}_1 = \mathrm{TS}_2$ we say that R is a bisimulation on TS_1. Two states q and q' are bisimilar, $q \sim q'$, if there exists a bisimulation R such that $(q, q') \in R$.

2.2 Finite place/transition Petri nets

We recall some basic notions on finite P/T Petri nets (see, e.g., [7,30–32] for an introduction). We use here a non-standard notation that better suits our needs.

Definition 3 (*Multisets*) Let $\mathbb{N}$ be the set of natural numbers. Given a set S, a *finite multiset* over S is a function $m : S \rightarrow \mathbb{N}$ such that $\mathrm{dom}(m) = \{s \in S \mid m(s) \neq 0\}$ is finite. The set of all finite multisets over S, $\mathcal{M}_{\mathrm{fin}}(S)$, is ranged over by m. A multiset m such that $\mathrm{dom}(m) = \emptyset$ is called *empty* and is denoted with $\emptyset$, with abuse of notation. We write $m \subseteq m'$ if $m(s) \leq m'(s)$ for all $s \in S$. The operator $\oplus$ denotes *multiset union*: $(m \oplus m')(s) = m(s) + m'(s)$. The operator $\ominus$ denotes *multiset difference*: if $m' \subseteq m$, then $(m \ominus m')(s) = m(s) - m'(s)$. The *scalar product* of a natural j with m is $(j \cdot m)(s) = j \cdot (m(s))$. A finite multiset m over a finite set $S = \{s_1, \ldots, s_n\}$ can be represented also as $k_1 \cdot s_1 \oplus k_2 \cdot s_2 \oplus \cdots \oplus k_n \cdot s_n$, where $k_j = m(s_j) \geq 0$ for $j = 1, \ldots, n$.

Definition 4 (*Finite P/T Petri nets*) A labeled *finite Place/Transition Petri net* is a tuple $N = (S, A, T)$, where

- S is the finite set of *places*, ranged over by s (possibly indexed),
- A is the finite set of *labels*, ranged over by a (possibly indexed), and
- $T \subseteq (\mathcal{M}_{\mathrm{fin}}(S)\backslash\emptyset) \times A \times \mathcal{M}_{\mathrm{fin}}(S)$ is the finite set of *transitions*, ranged over by t (possibly indexed), such that $\forall a \in A\, \exists t \in T$ with $l(t) = a$.

A finite multiset over the set S of places is called a *marking*. Given a marking m and a place s, we say that the place s contains $m(s)$ *tokens*. Given a transition $t = (m, a, m')$, we use the notation ${}^\bullet t$ to denote its *pre-set* m (which cannot be an empty marking), $t^\bullet$ for its *post-set* m' and $l(t)$ for its label a. Hence, transition t can be also represented as ${}^\bullet t \xrightarrow{l(t)} t^\bullet$. A *P/T system* is a tuple $N(m_0) = (S, A, T, m_0)$, where (S, A, T) is a P/T net and m_0 is a finite multiset over S, called the *initial marking*.

Our definition of T as a set of triples ensures that the net is *transition simple*: for any $t_1, t_2 \in T$, if ${}^\bullet t_1 = {}^\bullet t_2$ and $t_1^\bullet = t_2^\bullet$ and $l(t_1) = l(t_2)$, then $t_1 = t_2$. We are also assuming that a transition has a nonempty pre-set. These are the only constraints we impose over the definition of P/T net. The additional condition that A is covered by T (i.e., $\forall a \in A\, \exists t \in T$ with label a) is just for economy.

Definition 5 (*Net isomorphism*) Two P/T nets $N_1 = (S_1, A, T_1)$ and $N_2 = (S_2, A, T_2)$ are *isomorphic* if there exists a bijection $f : S_1 \to S_2$, homomorphically extended to markings, such that $(m, a, m') \in T_1$ iff $(f(m), a, f(m')) \in T_2$. Two systems $N_1(m_1)$ and $N_2(m_2)$ are *isomorphic* if N_1 and N_2 are isomorphic by f, which, additionally, preserves the initial markings: $f(m_1) = m_2$.

Definition 6 Given a labeled P/T net $N = (S, A, T)$, we say that a transition t is *enabled* at marking m, written as $m[t\rangle$, if ${}^\bullet t \subseteq m$. The execution of t enabled at m produces the marking $m' = (m \ominus {}^\bullet t) \oplus t^\bullet$, denoted by $m[t\rangle m'$. The set of markings *reachable* from m, denoted by $[m\rangle$, is defined as the least set such that

- $m \in [m\rangle$ and
- if $m_1 \in [m\rangle$ and, for some transition $t \in T$, $m_1[t\rangle m_2$, then $m_2 \in [m\rangle$.

Given a P/T system $N(m_0) = (S, A, T, m_0)$, we say that m is *reachable* if m is reachable from the initial marking m_0. A P/T system $N(m_0) = (S, A, T, m_0)$ is said *safe* if for all $m \in [m_0\rangle$ and for all $s \in S$ we have that $m(s) \leq 1$.

Definition 7 Given a P/T system $N(m_0) = (S, A, T, m_0)$, the *interleaving marking graph* of $N(m_0)$ is the rooted LTS $\mathrm{IMG(N(m_0))} = ([m_0\rangle, A, \to, m_0)$, where m_0 is the initial state and the transition relation $\to \subseteq \mathcal{M}_{\mathrm{fin}}(S) \times A \times \mathcal{M}_{\mathrm{fin}}(S)$ is defined by $m \xrightarrow{a} m'$ if and only if there exists a transition $t \in T$ such that $m[t\rangle m'$ and $l(t) = a$. The P/T systems $N_1(m_1)$ and $N_2(m_2)$ are *interleaving bisimilar*—denoted by $N_1(m_1) \sim N_2(m_2)$—if and only if there exists a bisimulation $R \subseteq [m_1\rangle \times [m_2\rangle$ such that $(m_1, m_2) \in R$.

Definition 8 (*Dynamically reduced*) A P/T system $N(m_0) = (S, A, T, m_0)$ is dynamically reduced if

- $\forall s \in S\, \exists m \in [m_0\rangle$ such that $m(s) \geq 1$, and
- $\forall t \in T\, \exists m, m' \in [m_0\rangle$ such that $m[t\rangle m'$.

Definition 9 (*Statically reduced*) Given a finite P/T net $N = (S, A, T)$, we say that a transition t is *statically enabled* by a set of places $S' \subseteq S$, denoted by $S'[\![t\rangle$, if $\mathrm{dom}({}^\bullet t) \subseteq S'$. Given two sets of places $S_1, S_2 \subseteq S$, we say that S_2 is *statically reachable in one step* from S_1 if there exists $t \in T$, such that $S_1[\![t\rangle$, $\mathrm{dom}(t^\bullet) \not\subseteq S_1$ and $S_2 = S_1 \cup \mathrm{dom}(t^\bullet)$; this is denoted by $S_1 \stackrel{t}{\Longrightarrow} S_2$. The *static reachability relation* $\Longrightarrow^* \subseteq \wp(S)_{\mathrm{fin}} \times \wp(S)_{\mathrm{fin}}$ is the least relation such that

- $S_1 \Longrightarrow^* S_1$ and
- if $S_1 \Longrightarrow^* S_2$ and $S_2 \stackrel{t}{\Longrightarrow} S_3$, then $S_1 \Longrightarrow^* S_3$.

A set of places $S_k \subseteq S$ is the *largest* set statically reachable from S_1 if $S_1 \Longrightarrow^* S_k$ and for all $t \in T$ such that $S_k[\![t\rangle$, we have that $\mathrm{dom}(t^\bullet) \subseteq S_k$.

Given a finite P/T system $N(m_0) = (S, A, T, m_0)$, we denote by $[\![\mathrm{dom}(m_0)\rangle$ the largest set of places statically reachable from $\mathrm{dom}(m_0)$, i.e., the largest S_k such that $\mathrm{dom}(m_0) \Longrightarrow^* S_k$. A finite P/T net system $N(m_0) = (S, A, T, m_0)$ is *statically reduced* if all the places are statically reachable from the places in the initial marking, i.e., if $[\![\mathrm{dom}(m_0)\rangle = S$.

Note that if $N(m_0) = (S, A, T, m_0)$ is statically reduced, then all the transitions in T are statically enabled by S. Note also that if $N(m_0) = (S, A, T, m_0)$ is dynamically reduced, then it is also statically reduced. However, there are statically reduced P/T systems that are not dynamically reduced. For instance, the statically reduced P/T system $N(s_1) = (\{s_1, s_2, s_3\}, \{a, b\}, \{(s_1, a, s_2), (2 \cdot s_1, b, s_3)\}, s_1)$ cannot reach dynamically place s_3.

3 Finite-net multi-CCS

Now we present finite-net multi-CCS: first its syntax, then the LTS operational semantics, followed by the definition of well-formedness; finally, an example.

3.1 Syntax

Let $\mathcal{L}$ be a denumerable set of names (inputs), ranged over by $a, b, \ldots$. Let $\overline{\mathcal{L}}$ be the set of co-names (outputs), ranged over by $\overline{a}, \overline{b}, \ldots$. The set $\mathcal{L} \cup \overline{\mathcal{L}}$, ranged over by $\alpha, \beta, \ldots$, is the set of visible actions. With $\overline{\alpha}$ we mean the complement of α, assuming that $\overline{\overline{\alpha}} = \alpha$. Let $\mathrm{Act} = \mathcal{L} \cup \overline{\mathcal{L}} \cup \{\tau\}$, such that $\tau \notin \mathcal{L} \cup \overline{\mathcal{L}}$, be the set of actions, ranged over by μ. Action τ denotes an invisible, internal activity. Let $\mathcal{C}$ be a denumerable set of process constants, disjoint from Act, ranged over by $A, B, C, \ldots$. The process terms are generated by the following abstract syntax

$$s ::= \mathbf{0} \mid \mu.t \mid \underline{\alpha}.s \mid s + s$$
$$t ::= s \mid t | t \mid C$$
$$p ::= t \mid (\nu a)p,$$

where we are using three syntactic categories: s, to range over sequential processes (i.e., processes that start sequentially), t, to range over restriction-free processes, and, finally p, to range over-restricted processes.

As for CCS [25], term $\mathbf{0}$ is the terminated process, $\mu.t$ is a normally prefixed process where action μ is first performed and then t is ready. Note that $s + s'$ is the sequential process obtained by the alternative composition of *sequential* processes s and s'; hence we are restricting the use of $+$ to so-called *guarded sum*. Term $t \mid t'$ is the parallel composition of t and t'. $(\nu a)p$ is process p where the name a is made private by applying the restriction operator over a. Finally, C is a process constant, equipped with a defining equation $C \stackrel{\text{def}}{=} t$, i.e., the body of a constant must be a restriction-free process. The only new operator of the calculus is *strong prefixing*: $\underline{\alpha}.s$ is a strongly prefixed process, where α is the first action of a transaction that continues with the *sequential* process s (provided that s can complete the transaction).

We sometimes use the syntactic convention of writing $(\nu a)((\nu b)p))$ as $(\nu a, b)p$. Generalizing this convention, a finite-net multi-CCS process may be represented as $(\nu L)t$, where L is a set of actions (if L is empty, the restriction operator is not present) and t is a restriction-free process.

The set $\mathcal{P}$ of *processes* contains those terms which use *finitely many* constants only and are, w.r.t. the constants they use, *closed* (all possess a defining equation) and *guarded* (for any defining equation $C \stackrel{\text{def}}{=} t$, any occurrence of a constant in t is within a *normally prefixed* subprocess $\mu.t'$ of t). $\mathcal{P}_{\text{seq}}$ is the set of *sequential processes*, i.e., those of syntactic category s. Note that the restriction operator cannot occur syntactically in any term of $\mathcal{P}_{\text{seq}}$. With abuse of notation, $\mathcal{P}$ will be ranged over by $p, q, r, \ldots$ (hence p may denote any kind of process terms, also sequential ones), possibly indexed.

Definition 10 For any finite-net multi-CCS process p, the set of its sequential subterms $\text{sub}(p)$ is defined by means of the auxiliary function (with the same name, with abuse of notation) $\text{sub}(p, \emptyset)$, whose second parameter is a set of already known constants, initially empty, described in Table 1.

Proposition 1 *For any finite-net multi-CCS process p, the set of its sequential subterms $\text{sub}(p)$ is finite.*

Proof By induction on the definition of $\text{sub}(p, \emptyset)$. The base cases are $\text{sub}(\mathbf{0}, I)$ and $\text{sub}(A, I)$ when $A \in I$. Note that induction will end eventually because the constants that a finite-net multi-CCS process may use are finitely many. □

Table 1 Sequential subterms of a process

$$\text{sub}(\mathbf{0}, I) = \{\mathbf{0}\} \qquad \text{sub}(\mu.p, I) = \{\mu.p\} \cup \text{sub}(p, I)$$
$$\text{sub}((\nu a)p, I) = \text{sub}(p, I) \qquad \text{sub}(\underline{\alpha}.p, I) = \{\underline{\alpha}.p\} \cup \text{sub}(p, I)$$
$$\text{sub}(p_1 + p_2, I) = \{p_1 + p_2\} \cup \text{sub}(p_1, I) \cup \text{sub}(p_2, I)$$
$$\text{sub}(p_1 \mid p_2, I) = \text{sub}(p_1, I) \cup \text{sub}(p_2, I)$$
$$\text{sub}(A, I) = \begin{cases} \emptyset & A \in I, \\ \text{sub}(p, I \cup \{A\}) & A \notin I \wedge A \stackrel{\text{def}}{=} p \end{cases}$$

Table 2 Operational rules [symmetric rule (Sum$_2$) omitted]

$$\text{(Pref)}\ \frac{}{\mu.p \xrightarrow{\mu} p} \qquad \text{(Cong)}\ \frac{p \equiv p' \xrightarrow{\sigma} q' \equiv q}{p \xrightarrow{\sigma} q} \qquad \text{(Sum}_1\text{)}\ \frac{p \xrightarrow{\sigma} p'}{p + q \xrightarrow{\sigma} p'}$$

$$\text{(Par)}\ \frac{p \xrightarrow{\sigma} p'}{p \mid q \xrightarrow{\sigma} p' \mid q} \qquad \text{(S-Pref)}\ \frac{p \xrightarrow{\sigma} p'}{\underline{\alpha}.p \xrightarrow{\alpha \diamond \sigma} p'} \quad \alpha \diamond \sigma = \begin{cases} \alpha & \text{if } \sigma = \tau, \\ \alpha\sigma & \text{otherwise} \end{cases}$$

$$\text{(S-Res)}\ \frac{p \xrightarrow{\sigma} p'}{(\nu a)p \xrightarrow{\sigma} (\nu a)p'} \quad a, \overline{a} \notin n(\sigma)$$

$$\text{(S-Com)}\ \frac{p \xrightarrow{\sigma_1} p' \quad q \xrightarrow{\sigma_2} q'}{p \mid q \xrightarrow{\sigma} p' \mid q'} \quad \text{Sync}(\sigma_1, \sigma_2, \sigma)$$

Remark 1 Note that for any processes p and q, if the sequential process p is such that $p \in \text{sub}(q)$, then $\text{sub}(p) \subseteq \text{sub}(q)$. This is because the definition of $\text{sub}(q)$ recursively calls itself on all of its sequential subterms.

3.2 Operational semantics with LTSs

The operational semantics for finite-net multi-CCS is given by the labeled transition system $(\mathcal{P}, \mathcal{A}, \longrightarrow)$, where the states are the processes in $\mathcal{P}$, $\mathcal{A} = \{\tau\} \cup (\mathcal{L} \cup \overline{\mathcal{L}})^+$ is the set of labels (ranged over by σ and composed of the invisible action τ and by sequences of visible actions), and $\longrightarrow \subseteq \mathcal{P} \times \mathcal{A} \times \mathcal{P}$ is the minimal transition relation generated by the rules listed in Table 2.

We briefly comment on the rules that are less standard. Rule (S-pref) allows for the creation of transitions labeled by nonempty sequences of actions. In order for $\underline{\alpha}.p$ to make a move, it is necessary that p be able to perform a transition, i.e., the rest of the transaction. Hence, if $p \xrightarrow{\sigma} p'$ then $\underline{\alpha}.p \xrightarrow{\alpha \diamond \sigma} p'$, where the label $\alpha \diamond \sigma = \alpha$ if $\sigma = \tau$, $\alpha \diamond \sigma = \alpha\sigma$ otherwise. Note that $\underline{\alpha}.\mathbf{0}$ cannot execute any action, as $\mathbf{0}$ is terminated. If a transition is labeled with $\sigma = \alpha_1 \ldots \alpha_{n-1}\alpha_n$, then all the actions $\alpha_1 \ldots \alpha_{n-1}$ are due to strong prefixes, while α_n is due to a normal prefix (or α_n is a strong prefix followed by a normal prefix τ). Rule (S-Com) has a side-condition on the possible synchronizability of σ_1 and σ_2. Relation $\text{Sync}(\sigma_1, \sigma_2, \sigma)$, defined by the axioms of Table 3, holds if at least one of the two sequences is a single action, say $\sigma_1 = \overline{\alpha}$, and the other starts with the complementary action

Table 3 Synchronization relation Sync

$$\frac{}{\mathrm{Sync}(\alpha, \overline{\alpha}, \tau)} \qquad \frac{\sigma \neq \epsilon}{\mathrm{Sync}(\alpha\sigma, \overline{\alpha}, \sigma)} \qquad \frac{\sigma \neq \epsilon}{\mathrm{Sync}(\overline{\alpha}, \alpha\sigma, \sigma)}$$

α. Note that it is not possible to synchronize two sequences. This means that, usually, a multi-party synchronization can take place only among one *leader*, i.e., the process performing the atomic sequence, and as many other components (the *servants*), as is the length of the atomic sequence, where each servant executes one visible action. This is strictly the case for so-called *well-formed processes*, i.e., processes that do not allow for the synchronization of two sequences, not even indirectly. However, more elaborate forms of synchronization are possible, as illustrated in Sect. 3.3, for non-well-formed processes. Rule (S-Res) is slightly more general than the corresponding one for CCS, as it requires that no action in σ can be a or $\overline{a}$. With $n(\sigma)$ we denote the set of all actions occurring in σ. Formally: $n(\mu) = \{\mu\}$, $n(\alpha\sigma) = \{\alpha\} \cup n(\sigma)$.

There is one further rule, called (Cong), which makes use of the structural congruence $\equiv$, induced by the three axioms in Table 4. Axioms **E1** and **E2** are for associativity and commutativity, respectively, of the parallel operator. Axiom **E3** is for unfolding and explains why we have no explicit operational rule for handling constants in Table 2: the transitions derivable from C are those transitions derivable from the structurally congruent term p if $C \stackrel{\mathrm{def}}{=} p$. Rule (Cong) enlarges the set of transitions derivable from a given process p, as the following example shows. The intuition is that, given a process p, a transition is derivable from p if it is derivable from any p' obtained as a rearrangement in any order (or association) of all of its sequential subprocesses.

Example 1 (Associativity and commutativity) Consider $(\underline{a}.b.p \mid \overline{a}.q) \mid \overline{b}.r$. The ternary synchronization among them, $(\underline{a}.b.p \mid \overline{a}.q) \mid \overline{b}.r \xrightarrow{\tau} (p \mid q) \mid r$, can take place, as proved in Table 5, without using rule (Cong). However, if we consider the very similar process $\underline{a}.b.p \mid (\overline{a}.q \mid \overline{b}.r)$, then we can see that $\underline{a}.b.p$ is able to synchronize with both $\overline{a}.q$ and $\overline{b}.r$ only by using rule (Cong), as follows:

$$\frac{\underline{a}.b.p \mid (\overline{a}.q \mid \overline{b}.r) \equiv (\underline{a}.b.p \mid \overline{a}.q) \mid \overline{b}.r \xrightarrow{\tau} (p \mid q) \mid r \equiv p \mid (q \mid r)}{\underline{a}.b.p \mid (\overline{a}.q \mid \overline{b}.r) \xrightarrow{\tau} p \mid (q \mid r)}$$

If we consider the slightly different variant process $(\underline{a}.b.p \mid \overline{b}.r) \mid \overline{a}.q$, we see easily that, without rule (Cong), no ternary synchronization is possible, because Sync(ab, $\overline{\mathrm{b}}$, a) does not hold. This example shows that, by using the axioms **E1** and **E2**, it is possible to reorder the servant subcomponents (in this example, subprocesses $\overline{a}.q$ and $\overline{b}.r$) in such a way that the actions they offer are in the expected order by the leader process (in this example, $\underline{a}.b.p$).

Two processes p and q are *bisimilar*, $p \sim q$, if there exists a bisimulation $R \subseteq \mathcal{P} \times \mathcal{P}$ such that $(p, q) \in R$. The following obvious result holds.

Proposition 2 *If $p \equiv q$ then $p \sim q$.*

3.3 Well-formed processes

We propose a syntactic condition on a process p, ensuring that, during its execution, p is unable to synchronize two atomic sequences, not even indirectly; a process satisfying such a syntactic condition will be called *well-formed*. The restriction to well-formed processes will be crucial in the following sections.

The definition of relation Sync$(\sigma_1, \sigma_2, \sigma)$ requires that at least one of σ_1 or σ_2 be a single action; this is not enough to prevent that two sequences may synchronize, even if indirectly. For instance, assume we have three processes $p_1 = \underline{a}.b.\mathbf{0}$, $p_2 = \overline{a}.\mathbf{0}$ and $p_3 = \underline{\overline{b}}.c.\mathbf{0}$, which may perform the sequences ab, $\overline{a}$, $\overline{b}c$, respectively; then a ternary synchronization is possible, because first we synchronize p_1 and p_2, by Sync(ab, $\overline{\mathrm{a}}$, b), getting a single action b, which can be then used for a synchronization with p_3, by Sync(b, $\overline{\mathrm{b}}$c, c); in such a way, the two atomic sequences ab and $\overline{b}c$ have been synchronized, by means of the single action $\overline{a}$. So, we would like to mark $(p_1 \mid p_2) \mid p_3$ as not well-formed. In order to define well-formed multi-CCS processes, some auxiliary definitions are needed.

Definition 11 (*Initials for sequential processes*) For any sequential process p, $In(p) \subseteq \mathcal{A}$ is the set of *initials* of p, defined inductively as

$$\mathrm{In}(\mathbf{0}) = \emptyset \qquad \mathrm{In}(\mu.p) = \{\mu\}$$
$$\mathrm{In}(\underline{\alpha}.p) = \alpha \diamond \mathrm{In}(p) \qquad \mathrm{In}(p_1 + p_2) = \mathrm{In}(p_1) \cup \mathrm{In}(p_2)$$

where $\alpha \diamond \mathrm{In}(p) = \{\alpha \diamond \sigma \mid \sigma \in \mathrm{In}(p)\}$.

Table 4 Axioms generating the structural congruence $\equiv$

E1	$(p \mid q) \mid r = p \mid (q \mid r)$	
E2	$p \mid q = q \mid p$	
E3	$A = q$	if $A \stackrel{\mathrm{def}}{=} q$

Table 5 Multi-party synchronization among three processes

$$\frac{\dfrac{\dfrac{\dfrac{}{b.p \xrightarrow{b} p}}{\underline{a}.b.p \xrightarrow{ab} p} \qquad \dfrac{}{\overline{a}.q \xrightarrow{\overline{a}} q}}{\underline{a}.b.p \mid \overline{a}.q \xrightarrow{b} p \mid q} \qquad \dfrac{}{\overline{b}.r \xrightarrow{\overline{b}} r}}{(\underline{a}.b.p \mid \overline{a}.q) \mid \overline{b}.r \xrightarrow{\tau} (p \mid q) \mid r}$$

Table 6 Names in sequences of a process

$$\mathrm{ns}(\mathbf{0}, I) = \emptyset \qquad \mathrm{ns}(p_1 + p_2, I) = \mathrm{ns}(p_1, I) \cup \mathrm{ns}(p_2, I)$$
$$\mathrm{ns}(\mu.p, I) = \mathrm{ns}(p, I) \qquad \mathrm{ns}(p_1 \mid p_2, I) = \mathrm{ns}(p_1, I) \cup \mathrm{ns}(p_2, I)$$
$$\mathrm{ns}(\underline{\alpha}.p, I) = \mathrm{ns}(p, I) \cup \{\alpha\} \cup \textstyle\bigcup_{\sigma \in \mathrm{In}(p) \wedge \sigma \neq \tau} n(\sigma)$$
$$\mathrm{ns}((\nu a)p, I) = \mathrm{ns}(p, I) \setminus \{a, \overline{a}\}$$
$$\mathrm{ns}(A, I) = \begin{cases} \emptyset & A \in I, \\ \mathrm{ns}(p, I \cup \{A\}) & A \notin I \wedge A \stackrel{\mathrm{def}}{=} p \end{cases}$$

Table 7 Well-formedness predicate

$$\frac{}{\mathrm{wf}(\mathbf{0}, I)} \qquad \frac{\mathrm{wf}(p, I)}{\mathrm{wf}(\mu.p, I)} \qquad \frac{\mathrm{wf}(p, I) \quad \nexists \beta.\beta \in \mathrm{ns}(\underline{\alpha}.p, I) \wedge \overline{\beta} \in \mathrm{ns}(\underline{\alpha}.p, I)}{\mathrm{wf}(\underline{\alpha}.p, I)}$$
$$\frac{\mathrm{wf}(p, I)}{\mathrm{wf}((\nu a)p, I)} \qquad \frac{A \in I}{\mathrm{wf}(A, I)} \qquad \frac{\mathrm{wf}(p, I \cup \{A\}) \quad A \stackrel{\mathrm{def}}{=} p \quad A \notin I}{\mathrm{wf}(A, I)}$$
$$\frac{\mathrm{wf}(p_1, I) \quad \mathrm{wf}(p_2, I) \quad \nexists \beta.\beta \in \mathrm{ns}(p_1, I) \wedge \overline{\beta} \in \mathrm{ns}(p_2, I)}{\mathrm{wf}(p_1 \mid p_2, I) \quad \mathrm{wf}(p_1 + p_2, I)}$$

Definition 12 (*Names in sequences of a process*) Let $\mathrm{ns}(p) \subseteq \mathcal{L} \cup \overline{\mathcal{L}}$ be the set of (free) names occurring in sequences *of length two or more* of p. Set $\mathrm{ns}(p)$ is defined by means of the auxiliary function (with the same name, with abuse of notation) $\mathrm{ns}(p, \emptyset)$, whose second parameter is a set of constants, where $\mathrm{ns}(p, I)$ is defined in Table 6.

A process p is well-formed if $\mathrm{wf}(p)$ holds, and $\mathrm{wf}(p)$ holds if the auxiliary relation (with the same name, with abuse of notation) $\mathrm{wf}(p, \emptyset)$ holds; the auxiliary relation $\mathrm{wf}(p, I)$, where the second parameter is a set of constants, is defined as the least relation induced by the axioms and rules of Table 7. The assumption that any process uses finitely many constants ensures that the well-formedness predicate is well-defined.

Example 2 Let us consider processes $p_1 = \underline{a}.b.\mathbf{0}$, $p_2 = \overline{a}.\mathbf{0}$ and $p_3 = \underline{\overline{b}}.c.\mathbf{0}$. Note that $\mathrm{wf}(p_2)$, because $\mathrm{wf}(\mathbf{0})$ holds; similarly, $\mathrm{wf}(b.\mathbf{0})$; as a consequence, $\mathrm{wf}(p_1)$ holds, because $\mathrm{ns}(p_1) = \{a, b\}$ does not contain a pair of complementary actions. In the same way, we can prove that $\mathrm{wf}(p_3)$ holds, with $\mathrm{ns}(p_3) = \{\overline{b}, c\}$. We also have that $\mathrm{wf}(p_1 \mid p_2)$, as no action of $\mathrm{ns}(p_1)$ occurs complemented in $\mathrm{ns}(p_2) = \emptyset$. However, it is not the case that $\mathrm{wf}((p_1 \mid p_2) \mid p_3)$, because there exists an action, namely b, such that $b \in \mathrm{ns}(p_1 \mid p_2)$ and $\overline{b} \in \mathrm{ns}(p_3)$.

To conclude this section, we comment on the well-formedness relation: if a process is well-formed, then it is not possible to synchronize two sequences, not even indirectly. Theorem 2 will prove this fact on the net semantics. A direct proof on the LTS semantics is reported in [19].

3.4 An example: concurrent readers and writers

In this problem, originally introduced in [6], there are two types of processes: reader processes and writer processes. All processes share a common file; so, each writer process must exclude all the other writers and all the readers while writing on the file, while multiple reader processes can access the shared file simultaneously. The problem is to define a control structure that does not deadlock or allow violations of the mutual exclusion criteria.

Assume we have n readers and m writers and that at most $k \leq n$ readers can read simultaneously. We can assume we have k lock resources such that a reader can read if at least one lock is available, while a writer can write if all the k locks are available, so that it prevents all the k possible concurrent reading operations. In a naïve CCS solution to this problem, a deadlock may occur when two writers are competing for the acquisition of the k locks, so that one has acquired i locks and the other one $k - i$, for some $0 < i < k$; in such a situation, both writers are stuck, waiting for the missing locks, and all the readers are not allowed to read as no lock is available. A simple multi-ccS solution to this coordination problem is forcing atomicity on the writer's acquisition of the k locks, so that either all or none are taken. To make the presentation simple, assume that $n = 4$, $k = 3$, $m = 2$. Each reader process R, each lock process L, each writer W can be represented as follows, where action l stands for lock and u for unlock:

$$R \stackrel{\mathrm{def}}{=} l.\mathrm{read}.u.R \quad L \stackrel{\mathrm{def}}{=} \overline{l}.\overline{u}.L \quad W \stackrel{\mathrm{def}}{=} \underline{l}.\underline{l}.l.\mathrm{write}.\underline{u}.\underline{u}.u.W$$

The whole system CRW is defined as

$$\mathrm{CRW} \stackrel{\mathrm{def}}{=} (\nu l, u)(R \mid R \mid R \mid R \mid W \mid W \mid L \mid L \mid L),$$

where parentheses are omitted as $\mid$ is associative. Note that a writer W executes a four-way synchronization with the three instances of the lock process L in order to get permission to write:

$$\mathrm{CRW} \xrightarrow{\tau} (\nu l, u)(R \mid R \mid R \mid R \mid W' \mid W \mid L' \mid L' \mid L'),$$

where $W' = \mathrm{write}.\underline{u}.\underline{u}.u.W$ and $L' = \overline{u}.L$. The LTS for CRW is finite-state. Note that, to ensure correctness, it is not necessary to require atomicity on the release of the locks: This choice is only done in order to have a smaller model.

4 Operational net semantics

4.1 Places and markings

The finite-net multi-CCS processes are built upon the set $\mathcal{L} \cup \overline{\mathcal{L}}$, ranged over by α, of visible actions. We assume we have also sets $\mathcal{L}' = \{a' \mid a \in \mathcal{L}\}$ and $\overline{\mathcal{L}'} = \{\overline{a'} \mid \overline{a} \in \overline{\mathcal{L}}\}$, where $\mathcal{L}' \cup \overline{\mathcal{L}'}$, ranged over by α', is the set of auxiliary *restricted* actions; by definition, each restricted action α' corresponds

Table 8 Decomposition function

$\text{dec}(\mathbf{0}, I) = \emptyset$	$\text{dec}(\mu.p, I) = \{\mu.p\}$
$\text{dec}(\underline{\gamma}.p, I) = \{\underline{\gamma}.p\}$	$\text{dec}(p + p', I) = \{p + p'\}$
$\text{dec}(p \mid p', I) = \text{dec}(p, I) \oplus \text{dec}(p', I)$	$\text{dec}(A, I) = \begin{cases} \emptyset & A \in I, \\ \text{dec}(p, I \cup \{A\}) & A \notin I \wedge A \overset{\text{def}}{=} p \end{cases}$
$\text{dec}((\nu a)p, I) = \text{dec}(p, I)\{a'/a\}$	$a' \in \mathcal{L}'$ is the restricted action corresponding to a

exactly to one visible action α. Set $\mathcal{G} = \mathcal{L} \cup \overline{\mathcal{L}} \cup \mathcal{L}' \cup \overline{\mathcal{L}'}$ is ranged over by γ. The set of all actions $\text{Act}_\gamma = \mathcal{G} \cup \{\tau\}$, ranged over by μ (with abuse of notation), is used to build the set of *extended*, finite-net multi-CCS processes $\mathcal{P}^\gamma$. The infinite set of places, ranged over by s, is $S_{\text{MCCS}} = \mathcal{P}^\gamma_{\text{seq}} \setminus \{\mathbf{0}\}$, i.e., the set of all sequential processes (except $\mathbf{0}$) whose prefixes are in Act_γ and whose strong prefixes are in $\mathcal{G}$.

Function dec : $\mathcal{P}^\gamma \times \wp(\mathcal{C}) \to \mathcal{M}_{\text{fin}}(S_{\text{MCCS}})$ defines the decomposition of extended processes into markings (see Table 8), where the second argument is the set of already known constants, initially empty. For simplicity sake, we often omit the second argument when it is empty or inessential. Process $\mathbf{0}$ generates no places. The decomposition of a sequential process p produces one place with name p. This is the case of $\mu.p$ (where μ can be any action in Act_γ), $\underline{\gamma}.p$ and $p + p'$. Parallel composition is interpreted as multiset union; e.g., the decomposition of $a.\mathbf{0} \mid a.\mathbf{0}$ produces the marking $a.\mathbf{0} \oplus a.\mathbf{0} = 2 \cdot a.\mathbf{0}$. The decomposition of a restricted process $(\nu a)p$—where $a \in \mathcal{L}$—generates the multiset obtained from the decomposition of p, to which the substitution $\{a'/a\}$ is applied; the application of the substitution $\{a'/a\}$ to a multiset is performed elementwise, as shown in the example below. Finally, a process constant A is first unwound once (according to its defining equation) and then decomposed, if A is not known yet.

We assume that, in decomposing $(\nu a)p$, the choice of the restricted name is fixed by the rule that associates to a visible action a its *unique* corresponding restricted action a'. As a process is of the form $(\nu L)t$ with $L = \{a_1, a_2, \ldots, a_n\}$, it can be first translated to the restriction-free process $t\{a_1'/a_1\} \ldots \{a_n'/a_n\}$ (shortened as $t\{L'/L\}$, for $L' = \{a_1', \ldots, a_n'\} \subseteq \mathcal{L}'$), and then decomposed to obtain a multiset. Function dec essentially performs this decomposition, by removing the restriction (which can occur only externally, by syntactic definition) and by replacing the bound names in L with the corresponding restricted names in L'.

Proposition 3 *For any restriction-free* $t \in \mathcal{P}$, $\text{dec}((\nu L)t) = \text{dec}(t\{L'/L\})$.

This means that we can restrict our attention to restriction-free processes built over Act_γ, as a restricted process $(\nu L)t$ in $\mathcal{P}$ is mapped via dec to the same marking of the restriction-free process $t\{L'/L\}$ in $\mathcal{P}^\gamma$.

Example 3 Consider the (non-well-formed) finite-net multi-CCS process $p = (\nu a)p'$, where $p' = (a.\mathbf{0} \mid (\underline{\overline{a}}.a.\mathbf{0} \mid \overline{a}.\mathbf{0}))$. Then,

$$\begin{aligned}
\text{dec}(p) &= \text{dec}(p')\{a'/a\} = \text{dec}(a.\mathbf{0} \mid (\underline{\overline{a}}.a.\mathbf{0} \mid \overline{a}.\mathbf{0}))\{a'/a\} \\
&= (\text{dec}(a.\mathbf{0}) \oplus \text{dec}(\underline{\overline{a}}.a.\mathbf{0} \mid \overline{a}.\mathbf{0}))\{a'/a\} \\
&= (\text{dec}(a.\mathbf{0}) \oplus \text{dec}(\underline{\overline{a}}.a.\mathbf{0}) \oplus \text{dec}(\overline{a}.\mathbf{0}))\{a'/a\} \\
&= (a.\mathbf{0} \oplus \underline{\overline{a}}.a.\mathbf{0} \oplus \overline{a}.\mathbf{0})\{a'/a\} \\
&= a'.\mathbf{0} \oplus \underline{\overline{a'}}.a'.\mathbf{0} \oplus \overline{a'}.\mathbf{0} \\
&= \text{dec}(a'.\mathbf{0} \mid \underline{\overline{a'}}.a'.\mathbf{0} \mid \overline{a'}.\mathbf{0}),
\end{aligned}$$

where a' is the corresponding restricted name in $\mathcal{L}'$.

Function dec is well-defined because the constants a process may use are finitely many. This also ensures the following fact.

Proposition 4 *For any* $p \in \mathcal{P}^\gamma$, $\text{dec}(p)$ *is a finite multiset of places.*

Of course, function dec is not injective, because it considers the parallel operator as commutative, associative, with $\mathbf{0}$ as neutral element. In fact, $\text{dec}((p \mid q) \mid r) = \text{dec}(p \mid (q \mid r))$, $\text{dec}(p \mid q) = \text{dec}(q \mid p)$, $\text{dec}(p \mid \mathbf{0}) = \text{dec}(p)$, etc. However, contrary to the decomposition functions in [8,28], one can prove that our dec is surjective. Take any finite multiset of places $m = k_1 \cdot s_1 \oplus \cdots \oplus k_n \cdot s_n$, for $n \geq 0$ ($m = \emptyset$ if $n = 0$), where each $s_i \in S_{\text{MCCS}}$, for $i = 1, \ldots, n$. Then, process $p = s_1^{k_1} \mid \cdots \mid s_n^{k_n}$, where $s^1 = s$ and $s^{n+1} = s \mid s^n$, is such that $\text{dec}(p) = m$. We can be even more demanding and prove that function dec is surjective even if we restrict ourselves to processes in $\mathcal{P}$.

Proposition 5 *Function* dec : $\mathcal{P} \to \mathcal{M}_{\text{fin}}(S_{\text{MCCS}})$ *is surjective.*

Proof Take any finite multiset of places $m = k_1 \cdot s_1 \oplus \cdots \oplus k_n \cdot s_n$, for $n \geq 0$ ($m = \emptyset$ if $n = 0$), where each $s_i \in S_{\text{MCCS}}$, for $i = 1, \ldots, n$. It is possible to find a substitution $\rho = \{a_1, \ldots, a_k/a_1', \ldots, a_k'\}$ (with $a_i' \in \mathcal{L}'$ and $a_i \in \mathcal{L}$) such that, for all $i = 1, \ldots, n$, $p_i = s_i\rho$ and $p_i \in \mathcal{P}_{\text{seq}}$. Take process $p = (\nu a_1 a_2 \ldots a_k)(p_1^{k_1} \mid \cdots \mid p_n^{k_n})$, assuming that no restriction is present if $k = 0$ and that, if $n = 0$, $(p_1^{k_1} \mid \cdots \mid p_n^{k_n}) = \mathbf{0}$. It is easy to observe that $\text{dec}(p) = m$. □

4.2 Properties of places and markings

We now list some useful properties of places and markings. First, we extend the definition of sequential subterm of a process p to a set of places S. The goal is to prove that the sequential subterms of dom(dec(p)) are essentially the same sequential subterms of p. This property will be useful in proving (Theorem 3) that each place statically reachable from dom(dec(p)) is a sequential subterm of p (up to a possible renaming of bound names to the corresponding restricted names), so that, since sub(p) is finite for any p (Proposition 1), the set of all the places statically reachable from dom(dec(p)) is finite as well.

Definition 13 Function sub($-$), defined over finite-net multi-CCS processes in Definition 10, can be extended to a finite set S of places (i.e., of sequential processes) as follows: $\mathrm{sub}(\emptyset) = \emptyset$ and $\mathrm{sub}(S) = \bigcup_{s \in S} \mathrm{sub}(s)$.

Proposition 6 *For any finite set of places S_1 and S_2, if $S_1 \subseteq \mathrm{sub}(S_2)$, then $\mathrm{sub}(S_1) \subseteq \mathrm{sub}(S_2)$.*

Proof By induction on the cardinality of S_1, using Remark 1. □

Proposition 7 *For any set of places S, $S \subseteq \mathrm{sub}(S)$.*

Proof For any sequential process s, Definition 10 ensures that $s \in \mathrm{sub}(s)$; hence, the thesis follows trivially. □

Proposition 8 *If p is restriction-free, then $\mathrm{sub}(\mathrm{dom}(\mathrm{dec}(p))) \subseteq \mathrm{sub}(p)$, while if $p = (\nu L)t$, then $\mathrm{sub}(\mathrm{dom}(\mathrm{dec}(p))) \subseteq \mathrm{sub}(p)\{L'/L\}$. Hence, for any p, $|\mathrm{sub}(p)| \geq |\mathrm{sub}(\mathrm{dom}(\mathrm{dec}(p)))|$.*

Proof By induction on the definitions of $\mathrm{sub}(p, I)$ and $\mathrm{dec}(p, I)$.

The first base case is when $p = \mathbf{0}$; in such a case $\mathrm{sub}(\mathbf{0}, I) = \{\mathbf{0}\}$; as $\mathrm{dec}(\mathbf{0}, I) = \emptyset$, the thesis follows trivially. The second base case is when $p = A$ and $A \in I$; in such a case, $\mathrm{sub}(A, I) = \emptyset$; as $\mathrm{dec}(A, I) = \emptyset$, the thesis follows trivially. The other simple case is when p is sequential (and not $\mathbf{0}$); in such a case, $\mathrm{dec}(p, I) = \{p\}$ and the thesis follows trivially.

Now the inductive cases. If $p = p_1 \mid p_2$, then $\mathrm{sub}(p, I) = \mathrm{sub}(p_1, I) \cup \mathrm{sub}(p_2, I)$ and $\mathrm{sub}(\mathrm{dom}(\mathrm{dec}(p, I))) = \mathrm{sub}(\mathrm{dom}(\mathrm{dec}(p_1, I)) \cup \mathrm{sub}(\mathrm{dom}(\mathrm{dec}(p_2, I))$; by induction, we have that $\mathrm{sub}(\mathrm{dom}(\mathrm{dec}(p_i, I)) \subseteq \mathrm{sub}(p_i, I)$, for $i = 1, 2$; hence, the thesis follows trivially. If $p = A$, with $A \notin I$ and $A \stackrel{\mathrm{def}}{=} t$, then $\mathrm{sub}(A, I) = \mathrm{sub}(t, I \cup \{A\})$ and $\mathrm{dec}(A, I) = \mathrm{dec}(t, I \cup \{A\})$; by induction, we have $\mathrm{sub}(\mathrm{dom}(\mathrm{dec}(t, I \cup \{A\})) \subseteq \mathrm{sub}(t, I \cup \{A\}))$, and so $\mathrm{sub}(\mathrm{dom}(\mathrm{dec}(A, I)) \subseteq \mathrm{sub}(A, I)$, as required. Finally, if $p = (\nu L)t$, then $\mathrm{sub}(p, I) = \mathrm{sub}(t, I)$, while $\mathrm{sub}(\mathrm{dom}(\mathrm{dec}((\nu L)t, I))) = \mathrm{sub}(\mathrm{dom}(\mathrm{dec}(t, I)\{L'/L\})) = \mathrm{sub}(\mathrm{dom}(\mathrm{dec}(t, I)))\{L'/L\}$; by induction, we have that $\mathrm{sub}(\mathrm{dom}(\mathrm{dec}(t, I)) \subseteq \mathrm{sub}(t, I)$, and therefore also $\mathrm{sub}(\mathrm{dom}(\mathrm{dec}(t, I)))\{L'/L\} \subseteq \mathrm{sub}(t, I)\{L'/L\}$, from which the thesis follows. □

Now we want to extend the definition of well-formed processes to sets of places. To this aim, we define a notion of *well-behaved* set of places, which will be useful in the next section in proving that any transition statically enabled by a well-behaved set S is such that no synchronization of sequences is possible (Theorem 2); first, we prove that a well-formed process p generates a marking dec(p) such that dom(dec(p)) is well-behaved (Theorem 1).

Definition 14 Function ns($-$) of Definition 12 is defined over a set S of places as $\mathrm{ns}(S) = \mathrm{ns}(S, \emptyset)$, where $\mathrm{ns}(S, I) = \bigcup_{s \in S} \mathrm{ns}(s, I)$ and $\mathrm{ns}(\emptyset, I) = \emptyset$.

Lemma 1 *If p is restriction-free, then* $\mathrm{ns}(p, I) = \mathrm{ns}(\mathrm{dom}(\mathrm{dec}(p, I)), I)$.

Proof By induction on the definitions of $\mathrm{ns}(p, I)$ and $\mathrm{dec}(p, I)$. The proof is very similar to that of Proposition 8, hence omitted. □

Definition 15 (*Well-behaved*) A set of places S is *well-behaved* if there exist no $\beta \in \mathcal{G}$ such that $\beta \in \mathrm{ns}(S)$ and $\overline{\beta} \in \mathrm{ns}(S)$.

Theorem 1 *If p is well-formed, then dom(dec(p)) is well-behaved.*

Proof By induction on the proof of $\mathrm{wf}(p, I)$. The first base case is $p = \mathbf{0}$, and the thesis trivially holds. The second base case is when $p = A$ and $A \in I$; in such a case, $\mathrm{wf}(A, I)$ holds and $\mathrm{dom}(\mathrm{dec}(A, I)) = \emptyset$, hence the thesis trivially holds.

Now the inductive cases. If $p = \mu.p'$, then $\mathrm{wf}(p, I)$ holds only if $\mathrm{wf}(p', I)$ holds. By induction, we have that $\mathrm{dom}(\mathrm{dec}(p', I))$ is well-behaved. Hence, also $\mathrm{dom}(\mathrm{dec}(\mu.p', I))$ is well-behaved, as $\mathrm{ns}(\mathrm{dom}(\mathrm{dec}(\mu.p', I)), I) = \mathrm{ns}(\{\mu.p'\}, I) = \mathrm{ns}(\mu.p', I) = \mathrm{ns}(p', I)$ and $\mathrm{ns}(p', I) = \mathrm{ns}(\mathrm{dom}(\mathrm{dec}(p', I)), I)$ by Lemma 1.

If $p = \underline{\alpha}.p'$, then $\mathrm{wf}(p, I)$ holds if there exists no $\beta \in \mathcal{G}$ such that $\beta \in \mathrm{ns}(p, I)$ and $\overline{\beta} \in \mathrm{ns}(p, I)$; by Lemma 1, $\mathrm{ns}(p, I) = \mathrm{ns}(\mathrm{dom}(\mathrm{dec}(p, I)), I)$, and so the thesis follows trivially.

If $p = p_1 + p_2$, then $\mathrm{wf}(p, I)$ holds only if $\mathrm{wf}(p_1, I)$ and $\mathrm{wf}(p_2, I)$ hold and, additionally, there exists no $\beta \in \mathcal{G}$ such that $\beta \in \mathrm{ns}(p_1, I)$ and $\overline{\beta} \in \mathrm{ns}(p_2, I)$. By induction, we have that $\mathrm{dom}(\mathrm{dec}(p_i, I))$ is well-behaved, for $i = 1, 2$; so, there exists no $\beta \in \mathcal{G}$ such that $\beta \in \mathrm{dom}(\mathrm{dec}(p_i, I))$ and $\overline{\beta} \in \mathrm{dom}(\mathrm{dec}(p_i, I))$, for $i = 1, 2$. By Lemma 1, $\mathrm{ns}(\mathrm{dom}(\mathrm{dec}(p_i, I)), I) = \mathrm{ns}(p_i, I)$ for $i = 1, 2$, and so there exists no $\beta \in \mathcal{G}$ such that $\beta \in \mathrm{ns}(p_i, I)$ and $\overline{\beta} \in$

Table 9 Rules for net transitions [symmetric rule (sum_2) omitted]

$$(\text{pref})\ \frac{}{\{\mu.p\} \xrightarrow{\mu} \text{dec}(p)} \qquad (\text{sum}_1)\ \frac{\{p\} \xrightarrow{\sigma} m}{\{p+p'\} \xrightarrow{\sigma} m}$$

$$(\text{s-pref})\ \frac{\{p\} \xrightarrow{\sigma} m}{\{\underline{\gamma}.p\} \xrightarrow{\gamma \circ \sigma} m} \qquad (\text{s-com})\ \frac{m_1 \xrightarrow{\sigma_1} m_1' \quad m_2 \xrightarrow{\sigma_2} m_2'}{m_1 \oplus m_2 \xrightarrow{\sigma} m_1' \oplus m_2'}\ \text{Sync}(\sigma_1, \sigma_2, \sigma)$$

Table 10 The proof of a net transition

$$(\text{s-com})\ \dfrac{(\text{s-com})\ \dfrac{(\text{s-pref})\ \dfrac{(\text{pref})\ \dfrac{}{\{b'.p\} \xrightarrow{b'} dec(p)}}{\{\underline{a}.b'.p\} \xrightarrow{ab'} dec(p)} \quad (\text{pref})\ \dfrac{}{\{\overline{a}.q\} \xrightarrow{\overline{a}} dec(q)}}{\{\underline{a}.b'.p, \overline{a}.q\} \xrightarrow{b'} dec(p) \oplus dec(q)} \quad (\text{pref})\ \dfrac{}{\{\overline{b'}.r\} \xrightarrow{\overline{b'}} dec(r)}}{\{\underline{a}.b'.p, \overline{a}.q, \overline{b'}.r\} \xrightarrow{\tau} dec(p) \oplus dec(q) \oplus dec(r)}$$

$\text{ns}(p_i, I)$, for $i = 1, 2$. Therefore, $\text{dom}(\text{dec}(p_1 + p_2, I)) = \{p_1 + p_2\}$ is well-behaved, too, because $\text{ns}(p_1 + p_2, I) = \text{ns}(p_1, I) \cup \text{ns}(p_2, I)$, and then there exists no $\beta \in \mathcal{G}$ such that $\beta \in \text{ns}(p_1 + p_2, I)$ and $\overline{\beta} \in \text{ns}(p_1 + p_2, I)$, as required. The case when $p = p_1 \mid p_2$ is similar to the above, hence omitted.

If $p = (\nu a)p'$, then $\text{wf}(p, I)$ holds only if $\text{wf}(p', I)$ holds. By induction, we have that $\text{dom}(\text{dec}(p', I))$ is well-behaved. It is easy to see that $\text{dom}(\text{dec}(p', I))\{a'/a\}$ is well-behaved too, as the substitution replaces action a with a new name a' not in use. Hence, as $\text{dom}(\text{dec}(p', I))\{a'/a\} = \text{dom}(\text{dec}(p', I)\{a'/a\}) = \text{dom}(\text{dec}(p, I))$, also $\text{dom}(\text{dec}(p, I))$ is well-behaved.

If $p = A$, with $A \notin I$ and $A \stackrel{\text{def}}{=} q$, then $\text{wf}(A, I)$ holds only if $\text{wf}(q, I \cup \{A\})$ holds. By induction, $\text{dom}(\text{dec}(q, I \cup \{A\}))$ is well-behaved. Since $\text{dec}(A, I) = \text{dec}(q, I \cup \{A\})$, also $\text{dom}(\text{dec}(A, I))$ is well-behaved. □

4.3 Net transitions

Let $\mathcal{A}^\gamma = \{\tau\} \cup \mathcal{G}^+$, ranged over by σ with abuse of notation, be the set of labels, and let $\rightarrow \subseteq \mathcal{M}_{\text{fin}}(S_{\text{MCCS}}) \times \mathcal{A}^\gamma \times \mathcal{M}_{\text{fin}}(S_{\text{MCCS}})$, be the least set of transitions generated by the axiom and rules in Table 9, where in a transition $m_1 \xrightarrow{\sigma} m_2$, m_1 is the pre-set, σ is the label and m_2 is the post-set.

Axiom (pref) states that if one token is present in the place $\mu.p$ then a μ-labeled transition is derivable from marking $\{\mu.p\}$, producing the marking $\text{dec}(p)$. This holds for any μ, i.e., for the invisible action τ, for any visible action α as well as for any restricted action α'. In rule (s-pref), γ ranges over visible actions α and *restricted* ones α'. This rule requires that the premise transition $\{p\} \xrightarrow{\sigma} m$ be derivable by the rules, starting form the sequential process p. Rule (sum_1) and its symmetric (sum_2) are as expected: the transition from place $p + p'$ are those from places p and p', as both p and p' are sequential. Finally, rule (s-com) explains how synchronization takes place: it is needed that m_1 and m_2 perform synchronizable sequences σ_1 and σ_2, producing σ; here we assume that Sync has been extended also to restricted actions in the obvious way, i.e., a restricted action $\overline{\alpha'}$ can be synchronized only with its complementary restricted action α' or with a sequence beginning with α'. As an example, net transition $\{\underline{a}.b'.p, \overline{a}.q, \overline{b'}.r\} \xrightarrow{\tau} \text{dec}(p) \oplus \text{dec}(q) \oplus \text{dec}(r)$ is derivable (see Table 10).

Transitions with labels containing restricted actions should not be taken in the resulting net, as we accept only transitions labeled on $\mathcal{A} = \{\tau\} \cup (\mathcal{L} \cup \overline{\mathcal{L}})^+$. However, they are useful in producing acceptable transitions, as two complementary restricted actions can synchronize, producing a τ-labeled transition or shortening the synchronized sequence: e.g., in the example above, the derivable transition $\{b'.p\} \xrightarrow{b'} \text{dec}(p)$ is not an acceptable transition because its label is not in $\mathcal{A}$, while $\{\underline{a}.b'.p, \overline{a}.q, \overline{b'}.r\} \xrightarrow{\tau} \text{dec}(p) \oplus \text{dec}(q) \oplus \text{dec}(r)$ is so. Hence, the P/T net for finite-net multi-CCS is the triple $N_{\text{MCCS}} = (S_{\text{MCCS}}, \mathcal{A}, T_{\text{MCCS}})$, where the set $T_{\text{MCCS}} = \{(m_1, \sigma, m_2) \mid m_1 \xrightarrow{\sigma} m_2$ is derivable by the rules and $\sigma \in \mathcal{A}\}$ is obtained by filtering out those transitions derivable by the rules such that no restricted name α' occurs in σ.

4.4 Properties of net transitions

Some useful properties of net transitions are listed here. First, given a transition $t = (m_1, \sigma, m_2)$, derivable by the rules in Table 9, we show that the marking m_2 generates subterms that are already present in the marking m_1.

Proposition 9 *Let* $t = m_1 \xrightarrow{\sigma} m_2$ *be a transition derivable by the rules in Table* 9. *Then,* $sub(dom(m_2)) \subseteq \text{sub}(\text{dom}(m_1))$.

Proof By induction on the proof of t. □

Lemma 2 *Let* $t = m_1 \xrightarrow{\sigma} m_2$ *be a transition derivable by the rules in Table* 9. *Then,* $\text{ns}(\text{dom}(m_2)) \subseteq \text{ns}(\text{dom}(m_1))$.

Proof By induction on the proof of t. □

Proposition 10 *If* $t = m_1 \xrightarrow{\sigma} m_2$ *is derivable by the rules and* $\mathrm{dom}(m_1)$ *is well-behaved, then* $\mathrm{dom}(m_2)$ *is well-behaved.*

Proof By Lemma 2, we know that $\mathrm{ns}(\mathrm{dom}(m_2)) \subseteq \mathrm{ns}(\mathrm{dom}(m_1))$. Therefore, if $\mathrm{dom}(m_1)$ is well-behaved, then $\mathrm{dom}(m_2)$ is well-behaved, too. □

Corollary 1 *If* S_1 *is well-behaved and* $S_1 \Longrightarrow^* S_k$*, then* S_k *is well-behaved.*

Proof By induction on the static reachability relation $\Longrightarrow^*$. The base case is $S_1 \Longrightarrow^* S_1$ and it is trivial. The inductive case is $S_1 \Longrightarrow^* S_{k-1} \stackrel{t}{\Longrightarrow} S_k$. By induction we can assume that S_{k-1} is well-behaved. Let $t = m_1 \xrightarrow{\sigma} m_2$ be a transition in T_{MCCS}. The set $\mathrm{ns}(S_{k-1})$ is $\mathrm{ns}(S_{k-1} \backslash \mathrm{dom}(m_1)) \cup \mathrm{ns}(\mathrm{dom}(m_1))$. The set $\mathrm{ns}(S_k)$ is $\mathrm{ns}(S_{k-1}) \cup \mathrm{ns}(\mathrm{dom}(m_2))$. By Lemma 2, we have $\mathrm{ns}(\mathrm{dom}(m_2)) \subseteq \mathrm{ns}(\mathrm{dom}(m_1))$. Therefore, $\mathrm{ns}(S_k) = \mathrm{ns}(S_{k-1}) \cup \mathrm{ns}(\mathrm{dom}(m_2)) \subseteq \mathrm{ns}(S_{k-1}) \cup \mathrm{ns}(\mathrm{dom}(m_1)) = \mathrm{ns}(S_{k-1})$; hence, also S_k is well-behaved. □

Now we want to prove that when a transition $m \xrightarrow{\sigma} m'$, whose label $\sigma \neq \tau$, involves in its proof some sequence of length greater than one, then the names of σ are all contained in $\mathrm{ns}(\mathrm{dom}(m))$.

Lemma 3 *If* $t = (m, \sigma, m')$ *is derivable by the rules of Table 9, and either* $|\sigma| \geq 2$ *or* $\sigma \neq \tau$ *and there exists a transition label* σ' *in its proof tree with* $|\sigma'| \geq 2$*, then* $n(\sigma) \subseteq \mathrm{ns}(\mathrm{dom}(m))$.

Proof By induction on the proof of transition t. If $m = \{\mu.p\}$, then, by axiom (pref), $t = (m, \mu, \mathrm{dec}(p))$. This case is vacuous as the only transition label in the proof tree is μ. If $m = \{\underline{\gamma}.p\}$, then $t = (m, \sigma, m')$ is derivable only if $(\{p\}, \sigma', m')$ is derivable, with $\sigma = \gamma \diamond \sigma'$. If $|\sigma'| \geq 2$, then induction can be applied to conclude that $n(\sigma') \subseteq \mathrm{ns}(\mathrm{dom}(\{p\})) = \mathrm{ns}(\{p\}) = \mathrm{ns}(p)$; hence, $n(\sigma) = \{\gamma\} \cup n(\sigma') \subseteq \{\gamma\} \cup \mathrm{ns}(p)$. Since $\mathrm{ns}(m) = \mathrm{ns}(\{\underline{\gamma}.p\}) = \mathrm{ns}(\underline{\gamma}.p)$ and $\{\gamma\} \cup \mathrm{ns}(p) \subseteq \mathrm{ns}(\underline{\gamma}.p)$, the thesis $n(\sigma) \subseteq n(m)$ follows trivially. If $|\sigma'| = 1$, then two further subcases are possible: either $\sigma' = \tau$ or $\sigma' = \gamma'$; in the former subcase, this is possible only if p, being sequential, has performed a prefix τ via (pref), so that no transition label in the proof tree is longer than one, hence this subcase is vacuous; in the latter subcase, $\sigma = \gamma\gamma'$ and $n(\sigma) \subseteq \mathrm{ns}(\underline{\gamma}.p)$, because $\gamma' \in \mathrm{In}(p)$.

If $m = \{p_1 + p_2\}$, then $t = (m, \sigma, m')$ is derivable only if $(\{p_1\}, \sigma, m')$ or $(\{p_2\}, \sigma, m')$ are derivable. W.l.o.g., assume that $(\{p_1\}, \sigma, m')$; then, if the hypothesis holds for this premise, by induction, we have $n(\sigma) \subseteq \mathrm{ns}(\{p_1\}) = \mathrm{ns}(p_1)$. Since $\mathrm{ns}(p_1) \subseteq \mathrm{ns}(p) = \mathrm{ns}(m)$, the thesis follows by transitivity.

If t is derived by rule (s-com), then $m = m_1 \oplus m_2$, $m' = m_1' \oplus m_2'$ and transitions $t_1 = (m_1, \sigma_1, m_1')$ and $t_2 = (m_2, \sigma_2, m_2')$ are derivable, with $\mathrm{Sync}(\sigma_1, \sigma_2, \sigma)$. As by hypothesis $\sigma \neq \tau$, then σ_1 or σ_2 must be of length greater than one. W.l.o.g., assume $|\sigma_1| \geq 2$. Since $\mathrm{Sync}(\sigma_1, \sigma_2, \sigma)$, necessarily $n(\sigma) \subseteq n(\sigma_1)$. By induction, $n(\sigma_1) \subseteq \mathrm{ns}(\mathrm{dom}(m_1))$; as $\mathrm{ns}(\mathrm{dom}(m_1)) \subseteq \mathrm{ns}(\mathrm{dom}(m_1 \oplus m_2))$, the thesis follows by transitivity. □

Proposition 11 *If* $t = (m, \gamma, m')$ *is derivable by the rules of Table 9 by using rule (s-com), then* $\gamma \in \mathrm{ns}(\mathrm{dom}(m))$.

Proof By induction on the proof of t. If rule (s-com) occurs in the proof of t, then m cannot be a sequential process. Therefore, the first rule must be (s-com), and so $m = m_1 \oplus m_2$, $m' = m_1' \oplus m_2'$, $t_1 = (m_1, \sigma_1, m_1')$ and $t_2 = (m_2, \sigma_2, m_2')$ are derivable, with $\mathrm{Sync}(\sigma_1, \sigma_2, \gamma)$. So, σ_1 or σ_2 must be a sequence of length greater than one, and so by Lemma 3, it follows that $\gamma \in \mathrm{ns}(\mathrm{dom}(m))$. □

Theorem 2 *If* $t = (m, \sigma, m')$ *is derivable by the rules and* $\mathrm{dom}(m)$ *is well-behaved, then the proof of t never synchronizes two sequences, not even indirectly.*

Proof By induction on the proof of t. If m is a singleton, then rule (s-com) is never used, and so no synchronization of sequences is possible. Otherwise, the first rule must be (s-com), and so $m = m_1 \oplus m_2$, $m' = m_1' \oplus m_2'$, $t_1 = (m_1, \sigma_1, m_1')$ and $t_2 = (m_2, \sigma_2, m_2')$ are derivable, with $\mathrm{Sync}(\sigma_1, \sigma_2, \sigma)$. As $\mathrm{dom}(m)$ is well-behaved, so are also $\mathrm{dom}(m_1)$ and $\mathrm{dom}(m_2)$; therefore, by induction, we know that in the proofs of transitions t_1 and t_2 two sequences are never synchronized. So, it remains to prove that the thesis holds for the resulting σ. By definition of Sync, if $\sigma = \tau$, then both σ_1 and σ_2 are complementary actions, say $\sigma_1 = \gamma$ and $\sigma_2 = \overline{\gamma}$. If both t_1 and t_2 are derived by using rule (s-com), then t synchronizes two sequences, even if indirectly; however, this is not possible, because Proposition 11 would ensure that $\gamma \in \mathrm{ns}(\mathrm{dom}(m_1))$ and $\overline{\gamma} \in \mathrm{ns}(\mathrm{dom}(m_2))$, contradicting that $\mathrm{dom}(m_1 \oplus m_2)$ be well-behaved. Therefore, t_1 or t_2 is derived without using rule (s-com) and so no synchronization of sequences is produced. By definition of Sync, if $\sigma \neq \tau$, then either σ_1 or σ_2 is a sequence of length greater than one; w.l.o.g. assume that $|\sigma_1| \geq 2$ and $\sigma_2 = \overline{\gamma}$. By Lemma 3, $n(\sigma_1) \subseteq \mathrm{ns}(\mathrm{dom}(m_1))$, in particular, $\gamma \in \mathrm{ns}(\mathrm{dom}(m_1))$. If t_2 is derived by using rule (s-com), then Proposition 11 would ensure that $\overline{\gamma} \in \mathrm{ns}(\mathrm{dom}(m_2))$, contradicting that $\mathrm{dom}(m_1 \oplus m_2)$ be well-behaved. Therefore, t_2 is derived without using rule (s-com) and so no synchronization of sequences is produced. □

Remark 2 By the proof of the prop above, it is clear that any transition $t = m_1 \xrightarrow{\sigma} m_2$ derivable from a *well-behaved* set of places $\mathrm{dom}(m_1)$ is such that in the proof tree for t, whenever rule (s-com) is used with premise transitions t_1 and t_2, at least one of the two, say t_1 w.l.o.g., is such that $^\bullet t_1$ is a singleton and $l(t_1)$ is a single action in Act^γ. That is, any derivable transition t from a well-behaved set of places $\mathrm{dom}(m_1)$ is such that one sequential process $s \in \mathrm{dom}(m_1)$ acts as the *leader* of the multi-party synchronization, while the other sequential components contribute each with a single action, acting as *servants*.

4.5 The reachable subnet Net(p)

The P/T system associated to $p \in \mathcal{P}^\gamma$ is the subnet of N_{MCCS} statically reachable from the initial marking $\mathrm{dec}(p)$. We indicate with $\mathrm{Net}(p)$ such a subnet.

Definition 16 Let p be a process in $\mathcal{P}^\gamma$. The P/T net system statically associated to p is $\mathrm{Net}(p) = (S_p, A_p, T_p, m_0)$, where $m_0 = \mathrm{dec}(p)$ and

$$S_p = [\![\mathrm{dom}(m_0)\rangle \text{ computed in } N_{\mathrm{MCCS}},$$
$$T_p = \{t \in T_{\mathrm{MCCS}} \mid S_p[\![t\rangle\}$$
$$A_p = \{\sigma \in \mathcal{A} \mid \exists t \in T_p \text{ such that } l(t) = \sigma\}.$$

The following three propositions present facts that are obviously true by construction of the net $\mathrm{Net}(p)$ associated to a finite-net multi-CCS process p.

Proposition 12 *For any $p \in \mathcal{P}$, Net(p) is a statically reduced P/T net.*

Proposition 13 *If* $\mathrm{dec}(p) = \mathrm{dec}(q)$, *then Net(p)* $= \mathrm{Net}(q)$.

Proposition 14 *For any $t \in \mathcal{P}$, let Net(t) $= (S, A, T, m_0)$. Then, for any $n \geq 1$, Net(t^n) $= (S, A, T, n \cdot m_0)$, where $t^1 = t$ and $t^{n+1} = t \mid t^n$.*

For any $(\nu L)t \in \mathcal{P}$, let Net($(\nu L)t$) $= (S, A, T, m_0)$. Then, for any $n \geq 1$, Net($(\nu L)(t^n)$) $= (S, A, T, n \cdot m_0)$.

Definition 16 suggests a way of generating $\mathrm{Net}(p)$ with an algorithm based on the inductive definition of the static reachability relation (see Definition 9): start by the initial set of places $\mathrm{dom}(\mathrm{dec}(p))$, and then apply the rules in Table 9 in order to produce the set of transitions (labeled on $\mathcal{A}$) statically enabled at $\mathrm{dom}(\mathrm{dec}(p))$, as well as the additional places statically reachable by means of such transitions. Then repeat this procedure from the set of places statically reached so far. The problems with this algorithm are two:

- the obvious *halting condition* is "until no new places are statically reachable"; of course, the algorithm terminates if we know that the set S_p of places statically reachable from $\mathrm{dom}(\mathrm{dec}(p))$ is finite; additionally,
- at each step of the algorithm, we have to be sure that the set of transitions derivable from the current set of statically reachable places is finite.

We are going to prove these two facts: (i) S_p is finite for any $p \in \mathcal{P}$, and (ii) for any *well-formed* process p, and for any set of places S, statically reachable from $\mathrm{dom}(\mathrm{dec}(p))$, the set of transitions statically enabled at S is finite.

Theorem 3 *For any $p \in \mathcal{P}$, let Net(p) $= (S_p, A_p, T_p, m_0)$ be defined as in Definition* 16. *Then, set S_p is finite.*

Proof We prove, by induction on the static reachability relation $\Longrightarrow^*$, that any set S_i of places, statically reachable from $\mathrm{dom}(m_0)$, is a subset of $\mathrm{sub}(\mathrm{dom}(m_0))$. This is enough as, by Proposition 8, we know that $|\mathrm{sub}(p)| \geq |\mathrm{sub}(\mathrm{dom}(m_0))|$; moreover, by Proposition 1, $\mathrm{sub}(p)$ is finite and so the thesis follows trivially.

The base case is $\mathrm{dom}(m_0) \Longrightarrow^* \mathrm{dom}(m_0)$. By Proposition 7, we have the required $\mathrm{dom}(m_0) \subseteq \mathrm{sub}(\mathrm{dom}(m_0))$.

Now, let us assume that S_i is a set of places statically reachable from $\mathrm{dom}(m_0)$ and let $t = m_1 \xrightarrow{\sigma} m_2$ be such that $S_i \stackrel{t}{\Longrightarrow} S_{i+1}$. By induction, we know that $S_i \subseteq \mathrm{sub}(\mathrm{dom}(m_0))$. So, we have to prove that the new places reached via t are in $\mathrm{sub}(\mathrm{dom}(m_0))$. Note that since $\mathrm{dom}(m_1) \subseteq S_i$, it follows that $\mathrm{dom}(m_1) \subseteq \mathrm{sub}(\mathrm{dom}(m_0))$ and also that $\mathrm{sub}(\mathrm{dom}(m_1))) \subseteq \mathrm{sub}(\mathrm{dom}(m_0))$, by Proposition 6. By Proposition 7, we have that $\mathrm{dom}(m_2) \subseteq \mathrm{sub}(\mathrm{dom}(m_2)$; by Proposition 9, we have that $\mathrm{sub}(\mathrm{dom}(m_2)) \subseteq \mathrm{sub}(\mathrm{dom}(m_1))$; by transitivity, $\mathrm{dom}(m_2) \subseteq \mathrm{sub}(\mathrm{dom}(m_0))$, and so $S_{i+1} = S_i \cup \mathrm{dom}(m_2) \subseteq \mathrm{sub}(\mathrm{dom}(m_0))$, as required.

Summing up, any place statically reachable from $\mathrm{dom}(m_0)$ is a (possibly, one-time renamed) sequential subterm of p. As by Proposition 1, $\mathrm{sub}(p)$ is finite, then also S_p (the largest set of places statically reachable from $\mathrm{dom}(m_0)$) is finite. □

We now want to prove that for any *well-formed* finite-net multi-CCS process p, and for any set of places $S \subseteq S_{\mathrm{MCCS}}$, statically reachable from $\mathrm{dom}(\mathrm{dec}(p))$, the set of transitions statically enabled at S is finite. Some auxiliary definitions and results are necessary. Given a single place $s \in S$, by $s \vdash t$ we mean that transition $t = (\{s\}, \sigma, m)$ is derivable by the rules in Table 9, hence with $\sigma \in \mathcal{A}^\gamma$.

Lemma 4 *Set $T_s = \{t \mid s \vdash t\}$ is finite, for any $s \in S_{\mathrm{MCCS}}$.*

Proof By induction on the structure of the sequential process s and then by induction on the rules in Table 9.

Given a finite set of places $S \subseteq S_{\mathrm{MCCS}}$, let T_1 be $\bigcup_{s \in S} T_s$, i.e., the set of all transitions, with a singleton preset in S, derivable by the rules with labeling in $\mathcal{A}^\gamma$. Set T_1 is finite, being the finite union (as S is finite) of finite sets (as T_s is finite for any s).

If p is well-formed, then $\mathrm{dom}(\mathrm{dec}(p))$ is well-behaved by Theorem 1. If S is statically reachable from $\mathrm{dom}(\mathrm{dec}(p))$, then S is well-behaved by Corollary 1. Let $k \in \mathbb{N}$ be the length of the longest label of any transition in T_1. Remark 2 explains that if a multi-party transition t is derivable by the rules from the well-behaved set $\mathrm{dom}(^\bullet t) \subseteq S$, then its proof contains $k+1$ synchronizations at most, each one between a transition (labeled with a sequence) and a *singleton-preset* transition (labeled with a *single* action). Therefore, the set of all the transitions statically enabled at a well-behaved set S can be defined by means of a sequence of sets T_i of transitions, for $2 \leq i \leq k+1$, where each transition $t \in T_i$ has a preset $^\bullet t$ composed of i tokens, as follows:

$$\begin{aligned} T_i = \{&(m_1 \oplus m_2, \sigma, m_1' \oplus m_2') \mid \\ &\exists \sigma_1 \exists \gamma.(m_1, \sigma_1, m_1') \in T_{i-1}, \\ &(m_2, \gamma, m_2') \in T_1, \mathrm{Sync}(\sigma_1, \gamma, \sigma)\} \end{aligned}$$

Note that T_2 is finite, because T_1 is finite; inductively, T_{i+1}, for $2 \leq i \leq k$ is finite, because T_i and T_1 are finite. The set T_S of all the transitions statically enabled at S is $\{t \mid t \in \bigcup_{i=1}^{k+1} T_i \wedge l(t) \in \mathcal{A}\}$, where only transitions labeled on $\mathcal{A}$ are considered. T_S is finite, being a finite union of finite sets; therefore, we have the following result.

Proposition 15 *If $S \subseteq S_{\mathrm{MCCS}}$ is a well-behaved, finite set of places, then set T_S of all the transitions enabled at S is finite.*

Example 4 Consider the non-well-formed process $p = (\nu a)(a.\mathbf{0} \mid (\underline{\overline{a}}.a.\mathbf{0} \mid \overline{a}.\mathbf{0}))$, discussed in Example 3. We have that $\mathrm{dec}(p) = a'.\mathbf{0} \oplus \underline{\overline{a'}}.a'.\mathbf{0} \oplus \overline{a'}.\mathbf{0}$, which is not well-behaved because $a' \in \mathrm{ns}(\mathrm{dom}(\mathrm{dec}(p)))$ and $\overline{a'} \in \mathrm{ns}(\mathrm{dom}(\mathrm{dec}(p)))$. It is easy to observe that transition $t_1 = a'.\mathbf{0} \oplus \underline{\overline{a'}}.a'.\mathbf{0} \oplus \overline{a'}.\mathbf{0} \xrightarrow{\tau} \emptyset$ is derivable, because first we synchronize $\overline{a'}a'$ with a', yielding a', which is then synchronized with $\overline{a'}$, yielding τ. However, the occurrence of action a' produced by the first synchronization may be used to synchronize an additional sequence $\overline{a'}a'$, yielding a' again. Therefore, it is not difficult to see that also $t_n = a'.\mathbf{0} \oplus n \cdot \underline{\overline{a'}}.a'.\mathbf{0} \oplus \overline{a'}.\mathbf{0} \xrightarrow{\tau} \emptyset$, is statically enabled at $\mathrm{dom}(\mathrm{dec}(p))$, for any $n \geq 1$. Hence, the set of transitions statically enabled at $\mathrm{dom}(\mathrm{dec}(p))$ is infinite.

Theorem 4 *For any well-formed, finite-net multi-CCS process p, $Net(p) = (S_p, A_p, T_p, \mathrm{dec}(p))$ is a finite P/T net.*

Proof If p is well-formed, then $\mathrm{dom}(\mathrm{dec}(p))$ is well-behaved, by Theorem 1, and finite, by Proposition 4. By Proposition 15, set $T_{\mathrm{dom}(\mathrm{dec}(p))}$ is finite. Let S_1 be the set of places $\mathrm{dom}(\mathrm{dec}(p)) \cup \bigcup_{t \in T_{\mathrm{dom}(\mathrm{dec}(p))}} \mathrm{dom}(t^\bullet)$. If $S_1 = \mathrm{dom}(\mathrm{dec}(p))$, then $S_p = \mathrm{dom}(\mathrm{dec}(p))$ and $T_p = T_{\mathrm{dom}(\mathrm{dec}(p))}$. Otherwise, repeat the step above for S_1; in fact, S_1 is a finite set of places, because $\mathrm{dom}(\mathrm{dec}(p))$ is finite, set $T_{\mathrm{dom}(\mathrm{dec}(p))}$ is finite and each transition has a finite post-set; moreover, S_1 is well-behaved by Corollary 1. By repeating the step above for S_1, we compute a new finite set T_{S_1} of transitions statically enabled at S_1, and a new finite set S_2 of places statically reachable from S_1 via the transitions in T_{S_1}; if $S_2 = S_1$, then $S_p = S_1$ and $T_p = T_{S_1}$. Otherwise, repeat the step above for S_2. This procedure will end eventually because, by Theorem 3, we are sure that S_p is a finite set. □

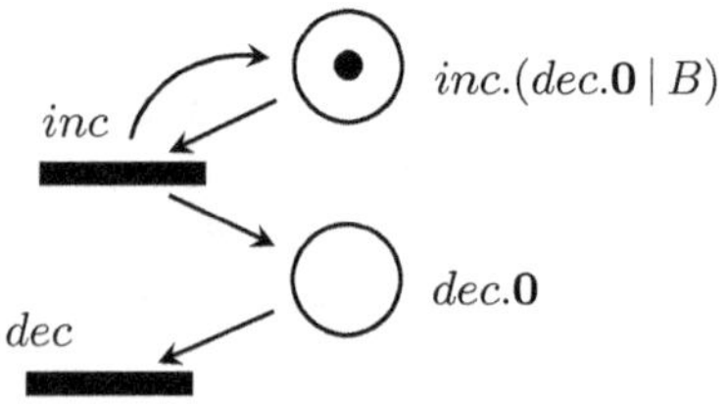

Fig. 1 The finite P/T system for a semi-counter

Example 5 (*Semi-counter*) A semi-counter, i.e., a counter that cannot test for zero, can be described by the finite-net multi-CCS process $B \stackrel{\mathrm{def}}{=} \mathrm{inc}.(\mathrm{dec}.\mathbf{0} \mid B)$. Net($B$) is the net (S_B, A_B, T_B, m_0) we are going to construct, where the initial marking m_0 is $\mathrm{dec}(B) = \{\mathrm{inc}.(\mathrm{dec}.\mathbf{0} \mid B)\}$. Then, the only enabled transition is

$$t_1 = \{\mathrm{inc}.(\mathrm{dec}.\mathbf{0} \mid B)\} \xrightarrow{\mathrm{inc}} \{\mathrm{dec}.\mathbf{0}, \mathrm{inc}.(\mathrm{dec}.\mathbf{0} \mid B)\}$$

and the set S_1 of places statically reachable in one step from $\mathrm{dom}(m_0)$ is $S_1 = \{\mathrm{dec}.\mathbf{0}, \mathrm{inc}.(\mathrm{dec}.\mathbf{0} \mid B)\}$. From S_1, besides transition t_1 above, also transition $t_2 = \{\mathrm{dec}.\mathbf{0}\} \xrightarrow{\mathrm{dec}} \emptyset$ is derivable, which however does not add any new reachable place. So, S_1 is the set S_B, $\{t_1, t_2\}$ is the set T_B and $\{\mathrm{inc}, \mathrm{dec}\}$ is the set A_B. The resulting net Net(B) is outlined in Fig. 1. □

Example 6 (*1/3 Semi-counter*) For the well-formed process $p = (\nu c)A$, where $A \stackrel{\mathrm{def}}{=} \mathrm{inc}.(A \mid (\underline{c}.\underline{c}.\mathrm{dec}.\mathbf{0} + \overline{c}.\mathbf{0}))$, three occurrences of inc are needed to enable one dec. Net(p) is the net (S_p, A_p, T_p, m_0) we are going to construct, where the initial marking m_0 is $\mathrm{dec}(p) = \mathrm{dec}((\nu c)A) = \mathrm{dec}(A)\{c'/c\} = \{\mathrm{inc}.(A \mid (\underline{c}.\underline{c}.\mathrm{dec}.\mathbf{0} + \overline{c}.\mathbf{0}))\}\{c'/c\} = \{s_1\}$; place s_1 is $\mathrm{inc}.(A_{\{c'/c\}} \mid (\underline{c'}.\underline{c'}.\mathrm{dec}.\mathbf{0} + \overline{c}'.\mathbf{0}))$, where the new constant $A_{\{c'/c\}}$ is obtained by applying the substitution $\{c'/c\}$ to the body of A: $A_{\{c'/c\}} \stackrel{\mathrm{def}}{=} \mathrm{inc}.(A_{\{c'/c\}} \mid (\underline{c'}.\underline{c'}.\mathrm{dec}.\mathbf{0} + \overline{c'}.\mathbf{0}))$. Now, only transition $t_1 = \{s_1\} \xrightarrow{\mathrm{inc}} \{s_1, s_2\}$ is derivable from $\mathrm{dom}(m_0) = \{s_1\}$, where $s_2 = \underline{c'}.\underline{c'}.\mathrm{dec}.\mathbf{0} + \overline{c}'.\mathbf{0}$ is a new statically reachable place. Note that s_2 can produce two transitions in T_{s_2}, namely $t' = \{s_2\} \xrightarrow{c'c'\mathrm{dec}} \emptyset$ and

Table 11 The proof of a net transition, where $s_2 = \underline{c'}.\underline{c'}.\text{dec}.\mathbf{0} + \overline{c'}.\mathbf{0}$

$$
\text{(s-com)}\ \dfrac{
\text{(s-com)}\ \dfrac{
\text{(sum}_1\text{)}\ \dfrac{\text{(s-pref)}\ \dfrac{\text{(s-pref)}\ \dfrac{\text{(pref)}\ \dfrac{}{\{dec.\mathbf{0}\} \xrightarrow{dec} \emptyset}}{\{\underline{c'}.dec.\mathbf{0}\} \xrightarrow{c'dec} \emptyset}}{\{\underline{c'}.\underline{c'}.dec.\mathbf{0}\} \xrightarrow{c'c'dec} \emptyset}}{\{s_2\} \xrightarrow{c'c'dec} \emptyset}
\quad
\text{(sum}_2\text{)}\ \dfrac{\text{(pref)}\ \dfrac{}{\{\overline{c'}.\mathbf{0}\} \xrightarrow{\overline{c'}} \emptyset}}{\{s_2\} \xrightarrow{\overline{c'}} \emptyset}
}{\{s_2, s_2\} \xrightarrow{c'dec} \emptyset}
\quad
\text{(sum}_2\text{)}\ \dfrac{\text{(pref)}\ \dfrac{}{\{\overline{c'}.\mathbf{0}\} \xrightarrow{\overline{c'}} \emptyset}}{\{s_2\} \xrightarrow{\overline{c'}} \emptyset}
}{\{s_2, s_2, s_2\} \xrightarrow{dec} \emptyset}
$$

$t'' = \{s_2\} \xrightarrow{\overline{c'}} \emptyset$, but both are not labeled with a sequence in $\mathcal{A}$. However, these transitions can be composed by means of rule (s-com), as shown in Table 11, to produce transition $t_2 = 3 \cdot s_2 \xrightarrow{\text{dec}} \emptyset$, which does not add any new reachable place. So, $S_p = \{s_1, s_2\}$ and $T_p = \{t_1, t_2\}$.

4.6 The CRW example

Let us consider process CRW of Sect. 3.4. The net associated to CRW is $\text{Net}(\text{CRW}) = (S_{\text{CRW}}, A_{\text{CRW}}, T_{\text{CRW}}, m_0)$ we are going to construct, where the initial marking is $m_0 = \text{dec}(\text{CRW}) = \text{dec}((\nu l, u)(R \mid R \mid R \mid R \mid W \mid W \mid L \mid L \mid L)) = \text{dec}(R \mid R \mid R \mid R \mid W \mid W \mid L \mid L \mid L)\{l'/l\}\{u'/u\} = 4 \cdot rd \oplus 3 \cdot lk \oplus 2 \cdot wr$, where $rd = l'.\text{read}.u'.R'$ (with $R' \stackrel{\text{def}}{=} l'.\text{read}.u'.R'$), $lk = \overline{l'}.\overline{u'}.L'$ (with $L' \stackrel{\text{def}}{=} \overline{l'}.\overline{u'}.L'$) and $wr = \underline{l'}.\underline{l'}.l'.\text{write}.\underline{u'}.\underline{u'}.u'.W'$ (with $W' \stackrel{\text{def}}{=} \underline{l'}.\underline{l'}.l'.\text{write}.\underline{u'}.\underline{u'}.u'.W'$).

One of the two possible initial transitions is $wr \oplus 3 \cdot lk \xrightarrow{\tau} wr' \oplus 3 \cdot lk'$, where $wr' = \text{write}.\underline{u'}.\underline{u'}.u'.W'$ and $lk' = \overline{u'}.L'$. After such a transition, no reader can read, as all the locks are busy. The other possible initial transition is $rd \oplus lk \xrightarrow{\tau} rd' \oplus lk'$, where $rd' = \text{read}.u'.R'$. From place wr', one transition is derivable, namely $wr' \xrightarrow{\text{write}} wr''$, where $wr'' = \underline{u'}.\underline{u'}.u'.W'$. From place rd', one transition is derivable, namely $rd' \xrightarrow{\text{read}} rd''$, where $rd'' = u'.R'$. Finally, two further transitions are derivable: $rd'' \oplus lk' \xrightarrow{\tau} rd \oplus lk$ and $wr'' \oplus 3 \cdot lk' \xrightarrow{\tau} wr \oplus 3 \cdot lk$. The resulting P/T Petri net Net(CRW) is depicted in Fig. 2.

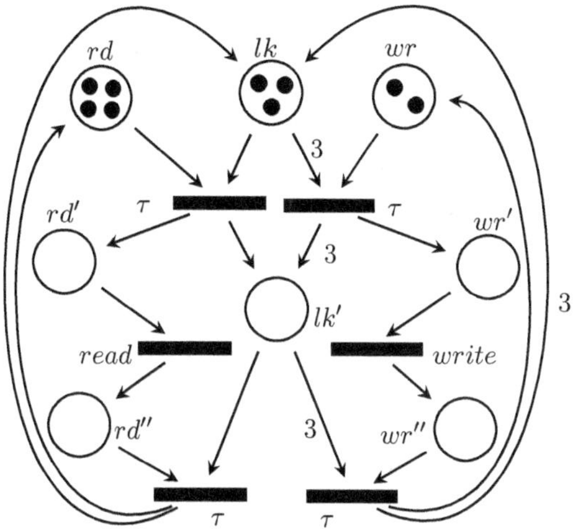

Fig. 2 The net for the concurrent readers/writers problem

Proof By induction on the proof of t. □

Lemma 6 *Let $t_1 = (m_1, \sigma, m_1')$ be derivable by the rules in Table 9, and let p be a process such that $\text{dec}(p)[t_1\rangle\text{dec}(p')$. If $p \equiv q$, then there exists a transition $t_2 = (m_2, \sigma, m_2')$ such that $\text{dec}(q)[t_2\rangle\text{dec}(q')$, with $q' \equiv p'$.*

Proof By induction on the proof of $q \equiv p$ and then on the proof of t_1. The base cases are the three axioms in Table 4. For axiom **E1** (associativity), we have that $\text{dec}(p \mid (q \mid r)) = \text{dec}(p) \oplus \text{dec}(q) \oplus \text{dec}(r) = \text{dec}((p \mid q) \mid r)$, so that transition t_2 is exactly t_1. Similarly, $\text{dec}(p \mid q) = \text{dec}(p) \oplus \text{dec}(q) = \text{dec}(q \mid p)$ and $\text{dec}(A) = \text{dec}(q)$ if $A \stackrel{\text{def}}{=} q$. So, for the base cases, the thesis follows trivially. For substitutivity of prefixing, we assume that $p = \mu.p_1$, $q = \mu.q_1$ and $p_1 \equiv q_1$; in such a case, $t_1 = (\{\mu.p_1\}, \mu, \text{dec}(p_1))$ is the only transition enabled at $\text{dec}(p)$; the required transition t_2 is $(\{\mu.q_1\}, \mu, \text{dec}(q_1))$. For substitutivity of strong prefixing, we assume that $p = \underline{\alpha}.p_1$, $q = \underline{\alpha}.q_1$ and $p_1 \equiv q_1$; in such a case, $t_1 = (\{\underline{\alpha}.p_1\}, \alpha \diamond \sigma', \text{dec}(p_1'))$ is derivable if $t_1' = (\{p_1\}, \sigma', \text{dec}(p_1'))$ is derivable; by induction, as $p_1 \equiv q_1$, there exists transition $t_2' = (\{q_1\}, \sigma', \text{dec}(q_1'))$, with $p_1' \equiv q_1'$; then, by (s-pref), also transition $t_2 = (\{\underline{\alpha}.q_1\}, \alpha \diamond \sigma', \text{dec}(q_1'))$ is derivable, as required. For substitutivity of choice, we assume that $p = p_1 + p_2$, $q = q_1 + q_2$ and $p_i \equiv q_i$, for $i =$

5 Soundness

In this section, we prove that the operational net semantics is sound w.r.t. the operational LTS semantics: for any process $p \in \mathcal{P}$, the LTS rooted in p is bisimilar to the rooted LTS $\text{IMG}(\text{Net}(\text{dec}(p)))$. First, some auxiliary lemmata.

Lemma 5 *Transition $t = (m, \sigma, m')$ is derivable by the rules in Table 9 if and only if transition $t' = (m\{a'/a\}, \sigma\{a'/a\}, m'\{a'/a\})$ is derivable by the rules.*

$1, 2$; in such a case, $t_1 = (\{p_1 + p_2\}, \sigma, \mathrm{dec}(p'_1))$ is derivable if (w.l.o.g., we assume p_1 moves) $t'_1 = (\{p_1\}, \sigma, \mathrm{dec}(p'_1))$ is derivable by (sum$_1$); by induction, as $p_1 \equiv q_1$, there exists transition $t'_2 = (\{q_1\}, \sigma, \mathrm{dec}(q'_1))$, with $p'_1 \equiv q'_1$; then, by (sum$_1$), also transition $t_2 = (\{q_1 + q_2\}, \sigma, \mathrm{dec}(q'_1))$ is derivable, as required.

For substitutivity of parallel composition, we assume that $p = p_1 \mid p_2$, $q = q_1 \mid q_2$, $p_i \equiv q_i$ for $i = 1, 2$, and $\mathrm{dec}(p)[t_1\rangle\mathrm{dec}(p')$. We have three subcases: (i) $\mathrm{dec}(p_1)[t_1\rangle\mathrm{dec}(p'_1)$, with $p' = p'_1 \mid p_2$; or (ii) $\mathrm{dec}(p_2)[t_1\rangle \mathrm{dec}(p'_2)$, with $p' = p_1 \mid p'_2$; or (iii) neither of the previous two cases, i.e., ${}^\bullet t_1$ is not contained in $\mathrm{dec}(p_1)$ or $\mathrm{dec}(p_2)$. In the first case, by induction (since $p_1 \equiv q_1$), there exists t_2 such that $\mathrm{dec}(q_1)[t_2\rangle\mathrm{dec}(q'_1)$, with $p'_1 \equiv q'_1$, and so $\mathrm{dec}(q)[t_2\rangle\mathrm{dec}(q'_1 \mid q_2)$, with $q'_1 \mid q_2 \equiv p'_1 \mid p_2$; the second case is symmetric, hence omitted.

In the third case, there exist two transitions, say t'_1 and t'_2, with $l(t'_1) = \sigma_1$, $l(t'_2) = \sigma_2$ and $\mathrm{Sync}(\sigma_1, \sigma_2, \sigma)$, such that, by rule (s-com), t_1 is $t'_1|t'_2 = ({}^\bullet t'_1 \oplus {}^\bullet t'_2, \sigma, t'^\bullet_1 \oplus t'^\bullet_2)$. By using the three axioms of the structural congruence $\equiv$ at the top level only (that we know can be used safely), we can find two processes $\overline{p}_1, \overline{p}_2$ such that $p \equiv \overline{p}_1 \mid \overline{p}_2$, $\mathrm{dec}(\overline{p}_1)[t'_1\rangle\mathrm{dec}(\overline{p}'_1)$, $\mathrm{dec}(\overline{p}_2)[t'_2\rangle\mathrm{dec}(\overline{p}'_2)$. Since $p \equiv q$, we can find two processes $\overline{q}_1, \overline{q}_2$ such that $q \equiv \overline{q}_1 \mid \overline{q}_2$ and $\overline{p}_i \equiv \overline{q}_i$ for $i = 1, 2$. Then, induction can be applied to conclude that there exist two transitions t''_1 and t''_2 such that $\mathrm{dec}(\overline{q}_1)[t''_1\rangle\mathrm{dec}(\overline{q}'_1)$, $\mathrm{dec}(\overline{q}_2)[t''_2\rangle\mathrm{dec}(\overline{q}'_2)$, with $\overline{p}'_i \equiv \overline{q}'_i$ for $i = 1, 2$. So, by rule (s-com), transition $t_2 = t''_1|t''_2 = ({}^\bullet t''_1 \oplus {}^\bullet t''_2, \sigma, t''^\bullet_1 \oplus t''^\bullet_2)$ is derivable; hence, $\mathrm{dec}(q) = \mathrm{dec}(\overline{q}_1) \oplus \mathrm{dec}(\overline{q}_2)[t_2\rangle\mathrm{dec}(\overline{q}'_1 \mid \overline{q}'_2)$, with $\overline{q}'_1 \mid \overline{q}'_2 \equiv \overline{p}'_1 \mid \overline{p}'_2 \equiv p'$.

For substitutivity of restriction, we assume that $p = (\nu a)p_1$, $q = (\nu a)q_1$, $p_1 \equiv q_1$, and $\mathrm{dec}(p)[t_1\rangle \mathrm{dec}(p')$, with $l(t_1) = \sigma$ and $a, \bar{a} \notin n(\sigma)$. Since $\mathrm{dec}(p) = \mathrm{dec}(p_1)\{a'/a\}$, t_1 has the form $(m_1\{a'/a\}, \sigma, m'_1\{a'/a\})$, and $t'_1 = (m_1, \sigma, m'_1)$ is derivable by Lemma 5; moreover, $\mathrm{dec}(p_1)[t'_1\rangle\mathrm{dec}(p'_1)$, with $\mathrm{dec}(p') = \mathrm{dec}(p'_1)\{a'/a\} = \mathrm{dec}((\nu a)p'_1)$. By induction, as $p_1 \equiv q_1$, there exists $t'_2 = (m_2, \sigma, m'_2)$ such that $\mathrm{dec}(q_1)[t'_2\rangle\mathrm{dec}(q'_1)$, with $q'_1 \equiv p'_1$. By Lemma 5, also $t_2 = (m_2\{a'/a\}, \sigma, m'_2\{a'/a\})$ is derivable, with $\mathrm{dec}(q) = \mathrm{dec}(q_1)\{a'/a\}\,[t_2\rangle\, \mathrm{dec}(q'_1)\{a'/a\} = \mathrm{dec}((\nu a)q'_1)$, where $(\nu a)q'_1 \equiv (\nu a)p'_1$ as required. □

Proposition 16 *For any process $p \in \mathcal{P}$, if $p \xrightarrow{\sigma} p'$ then there exist $t \in T_p$ and $p'' \equiv p'$ such that $\mathrm{dec}(p)[t\rangle\mathrm{dec}(p'')$ with $l(t) = \sigma$.*

Proof The proof is by induction on the proof of $p \xrightarrow{\sigma} p'$. The base case is axiom (Pref), hence $p = \mu.q$, $\sigma = \mu$ and $p' = q$. The thesis follows by noting that axiom (pref) ensures that $\mathrm{dec}(p) = \{\mu.q\} \xrightarrow{\mu} \mathrm{dec}(q) = \mathrm{dec}(p')$ is in T_p.

If rule (S-pref) is the last rule used to derive $p \xrightarrow{\sigma} p'$, then $p = \underline{\alpha}.q$, $q \xrightarrow{\sigma'} p'$ and $\sigma = \alpha \diamond \sigma'$. The inductive hypothesis on the premise of rule (S-pref) ensures that there exist a transition $t = (m, \sigma', m')$ and a process $p'' \equiv p'$ such that $\mathrm{dec}(q)[t\rangle\mathrm{dec}(p'')$ with $l(t) = \sigma'$. Since q must be sequential, then $m = \mathrm{dec}(q) = \{q\}$ and $m' = \mathrm{dec}(p'')$. Hence the thesis follows by rule (s-pref): $t = (\{q\}, \sigma', \mathrm{dec}(p''))$ implies $\mathrm{dec}(p) = \{\underline{\alpha}.q\} \xrightarrow{\alpha\diamond\sigma'} \mathrm{dec}(p'')$.

If rule (Sum$_1$) is the last rule applied to derive transition $p \xrightarrow{\sigma} p'$, then $p = p_1 + p_2$ and $p_1 \xrightarrow{\sigma} p'$. The inductive hypothesis on the premise of rule (Sum$_1$) ensures that there exist a transition $t = (m, \sigma', m')$ and a process $p'' \equiv p'$ such that $\mathrm{dec}(p_1)[t\rangle\mathrm{dec}(p'')$ with $l(t) = \sigma$. Since p_1 is sequential, $m = \mathrm{dec}(p_1) = \{p_1\}$ and $m' = \mathrm{dec}(p'')$. Hence, the thesis follows by rule (sum$_1$): t implies $\mathrm{dec}(p_1 + p_2) \xrightarrow{\sigma} \mathrm{dec}(p'')$. Symmetrically, if (Sum$_2$) is the last rule applied.

If rule (Par$_1$) is the last rule used to derive $p \xrightarrow{\sigma} p'$, then $p = p_1 \mid p_2$ and $p_1 \xrightarrow{\sigma} p'_1$. The inductive hypothesis on the premise of (Par$_1$) ensures that there exist a transition $t = (m_1, \sigma, m'_1)$ and a process $p''_1 \equiv p'_1$ such that $\mathrm{dec}(p_1)[t\rangle\mathrm{dec}(p''_1)$ with $l(t) = \sigma$. Hence, the thesis then follows by additivity: $\mathrm{dec}(p_1 \mid p_2) = \mathrm{dec}(p_1) \oplus \mathrm{dec}(p_2)[t\rangle\mathrm{dec}(p''_1) \oplus \mathrm{dec}(p_2) = \mathrm{dec}(p''_1 \mid p_2)$, with $p''_1 \mid p_2 \equiv p'_1 \mid p_2$. Symmetrically, if rule (Par$_2$) is the last rule applied.

If rule (S-Com) is the last rule used to derive $p \xrightarrow{\sigma} p'$, then $p = p_1 \mid p_2$, $p' = p'_1 \mid p'_2$, $p_1 \xrightarrow{\sigma_1} p'_1$, $p_2 \xrightarrow{\sigma_2} p'_2$ and $\mathrm{Sync}(\sigma_1, \sigma_2, \sigma)$. The inductive hypothesis on the premises of (S-Com) ensures that there exist two transitions, t_1 and t_2, and two processes, $p''_1 \equiv p'_1$ and $p''_2 \equiv p'_2$, such that $\mathrm{dec}(p_1)[t_1\rangle\mathrm{dec}(p''_1)$ with $l(t_1) = \sigma_1$, and $\mathrm{dec}(p_2)[t_2\rangle\mathrm{dec}(p''_2)$ with $l(t_2) = \sigma_2$. Hence, by rule (s-com), t_1 and t_2 imply transition $t_1|t_2 = ({}^\bullet t_1 \oplus {}^\bullet t_2, \sigma, t_1^\bullet \oplus t_2^\bullet)$; note that we are sure that the executability of t_1 and t_2 on their respective markings ensures that also the compound transition $t_1|t_2$ is executable on the union of the two markings, i.e., $\mathrm{dec}(p_1) \oplus \mathrm{dec}(p_2)[t_1|t_2\rangle\mathrm{dec}(p''_1) \oplus \mathrm{dec}(p''_2)$. Hence: $\mathrm{dec}(p_1 \mid p_2)[t_1|t_2\rangle\mathrm{dec}(p''_1 \mid p''_2)$, with $p''_1 \mid p''_2 \equiv p'_1 \mid p'_2$.

If rule (S-Res) is the last rule used to derive $p \xrightarrow{\sigma} p'$, then $p = (\nu a)p_1$, $p' = (\nu a)p'_1$, $p_1 \xrightarrow{\sigma} p'_1$ and $a, \bar{a} \notin n(\sigma)$. The inductive hypothesis on the premise of rule (S-Res) ensures that there exist a transition $t = (m, \sigma, m')$ and a process $p''_1 \equiv p'_1$ such that $\mathrm{dec}(p_1)[t\rangle\mathrm{dec}(p''_1)$ with $l(t) = \sigma$. Note that $\mathrm{dec}((\nu a)p_1) = \mathrm{dec}(p_1)\{a'/a\}$ for a' restricted. Note also that, by Lemma 5, if t is derivable by the net rules, then also transition $t' = (m\{a'/a\}, \sigma, m'\{a'/a\})$ is derivable by the net rules. Therefore, since $m\{a'/a\} \subseteq \mathrm{dec}(p_1)\{a'/a\}$, we have that $\mathrm{dec}((\nu a)p_1) = \mathrm{dec}(p_1)\{a'/a\}\,[t'\rangle\, \mathrm{dec}(p''_1)\{a'/a\} = \mathrm{dec}((\nu a)p''_1)$, with $(\nu a)p''_1 \equiv (\nu a)p'_1$.

If rule (Cong) is the last rule used to derive $p \xrightarrow{\sigma} p'$, then $p \equiv q$, $q \xrightarrow{\sigma} q'$ and $q' \equiv p'$. The inductive hypothesis on the premise ensures the existence of a transition $t' = (m', \sigma, m'')$

and a process $q'' \equiv q'$ such that $\text{dec}(q)[t'\rangle\text{dec}(q'')$ with $l(t') = \sigma$. By Lemma 6, there exists a transition t, with $l(t) = \sigma$, such that $\text{dec}(p)[t\rangle\text{dec}(p'')$ and $p'' \equiv q''$, hence, by transitivity, $p'' \equiv p'$. □

Proposition 17 *For any process $p \in \mathcal{P}$, if there exists $t \in T_p$ such that* $\text{dec}(p)[t\rangle\text{dec}(p')$ *with $l(t) = \sigma$, then $p \xrightarrow{\sigma} p'$.*

Proof By induction on the definition of $\text{dec}(p, I)$ and then by induction on the proof of t. The base cases are empty. The first base case is $\text{dec}(\mathbf{0}, I) = \emptyset$ and so no transition t is enabled. Similarly, the second base case is $p = A$, with $A \in I$ (hence, $\text{dec}(A, I) = \emptyset$). The other cases follow.

$\text{dec}(\mu.q, I) = \{\mu.q\}$. By axiom (pref), the only derivable transition is $t = (\{\mu.q\}, \mu, \text{dec}(q))$. By axiom (Pref), $\mu.q \xrightarrow{\mu} q$, and so the thesis follows trivially.

$\text{dec}(\underline{\alpha}.q, I) = \{\underline{\alpha}.q\}$. By rule (s-pref), a transition $t = (\{\underline{\alpha}.q\}, \alpha \diamond \sigma', \text{dec}(q'))$ is derivable only if a transition $t' = (\{q\}, \sigma', \text{dec}(q'))$ is derivable. The inductive hypothesis on the premise t' of the rule (s-pref) ensures that $q \xrightarrow{\sigma'} q'$. By rule (S-Pref), $\underline{\alpha}.q \xrightarrow{\alpha\diamond\sigma'} q'$, as required.

$\text{dec}(p_1 + p_2, I) = \{p_1 + p_2\}$. By rule (sum$_1$), transition $t = (\{p_1 + p_2\}, \sigma, \text{dec}(p'))$ is derivable only if transition $t' = (\{p_1\}, \sigma, \text{dec}(p'))$ is derivable. The inductive hypothesis on the premise t' of the rule (sum$_1$) ensures that $p_1 \xrightarrow{\sigma} p'$. By rule (Sum$_1$), $p_1 + p_2 \xrightarrow{\sigma} p'$, as required. Symmetrically, if rule (sum$_2$) is used.

$\text{dec}(p_1 \mid p_2, I) = \text{dec}(p_1, I) \oplus \text{dec}(p_2, I)$. Given a transition t, with $l(t) = \sigma$, such that $\text{dec}(p_1 \mid p_2, I)[t\rangle\text{dec}(p')$, three cases are possible. If t is enabled at $\text{dec}(p_1, I)$ and so $\text{dec}(p_1, I)[t\rangle\text{dec}(p_1')$, then $p' = p_1' \mid p_2$ and, by induction, we know that $p_1 \xrightarrow{\sigma} p_1'$. Hence the thesis follows by rule (Par). Symmetrically, if t is enabled at $\text{dec}(p_2)$. The third case is when transition t is such that $^\bullet t$ is not contained in $\text{dec}(p_1, I)$ or in $\text{dec}(p_2, I)$. In such a case, there exist two transitions, say t_1 and t_2, with $l(t_1) = \sigma_1$, $l(t_2) = \sigma_2$ and $\text{Sync}(\sigma_1, \sigma_2, \sigma)$, such that, by rule (s-com), t is $t_1 | t_2 = (^\bullet t_1 \oplus {}^\bullet t_2, \sigma, t_1^\bullet \oplus t_2^\bullet)$. The marking $\text{dec}(p_1, I) \oplus \text{dec}(p_2, I)$ can be equivalently represented as $\text{dec}(q_1, I) \oplus \text{dec}(q_2, I)$ such that $p_1 \mid p_2 \equiv q_1 \mid q_2$, $\text{dec}(q_1, I)[t_1\rangle\text{dec}(q_1')$ and $\text{dec}(q_2, I)[t_2\rangle\text{dec}(q_2')$. Then, induction can be applied to conclude that $q_1 \xrightarrow{\sigma_1} q_1'$ and $q_2 \xrightarrow{\sigma_2} q_2'$; hence, by rule (S-Com), also $q_1 \mid q_2 \xrightarrow{\sigma} q_1' \mid q_2'$ is derivable, and by rule (Cong), $p_1 \mid p_2 \xrightarrow{\sigma} q_1' \mid q_2'$, as required.

$\text{dec}((\nu a)p_1, I) = \text{dec}(p_1, I)\{a'/a\}$. A transition t, with $l(t) = \sigma \in \mathcal{A}$ and $a, \bar{a} \notin n(\sigma)$, is such that $\text{dec}(p_1, I)\{a'/a\}[t\rangle\text{dec}(p_1')\{a'/a\}$ if transition t has the form $(m\{a'/a\}, \sigma, m'\{a'/a\})$; so transition $t' = (m, \sigma, m')$ is derivable by Lemma 5 and $\text{dec}(p_1, I)[t'\rangle\text{dec}(p_1')$. By induction, we have $p_1 \xrightarrow{\sigma} p_1'$, and so by rule (S-Res), also $(\nu a)p_1 \xrightarrow{\sigma} (\nu a)p_1'$ is derivable, as required.

$\text{dec}(A, I) = \text{dec}(p, I \cup \{A\})$ if $A \stackrel{\text{def}}{=} p$ and $A \notin I$. Then, if there exists t, with $l(t) = \sigma$, such that $\text{dec}(A, I)[t\rangle\text{dec}(p')$, then also $\text{dec}(p, I \cup \{A\})[t\rangle\text{dec}(p')$. By induction, we can assume that transition $p \xrightarrow{\sigma} p'$ is derivable. Hence, by rule (Cong), also $A \xrightarrow{\sigma} p'$ is derivable, too. □

We are now ready to state the soundness theorem: the interleaving marking graph associated to $Net(p)$ is bisimilar to the LTS rooted in p.

Theorem 5 (Soundness) *For any process $p \in \mathcal{P}$, $p \sim$* $\text{dec}(p)$.

Proof If the relation $R = \{(p, \text{dec}(q)) \mid p, q \in \mathcal{P} \wedge p \equiv q\}$ is a bisimulation, then the thesis follows trivially, as $p \equiv p$. On the one hand, if $p \xrightarrow{\sigma} p'$, then, by Proposition 16, there exist a transition t, with $l(t) = \sigma$, and a process p'', with $p'' \equiv p'$, such that $\text{dec}(p)[t\rangle\text{dec}(p'')$, and $(p', \text{dec}(p'')) \in R$. On the other hand, if $\text{dec}(q)[t\rangle\text{dec}(q')$, with $l(t) = \sigma$, then, by Proposition 17, we have $q \xrightarrow{\sigma} q'$; as $p \equiv q$, by rule (Cong), $p \xrightarrow{\sigma} q'$, and $(q', \text{dec}(q')) \in R$, as required.

6 A process term for any finite P/T net

In this section we address the following problem: given a finite, statically reduced, P/T Petri net system $N(m_0)$, labeled on $\mathcal{L} \cup \{\tau\}$, can we single out a finite-net multi-CCS process $p_{N(m_0)}$ such that $\text{Net}(p_{N(m_0)})$ and $N(m_0)$ are isomorphic? The answer to this question is positive; hence, finite-net multi-CCS can represent all finite, statically reduced, P/T Petri nets, up to net isomorphism.

The translation from nets to processes we are going to present defines a constant C_i in correspondence to each place s_i; the definition of the constant C_i contains an addend composed of a new bound name y_i, which is used in order to distinguish syntactically all the constants bodies, so that no fusion of two constants to the same place is possible when applying the reverse step from the generated process term to its associated net (see Example 8). Moreover, the translation considers a bound name x_i^j for each pair (s_i, t_j), where s_i is a place and t_j is a transition; such bound names are used to synchronize all the components participating in transition t_j. The constant C_i, associated to place s_i, has a summand c_i^j for each transition t_j, which may be $\mathbf{0}$ when s_i is not in the pre-set of t_j. Among the many places in the pre-set of t_j, the one with minimal index (as we assume that places are indexed) plays the role of *leader* of the multi-party synchronization (i.e., the process performing the atomic sequence of inputs x_i^j to be synchronized with single outputs $\bar{x}_i^j$ performed by the other *servant* participants).

Definition 17 Let $N(m_0) = (S, A, T, m_0)$—with $S = \{s_1, \dots, s_n\}$, $A \subseteq \mathcal{L} \cup \{\tau\}$, $T = \{t_1, \dots, t_k\}$, and $l(t_j) = a_j$

for $j = 1, \dots, k$—be a finite P/T net system. Function $\mathrm{INet}(-)$, from finite P/T net systems to well-formed, finite-net multi-CCS processes is defined as

$$\mathrm{INet}(N(m_0)) = (\nu L)(\underbrace{C_1 | \cdots | C_1}_{m_0(s_1)} | \cdots | \underbrace{C_n | \cdots | C_n}_{m_0(s_n)})$$

where $L = \{y_1, \dots, y_n\} \cup \{x_1^1, \dots, x_n^1, x_1^2, \dots, x_n^2, \dots, x_1^k, \dots, x_n^k\}$, and each C_i has a defining equation

$$C_i \stackrel{\mathrm{def}}{=} c_i^1 + \cdots + c_i^k + y_i.\mathbf{0}$$

where each c_i^j, for $j = 1, \dots, k$, is equal to

- $\mathbf{0}$, if $s_i \notin {}^\bullet t_j$;
- $a_j.\Pi_j$, if ${}^\bullet t_j = \{s_i\}$;
- $\overline{x}_i^j.\mathbf{0}$, if ${}^\bullet t_j(s_i) > 0$ and ${}^\bullet t_j(s_{i'}) > 0$ for some $i' < i$ (i.e., s_i is not the leader for the synchronization on t_j);
- $\underbrace{\underline{x}_{i+1}^j.\cdots.\underline{x}_{i+1}^j}_{{}^\bullet t_j(s_{i+1})}.\cdots.\underbrace{\underline{x}_n^j.\cdots.\underline{x}_n^j}_{{}^\bullet t_j(s_n)}.a_j.\Pi_j$, if ${}^\bullet t_j(s_i) = 1$ and s_i is the leader of the synchronization (i.e., ${}^\bullet t_j(s_{i'}) > 0$ for no $i' < i$, while ${}^\bullet t_j(s_{i'}) > 0$ for some $i' > i$);
- $\overline{x}_i^j.\mathbf{0} + \underbrace{\underline{x}_i^j.\cdots.\underline{x}_i^j}_{{}^\bullet t_j(s_i)-1}.\underbrace{\underline{x}_{i+1}^j.\cdots.\underline{x}_{i+1}^j}_{{}^\bullet t_j(s_{i+1})}.\cdots.\underbrace{\underline{x}_n^j.\cdots.\underline{x}_n^j}_{{}^\bullet t_j(s_n)}.a_j.\Pi_j$, otherwise (i.e., s_i is the leader and ${}^\bullet t_j(s_i) \geq 2$).

Finally, process Π_j is defined as $\Pi_j = \underbrace{C_1 | \cdots | C_1}_{t_j^\bullet(s_1)} | \cdots | \underbrace{C_n | \cdots | C_n}_{t_j^\bullet(s_n)}$, meaning that $\Pi_j = \mathbf{0}$ if $t_j^\bullet = \emptyset$.

Example 7 Consider the net $N(m_0)$ of Fig. 3, where transition t_1 is labeled with a, t_2 with b and t_3 with c. Applying the translation above, we obtain the well-formed, finite-net multi-CCS process

$$\mathrm{INet}(N(m_0)) = (\nu L)(C_1 \,|\, C_1 \,|\, C_1 \,|\, C_2 \,|\, C_2)$$

where $L = \{y_1, y_2, y_3\} \cup \{x_1^1, x_2^1, x_3^1, x_1^2, x_2^2, x_3^2, x_1^3, x_2^3, x_3^3\}$, and

$$C_1 \stackrel{\mathrm{def}}{=} (\overline{x}_1^1.\mathbf{0} + \underline{x}_1^1.a.C_1) + (\overline{x}_1^2.\mathbf{0} + \underline{x}_1^2.\underline{x}_1^2.\underline{x}_2^2.b.\mathbf{0}) + \underline{x}_2^3.\underline{x}_2^3.c.C_3 + y_1.\mathbf{0}$$

$$C_2 \stackrel{\mathrm{def}}{=} \mathbf{0} + \overline{x}_2^2.\mathbf{0} + \overline{x}_2^3.\mathbf{0} + y_2.\mathbf{0}$$

$$C_3 \stackrel{\mathrm{def}}{=} \mathbf{0} + \mathbf{0} + \mathbf{0} + y_3.\mathbf{0}$$

Note that $\mathrm{INet}(N(m_0))$ is a *finite-net multi-CCS process*: in fact, the restriction operator occurs only at the top level, applied to the parallel composition of a number of constants; each constant has a body that is sequential and restriction-free. Note also that $\mathrm{INet}(N(m_0))$ is a *well-formed* process: in fact, each *strong prefix* is an input x_i^j, and any sequence ends with an action $a_j \in A$ which is either an input or τ; hence, no synchronization of sequences is possible. Therefore, the following proposition holds by Theorem 4 and Proposition 12.

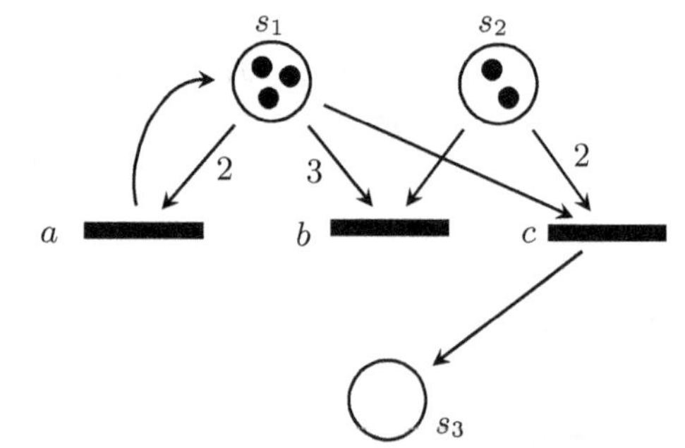

Fig. 3 A simple net

Proposition 18 *For any finite P/T Petri net $N(m_0) = (S, A, T, m_0)$, the net Net(INet($N(m_0)$)) is a finite, statically reduced, P/T net.*

Example 8 In order to explain the role of addend y_i in the body of constant C_i, for $i = 1, \dots, n$, let us assume that they are omitted in Definition 17. Now, let us consider the net $N(\{s_1, s_2\}) = (\{s_1, s_2, s_3, s_4\}, \{a\}, \{(s_1, a, s_3), (s_2, a, s_4)\}, \{s_1, s_2\})$, which has four places and two transitions. The finite-net multi-CCS term $\mathrm{INet}(N(\{s_1, s_2\}))$ would be $(\nu L)(C_1 \,|\, C_2)$, where $L = \{x_1^1, x_2^1, x_1^2, x_2^2\}$ and

$$C_1 \stackrel{\mathrm{def}}{=} a.C_3 + \mathbf{0} \qquad C_2 \stackrel{\mathrm{def}}{=} \mathbf{0} + a.C_4$$

$$C_3 \stackrel{\mathrm{def}}{=} \mathbf{0} + \mathbf{0} \qquad C_4 \stackrel{\mathrm{def}}{=} \mathbf{0} + \mathbf{0}$$

but now Net(INet($N(\{s_1, s_2\})$)) is the net $(\{a.C_3 + \mathbf{0}, \mathbf{0} + a.C_4, \mathbf{0} + \mathbf{0}\}, \{a\}, \{(a.C_3 + \mathbf{0}, a, \mathbf{0} + \mathbf{0}), (\mathbf{0} + a.C_4, a, \mathbf{0} + \mathbf{0})\}, \{a.C_3 + \mathbf{0}, \mathbf{0} + a.C_4\})$, which has three places only, as the two distinct places s_3 and s_4 are now mapped to the same place $\mathbf{0} + \mathbf{0}$. This fusion cannot happen when we include the additional addend y_i in the body of each constant C_i.

Now we are ready to state our main result, the so-called *representability theorem*.

Theorem 6 *(Representability theorem) Let $N(m_0) = (S, A, T, m_0)$ be a finite, statically reduced, P/T net system such that $A \subseteq \mathcal{L} \cup \{\tau\}$, and let $p = \mathrm{INet}(N(m_0))$. Then, Net($p$) is isomorphic to $N(m_0)$.*

Proof Let $N(m_0) = (S, A, T, m_0)$ be a finite, statically reduced, P/T net system, with $S = \{s_1, \dots, s_n\}$, $A \subseteq \mathcal{L} \cup \{\tau\}$,

$T = \{t_1, \dots, t_k\}$ and $l(t_j) = a_j$ for $j = 1, \dots, k$. The associated finite-net multi-CCS process is

$$\mathrm{INet}(N(m_0)) = (\nu L)(\underbrace{C_1|\cdots|C_1}_{m_0(s_1)}|\cdots|\underbrace{C_n|\cdots|C_n}_{m_0(s_n)})$$

where $L = \{y_1, \dots, y_n\} \cup \{x_1^1, \dots, x_n^1, x_1^2, \dots, x_n^2, \dots, x_1^k, \dots, x_n^k\}$, and for each place s_i we have a corresponding constant $C_i \stackrel{\mathrm{def}}{=} (\sum_{j=1}^{k} c_i^j) + y_i.\mathbf{0}$, defined as in Definition 17. For notational convenience, $(\sum_{j=1}^{k} c_i^j) + y_i.\mathbf{0}$ is denoted by p_i, i.e., $C_i \stackrel{\mathrm{def}}{=} p_i$; for the same reason, we use p to denote $\mathrm{INet}(N(m_0))$.

Let $\rho = \{L'/L\}$ be a substitution that maps each bound name x_i^j (or y_i) to its corresponding restricted name $x_i'^j$ (or y_i') in $\mathcal{L}'$, for $i = 1, \dots, n$ and $j = 1, \dots, k$. Let $\mathrm{Net}(p) = (S', A', T', m_0')$. Then, $m_0' = \mathrm{dec}(p)$ is the multiset

$$\begin{aligned}
&\mathrm{dec}((\nu L)(\underbrace{C_1|\cdots|C_1}_{m_0(s_1)}|\cdots|\underbrace{C_n|\cdots|C_n}_{m_0(s_n)})) \\
&= \mathrm{dec}(\underbrace{C_1|\cdots|C_1}_{m_0(s_1)}|\cdots|\underbrace{C_n|\cdots|C_n}_{m_0(s_n)})\rho \\
&= m_0(s_1) \cdot p_1\rho \oplus \cdots \oplus m_0(s_n) \cdot p_n\rho.
\end{aligned}$$

because $C_i \stackrel{\mathrm{def}}{=} p_i$ for $i = 1, \dots n$ and so $\mathrm{dec}(C_i) = \{p_i\}$. Hence, the initial places are all of the form $p_i\rho$, where such a place is present in m_0' only if $m_0(s_i) > 0$.

Note that, by Definition 17, any transition $t' \in T'$ is such that $t'^{\bullet} = \mathrm{dec}(\Pi_j)$ for some suitable j, so that each statically reachable place s_i' in S' is of the form $p_i\rho$, which are all distinct because each p_i contains one distinguishing summand $y_i.\mathbf{0}$. Hence, there is a bijection $f : S \to S'$ defined by $f(s_i) = s_i' = p_i\rho$, which is the natural candidate isomorphism function. To prove that f is an isomorphism, we have to prove that:

1. $f(m_0) = m_0'$,
2. $t = (m, a, m') \in T$ implies $f(t) = (f(m), a, f(m')) \in T'$, and
3. $t' = (m_1', a, m_2') \in T'$ implies there exists $t = (m_1, a, m_2) \in T$ such that $f(t) = t'$, i.e., $f(m_1) = m_1'$ and $f(m_2) = m_2'$.

From items (2) and (3) above, it follows that $A = A'$.

Proof of 1: Let $m_0 = k_1 \cdot s_1 \oplus k_2 \cdot s_2 \oplus \cdots \oplus k_n \cdot s_n$, where $k_i = m_0(s_i) \geq 0$ for $i = 1, \dots, n$. The mapping via f of the initial marking m_0 is $f(m_0) = k_1 \cdot f(s_1) \oplus k_2 \cdot f(s_2) \oplus \cdots \oplus k_n \cdot f(s_n) = k_1 \cdot p_1\rho \oplus k_2 \cdot p_2\rho \oplus \cdots \oplus k_n \cdot p_n\rho = \mathrm{dec}(\underbrace{C_1|\cdots|C_1}_{k_1 \text{ times}}|\cdots|\underbrace{C_n|\cdots|C_n}_{k_n \text{ times}})\rho = \mathrm{dec}(p) = m_0'$.

Proof of 2: we prove that, for $j = 1, \dots, k$, if $t_j = (m, a, m') \in T$, then $t_j' = (f(m), a, f(m')) \in T'$. From transition t_j, we can derive the two processes $P_j = (\underbrace{C_1\rho|\cdots|C_1\rho}_{^{\bullet}t_j(s_1)}|\cdots|\underbrace{C_n\rho|\cdots|C_n\rho}_{^{\bullet}t_j(s_n)})$ and $P_j' = (\underbrace{C_1\rho|\cdots|C_1\rho}_{t_j^{\bullet}(s_1)}|\cdots|\underbrace{C_n\rho|\cdots|C_n\rho}_{t_j^{\bullet}(s_n)})$ such that $f(^{\bullet}t_j) = \mathrm{dec}(P_j)$ and $f(t_j^{\bullet}) = \mathrm{dec}(P_j')$. According to Definition 17, for each $C_i = p_i$, we have a summand c_i^j in p_i, with $Q_j = (\underbrace{c_1^j\rho|\cdots|c_1^j\rho}_{^{\bullet}t_j(s_1)}|\cdots|\underbrace{c_n^j\rho|\cdots|c_n^j\rho}_{^{\bullet}t_j(s_n)})$. By inspecting the shape of t_j and the definition of the various c_i^j's, one can get convinced that $(\mathrm{dec}(Q_j), l(t_j), \mathrm{dec}(P_j'))$ is a derivable transition. Hence, since each p_i is a summation containing the summand c_i^j, also $(\mathrm{dec}(P_j), l(t_j), \mathrm{dec}(P_j'))$ is a derivable transition and belongs to T', as required.

Proof of 3: We prove that if $t_j' = (m_1', a, m_2') \in T'$, then there exists a transition $t_j = (m_1, a, m_2) \in T$ such that $f(m_1) = m_1'$ and $f(m_2) = m_2'$. This is proved by case analysis on the shape of the marking m_1'.

If m_1' is a singleton, then $m_1' = \{p_i\rho\}$ for some $i = 1, \dots, n$, and so $t_j' = \{p_i\rho\} \xrightarrow{a} m_2'$. According to Definition 17, such a transition is derivable by the rules only if, among the many summands composing $p_i\rho$, there exists a summand $c_i^j\rho = a.\Pi_j\rho$, which is possible only if in $N(m_0)$ we have a transition t_j with $^{\bullet}t_j = \{s_i\}$, $f(\{s_i\}) = \{p_i\rho\}$, $f(t_j^{\bullet}) = \mathrm{dec}(\Pi_j\rho) = m_2'$ and $l(t_j) = a$, as required.

Otherwise, if $m_1' = k_1 \cdot p_1\rho \oplus \cdots \oplus k_n \cdot p_n\rho$ and i is the least index such that $k_i > 0$, then in deriving transition $t_j' = m_1' \xrightarrow{a} m_2'$, one of the k_i processes $p_i\rho$ acts as the leader of the synchronization, and all the other participants are servants. If $k_i = 1$, then, by Definition 17, p_i has a summand c_i^j defined as $\underbrace{\underline{x}_{i+1}^j.\cdots.\underline{x}_{i+1}^j}_{k_{i+1} \text{ times}}.\cdots.\underbrace{\underline{x}_n^j.\cdots.\underline{x}_n^j}_{k_n \text{ times}}.a_j.\Pi_j$, where $\Pi_j = \underbrace{C_1|\cdots|C_1}_{h_1 \text{ times}}|\cdots|\underbrace{C_n|\cdots|C_n}_{h_n \text{ times}}$..

This summand c_i^j will synchronize with all the other components of m_1', as each other may only contribute with an action of the form $\overline{x}_k^j$ for $k = i + 1, \dots, n$, being the unique synchronizable summand of p_k. Therefore, transition t_j' is possible only if transition $t_j = (m_1, a, m_2)$ is in T, where $m_1 = k_1 \cdot s_1 \oplus \cdots \oplus k_n \cdot s_n$, with $f(m_1) = m_1'$, and $m_2 = h_1 \cdot s_1 \oplus \cdots \oplus h_n \cdot s_n$ is such that $f(m_2) = \underbrace{C_1\rho|\cdots|C_1\rho}_{h_1\,times}|\cdots|\underbrace{C_n\rho|\cdots|C_n\rho}_{h_n\,times}$, as required.

Similarly, if $k_i \geq 2$, then p_i has a summand c_i^j defined as

$\overline{x}_i^j.\mathbf{0} + \underbrace{\underline{x}_i^j \cdot \cdots \cdot \underline{x}_i^j}_{k_i - 1 \text{ times}} \cdot \underbrace{\underline{x}_{i+1}^j \cdot \cdots \cdot \underline{x}_{i+1}^j}_{k_{i+1} \text{ times}} \cdot \cdots \cdot \underbrace{\underline{x}_n^j \cdot \cdots \cdot \underline{x}_n^j}_{k_n \text{ times}} .a_j.\Pi_j$, such that the other $k_i - 1$ instances of p_i can contribute to a synchronization with the first p_i by means of the summand $\overline{x}_i^j.\mathbf{0}$ in c_i^j. □

Example 9 Function INet(−) can be applied to any finite P/T net $N(m_0)$. However, if $N(m_0)$ is not *statically reduced*, the representability theorem does not hold. Let us consider the net $N(\{s_1\}) = (\{s_1, s_2\}, \{a\}, \{(s_1, a, \emptyset), (s_2, a, \emptyset)\}, \{s_1\})$. Clearly such a net is not statically reduced because place s_2 is not statically reachable from the initial marking. The finite-net multi-CCS term INet($N(\{s_1\})$) would be $(\nu L)(C_1)$, where $L = \{y_1, y_2\} \cup \{x_1^1, x_2^1, x_1^2, x_2^2\}$ and

$$C_1 \stackrel{\text{def}}{=} a.\mathbf{0} + \mathbf{0} + y_1.\mathbf{0} \qquad C_2 \stackrel{\text{def}}{=} \mathbf{0} + a.\mathbf{0} + y_2.\mathbf{0}$$

but now Net(INet($N(\{s_1\})$)) is the net $(\{a.\mathbf{0}+\mathbf{0}+y_1.\mathbf{0}\}, \{a\}, \{(a.\mathbf{0} + \mathbf{0} + y_1.\mathbf{0}, a, \emptyset)\}, \{a.\mathbf{0} + \mathbf{0} + y_1.\mathbf{0}\})$, which has one place and one transition only, i.e., it is isomorphic to the subnet of $N(\{s_1\})$ statically reachable from the initial marking $\{s_1\}$.

Remark 3 In the classic definition of Petri nets (see, e.g., [7,30,31]), the transition labeling is given with actions taken from a set A of *unstructured* actions; hence, our assumption that $A \subseteq \mathcal{L} \cup \{\tau\}$ is in analogy with this tradition.

However, if we want to be more generous and consider Petri nets labeled over the set Act $= \mathcal{L} \cup \overline{\mathcal{L}} \cup \{\tau\}$ of *structured* actions and co-actions, the extension of the representability theorem to this larger class of nets is not trivial. First of all, we note that the translation in Definition 17 is no longer accurate; consider the Petri net $N(\{s_1, s_2\}) = (\{s_1, s_2\}, \{a, \bar{a}\}, \{(s_1, a, \emptyset), (s_2, \bar{a}, \emptyset)\}, \{s_1, s_2\})$, then INet($N(\{s_1, s_2\})$) is $(\nu L)(C_1 \,|\, C_2)$, with $L = \{y_1, y_2\} \cup \{x_1^1, x_2^1, x_1^2, x_2^2\}$ and

$$C_1 \stackrel{\text{def}}{=} a.\mathbf{0} + \mathbf{0} + y_1.\mathbf{0} \qquad C_2 \stackrel{\text{def}}{=} \mathbf{0} + \bar{a}.\mathbf{0} + y_2.\mathbf{0},$$

but now Net(INet($N(\{s_1, s_2\})$)) contain also an additional synchronization transition $(\{a.\mathbf{0} + \mathbf{0} + y_1.\mathbf{0}, \mathbf{0} + \bar{a}.\mathbf{0} + y_2.\mathbf{0}\}, \tau, \emptyset)$, which has no counterpart in the original net $N(\{s_1, s_2\})$. We conjecture that a possible solution is to be based on the introduction an additional operator in the language: the relabeling operator of CCS [25]—$[b_1/a_1, \ldots, b_n/a_n]$, which relabels each action a_i into b_i—to be used only at the top level. The procedure is as follows:

- First, relabel each transition t_j of the original net $N(m_0)$, labeled with an input action a_j, to a new, not in use, input action a_j^j, yielding a new renamed net $N'(m_0)$.
- Then, compute the associated process INet($N'(m_0)$), according to Definition 17; note that in Net(INet($N'(m_0)$)) no additional synchronization transitions are introduced, because, by renaming, no pair of transitions in $N'(m_0)$ are labeled with a matching pair of actions/co-actions.
- Then, consider the process INet($N'(m_0)$)$[a_1/a_1^1, \ldots, a_k/a_k^k]$ and compute its associated net: it will be isomorphic to the original net $N(m_0)$. □

7 Conclusion

The class of finite-net multi-CCS processes represents a language for describing finite, statically reduced, P/T Petri nets. This is not the only language expressing finite P/T nets: the first (and only other) one is Mayr's PRS [22], which however is rather far from a typical process algebra as its basic building blocks are rewrite rules (or net transitions) instead of actions and, for instance, it does not contain any scope operator like restriction.

A bit pretentiously, we claim that well-formed, finite-net Multi-CCS is *the* language for finite Petri nets. The main argument defending this claim is that the parallel operator $- \parallel -$ of a language able to express Petri nets has to be

- *permissive*: in a process $p \parallel q$, the actions p can perform cannot be prevented by q. This requirement is necessary because P/T Petri nets are permissive as well, meaning that if a transition t is enabled at a marking m, then t is also enabled at a marking $m' \supseteq m$; the parallel operator of Multi-CCS is permissive, while this is not the case for other parallel operators, such as the CSP one $p \parallel_A q$ [20];
- Moreover, the parallel operator $- \parallel -$ is to be ACI (*associative, commutative, with an identity*), because the decomposition of a parallel process into a marking has to reflect that a marking is a (finite) *multiset*; also in this case, the parallel operator of Multi-CCS is ACI, while this is not the case for other parallel operators, notably the CSP one.
- Moreover, the parallel operator should be able to express multi-party synchronization, because a net transition, which may have a preset of any size, can be generated by means of a synchronization among many participants, actually as many as are the tokens in its preset. The Multi-CCS parallel operator can model multi-party synchronization, by means of the interplay with the strong prefixing operator. Other process algebras offer parallel operators with multi-party synchronization capabilities, but in Multi-CCS multi-party synchronization is "programmable", meaning that we can prescribe the order in which the various participants are to interact, independently of the syntactic position they occupy within the global term and without resorting to a global synchro-

nization function, as in the case of some ACP dialects [2].

The multi-party synchronization discipline has been chosen as simple as possible: a sequence can synchronize with a complementary action at a time, in the exact order they occur in the sequence. About sequentialization operators, we note that prefixing cannot be replaced by ACP-like sequential composition, because a language with recursion and sequential composition can express all the context-free languages, while finite P/T nets cannot [19,30]; hence, sequential composition is too powerful to express only finite P/T nets. As we have chosen a CCS-like naming convention, the scoping operator, which can occur syntactically only at the top level, is the CCS restriction operator.

Summing up, any other language, if any, able to represent all and only finite P/T Petri nets should possess these necessary features, which, altogether, seem to be exclusive of finite-net Multi-CCS, or that at least are very rare in the panorama of process algebras.

Our calculus is given a net semantics in terms of *unsafe*, finite P/T nets, improving over previous work. Degano et al. [8] and Olderog's approach [28] is operational like ours, but somehow complementary in style, as it builds directly over the SOS semantics of CCS. Their construction generates *safe* P/T nets which are finite only for regular CCS processes (i.e., processes where restriction and parallel composition cannot occur inside recursion). On the contrary, here we give finite P/T net semantics to a calculus strictly larger than regular CCS, as parallel composition can occur in the body of recursively defined constants. Similar concerns are for PBC [4], whose semantics is given in terms of *safe* P/T nets only. Nonetheless, PBC can express multiway synchronization by means of its relabeling operators, and so, in principle, if equipped with an unsafe semantics, it might also serve as a language expressing all unsafe, finite P/T nets. The first paper defining a net semantics in terms of *unsafe* P/T nets is [13], where the approach is denotational and the considered language is limited to CCS without restriction. Our technique is somehow indebted to the earlier work of Busi and Gorrieri [5] on giving labeled net semantics to the π-calculus [26] in terms of P/T nets with inhibitor arcs; our solution simplifies their approach for finite-net Multi-CCS because we do not need inhibitors. In particular, already in that paper it is observed that finite-net π-calculus processes originate finite P/T net systems (with inhibitor arcs). Similar observations on the interplay between parallel composition and restriction in recursive definitions, in different contexts, has been done also by others, e.g., [1]. Also important is the work of Meyer [23,24] in providing an unlabeled P/T net semantics for a fragment of the π-calculus; the main difference is that his semantics may offer a finite net representation also for some processes where restriction occurs inside recursion, but the price to pay is that the resulting net semantics may be incorrect from a causality point of view; for instance, in process $(\nu c)(a.c.\mathbf{0} \mid b.\bar{c}.\mathbf{0}) \mid (\bar{a}.\mathbf{0} \mid \bar{b}.\mathbf{0})$ the two synchronizations on a and b are causally dependent in his semantics.

Denotational net semantics for unsafe Petri nets are rare. Besides the work by Goltz [13] mentioned above, we know also of [3], where CSP [20] is given a denotational net semantics in terms of so-called *open* nets, a reactive extension of ordinary Petri nets, with the limitation that parallel composition is modeled by disjoint union and arc weight can only be 1. Future work will be devoted to define compositional (i.e., denotational in style) unsafe P/T net semantics for finite-net Multi-CCS, generalizing work of Goltz [13] and Taubner [33].

We conclude this overview of related literature by noting the differences of this paper with respect to its earlier version [18]. First, the definition of finite-net Multi-CCS is a bit simpler now, in order to capture the minimal language capable of representing all and only finite P/T nets. Second, the net $\text{Net}(p)$ associated to a process p is statically reduced: this ensures that $\text{Net}(p)$ and $\text{Net}(p \mid p)$ are the same unmarked net, but with a different initial marking; on the contrary, in [18] $\text{Net}(p)$ was only dynamically reduced. Third, the finiteness theorem was wrongly stated in [18]: in fact, $\text{Net}(p)$ is finite not for all finite-net processes, but only for *well-formed* finite-net processes. Fourth, the construction of the finite-net process $p = \text{INet}(N(m_0))$ from the finite P/T net system $N(m_0)$ is inaccurate in [18], as $\text{Net}(p)$ may have more transitions than $N(m_0)$; as the previous construction used too few bound names, it was impossible to link precisely the tokens consumed by a transition to the actual place from which these tokens are to be consumed.

Finally, an open problem for future research. Compositional equivalence-checking on finite-state process algebras, such as regular CCS, is a viable technique because the used equivalence (typically, some form of bisimilarity over finite-state LTSs) is decidable and also a congruence for the operators of regular CCS. In desire of a similar technique for finite-net Multi-CCS, one has to find an equivalence relation which is decidable over finite P/T nets and a congruence for the operators of Multi-CCS. This is not easy. Let us examine three well-known equivalences over finite P/T nets: interleaving bisimilarity (Definition 7), step bisimilarity [27] and net isomorphism (Definition 5). On the one hand, only net isomorphism is decidable for finite P/T nets, while interleaving bisimilarity and step bisimilarity are undecidable [12,21]. On the other hand, net isomorphism is not a congruence for $+$: for instance, $p = a.(\mathbf{0} + \mathbf{0})$ and $q = a.(\mathbf{0} + \mathbf{0} + \mathbf{0})$ are such that $\text{Net}(p) \cong \text{Net}(q)$ (both nets have only two places and one transition), but $\text{Net}(p + p) \ncong \text{Net}(q + p)$, as $\text{Net}(p + p)$ is isomorphic to $\text{Net}(p)$, while $\text{Net}(q + p)$ has three places and two transitions. Moreover, interleaving bisimilarity is not a congruence for Multi-CCS parallel composition [19], while step bisimilarity is a congruence for all the operators of Multi-CCS [19]. Summing up, none of these three equivalences satisfies both properties: being decidable and a congruence. Of course, if we restrict our attention to finite, *bounded* nets, the situation is much better and step bisimilarity can be used to this aim, being decidable and a congruence. However, for general, unbounded finite P/T nets it is a challenging open problem to find an equivalence relation which satisfies both properties.

Acknowledgments The anonymous referees are thanked for their detailed comments and suggestions. Massimo Morara is thanked for pointing out the inaccuracy in the definition of the process $\mathrm{INet}(N(m_0))$ in [18].

References

1. Aranda, J., Valencia, F., Versari, C.: On the expressive power of restriction and priorities in CCS with replication. In: Proceedings of the FOSSACS 2009. LNCS, vol. 5504, pp. 242–256. Springer, New York (2009)
2. Baeten, J.C.M., Basten, T., Reniers, M.A.: Process algebra: equational theories of communicating processes. In: Cambridge Tracts in Theoretical Computer Science, vol. 50. Cambridge University Press, Cambridge (2010)
3. Baldan, P., Bonchi, F., Gadducci, F., Monreale, G.: Encoding synchronous interactions using labelled Petri nets. In: Proceedings of the Coordination'14. LNCS, vol. 8459, pp. 1–16. Springer, New York (2014)
4. Best, E., Devillers, R., Koutny, M.: The box algebra = Petri nets + process expressions. Inf. Comput. **178**(1), 44–100 (2002)
5. Busi, N., Gorrieri, R.: Distributed semantics for the π-calculus based on Petri nets with inhibitor arcs. J. Logic Algebraic Program. **78**(3), 138–162 (2009)
6. Courtois, P., Heymans, F., Parnas, D.: Concurrent control with readers and writers. Commun. ACM **14**(10), 667–668 (1971)
7. Desel, J., Reisig, W.: Place/Transition Petri Nets. In: Reisig, W., Rozenberg, G. (eds.) Lectures on Petri Nets I: Basic Models. LectureNotes in Computer Science, vol. 1491, pp. 122–173. Springer, New York (1998)
8. Degano, P., De Nicola, R., Montanari, U.: A distributed operational semantics for CCS based on C/E systems. Acta Inform. **26**(1–2), 59–91 (1988)
9. Degano, P., De Nicola, R., Montanari, U.: Partial ordering descriptions and observations of nondeterministic concurrent systems. In: Lecture Notes in Computer Science, vol. 354, pp. 438–466. Springer, New York (1989)
10. Degano, P., Gorrieri, R., Marchetti, S.: An exercise in concurrency: a CSP process as a condition/event system. Adv. Petri Nets (LNCS, Springer) **340**, 85–105 (1988)
11. Degano, P., Meseguer, J., Montanari, U.: Axiomatizing the algebra of net computations and processes. Acta Inform. **33**(7), 641–667 (1996)
12. Esparza, J.: Decidability and complexity of Petri net problems: an introduction. In: Reisig, W., Rozenberg, G. (eds.) Lectures on Petri Nets I: Basic Models. LectureNotes in Computer Science, vol. 1491, pp. 374–428. Springer, New York (1998)
13. Goltz, U.: On representing CCS programs by finite Petri nets. In: Proceedings of the MFCS'88. LNCS, vol. 324, pp. 339–350. Springer, New York (1988)
14. Gorrieri, R.: Language representability of finite P/T nets. In:Programming Languages with Applications to Biology and Security—Colloquium in Honour of Pierpaolo Degano for His 65th Birthday, (PLABS 2015). LNCS, vol. 9465. Springer, New York (2015) (being printed)
15. Gorrieri, R., Montanari, U.: SCONE: a simple calculus of nets. In: Proceedings of the CONCUR'90. LNCS, vol. 458, pp. 2–30. Springer, New York (1990)
16. Gorrieri, R., Montanari, U.: Towards hierarchical specification of systems: a proof system for strong prefixing. Int. J. Found. Comput. Sci. **1**(3), 277–293 (1990)
17. Gorrieri, R., Marchetti, S., Montanari, U.: A^2CCS: atomic actions for CCS. Theor. Comput. Sci. **72**(2–3), 203–223 (1990)
18. Gorrieri, R., Versari, C.: A process calculus for expressing finite place/transition Petri nets. In: Proceedings of the EXPRESS'10, EPTCS, 2010. doi:10.4204/EPTCS.41.6. arXiv:1011.6433v1
19. Gorrieri, R., Versari, C.: EATCS Text in Computer Science. Introduction to concurrency theory: transition systems and CCS. Springer, New York (2015)
20. Hoare, C.A.R.: Communicating Sequential Processes. Prentice-Hall, New York (1985)
21. Jančar, P.: Undecidability of bisimilarity for Petri nets and some related problems. Theor. Comput. Sci. **148**(2), 281–301 (1995)
22. Mayr, R.: Process rewrite systems. Inf. Comput. **156**(1–2), 264–286 (2000)
23. Meyer, R.: A theory of structural stationarity in the π-calculus. Acta Inform. **46**(2), 87–137 (2009)
24. Meyer, R., Gorrieri, R.: On the relationship between pi-calculus and finite place/transition Petri nets. In: Proceedings of the CONCUR 2009. LNCS, vol. 5710, pp. 463–480. Springer, New York (2009)
25. Milner, R.: Communication and Concurrency. Prentice-Hall, New York (1989)
26. Milner, R.: Communicating and Mobile Systems: Theπ-Calculus. Cambridge University Press, Cambridge (1999)
27. Nielsen, M., Thiagarajan, P.S.: Degrees of non-determinism and concurrency: a Petri net view. In: Proceedings of the Fourth Conference on Foundations of Software Technology and Theoretical Computer Science (FSTTCS'84). LNCS, vol. 181, pp. 89–117. Springer, New York (1984)
28. Olderog, E.R.: Nets, terms and formulas. In: Cambridge Tracts in Theoretical Computer Science, vol. 23. Cambridge University Press, Cambridge (1991)
29. Pomello, L., Rozenberg, G., Simone, C.: A survey of equivalence notions for net based systems. Lect. Notes Comput. Sci. **609**, 410–472 (1992)
30. Peterson, J.L.: Petri Net Theory and the Modeling of Systems. Prentice-Hall, New York (1981)
31. Reisig, W.: EATCS Monographs on TCS. Petri Nets: An Introduction. Springer, New York (1985)
32. Reisig, W., Rozenberg, G. (eds.) Lectures on Petri Nets I: Basic Models. Lecture Notes in Computer Science, vol. 1491. Springer, New York (1998)
33. Taubner, D.: Finite representations of CCS and TCSP programs by automata and Petri nets. In: Lecture notes in computer science, vol. 369. Springer, New York (1989)

12

A software reliability model with time-dependent fault detection and fault removal

Mengmeng Zhu[1] · Hoang Pham[1]

Abstract The common assumption for most existing software reliability growth models is that fault is independent and can be removed perfectly upon detection. However, it is often not true due to various factors including software complexity, programmer proficiency, organization hierarchy, etc. In this paper, we develop a software reliability model with considerations of fault-dependent detection, imperfect fault removal and the maximum number of faults software. The genetic algorithm (GA) method is applied to estimate the model parameters. Four goodness-of-fit criteria, such as mean-squared error, predictive-ratio risk, predictive power, and Akaike information criterion, are used to compare the proposed model and several existing software reliability models. Three datasets collected in industries are used to demonstrate the better fit of the proposed model than other existing software reliability models based on the studied criteria.

Keywords Non-homogeneous Poisson process (NHPP) · Software reliability growth · Fault-dependent detection · Imperfect fault removal · The maximum number of software faults

1 Introduction

Reliability research has been studied over the past few decades. Also, considerable research has been done in the hardware reliability field. The increasing significant impact on software has shifted our attention to software reliability, owing to the fact that software developing cost and software failure penalty cost are becoming major expenses during the life cycle of a complex system for a company [1]. Software reliability models can provide quantitative measures of the reliability of software systems during software development processes [2]. Most software bugs only produce inconvenient experiences to customers, but some may result in a serious consequence. For instance, because of a race condition in General Energy's monitoring system, the 2003 North America blackout was triggered by a local outage. From the latest report, Toyota's electronic throttle control system (ETCS) had bugs that could cause unintended acceleration. At least 89 people were killed as a result.

Software reliability is a significant measurement to characterize software quality and determine when to stop testing and release software upon the predetermined objectives [3]. A great number of software reliability models also have been proposed in the past few decades to predict software failures and determine the release time based on a non-homogeneous Poisson process (NHPP). Some software reliability models consider perfect debugging, such as [4–7]; some assume imperfect debugging [6–10]. The fault detection rate, described by a constant [4,6,11] or by learning phenomenon of developers [3,8,12–16], is also studied in literature. However, lots of difficulties are also generated from model assumptions when applying software reliability models on real testing environment. These non-significant assumptions have limited their usefulness in the real-world application [17]. For most software reliability models in literature, software faults are assumed to be removed immediately and perfectly upon detection [9,17,18]. Additionally, software faults are assumed to be independent for simplicity reason. Several studies including [3,19,20] incorporate fault removal efficiency and imperfect debugging into the modeling consideration. Also, Kapur et al. [21] consider that the

✉ Hoang Pham
hopham@rci.rutgers.edu

[1] Department of Industrial and Systems Engineering, Rutgers University, New Brunswick, NJ 08854, USA

delay of the fault removal efficiency depends on their criticality and urgency in the software reliability modeling in the operation phase. However, we have not seen any research incorporate fault-dependent detection and imperfect fault removal based on our knowledge.

Why do we need to address imperfect fault removal and fault-dependent detection in the software development process? Firstly, in practice, the software debugging process is very complex [14,22]. When the software developer needs to fix the detected fault, he/she will report to the management team first, get the permission to make a change, and submit the changed code to fix a fault [17]. In most cases, we assume that the submitted fix at the first attempt is able to perfectly remove the faults. But this perfect fault removal assumption is not realistic due to the complexity of coding and different domain knowledge level for the software developer, since domain knowledge has become a significant factor in the software development process based on the newly revisited software environmental survey analysis [14].

Moreover, the proficiency of domain knowledge has a direct impact on the fault detection and removal efficiency [14]. If the submitted fix cannot completely remove the fault, the number of actual remaining errors in the software is higher than what we estimated. These remaining faults contained in the software, indeed, affect the quality of the product. The company will release the software based on the scheduled date and pre-determined software reliability value; however, the actual quality of the software product is not as good as what we expect. Hence, the amount of complaints from the end-user may be above expectations, and the penalty cost to fix the faults through an operation phase will be much higher than in an in-house environment [23]. In consequence, the software organization has to release the updated version of the software product earlier than determined, if they want to lower the fixing cost of software faults existing in the current release. Therefore, it is plausible to incorporate imperfect fault removal into software reliability modeling for consideration in the long run.

Furthermore, software faults can be classified depending on the kind of failures they induce [24]. For instance, Bohrbug is defined as a design error and always causes a software failure when the operation system is functioning [25]. Bohrbugs are easy to be detected and removed in the very early stage of software developing or testing phase [26]. In contrast, a bug that is complex and obscure and may cause chaotic or even non-deterministic behaviors is called Mandelbug [27]. Often, Mandelbug is triggered by a complex condition [28], such as an interaction of hardware and software, or a different application field. Thus, it is difficult to remove or completely remove Mandelbugs in the testing phase due to the non-deterministic behaviors of Mandelbugs [26]. Most importantly, the detection of this type of fault is not independent and relies on the previously detected software errors. Hence, including fault-dependent detection is desirable in model development. Of course, imperfect fault removal provides more realistic explanation for this type of software faults.

What is the maximum number of software faults and why do we incorporate them in this study? Due to the fact that software fault removal is not perfect in reality and new faults will be introduced in debugging, there is always a portion of software faults left in the software product after every debugging effort. These non-removed software faults and newly generated faults, which are caused by the interaction of new faults and existing faults, cumulate in the current version and will be carried into the next phase. Hence, the maximum number of software faults is defined in this paper, also an unknown parameter, which can be interpreted as the maximum number of faults that the software product can carry while under the designed function. If the number of faults that the software contains is larger than the maximum number, the software product will stop the designed function.

In this paper, we propose a model with considerations of fault-dependent detection, imperfect fault removal, the maximum number of software faults and logistic failure growth to predict software failures and estimate software reliability during the software development process.

Section 2 describes the software reliability modeling development and the interpretation of practical application. Section 3 states four goodness-of-fit criteria. Section 4 compares the proposed model with existing software reliability models based on the goodness-of-fit criteria described in Sect. 3, using three datasets collected from real software applications. Section 5 draws the conclusion of the proposed model and points out the future research with the application of the proposed model.

Notation $N(t)$ The total number of software failures by time t based on NHPP.

$m(t)$ The expected number of software failures by time t, i.e., $m(t) = E[N(t)]$.

$a(t)$ Fault content function.

L The maximum number of faults software is able to contain.

$b(t)$ Software fault detection rate per fault per unit of time.

$c(t)$ Non-removed error rate per unit of time.

$\lambda(t)$ Failure intensity function.

$R(x|t)$ Software reliability function by time x given a mission time t.

2 Software reliability modeling

It is commonly assumed that the software failure intensity is proportional to the remaining faults contained in the software in most existing NHPP models. Moreover, software faults are independent and can be removed perfectly upon detection.

Table 1 Summary of software reliability models

Model name	Model type	MVF (m(t))
Goel–Okumoto (G–O) model [4]	Concave	$m(t) = a(1 - e^{bt})$
Delayed S-shaped model [6]	S-shaped	$m(t) = a(1 - (1 + bt)e^{-bt})$
Inflection S-shaped model [7]	S-shaped	$m(t) = \frac{a(1-e^{-bt})}{1+\beta e^{-bt}}$
Yamada imperfect debugging model [29]	Concave	$m(t) = a\left[1 - e^{-bt}\right]\left[1 - \frac{\alpha}{b}\right] + \alpha a t$
PNZ model [8]	S-shaped and concave	$m(t) = \frac{a[(1-e^{-bt})(1-\frac{\alpha}{b})+\alpha t]}{1+\beta e^{-bt}}$
Pham-Zhang model [30]	S-shaped and concave	$m(t) = \frac{1}{1+\beta e^{-bt}}[(c + a)(1 - e^{-bt}) - \frac{ab}{b-\alpha}(e^{-\alpha t} - e^{-bt})]$
Dependent-parameter model [31]	S-shaped and concave	$m(t) = \alpha(1 + \gamma t)(\gamma t + e^{-\gamma t} - 1)$
Dependent-parameter model with $m(t_0) \neq 0$, $t_0 \neq 0$ [32]	S-shaped and concave	$m(t) = m_0(\frac{\gamma t+1}{r t_0+1})e^{-\gamma(t-t_0)} + \alpha(\gamma t + 1)[\gamma t - 1 + (1 - \gamma t_0)e^{-\gamma(t-t_0)}]$
Loglog fault-detection rate model [18]	Concave	$m(t) = N(1 - e^{-(a^{t^b}-1)})$
Proposed model	S-shaped and concave	$m(t) = \frac{\beta+e^{bt}}{\frac{b}{L(b-c)}[e^{bt}-e^{ct}]+\frac{1+\beta}{m_0}e^{ct}}$

Therefore, a general NHPP software mean value function (MVF) by considering time-dependent failure detection rate is given as

$$m(t) = N\left[1 - e^{-\int_0^t b(x)\mathrm{d}x}\right]. \qquad (1)$$

However, nowadays, the above software mean value function is not adequate to describe more complex software product. In reality, software faults cannot be completely removed upon detection due to the programmer's level of proficiency and the kind of faults. Some software faults may not appear in the testing phase, but could manifest in the operation field. The detection for software faults is not independent, but depends on the previously detected errors. Debugging is an error-removal process, as well as an error-induction process. In other words, we can treat it as a fault-growing process, since all the leftover (unremovable) faults cumulate in the software. Hence, a maximum number of software faults are introduced.

An NHPP software reliability model, which not only considers fault-dependent detection and imperfect fault removal process, but also takes into account the maximum number of faults in the software, is proposed in this paper. The assumptions for this proposed NHPP model are given as follows:

1. The software failure process is a non-homogeneous Poisson process (NHPP).
2. This is a fault-dependent detection process.
3. Fault detection is a learning curve phenomenon process.
4. Fault is not removed perfectly upon detection.
5. The debugging process may introduce new errors into the software. This is an imperfect debugging process, but the maximum faults contained in the software is L.
6. The software failure intensity $\lambda(t)$ is explained as the percentage of the removed errors in the software product.
7. The non-removed software error rate is assumed to be a constant.

An NHPP software reliability model with fault-dependent detection, imperfect fault removal and the maximum number of faults can be formulated as follows:

$$\frac{\mathrm{d}m(t)}{\mathrm{d}t} = b(t)m(t)\left[1 - \frac{m(t)}{L}\right] - c(t)m(t). \qquad (2)$$

The marginal condition for the above equation is given as

$$m(t_0) = m_0, \quad m_0 > 0. \qquad (3)$$

Usually, the software tester performs a pre-analysis test to eliminate the most trivial errors before officially starting the testing phase. Thus, most of the existing models consider $m_0 = 0$. In this paper, we assume $m_0 > 0$ by taking into consideration those trivial errors.

The general solution for (2) can be easily obtained:

$$m(t) = \frac{e^{\int_{t_0}^t (b(\tau)-c(\tau))\mathrm{d}\tau}}{\frac{1}{L}\int_{t_0}^t e^{\int_{t_0}^\tau (b(s)-c(s))\mathrm{d}s} b(\tau)\mathrm{d}\tau + \frac{1}{m_0}}, \qquad (4)$$

where $m(t)$ represents the expected number of software failures detected by time t, L denotes the maximum number of software faults, $b(t)$ is the fault detection rate per individual

Table 2 Phase I system test data [34]

Week index	Exposure time (cumulative system test hours)	Fault	Cumulative fault
1	356	1	1
2	712	0	1
3	1068	1	2
4	1424	1	3
5	1780	2	5
6	2136	0	5
7	2492	0	5
8	2848	3	8
9	3204	1	9
10	3560	2	11
11	3916	2	13
12	4272	2	15
13	4628	4	19
14	4984	0	19
15	5340	3	22
16	5696	0	22
17	6052	1	23
18	6408	1	24
19	6764	0	24
20	7120	0	24
21	7476	2	26

Table 3 Phase II system test data [34]

Week index	Exposure time (cumulative system test hours)	Fault	Cumulative fault
1	416	3	3
2	832	1	4
3	1248	0	4
4	1664	3	7
5	2080	2	9
6	2496	0	9
7	2912	1	10
8	3328	3	13
9	3744	4	17
10	4160	2	19
11	4576	4	23
12	4992	2	25
13	5408	5	30
14	5824	2	32
15	6240	4	36
16	6656	1	37
17	7072	2	39
18	7488	0	39
19	7904	0	39
20	8320	3	42
21	8736	1	43

fault per unit of time and $c(t)$ represents the non-removed error rate per unit of time.

$(1 - \frac{m(t)}{L})$ indicates the proportion of available resources that can be used in the future, which can also be interpreted as the proportion of software faults detected in every debugging effort. $b(t)m(t)\left[1 - \frac{m(t)}{L}\right]$ is the percentage of detected dependent errors by time t. $c(t)m(t)$ represents the non-removed errors by time t. Hence, $b(t)m(t)\left[1 - \frac{m(t)}{L}\right] - cm(t)$ represents the proportion of the removed errors in the software by time t. $\lambda(t) = \frac{\mathrm{d}m(t)}{\mathrm{d}t}$ is the failure intensity function for the whole software system by time t.

Assume that fault detection is a learning process which can be addressed in Eq. (5) and non-removed rate $c(t)$ is a constant,

$$b(t) = \frac{b}{1 + \beta e^{-bt}}, \quad b > 0, \quad \beta > 0, \tag{5}$$

$$c(t) = c, \quad c > 0. \tag{6}$$

Substitute (5) and (6) into (4), we obtain

$$m(t) = \frac{\beta + e^{bt}}{\frac{b}{L(b-c)}\left[e^{bt} - e^{ct}\right] + \frac{1+\beta}{m_0} e^{ct}}. \tag{7}$$

The software reliability function within $(t, t + x)$ based on the proposed NHPP is given by

$$R(x|t) = e^{-[m(t+x)-m(t)]}. \tag{8}$$

Table 1 summarizes the features and mean value function of the proposed model and existing models.

3 Parameter estimation and goodness-of-fit criteria

We apply the genetic algorithm (GA) to obtain the parameter estimates of the proposed model and other models as mentioned in Table 1. To compare the goodness of fit for all models, we apply four criteria in this paper described as follows. The mean-squared error (MSE) refers to the mean value of the deviation between the prediction value and the observation value as follows:

$$\mathrm{MSE} = \frac{\sum_{i=1}^{n} (\hat{m}(t_i) - y_i)^2}{n - N},$$

where $\hat{m}(t_i)$ represents the estimated expected number of faults detected by time t; y_i represents the observation value;

Table 4 Parameter estimation and comparison (Phase I system test data)

Model name	MSE	PRR	PP	AIC	Parameter estimate
Goel–Okumoto (G–O)	5.944	1.818	8.165	66.211	$\hat{a} = 62.0395$ $\hat{b} = 0.0243$
Delayed S-shaped	1.609	14.546	0.981	64.230	$\hat{a} = 44.221$ $\hat{b} = 0.1007$
Inflection S-shaped	0.709	1.714	0.512	63.938	$\hat{a} = 27.247$ $\hat{b} = 0.269$ $\hat{\beta} = 17.255$
Yamada imperfect debugging	2.602	0.840	0.757	66.710	$\hat{a} = 1.8643$ $\hat{b} = 0.25$ $\hat{\alpha} = 0.8418$
PNZ Model	2.479	2.954	0.690	68.611	$\hat{a} = 1.5556$ $\hat{b} = 0.3239$ $\hat{\alpha} = 0.9689$ $\hat{\beta} = 0.9999$
Pham-Zhang model	3.429	1.982	1.187	70.617	$\hat{a} = 13.394$ $\hat{b} = 0.2671$ $\hat{\alpha} = 0.5113$ $\hat{\beta} = 9.0131$ $\hat{c} = 12.0336$
Dependent-parameter model	15.741	287.191	3.768	77.541	$\hat{\alpha} = 0.0872$ $\hat{\gamma} = 0.9523$
Dependent-parameter model with $m_0 \neq 0$, $t_0 \neq 0$	13.477	2.136	1.189	77.621	$\hat{\alpha} = 6206$ $\hat{\gamma} = 0.0048$ $t_0 = 1$ $m_0 = 1$
Loglog fault-detection rate model	71.241	11.736	15.475	93.592	$\hat{N} = 15.403$ $\hat{a} = 1.181$ $\hat{b} = 0.567$
Proposed model	0.630	0.408	0.526	65.777	$\hat{m}_0 = 1$ $\hat{L} = 49.7429$ $\hat{\beta} = 0.2925$ $\hat{b} = 0.6151$ $\hat{c} = 0.292$

and n and N are the number of observations and the number of parameters, respectively.

The predictive-ratio risk (PRR) represents the distance of the model estimates from the actual data against the model estimates and is defined as [33]:

$$\mathrm{PRR} = \sum_{i=1}^{n} \left(\frac{\hat{m}(t_i) - y_i}{\hat{m}(t_i)} \right)^2 .$$

It is noticeable that the PRR value will assign a larger penalty to a model which has underestimated the cumulative number of failures.

The predictive power (PP) measures the distance of the model estimates from the actual data against the actual data, which is defined as [34]:

$$\mathrm{PP} = \sum_{i=1}^{n} \left(\frac{\hat{m}(t_i) - y_i}{y_i} \right)^2 .$$

To compare the model's ability in terms of maximizing the likelihood function while considering the degrees of freedom, Akaike information criterion (AIC) is applied.

$$\mathrm{AIC} = -2 \log |\mathrm{MLF}| + 2 * N,$$

where N represents the number of parameters in the model and MLF is the maximum value of the model's likelihood function.

For all four goodness-of-fit criteria described above, the smaller the value, the better is the goodness of fit for the software reliability model.

4 Model evaluation and comparison

4.1 Software failure data description

Telecommunication system data reported by Zhang in 2002 [34] are applied to validate the proposed model. System test

Table 5 Parameter estimation and comparison (Phase II system test data)

Model name	MSE	PRR	PP	AIC	Parameter estimate
Goel–Okumoto (G–O)	6.607	0.687	1.099	74.752	$\hat{a} = 98295$ $\hat{b} = 5.2E-8$
Delayed S-shaped	3.273	44.267	1.429	77.502	$\hat{a} = 62.3$ $\hat{b} = 2.85E-4$
Inflection S-shaped	1.871	5.938	0.895	73.359	$\hat{a} = 46.6$ $\hat{b} = 5.78E-4$ $\hat{\beta} = 12.2$
Yamada imperfect debugging	4.982	4.296	0.809	78.054	$\hat{a} = 1.5$ $\hat{b} = 1.1E-3$ $\hat{\alpha} = 3.8E-3$
PNZ Model	1.994	6.834	0.957	75.501	$\hat{a} = 45.99$ $\hat{b} = 6.0E-4$ $\hat{\alpha} = 0$ $\hat{\beta} = 13.24$
Pham-Zhang model	2.119	6.762	0.952	77.502	$\hat{a} = 0.06$ $\hat{b} = 6.0E-4$ $\hat{\alpha} = 1.0E-4$ $\hat{\beta} = 13.2$ $\hat{c} = 45.9$
Dependent-parameter model	43.689	601.336	4.530	101.386	$\hat{\alpha} = 3.0E-6$ $\hat{\gamma} = 0.49$
Dependent-parameter model with $m_0 \neq 0, t_0 \neq 0$	35.398	2.250	1.167	87.667	$\hat{\alpha} = 890996$ $\hat{\gamma} = 1.2E-6$ $t_0 = 832$ $m_0 = 4$
Loglog fault-detection rate model	219.687	13.655	4.383	114.807	$\hat{N} = 231.92$ $\hat{a} = 1.019$ $\hat{b} = 0.489$
Proposed model	1.058	0.163	0.144	68.316	$\hat{m}_0 = 3$ $\hat{L} = 59.997$ $\hat{\beta} = 0.843$ $\hat{b} = 0.409$ $\hat{c} = 0.108$

data consist of two phases of test data. In each phase, the system records the cumulative number of faults by each week. 356 system test hours were observed in each week for Phase I data, as shown in Table 2; 416 system test hours were observed in each week for Phase II data, as shown in Table 3. Parameter estimate was carried out by the GA method. To provide a better comparison of our proposed model with the other existing models, we analyzed Phase I as well as Phase II system test data in this section.

4.2 Model comparison

In the proposed model, when $t = 0$, the initial number of faults in the software satisfies $0 < m_0 \leq y_1$, where y_1 is the number of observed failures at time $t = 1$; at the same time, m_0 must be an integer. The interpretation of this constraint is that the software tester often completes pre-analysis to eliminate trivial errors existing in the software before officially starting testing. The cause of these trivial errors could be human mistakes or other simple settings. Since we consider the maximum number of faults that the software is able to contain in the modeling, these eliminated trivial errors will be counted into the total number of faults.

Tables 4 and 5 summarize the results of the estimated parameters and corresponding criteria value (MSE, PRR, PP, AIC) for the proposed model and other existing models. Both two-phase system test data present as an S-shaped curve; therefore, existing models such as Goel–Okumoto model is not able to perfectly capture the characteristic of the two system test datasets.

For Phase I system test data, the estimated parameters are $\hat{m}_0 = 1, \hat{L} = 49.7429, \hat{\beta} = 0.2925, \hat{b} = 0.6151, \hat{c} = 0.292$. As seen in Table 4, MSE and PRR values for the proposed model are 0.630 and 0.408, which are the smallest among all ten models listed here. Inflection S-shaped model has the smallest PP value. However, the PP value for the proposed model is 0.526, which is only slightly higher than 0.512. Moreover, the PRR value for the inflection S-shaped model is much higher than that of the proposed model. The

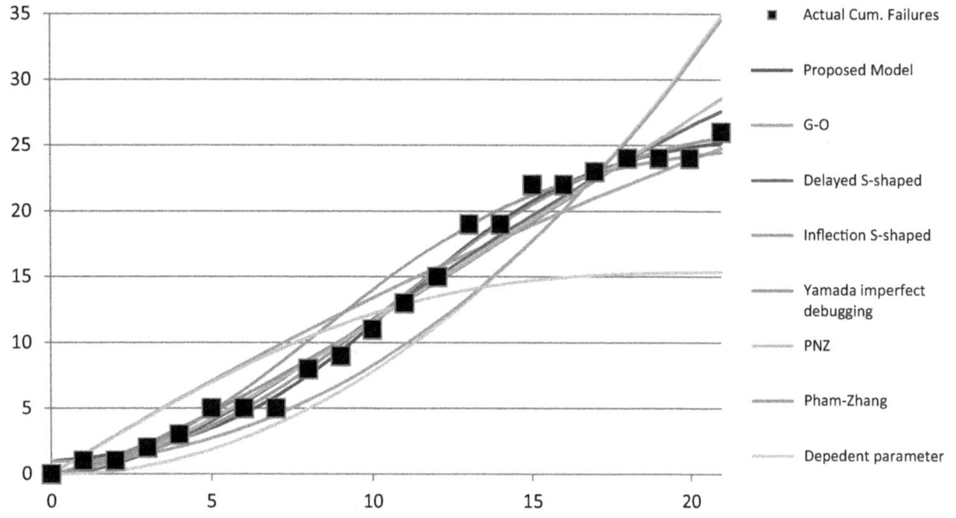

Fig. 1 Comparison of actual cumulative failures and cumulative failures predicted by software reliability models (Phase I system test data)

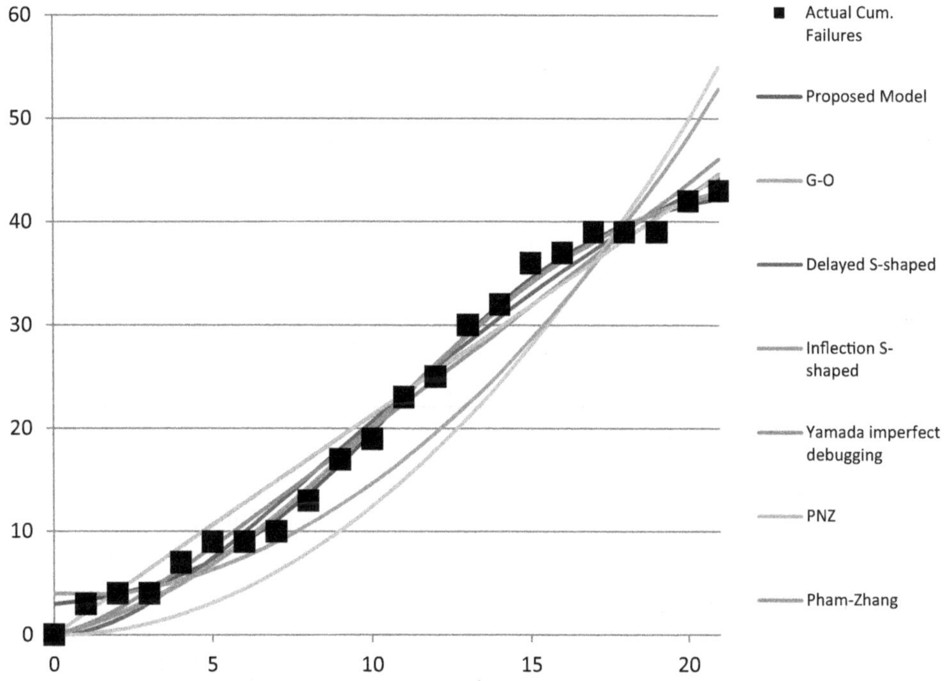

Fig. 2 Comparison of actual cumulative failures and cumulative failures predicted by software reliability models (Phase II system test data)

AIC value for the proposed model is 65.777, which is just slightly higher than the smallest AIC value, 63.938. Thus, we conclude that the proposed model is the best fit for Phase I system test data compared with the other nine models in Table 1. Figure 1 shows the comparison of actual cumulative failures and cumulative failures predicted by ten software reliability models.

For Phase II system test data, the estimated parameters are $\hat{m}_0 = 3$, $\hat{L} = 59.997$, $\hat{\beta} = 0.843$, $\hat{b} = 0.409$, $\hat{c} = 0.108$. The proposed model presents the smallest MSE, PRR, PP and AIC value in Table 5. Thus, we conclude that the proposed model is the best fitting for Phase II test data among all other models in Table 1. Figure 2 plots the comparison of the actual cumulative failures and cumulative failures predicted by ten software reliability models.

Moreover, the proposed model provides the maximum number of faults contained in software, for instance, $L = 60$ for Phase II test data. Assume that the company releases software at week 21, 43 faults will be detected upon this time based on the actual observations; however, the fault may not be perfectly removed upon detection as discussed in Sect. 2. The remaining faults shown in the operation field, mostly, are Mandelbugs [27]. Given the maximum number of faults in the software, it is very helpful for the software developer

Table 6 Comparison of G-O, Zhang–Teng–Pham model and the proposed model using tandem computer software failure data

Testing time (weeks)	CPUhours	Defects found	Predicted total defects by G-O	Predicted total defects by Zhang–Teng–Pham model	Predicted total defects by proposed model
1	519	16	–	–	–
2	968	24	–	–	–
3	1430	27	–	–	–
4	1893	33	–	–	–
5	2490	41	–	–	–
6	3058	49	–	–	–
7	3625	54	–	–	–
8	4422	58	–	–	–
9	5218	69	–	–	–
10	5823	75	98	74.7	75.5
11	6539	81	107	80.1	80.8
12	7083	86	116	85.2	85.1
13	7487	90	123	90.1	88.5
14	7846	93	129	94.6	91.2
15	8205	96	129	98.9	93.2
16	8564	98	134	102.9	94.7
17	8923	99	139	106.8	95.8
18	9282	100	138	110.4	96.6
19	9641	100	135	111.9	97.2
20	10,000	100	133	112.2	97.6
Predicted MSE			1359.222	82.66	10.120
Predicted AIC			149.60	186.468	169.667
Predicted PRR			0.756	0.041	0.007
Predicted PP			1.395	0.050	0.006

to better predict the remaining errors and decide the release time for the next version.

4.3 Software failure data from a tandem computer project

Wood [35] provides software failure data including four major releases of software products at Tandem Computers. Eight NHPP models were studied in Wood [35] and it was found that the G-O models provided the best performance in terms of goodness of fit. By fitting our model into the same subset of data, from week 1 to week 9, we predict the cumulative number of faults from week 10 to week 20, and compare the results with the G-O model and Zhang–Teng–Pham model [3]. Table 6 describes the predicted number of software failures from each model. The AIC value for the proposed model is not the smallest AIC value present in Table 6; however, we still conclude that the proposed model is the best fit for this dataset, since the other three criteria (MSE, PRR and PP) indicate that the proposed model is significantly better than other models. The GA method is applied here to estimate the parameter. Parameter estimates for the proposed model are given as $\hat{m}_0 = 3, \hat{L} = 181, \hat{\beta} = 0.5001, \hat{b} = 0.602, \hat{c} = 0.274$.

5 Conclusions

In this paper, we introduce a new NHPP software reliability model that incorporates fault-dependent detection and imperfect fault removal, along with the maximum number of faults contained in the software. In light of the proficiency of the programmer, software faults classification, and programming complexity, we consider software fault-dependent detection and imperfect fault removal process. To our knowledge, however, not many researches have been done on estimating the maximum number of faults that can be carried in a software. We estimate the maximum number of faults in the software considering fault-dependent detection and imperfect fault removal to provide software measurement metrics, such as remaining errors, failure rate and software reliability. Hence, when to release the software and how to arrange multi-release for a software product will be addressed in future research, since we have obtained the maximum number of faults in this study.

References

1. Pham, H.: Software reliability and cost models: perspectives, comparison, and practice. Eur. J. Oper. Res. **149**(3), 475–489 (2003)
2. Pham, H., Zhang, X.: NHPP software reliability and cost models with testing coverage. Eur. J. Oper. Res. **145**, 443–454 (2003)
3. Zhang, X., Teng, X., Pham, H.: Considering fault removal efficiency in software reliability assessment. In: IEEE Transactions on Systems, Man and Cybernetics, Part A: Systems and Humans, vol. 33, no. 1, pp. 114–120 (2003)
4. Goel, A.L., Okumoto, K.: Time-dependent error-detection rate model for software reliability and other performance measures. IEEE Trans. Reliab. **28**(3), 206–211 (1979)
5. Hossain, S.A., Dahiya, R.C.: Estimating the parameters of a non-homogeneous Poisson-process model for software reliability. IEEE Trans. Reliab. **42**(4), 604–612 (1993)
6. Ohba, M., Yamada, S.: S-shaped software reliability growth models. In: International Colloquium on Reliability and Maintainability, 4th, Tregastel, France, pp. 430–436 (1984)
7. Ohba, M.: Inflection S-shaped software reliability growth model. Stochastic Models in Reliability Theory, pp. 144–162. Springer (1984)
8. Pham, H., Nordmann, L., Zhang, X.: A general imperfect-software-debugging model with S-shaped fault-detection rate. IEEE Trans. Reliab. **48**(2), 169–175 (1999)
9. Xie, M., Yang, B.: A study of the effect of imperfect debugging on software development cost. IEEE Trans. Softw. Eng. **29**(5), 471–473 (2003)
10. Pham, H., Zhang, X.: An NHPP software reliability model and its comparison. Int. J. Reliab. Qual. Saf. Eng. **4**(3), 269–282 (1997)
11. Pham, L., Pham, H., et al.: Software reliability models with time-dependent hazard function based on Bayesian approach. IEEE Trans. Syst. Man Cybern. Part A Syst. Hum. **30**(1), 25–35 (2000)
12. Pham, H., Wang, H.: A quasi-renewal process for software reliability and testing costs. In: IEEE Transaction on Systems, Man and Cybernetics, Part A: Systems and Humans, vol. 31, no. 6, pp. 623–631 (2001)
13. Jones, C.: Software defect-removal efficiency. Computer **29**(4), 94–95 (1996)
14. Zhu, M., Zhang, X., Pham, H.: A comparison analysis of environmental factors affecting software reliability. J. Syst. Softw. **109**, 150–160 (2015)
15. Pham, H., Pham, D.H., Pham, H.: A new mathematical logistic model and its applications. Int. J. Inf. Manag. Sci. **25**(2), 79–99 (2014)
16. Fang, C.-C., Chun-Wu, Y.: Effective confidence interval estimation of fault-detection process of software reliability growth models. J. Syst. Sci (2015). doi:10.1080/00207721.2015.1036474
17. Ho, S.L., Xie, M., Goh, T.N.: A study of the connectionist models for software reliability prediction. Comput. Math. Appl. **46**(7), 1037–1045 (2003)
18. Pham, H.: Loglog fault-detection rate and testing coverage software reliability models subject to random environments. Vietnam J. Comput. Sci. **1**(1), 39–45 (2014)
19. Zhang, X., Pham, H.: Software field failure rate prediction before software deployment. J. Syst. Softw. **79**(3), 291–300 (2006)
20. Zhang, X., Jeske, D.R., Pham, H.: Calibrating software reliability models when the test environment does not match the user environment. Appl. Stoch. Models Bus. Ind. **18**(1), 87–99 (2002)
21. Kapur, P.K., Gupta, A., Jha, P.C.: Reliability analysis of project and product type software in operational phase incorporating the effect of fault removal efficiency. Int. J. Reliab. Qual. Saf. Eng. **14**(3), 219–240 (2007)
22. Lyu, M.R.: Handbook of Software Reliability Engineering. vol. 222, IEEE computer society press (1996)
23. Grottke, M., Trivedi, K.S.: Fighting bugs: Remove, retry, replicate, and rejuvenate. Computer **40**(2), 107–109 (2007)
24. Grottke, M., Trivedi, K.S.: A classification of software faults. J. Reliab. Eng. Assoc. Jpn. **27**(7), 425–438 (2005)
25. Shetti, N.M.: Heisenbugs and Bohrbugs: Why are they different. Techn. Ber. Rutgers, The State University of New Jersey (2003)
26. Alonso, J., Grottke, M., Nikora, A.P., Trivedi, K.S.: An empirical investigation of fault repairs and mitigations in space mission system software. In: 2013 43rd Annual IEEE/IFIP International Conference on Dependable Systems and Networks (DSN), pp. 1–8 (2013)
27. Vaidyanathan, K., Trivedi, K.S.: Extended classification of software faults based on aging. In: IEEE International Symposium on Software Reliability Engineering, ISSRE (2001)
28. Carrozza, G., Cotroneo, D., Natella, R., Pietrantuono, R., Russo, S.: Analysis and prediction of mandelbugs in an industrial software system. In: IEEE Sixth International Conference on Software Testing, Verification and Validation, pp. 262–271 (2013)
29. Pham, H.: A new software reliability model with Vtub-shaped fault-detection rate and the uncertainty of operating environments. Optimization **63**(10), 1481–1490 (2014)
30. Chang, I.H., et al.: A testing-coverage software reliability model with the uncertainty of operating environments. Int. J. Syst. Sci. Oper. Logist. **1**(4), 220–227 (2014)
31. Yamada, S., Tokuno, K., Osaki, S.: Imperfect debugging models with fault introduction rate for software reliability assessment. Int. J. Syst. Sci. **23**(12), 2241–2252 (1992)
32. Pham, H.: An imperfect-debugging fault-detection dependent-parameter software. Int. J. Autom. Comput. **4**(4), 325–328 (2007)
33. Pham, H., Deng, C.: Predictive-ratio risk criterion for selecting software reliability models. In: Proceedings of the 9th International Conference on Reliability and Quality in Design, pp. 17–21 (2003)
34. Pham, H.: System Software Reliability. Springer (2007)
35. Wood, A.: Predicting software reliability. Computer **29**(11), 69–77 (1996)

13

$\mathcal{IRORS}$: intelligent recommendation of RSS feeds

Nedia Araibi[1] · Eya Ben Ahmed[2] · Wahiba Karaa Ben Abdessalem[1]

Abstract The abundance of information prohibits getting relevant results on online social researches. Thus, RSS feeds appear as monitoring tool of current events according to users preferences. However, the user is flooded by the amount of such RSS feeds. For that reason, any analysis of RSS feeds seems effortful and complex. In this paper, we aim to improve the effectiveness and swiftness of pertinent RSS feeds analysis through recommending suitable fragments of queries during the analysis process of events. Accordingly, we propose an innovative architecture of our new active RSS feeds warehouse. Additionally, we introduce a new recommender system to improve the querying expression of RSS feeds. Our experiment results show the robustness and efficiency of our approach.

Keywords Data warehouse · OLAP query log · Recommender system · RSS feeds

1 Introduction

The social media is becoming increasingly popular. Hence, the need to provide pertinent results on information retrieval proliferates. In this context, really simple syndication (RSS) is among the dedicated solutions for news monitoring according to various topics.

There is a large amount of previous work on processing RSS feeds from the user side through refining the RSS feeds according to the user requirements [6,7]. However, few works shed the light on analyzing the RSS feeds by decision makers to answer many questions, such as: Which is the most attention-grabbing RSS feeds topic? and How many RSS feeds are daily received? in order to undertake the compulsory actions.

Alongside, the set of RSS can be considered as a multidimensional data stored in a data warehouses (DW). In fact, due to the multiplicity of the analysis axis of RSS feeds, we opt for multidimensional modeling as a data warehouse in order to perform better-quality analysis. Indeed, according to Inmon [15], the data warehouse is an integrated collection of subject oriented, nonvolatile, historized, summarized and available data for analysis. Indeed, such data are organized according to analysis subjects in order to facilitate the extraction of relevant information. In such a context, OLAP operations can be performed in data warehouse to assist the decision maker [14]. The latter can ignore accurately the data warehouse schema, or the generated results of launched OLAP operations are distinct from the analysts expectations. Hence, the assistance of the analysis process arises through suggesting the MDX queries or OLAP fragments according to the analyst preferences.

In order to propose multidimensional recommendation, several approaches for OLAP recommender system have been proposed [3]. Among all these approaches, two main pools can be distinguished. The first pool approaches produce individual user recommendation based on graph models [16,17]. However, such approaches may lead to irrelevant recommendations when the number of analysts is so abundant. Hence, the second pool of approaches is introduced

✉ Eya Ben Ahmed
eya.benahmed@gmail.com

Nedia Araibi
nediaar@gmail.com

Wahiba Karaa Ben Abdessalem
wahiba.benabdessalem@isg.rnu.tn

1 High Institute of Management of Tunis, University of Tunis, Tunis, Tunisia

2 Miracl Laboratory, University of Sfax, Sfax, Tunisia

to suggest group recommendation through performing data mining techniques on users navigation histories to scrutinize the similarity between users [8–10, 19].

Unfortunately, those approaches are not suitable for active data warehouse such as our RSS multidimensional modeling, and any eventual generated recommendation from classical strategies will be obsolete compared to our active context. Indeed, any extracted recommendation should have a feature that can integrate data changes while maintaining or scheduled cycle refreshes.

In this paper, we investigate another way aiming at introducing refined RSS recommendations based on a data warehouse perspective. Thus, we introduce a new RSS recommender system.

In summary, our major contributions are:

1. We formalize the problem of active data warehouse, and we introduce a new architecture for active data warehouse establishment;
2. We investigate the optimized RSS feeds modeling, and we define its multidimensional representation through introducing our active RSS warehouse functional architecture;
3. We sketch the active multidimensional modeling profile, and we propose an efficient devoted algorithm for drawing such a profile;
4. We shed the light on active recommendations issue, and we consolidate our proposal through introducing an IRORS recommender system;
5. We conduct a comprehensive experimental study to evaluate the performance of our system.

The remainder of the paper is organized as follows: Sect. 2 motivates our proposal through an inspiring example. Section 3 sketches a thorough study of the related work to the active data warehouse and multidimensional recommender system. Section 4 recalls formal preliminaries. Section 5 details our approach. Section 6 reports the experimental results, showing the soundness of our system. Finally, Sect. 7 concludes our paper and outlines avenues of future work.

2 Motivating example

We consider a motivating example from the social media area, namely the really simple syndication (RSS). Indeed, the RSS benefits [25] from a range of standard Web feed formats to bring out regularly updated information, such as news titles and, audio or video headlines. Therefore, an RSS feed incorporates relevant characteristics of news, namely the source or the channel providing such information, the publishing date and the news title.

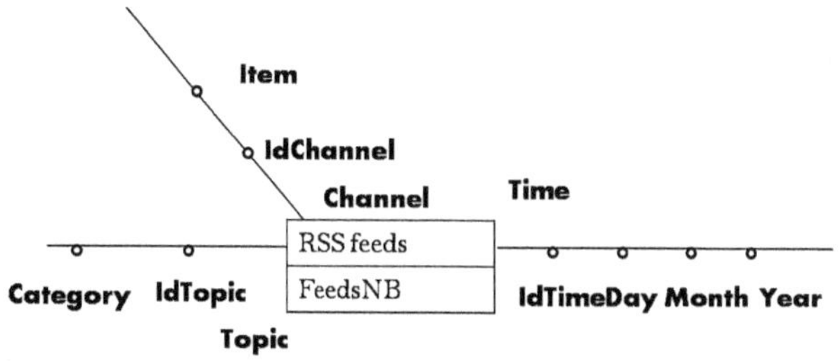

Fig. 1 A part of our RSS feeds data warehouse logical schema

Both publishers and users take advantages from RSS feeds. In fact, the latter facilitates for publishers to automatically organize data. Additionally, RSS feeds allow users to be up-to-date through getting timely updates from preferred Web sites avoiding to manually checking the Web site for novel content.

In this context, we propose an RSS feeds warehousing aiming to scrutinize the RSS feeds. The main goal behind new active RSS feeds modeling is to evaluate the progress of the news contents. Not only such carried out analysis of feeds allows an accurate identification of peaks periods and undertakes the required measures, but also it may stimulate feeds organized in subjects in order to permit a refined recommendation according to the users interests and avoid any overabundance of excessive flow.

A part of our logical data warehouse schema is depicted in Fig. 1. The adopted notations are similar to notations of [11]. Indeed, our schema includes a fact called RSS feeds which is measured using the number of feeds denoted as $FeedsNB$. It can be analyzed through various dimensions such as the channel, the topic and the time.

In this respect, according to Fig. 2, an analyst may launch a real-time query to discern in June 2015 the number of feeds related to the baccalaureate degree. Particularly, a more refined query can handle the numbers of feeds subject of declaration of results of baccalaureate degree in June 2015. Such a session may be used to establish the analyst profile interested on baccalaureate degree 2015, and we can recommend in real-time updated analysis of queries such as investigation of the success of baccalaureate degree in June 2015.

3 Related work

In this section, we present an overview of the previous work that has been done in active data warehouse and multidimensional recommender system.

3.1 Active data warehouse

Active data warehousing has appeared as an option to usual warehousing practices in order to converge the criti-

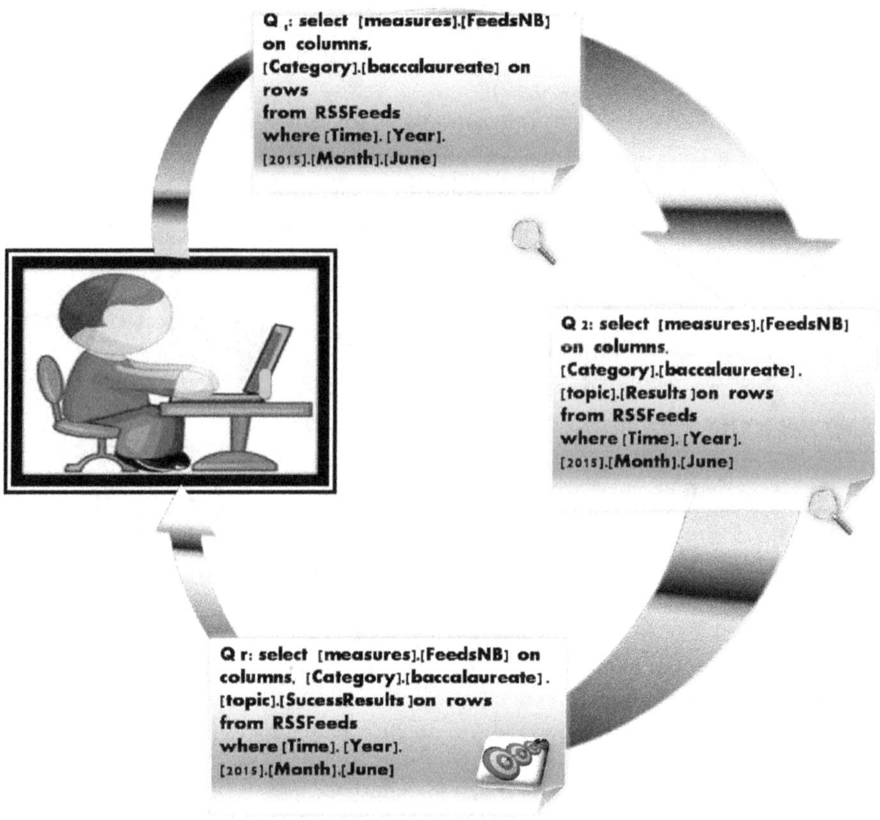

Fig. 2 An illustration of our recommender system process

cal request of applications for the newest information [21]. In this respect, in the literature, we distinguish two main trends of active data warehouse approaches. The first trend is principally based on the warehousing process analysis, and the second trend is essentially backboned on the ETL process.

In the first category, the usual data warehouse architecture is extended with analysis rules that imitate the activity of an analyst during decision making. Indeed [23], proposes a multidimensional analysis approach to define the analysis rules and to help analysts to change the values of given dimensions in order to improve the fact table.

However, in the second family of approaches [18,24], propose to follow updated tuples using messages holders of time indicators. The loading operation is performed continuously and must be done in real time admitting a consultation of data in parallel.

To the best of our knowledge, no method has incorporated both alimentation side and analysis side in the instauration of an active data warehouse. However, the update operation should impact both steps as new data will be considered during the alimentation step, but will affect the analysis stage in all cases. Hence, the need to introduce a new active data warehouse architecture that merges both steps is amplified.

3.2 Multidimensional recommender system

Recently, recommender systems have grabbed the attention of research society in data warehouse area. Indeed, Jerbi et al. [16,17] presented a framework for anticipatory OLAP recommendations in order to guide the user during his OLAP analysis through providing the imminent analysis step. To this end, a context-aware preference model has been introduced and applied to draw personalized anticipatory recommendations.

Along with the same preoccupation, Giacometti introduced a multidimensional recommender system taking benefits from the past querying experiences of analysts [8–10]. Its basic idea is to infer from the log of the OLAP server the activities of previous users to offer suitable recommendations to assist the user on his cube navigating.

Khemiri and bentayeb [19] presented a new approach to help the decision makers on constructing their analytical queries through investigating their past querying experiences. Indeed, the authors extracted frequent itemsets from the historical log files and used them to suggest pertinent recommendations, assuming that the significance of a recommended item wholly associated with its occurrence in the workload's queries.

More recently, Amo and Oliveira [2] presented a general framework for suggesting hybrid recommendations using preference mining and aggregation techniques. Indeed, they applied pairwise preference mining techniques to predict the favorite item for resolving the cold-start dilemma.

Moreover, Ben Ahmed et al. [4] introduced the semantic multidimensional group recommendations. Indeed, they presented the group profiling by means of an ontology on which they spread the analysts activities. Consequently, such profiling is exploited to develop semantic recommendations, namely fragments and complete queries. More recently, Aligon et al. [1] suggested recommending not single OLAP queries but whole OLAP sessions. First, the introduced recommender system recognized the most similar sessions with the current one. Then, the most significant subsessions derived and adapted to the current session.

Comparing the surveyed approaches in Table 1, we make out several analytical criteria, such as profiling source (behavior, external sources), user intervention (manual, automatic), profiling formulation (qualitative, quantitative), recommendation source (profile, external sources), recommendation strategy (language, method), type of recommendation (collaborative filtering [22], content-based), recommended object (fragment of query, complete query) and application domain (social media, movie, stock market, commercial).

It can be highlighted that all recommender systems are backboned on passive data warehouse. No consideration of real-time feature is involved. However, such a characteristic is fundamental in many domains such as social media where the speed of producing information is highly expedited and requires an instantaneous update of data warehouse.

Therefore, to the best of our knowledge, no strategy to suggest active recommendations is proposed in the literature. Thus, we introduce, in this paper, an innovative active data warehouse for RSS feeds modeling. From which, the users OLAP sessions are investigated to draw an efficient profiling of decision makers. Such a profiling is exploited to offer active recommendations of RSS feeds.

4 Preliminaries

In this section, we define the multidimensional model we will use to formalize our approach and illustrate it using our working example.

Definition 1 Multidimensional schema A multidimensional schema MS is a triple MS = (L, H, M) with:

- L is a finite set of levels, each level l ∈ L defined on a categorical domain Dom(l);
- H = h_1, ..., h_n is a restricted set of hierarchies, each characterized by: (*i*) a subset $L_i \subseteq$ L of levels (all L_i)'s are disjoint; (*ii*) a rollup total order > L_i of level (L_i);
- M is a limited set of measures, each defined on a numerical attribute.

Example 1 Figure 1 illustrates an example of multidimensional schema related to RSS feeds. Indeed, our schema MS= (L, H, M) is composed of:

- L is the set of levels related to all hierarchies, i.e., Year is a level of the time hierarchy;
- H is the set of hierarchies dedicated to all considered dimensions, namely Time, Topic and Channel;
- M is our measure, *i.e.*, FeedsNB.

Definition 2 OLAP query fragment
Given a multidimensional schema MS = (L, H, M), a query fragment f is either a level in L, a measure in M, or a simple boolean predicate involving a level and/or a measure.

Example 2 In our working example, a representative example of a query fragment is FeedsNB.

Definition 3 OLAP query
An OLAP query is a collection of OLAP query fragments with at least one level for each hierarchy in H and at least one measure in M.

Example 3 In our working example, an example of OLAP query expressed in MDX language incorporating diverse fragments (i.e., fragment as a measure and fragment as a level) is

SELECT [measures].[FeedsNB] **ON COLUMNS**, [Category].[baccalaureate] **ON ROWS FROM** RSSFeeds;

5 Our approach

In this section, we present our innovative concepts. Then, we describe our new recommender system.

5.1 Active preference aggregation model

Definition 4 Active preference P_i
Given a multidimensional schema MS of an active data warehouse, an active preference P_i is a fragment of OLAP query.

Example 4 A typical example of an active preference is FeedsNB in our working example.

Definition 5 Cadency of active preference
Let P_i be an active preference; the cadency of P_i in the context C, denoted as C(P_i), is defined as the number of occurrence of P_i in C.

Example 5 Given a context containing the active preference P_1= FeedsNB in three OLAP queries, the cadency of C(P_1= FeedsNB) is 3.

Table 1 Comparison of multidimensional recommender systems

Context		Approach	Profiling						Recommendation			
			Source		User intervention		Formulation		Source		Strategy	
			Behavior	External sources	Automatic	Manual	Quantitative	Qualitative	Profile	External sources	Language	Method
Multidimensional	Passive	Jerbi et al. [16,17]	X			X		X	X			X
		Khemeri and bentayab [19]	X		X		X		X			X
		Giaco-metti et al. [8–10]	X		X		X		X			X
		Ben Ahmed et al. [4]	X		X			X	X			X
		Amo et Oliveira [2]	X	X	X							
		Aligon et al. [1]	X		X		X		X			X
	Active	Our proposal	X		X		X		X			X
Multidimensional	Passive	Jerbi et al. [16,17]		X		X						X
		Khemeri and bentayab [19]	X			X						X
		Giaco-metti et al. [8–10]		X			X					X
		Ben Ahmed et al. [4]	X			X	X				X	
		Amo et Oliveira [2]			X					X		
		Aligon et al. [1]	X					X				
	Active	Our proposal		X		X			X			

Definition 6 Multidimensional active profile model
Let u be a user and P_i be an active preference; the multidimensional active profile model is denoted as MAP (u), and it is equal to the set of active preferences:
MAP $(u) = \cup P_i$.

5.2 Two-layered active data warehouse: RSS feeds case study

As shown in Fig. 3, our active data warehouse architecture enriches the classical data warehouse architecture through an innovative extension which consists on a novel layer to handle the update process in our data warehouse. In this subsection, we first introduce the classical modeling of our multidimensional data warehouse dedicated to RSS feeds in our case of study. Then, we detail our extended layer for insuring update operations.

5.2.1 Layer of RSS feeds modeling

We propose to model the RSS feeds data as a multidimensional structure based on the STAR schema shown in Fig. 1. Indeed, the fact table RSS feeds includes the attribute FeedsNB that measures the number of RSS feeds. The latter can be analyzed from different perspectives, which are our dimensions. Thus, we introduce the Time dimension to report information about the date and the time when the RSS feed was delivered. Besides, the Topic dimension describes the topic of the RSS feed and its related category. Likewise, the Channel dimension depicts the metadata of the feed such as the item, the title and the associated URL. Moreover, hierarchies are used to aggregate the measure values. Therefore, we introduce a concept hierarchy for each dimension. For instance, Time [Day] Time [Month] Time [Year] is the hierarchy on the Time dimension, Topic [Name] Topic [Category] is the hierarchy on the Topic dimension, and Channel [Name] Channel [Item] is the hierarchy on the Channel dimension. Such aggregated hierarchies of dimensions can be used to sum up the measure values using operators like SUM, COUNT or AVG.

Aggregating measure values along the hierarchies of diverse dimensions (i.e., rollup) generates a multidimensional sight on data, which is recognized as data cube or cube. Deaggregating the measures of a cube to a lower dimension level (i.e., drilldown) provides a more detailed cube. Selecting the subset of a cubes cells that respect a given selection condition (i.e., slicing) also develops a more detailed cube. Such modeled layer must be maintained using our two-state update layer.

5.2.2 Two-state update layer

Regarding the update side, we introduce a two-state solution. Those states are the data warehouse positions during any maintenance operation. As soon as new data arises, the data warehouse mutates in the wait state where the alimentation of the new data is performed and any analysis operation is blocked in order to avoid any inconsistency in generated results. Once this maintenance is accomplished, the data warehouse moves to the signal state where analysis tasks

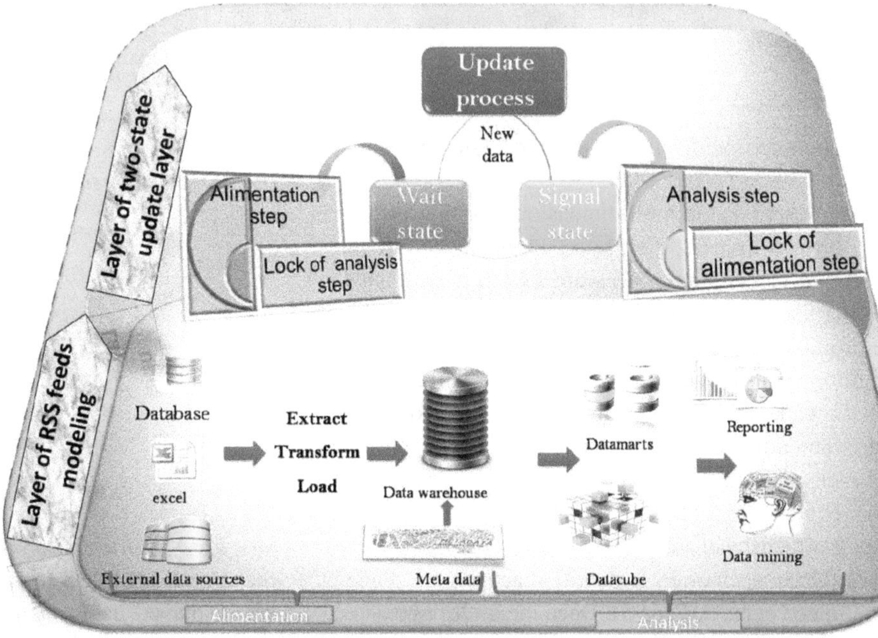

Fig. 3 Two-layered active data warehouse architecture

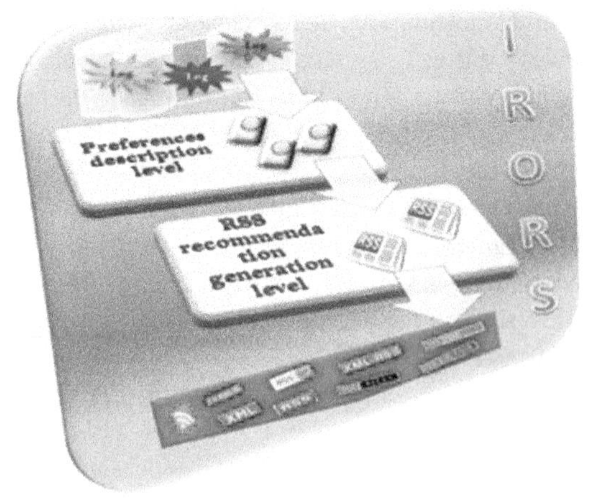

Fig. 4 IRORS architecture

can be performed at the moment that any update operation is blocked.

5.3 IRORS system architecture

Our new recommender system consists of two levels as shown in Fig. 4. The first level, known as multidimensional active profile model description level, handles the analyst preference modeling in our system. At the generation level, such modeled preferences are managed to draw appropriate RSS feeds recommendation using our new innovative strategy.

5.3.1 Multidimensional active profile model description

This level describes the multidimensional profile of active analyst through drawing his preferences. Indeed, all multidimensional active preferences are investigated from the OLAP log files and are used to draw the multidimensional active profile model of the decision maker. The key idea of our multidimensional active profile building is the computing of the cadency of each active preference. To do this, we introduce a new algorithm called ACTIF for automatic multidimensional active profile modeling. First, we scan the analysis context (Line 2), and we identify the category of each multidimensional active preference (Line 4). Then, we compute the cadency of each identified active preference in the scrutinized context (Line 5). Once the multidimensional active preferences Pi are collected in the multidimensional active profile MAP, the extracted profile is drawn (Line 8).

Algorithm 1 : ACTIF : multidimensional ACTIve proFile building algorithm
Input : Multidimensional schema MS, Analysis Context AC
Output : Multidimensional active profile MAP

```
1 Begin
2   Foreach query q in AC do
3       Foreach fragment f in q do
4           Identify the type of f
5           Pi → f
6           C(Pi) → C(Pi) +1
7           MAP → MAP U Pi
8   Return MAP
9 End
```

5.3.2 Generation of RSS recommendation level

At this level, based on identified multidimensional active preferences, our system generates the k candidate RSS recommendations. Finally, the display of generated recommendations is accomplished.

Extraction of RSS candidate recommendations Let X be an analyst who starts his query formulation. In addition, our algorithm ECAR takes as input the multidimensional active profile and the number of generated active recommendations k. First, ECAR captures the missing fragments on the current query MF (Line 4). For each missed fragment, it scans the multidimensional active preferences including in MAP (Line 5). When the type of the active preference corresponds to MF, it generates the current preference (Line 8). After that, it increments the flag variable A (Line 9). Such operation is stopped when our flag variable reaches the k parameter (Line 10).

Algorithm 2 : ECAR : ExtraCtion of Active Recommendation algorithm
Input : Multidimensional active profile MAP k number of generated active recommendations
Output : Set of active recommendation R

```
1  Begin
2      a← 0
3    Foreach query q do
4        MF ← Identify the type of missing fragment
5        Foreach Preference Pi in MAP do
6            Do
7                If Type(Pi)= MF then
8                    R← R U Pi
9                    a← a+1
10           Until (a=k)
11   Return R
12 End
```

Display of extracted RSS candidate recommendations After the extraction of RSS candidate recommendations, the results are displayed using matrix according to his requirements. Each cell of this matrix represents the related fact using the dedicated measure.

6 Experimental study

This section presents an experimental evaluation of the proposed system. First, we report our data description. Then, we discuss our experimental results.

6.1 Data description

All experiments have been performed on a system equipped with a 3-GHz CPU and 2 GB of main memory. In addition, they were conducted on real data warehouse built to support the analysis of RSS feeds. Undoubtedly, we collect 100 OLAP log files related to RSS feeds log files. Each log file contains 30 MDX queries. The whole size of analyzed files is about 3000 queries. For each query, we have identified the analyst preferences using his built profile.

In order to evaluate our proposal, we considered three quality measures broadly used, namely the recall, the precision and the F-measure [11,12]. We denote the number of recommended queries by card(R), the number of recommended significant queries by card(Rs) and the number of total significant recommended queries by card(RsT). Indeed, the precision describes the proportion of top results that are significant:

$$\text{Precision} = \frac{\text{Card}(Rs)}{\text{Card}(R)}. \tag{1}$$

However, the recall computes the proportion of all significant queries incorporated in the top results:

$$\text{Recall} = \frac{\text{Card}(RT)}{\text{Card}(RsT)}. \tag{2}$$

To assess the global accuracy, we apply the F-measure metric, computed as follows:

$$\text{F-Measure} = 2\frac{(\text{Precision} \times \text{recall})}{(\text{Precision} + \text{recall})}. \tag{3}$$

6.2 Results and discussion

This subsection describes the results of the experimental tests we performed. First, we report the scalability of our new recommender system. Then, to show the parameter sensitiveness and efficiency of the proposed system, we examine the correlation between the performance of IRORS and the cadency variation of multidimensional fragments. After that, we assess the pertinence of our IRORS system. Finally, the accuracy is discussed.

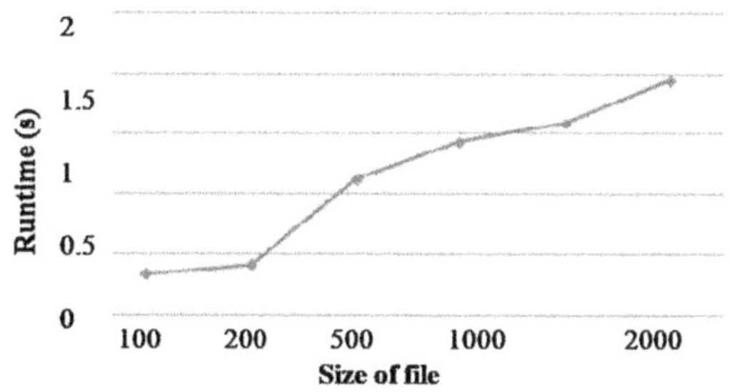

Fig. 5 Scalability of our IRORS system

6.2.1 Scalability analysis

In this subsection, we put the focus on the scalability of our system which describes the ability of our system to react facing the size variation of OLAP log files. To do so, we compare the runtime of our IRORS system versus the variation of OLAP log file size. The time of the recommendation increases regularly with the number of handled OLAP log queries. For example, if we handle 100 MDX queries, the required runtime of recommendations is 0.334 s. Regularly, an OLAP log file containing 300 queries needs 1.706 s in our recommendation process as depicted in Fig. 5. This can be explained by the increase in the size file engendering additional time for active profile building so that the recommendation process will exploit such a huge profile to generate active recommendations. Hence, more required time will be involved. These first results are intended to show the feasibility of our approach. They are encouraging as we do not observe notable changes in the recommender system runtime.

6.2.2 Performance analysis

To demonstrate the performance of our system, we scrutinized the impact of the cadencies variation. In fact, we have introduced randomly values of minimum confidence criteria denoted as MinC. Figure 6 sketches the statistics for the runtime obtained by IRORS versus the variation of the MinC values. In fact, we can point out that the MinC value influences the performance of our system, i.e., the runtime decreases as long as the MinC value increases. For example,

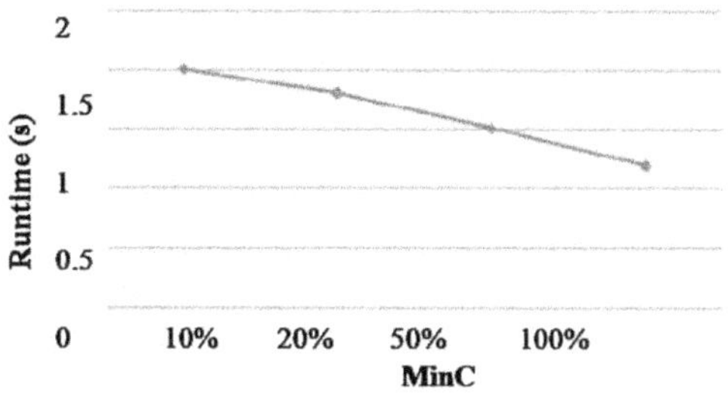

Fig. 6 Evaluation of IRORS performance

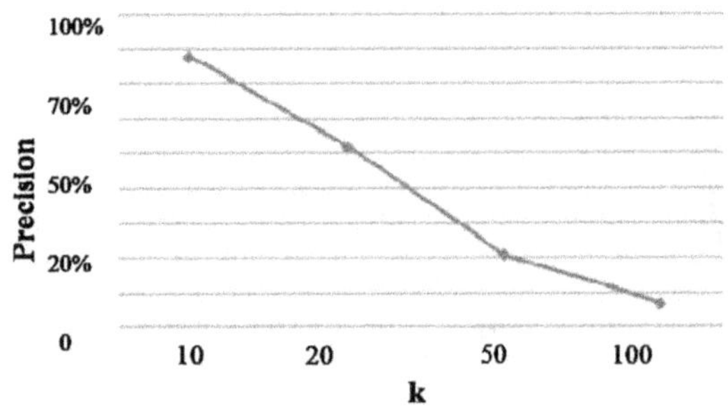

Fig. 7 Evaluation of the IRORS precision

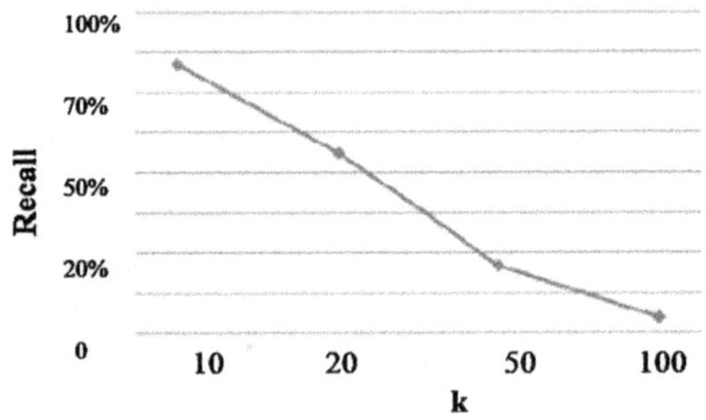

Fig. 8 Evaluation of the IRORS recall

a MinC value equal to 10 % engenders a runtime equal to 2 s. However, if we higher the MinC to 100 %, then we remark that the runtime decreases to 1.1 s. This can be explained by the fact that any rise of the MinC value leads to the vanishing of certain values, which became infrequent. This can hamper the performance of our recommender system.

6.2.3 Pertinence analysis

For each analyst, we extract k active recommendations dedicated to RSS feeds. We investigate the sensitiveness of this parameter on our IRORS system through varying its value from 5 to 100. Figure 7 shows the precision of our system according to the number of extracted recommendations.

In the resulting curve, presented in Fig. 7, we notice that the precision of our system gradually decreases when the number of generated RSS recommendations increases. This may be explained by the accuracy to recommend a restricted number of RSS recommendations.

Similarly, the recall, shown in Fig. 8, decreases when the number of suggested RSS feeds rises. It is important to mention that the recall deeply depends on the number of generated recommendations.

6.2.4 Accuracy analysis

The results in Fig. 9 show how the accuracy changes while the number of generated MDX query fragments k increases. When the number of candidate recommendations is 5, the

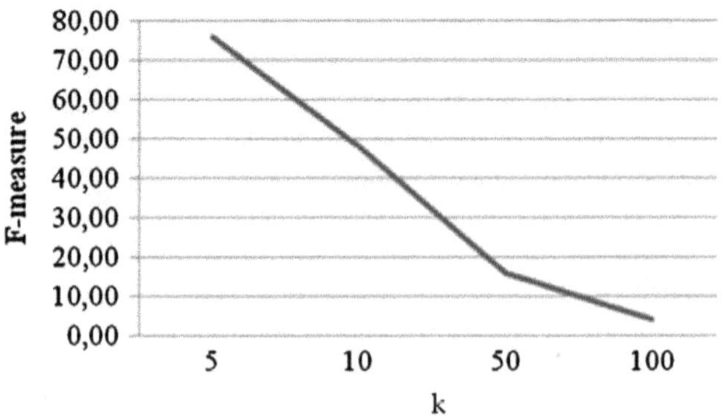

Fig. 9 Evaluation of IRORS accuracy

best overall F-measure is achieved, meaning that the curve for precision clearly shows that our recommender system is well capable of delivering good recommendations when the low number of generated recommendations is input.

7 Conclusion

In this paper, we proposed a new active data warehouse architecture involved by two dedicated layers. Based on this, a new recommender system to assist the OLAP analysis of RSS feeds is proposed. Such a proposal is managed by three-step process: (i) modeling of the active user profile from OLAP log files using our ACTIF algorithm; (ii) extraction of candidate recommendations from the identified active preferences using our new algorithm ECAR; and (iii) display of relevant RSS recommendations. To evaluate our approach, we conducted several experiments that have highlighted the performance of our recommender system.

As future work, we finally plan to: (1) evaluate the recommender system quality that determinates the recommendation reliability, and (2) integrate the uncertainty aspect to deal with our imperfect context.

References

1. Aligon, J., Gallinucci, E., Golfarelli, M., Marcel, P., Rizzi, S.: A collaborative ltering approach for recommending OLAP sessions. Decis. Support Syst. **69**, 20–30 (2015)
2. Amo, S., Oliveira, C.G.: Towards a Tunable Framework for Recommendation Systems Based on Pairwise Preference Mining Algorithms, 27th Canadian Conference on Artificial Intelligence, Canadian AI 2014, Montral, QC, Canada (2014)
3. Ben, Ahmed E., Nabli, A., Gargouri, F.: A survey of user-centric data warehouses: from personalization to recommendation. Int. J. Database Manag. Syst. **3**(2), 59–71 (2011)
4. Ben Ahmed, E., Tebourski, W., Ben Abdesselam, W., Gargouri, F.: SMART: semantic multidimensionAl gRroup recommendations. Multimed. Tools Appl. **74**(23), 10419–10437 (2014)
5. Burke, R.: Hybrid recommender systems : survey and experiments. User Model. User-Adap. Inter. **12**(4), 331–370 (2002)

6. Creus, J., Amann, B., Travers, N., Vodislav, D.: RoSeS: a continuous content-based query engine for RSS feeds. In: Proceedings of 21th International Conference on Database and Expert Systems Applications DEXA11, LNCS, Toulouse, pp. 203–218 (2011)
7. Creus, J., Amann, B., Travers, N., Vodislav, D.: Un agrgateur de ux rss avanc, 26 me Journes Bases de Donnes Avances (2010)
8. Giacometti, A., Marcel, P., Negre, E., Soulet, A.: Query recommendations for OLAP discovery-driven analysis. Int. J. Data Warehouse. Min. **7**(2), 1–25 (2011)
9. Giacometti, A., Marcel, P., Negre, E., Soulet, A. : Query recommendations for OLAP discovery-driven analysis. In: International Workshop on Data Warehousing and OLAP (DOLAP), pp. 81–88 (2009)
10. Giacometti, A., Marcel, P., Negre, E. : Recommending multidimensional queries. In: International Conference on Data Warehousing and Knowledge Discovery (DaWaK), pp. 453–466 (2009)
11. Golfarelli, M.: From user requirements to conceptual design in data warehouse design—a survey. Data Warehous. Design Adv. Eng. Appl. Methods Complex Constr. **23**(1), 1–16 (2008)
12. Gunawardana, A., Shani, G.: A survey of accuracy evaluation metrics of recommendation tasks. J. Mach. Learn. Res. **10**, 2935–2962 (2009)
13. Ge, M., Delgado-Battenfeld, C., Jannach, D.: Beyond accuracy: evaluating recommender systems by coverage and serendipity, pp. 257–260. Barcelona, Spain, Proc. RecSys (2010)
14. Han, J., Kamber, M., Pei, J.: Data Mining: Concepts and Techniques, Series in Data Management Systems. Morgan Kaufmann Publishers, Burlington(2011)
15. Inmon, W.B.: Building the Data Warehouse, 4th edn. Wiley, New Delhi, India (2005)
16. Jerbi, H., Ravat, F., Teste, O., Zuruh, G.: Applying Recommendation Technology in OLAP Systems. In: ICEIS Conference Proceedings, pp. 220–233 (2009)
17. Jerbi, H., Ravat, F., Teste, O., Zuruh, G.: Preference-based recommendations for OLAP analysis. In: DaWaK Conference Proceedings, pp. 467–478 (2009)
18. Karakasidis, A., Vassiliadis, P., Pitoura, E.: ETL Queues for Active Data Warehousing. In: IQIS05: Proceedings of the 2nd International Workshop on Information Quality in Information Systems. ACM Press, New York, NY, pp. 28–39(2005)
19. Khemiri, R., Bentayeb, F.: Interactive query recommendation assistant. In: The 23rd International Workshop on Database and Expert Systems Applications (DEXA), pp. 93–97 (2012)
20. Lops, P., de Gemmis, M., Semeraro, G.: Content-based recommender systems: state of the art and trends. In: Ricci, F., Rokach, L., Shapira, B., Kantor, P.B. (eds.) Recommender Systems Handbook pp. 73–105. Springer, USA (2011)
21. Mohania, M., Nambiar, U., Schrefl, M., Vincent, M.: Active and Real-Time Data Warehousing. Encyclopedia of Database Systems. Springer, USA (2009)
22. Su, X., Khoshgoftaar, T.M.: A survey of collaborative ltering techniques. Adv. Artif. Intell. **2009**, 421425 (2009)
23. Thalhammer, T., Schre, M., Mohania, M.K.: Active data warehouses: complementing OLAP with analysis rules. Data Knowl. Eng. **39**(3), 241–269 (2001)
24. Tho, M.N., Tjoa, A.M.: Zero-latency data warehousing for heterogeneous data sources and continuous data streams. Services Computing, pp. 357–365 (2004)
25. Travers, N., Hmedeh, Z., Vouzoukidou, N., Mouza, C., Christophide, C., Scholl, M.: RSS feeds behavior analysis, structure and vocabulary. Int. J. Web Inf. Syst. **10**(3), 291–320 (2014)

14

Algorithm of computing verbal relationships for generating Vietnamese paragraph of summarization from the logical expression of discourse representation structure

Trung Tran[1] · **Dang Tuan Nguyen**[1]

Abstract This paper presents an important phase of our new approach for summarizing the given Vietnamese paragraph. The central of this phase is an algorithm for computing verbal relationships in the process of generating the Vietnamese paragraph from the logical expression of discourse representation structure (DRS), which is the first-order logic expressions without explicit quantifiers, and represents the meaning as well as reflects the potential contexts of a given discourse or a sequence of sentences. By defining elements to describe the appropriate information in each predicate of the logical expression (or can be called "DRS-conditions"), the algorithm is based on in turn considering three consecutive predicates in a logical expression for determining: the relationship between the first and second sentence, the relationship between the second and third sentence, and the priority when comparing these two relationships. The evaluation achieves two given criteria: the semantic completeness of summarization, and the natural quality of new reduced paragraph.

Keywords Logical expression · Discourse representation structure · Sentence generation · Predicate relationship

1 Introduction

In general, the study of transforming a given paragraph to a new summary (Das and Martins [7], Lloret [20], Mani and Mayburi [21], Jezek and Steinberger [13], Jones [14,15]) has to answer three important questions (Jones [14,15]): (i) how to represent the meaning of the source paragraph; (ii) how to construct a computing representation form of the destination paragraph by transforming the source computing representation form; (iii) how to transform the destination computing representation form into the complete paragraph. These lead to two main approach directions: (i) extract some sentences which have highest benchmarks to produce the summary—this direction is called "extraction"; (ii) construct a summary based on understanding the meaning of the source paragraph—this direction is called "abstraction".

Follow the idea of "abstraction", this paper addresses an important problem in our new approach for summarizing the given Vietnamese paragraph having more than two simple sentences: generate the new reduced Vietnamese paragraph from the logical expression of discourse representation structure (DRS) (Kamp [16], Covington and Schmitz [5], Covington et al. [6], Blackburn and Bos [1])—under the form of expressions without explicit quantifiers in first-order logic (FOL). To limit the scope of this article, we assume that there were the methods for mapping the original paragraphs to the logical expressions encodings of their meanings (Zettlemoyer and Collins [34,35]). Using the logical expression representing the semantic of the paragraph, our objective is to propose a solution for transforming this logical expression into a new reduced complete Vietnamese paragraph.

As an example, consider the following original Vietnamese paragraph consisting of four simple sentences:

Example 1 *"Lan vui vẻ. Cô học cùng con trai. Nó khoái chí. Nó được điểm cao."*

✉ Trung Tran
ttrung@nlke-group.net

Dang Tuan Nguyen
dangnt@uit.edu.vn

1 Faculty of Computer Science, University of Information Technology, VNU-HCM, Ho Chi Minh City, Vietnam

(English: "Lan is happy. She studies with son. He is overjoyed. He takes high mark.")

The logical expression representing the semantic of paragraph in Example 1 is illustrated in two forms:

- DRS form:

```
[x,y,z]
------------------
lan (x)
vui_vẻ (x)
con_trai (y)
học_cùng (x,y)
khoái_chí (y)
điểm_cao (z)
đư'ợ'c (y,z)
```

- FOL form:

`∃x∃y∃z[lan(x) & vui_vẻ (x) &con_trai (y) & học_cùng (x,y) &khoái_chí (y) &điểm_cao (z) & được (y,z)].`

With this logical expression, we transform into the new reduced Vietnamese paragraph as follows:

"Lan vui vẻ vì học cùng con trai. Con trai khoái chí vì được điểm cao."

(English: "Lan is happy because of studying with son. The son is overjoyed because of taking high mark.")

In the logical expression, in which two representation forms are equivalent, the DRS form represents the meaning as well as reflects the context change potential of the given discourse. The FOL form is used for expressing the semantic for DRS form. In the above case, the logical expression represents:

- Instances "lan", "con trai" (the son) and "điểm cao" (high mark) by predicates which associated with variables `x, y` and `z: lan (x), con_trai (y), điểm_cao (z)`.
- Actions and states of these instances through predicates which associated with variables `x, y, z` appropriately: `vui_vẻ (x), học_cùng (x,y), khoái_chí (y), đư'ợ'c (y,z)`.

The considered objects in this research are complete logical expressions encoding the semantics of Vietnamese paragraphs.

The heart of the proposed solution is an algorithm that auto generates the new reduced Vietnamese paragraph from the logical expression. With the given requirement that the generated paragraph has to satisfy the universality in common Vietnamese communication, our algorithm in turn considers three consecutive predicates representing actions and states of instances. The algorithm compares two predicate pairs `[predicate (1), predicate (2)]` and `[predicate (2), predicate (3)]` in considered three predicates based on the sustainable priority factor which proposed by us. The pair having the higher priority will be used for generating the syntactic structure of a new Vietnamese sentence, then combined with lexicons for completing. The remaining predicate is handled in two ways: re-create the original Vietnamese sentence or combine consideration with next two predicates in the logical expression. The algorithm is performed based on our assumption that a paragraph has the natural quality if each sentence in this has the natural quality.

To evaluate the effectiveness of the generating solution in this study, we establish two criteria: (i) the first criteria is the semantic completeness—in the sense of the generated paragraph has the content which correctly summarizes the meaning of the source paragraph; (ii) the second criteria is the natural quality—in the sense of each sentence in the generated paragraph has the native form of Vietnamese usage.

The organization of this paper is as follows. Section 2 provides a literature review of abstraction summarization direction. Section 3 presents an overview of our works with the new approach based on abstraction direction. The main content in Sect. 4 is about the heart of our solution which is the algorithm of computing verbal relationships for generating the new reduced Vietnamese paragraph. Next, in Sect. 5, we describe the experiment and indicate some analysis according to the results. Finally, Sect. 6 concludes this paper and presents future research directions.

2 Abstraction summarization literature review

Generally, the methods in abstraction direction can be classified into two categories (Kasture et al. [17], Khan and Salim [18], Saranyamol and Sindhu [25]): (i) structured based in which the researcher tried to determine the most important content using some structures such as tree, template, ontology, …; (ii) semantic based in which the authors introduced some methods in natural language generation (NLG) to make the semantic representation.

2.1 Structured-based approach

2.1.1 Tree-based method

Researchers following this method illustrated the content of given document using a dependency tree. This method is often applied for summarizing multi-documents.

Barzilay et al. [2] proposed a solution in which firstly they preprocessed the similar sentences in some news articles. Then, a theme intersection algorithm had been used for determining the common phrases which will be transferred to FUF/SURGE language generator so that the new summary sentences were created. Although using a language generator help for reducing repetitions and increasing fluency, there was lacking in the context in which similar sentences in different document appeared while determining the intersected phrase.

In another research, Barzilay and McKeown [3] worked on sentence fusion by integrating information in overlapping sentences. Firstly, they analyzed the sentences and illustrated by the dependency trees. They determined the centroid of these trees to build a main tree and then augmented with the sub-trees of other sentences. The main drawback of this approach is that a complete model to present the abstract representation of selected content was not proposed.

2.1.2 Template-based method

In this approach, the researcher built a template which is text snippets to represent the given documents and generate the summary. They applied rules in an Information Extraction system (Harabagiu and Lacatusu [12]) to extract information from multiple documents. This information was used to fill the template and then generate coherent, informative multi-document summaries. The limitation of this approach is that it requires the summary sentences that are already present in the source documents and cannot identify the similar and different information across multiple documents.

2.1.3 Ontology-based method

Applying ontology, especially fuzzy ontology, to improve the process of summarization is one of the most interesting method. This helps for handling the uncertain data and well summarizing documents on websites which have own knowledge structure. However, because the domain experts had to make a lot of effort to define dictionary and news corpus, up to now, this approach is limited to Chinese news (Lee et al. [19]).

2.1.4 Lead and body phrase method

Studies in this approach focused on rewriting the lead sentence using inserting and substituting phrases in the lead and body sentences which have same syntactic head chunk. Tanaka et al. [26] proposed a method following this approach in broadcast news. They determined the maximum phrases of each same chunk in the lead and body sentences. The substitution and insertion operations were applied to these phrase in order to revise the lead sentence. By using this method, they could find the semantically appropriate revisions. However, similar to other structure-based methods, it is the lack of a complete model.

2.1.5 Rule-based method

Genest and Lapalme [8] presented a method with three main modules: (i) information extraction determined several candidate rules for each aspect of verbs and nouns; (ii) content selection selected the best rule for each aspect; (iii) summary generation formed the output text using generation patterns. With this method, the researchers created summaries with greater information. On the other hand, they had to make a lot of effort to manually write all the rules and patterns.

2.2 Semantic-based approach

2.2.1 Multimodal semantic model

A framework was proposed by Greenbacker [10] for generating abstractive summary with three main steps: (i) they used ontology to build a semantic model representing the contents of multimodal documents; (ii) the metric rated the concepts in ontology with several factors such as the completeness of attributes, the number of relationships with other concepts, ...; (iii) the generator built the summary with the most important concepts. The idea of producing the abstract summary is the most important distribution of this framework, because it includes salient textual and graphical content. One point that needs to be deeply researched is that the evaluation for this framework is manually handled by human.

2.2.2 Information item-based method

Another research in multi-document abstraction summarization worked by Genest and Lapalme [9] focuses on generating the summary from the abstract representation of original documents called information item. They introduced a framework for summarizing with main modules: (i) information item retrieval module parsed source text and extracted subjects of verb and objects; (ii) sentence generation module creates a new sentence; (iii) sentence selection module evaluated the generated sentences generated with appropriate score; (iv) summary generation module combined highly scored generated sentences with information about dates and location to construct the whole summary.

Although the summary is short, coherent, information rich and less redundant, there are some limitations in this method: some information items which are difficult for creating meaningful and grammatical sentences can be eliminated; in information item retrieval module, if the parser could not parse correctly the syntactic tree, then the linguistic quality of summaries is low.

2.2.3 Semantic graph-based method

Moawad and Aref [22] constructed a semantic graph called rich semantic graph to represent the semantic of source document. This graph was then reduced using some heuristic rules and transformed to the abstractive summary. The output summary of this method could be concise, coherent and less redundant. However, this method lacked of knowledge about linguistic theories, then the summary may be not grammatically and naturally correct in applied languages.

3 Overview of paragraph summarization by generating reduced paragraph

Follow the idea of "abstraction" but with the approach which is to combine the knowledge and techniques in text understanding and representing, text generation (Reiter and Dale [23,24]) as well as functional grammar linguistic theory (Cao [4], Halliday and Matthiessen [11]), we proposed in [30] a specification model called Verbal Relationship-based Computational Model (VRBCM) to formalize the main idea of our summarization solution. This model consists of four main components: The first three sets help for specifying understanding the meaning of the original paragraph—set of lexical information representations, set of inner relationships of each sentence, set of inter-sentential relationships between each pair of consecutive sentences; the last set helps for specifying generating the new paragraph—this set contains syntactic structures of sentences of the summary. The foundation of this model is the hypotheses about four types of inter-sentential relationships between each pair of consecutive sentences in the original paragraph: objective, cause, consequence, concurrence.

Implementing and applying model VRBCM, focusing on the phase of transforming the source representation form to summary, we based on considering objective and consequence inter-relationships between two sentences to propose in [27–29,33] methods and techniques to summarize some pair types of Vietnamese sentences having suitable characteristics.

At the phase of understanding the meaning of the source pair of Vietnamese sentences, we proposed in [31,32] strategies for resolving the ambiguity when considering inter-anaphoric pronouns appearing in some pair types of Vietnamese sentences having special characteristics.

4 Generation of summarizing paragraphs

In this section, we present the heart of our solution which is the algorithm of computing verbal relationships for generating the new reduced Vietnamese paragraph. The input of the algorithm is predicates representing actions or states in the logical expression. The main idea of the algorithm is to consider, in turn, three consecutive predicates, determine the pair of predicates having the higher relationship priority and generate the syntactic structure of the new Vietnamese sentence based on the relationship of this pair. Thus, at a high level, the algorithm will involve the following three sub-problems:

- Determine predicates representing actions or states.
- Generate the syntactic structure of the new Vietnamese sentence based on the relationship of one pair of predicates.
- Determine the relationship priority in comparison between two pairs of predicates.

In the remainder of this section, we describe an overall strategy for these three problems. Section 4.1 presents the characteristic structure of one predicate which is defined for this research and the algorithm for selecting predicates representing actions or states. In Sect. 4.2, we synthesize relationship types between two predicates representing actions or states based on considering the characteristic structure. Also in this section, corresponding to each relationship type, we present constructing the syntactic structure of the new Vietnamese sentence. Finally, in Sect. 4.3, we present handling the third problem and describe in general the algorithm for generating the new Vietnamese paragraph.

4.1 Predicate characteristic structure

In this research, we limit the consideration of action or state sentences. The verbs indicating actions or states belong to one of the four categories with meanings (based on the categorization in theory functional grammar [4,11]):

- The first category is called action "intransitive". The verbs belonging to this category indicate an action which associates to only one actor.
- The second category is called action "transitive". The verbs belonging to this category indicate an action which associates to one actor and one goal.
- The third category is called state "status". The verbs belonging to this category indicate existing temporary status of a subject.
- The forth category is called state "property". The verbs belonging to this category indicate a property inside a subject.

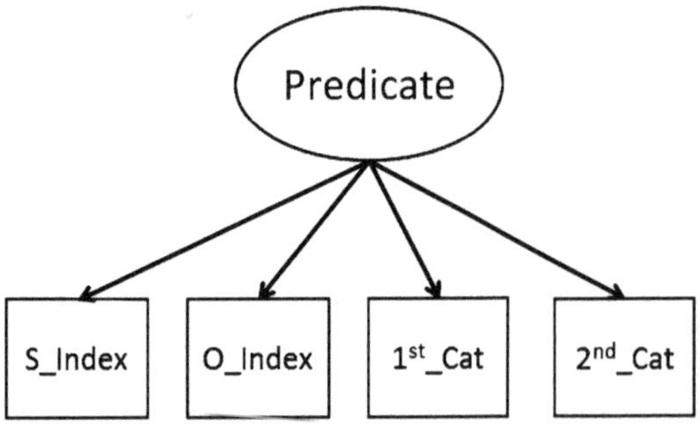

Fig. 1 The characteristic structure of a predicate in the logical expression

Based on the above categorization, we define the characteristic structure of a predicate in the logical expression composing components in Fig. 1:

In this structure, each component takes value as follows:

- Component `S_Index` taking the value as an index (represented by one bound variable) indicates the instance taking the subject role.
- Component `O_Index` taking the value as an index (represented by one bound variable) indicates the instance taking the object role.
- Component `1st_Cat` taking the value as an index (represented by one bound variable) indicates the category at the first level: object/action/state.
- Component `2nd_Cat` taking the value as an index (represented by one bound variable) indicates the category at the second level: proper/common/intransitive/transitive/status/property.

As an example, consider the logical expression in Sect. 1. The predicates in this expression have the characteristic structure with components taking values as follows:

lan	:={S_Index → x; O_Index; 1st_Cat → object; 2nd_Cat → proper}
vui_vẻ	:={S_Index → x; O_Index; 1st_Cat → state; 2nd_Cat → status}
con_trai	:={S_Index → y; O_Index; 1st_Cat → object; 2nd_Cat → common}
học_cùng	:={S_Index → x; O_Index → y; 1st_Cat → action; 2nd_Cat → transitive}
khoái_chí	:={S_Index → y; O_Index; 1^{st}_Cat → state; 2nd_Cat → status}
điểm_cao	:={S_Index → z; O_Index; 1st_Cat → object; 2nd_Cat → common}
được	:={S_Index → y; O_Index → z; 1st_Cat → action; 2nd_Cat → transitive}

We classify into two lists: `O_List` consists of predicates representing instances, `AS_List` consists of predicates representing actions or states. The main idea of this classification is based on the value of component `1st_Cat` in each predicate. The classification algorithm:

Algorithm 1: Classify predicates representing instances and predicates representing actions or states.

Input: `P_List` = List of predicates in the logical expression.
Output: `O_List` = List of predicate representing instances; `AS_List` = List of predicates representing actions or states.

```
n = |P_List|;
For i = 1 to n Do
   If 1st_Cat(predicate(i)) == "object"
Then
      Put predicate(i) into O_List;
   Else Then
      Put predicate(i) into AS_List;
   End If
End For
```

Apply Algorithm 1 for predicates in the logical expression in Fig. 1, we obtain the result with two lists `O_List` and `AS_List`:

- `O_List: lan, con_trai, điểm_cao.`
- `AS_List: vui_vẻ, học_cùng, khoái_chí, được.`

4.2 Predicate relationships and sentence structure generation

The main content of this section is to present establishing the assumption about relationship types between two predicates representing actions or states. Therefrom, we present generated syntactic structures of new Vietnamese sentences suitable for each relationship type. The main idea for implementing is based on the verbal categorization in Sect. 4.1.

An important requirement in this study is that the generated paragraph has to satisfy the universality in common Vietnamese communication. We accept that in order to meet this requirement, each generated Vietnamese sentence has to satisfy the universality. Generating the new sentence having this characteristic needs to be based on considering relationships in a certain context between two original sentences. In this research, our solution is to establish an order priority for considering predicates representing actions or states. Therefrom, we propose relationship types between pairs of predicates which represent relationships between original pairs of sentences.

According to categorizing verbs indicating actions or states in Sect. 4.1, we assume a considering order priority. The basis for establishing the assumption is based on the sustainable level in the context: if the sustainable level is longer, then the considering priority is lower. Concretely, the order priority of each verbal category is as follows:

- Verbs indicating state status take the highest considering priority is (1).
- Next, verbs indicating action intransitive and action transitive in turn take the considering priority are (2) and (3).
- Lastly, verbs indicating state property take the lowest considering priority is (4).

Consider each pair of predicates representing actions or states (Pas_i–Pas_j), there are four relationship types when comparing the priority of Pas_i and Pas_j:

(i) Pas_i having priority (2) is performed so that can perform Pas_j having priority (2) or (3);
(ii) Pas_j having the lower priority takes the role as a cause of Pas_i;
(iii) Pas_j having the higher priority takes the role as consequence of Pas_i;
(iv) Pas_i and Pas_j occur simultaneously if have the equal priority.

In Table 1, we synthesize all cases of these four relationship types:

We generate the syntactic structure of the new reduced Vietnamese sentence for each pair of predicates representing actions or states (Pas_i–Pas_j) based on each relationship type in Table 1. The main idea for implementing consists of the following main steps:

- *Step 1* In turn determine predicates representing instances which have the relationship with each predicate Pas_i and Pas_j. The relationship here is understood that component `S_Index` in the predicate indicating instance takes the value which is identical with the value of component `S_Index` or `O_Index` of Pas_i or Pas_j. Therefrom, construct two syntactic structures according to Pas_i and Pas_j. Each this syntactic structure is the structure of one sentence in the source paragraph and belongs to one of two form:
  - *Case 1* Component `2nd_Cat` of predicate representing action or state Pas takes value "transitive". There are two predicates representing instance which are Po1(x) and Po2(y) which have the relationship with Pas. The structure form is:

    `Form_1 := Po1(x) + Pas(x, y) + Po2(y)`

  - *Case 2* Component `2nd_Cat` of predicate representing action or state Pas takes other values. There is one predicate representing instance which is Po1(x) which have the relationship with Pas. The structure form is:

    `Form_2 := Po1(x) + Pas(x, y).`

- *Step 2* Merge two syntactic structures according to Pas_i and Pas_j to construct the syntactic structure of the new reduced Vietnamese sentence. The merging rule consists of the following steps:
  - *Step 2.1* Add elements in the syntactic structure according to Pas_i into the new structure.
  - *Step 2.2* Add the relationship factor belonging to one of relationship types in Table 1 into the new structure.
  - *Step 2.3* Determine the context is active or passive voice for the syntactic structure according to Pas_j.
  - *Step 2.4* Add elements in the syntactic structure according to Pas_j into the new structure.

Table 1 Classify relationship types for each pair of predicates

Type	Meaning	Priority of Pas_i	Priority of Pas_j
i	Pas_i is performed so that can perform Pas_j	(2)	(2)
		(2)	(3)
ii	Pas_j is the cause of Pas_i	(1)	(4)
		(1)	(2)
		(1)	(3)
		(2)	(4)
		(3)	(4)
iii	Pas_j is the consequence of Pas_i	(4)	(1)
		(4)	(2)
		(4)	(3)
		(2)	(1)
		(3)	(1)
		(3)	(2)
iv	Pas_i and Pas_j occur simultaneously	(4)	(4)
		(1)	(1)
		(3)	(3)

Table 2 The syntactic structure of the new reduced Vietnamese sentence according to relationship type ⟨i⟩

Priority of Pas$_i$	Priority of Pas$_j$	Syntactic structure
(2)	(2)	[Po1] + [Pas$_i$] + ⟨i⟩ + [Pas$_j$]
(2)	(3)	[Po1] + [Pas$_i$] + ⟨i⟩ + [Pas$_j$] + [Po2]
		[Po1] + [Pas$_i$] + ⟨i⟩ + "is"[Pas$_j$] + "by" + [Po2]

Table 3 The syntactic structure of the new reduced Vietnamese sentence according to relationship type ⟨iii⟩

Priority of Pas$_i$	Priority of Pas$_j$	Syntactic structure
(4)	(1)	[Po1] + [Pas$_i$] + ⟨iii⟩ + [Pas$_j$]
(4)	(2)	[Po1] + [Pas$_i$] + ⟨iii⟩ + [Pas$_j$]
(4)	(3)	[Po1] + [Pas$_i$] + ⟨iii⟩ + [Pas$_j$] + [Po2]
		[Po1] + [Pas$_i$] + ⟨iii⟩ + "is" + [Pas$_j$] + "by" + [Po2]
(2)	(1)	[Po1] + [Pas$_i$] + ⟨iii⟩ + [Pas$_j$]
(3)	(1)	[Po1] + [Pas$_i$] + [Po2] + ⟨iii⟩ + [Pas$_j$]
		[Po1] + [Pas$_i$] + [Po2] + ⟨iii⟩ + [Po2] + [Pas$_j$]
(3)	(2)	[Po1] + [Pas$_i$] + [Po2] + ⟨iii⟩ + [Pas$_j$]
		[Po1] + [Pas$_i$] + [Po2] + ⟨iii⟩ + [Po2] + [Pas$_j$]

Perform step 1 and step 2, we synthesize syntactic structure forms of new Vietnamese sentences according to each relationship type in Table 1:

- Relationship type ⟨i⟩ (Table 2)
- Relationship type ⟨ii⟩ (Table 8)
- Relationship type ⟨iii⟩ (Table 3)
- Relationship type ⟨iv⟩ (Table 4).

4.3 The Vietnamese paragraph generation algorithm

The algorithm for generating the new reduced Vietnamese paragraph takes the input as two lists: `AS_List` contains predicates representing actions or states and `O_List` contains predicates representing instances (described in Sect. 4.1). The output of the algorithm is an ordered list `S_StructureList` containing syntactic structures of sentences in the new paragraph.

At all stages, the algorithm considers three consecutive predicates ($\text{Pas}_{i-1}, \text{Pas}_i, \text{Pas}_{i+1}$) in `AS_List`. The algorithm compares the priority between two pairs ($\text{Pas}_{i-1} - \text{Pas}_i$) and ($\text{Pas}_i$–$\text{Pas}_{i+1}$) and generates the syntactic structure of the new Vietnamese sentence for the pair having higher priority. With the remaining predicate, the algorithm performs one of two ways: (i) construct the syntactic structure according to this predicate—is the structure of one sentence in the original paragraph; or (ii) consider this predicate with two next predicates in `AS_List`.

Based on classifying relationship types in Table 1, we determine priority cases between two pairs (Pas_{i-1}–Pas_i) and (Pas_i–Pas_{i+1}) as follows [in which $(X), (Y), (Z)$, respectively, indicate the priority of $\text{Pas}_{i-1}, \text{Pas}_i, \text{Pas}_{i+1}$]:

- The priority of (Pas_{i-1}–Pas_i) is higher than the priority of (Pas_i–Pas_{i+1}) (Table 5)
- Two priorities are equal (Table 7)

Table 4 The syntactic structure of the new reduced Vietnamese sentence according to relationship type ⟨iv⟩

Priority of Pas$_i$	Priority of Pas$_j$	Syntactic structure
(4)	(4)	[Po1] + [Pas$_i$] + ⟨iv⟩ + [Pas$_j$]
(1)	(1)	[Po1] + [Pas$_i$] + ⟨iv⟩ + [Pas$_j$]
(3)	(3)	[Po1] + [Pas$_i$] + [Po2] + ⟨iv⟩ + [Pas$_j$] + [Po3]
		[Po1] + [Pas$_i$] + [Po2] + ⟨iv⟩ + "is" + [Pas$_j$] + "by" + [Po3]
		[Po1] + [Pas$_i$] + [Po2] + ⟨iv⟩ + [Po2] + [Pas$_j$] + [Po3]
		[Po1] + [Pas$_i$] + [Po2] + ⟨iv⟩ + [Po2] + "is" + [Pas$_j$] + "by" + [Po3]
		[Po1] + [Pas$_i$] + ⟨iv⟩ + [Pas$_j$] + [Po2]
		[Po1] + [Pas$_i$] + ⟨iv⟩ + "is" + [Pas$_j$] + "by" + [Po2]

Table 5 The priority of (Pas_{i-1}–Pas_i) is higher than the priority of (Pas_i–Pas_{i+1})

Case	Priority of Pas_{i-1}	Priority of Pas_i	Priority of Pas_{i+1}
1	$(X) = (1)$	(Y)	$(Z) > (X)$
2	$(X) = (2)$	(Y)	$(Z) > (X)$
3	$(X) = (3)$	(Y)	$(Z) > (X)$

Table 6 The priority of (Pas_{i-1}–Pas_i) is lower than the priority of (Pas_i–Pas_{i+1})

Case	Priority of Pas_{i-1}	Priority of Pas_i	Priority of Pas_{i+1}
1	$(X) = (4)$	(Y)	$(Z) < (X)$
2	$(X) = (3)$	(Y)	$(Z) < (X)$
3	$(X) = (2)$	(Y)	$(Z) < (X)$

- The priority of (Pas_{i-1}–Pas_i) is lower than the priority of (Pas_i–Pas_{i+1}) (Table 6).

The algorithm for generating `S_StructureList` concretely as follows:

- Component `S_Index` in P_x takes the value which is identical with the value of component `S_Index` in P_y.
- Component `S_Index` in P_x takes the value which is identical with the value of component `O_Index` in P_y.

Algorithm 2: Generate `S_StructureList`.

Input: `O_List` = List of predicates representing instances; `AS_List` = List of predicates representing actions or states.
Output: `S_StructureList` = List of syntactic structures of sentences in the new paragraph.

```
i = 2; n = |AS_List|;
While i < n Do
  Consider Pi-1, Pi, Pi+1 ∈ AS_List;
  C_IAP_1 = check_inter-sentential_anaphoric_pronoun(Pi-1, Pi);
  C_IAP_2 = check_inter-sentential_anaphoric_pronoun(Pi, Pi+1);
  If ((C_IAP_1 == TRUE) and (C_IAP_2 == TRUE)) Then
    If (level_priority(Pi-1, Pi) >= level_priority(Pi, Pi+1)) Then
      new_structure = summarize(Pi, Pi+1);
      Put new_structure into S_StructureList;
      i = i + 2;
    Else
      new_structure = re_create(Pi-1);
      Put new_structure into S_StructureList;
      i = i + 1;
    End
  Else If (C_IAP_1 == TRUE) Then
    new_structure = summarize(Pi, Pi+1);
    Put new_structure into S_StructureList;
    i = i + 2;
  Else If (C_IAP_2 == TRUE) Then
    new_structure = re_create(Pi-1);
    Put new_structure into S_StructureList;
    i = i + 1;
  Else
    new_structure = re_create(Pi-1);
    Put new_structure into S_StructureList;
    new_structure = re_create(Pi);
    Put new_structure into S_StructureList;
    i = i + 2;
  End If
End While
If (i == n+1) Then
  new_structure = re_create(Pi-1);
  Put new_structure into S_StructureList;
Else If (i == n) Then
  C_IAP = check_inter-sentential_anaphoric_pronoun(Pi-1, Pi);
  If (C_IAP == TRUE) Then
    new_structure = summarize(Pi-1, Pi);
    Put new_structure into S_StructureList;
  Else
    new_structure = re_create(Pi-1);
    Put new_structure into S_StructureList;
    new_structure = re_create(Pi);
    Put new_structure into S_StructureList;
  End If
End If
```

In Algorithm 2, there are three important functions:

- Function `check_inter − sentential_anaphoric_pronoun`(P_x, P_y) is performed to examine the inter-sentential anaphoric pronoun relationship between two sentences. This function returns TRUE if there is one in four cases:
- Component `O_Index` in P_x takes the value which is identical with the value of component `S_Index` in P_y.
- Component `O_Index` in P_x takes the value which is identical with the value of component `O_Index` in P_y.

- Function `summarize(Px, Py)` generates the syntactic structure of the new Vietnamese sentence for pair of predicates P_x, P_y.
- Function `re_create(Px)` constructs the syntactic structure according to predicate P_x.

To complete the new reduced Vietnamese paragraph, we replace syntactic structures by appropriate lexicon set with the following general algorithm:

Algorithm 3: Complete the new Vietnamese paragraph.
Input: `S_StructureList` = List of syntactic structures of sentences in the new paragraph.
Output: The complete new Vietnamese paragraph.

```
For structure(i) in S_StructureList Do
   For element(j) in structure(i) Do
      If element(j) is predicate Then
         Replace element(j) by its
represented lexicon;
      Else If element(j) is relationship
type Then
         Replace element(j) by appropriate
lexicon set in Vietnamese;
      End If
   End For
End For
```

In this research, we use the Vietnamese lexicon set suitable for each relationship type in Table 1 as follows:

- Relationship type ⟨i⟩: "để" (English: for).
- Relationship type ⟨ii⟩: "vì" (English: because/because of).
- Relationship type ⟨iii⟩: "nên" (English: so).
- Relationship type ⟨iv⟩: "và" (English: and).

Apply Algorithm 2 for `O_List` and `AS_List` containing predicates of the logical expression in Sect. 1 (described in Sect. 4.1) as follows:

- $n = |$`AS_List`$| \rightarrow 4$;
- $i = 2 < n$;
  - Consider three predicates:
    - P_1 = `vui_vẻ (x, state, status)`
    - P_2 = `học_cúng (x, y, action, transitive)`
    - P_3= `khoái_chí (y, state, status)`.
  - Check inter-sentential anaphoric pronoun:
    - C_IAP_1 = TRUE because component `S_Index` in P_1 takes the value which is identical with the value of component `S_Index` in P_2.

Table 7 Two priorities are equal

Case	Priority of Pas_{i-1}	Priority of Pas_i	Priority of Pas_{i+1}
1	(X)	(Y)	$(Z) = (X)$

    - C_IAP_2 = TRUE because component `O_Index` in P_2 takes the value which is identical with the value of component `S_Index` in P_3.
  - According to Table 7: level_priority(P_1, P_2) = level_priority(P_2, P_3).
  - new_structure = summarize(P_1, P_2).
    - According to Table 8: new_structure = `[lan (x)]+[vui_vẻ(v)] + <ii>+ [học_cùng (x, y)] + [con_trai (y)]`.
  - Put new_structure into `S_StructureList`;
  - $i = i + 2 \rightarrow 4$;
- $i = 4 = n$;
  - Consider two predicates:
    - P_3 = `khoái_chí (y, state, status)`
    - P_4 = `được (y, z, action, transitive)`.
  - Check inter-sentential anaphoric pronoun:
    - C_IAP = TRUE because component `S_Index` in P_3 takes the value which is identical with the value of component `S_Index` in P_4.
  - new_structure = summarize(P_3, P_4).
    - According to Table 8: structure = `[con_trai (y)] + [khoái_chí (y)] +<ii> + [đu'ọ'c (y, z)] + [điểm_cao(z)]`.
  - Put new_structure into `S_StructureList`;
- Apply Algorithm 3, we obtain the result is the new reduced Vietnamese paragraph:

"Lan vui vẻ vì học cùng con trai. Con trai khoái chí vì được điểm cao."
(English: "Lan is happy because of studying with the son. The son is overjoyed because of taking high mark.").

5 Experiment and analysis

To perform the experiment and evaluate the success rate, we establish two criteria with concrete marks:

Table 8 The syntactic structure of the new reduced Vietnamese sentence according to relationship type ⟨ii⟩

Priority of Pas_i	Priority of Pas_j	Syntactic structure
(1)	(4)	`[Po1]` + `[Pasi]` + ⟨ii⟩ + `[Pasj]`
(1)	(2)	`[Po1]` + `[Pasi]` + ⟨ii⟩ + `[Pasj]`
(1)	(3)	`[Po1]` + `[Pasi]` + ⟨ii⟩ + `[Pasj]` + `[Po2]`
		`[Po1]` + `[Pasi]` + ⟨ii⟩ + "is"`[Pasj]` + "by" + `[Po2]`
(2)	(4)	`[Po1]` + `[Pasi]` + ⟨ii⟩ + `[Pasj]`
(3)	(4)	`[Po1]` + `[Pasi]` + `[Po2]` + ⟨ii⟩ + `[Pasj]`
		`[Po1]` + `[Pasi]` + `[Po2]` + ⟨ii⟩ + `[Po2]` + `[Pasj]`

Table 9 The testing results

Case	Number	/No1	/No2	/No3
The number (No1) of logical expressions	500			
The number (No2) of new reduced paragraphs	428	0.856		
The number (No3) of new reduced paragraphs satisfying mark 1 of the first criteria	397	0.794	0.928	
The number (No4) of new reduced paragraphs satisfying mark 1 of the second criteria	136		0.318	0.343
The number (No5) of new reduced paragraphs satisfying mark 2 of the second criteria	234		0.547	0.589

- The first criterion is the semantic correctness with two marks: 1—correctness; 0—not correctness. This criterion is evaluated based on manually considering that the new reduced paragraph correctly summarizes the meaning of the original paragraph or not.
- The second criteria are the universality in Vietnamese with three marks: 2—universality if every sentences in the new reduced paragraph have the universality; 1—acceptable if there is one sentence in the new reduced paragraph which does not totally have the universality; 0—do not have the universality when there are two or more sentences which do not have the universality.

Based on these two criteria, we built the testing data set consisting of Vietnamese paragraphs according to the rule with the following points:

- Each paragraph is composed of 3–5 Vietnamese sentences having simple structure.
- If there are three or more consecutive sentences in which each pair of sentences does not have the inter-sentential anaphoric pronoun relationship, then the paragraph is fairly trivial to summary. Therefore, we require at least at the second and the forth sentence there are the occurrences of the anaphoric pronouns.

With the above rule, we collected 500 Vietnamese paragraphs and constructed 500 logical expressions for testing. The results are presented in Table 9 as follows:

Analyzing the results in Table 9, we see that

- With the central is Algorithm 2, the solution showed the effectiveness in generating new reduced paragraphs which satisfy the above criteria.
- There are some limitations with causes:
  - Because there is no additional factor showing the context about space and time in which the fact happened, therefore, we determined the inter-sentential relationships based on the assumption in Sect. 2.2. This leads to the generated paragraph may not have totally semantic correctness or universality in a reality context.
  - In some logical expressions, there are predicates representing actions or states which have component `S_Index` or `O_Index` taking the value which does not indicate the correct object. This leads to cannot generate or the new generated paragraph does not have the semantic correctness.

These limitations will become our main objectives in the next researches.

6 Discussion and conclusion

In this paper, we presented the algorithm of generating the new reduced Vietnamese paragraph from the logical expression of DRS encoding the semantics of the source paragraph. This algorithm computes the verbal relationships between related sentences, based on the proposed assumptions. The experiment shows that the quality of new summarization paragraphs is enhanced and considerably conformable to Vietnamese native speakers.

We also pointed out some limitations of this solution. These limitations will be studied and overcome in future researches, focused on following main points: consider paragraphs having more complex structure, and try to find other assumptions which are more universal in Vietnamese.

References

1. Blackburn, P., Bos, J.: Representation and Inference for Natural Language—Volume II: Working with Discourse Representation Structures. Department of Computational Linguistics, University of Saarland, Saarbrücken (1999)
2. Barzilay, R., et al.: Information fusion in the context of multi-document summarization. In: Proceedings of the 37th Annual Meeting of the Association for Computational Linguistics on Computational Linguistics, pp. 550–557 (1999)
3. Barzilay, R., McKeown, K.R.: Sentence fusion for multidocument news summarization. Comput. Linguist. **31**, 297–328 (2005)
4. Cao, H.X.: Tiếng Việt: Sơ thảo ngữ pháp chức năng [Vietnamese: Brief of Functional Grammar]. Nhà xuất bản giáo dục [Education Publisher] (2006)
5. Covington M.A., Schmitz, N.: An Implementation of Discourse Representation Theory. ACMC Research Report Number: 01-0023. Advanced Computational Methods Center, The University of Georgia, Athens (1989)
6. Covington, M.A., Nute, D., Schmitz, N., Goodman, D.: From English to Prolog Via Discourse Representation Theory. ACMC Research Report Number: 01-0024. Advanced Computational Methods Center, University of Georgia, Athens (1988)
7. Das, D., Martins, A.F.T.: A Survey on Automatic Text Summarization. Language Technologies Institute, Carnegie Mellon University, Pittsburgh (2007)
8. Genest, P.E., Lapalme, G.: Fully abstractive approach to guided summarization. In: Proceedings of the 50th Annual Meeting of the Association for Computational Linguistics: Short Papers, vol. 2, pp. 354–358 (2012)
9. Genest, P.E., Lapalme, G.: Framework for abstractive summarization using text-to-text generation. In: Proceedings of the Workshop on Monolingual Text-To-Text Generation, pp. 64–73 (2011)
10. Greenbacker, C.F.: Towards a framework for abstractive summarization of multimodal documents. ACL HLT **2011**, 75 (2011)
11. Halliday, M.A.K., Matthiessen, C.M.I.M.: An Introduction to Functional Grammar, 3rd edn. Hodder Arnold, London (2004)
12. Harabagiu, S.M., Lacatusu, F.: Generating single and multi-document summaries with gistexter. In: Document Understanding Conferences (2002)
13. Jezek, K., Steinberger, J.: Automatic text summarization. In: Snasel, V. (ed.): Znalosti 2008, ISBN 978-80-227-2827-0, FIIT STU Brarislava, Ustav Informatiky a softveroveho inzinierstva, pp. 1–12 (2008)
14. Jones, K.S.: Automatic summarizing: factors and directions. In: Mani, I., Marbury, M. (eds.): Advances in Automatic Text Summarization. MIT Press, Cambridge (1999)
15. Jones, K.S.: Automatic Summarising: A Review and Discussion of the State of the Art. Technical Report 679. Computer Laboratory, University of Cambridge, Cambridge (2007)
16. Kamp, H.: A theory of truth and semantic representation. In: Groenendijk, J., Janssen, T.M.V., Stokhof, M. (eds.): Formal Methods in the Study of Language, Part 1. Mathematical Centre Tracts. Mathematical Centre Tracts, pp. 277–322 (1981)
17. Kasture, N.R., Yargal, N., Singh, N.N., Kulkarni, N., Mathur, V.: A survey on methods of abstractive text summarization. Int. J. Res. Merg. Sci. Technol. **1**(6), 53–57 (2014)
18. Khan, A., Salim, N.: A review on abstractive summarization methods. J. Theor. Appl. Inf. Technol. **59**(1), 64–72 (2014)
19. Lee, C.S., et al.: A fuzzy ontology and its application to news summarization. IEEE Trans. Syst. Man Cybern. Part B Cybern. **35**, 859–880 (2005)
20. Lloret, E.: Text summarization: an overview. In: Paper Supported by the Spanish Government Under the Project TEXT-MESS (TIN2006-15265-C06-01) (2008)
21. Mani, I., Maybury, M.T.: Advances in Automatic Text Summarization. MIT Press, Cambridge (1999)
22. Moawad, I.F., Aref, M.: Semantic graph reduction approach for abstractive text summarization. In: Seventh International Conference on Computer Engineering and Systems (ICCES), pp. 132–138 (2012)
23. Reiter, E., Dale, R.: Building Natural Language Generation System. Cambridge University Press, Cambridge (1997)
24. Reiter, E., Dale, R.: Building applied natural language generation systems. Nat. Lang. Eng. **3**(1), 57–87 (1997)
25. Saranyamol, C.S., Sindhu, L.: A survey on automatic text summarization. Int. J. Comput. Sci. Inf. Technol. **5**(6), 7889–7893 (2014)
26. Tanaka, H., et al.: Syntax-driven sentence revision for broadcast news summarization. In: Proceedings of the 2009 Workshop on Language Generation and Summarisation, pp. 39–47 (2009)
27. Tran, T., Nguyen, D.T.: Merging two Vietnamese sentences related by inter-sentential anaphoric pronouns for summarizing. In: Proceedings of the 1st NAFOSTED Conference on Information and Computer Science (NICS'14), Hanoi, pp. 371–381 (2014)
28. Tran, T., Nguyen, D.T.: Improving techniques for summarizing the meaning of two Vietnamese sentences by adding a meaningful relationship between two actions. In: Proceedings of the 16th ACM International Conference on Information Integration and Web-based Applications and Services (iiWAS'14), Hanoi, pp. 484–488 (2014)
29. Tran, T., Nguyen, D.T.: Enhancement of sentence-generation based summarization method by modelling inter-sentential consequent-relationships. In: Proceedings of the 16th ACM International Conference on Information Integration and Web-Based Applications and Services (iiWAS'14), Hanoi, pp. 302–309 (2014)
30. Tran, T., Nguyen, D.T.: Specification model of paragraph summarization by verbal relationships: objective, cause, consequence, concurrence. In: Proceedings of the 2nd IEEE International Conference on Artificial Intelligence, Modelling and Simulation (AIMS'14), Madrid, pp. 205–210 (2014)
31. Tran, T., Nguyen, D.T.: Semantic predicative analysis for resolving some cases of ambiguous referents of pronoun "Nó" in summarizing meaning of two Vietnamese sentences. In: Proceedings of the 17th UKSIM-AMSS International Conference on Modelling and Simulation (UKSIM'15), Cambridge, pp. 340–345 (2015)
32. Tran, T., Nguyen, D.T.: Combined method of analyzing anaphoric pronouns and inter-sentential relationships between transitive verbs for enhancing pairs of sentences summarization. In: Silhavy, R. (eds.): Proceedings of the 4th Computer Science On-line Conference (CSOC'15)—Vol 1: Artificial Intelligence Perspectives and Applications. Advances in Intelligent Systems and Computing, vol. 347, pp. 67–77. Faculty of Applied Informatics, Tomas Bata University in Zlin, Czech Republic (2015)
33. Tran, T., Nguyen, D.T.: Modelling consequence relationships between two action, state or process Vietnamese sentences for improving the quality of new meaning-summarizing sentence. Int. J. Pervasive Comput. Commun. **11**(2), 169–190 (2015). (Emerald Group Publishing Limited. ISBN 1742-7371)
34. Zettlemoyer, L.S., Collins, M.: Learning to map sentences to logical form: structured classification with probabilistic categorial grammars. In: Proceedings of the 21st Conference on Uncertainty in Artificial Intelligence (UAI'05), pp. 658–666 (2005)

35. Zettlemoyer, L.S., Collins, M.: Online learning of relaxed CCG grammars for parsing to logical form. In: Proceedings of the 2007 Joint Conference on Empirical Methods in Natural Language Processing and Computational Natural Language Learning (EMNLP-CoNLL'07), pp. 678–687 (2007)

Further Readings

36. Covington, M.A.: GULP 4: An Extension of Prolog for Unification Based Grammar. Research Report Number: AI-1994-06. Artificial Intelligence Center, The University of Georgia, USA (2007)
37. Gupta, V., Lehal, G.S.: A survey of text summarization extractive techniques. J. Emerg. Technol. Web Intel. **2**(3), 258–268 (2010)
38. Le, H.T., Le, T.M.: An approach to abstractive text summarization. In: Proceedings of the 5th International Conference of Soft Computing and Pattern Recognition (SoCPaR'13), Hanoi, pp. 372–377 (2013)
39. Le, H.T., Sam, R.C., Nguyen, P.T.: Extracting phrases in Vietnamese document for summary generation. In: Proceedings of International Conference on Asian Language Processing (IALP), Harbin, pp. 207–210 (2010)
40. Tran, T., Nguyen, D.T.: Improve effectiveness resolving some inter-sentential anaphoric pronouns indicating human objects in Vietnamese paragraphs using finding heuristics with priority. In: Proceedings of the 10th IEEE RIVF International Conference on Computing and Communication Technologies–Research, Innovation, and Vision for the Future (RIVF'13), Hanoi, pp. 109–114 (2013)
41. Tran, T., Nguyen, D.T.: A solution for resolving inter-sentential anaphoric pronouns forVietnamese paragraphs composing two single sentences. In: Proceedings of the 5th International Conference of Soft Computing and Pattern Recognition (SoCPaR'13), Hanoi, pp. 172–177 (2013)
42. Tran, T., Nguyen, D.T.: Implementation of a discourse representation based approach for summarization of Vietnamese text paragraphs. In: Proceedings of the 3rd Asian Conference on Information Systems (ACIS'14), Nha Trang, pp. 275–282 (2014)

15

Application based brokering algorithm for optimal resource provisioning in multiple heterogeneous clouds

Thiruselvan Subramanian[1] · **Nickolas Savarimuthu**[1]

Abstract In recent years, adoption of cloud computing for computational needs is growing significantly due to various factors such as no upfront cost and access to latest service. In general, cloud infrastructure providers offer a wide range of services with different pricing models, instance types and a host of value-added features. Efficient selection of cloud services constitutes significant management challenges for cloud consumer, which is tedious and involves large information processing. To overcome this, the cloud brokers provide resource provisioning options that ease the task of choosing the best services based on consumers requirements and also provide a uniform management interface to access cloud services. This paper proposes a novel cloud brokering architecture that provides an optimal deployment plan for placement of virtual resources in multiple clouds. The objective of the deployment plan is to select the best cloud services with optimal cost, taking into account various attributes defined in service measurement index (SMI) with additional physical and logical constraints. The proposed cloud brokering architecture has been modeled using mixed integer programming formulation and Benders decomposition algorithm to solve efficiently. Efficacy of the proposed algorithm has been verified by extensive numerical studies and sensitivity analysis.

Keywords Cloud broker · Infrastructure as a service · Deployment plan · Service measurement index · Mixed integer programming · Optimization

✉ Thiruselvan Subramanian
thirulic@gmail.com

Nickolas Savarimuthu
nickolas@nitt.edu

1 Department of Computer Applications, National Institute of Technology, Tiruchirappalli 620015, India

1 Introduction

Cloud computing has emerged as a paradigm to deliver, on demand computing resources to cloud consumers, similar to other utilities (e.g., water, electricity and gas) [1]. The size of the cloud computing market is growing rapidly in recent years. In this huge cloud market, it is difficult for cloud users to deal with different types of virtual machines (configurations and virtualization software's running under them), interface managers, pricing schemes, levels of service quality, variation in availability of resources and other value-added services. Some cloud providers also enforce restrictions on the number of virtual machines (VMs) that a user can utilize. The complexity of selecting and provisioning right cloud services is intermediated by cloud broker services, which manages the use, performance and delivery of cloud services and often negotiates the relationships between cloud providers and cloud consumers [2]. Cloud broker eases the task of consumers to select suitable resources based on their computational needs.

A cloud broker has to provide the best deployment plan, where VMs are placed in an independent cloud or in multiple clouds based on the consumers requirements. To carry out this, the broker must take into account the attributes such as the configuration of resources, service performance, total cost, security. Also, the consumer can specify constraints regarding geographical locations, load balancing criteria, service configurations and legal regulations for data placement. The cloud broker synthesizes an optimized deployment plan for the placement of VMs among multiple clouds, which adheres to the user criteria and placement constraints. Deploying VMs over multiple clouds offers several benefits such as scalability of services, improved reliability cost reduction and avoid vendor lock-in. The cloud broker implicitly considers the possibility of multi-cloud deployment.

Based on the requirements, the cloud broker can provide a single-cloud or multi-cloud deployment plan. Usually, a multi-cloud deployment is preferred when consumers application has loosely coupled services with less communication overhead. In contrast, a single-cloud deployment plan is preferred when a tightly coupled set of application components with a high communication overhead is involved.

For optimal resource provision in heterogeneous cloud environments, a three-phase approach cloud broker architecture is proposed. In the first phase, the cloud broker has to get the service request description, and relative weights of the required service measurement index (SMI) attribute from the consumers. The service request description consists of the type of application, virtual machine configuration, number of VMs required, location, minimum required SMI score and other Quality-of-Service (QoS) parameters. The possible set of cloud resources and services satisfying service request is identified in the second phase. In the third phase, the cloud providers are evaluated based on SMI, developed by Cloud Service Measurement Index Consortium (CSMIC) [3], and a cost optimized deployment plan is developed.

In this paper, the resource provisioning over multiple clouds is addressed by mixed integer programming model formulation using AIMMS [4] modeling language, which provides access to a wide range of solvers including CPLEX and GUROBI. Benders decomposition [5] is discussed as a possible way to solve the optimization problem efficiently for a large number of cloud providers. The cloud broker limits the number of providers for provisioning resources based on application requirements or consumers specification. The consumer can specify minimum score for each SMI category and attributes along with their weights to enable the selection cloud provider for the optimal resource provisioning phase. The objective is to minimize the total cost of the deployment plan, which satisfies consumers requirements. To illustrate the effectiveness of the optimization mechanism, numerical analysis of the model is performed using a large synthetic data set involving one thousand cloud providers.

In this work, cloud brokering architecture for provisioning resources on multiple-cloud environments is considered, and the major contributions are as follows:

- The problem of minimizing the cost of resource provisioning in the multi-cloud environment is formulated as a mixed integer programming(MIP) problem, and its specification is modeled with AIMMS modeling language.
- Those cloud providers satisfying the consumers minimum requirement of SMI category and attribute score as per the metrics defined by CSMIC are evaluated for cost optimal deployment plan.
- Benders decomposition algorithm has been applied to the MIP formulation to solve the model efficiently and to prove the scalability of the model.
- Numerical evaluation and sensitivity analysis are performed to prove the effectiveness and scalability of the proposed model.

The rest of this paper is organized as follows. Related work is discussed in Sect. 2. The proposed cloud brokering architecture is described in Sect. 3. In Sect. 4, a mixed integer programming model formulation is presented. Benders decomposition algorithm is presented in Sect. 5. In Sect. 6, numerical evaluation and sensitivity analysis of the proposed model are presented. Finally, the conclusions and future research directions are discussed in Sect. 7.

2 Related work

In recent years, researchers and cloud brokers have focused on developing models and methods for federated cloud service and product selection based on either minimizing the total deployment cost or maximizing the QoS. Cloud service provisioning and cost optimization based on static demand, price and availability have been discussed in [6–11], where [12,13] deal with the uncertainty in the demand, price and availability of cloud services.

Tordsson et al. [6] proposed a cloud brokering mechanism that performs two operations: (i) the optimal placement of the virtual resources of a virtual infrastructure across a set of cloud providers and (ii) management and monitoring of these virtual resources by providing a unified management user interface. By considering the demand and price of resources to be static, a 0–1 integer programming model is developed to minimize the cost and maximize the performance. Experimental results confirm that multi-cloud deployment provides better performance and lower costs compared to the usage of a single-cloud deployment. Simarro et al. [7] provided a cloud brokering architecture that can work with different scheduling strategies for optimal deployment of virtual services across multiple clouds based on different optimization criteria and several user constraints. Binary integer programming formulation is used in [7].

Papagianni et al. [8] and Breitgand et al. [9] used integer linear programming with approximation algorithms to optimize the cost and improve the QoS. In [8], the authors focused on the benefits for cloud consumers in contrast to [9], where the focus is on maximizing profit and QoS of the cloud providers by utilizing the resources of partnering cloud providers to meet the peak demand. Malawski et al. [10] developed a mixed integer nonlinear programming model to optimize the total cost of resource provisioning under the time constraint. The authors also considered the maximum number of resources provided by a single-cloud provider. Wright et al. [11] introduced a two-phase constraint-based approach in a multi-cloud environment for discovering the most appropriate set of infrastructure resources for a given application. In the first phase, suitable resources are identified for the application, and in second phase, heuristic approach is used to select the best services based on cost and performance.

Simarro et al. proposed a methodology in [12] which considers the dynamic price and demand of cloud service in contrast to the static one in [7]. The authors also considered cloud migration overhead issues for service provisioning among multiple clouds. Chaisiri et al. [13] proposed an optimization of resource provisioning cost in the federated cloud with future demand and price uncertainty. There is a trade-off between reservation and on-demand pricing plan where the focus is on minimizing on-demand and over subscription cost [13].

Javadi et al. [14] consider the problem of QoS-based resource provisioning in a hybrid-cloud computing system where the private cloud is failure-prone and to overcome that they had developed a hybrid-cloud architecture. They proposed a brokering strategy in the hybrid-cloud system where an organization that operates its private cloud aims to improve the QoS by utilizing the public cloud resources.

In case of evaluation of infrastructure providers, proximity aware service selection methods for effective service selection for IaaS and geographically distributed clouds were proposed in [15,16]. The CSMIC [3,17] are developing a standard measurement framework for the cloud services, called the SMI. SMI compares cloud services with relevant and meaningful cloud characteristics. The cloud characteristics are categorized into seven categories such as accountability, agility, assurance, financial, performance, security and privacy, and usability. Each category has three or more attributes, and in total, SMI addresses 51 attributes. A framework for ranking IaaS cloud services using the AHP method considering the elements quantitative criteria has been developed by [18].

Wu et al. [19] proposed a service selection method based on qualitative evaluation criteria with quality-of-service aspects (such as response time and availability) as well as social perspectives of services. Rehman et al. [20] applied MCDM for service selection, which is effective for services offered with similar specifications but only differ in performance. User feedback-based MCDM approach for effective cloud service monitoring and selection has been proposed in [21]. Yan et al. [22] developed an MCDM approach for recommendation and selection of cloud services for hybrid-cloud computing environment. Cloud service evaluation and service selection method combining interval-valued fuzzy sets with VIKOR method for cloud services have been proposed in [23]. A fuzzy AHP-based service selection method has been proposed in [24].

In this work, the optimal resource provisioning over multiple clouds is addressed by evaluating the cloud providers using SMI attributes and final deployment plan using MIP formulation. The proposed approach considers both technical- and business-level criteria, while existing works consider only QoS attributes and cost for resource provisioning. Also, the model considers the location of service provided, jurisdictional regulations and the lower and upper bound for the number of VMs provided by a cloud provider. The proposed model considers families of VMs rather than individual VMs as such. It helps to overcome the minor variations among the VM configurations offered by various cloud providers in reality.

3 System model

3.1 Cloud broker architecture

Cloud brokering architecture outlined in Fig. 1 consists of three main actors, namely consumer, cloud provider and cloud broker. The consumer has the demand for computing infrastructure to execute jobs, which they can obtain from the cloud provider. Consumers request the cloud broker for virtualized infrastructure, with service request description. The service request description consists of a required set of VMs, optimization criteria, location of data center or availability zones (where VMs are placed) and required level of SMI attributes that may include performance, security level, accountability, usability.

The broker then filters the cloud providers that meet the criteria based on the consumers or applications requirements as described in service request description. The filtered cloud providers are ranked based on CSMIC SMI attributes on a 10-point scale, using weighted sum model [25]. After ranking the providers, the broker selects those providers who satisfy the minimum SMI score in either category, attribute, measure or total score based on consumers specification. Then, the broker implements an algorithm to make an optimal deployment plan to reduce the total infrastructure cost.

In this work, there are multiple VM classes that are used to categorize the different types of VMs. Let $i \in \mathbb{N}$ denote the set of VM classes. It is assumed that one VM class represents a family of VM configuration within a range. In real-world scenario, VMs are offered in both predefined and customized configurations to suit customer needs. Providers like Amazon [26] offer only predefined instances where ElasticHosts [27] offers only customized VMs. Customer may request the broker with different VM configurations to run their jobs. With this requirement, the cloud broker can select the best computing resources from the available cloud providers to cater the actual demand.

Let $p \in \mathbb{N}$ denote the set of cloud providers. Each cloud provider has a pool of resources with predefined or customizable VM class. Let r denote the set of resource types provided by the cloud providers. Resource types can be computing power, storage, memory, network bandwidth, etc. Each VM class has its specification of required resource type. Let b_{ir}

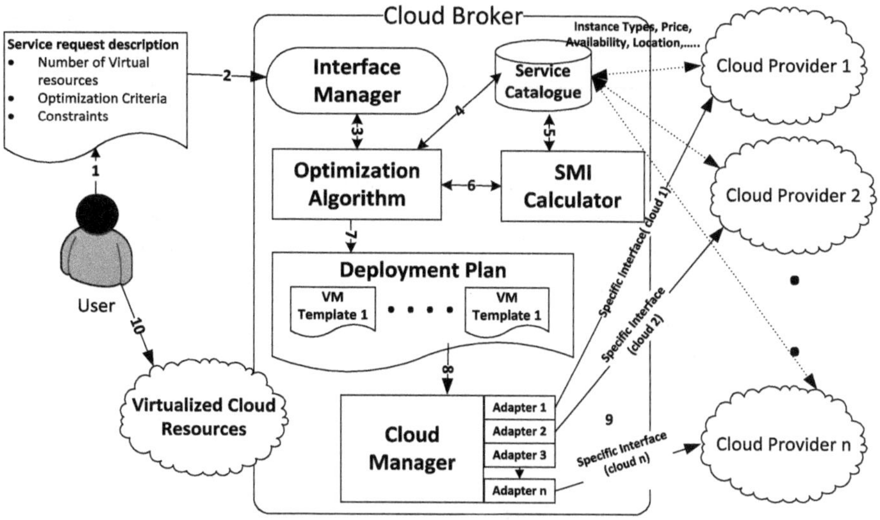

Fig. 1 Proposed cloud broker architecture

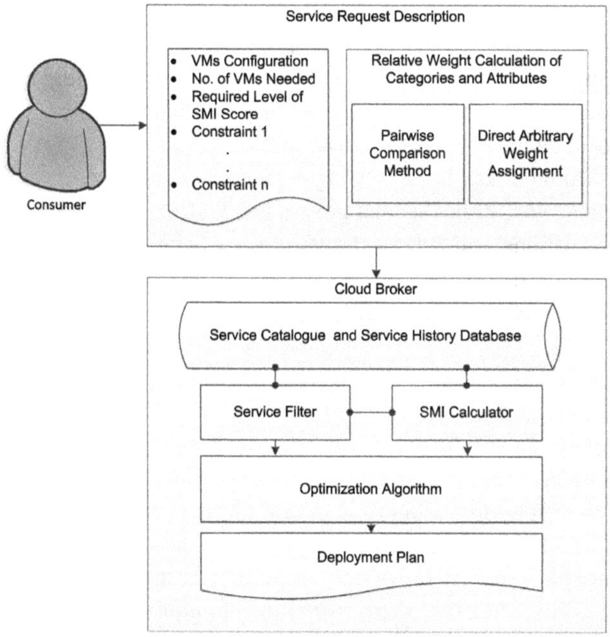

Fig. 2 Work flow of the cloud brokering approach

be the amount of resource type r required by the VM in class i. Let $l \in \mathbb{N}$ denote the set of geographical locations where the cloud provider offers services. It is assumed that every cloud provider prepares facilities such as virtualization management software, network facility and load balancer to support the consumer using the VMs. Schematic diagram of the proposed model is provided in Fig. 2. The key notations used in this paper are listed in Table 1.

3.2 Virtual machine cost

The cloud providers offer VMs either in predefined configurations or as customized configurations. Amazon EC2 [26] and GoGrid [28] offer VMs in predefined configurations. Amazon EC2 offerings are grouped into eight families: standard, micro, high-memory, high-CPU, cluster compute, cluster GPU and high I/O [26]. Each family has its configuration to cater the needs of different types of application requirements. When choosing VMs, the broker considers the characteristics of the application with regard to resource utilization and selects a suitable one. For example, cluster computer and cluster GPU family VMs are selected for high-performance computing (HPC) applications, while micro VMs are well suited for lower throughput applications and Web sites that consume significant compute cycles periodically. Cloud providers like ElasticHosts [27] offer customized VMs, where VMs are configured based on application needs.

In general, the cloud services are offered in nonlinear pricing plans to serve consumer heterogeneity. Cloud services are offered in one of the following ways.

Pay per use Pay per use component consists only of a per unit rate for every utilized unit (i.e., pay per hour), known as linear tariff, normally offered by many cloud providers. The pay per use tariff is also called as usage price, marginal price or per unit charge.

Flat rate The flat rate component with fixed fee is independent of the consumer's consumption that is charged on a regular seasonal basis (either monthly, quarterly, half yearly or yearly).

Two-part pricing The consumers have to pay an upfront cost for the period (either monthly, quarterly, half yearly or yearly) and will be charged with pay per usage unit rate for every utilized unit.

The VMs are charged based on the resource configuration (number of CPU cores, memory size, storage capacity and network bandwidth), licensing cost of the software running

Table 1 List of key notations

Symbol	Definition
i	Set of virtual machine classes
p	Set of cloud providers
l	Set of locations of data center or availability zones
c	Set of SMI categories
a	Set of SMI attributes
m	Set of SMI measures
r	Set of resources
j	Set of regulations and legal constraints
C^o_{ipl}	Price VM class i by cloud provider p in location l for pay per use plan
C^f_{ipl}	Price VM class i by cloud provider p in location l for flat rate plan
F_p	Fixed cost of cloud provider p for extra services
y_p	Decision variable representing the number providers p selected
Y_{jpl}	cloud provider p in location l is compliance with regulation j
x_{ipl}	Decision variable representing the number of VMs in class i provisioned
	by cloud provider p in location l
D_{il}	Number of VMs consumer required to execute class i in location l
A_{ipl}	Maximum capacity of VMs i offered by cloud provider p in location l
b_{ir}	Amount of resource type r required by VMs i
C_{rpl}	Unit price of resource type r provided by cloud provider p in location l
S_{pa}	Score of attribute a for the service offered by cloud provider p
S_{pc}	Score of category c for the service offered by cloud provider p
S_{pam}	Score of measure m for the service offered by cloud provider p which belong attribute a
TS_p	Total SMI score of a cloud provider p
u_c	Weight of category c
u_{am}	Weight of measure m belongs to attribute a
u_{ca}	Weight of attribute a belongs to category c
u_a	Minimum required SMI attribute score for attribute a by user
u_c	Minimum required SMI category score for category c by user
u_{ts}	Minimum required SMI total score for a cloud provider p
uw_a	Weight of the attribute a defined by user
uw_c	Weight of the category c defined by user
uw_{am}	Weight of the measure m belong attribute a defined by user

on them and location of the data center. Normally, VMs are charged per usage hour. The pricing charged by the cloud providers are in US dollars ($) per resource unit per usage hour. Let C_{rpl} denote the unit price of resource type r provided by cloud provider p in location l. The cost of VM class C_{ipl} is the cost for provisioning every resource type defined as follows:

$$C_{ipl} = \sum_r b_{ir} \, C_{rpl} \tag{1}$$

where b_{ir} is amount of resource type r required by VMs i.

3.3 Location and legal constrains

Data-center location of cloud services determines the performance of the service offered to the end user. The cloud providers build multiple data centers that are distributed geographically to meet the availability and reliability of the service. It plays an important role in the performance of the applications hosted. Response time is the key issue that can be reduced when the end user of the hosted applications has less geographical distance from the data center. Applications like telephony, video conferencing, online gaming and finance are delay sensitive, and they are benefited from the local data-center that is closer to the end user.

Another key issue is being the legal constraints and compliance requirements that govern the data. Local states have regulations and juristic limitations on where data can be stored and how data can be accessed. In the USA, regulations such as HIPAA [29], FERPA [30], PATRIOT Act [31] and GLBA [32] control how data can be stored, as well as who may access that data. In the European Union (EU), the Data Protection Directive (EUDPD) [33] governs sensitive private data and flatly forbids the transfer of data to other jurisdictions not explicitly approved [34]. Some state laws like Israeli law [35] permit data reside in other jurisdictions when adequate and sufficient levels of protection are met. The local jurisdictions have restrictions on permitting trans-border data crossing when the other jurisdiction has equivalent or better levels of protection. Many cloud providers started offering services in different geographical locations based on local state-specific regulations. Amazon offers AWS GovCloud [36] for US government agencies and contractors to move more sensitive workloads into the cloud by addressing their specific regulatory and compliance requirements.

The consumers should select the required regulations and compliance laws during service request description. Let $j \in \mathbb{N}_1$ be a juristic regulation and compliance laws for the data placement. Let Y_{jpl} be a binary decision variable representing the cloud provider p available in location l is compliance with data placement regulation j is defined as follows:

$$Y_{jpl} = \begin{cases} 1 & \text{if provider } p \text{ has compliance with} \\ & \text{regulation } j \text{ in location } 1 \\ 0 & \text{otherwise} \end{cases} \tag{2}$$

3.4 Service measurement index (SMI)

The SMI is a framework of critical characteristics, associated attributes, and measures that decision-makers may apply to enable comparison of cloud services available from multiple providers. SMI is devised to be a standard method to measure any cloud service based on critical business and technical requirements of the consumers. The SMI starts with a hierarchical framework. The top level divides into seven categories, where each category is further refined by three or more attributes as defined in Table 2. Then, within each attribute one or more measures are being defined to enable the use of cloud service provider data to inform selection decisions. Some of the attributes and measures will be service specific, while others such as the security, financial will apply to all types of cloud services [3,37]. The seven categories are defined below:

Accountability attributes used to measure the properties related to a service provider organization. These properties may be independent of the service being provided.

Agility attributes indicating the impact of a service upon the consumers ability to change direction, strategy or tactics quickly with minimal disruption.

Assurance attributes that indicate how likely it is that the service will be available as specified.

Table 2 SMI categories and attributes

Categories	Attributes
Accountability	Auditability; compliance; contracting experience; governance; ease of doing business; ownership; provider business stability; provider certifications; provider contract/SLA verification; provider ethicality; provider personnel requirements; provider supply chain; sustainability
Agility	Adaptability; elasticity; extensibility; flexibility; portability; scalability
Assurance	Availability; maintainability; recoverability; reliability; resiliency/fault tolerance; service stability; serviceability
Financial	Billing process; cost; financial agility; financial structure
Performance	Accuracy; functionality; suitability; interoperability; service response time
Security and privacy	Access control and privilege management; data integrity; data privacy and data loss; retention/disposition; physical and environmental security; security management; proactive threat and vulnerability management
Usability	Accessibility; client personnel requirements; installability; learnability; operability; transparency; understandability

Table 3 Rating formula for suitability attribute

Point scale	Condition
10	If all the essential features are satisfied
0	If any of the essential features is not satisfied
$fp/fr \times 10$	If all essential features are satisfied and some of the non-essential
	Features are not satisfied
	where:
	fp = number of essential and non-essential features provided by
	the service
	fr = number of essential and non-essential features required by
	the consumer

Financial the amount spent on the service by the consumer.

Performance attributes that indicate the performance characteristics of the provided services.

Security and privacy attributes that indicate the effectiveness of a service provider in controlling access to services, service data and physical facilities from which services are provided.

Usability the ease with which a service can be used by the consumers.

3.5 SMI score

SMI scores for the categories and attributes are rated from 0 to 10 where zero is the least score. The rating formula for attribute and measure is defined by CSMIC [38] and will change periodically based on the evolution of standards. SMI framework consists of both qualitative and quantitative measures. The score of the cloud provider is calculated using a weighted sum model [25], where each category, attribute and measure has their own weight based on consumer's preferences. This provides flexibility to the consumer who provides their weights based on importance. Comparison of points scored by providers of a particular attribute to the consumers required score for a particular category or attribute is done to select the providers who meet the minimum criteria. The rating formula for suitability attribute of performance category and learnability attribute of usability category is defined in Tables 3 and 4, respectively.

3.5.1 Relative weight calculation

SMI attribute scores are calculated using the weighted sum model of relevant measures. The weights are assigned to SMI attributes either based on predefined configuration settings

Table 4 Rating formula for learnability attribute

Point scale	Condition
10	If X is = or <10 min
8	If X is = or <20 min
6	If X is = or <30 min
4	If X is = or <40 min
2	If X is = or <50 min
0	If X is = or >60 min
	where:
	X = total elapsed time to learn use of new service

Table 5 Scale for pairwise comparisons

Intensity of importance	Definition
1	Equal importance
3	Moderate importance
5	Strong importance
7	Very strong importance
9	Extreme importance

(such as high performance, high security, cost-effective) or by using relative weights based on consumer preferences. For customization, they can either use pairwise comparison method proposed by Saaty [39,40] or can provide direct arbitrary weight.

Pairwise comparison The pairwise comparisons are made depending on the scale shown in Table 5. In the pairwise comparison matrix, the score of s_{uv} represents the relative importance of the component on row (u) over the component on column (v); i.e., $s_{uv} = w_u/w_v$. The reciprocal value of the expression ($1/s_{uv}$) is used when the component v is more important than the component u. The comparison matrix S is defined as

$$S = \begin{bmatrix} w_1/w_1 & w_1/w_2 & \cdots & w_1/w_n \\ w_2/w_1 & w_2/w_2 & \cdots & w_2/w_n \\ \vdots & \vdots & \ddots & \vdots \\ w_n/w_1 & w_n/w_2 & \cdots & w_n/w_n \end{bmatrix} = \begin{bmatrix} 1 & s_{12} & \cdots & s_{1n} \\ s_{21} & 1 & \cdots & s_{2n} \\ \vdots & \vdots & \ddots & \vdots \\ s_{n1} & s_{n2} & \cdots & 1 \end{bmatrix} \quad (3)$$

Then, a local priority vector (eigenvector) w is computed as an estimate of the relative importance accompanied by the elements being compared by solving the following equation:

$$Sw = \lambda_{\max} w, \quad (4)$$

where $\lambda_{\max}$ is the largest eigenvalue of matrix S.

Direct arbitrary consumer assigned weights The consumer can assign weights on their own scale rather than using the pairwise comparison. In this case, the weights are normalized. Let uw_c denote the user-assigned weight for category c, and then SMI category weights W_c is calculated as follows:

$$W_c = \frac{uw_c}{\sum_c uw_c}, \ \forall c \quad (5)$$

Let uw_{ca} denote the user-assigned weight for attribute a and uw_{am} denote the user-assigned weight for measures m. Let W_a and W_{am}, defined similarly as (1), which denote the normalized attribute and measure weight, respectively.

3.5.2 SMI score calculation

Let S_{pa} denote the SMI attribute score of an attribute a for a cloud provider p and S_{pam} denote the measure score of a measure m belong to attribute a. The attribute score S_{pa} for every attribute type is calculated as follows:

$$S_{pa} = \sum_m W_{am} \, S_{pam}, \ \forall (p, a) \quad (6)$$

subject to

$$\sum_m W_{am} = 1, \ \forall a \quad (7)$$

Let S_{pac} denote the score of the category c for the cloud provider p. The category score S_{pac} is calculated using weighted sum approach of relevant SMI attributes score S_{pa} and measures m. The SMI category score S_{pc} for every category type is defined as follows:

$$S_{pc} = \sum_a W_{ca} \, S_{pa}, \ \forall (p, c) \quad (8)$$

subject to

$$\sum_a W_{ca} = 1, \ \forall c \quad (9)$$

Let Ts_p denote the total SMI score for a cloud provider p. Total SMI score Ts_p is calculated by using weighted sum approach of all SMI category scores S_{pac}. The SMI total score for every cloud provider p is defined as follows.

$$Ts_p = \sum_c W_c \, S_{pc}, \ \forall p \quad (10)$$

subject to

$$\sum_{c} W_c = 1 \quad (11)$$

4 Mixed integer programming model

In this section, the mixed integer programming is presented as the core formulation.

Minimize:

$$\sum_{ipl} C^{o}_{ipl}\, x_{ipl} + \sum_{ipl} C^{f}_{ipl}\, x_{ipl} + \sum_{p} F_p y_p \quad (12)$$

subject to:

$$\sum_{p} x_{ipl} \geq D_{il},\ \forall (i, l) \quad (13)$$

$$x_{ipl} \leq A_{ipl},\ \forall (i, p, l) \quad (14)$$

$$\sum_{p} y_p \leq n,\ \forall p \quad (15)$$

$$Y_{jpl} \geq u y_{jl},\ \forall (j, p, l) \quad (16)$$

$$\underline{M}_{ipl} y_p \leq x_{ipl} \geq \overline{M}_{ipl} y_p,\ \forall (i, p, l) \quad (17)$$

$$S_{pc} \geq u_c,\ \forall (p, c) \quad (18)$$

$$S_{pa} \geq u_a,\ \forall (p, a) \quad (19)$$

$$TS_p \geq u_{ts},\ \forall p \quad (20)$$

$$x_{ipl} \in \mathbb{N}_0,\ \forall (i, p, l) \quad (21)$$

$$y_p \in \{0, 1\},\ \forall p \quad (22)$$

$$Y_{jpl} \in \{0, 1\},\ \forall (j, p, l) \quad (23)$$

The general form of the optimization algorithm is formulated in Eqs. (12) to (23). The goal of the objective function Eq. (12) is to minimize the total deployment cost of VMs among multiple-cloud providers. The decision variable x_{ipl} denotes the number of VMs provisioned, and C^{o}_{ipl} denotes the pay per use cost of the VMs i offered by the cloud provider p in location l. The parameter C^{f}_{ipl} denotes the flat rate cost of the VMs, and F_p denotes the fixed cost of the provider p. The constraint in Eq. (13) maintains that the consumers demand for VMs i in location l is satisfied. In Eq. (14), the constraint states that the allocation of resource for VMs must not exceed the maximum resource capacity offered by the cloud provider p in location l. Constraint Eq. (15) indicates that the number of cloud providers is limited for deployment of VMs according to the consumer specification and application requirements. The constraint in (16) ensures that the providers compliance with legal and juristic regulations is met. The minimum and maximum number of VMs that can be provisioned by the cloud provider p in location l is limited by the constraint Eq. (17). Constraints in Eqs. (18) and (19) ensure that the cloud providers are having SMI category and attribute score greater than or equal to the consumer requirement. In Eq. (20), the constraint implies that the cloud provider having a total SMI score greater than or equal to the consumer specified score alone is considered for resource provisioning. Constraint Eq. (21) indicates that the variables accept values from a set of nonnegative integers.

A multitude of modeling languages and solvers could be used to solve the specified optimization problem. Our choice of modeling language is AIMMS [4]. It offers some advanced modeling concepts not found in other languages, as well as a full graphical user interface for both developers and end users. It can be used with world class solvers and personal solvers. CPLEX [41] solver is used for MIP formulation in this paper. AIMMS modeler can be incorporated with existing cloud brokers using a Web service-based interface. External database and data sets can be incorporated with AIMMS, and it is adaptable to any architecture.

5 Benders decomposition

In this section, Benders decomposition algorithm [5] is applied to solve the mixed integer programming formulation. Benders decomposition is an approach to solve complicated mathematical programming problems by splitting them into a master problem and multiple subproblems that can be solved in parallel. The master problem contains integer variables while continuous variables become a part of the subproblem. The classic approach of Benders decomposition algorithm is implemented, and it solves an alternative sequence of master and subproblems.

To apply Benders decomposition, it is necessary to divide the variables and constraints of the MIP formulation $P(x, y)$ into two groups. The binary variable y_p, together with the constraint Eqs. (15)–(17) and (22), represents the set Y. The continuous variable x_{ipl}, together with the constraint Eqs. (13), (14) and (21), represents the linear part to be dualized. The flowchart of the benders decomposition algorithm is presented in Fig. 3.

The initial master problem $M(y, m = 0)$ does not contain any Benders cuts (i.e., $m = 0$) and can be stated as follows.

Minimize:

$$\sum_{p} F_p\, y_p \quad (24)$$

subject to : Eqs. (15)–(17), (22).

The problem to be dualized (i.e., linear formation), the equivalent of the inner optimization problem can be stated as follows.

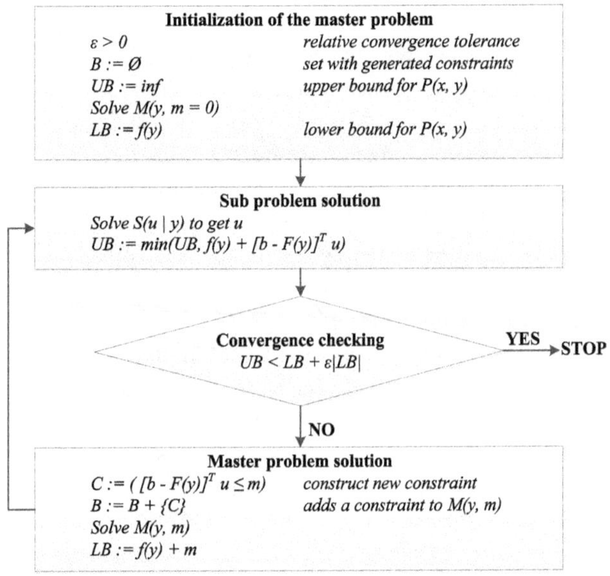

Fig. 3 Benders decomposition algorithm flowchart

Minimize:

$$\sum_{ipl} x_{ipl}\, C^{o}_{ipl} + \sum_{ipl} x_{ipl}\, C^{f}_{ipl} \tag{25}$$

subject to: Eqs. (13), (14), (21).

By introducing the dual variables [5] σ_{il} and π_{ipl} corresponding to the two constraints Eqs. (13) and (14), the dual formation $S(\sigma, \pi \,|\, y)$ of the problem in Eq. (25) can be written as follows.

Maximize:

$$\sum_{il} \sigma_{il}\, D_{il} + \sum_{ipl} \pi_{ipl}\, A_{ipl} \tag{26}$$

subject to:

$$\sigma_{il} + \pi_{ipl} \geq C^{o}_{ipl},\ \forall i, \forall p, \forall l \tag{27}$$

$$\sigma_{il} + \pi_{ipl} \geq C^{f}_{ipl},\ \forall i, \forall p, \forall l \tag{28}$$

$$\sigma_{il} \leq 0,\ \pi_{ipl} \geq 0. \tag{29}$$

The Benders cuts [5] added to master problem at each iteration are derived from the objective function of the subproblem $S(\sigma, \pi \,|\, y)$, and a new constraint is derived as follows.

$$\sum_{il} \sigma_{il}\, D_{il} + \sum_{ipl} \pi_{ipl}\, A_{ipl} \leq m \tag{30}$$

The relaxed master problem $M(y, m)$ can be obtained by adding the Benders cuts b to the initial master problem $M(y, m = 0)$ after introducing the set of Benders cuts B generated so far. The resulting master problem is developed by adding the variables stated as follows.

Minimize:

$$\sum_{p} F_p\, y_p + m \tag{31}$$

subject to: Eqs. (15)–(17), (22)

$$\sum_{il} \sigma_{bil}\, D_{il} + \sum_{ipl} \pi_{bipl}\, A_{ipl} \leq m, \forall b \tag{32}$$

6 Numerical evaluation

To validate the MIP formulation, numerical analysis is performed as follows. Due to the unavailability of benchmarking data sets, a synthetic data set is created using the uniform distribution function available in the AIMMS programming language. For the evaluation purpose, the set of cloud providers p is loaded with one thousand cloud providers (i.e., P-1 ... P-1000). The set locations l, set VM class i and set

Table 6 VM demand (D_{il})

	Loc-1	Loc-3
Vm-1	34	–
Vm-2	40	–
Vm-3	35	–
Vm-4	40	–
Vm-5	50	–
Vm-6	–	60
Vm-7	–	60
Vm-8	–	30
Vm-9	–	45

Table 7 Criteria for service selection

Aspects	Criteria	
Accountability	Compliance;	C_1
	Ease of doing business	C_2
	Provider business stability	C_3
Agility	Elasticity	C_4
	Portability	C_5
	Adaptability	C_6
Assurance	Service stability	C_7
	Reliability	C_8
Financial	Cost	C_9
Security and privacy	Access control and privilege	C_{10}
	Security management	C_{11}
Usability	Training and support	C_{12}
Performance	Service response time	C_{13}

Table 8 Pairwise comparison

	C_1	C_2	C_3	C_4	C_5	C_6	C_7	C_8	C_9	C_{10}	C_{11}	C_{12}	C_{13}	Geo mean	Weight
C_1	1.00	7.00	5.00	0.33	0.33	0.20	0.14	1.00	0.11	0.14	0.14	7.00	5.00	0.69	0.04
C_2	0.14	1.00	0.20	0.11	0.14	0.20	0.33	0.20	0.14	0.11	0.11	1.00	1.00	0.24	0.01
C_3	0.20	5.00	1.00	0.20	0.14	0.20	0.20	0.33	0.20	0.14	0.14	5.00	5.00	0.46	0.02
C_4	3.00	9.00	5.00	1.00	1.00	1.00	1.00	3.00	1.00	1.00	0.33	9.00	9.00	2.04	0.11
C_5	3.00	7.00	7.00	1.00	1.00	1.00	1.00	1.00	1.00	1.00	1.00	9.00	9.00	2.06	0.11
C_6	5.00	5.00	5.00	1.00	1.00	1.00	0.33	0.33	0.20	0.33	0.33	5.00	7.00	1.20	0.06
C_7	7.00	3.00	5.00	1.00	1.00	3.00	1.00	1.00	0.33	1.00	1.00	9.00	7.00	1.97	0.10
C_8	1.00	5.00	3.00	0.33	1.00	3.00	1.00	1.00	0.20	0.20	0.20	9.00	7.00	1.17	0.06
C_9	9.00	7.00	5.00	1.00	1.00	5.00	3.00	5.00	1.00	0.33	0.33	5.00	5.00	2.35	0.12
C_{10}	7.00	9.00	7.00	1.00	1.00	3.00	1.00	5.00	3.00	1.00	1.00	9.00	9.00	3.00	0.16
C_{11}	7.00	9.00	7.00	3.00	1.00	3.00	1.00	5.00	3.00	1.00	1.00	9.00	9.00	3.27	0.17
C_{12}	0.14	1.00	0.20	0.11	0.11	0.20	0.11	0.11	0.20	0.11	0.11	1.00	0.14	0.19	0.01
C_{13}	0.20	1.00	0.20	0.11	0.11	0.14	0.14	0.14	0.20	0.11	0.11	7.00	1.00	0.26	0.01

Table 9 Attribute score of providers

	P_1	P_2	P_3	P_4	P_5	P_6
C_1	9	3	7	3	9	9
C_2	5	7	5	5	9	5
C_3	3	1	3	9	3	7
C_4	3	3	5	9	9	3
C_5	9	5	5	5	7	9
C_6	3	7	9	9	5	9
C_7	7	5	5	7	3	5
C_8	5	9	3	5	5	3
C_9	3	5	7	9	5	7
C_{10}	7	3	5	3	9	1
C_{11}	9	1	3	9	5	5
C_{12}	7	7	9	5	3	7
C_{13}	7	5	9	9	3	1

Table 10 The weighted attribute score of providers

	P_1	P_2	P_3	P_4	P_5	P_6
C_1	0.065	0.022	0.050	0.022	0.065	0.065
C_2	0.002	0.002	0.002	0.002	0.003	0.002
C_3	0.001	0.000	0.001	0.002	0.001	0.001
C_4	0.007	0.007	0.011	0.020	0.020	0.007
C_5	0.018	0.010	0.010	0.010	0.014	0.018
C_6	0.010	0.023	0.030	0.030	0.016	0.030
C_7	0.023	0.016	0.016	0.023	0.010	0.016
C_8	0.030	0.053	0.018	0.030	0.030	0.018
C_9	0.019	0.011	0.008	0.006	0.011	0.008
C_{10}	0.006	0.003	0.005	0.003	0.008	0.001
C_{11}	0.131	0.015	0.044	0.131	0.073	0.073
C_{12}	0.003	0.003	0.003	0.002	0.001	0.003
C_{13}	0.005	0.003	0.006	0.006	0.002	0.001

Table 11 Deployment plan (x_{ipl})

VM class (i)	Provider (p)	Location (l)	(x_{ipl})
Vm-1	P-367	Loc-1	34
Vm-2	P-367	Loc-1	40
Vm-3	P-416	Loc-1	35
Vm-4	P-367	Loc-1	40
Vm-5	P-367	Loc-1	47
Vm-5	P-416	Loc-1	3
Vm-6	P-367	Loc-3	12
Vm-6	P-416	Loc-3	48
Vm-7	P-367	Loc-3	47
Vm-7	P-416	Loc-3	13
Vm-8	P-367	Loc-3	30
Vm-9	P-416	Loc-3	45

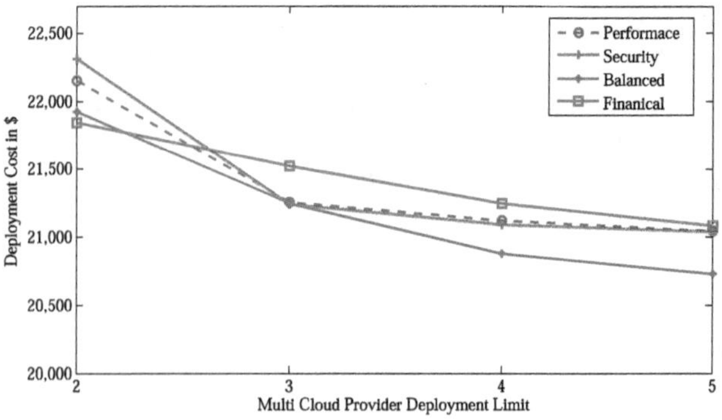

Fig. 4 Optimal deployment plan with various required SMI levels and multi-cloud provider deployment limit

regulation j are loaded with nine locations (i.e., Loc-1 ... Loc-9), nine VM classes (i.e., VM-1 ... VM-9) and nine regulations (i.e., R-1 ... R-9), respectively. The parameter VM availability A_{ipl} is generated by using pseudo random number generator based on uniform distribution with lower bound set to 40 and an upper bound of 50. The data for parameter S_{pc} are generated using normal distribution with lower and upper bound set to 4 and 10, respectively. The cost of VM class for per hour usage C^o_{ipl} in $ is derived using uniform distribution with lower and upper bound to be 1 and 4, respectively. The values of parameters C^r_{ipl}, C^f_p and Y_{jpl} have been generated using uniform distribution with range of (50, 80), (40, 60) and (0, 1), respectively. The VM demand parameter D_{il} is defined as in Table 6. The parameter u_{ts} user required minimum SMI score is set to eighty. For the illustrative purpose, thirteen SMI criteria (in Table 7) and six cloud service providers are considered. The relative weight of the criteria is computed using pairwise comparison method as shown in Table 8. SMI score and the normalized weighted score of the cloud service provider are shown in Tables 9 and 10, respectively. Then, the objective function is solved using Benders decomposition method. The final optimal deployment plan x_{ipl} is listed in Table 11.

The evaluation is performed with combinations of different required SMI level and limiting resource provisioning in multiple clouds. The required SMI levels such as high performance, high security, balanced and financial stability are considered, while multi-cloud provider deployment limit is varied from 2 to 5. The final results are shown in Fig. 4.

6.1 Comparison with other resource provisioning algorithms

In this section, the proposed resource provisioning method is compared with existing resource provisioning algorithms (i.e., SMICloud [18], OCRP [13], Tordsson et al. [6], Breitgand et al. [9] and Wright et al. [11]). In SMICloud, the cloud providers are evaluated using analytical network processing (AHP) for quantitative attributes, and finally, the service provisioning is done based on value/cost ratio. ORCP considers the trade-off between pay per use and reservation pricing plan with uncertain demand. Tordsson method uses integer programming by considering the hardware configuration, minimum and a maximum number of VMs allocation and load balancing constraints. Policy-based resource provisioning is performed by Breitgand et al. [9]. Wright et al. [11] use constraint optimization engine with two-phase constraint-based discovery approach.

All the methods are coded in AIMMS modeling language with defined input parameters in the above section. The solution from each method yields the deployment plan with optimal provisioning costs. A simulation program is developed to evaluate the solution of each method. The simulation contains multiple iterations of three scenarios. In the first scenario, these methods are evaluated with various SMI requirement levels such as high performance, high security, balanced and financial stability. The optimal deployment plan of the first scenario is shown in Fig. 5. The proposed approach yields cost-effective deployment plan in the least computational time compared to other methods and considers all the attributes and measures to evaluate the providers. The second evaluation scenario is based on the limiting number of cloud providers for resource provisioning. The limit is initially set to two providers and increased up to five and evaluated for all the algorithms and is shown in Fig. 6. Proposed approach and Tordsson method provide the best optimal deployment plan compared to other methods. Finally, these methods are evaluated with different types of jurisdiction and legal regulation requirements which is shown in Fig. 7. For most of the evaluation scenarios, the proposed approach provides best optimal deployment plan in the least time compared to other methods.

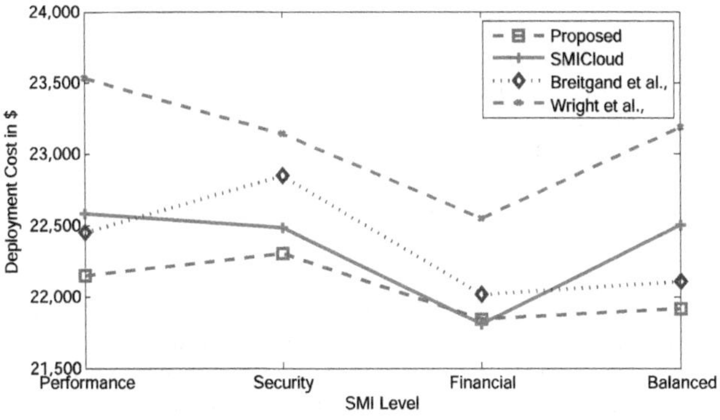

Fig. 5 SMI evaluation level

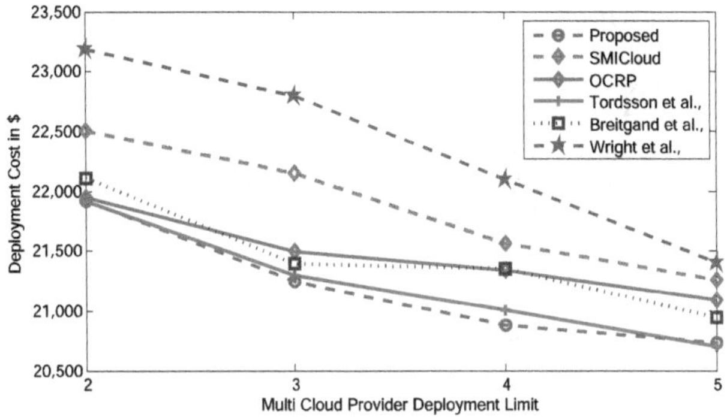

Fig. 6 Cloud provider limit

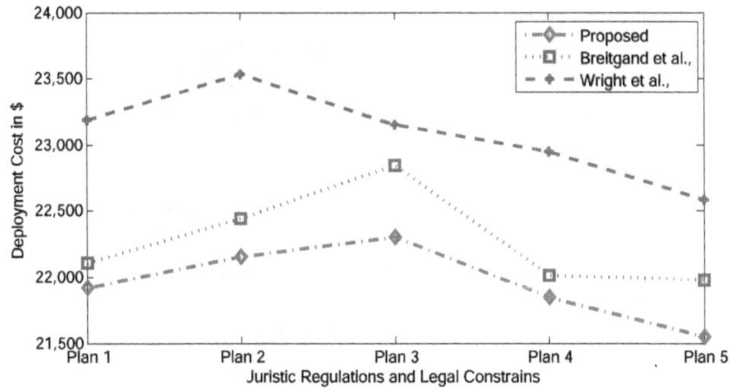

Fig. 7 Legal regulation requirements

6.2 Sensitivity analysis

Sensitivity analysis investigates the changes in the objective function value of a model as the result of changes in the input data. The marginal values derived from simplex algorithm give the additional information on the variability of an optimal solution of the model to changes in the data. The marginal values are divided into shadow prices (associated with constraints and their right-hand side) and reduced costs (associated with the decision variables and their bounds) [42].

Shadow price Defined as the rate of change of the objective function from a unit increase in the right-hand side. A positive shadow price of the constraint indicates that the objective function will increase with a unit increase in the right-hand side of the constraint, while negative shadow price indicates that the objective will decrease. The shadow price will be zero for a non-binding constraint since its right-hand side is not constraining the optimal solution [42].

Reduced costs Defined as the rate of change of the objective function for a unit increase in the bounds of a variable. A positive reduced cost of a non-basic variable increases the objective function with a unit increase in the binding domain. The objective function will decrease if a non-basic variable has a negative reduced cost. The reduced cost of a basic variable is zero since its bounds are non-binding and, therefore, do not constrain the optimal solution [42].

In the proposed MIP formulation, sensitivity analysis is done on continuous variables by fixing all the integer variables to an optimal solution. The decision variable x_{ipl} has positive reduced cost for non-basic variables and zero for the basic variables since its bounds are non-binding. The shadow price of the constraint in Eq. (13) is positive which indicates that the objective will increase with a unit increase in the right-hand side of the constraint (i.e., D_{il}). The shadow prices of the other constraints are zero since the right-hand side is not constraining the optimal solution.

7 Conclusion and future work

In this work, a novel cloud brokering architecture for optimal deployment of resources among multiple-cloud providers has been proposed. The consumer sends the service request description, which contains required configuration and quantity of virtual machines along with constraints such as location, performance, legal and jurisdictional regulations. Furthermore, consumer assigns weight for the SMI categories and attributes, either by pairwise comparison method or by direct arbitrary weighting method. They also define the required SMI total, category or attribute score based on their application requirement. The proposed broker filters the cloud services based on the constraints given in the service request description. Then, the SMI score for the filtered cloud services is calculated. Optimal deployment plan is obtained by formulating and solving the mixed integer programming. The efficiency of the model is improved by implementing the Benders decomposition algorithm by decomposing into multiple smaller problems and solving it in parallel solver sessions. The evaluation of the proposed model has been performed using numerical analysis and sensitivity analysis to show the robustness and scalability of the proposed model.

In future, dynamic cloud deployment plan for applications with dynamic workloads will be investigated. One such example is a Web server, where the load for the server can vary significantly over time. Another aspect of the study is to minimize the effect of virtual machine migrations, as it involves performance degradation and incurs migration cost.

References

1. Buyya, R., Yeo, C.S., Venugopal, S., Broberg, J., Brandic, I.: Cloud computing and emerging IT platforms: vision, hype, and reality for delivering computing as the 5th utility. Future Gener. Comput. Syst. **25**(6), 599–616 (2009)
2. Liu, F., Tong, J., Mao, J., Bohn, R., Messina, J., Badger, L., Leaf, D.: NIST cloud computing reference architecture. NIST Spec. Publ. **500**, 292 (2011)
3. Cloud Services Measurement Initiative Consortium. http://csmic.org/. Accessed 1 June 2014
4. Bisschop J, Roelofs M.: AIMMS-Language Reference (2006)
5. Conejo, A. J., Castillo, E., Mnguez, R., Garca-Bertrand, R.: Decomposition in linear programming: complicating variables. In: Decomposition Techniques in Mathematical Programming, pp. 107–139 (2006)
6. Tordsson, J., Montero, R.S., Moreno-Vozmediano, R., Llorente, I.M.: Cloud brokering mechanisms for optimized placement of virtual machines across multiple providers. Future Gener. Comput. Syst. **28**(2), 358–367 (2012)
7. Lucas-Simarro, J.L., Moreno-Vozmediano, R., Montero, R.S., Llorente, I.M.: Scheduling strategies for optimal service deployment across multiple clouds. Future Gener. Comput. Syst. **29**(6), 1431–1441 (2013)
8. Papagianni, C., Leivadeas, A., Papavassiliou, S., Maglaris, V., Cervello-Pastor, C., Monje, A.: On the optimal allocation of virtual resources in cloud computing networks. Comput. IEEE Trans. **62**(6), 1060–1071 (2013)
9. Breitgand, D., Marashini, A., Tordsson, J.: Policy-driven service placement optimization in federated clouds. IBM Res. Div.Tech. Rep. **9**, 11–15 (2011)
10. Malawski, M., Figiela, K., Nabrzyski, J.: Cost minimization for computational applications on hybrid cloud infrastructures. Future Gener. Comput. Syst. **29**(7), 1786–1794 (2013)
11. Wright, P., Sun, Y.L., Harmer, T., Keenan, A., Stewart, A., Perrott, R.: A constraints-based resource discovery model for multi-provider cloud environments. J. Cloud Comput. **1**(1), 1–14 (2012)
12. Lucas-Simarro, J.L., Moreno-Vozmediano, R., Montero, R.S., Llorente, I.M.: Cost optimization of virtual infrastructures in dynamic multi-cloud scenarios. Concurr. Comput.: Pract. Exp. **27**(9), 2260–2277 (2015). doi:10.1002/cpe.2972
13. Chaisiri, S., Lee, B.S., Niyato, D.: Optimization of resource provisioning cost in cloud computing. Serv. Comput. IEEE Trans. **5**(2), 164–177 (2012)
14. Javadi, B., Abawajy, J., Buyya, R.: Failure-aware resource provisioning for hybrid cloud infrastructure. J. Parallel Distrib. Comput. **72**(10), 1318–1331 (2012)
15. Qian, H., Wang, Q.: Towards proximity-aware application deployment in geo-distributed clouds. Adv. Comput. Sci. Appl. **2**(3), 416–424 (2013)
16. Qian, H., Zu, H., Cao, C., Wang, Q.: CSS: Facilitate the cloud service selection in IaaS platforms. In: International Conference on Collaboration Technologies and Systems (CTS), pp. 347–354 (2013). doi:10.1109/CTS.2013.6567253
17. Siegel J, Perdue J(2012) Cloud services measures for global use: the service measurement index (SMI). In: SRII Global Conference (SRII), pp. 411–415
18. Garg, S.K., Versteeg, S., Buyya, R.: A framework for ranking of cloud computing services. Future Gener. Comput. Syst. **29**(4), 1012–1023 (2013)
19. Wu, Q., Iyengar, A., Subramanian, R., Rouvellou, I., Silva-Lepe, I., Mikalsen, T.: Combining quality of service and social information for ranking services. In: Service-Oriented Computing, pp. 561–575 (2009)
20. Rehman, Z. U., Hussain, F. K., Hussain, O. K.: Towards multi-criteria cloud service selection. In: Fifth International Conference on Innovative Mobile and Internet Services in Ubiquitous Computing, pp. 44–48 (2011). doi:10.1109/IMIS.2011.99
21. Rehman, Z. U., Hussain, O. K., Parvin, S., Hussain, F. K.: A framework for user feedback based cloud service monitoring. In: Sixth International Conference on Complex, Intelligent and Software Intensive Systems (CISIS), pp. 257–262 (2012). doi:10.1109/CISIS.2012.157
22. Yan, S., Chen, C., Zhao, G., Lee, B. S.: Cloud service recommendation and selection for enterprises. In: 8th International Conference on Network and Service Management (CNSM) and Workshop on Systems Virtualiztion Management (svm), pp. 430–434 (2012)
23. Chen, C. T., Hung, W. Z., Zhang, W. Y.: Using intervalvalued fuzzy VIKOR for cloud service provider evaluation and selection. In: Proceedings of the International Conference on Business and Information (BAI13) (2013)
24. Patiniotakis, I., Rizou, S., Verginadis, Y., Mentzas, G.: Managing imprecise criteria in cloud service ranking with a fuzzy multi-criteria decision making method. In: Service-Oriented and Cloud Computing, p. 34 (2013)
25. Triantaphyllou, E.: Multi-Criteria Decision Making Methods: A Comparative Study. Springer Science & Business Media, Berlin (2013)
26. Amazon EC2 Instances. http://aws.amazon.com/ec2/instance-types/. Accessed 26 July 2014
27. ElasticHosts Ltd. http://www.elastichosts.com/cloud-servers-quote/. Accessed 26 July 2014
28. GoGrid. http://www.gogrid.com/products/pricing. Accessed 26 July 2014
29. The Health Insurance Portability and Accountability Act of 1996. http://www.gpo.gov/fdsys/pkg/PLAW-104publ191/content-detail.html. Accessed 2 June 2014
30. FERPA Final Regulations Note. http://www.ofr.gov/OFRUpload/OFRData/2011-30683_PI.pdf. Accessed 1 June 2014
31. USA Patriot Act comes under fire in B.C. report. CBSNews. http://www.cbc.ca/news/canada/usa-patriot-act-comes-under-fire-in-b-c-report-1.487630. Accessed 2 June 2014
32. GrammLeachBliley Act. http://www.gpo.gov/fdsys/pkg/PLAW-106publ102/content-detail.html. Accessed 2 June 2014
33. EU Data Protection. http://ec.europa.eu/justice/policies/privacy/index_en.htm. Accessed 2 June 2014
34. Commission decisions on the adequacy of the protection of personal data in third countries - Justice. http://ec.europa.eu/justice/data-protection/document/international-transfers/adequacy/index_en.htm. Accessed 13 July 2013
35. Kuner, C.: Regulation of transborder data flows under data protection and privacy law: past, present, and future. TILT Law and Technology Working Paper. 016 (2010)
36. AWS GovCloud Region. http://aws.amazon.com/govcloud-us/. Accessed 13 May 2014
37. Service Measurement Index. Framework Version 2.0 draf. http://csmic.org/wp-content/uploads/2013/08/SMI_Overview_1308151.pdf. Accessed 13 May 2014
38. Service Measurement Index. http://csmic.org/resources/downloads. Accessed 13 May 2014
39. Saaty, T.L.: The Analytic Hierarchy Process: Planning, Priority Setting, Resources Allocation. McGraw, New York (1980)
40. Saaty, T.L.: Theory and Applications of the Analytic Network Process: Decision Making with Benefits, Opportunities, Costs, and Risks. RWS publications, Pittsburgh (2005)
41. Optimizer I.I.C.12.4. www.ibm.com/software/integration/optimization/cplex-optimizer.(2013). Accessed 12 April 2014
42. Bisschop, J.: Sensitivity analysis. AIMMS-optimization modeling. http://www.aimms.com/downloads/manuals/optimization-modeling. (2013). Accessed 25 January 2014

Permissions

All chapters in this book were first published in VJCS, by Springer International Publishing AG.; hereby published with permission under the Creative Commons Attribution License or equivalent. Every chapter published in this book has been scrutinized by our experts. Their significance has been extensively debated. The topics covered herein carry significant findings which will fuel the growth of the discipline. They may even be implemented as practical applications or may be referred to as a beginning point for another development.

The contributors of this book come from diverse backgrounds, making this book a truly international effort. This book will bring forth new frontiers with its revolutionizing research information and detailed analysis of the nascent developments around the world.

We would like to thank all the contributing authors for lending their expertise to make the book truly unique. They have played a crucial role in the development of this book. Without their invaluable contributions this book wouldn't have been possible. They have made vital efforts to compile up to date information on the varied aspects of this subject to make this book a valuable addition to the collection of many professionals and students.

This book was conceptualized with the vision of imparting up-to-date information and advanced data in this field. To ensure the same, a matchless editorial board was set up. Every individual on the board went through rigorous rounds of assessment to prove their worth. After which they invested a large part of their time researching and compiling the most relevant data for our readers.

The editorial board has been involved in producing this book since its inception. They have spent rigorous hours researching and exploring the diverse topics which have resulted in the successful publishing of this book. They have passed on their knowledge of decades through this book. To expedite this challenging task, the publisher supported the team at every step. A small team of assistant editors was also appointed to further simplify the editing procedure and attain best results for the readers.

Apart from the editorial board, the designing team has also invested a significant amount of their time in understanding the subject and creating the most relevant covers. They scrutinized every image to scout for the most suitable representation of the subject and create an appropriate cover for the book.

The publishing team has been an ardent support to the editorial, designing and production team. Their endless efforts to recruit the best for this project, has resulted in the accomplishment of this book. They are a veteran in the field of academics and their pool of knowledge is as vast as their experience in printing. Their expertise and guidance has proved useful at every step. Their uncompromising quality standards have made this book an exceptional effort. Their encouragement from time to time has been an inspiration for everyone.

The publisher and the editorial board hope that this book will prove to be a valuable piece of knowledge for researchers, students, practitioners and scholars across the globe.

List of Contributors

Hazra Imran, Mohammad Belghis-Zadeh, Kinshuk and Sabine Graf
Athabasca University, Edmonton, Canada

Ting-Wen Chang
Beijing Normal University, Beijing, China

Truong Chi Tin, Duong Van Hai and Hoang Nguyen Thuy Ngan
Department of Mathematics and Informatics, University of Dalat, Dalat, Vietnam

Andrzej Siemiński
Faculty of Computer Science and Management, Wroclaw University of Technology, Wroclaw, Poland

Thi Ngoc Chau Vo and Hua Phung Nguyen
Faculty of Computer Science and Engineering, Ho Chi Minh City University of Technology, Vietnam National University, Ho Chi Minh City, Vietnam

Thi Ngoc Tran Vo
School of Industrial Management, Ho Chi Minh City University of Technology, Vietnam National University, Ho Chi Minh City, Vietnam

Bui Cong Giao, Duong Tuan Anh
Faculty of Computer Science and Engineering, Ho Chi Minh City University of Technology, Ho Chi Minh City, Vietnam

Duc-Hau Le
School of Computer Science and Engineering, Water Resources University, 175 Tay Son, Dong Da, Hanoi, Vietnam

Vu-Tung Dang
Department of Information Technology, Vietnam Youth Academy, 58 Nguyen Chi Thanh, Dong Da, Hanoi, Vietnam

Fabian Schomm and Lara Vomfell
ERCIS, University of Münster, Münster, Germany

Florian Stahl and Gottfried Vossen
ERCIS, University of Münster, Münster, Germany
The University of Waikato Management School, Hamilton, New Zealand

Natarajan Meghanathan
Jackson State University, Jackson, MS 39217, USA

Jan Treur
VU University Amsterdam, Behavioral Informatics Group, Amsterdam, The Netherlands

Duy Nguyen, Vinh Lai, Khanh Nguyen and Trung Le
Faculty of Information Technology, HCMc University of Pedagogy, Ho Chi Minh City, Vietnam

Roberto Gorrieri
Dipartimento di Informatica, Scienza e Ingegneria, Università di Bologna, Mura A. Zamboni, 7, 40127 Bologna, Italy

Mengmeng Zhu and Hoang Pham
Department of Industrial and Systems Engineering, Rutgers University, New Brunswick, NJ 08854, USA

Nedia Araibi and Wahiba Karaa Ben Abdessalem
High Institute of Management of Tunis, University of Tunis, Tunis, Tunisia

Eya Ben Ahmed
Miracl Laboratory, University of Sfax, Sfax, Tunisia

Trung Tran and Dang Tuan Nguyen
Faculty of Computer Science, University of Information Technology, VNU-HCM, Ho Chi Minh City, Vietnam

Thiruselvan Subramanian and Nickolas Savarimuthu
Department of Computer Applications, National Institute of Technology, Tiruchirappalli 620015, India

Index

O

P

R

S

T

V

CPSIA information can be obtained
at www.ICGtesting.com
Printed in the USA
LVHW060816140920
665711LV00034B/12

9 781632 407801